THE
PHILOSOPHY
OF
HISTORIOGRAPHY

E-Rights/E-Reads, Ltd. Publishers
171 East 74th Street, New York, NY 10021

www.ereads.com

Copyright © 2010 by John Lange.

The Author asserts the moral right to be identified as author of this work.

All rights reserved. No part of this book may be reproduced or transmitted in any form or by any means, electronic, or mechanical, including photocopy, recording, scanning or any information storage retrieval system, without explicit permission in writing from the Author or Publishers.

*To James N. Jordan —
Friend and colleague
of many years. With best wishes,
John Lange*

THE PHILOSOPHY OF HISTORIOGRAPHY

by JOHN LANGE

[e-reads]

Contents

Prologue ... 1

Part One: Preliminary Considerations ... 3
I. Introduction 5
    1. The Proximity of the Past ... 7
    2. The Limitations of the Individual ... 8
    3. The Inducing Brain ... 12
    4. Trajectory and the 5-D Map ... 14
    5. The Importance of Comprehension ... 16
  6. The Urgency of Comprehension ... 22
II. Some Distinctions ... 27
    1. *Historia* ... 27
    2. History ... 29
    3. History, again. ... 31
    4. Historiography ... 37
III. Studies and Metastudies ... 39
IV. Analytic vs. Speculative Philosophy of History ... 47
V. Varieties of History ... 49
    1. Types ... 49
    2. Agendas ... 51
        1. Reportorial ... 52
        2. Explanatory ... 54
        3. Didactic ... 55
    4. Inspirational ... 57
    5. Polemical ... 58
    6. Hagiographical ... 60
    7. Judgmental ... 61
    8. Illuminative ... 63
    9. Recollective ... 65
    10. Protective ... 65
    11. Entertainment ... 66
    12. Response to Life ... 67
    13. Contextualization ... 69
    14. The Satisfaction of Curiosity ... 71

Part Two: Logic and Semantics   73
I. Logic   75
II. Semantics   87

Part Three: Metaphysics   131
I. Monisms and Dualisms   133
II. Ontology: The Basic Ontic Hypothesis   139
    1. Problematicities of Time   139
    2. Past, Present, and Future   155
III. Causality: The Roots of Why   187
IV. Progress, Plan, and Pattern   235
    1. Progress   238
        1. Means/Ends Sufficiencies   238
        2. Not all change is progress.   239
        3. Criteria-relevant Considerations   240
        4. Some Concepts of Progress   242
        5. Some Challenges to Progress Theory   245
        6. Some Dangers of Progress Theory   251
    2. Plan   254
    3. Pattern   268
        1. Prolegomena.   268
        2. Pattern Potentiality   271
        3. Pattern Triviality   275
        4. Relevant Pattern   276
        5. Varieties of Pattern   279
        6. Detectability   294

Part Four: Epistemology   303
I. Historical Statements   305
II. A Theory of Historical Statements   351
III. Ancillary Observations: Historical Process
    and Historical Event   355
IV. Truth   363
V. Skepticism   385
VI. Evidence: Some General Considerations   389
    1. The Person   390
    2. The Process   391
    3. Selection   393

VII. The Dubiety Dilemma	397
VIII. Knowledge	403
1. Problematicities	403
2. Evidence: Some Particular Considerations	408
1. The Evidence Predicate	408
2. The Transcendence of Evidence	410
3. Evidential Conflict	410
4. Evidential Change	412
5. The Assessor of Evidence	412
6. The Assessment of Evidence	413
3. Levels of Knowledge	415
IX. Explanation	425
1. Causal-Thread Analysis	425
2. Elucidation	428
3. Explaining How	429
4. Colligation	429
5. Deductive/Nomological Explanation	435
1. Impracticality	447
2. Unnecessary	449
3. Untestable.	449
4. Appropriateness?	450
6. Rational Explanation	453
1. A theory of reason.	467
2. Explanation in terms of reasons.	472
3. The indispensability of rational explanation.	474
4. Addendum: Multiply Explanatory Prose	481
X. Historiography and Objectivity	485
XI. The Cognitivity Status of Historiography	511
1. Preliminary Considerations	511
2. Particular Considerations	519
1. Methodology	519
2. Intent	526
3. Time-and-Place Stance.	527
4. Subject Matter	528
5. Law-Boundedness	528
6. Explanations	530
7. Outcome statements	531

8. The Objectivity Problem	532
9. Accessibility	537
3. The Classification of Historiography	539

Part Five: Axiology — 549
I. Preliminary Considerations — 551
II. Ethical Taxonomy — 561
III. Systemic-Process Morality — 571
IV. An Examination of Some Arguments Pertinent to the Cognitivity of Value Judgments — 577
    1. Background Considerations — 577
        1. Fact/Value Dichotomization — 577
        2. Is/Ought — 578
        3. Open-Question Argumentation — 581
    2. Some Arguments — 584
        1. Linguistic — 584
        2. Intuitional — 586
        3. Anthropological — 589
        4. Species Relativity — 592
        5. Presupposition of Science and Technology — 602
        6. Human Consciousness and the Imperative to Action — 603
        7. The Possibility of Axiological Error — 607
        8. Nonaxiological/Axiological Belief Convergence — 607
        9. Societal Prerequisites — 610
        10. The Implausibility of an Alternative — 612
    3. The Relevance of Axiology to Historiography — 613

Part Six: Aesthetics — 619

Epilogue — 651

Prologue

There are these passengers on a ship, you see. It might be a ship, but perhaps not. If it is a ship, it is not clear it has a rudder. It may drift with currents, responsive to dynamics with which we are not familiar. Is the ship on some course, arranged on a captain's bridge, to which we have no access? Could we ourselves take the helm? We have some sense of where the ship has been, put together from fragments, abetted by shrewd guesswork. But we cannot, as yet, find the helm, and if this were managed, somehow, it is not clear what course we might chart, or if, given the sea, the winds, and such, we might inadvertently guide the ship into waters unforeseen and best avoided. Perhaps most interestingly, most of our fellow passengers are unaware of the existence of the ship, and live, and replicate, and die, in their cabins, unconcerned with the ship and its course, or whether it has a course. Perhaps they are the wisest of all. But that is not clear.

Part One: Preliminary Considerations

I. Introduction

It is amazing that one of the most neglected domains of philosophical inquiry is that to which one would expect to find addressed constant and profound attention, namely, the multiplex histories of which we find ourselves the product.
It is not altogether obvious why this should be the case.
Consider, for example, the philosophy of science. That is, assuredly, an important and justifiably prestigious discipline within the philosophical enterprise; it is honored with considerable and well-deserved attention, and has profited, happily, from the labors of a number of unusually gifted philosophers. One begrudges her nothing, but her eminence does, given inevitable comparisons, surprise one. Why so much interest there? Or, perhaps better, why not similar interest elsewhere? Certainly science affects our lives and illuminates our understanding; it gives us aspirin and atomic weaponry, jet engines and drip-dry shirts, fountain pens, if anyone remembers such things, and computers, and life-saving surgery and poison gas. It improves immeasurably the quality of our lives and puts the means of universal extermination in the hands of sociopathic lunatics. Surely it deserves philosophical attention, and who has not wondered about stars and space, galaxies and quarks, such things. To try to philosophically grasp such an endeavor, to consider this remarkable path to knowledge, is an estimable inquiry. On the other hand, science has a bottom, so to speak, regardless of whether or not one gets there. It ends somewhere; it is finite. Somewhere the last fact lurks. Perhaps

history has, too, so to speak, a bottom, but the complexities of understanding her are immeasurably deeper, and, perhaps, of greater importance. In history there may be no last fact. And, if there is, it is unlikely to be found. Atoms were presumably no more about in the time of Sargon of Akkad than they are today. But history's lessons of aggression and imperialism may weigh more heavily in speculations concerning human survival than valence bonds and molecules. Quarks were about when Buddha sat beneath a shade-giving tree and Jesus preached in Galilee. Quarks were doubtless much the same then as now, but history is different. Perhaps the prestige of science redounds to the prestige of the philosophy of science. Or perhaps the comparative simplicity of science encourages the moths of scholarship. It may be something one can get one's hands on. Perhaps it is a bit like the wonders and glories of mathematics, so attractive to fine minds searching for stability, beauty, and a refuge from a messier, more dangerous world. The number two, for example, is congenial. It can be relied on. It stands still, so to speak, and exceeds one and refuses to invade three. It is always there. You can count on it. In any event, whatever may be the causes here, whether psychologically explicable or a simple matter of a planet's biographical idiosyncrasies, we confront the anomaly that an area which is most telling, and the most undeniably momentous, seems remarkably, and perhaps unconscionably, comparatively neglected. There are, of course, philosophical intrusions into the human past, and its endemic problematicities, studies undertaken by vital and astute minds, but there are too few troves in this area, certainly proportionately, and those that exist are today commonly neglected. Ratios are involved, of course. My claim here is twofold, first, history, as a discipline, is enormously important, even cognitively fundamental, and, secondly, she is woefully undervalued and understood. It is the philosopher's job to remedy to some extent, subject to his limitations, this defect. This is not to compete with the historian, no more than the philosopher of science competes with the scientist. The point here is to try to understand history, and historiography. Thus the title of this book, the Philosophy of Historiography.

My general approach is as follows. Classically the five major branches of philosophy are logic and semantics; metaphysics; epistemology; axiology, and aesthetics. Accordingly, I would like to devote some attention to the logic and semantics, the metaphysics, the epistemology, the axiology, and the aesthetics of historiography. To be sure, given the constraints of time and space, the implementation of this program will be highly selective. We do hope, on the other hand, to do more than point some directions and open a few roads. In the end of course, this country, like the night, is "large and full of wonders." Certainly exploration is welcome and invited. Portions of this work are, as far as I know, quite original. On the other hand, many points are familiar from the literature, and I think it is important to deal with them. We are not out to invent the philosophy of historiography here, or to pretend to invent it, but to deal with it, hopefully in a way that the reader, whom the author supposes to be generally unfamiliar with the subject matter, may find interesting and informative.

1. The Proximity of the Past

"That's history" is commonly a disparagement. It is interesting to note that "That's science" is commonly a compliment. Whereas I would not have written this book if I did not think it important, and that it would fill a woeful lacuna in the intellectual landscape, and that history is terribly important, and so on, I think that many people do not realize how close much of history is to us. Much of it is not that faraway, and even much of it that is faraway isn't really that faraway. Let us suppose a lifetime of something like seventy years or so. On this scale, the regime of National Socialism in Germany, for example, is still within the living memory of many individuals, including the author. Within two lifetimes the wounds of the American Civil War were still fresh, wounds that left scars still visible. Some three lifetimes ago the Bastille had recently fallen and Waterloo lay in the future. Some seven lifetimes or so ago Columbus thought he had discovered a new route to India. Some ten generations ago Crusaders were disembarking at Acre. Some thirty generations ago Caesar crossed the Rubicon, and marched on Rome.

The caves are a long time behind us, but most of history is not.

2. The Limitations of the Individual

Knowledge is not easily achieved. And it is, commonly, an achievement. That should be clearly recognized. Too, all knowledge is the knowledge of individuals. It is not in books. Ink marks are in books, films are in cans, and so on. How impressive that the individual should strive to know, and how much more impressive that he occasionally seems to be successful.

Consider the difficulties, the limitations of the individual. First, he is a member of a species. Each species has its limitations. The human, for example, is unable to experience through antennae, something that is no problem for something like eight-hundred thousand other species. Consider the radiation of the electromagnetic spectrum. Here there are wave lengths ranging from trillionths of an inch, as in Gamma rays, to miles in length, as in some radio waves. How much of that spectrum is available to the human being, something between sixteen to thirty-two millionths of an inch. We build our entire world of vision on that narrow window to the world, all the colors, and, within each, the infinite varieties of brilliance, saturation, and hue. Bees can see in ultraviolet light. We cannot. The difference between violet and ultraviolet light is negligible in the spectrum, but, to us, it is the difference between seeing and not seeing, between, in its way, light and darkness. We hear sound and feel heat, both movements in the atmosphere. Were we differently constituted, and there were no survival liabilities involved, we might feel sound and hear heat. What is the visual experience of the whale, with its tiny eyes separated by several feet? Does the bat have visual experiences, transducing reflected sound waves into visual data, or does it experience in an altogether different way, which would make no sense to us, which we could not even imagine? One does not know. And these limitations, and such, deal only with sensory apparatus.

We are also limited, as a species, cognitively.

Intelligence was not evolved for the purposes of contemplation, for doing mathematics, for the analysis of the cosmos, for inquiring into the mysteries of existence, and such. In fact, it was not evolved, even, for the enablement of survival, gene replication, and such. It had no purpose; it discovered purposes. It was not evolved to work, but it worked, and so it survived. As the saying goes, genetics cast the dice, and the environment selected the winning numbers. Intelligence was, happily, a winning number. Intelligence was preserved because it was an excellent tool for a fragile species at risk in a precarious environment. As it turned out, it was superior to horns, hoofs, fangs, and claws, to toughness of hide and fleetness of foot, to wings, keenness of vision, of hearing, and scent, even to strength and agility. But its primary value was pragmatic; it was a tool, one useful in acquiring food, clothing, shelter, safety, and mates. It was useful, too, obviously, for purposes of social organization and coordinated activity. It was not designed to do science, or write history. Quite possibly the human mind is not equipped, for example, to understand the nature of space, to unravel its riddles and paradoxes; nor to understand what took place before the first moment, and before that; nor the nature of a last moment; nor to comprehend a succession of causes, receding endlessly into a night of negative numbers. Perhaps there is a ground of being spewing forth universes from dimensions inconceivable to a roving, inquisitive hominid, with a world limited to his now and then, his up and down, and back and forth. One hears that dimensions may come in crates and bundles, far exceeding a puny three or four, or five, and that it takes some twenty-six of them to account for the counter-clockwise vibrations of this or that, which thises or thats may not exist in the first place. One hears elsewhere that physics proclaims the empirical feasibility of time travel. That should intrigue historians. Too bad one may need the energy of a galaxy to bring it about. Do not hasten to submit travel requests to the dean. One suspects no more here, really, than a dazzling form of mathematical play. But these people are serious, one supposes. They say they are. How about an infinite set of universes, a geometrical progression along an infinite set of world lines? What about Schrödinger's cat, which is neither alive nor dead, until one looks, a lovely metaphor for reality's observer dependence. The particle or wave is neither here nor there, nor doing this or that, until you check up on it. Let us suppose some of this, if intelligible at all, is true. Our world then would surely be quite different from the world of our experience, which we usually suppose is the real world, except for the little stuff you can't see. It is difficult to do a good job with the wrong tool. Squirrels are unlikely to do well in rocket science, and the world is still waiting for first raccoon to excel in econometrics. Skills and competencies exist in hierarchies and those of paramecia are excelled by those of coelenterates, and theirs by a variety of successors in the phylogenetic scale, and so on, and we may or may not be at the epistemological summit of the universe. It would be quite a tragedy if we were, but, clearly, there must be much beyond us cognitively, and perhaps much beyond minds as far beyond ours as ours is, hopefully, beyond those of mice and rabbits. There is no guarantee that the world will produce minds capable of comprehending it. J.B.S. Haldane is alleged to have remarked that the universe may not only be queerer than we think, but queerer than we can think. One suspects he is right, but one keeps trying. Why not? There is no point in stopping until one hits the wall, or, say, meets oneself on the way back.

The point of these remarks is to make certain that we are well aware of the difficulties which must beset and condition cognitivity.

Our knowledge is not only difficult to come by, but it may be somewhat unrelated to how things are.

Presumably there is but one reality, but it is not clear that an intelligent insect, an intelligent fish, an intelligent bat, and an intelligent primate, would all come up with the same science.

If they did, terrific.

What they would come up with would be sciences that would work more or less well for them, and sciences which each species would presumably take for the indisputable, exact, proven nature of reality.

More power to them; let them sleep well at night.

These limitations of the species, sensory and cognitive, must obviously afflict the individual generically. Beyond them, however, are limitations which are nongeneric, but specific. Each individual, *qua* individual, has his personal limitations of sensory acuity, intelligence, imagination, education, experience, background, situation, family, judgment, and so on. He occupies a particular place and a particular time, which will affect what he can know, and what he will be, and can be. There is a sense in which the Paleolithic worker of flint, the infantryman of Assurbanipal, the mendicant friar, the Napoleonic grenadier, the Victorian biologist or diplomat, and so on, all live in different worlds, psychologically, sociologically, politically, and so on. This will affect their memories, and what they might record, if so inclined. As the saying has it, there is no view from nowhere. This is less a limitation, actually, than an inevitability, a natural and unobjectionable fact of life. One cannot write from somewhere, unless one is somewhere from which to write. Relativity is a reality.

Now consider the problem of the historiographer, or that of anyone who might address himself to that sort of work.

He has the task of delineating and explaining the past.

Any moment is presumably the precipitate of hundreds of thousands of intersecting causal lines, coming from a diversity of directions, and fading into a past which fades into mystery after a few billion years.

Our historian may limit himself to the history of last Tuesday in Minneapolis or, like a Vico, a Spengler or Toynbee, address his attention to pageants and panoramas, redolent of trajectories, seeming to steam with meaning, telling us stories which illuminate, or pretend to, wisely or not, the records of empires, the nature of thriving and dying worlds.

In any event, as we shall see, the historian, even of last Tuesday, addresses himself to a task of enormous subtlety and complexity, most of which, thoughtfully, depending on his agenda, he has no choice but to ignore.

And yet there are few thing a human being could do which are more relevant to life, and more revelatory of human significance, meaning, and possibility than historiography.

They are treasurers of our species, without which, in a fully human sense, we could not understand ourselves.

3. The Inducing Brain

The inducing brain has been selected for. It is endemic in the animal world. Briefly, this is the supposition to believe, or to act as though one believed, that the future will resemble the past, that regularities obtain, and that patterns exist. Long ago David Hume pointed out, in effect, that induction was not deduction, and that inductive argumentation was deductively invalid. One supposes this was clear enough to anyone who spent a second or so thinking about it, but it inaugurated a literature of attempts to justify induction. A pragmatic justification, in terms of its working, for example, could only show that it had worked up to now, and what guarantee was there that tomorrow fire might not freeze, snow might not burn, and rodents might not begin to sing Italian opera, and so on? There are many philosophical twists and turns in these woods, and the intellectual scenery is well worth the trip, but our concerns here are not with the justification of induction, the nature of causality, and so on, but with the simple recognition that the inducing brain exists, and what effect this might have on the nature of science, and, in particular, historiography.

The human being, as several other species, is a pattern-seeking animal. It wants to make sense out of the world. It seeks meaning and it is likely to find it, whether it is there or not.

The human being, if necessary, will impose meaning on the world. It is his nature.

This is something important to understand as we delve farther into historiography. The historian is going to make sense out of what he is working with, and won't stop until it does make sense. Putting aside the explanation of chancery seals, giving accounts of the rules for dynastic succession, exposing forged documents, and such, the historian is out to tell a story, and, hopefully, one which is true, or more likely, true enough, or not all that far off from what really happened.

In short, we expect the historian, and he expects himself, to find meaning, and pattern, in history. He wants it there. He demands that it be there. It must be there. And he is going to find it there, whether it is there or not. We expect him not merely to recount, but to explain, and one can only explain by making sense out of things. He has, and I suppose most of us have, what Charles Sanders Peirce referred to as "the irritation of doubt," and what scratches that itch is a fixed belief, one we are satisfied with. When we are satisfied, we stop looking. The fixed belief, obviously, from a common-sense point of view, may be fixed, but false. Peirce went on to try to give an account of truth in terms of a sort of idealized fixed belief that was fated to be the fixed belief to be arrived at under an ideality of conditions, and such, but that is not much help here, or not of obviously much help here.[1]

The notion that things should make sense is not only native to many species, but seems to constitute a compulsion of sorts. Things may, of course, make sense. But then, again, they might not. The world may not be a mistake, but it is not clear it is on purpose either. One of the philosopher's jobs, or, at any rate, common employments, at least in the old days, was to construct, or borrow, a *Weltanschauung*, which is a world view, or, better, given the meaning of '*Anschauung*', a world *vision*. How do things fit together? The philosopher usually had this presupposition, like most folks, that things did fit together. On the other hand, a *Weltanschauung* need not be this optimistic. It would be enough if it was right. For example, one can conceive of a *Weltanschauung* in which the notion was that the world was a sort of meaningless happenstance, and it was our job not to betray it with rationalizations, but to make the best of it, as we could. If the world doesn't make sense, it would be nice to know that, as well. The historian, on the other hand, is expected to make sense of his world, whether it makes sense or not. To be sure, the scientist seems to labor under a similar cultural obligation.

The inducing brain seems to be at work everywhere. Folks ask what is the meaning of existence, of the universe, of life, of history, of Timmy's dog having a broken leg, and so on. Some fellow has a narrow escape, and then begins to ponder why, and what this

---

[1] This approach to matters is far more interesting, valuable, and plausible, at least in my view, if one is attempting to work out a theory of philosophical truth, as opposed to, say, one of logical or empirical truth. Cf. *The Cognitivity Paradox: An Inquiry Concerning the Claims of Philosophy* (Princeton University Press, 1970).

means he should do with the rest of his life, and so on. Some people seem to think that everything happens for a purpose, which puts quite a burden on everything. People used to look for clues in herbs, as to their medical value. Surely that kidney-shaped structure was a hint, etc. Some people seemed to think the main point of the Roman empire, the pervasiveness of Latin, the absence of borders, the excellent system of roads, and such, was intended to facilitate the spread of a particular religion, their own, and such. What was the meaning of wings? Surely that the bird could get off the ground, and elude cats. And what was the meaning of the cat's fangs and claws, that it could catch birds, and such. Aristotle seemed to think that the meaning, or end, or teleology, of the acorn was to produce an oak tree, and such. And he was about as smart as one can get.

So we should keep the inducing brain in mind when thinking about historiography. It is a blessing, is it not, which may lead us to insights and discoveries, and, is it not, sometimes a lure and menace, which may dazzle, beckon, and befuddle us into stupidities which, perhaps mercifully, we may never detect. Truth crushed to earth may rise again, but, if it didn't, we wouldn't find out about it.

4. Trajectory and the 5-D Map

From our own point of view, we are for the most part, our memories. Without these memories, recent and those acquired over years, we would have very little sense of ourselves. Without them we would be a stranger to ourselves, the inhabitant of a mysterious alien body. We would be as Adam awakening, and wondering, following Milton, "How came I thus, how here?" Except that there would be no language, and no sense of "I." At best there would be a cloud of wonder dissociated from a source. So we have this sense of self, largely constituted by memory, and an awareness of a moment, seemingly taken up and extended, a sense of a "now," a sense of our whereabouts, and a sense of direction, of anticipation, of the future. These are the three conscious ingredients of our being, whatever may be the cellular foundations, the unnoted motivations, the unseen engines, which lift this surprising phenomenon out of a subterranean nature into the sunlight of awareness. And so in this remarkable moment we have memory, awareness, and projection. We have a sense of past, present, and future. We are on the road. We are going somewhere. We have directionality. We have a sense of where we have been, where we are, and how things might be, where we might go, and what we might do. The bird of consciousness is always in flight. Note that each of these remarkable, hastening, fused ingredients, which in their reality elude the language, the clumsy counters, in which we must describe them, is essential to the whole. Without memory our reality would be unintelligible; so, too, if we were limited to a single flash of consciousness, without a sense of past and future; and there could be no sense of a future, if there were no sense of a past and present. For our purposes here, let us call attention to what we might refer to as the trajectory of consciousness. Without this trajectory consciousness in the human sense could not exist; at best one would sustain incomprehensible sensations, pressures, perhaps some comforts, and discomforts.

Understanding needs this sense of trajectory.

The view of an instant is inadequate. We need this sense of direction. Imagine the impossibility of judging a fly ball if one could note it just once, as it might appear in a photograph. One would have no idea of its origin, its flight, its descent. It would make no sense. Not only could you not catch it; you would not even have an idea of where it is, because you can't really know where it is unless you know where it has been and where it seems to be going. Those things tell us where it is.

As the saying has it, analogies limp, but the analogy with historiography, lame or not, is clear.

The historian supplies us with an essential element in social and cultural consciousness. He gives us a sense of where we have been, without which we cannot understand, fully, where we are. He illuminates the present, giving us some sense of how we got where we are, and why. The analogy with the fly ball, of course, is quite imperfect. The fly ball is a simple thing, however difficult it may be to catch. It is subject to a limited number of comprehensible conditions. The historian's account of the past, however valuable, will be, and must be, grossly oversimplified, and doubtless, in many respects, just wrong.

The past is no fly ball. So our understanding of the present, based on his work, may be more useful, more seemingly enlightening, than true. Similarly, considering the dubious and unlikely foundations of conjectures based on an inevitably misunderstood past and present, one is not sanguine about the feasibility of prediction, and most historians wisely eschew soothsaying. They know, if we do not, the difficulties of judging complex, mysterious fly balls that one has never seen, based on fragmentary reports of its position, reports often supplied by sources which would rather you never caught it at all. Too, of course, knowledge enters the causal stream and cancels all bets. Many an individual may see where the ball is going and then intervene, to make sure it never gets there. The system is not isolated. Intrusions abound. And there is always the possibility, to be considered later, that the past is not a natural phenomenon, even a complex natural phenomenon. Not only may it not be a fly ball, but it may be something very different from stones and stars, from pendulums and gears, from thermodynamics and meteorology. That will be considered later.

If we are to understand the world, however inadequately, we must understand it as at least a five-dimensional structure. In short, to make sense of things, beyond the conveniences of mathematics and measurement, we need to add to the three dimensions of space and the one of time, another, one of history, a fifth dimension, without which the world is utterly incomprehensible.

As historical creatures we live in a five-dimensional world.

History is not an intellectual superfluity, a cognitive luxury; an inessential joy; it, like space and time, supplies us with coordinates, coordinates without which we cannot locate ourselves. Without the 5-D Map we do not know where we are.

5. The Importance of Comprehension

Analogous to the selections which favor certain genetic linkages, are social and historical selections which tend to favor certain ideological linkages. Some of these ideological linkages are quite tenacious and seem to promote themselves regardless of their dubious or negative effects on human welfare. Social psychoses are common. Part of the psychosis, of course, is that the terrified victim must inflict the same madness on his offspring, or supposedly suffer a fate too dire to contemplate. And so the contagion lingers and spreads. Certainly some clever fellows with an agenda, usually prestige, power, and a free ride through life, must have thought up this wisdom. If not, it seems in any event they profit nicely from it. One property of the poison syrup is that one must feed it to the innocent, wherever found, usually in the cradle. It seems important to comprehend this sort of thing, and history may furnish the antidote to insanity, by discovering its etiology and the utility it once served. The more one learns about poison the less likely one is to prescribe and dispense it.

Without history one is carried by the current. It would be nice to know how the current came about, and where it might be taking us.

Certainly any rational individual without an ax to grind would find this of interest.

The current, of course, might be complex and benign. Some of the most marvelous and intricate achievements of the human species worked themselves out, in virtue of countless interactions, billions of them, bit by bit, generation by generation, century by century. There are historical ecologies, and balances, and proportions, similar to, but less fearful and harrowing, than those of nature. The classical dichotomy between the natural and the artificial, or conventional, succumbs to the fallacy of incomplete division. This is called to the attention of those who are intellectually free enough to look into these matters by the analysts of systemic processes, by evolved-order theorists. Much that is of most value to humanity is "the product of human action but not of human design." These things are worked out in smithies few know exist. Consider the cornucopia of wealth consequent upon the division of labor; the market, developed over generations; the language you speak, with its incredible lexicon, its subtlety and sophistication; resulting from centuries of vitality and service; the structure of the law, raised over millennia, decision by decision, judgment by judgment; the morality you had best hope the majority of your fellow men continue to take seriously, and so on. These things work. They are mighty, awesome, and proven. It is not clear they can be judiciously discarded in favor of things worked out in libraries.

At least one might think a little.

Might not the historian legitimately take note of such things?

Might not the results of his researches serve a purpose, perhaps suggesting social or political caution?

Let the "thousand-year perspective" be celebrated. It is not obviously inferior to that of last Tuesday, or that of this afternoon.

Might not the efforts of the historian mitigate to some extent, in some minds, the arrogance of contemporary megalomaniacs. There are always costs, always trade-offs. The bridge built here is not built there. Economics is the study of scarce resources which have alternative uses. It is hard to predict the results of action. Martin Luther presumably did not intend to further a radical freedom of thought, freedom of the press, the liberation of peasants, the growth of democracy, and such. Nor, one supposes, did Hegel intend the Gestapo or Marx the KGB. But I am less sure about Marx. In any event the historian might encourage us, before we hurry to solve the latest problem, to look ahead, and sideways, as well. And remember that scarce resources always have alternative uses. His work might remind us to spend wisely. Is A really more important than B, or is A merely noisier?

The importance of comprehension might seem even more imperative, when we keep in mind the ideological utilities of history. History offers propaganda a remarkable and frightening weapon, and is easily abused, even by those whom one might hope would know better.

There is a story which has to do with the Prussian general staff, in the second half of the nineteenth century. As the story goes a young Prussian officer expresses his concern over what will be the judgment of history, if a particular morally suspect military operation is implemented. As the story goes, a senior officer puts his concerns to rest by reassuring him that they will write the history.

Winners usually write the histories.

This is not surprising.

Does it make a difference to our understanding of the past?

Perhaps.

Generals used to carry historians with them, as part of their baggage. What sort of history would they write? Hopefully one that would not leave them behind for the Parthians.

Antonio Gramsci was a brilliant Communist tactician. It was clear to him that as the productive bounty of capitalism, in which mass production serves the masses, or the capitalist goes out of business, was constantly and remarkably improving the quality of human life, that it was going to be progressively more and more difficult to get the worker to the barricades, to risk his life for a lower standard of living, to die for subservience to the state, and such, so a new tack was in order. The new tack was to infiltrate the media, education, unions, and even religion, so that the culture wars might be won. What could not be bought by bayonets and bullets might be bought in the newspapers, the class rooms, the pulpits, and such, with consequences, naturally, at the ballot box. Democracy may bear within itself the seeds of its own destruction. Democracy could be the road to statism. Did it not put Hitler into power? One might freely vote to end freedom. Has it not been done? This is what Gramsci called "the march through the institutions." I mention Gramsci here because he gives us a wonderful illustration of a marvelously contrived program for an ideological offensive, one declining to advertise its weaponry and carefully concealing both its mission and objective. And prominent and essential amongst all this legerdemain would be history, because we build our future on our understanding of the past. This sort of thing, of course, need not be limited to a particular political or religious program. This sort of thing is quite neutral. It, like a knife, or bomb, can be of service to any fanaticism.

What protection is there for us, except for the historian who is doing his best to tell the truth?

How tragic that he might congratulate himself on his treachery, and regard as his proper mission the betrayal of his discipline.

Imagine a Nazi history of the Holocaust. It would certainly be rationalized, if not justified. There was no choice. It had to be done, it should have been done, and so on. It wasn't as bad as some think, etc. Indeed, it might not even appear in a Nazi history.

There are individuals, in the Middle East, and elsewhere, one understands, who deny the Holocaust, or minimize it. To most informed individuals this seems incomprehensible, or preposterous, even morally hideous. But that is precisely because they are informed. What if they were not informed? One of the most common behaviors of any collectivism, statism, authoritarianism, or tyranny, historically, is to practice the ruthless suppression of whatever might, in its perception, appear to menace its power. One controls the human being, of course, by means of the mind of the human being. The vast majority of a population cannot very well be imprisoned or done away with. That only works with minorities. The key to control is to use the prisoner as his own jailer. Let us suppose that a planetary caliphate, or such, is eventually imposed on the human race. If it did not find the memory of the Holocaust congenial, or in its interest, that memory, for most people, would disappear. Jewish communities, if extant, would doubtless remember, for a long time. But eventually one might hear of such things only in darkened rooms in whispers, by candlelight, and perhaps, after a time, even Jewish youngsters would begin to wonder if the old stories might be exaggerated, or invented, perhaps for religious purposes. Have not such things been done, often enough, in the past?

We are at the mercy of our historians.

One hopes they will not abuse the trust we place in them.

Surely one of the most deplorable of intellectual crimes is the subversion of history to ideological purposes.

Or do we all do that, and it can't be otherwise, so let us all, our consciences now clear, enter the lists in the distortion wars.

We reject here, incidentally, what is, in effect, a Thrasymachian theory of truth, that truth is what those in power prefer. The best propaganda, of course, is that which is true, but is not the whole truth, namely, truths carefully selected to clip facts like hedges, creating desired shapes, or designed to spin real street signs, leading to predetermined addresses. Truths judiciously arranged will support the house of falsity. The scholar activist, much with us today, out of the orthodoxy of Marx's Eleventh Thesis on Feuerbach, has transcended the prosaic occupation of trying to understand the world, presumably a heritage of an unraised consciousness, and is now out to change it.[2] Understanding the world is not easy; and no one has really managed it yet, which is depressing; and why bother anyway; changing it is more fun. It is interesting that individuals who know enough not to tinker with an automobile engine, have so few reservations about transforming society. But this is supposing one bothers about truths, at all, even their misuse. Absolute falsity is welcome, as well, assuming it is difficult to detect. Is not the lie the ideal's best friend? Falsehood in the proper cause is the new name of truth. In any event, though we will consider these matters, our own project here is not conversion but comprehension. Whereas it may be politically judicious to substitute falsity for truth, one should at least, if only in the interests of civility, own up to what one is doing, or would that spoil the game? But then is not the respect for truth, and its pursuit, not merely another tactic of benighted oppressors, like their pursuit, however, imperfect, of logic , rationality, objectivity, and such? To be sure, an ideology which requires irrationality, fallacy, distortion, misrepresentation, subjectivity, relativism, and so on, and accepts these things as inevitable, and celebrates them as therapeutic and instrumental, is not likely to have universal appeal. Therefore, it will continue to talk about truth. It is hard to play chess with folks who are busy bowling or doing tennis with croquet mallets, or planting bombs, and think you are up to the same recreation. In short, for the most

---

2 If Marx is correct, of course, and historical developments are inevitable, and such, this encouragement to change the world is gratuitous. One might as well sit about and wait. Or was it merely determined that Marx was merely determined to utter such exhortations, and it was also merely determined that others would be merely determined to act or not act? What is the point of it all? And how can one "hasten birth pangs"? Can one hasten the tides or the phases of the moon? This is an example of the "Hortatory Paradox," where, say, a determinist urges you to believe in determinism, to adopt his deterministic faith, or philosophy, or such. It makes no sense. It's already all "in the can," laid out amongst the gas molecules of the primeval nebula, in the designs of a divine entity, in the insouciant, implacable teleology of *Geist*, or whatever. You cannot have it both ways. You have determinism or you don't. But consistency is a great deal to ask from any human being. Whoever asked Marx to be consistent? It wasn't Hegel. Scientific materialism, here, seems to be neither a materialism nor scientific, though one can appreciate the motivation for calling it both. It is, however, an excellent example of an ideology, complete with the usual pretensions.

part, we have an old-fashioned notion of truth in mind. If this is reactionary or insufficiently progressive, so be it. Why should truth be on the side of those who deny it?

6. The Urgency of Comprehension

There are various theories of organic evolution, whether Darwinian or Neo-Darwinian, whether incremental or cataclysmic, whether founded on micromutations or macromutations, and such, but they do have in common that they are all theories of organic evolution. Few folks today, statistically, even religious folks, believe in a wholesale or retail special creation. It would be much niftier, or more elegant, surely, for a divine entity to manufacture one primeval replicator and turn it loose than to bother with a large number of special creations. For example, there are some 800 thousand insect species. And that would take a lot of creating. A lesser god, for example, might have to spend all Tuesday afternoon on that job. It would be much more impressive, as the analogy goes, for the billiard champion to hit one ball, have that hit two, and so on. That would be a real shot. To be sure, as the vast majority of all species are extinct, a few of those shots may have gone wrong, unless, of course, that was the point of the shot, that it should go wrong. For the purposes of what we are doing here, we are supposing that some theory of organic evolution is correct, even if it has not yet been discovered. We are, further, supposing that natural selection is most pertinent to our purposes. We shall then ignore the other side of the coin, sexual selection, though this is not to be construed as any disparagement of its results, with many of which I am more than pleased.

The first point now is to consider what properties would be likely to bring a species to the top of the food chain. A moment's reflection will suggest that they may not be a universalized altruism, a generalized benignity, a noble tolerance of diversity, habitual passivity, cosmic love, a ready and unthinking penchant for self-sacrifice, and such. Presumably of greater utility would be intelligence, energy, aggression, ambition, self-seeking, egocentricity, a certain lack of scruples, and so on.

Here we might distinguish between organic evolution and technological, or superorganic evolution, the evolution of devices, tools, and such. Whereas there are many analogies between these forms of evolution, there is at least one characteristic in which they differ, radically. Organic evolution is, for most practical purposes, arithmetical, or incremental, even if it skips between two and five every so often. Technological, or superorganic evolution, for most practical purposes, proceeds differently, rather geometrically. Millions of years separates small, hairy, shambling creatures huddled at a squatting place from the first forms of life we might be willing, with reservations, to call human, and thousands of years later there is very little, if anything, probably nothing, which physically separates that form of life from the modern human being. It was "modern," except that it lived a long time ago, or, one supposes, we are "ancient," except that we are still around. Obviously technological, or superorganic, evolution, is quite different. Geologically, a blink of time separates the flint chip from the computer chip, the stone club from the intercontinental ballistic missile.

Konrad Lorenz, the naturalist, has noted that the dove, interestingly regarded as a symbol of peace, is a rather nasty, aggressive little fellow. He has a small beak and spends a certain amount of his time punching other doves in the head with that beak, which, happily, as a weapon, doesn't do much damage. On the other hand, the raven, which has a sharp, dangerous beak, is a gregarious fellow who spends very little time annoying his flock brothers. Now if the dove was equipped with the raven's beak there might be few doves about. The life of the average dove, if not solitary, would be likely to be, following Hobbes' speculations, prior to the social contract, nasty, brutish, and short. The moral of Lorenz's apprehensions is that, in effect, in the case of the human, the dove has, in virtue of technological, or superorganic, evolution, equipped himself with the raven's beak. Unless one is a trained martial-arts type, a commando, or such, it is not easy to kill another human being with one's hands. One has to get close, one might not manage it, the other human might object, and so on. On the other hand, with a stone club, a wooden spear, or a forty-five caliber bullet, there is no big problem. With a hydrogen bomb or a crafted virus there is even less of a problem. One does not even have to get close or pay attention to the results of one's work.

The next piece in this puzzle, which must be fitted in place, is what one might call "the Mystery of the Silent Sky." Probably everyone is familiar with, even if peripherally so, SETI, the Search for Extraterrestrial Intelligence. In this endeavor, one listens for, so to speak, signals, or evidence of rational life in the universe, perhaps having failed, as cynics might suggest, to find it at home. Before this is dismissed as mindless hokum, fascinating only to fourteen-year-old males with unusually high IQ's, it should be clearly understood, for a variety of reasons we do not have time to consider here, that there are many reasons, statistical, physical, biochemical, and meteoric, and so on, for conjecturing that life, rationality, culture, and technology would be common, even abundant, in the universe. This may be a serious mistake, of course. It may be that in a universe in which galaxies are as plentiful as blackberries, and more so, endless horizons of blackberries, we, on our small planet orbiting a minor star on the edge of one of the smaller galaxies are the only form of rational life in the entire universe, the best that the universe could manage. That is possible. On the other hand, given the supposition that that seems incredible, one is entitled to ask Fermi's question, "Where are they?" There are, of course, dozens of possibilities why we have not discovered empirical evidence of other forms of rational life, if it is there, for example, such forms of life might not be interested, philosophically, religiously, or socially in communicating; they might be afraid to do so; they might be isolationistic; their civilization might not be technological; if it is aquatic it would have difficulty lighting fires under water and smelting metals; it might be signaling vigorously, but in a manner we cannot detect, and have not yet discovered, and so on. On the other hand, one of the more plausible, and alarming theories, is the "theory of the bent arrow." The notion here is that the arrow of progress, sped by an energetic, intelligent, belligerent, acquisitive, xenophobic species, qualities which brought its competitive representatives to the point of planetary preeminence over other species, is likely to turn inward, and wreak its own destruction, and that of the civilizations which produced it. The dove forged for itself the raven's beak. The notion then is that violence and aggression, properties once useful in ascent, may, at a given point of technological sophistication, turn inward, and lead to an inevitable descent, to the destruction of civilizations, and perhaps of the species which formed them. Within the seed may lie the destiny of its own dissolution. The wings that enabled flight may eventually be folded in fiery sleep. Once more the flight of Icarus has carried him too near the sun.

Beyond the commendable efforts of the historian of last Tuesday, bless him, for he deserves and will get tenure, one hopes for something more from the students of the past. One would like to consider the geography of the forest, not merely speculations concerning particles of bark on the more accessible trees. Doubtless there is an important role for the historical microscope. That is not to be denied. But, too, is there not in the universe of history a role for a different instrument, the historical telescope, which would inquire into far things, and examine large spaces.

What of trajectory?
What of the silent sky?
What of the future?
What of the past? We learn what the human being is from what the human being has thought, and done. Are we to find encouragement here, or despair?

Can anything be learned from the lives of vanished societies, from the ruins of former civilizations? Are portents of decline about us, unnoticed, ignored, or brushed aside?

No one expects the historian to be a prophet, a prognosticator. One would like him, however, to be brave, and risk high limbs, from which more can be seen. Should he try to say something large or important, or meaningful, he is likely to be derided by his smaller brethren, but what better evidence is there of his having actually said, or having actually tried to say, something large or important, or meaningful?

Historians give society its memories, false or veridical; they illuminate our present; they help us to consider our future.

It is difficult to see how the importance of this discipline could be overestimated.

Let us now proceed, however imperfectly and inadequately, to consider its foundations, nature, and limitations; in short, let us proceed to the philosophy of historiography.

II. Some Distinctions

1. *Historia*

I think it would be well, initially, to sort out some of the things that might be meant by 'history', 'historiography', and 'philosophy of history.' Following that, we will have a better sense of our particular concerns, which might be referred to under the rubric of 'philosophy of historiography'.

The English word 'history' is derived ultimately from the Greek word which, transliterated into English letters, would be '*historia*'. The original meaning of the word seems to have been twofold, suggesting an intellectual project, wherein one learns by inquiring, and, secondly, a narrative. Whereas much of this is obscure, one might contrast a learning by inquiry, from a learning by, say, mathematical insight and proof construction, of which a paradigm case would be the thirteen books of Euclid. Many Greek philosophers, but certainly not all, were what might be called rationalists. The rationalist is not likely to inquire, in the sense of questioning eye witnesses, and such, but to draw inferences from what appear to him to be indubitable or necessary truths. This might be regarded as an inquiry of sorts, one supposes, into the bones of being, or such, but it is not like locating documents, interviewing old soldiers, visiting battlefields, and so on, hoping to construct a plausible account of, say, the Persian or Peloponnesian Wars. One hopes, then, that the notion of a learning by inquiry refers to a particular sort of intellectual endeavor, different from the usual pursuit of the rationalist. Greek intellectuals, if we may take Aristotle as a fair representative of the category, tended to regard history on the whole as inferior to, and less informative than, scouting about for forms, and such. Poetry, for Aristotle, was superior to history; for example, poetry dealt with kinds, with generalities, and thus its truth scope was broader and more profound than that of history, which just worried about what, say, Alcibiades, or someone, might have been up to at one time or another. The universal was usually regarded as more enlightening and significant than the particular. They believed in universals, forms, and such. Another encouragement to the neglect of history by rationalists was presumably their general lack of a historical consciousness. History was not going anywhere, unless in circles. Men were born, suffered, and died. Colonies were founded, cities were sacked, armies marched, battles were fought and won, and lost, and so on. It was all pretty much the same. What else was new? History was journalism, not science. Also, perhaps more piteously, history could not, by its very nature, achieve knowledge, because there could be no knowledge without necessity, that by definition. Apodictic reasoning guarantees truth, but empirical evidence, at best, can supply only probability. Indeed, it, following Plato, can supply nothing better than opinion, never knowledge. One can count on the sum of the interior angles of a triangle, provided it's not in this world, but Alcibiades was notoriously unreliable, and so, too, hearsay, reports, or guesses about his whereabouts, actions, and motivations. So we will suppose that "learning by inquiring" involved the sort of thing a historian might do, rather than the sort of thing a mathematician, a speculative physicist, theorizing from a marble armchair, a metaphysician, might do. The second meaning of 'historia', namely, a narrative, rings familiar bells. Whereas a historian is likely to do much more than construct narratives, that job is one with which he is commonly associated. It is important to keep in mind, of course, that a particular sort of narrative is in mind, namely, one which is the result of inquiring, a narrative which purports to be true.

2. History

The word 'history' in English has two reasonably clear senses, or sets of senses. There is history in the sense of what occurred, what was the case, and such, which might be called Alpha history, primary history, subject history, event history, deed history, or such, and history in the sense of dealing with the first sort of history, which one might call Beta history, secondary history, report history, inquiry history, account history, or such. Since the two senses of 'history' in English are not likely to be confused, and which is intended should be clear from a context, we will not bother to distinguish further between these two senses, as they are familiar, and unlikely to result in any confusion. Indeed, it might seem a bit pedantic to do so. At any rate, it is not necessary.

We do have, however, senses within each sense which might be important to sort out.

In what immediately follows, we are concerned with what we spoke of as the first sort of history, namely, that sort of history with which the second sort of history is concerned.

Whereas one can multiply these things well beyond semantic necessity, so to speak, there do seem to be three general categories involved here, which are often encountered.

These are each good senses of 'history' in English, but they are not, at least for the most part, the sort of thing with which the historian, *qua* historian, is likely to be concerned.

One sense of 'history' is very broad, the past, namely, whatever has taken place. In this sense one might speak of the history of the cosmos, the history of stars, the history of the earth, the history of animal life on the planet, the history of the horse, and so on.

The next sense of history is the human past. This, too, is quite broad. In one sense it is goes too far back, and in another sense it includes too much. Tracing the emergence of primitive hominids into primitive humans is certainly of great interest and importance, but it is unlikely the historian will be looking into this. Similarly, the rudiments of culture, the transition from Paleolithic to Neolithic technology, the transition from a hunting/gathering economy to a herding/agricultural economy, the management of fire, the invention of the lever and wheel, the working of metals, and such, while of great historical importance, are not what we expect our historian to be dealing with, or not much, at any rate. Similarly, this sense of history not only goes too far back, so to speak, but includes too much. Most of the human past is not likely have, or seem to have, historical importance. Hundreds of thousands of people, in the distant past, and later, in the less distant past, even yesterday, one supposes, have crossed the Rubicon, but history is not interested in most of them.

When the author was younger one could date history, if so inclined, from the first appearance of written records, say, about 3300 B.C. That was arbitrary, but it did give one a place to start, a way of drawing a distinction.

Historians, today, of course, would reject the notion that their work is founded exclusively on written sources. They profit from the labors of archaeologists, anthropologists, astronomers, linguists, physicists, and so on.

The third sense of the first sort of history is the *significant* human past. An inquiry into the origin of the pretzel or a concern with the history of buttons would probably be dismissed as antiquarianism. I myself am fond of pretzels and often rely on buttons, and would not mind learning more about them, but then I am not a historian. On the other hand, where it is reasonably clear what is involved in crossing a small stream it seems less clear what counts as the *significant* crossing of the stream. What are the criteria for *significance*? In a subsense of 'history' here, the historian wishes to be concerned with the *objectively* significant human past, presumably not with the mere *personally* or *subjectively* significant human past. I am not suggesting this is an unintelligible undertaking, the delineation of the *objectively* significant human past, but it seems obvious that legitimate differences of opinion might appear. For example, is it really important what side of the road one walks on or on which side of the shirt buttons are sewn? It seems not. Yet the English keep to the left side of the road. In this way, if one is right-handed, as are most folks, one's sword arm faces the oncoming stranger. Does this tell us something about Roman Britain, about Medieval

England? Similarly, the buttons on a man's shirt are on the right side. Is this a mere convenience? Perhaps. It also facilitates the natural across-the-body draw of an edged weapon. That, too, is interesting.

3. History, again.

So now we come to the second sort of history, with a set of senses similarly familiar, though obviously different from those of what we have spoken of as the first sort of history.

One sense of 'history' here is that of dealing with or engaging the past. For example, it is taken as a subject matter; it is a study; it is an investigation; it is an object of memory; and one might even speak of "teaching history," "taking a course in history;" "majoring in history," and so on.

A second set of senses here would be that of purportedly true accounts of the past. We might encounter along these lines narratives, articles, monographs, films, plays, tales, ballads, poems, perhaps the Song of Roland, and so on, such things. These need not be written down, of course. They could be oral in nature, as the chantings of skalds, the performances of minstrels, the tales of itinerant storytellers, and such. Note that we are suggesting that these accounts are purportedly true. They need not be true, of course. If truth requires the whole truth and nothing but the truth there are probably no true histories. The whole truth, for example, is never known. The most we can expect of the historian, morally, is that he does his best to be fair, and not to lie. Professionally we can expect much more. Even the maliciously contrived false history purports to be true. History is to be distinguished from the historical novel, even if the historical novel happens to be true. History purports to be true. The historical novel does not purport to be true.

Consider the following *Gedankenexperiment*.

A historical novelist, Person[1], writes a historical novel. He intends it to be, and believes it to be, a work of fiction. A madman, Person[2], during a succession of seizures, unaware of what he is doing, writes an extended piece of prose. A mystic, Person[3], seemingly receiving reports in a dream from a supposed eyewitness of certain historical events, who wishes the truth about them to be known, transcribes upon awakening the supposed eyewitness's accounts. Lastly, suppose that a historian, Person[4], after a considerable amount of diligent research, sifting through documents, and such, constructs a historical narrative pertaining to a series of events which seems to have taken place in the past. The work of the historian is undoubtedly history. Let us further suppose that the historian's account is true. Now suppose, as a logical possibility, that all four productions, those of the novelist, the madman, the mystic, and the historian are identical in content.

The question, then, might be, are the productions of the novelist, the madman, and the mystic also history? If so, why? If not, why not?

An excellent reason for taking all four accounts to be history, is that account Four, that of Person[4], the historian, is clearly history, even if totally false, and accounts One, Two, and Three, those respectively of Person[1], Person[2], and Person[3] are identical to it. It seems as though identity theory here might be regarded as not only embarrassing but insurmountable. For example, If A has property P, say, being history, and B, C, and D are identical with A, then it seems that B, C, and D must also possess property P, in this case, the property of being history. Certainly we cannot restrict the writing of history to historians, for anyone might write history, nor can we usefully beg the question, requiring that anyone who writes history, *ipso facto*, is, by definition, a historian. The main problem here is not that some dentists might turn out to be historians, which might be the case, or that Susan, recording last night's tussle with Bob in her diary, is a historian, but, rather that this approach, and identity theory, would seem to suggest that the accounts of Person[1], Person[2], and Person[3] must also be accepted as history. We are supposing, however, that this approach would produce cognitive discomfort and one must look further. Requiring that the account must purport to be true allows us to dismiss the account of Person[1] as history, for he is writing, and claims to be writing, a historical novel. This gives us an escape route from identity theory by enlarging our criteria for an historical account beyond the mere content of the account. Thus the accounts of Person[1], the historical novelist, and Person[4] are no longer identical. We may suppose that the work of Person[1], the novelist, is "true to the period," and such, but that does not count. He would not be much of a historical novelist, if it weren't. We might still have problems with Person[2], the madman, and Person[3], the mystic, of course, should both purport their accounts to be true. It seems likely they would do so.

Let us suppose that is the case, that both purport, or presume, their accounts to be true.

We might be able to eliminate Person[2], the madman, on the basis of a citable-evidence requirement. He produces no citable evidence, alleged, or otherwise. The truth of his account is not at issue, only whether or not it should count as history. It is certainly possible that, as logic is tolerant except where contradictions threaten its security, that the ravings of Person[2] might invariably prove to be true, stand up to subsequent empirical inquiry, might be invariably confirmed, and so on. If this should turn out to be the case we would have on our hands a remarkable epistemological phenomenon. Presumably such a phenomenon would be received with interest, and possibly elation, by parapsychologists. Perhaps not by others. Some might even claim, if only in an unguarded moment, that Person[2] somehow *knows* these things, that he has *knowledge*, even that he *must* have evidence, of a sort, and good evidence, given his high scores in this matter, though evidence of a sort which neither he nor we understand. We may rule against his account, then, either generally, because there is no evidence, or, in this case, no citable evidence. Obviously if there is no evidence, *simpliciter*, there is no citable evidence. Person[3], on the other hand, the mystic, does have citable evidence. He has an alleged eyewitness report, which he cites. This report, delivered in a dream, even if false, which, in this case, by supposition, it isn't, is citable. We need then an additional caveat here, in order to dismiss the mystic's account, and it is not far to seek. The evidence must be *public*.

Accordingly, our revised criterion for an account to qualify as history will be (1) that it is an account which pertains to history in the first sense of 'history', (2) it purports to be true, (3) it is founded on citable evidence, and (4) the evidence is public. On this basis we are justified in accepting the account of Person[4] as history, and rejecting the accounts of Person[1], Person[2], and Person[3] as history, which is what we wanted to do in the first place. In short, history goes beyond content, and has to do, as well, with how that content has come about.[3]

This is a broad notion of history, of course, and the historian might well prefer a narrower one, involving a reference to the objectively significant human past, or such. Here one might find a history of turtles, Susan's diary, and so on. We are interested in a generic concept of history here, of the second sort, however, not one more germane to the historian's customary concerns.

That can come later.

Whereas there are many problems involved here, for example, with respect to the nature of history in its several senses, and the nature of truth, evidence, citability, and such, we will limit the discussion to one additional point. When we require the evidence to be "public," this is understood in the sense that it is public in theory, to qualified interpreters, not in the sense that it requires general accessibility, or current availability. For example, the evidence of radioactive dating is public, but few people would be in a position to obtain and interpret that evidence. Similarly, even more typical chronological determinations might be beyond most people, say, those indexed to Athenian *archon* lists, and such, as might be much evidence in paleography, epigraphy, numismatics, philology, sigillography, and so on. Also, evidence, to be public, need not be publicly available. One individual might speak to another privately; that is acceptable because it is pubic in theory; another might have listened, as well. Similarly an individual might have had unique access to a document which

---

[3] The evidence-predicate is not a monadic, or a one-place, predicate, but a polyadic, in this case, a three-place predicate. Logically, the function would not be 'Ex' but 'Exyz'. In short, x is evidence of y to z. Something is evidence of something to someone. For example, the Lincoln penny might be evidence to someone of, say, metallurgy, dies and engraving, racial characteristics, barbering, clothing and tailoring, English and Latin, architecture, geography, political and religious views, chronology, economics, the decimal system, and so on. Consider the existence of a manuscript in a lost language. This is public, but, on the other hand, it is evidence of little more than the existence of a lost language. For most practical purposes it is not evidence. One might speak of potential evidence, but then it is hard to see what might not count as evidence.

was subsequently destroyed. This is acceptable, as others might have had the same access.

The major difficulty with this general approach, since we are rejecting the mystic's account, given the public unavailability of his evidence, even in theory, would seem to be that we must also reject an individual's private memories as evidence, and these are the foundation of all historical evidence. Similarly, I would like to think that an individual's memories constitute a form of history, an interesting one, for the evidence and the account seem to fuse. The evidence, the memories, seem to be the account. Strictly, however, it seems they may be distinguished, in two moments. The first moment is the evidence; the second moment is the taking of the evidence, the memories, as the account. For example, one might doubt the reliability or accuracy of the memory. This exemplifies a cognitive division, one often overlooked. Here one is clear on the nature of the memory, the evidence, but might doubt the account. There is no contradiction in saying I remember it in such-and-such a way, but I now realize it could not have happened in that way. Memory is notoriously unreliable. I suppose one could define memories as veridical, and dismiss misremembering, and such, as not really remembering, but there seems little justification for shaking up and revising psychiatry, clinical psychology, common sense, and so on. If one wishes to do so then one could contrast memories with *seeming* memories, and put things back in place under an alternative nomenclature. But there seems little point in doing so, so we won't.

I think the best way to proceed here, wishing to reconcile the importance of memory, which is private, and wishing to allow for an individual's "private history," based on memory, *with the publicness criterion*, is to recognize a distinction, which seems implicit in our practice, one between personal and interpersonal history, and note that the historian is concerned with interpersonal history, unless dealing with his own memories. This does not preclude the importance of individual memories; it only reminds us that they become of interpersonal importance only when shared, only when expressed, written down, or such.

On this approach we can accept the mystic's *explicit* account of the contents of the dream, based on his memories of the dream, as public evidence of the dream, supposing he is not lying, but we need not accept his account as a history of the alleged events recounted by the dream witness, with its battles, intrigues, alarms, or whatever. All we have evidence for, at best, is the dream. We do not have evidence of the alleged events. There may be independent evidence that the dream was true, but this evidence is not supplied by the dream. Thus we may continue to reject the mystic's account as history. At best it is a public history only of a dream.

As an account of actual events, it fails to meet the criterion of interpersonal corroboration.

Except in our own case, we must deal with externalities, externalities the value of which is largely to open speculative windows on conjecturable internalities, those of other human beings, of other times.

Two last points here:

First, if the "dream witness" had been an actual person, conveying his account to the dreamer, when the dreamer was awake, at, say, the corner of Fifteenth and Main Street yesterday afternoon, that would qualify as public evidence, even if no one else was in the vicinity, hard though that might be to believe at Fifteenth and Main. In such a case, given the accuracy of the report, one would suppose the informant well knew what he was talking about, and might be a valuable source. Once we are dealing with public evidence, it is the historian's task to see to its evaluation, its consistency, its plausibility, the likely soundness of its grounds, its honesty, its coherence with other matters, and so on.

Second, nothing is changed here, really, if the "dream witness" continues to appear to the mystic, and continues to reveal truths, or if the "dream witness" begins to appear in the dreams of several persons, revealing more truths. These accounts would still fail as history, lacking satisfaction of the criterion of publicness. They might constitute, of course, marvelous experiences, have heuristic value in developing hypotheses, suggest lines of research, and such, but they would not, in themselves, qualify as history. History requires more than truth; it requires that the truth be sought in particular ways. A simple consideration makes this clear: Let us suppose that several such accounts can be independently confirmed, for example, Accounts A_1 through A_n, but that all the evidence goes against Account A_{n+1}. This would undermine our confidence in Accounts A_1 through A_n. We might think coincidence; more likely we would think fraud. Perhaps the Cartesian demon had taken up history.

4. Historiography

The meaning of 'Historiography', as commonly understood, is trifold. First, it may mean the history of history, so to speak. In this sense it would be concerned with development of history as a discipline, how it began and changed over time, how notions differed from period to period, and place to place, as to what it should be concerned with, how it should treat its matters of concern, and so on. What should the historian be doing, how should he do it, as the time saw it, and, in fact, how did he do it, what were the results of his doing it, and so on. For example, a great deal of historical water has gone under the bridge between Herodotus and Charles Beard. Flavius Josephus and Livy are quite different. So, too, are Tacitus and Eusebius. And Gibbon is very different from both. Ranke is one thing, Karl Marx is another, and so on. The doing of history and the being of a historian differ from age to age.

A second meaning of 'historiography' is simply historical writings. In this sense it would be much like one of the senses of the second sort of history, which we considered earlier. It would be a bit narrower, however, if one were to be strict about it, as there we allowed for unwritten history, for example, songs, stories, and such. If one were to be a bit more charitable, as one supposes one should be, this sense of historiography might be construed broadly enough to include such things. If so, then we might regard it as identical to the aforementioned sense.

The third meaning of 'historiography' is the discipline of the historian. Here, for example, one might find much of the working equipment of the historian, his backgrounding, orientation, presuppositions, and such, the sort of thing which makes him a historian and not, for example, a physicist, a sociologist, a political scientist, an engineer, or such, for example, his projects, techniques, rules, procedures, practices, ethics, values, lore, and such. Each field has such things.

III. Studies and Metastudies

The philosophy of history has been variously understood. For example, in the Enlightenment the term 'philosophy of history' seemed to function rather analogously to the term 'philosophy of nature'. That term meant, in effect, "science." The "natural philosopher" then was, in effect, a scientist. The term 'science' was not always used for science. The term used to be 'the philosophy of nature'. Along these lines 'philosophy of history' came to mean scientific history, careful history, documented history, critical history, and such. Later, largely thanks to Hegel, for better or for worse, the expression 'philosophy of history' came to mean a profound grasp of the whole of history and a comprehension of its nature and direction. It involved, in theory, an understanding of, and an interpretation of, the whole of human history. That would be, of course, a very ambitious undertaking, but Hegel, happily, whose lacks did not include one of ambition, did not shrink from the task. Philosophy's job, following Hegel, was to comprehend the whole, to comprehend all time and existence, to understand it and its meaning. That is *Weltanschauung* with a vengeance. No wonder Hegel was a full professor. A part of this, obviously, would involve views pertaining to history. Hegel's particular views need not be mentioned here. It is easy for philosophical valets, so to speak, to amuse themselves with the Hegels of the discipline, but the discipline is the better, and the deeper and richer, for them. A value judgment is involved. Is it better to fail at large things, if one fails, or succeed in small things? Certainly large things are not likely to be achieved if they are not attempted; too, large things are seldom the results of small things arranged in careful piles. Large failures are instructive; from small failures one learns little. Presumably every discipline profits both from the bold and reckless and the careful and judicious. Should there not be diversity in the historical gene pool? Why not? Surely there must be a place for the historian of last Tuesday, in Minneapolis, but one might hope, too, that every discipline will be blessed by a few hardy souls who will have no compunction about rushing in where angels, timid angels at least, might fear to tread; there may be some very interesting things there; and why, for example, should some angels fear to enter? That, too, is interesting. Too, not everyone who fears to tread is an angel. Hegel thought he saw the track and where the train was going. There may have been no track and no train, but philosophy has never been the same since. Remarkable journeys may have beneficent effects. Perhaps history has no pattern, and no meaning. But, if so, that would be important to know, as well, and that, too, that view, one notes, involves a *Weltanschauung*, as much as that of Saint Paul or Karl Marx. If one has a brain of a certain level of complexity it is hard to do without a *Weltanschauung*. A third way of taking 'philosophy of history' would characterize the diaper days of sociology, and views commonly associated with the remarkable Auguste Compte. Here the philosophy of history might be contrasted with history. The historian, in the intellectual trenches, accumulates data. The theoretician, in a rather Baconian manner, inquires into this data, and discovers laws which describe, but do not produce, the phenomena of human life and action. History, thus, is a step on the road to sociology. An analogue to the Comptean program emerges in work by C. G. Hempel, to which it will later be instructive to turn.[4]

---

[4] Associated with Compte is one of the classical periodizations of human history, the law of the three stages, the first being the "theological stage," in which individuals commonly believed in one or more anthropomorphic gods or spirits and took them to be explicatory with respect to all or selected phenomena; the second being the "metaphysical stage," in which the anthropomorphic theoretical entities are replaced with theoretical entities of a less personal sort, say, atoms, forces, or such; and the third being the "positivistic stage," in which theoretical entities are abandoned, and one deals with the ascertainable, namely, phenomena

As it is commonly understood today, the philosophy of history is a metastudy, and so, too, would be the philosophy of historiography. I am generally preferring the latter term because, it seems to me, that the philosophy of history has usually been, in effect, the philosophy of historiography. An exception to the notion of the philosophy of history as a metastudy would be, however, the concept of the "speculative philosophy of history," a concept much closer to the Hegelian notion. We will later distinguish between the "analytic philosophy of history," which is a metastudy, and the "speculative philosophy of history," which is a form of history herself, one usually distinguished by its breadth of scope and interpretation.

The metastudy is the study of a study.

That may be helpful.

But not all that helpful, perhaps.

We assume that the notion of a "study" is reasonably clear, for example, physics, chemistry, astronomy, and such are studies. Following Wittgenstein one can recognize plants, and know what one is talking about, when one talks about plants, and so on, without being able to define 'plant'. If one is genuinely confused, and senses one is running into trouble, or talking at cross-purposes with an interlocutor, then one can worry about definitions. Definitions are important, but, like hammers and saws, one need not always draw them from the tool chest. They are not always needed. Socrates might have sought for definitions or forms but if he did not really, honestly, know what he was talking about to start with he would have no way of looking for a definition, or form, in the first place, nor would he have any device for deciding amongst competitive definitions, or forms. Again, following Wittgenstein, we will

---

and its laws. It was not recognized at the time that this would stop science in its tracks. Comptean positivism, incidentally, is not to be confused with the philosophical orientation usually spoken of as logical positivism, or logical empiricism. Compte took it for granted that philosophers would talk about the world, and it did not occur to him that they should, in effect, only talk about talk about the world, that they should limit themselves to projects of clarification, linguistic recommendation, and such.. One of the more interesting aspects of the Comptean philosophy was the invention of a new religion, complete with sacraments and priests. The object of worship here was to be "humanity." It never caught on, perhaps because most people knew more about humanity than Compte.

not spend much time looking for meanings here, necessary and sufficient conditions, or such, which may or may not exist, but will spend some time showing differences. Examples are a good place to start, and might even be where one has to end, unless one is prepared to resort to semantic tyranny, and stipulate, not that there is anything wrong with that, really.

The difference between a study and a metastudy has to do with the sort of questions involved in each, which tend to be different. Science and the philosophy of science are related as study and metastudy, as would be history and the philosophy of history.

Consider some questions in science, some in theoretical science, some in applied science, some simple, some complex, some rather limited, others more general.

What is the boiling point of mercury?
What are the properties of sulfuric acid?
How much does a given volume of air weigh?
How can we produce a stronger, lighter-weight aluminum?
How can we produce a dye that won't fade after repeated washings?
How can we build more efficient bombs?
Why does water boil?
Why does ice melt?
What is light?
Why does the earth move?
Why is it that when I wish to move my hand, my hand moves?

Heraclitus once remarked that he would rather discover one cause than be the King of Persia.

Consider some questions now in the philosophy of science.

What are the criteria for an acceptable scientific explanation?
What is a natural law?
What is the nature of a theory?
What types of entities may figure in scientific explanations?
What statements are allowed to be scientifically meaningful?
When is a hypothesis sufficiently established?

Should, ideally, a sense-data language or a physicalistic language be the base language for science?
Is predictive power a necessary condition for a scientific explanation?
What is a cause?
Is the concept of causality required for scientific explanation?
Is the uniformity of nature a presupposition of scientific inquiry?

Note that these questions cannot be answered by the results of observation and measurement. Microscopes and telescopes, meter sticks and scales, cyclotrons and electrostatic grids are unavailing. The most expensive and sophisticated apparatus and techniques are useless, and irrelevant. Yet the very existence of science, as a rational enterprise entered into by conscious practitioners, presupposes its philosophy, notions as to its presuppositions, purposes, subject matter, objectives, legitimate methodologies and techniques, criteria of assessment and confirmation, its ethics, and so on. Science cannot be coherently and intelligibly practiced, or get on with even its most basic work, without some conception, implicit or explicit, as to what counts as science, how it should proceed, and so on.

In order that this not be misunderstood, we are not supposing here that the typical practitioner of science, her infantryman, so to speak, has even heard of the philosophy of his discipline, has even thought what must be involved for science to be practicable, has given much, if any thought, to meaningfulness, explanation, causality, law, and so on. He does not have to be explicitly aware of these things. It would not occur to him to explain the results of titrations in terms of occult entities, combustion in terms of phlogiston, light in terms of ether, and so on. Nor why this is no longer done. He mixes A and B, and expects C, because that is what is supposed to show up, and regularly, and so on, without bothering himself with why, ultimately, and what can be known and what cannot be known, and so on. Some scientists, of course, are muchly aware of the philosophy of science, and its fascinations, and have written books on the subject. In doing this, of course, they are dealing with the philosophy of science, the logically prior foundations without which the structure of science either could not exist, or would be quite different from what we find it to be today. One could still explain disease in terms of the hostility of gods, who might use germs as their thunderbolts, but we do not, for the most part, at least. Why not? Occam might have a suggestion.

Here are some questions which might be regarded as questions *within* history.

> What were the politics of Egypt in the time of Ikhnaton?
> Who was the tutor of Alexander the Great?
> How did Rome become an empire?
> When was the Donation of Constantine written?
> What were the effects of the invention of the horse collar and the moldboard plow on the society of early Medieval Europe?
> What were the relations between the Papacy and the Holy Roman Empire in the 11th Century A.D.?
> How did the Crusades change Europe?
> Who invented the steam engine?
> What were the social and political effects of the Industrial Revolution in England?
> What were the causes of World War II?

One might then contrast the former set of questions, questions *in* history, with questions *about* history, or, better, with questions in the philosophy of history, or, say, that of historiography.

> Does the past exist? If so, in what sense? Does history need the hypothesis that the past exists?
> Is it possible to know the past, or to know that one knows the past?
> As evidence does not logically entail an account, what is the relationship between evidence and the construction of an account?
> As there are several theories of truth which is that of history, or does history have, or need, a theory of truth?
> What would be the criterion for historical truth?
> Are there historical facts, and, if so, what are they, and how are they to be ascertained?

Is history objective?
Can history be objective?
How is "importance" to be understood in historiography? Are some events more important than others? Suppose A and B are both necessary for C. Might A be more important than B?
What counts as history? What should count as history?
What is a document?
Does reciprocal documentation involve circularity and, if so, what effect might this have on an account?
What are causes in history? Are there unique historical causes?
Is historiographical construction theory-laden?
Does narration necessitate the distortion or falsification of history?
Is moral judgment legitimate in history?
What are the moral responsibilities, if any, of the historian?
As natural language is value-charged, does this jeopardize historiographical objectivity?
Is history relative, and, if so, to what, and does this jeopardize its cognitivity?
Can historical generalizations be obtained objectively?
Are there historical laws?
Are historical events predictable?
Are historiographical hypotheses testable and/or confirmable?
Is human nature an artifact of history?
Is it possible for human beings of one time or place to understand those of a quite different time and place? If not, what effect does this have on historiography? If so, how is that possible, and how could one determine that one is correct?
Is agenda historiography morally and scientifically justifiable, and if not, why not, and, if so, under what conditions?
Is history determined? Might it be determined? Could this be discovered, and confirmed?
Does history reveal a plan or pattern?
How important are individuals in history?
Is history a science?
What should we count as an explanation in history?
Are there irreducible historical categories?

What are the theoretical entities, if any, of history?
Are historical "constructs" real, scientifically acceptable?
Could there be a "Platonic Historian," that is, could there be, at least in theory, the ideal historian? If not, why not? If so, what would the entity be like

IV. Analytic vs. Speculative Philosophy of History

The "versus" in the preceding title is not intended to suggest that there is an incompatibility between the analytic philosophy of history and the speculative philosophy of history. There might too often exist suspicion, if not outright hostility, between the practitioners of these two crafts, the one regarding the other as an eccentric, pompous fraud and he regarding his fellow, in turn, as an unimaginative, bean-counting nincompoop, but the two endeavors in theory fit so nicely together that one might think of them more in terms of the two sides of an important and interesting coin, that of trying to understand history, rather than in terms of oil and water, cats and dogs, statement and negation. To be sure, different sorts of minds are likely to find one or the other more congenial, but it seems that each has its contribution to make, and that the analytic philosophy of history might sharpen the blade of speculation, and that the speculative philosophy of history might dignify and redeem her brother by putting the blade to work.

I think the nature of the analytic philosophy of history, or of historiography, is reasonably clear. At least we tried to make it so, reasonably so, in the preceding section of this work. That is a metastudy, the metastudy of history. On the other hand, the speculative philosophy of history, philosophy of history in its rather

Hegelian sense, is enormously important, even if merely because it might move peoples and societies, and its continent should be indicated, however briefly, on our map. The speculative philosophy of history is not a metastudy. It is history, and whoever does it is doing history. There are many examples of this form of history, to some of which we shall allude, at later times and points. The term will certainly come up in any attempt to deal with either pattern or plan in history, and, time permitting, one might call attention, however briefly and inadequately, to one or more examples of this type of ambitious program. Such histories are large in scope, perhaps dealing with the whole of history, or, in any event, with units of large size; similarly, they often tend to see history in terms of meaning, or direction; something interesting or important is being enacted; often there is a sense of metadynamics involved, namely, that something is working behind or through history; pulling strings, surreptitiously guiding the vessel, or such; and, also, not uncommonly, but not necessarily, such histories tend to anticipate, or predict, destinations. History is going somewhere, and the historian has an idea where. A few examples of such large-scale speculative interpretations of history would be a Christian or Moslem view that history reveals the plan and purposes of a divine entity; or that it manifests, say, the presence of a seemingly pantheistic Absolute Spirit, or *Geist*, intent on maximizing its own view of freedom, probably not ours; that it exemplifies, say, the juggernaut of economic necessity; or that it displays the lovely-in-their-way, aimless, predictable life-cycles of cultures and/or civilizations; or, say, that it heralds the inevitable, if chaotic, forward march of democracy, progress, material welfare, brotherhood, and such. To be sure, one might have philosophies of history which look forward not to a police-state utopia, a planetary universal religion, or such, but cycles of wars, destructions, savageries, barbarisms, and such, the means for which are already well in hand. We might manage to get back to the spear, and the bow and arrow. It is hard not to have a philosophy of history. Even the notion that history is "one damn thing after another," and entirely meaningless, and no more than a waste of cosmic time, is a philosophy of history. To be sure, it is not necessary to have philosophy of history. It might never have occurred to someone to think about such things, or, if it did, he may have made it a point to forgot about it as soon as possible.

V. Varieties of History

Here we wish to remind ourselves of the diversity, complexity, and wealth of historiography and the purposes it might serve. These two recollections, I think, will make clear something of the challenges which the discipline presents to a metastudy, attempting to comprehend it, however inauspiciously or hazardously, and justify to some extent the value and importance of attempting to do so.

1. Types

A useful way to graph the productions of historiography is to distinguish amongst longitudinal, latitudinal, and point studies. Consider a graph in which the y axis is indexed to time, earlier to later, and the x axis to, say, matters political, social, economic, intellectual, and such. The longitudinal, or vertical, study then is one which traces a phenomenon over time, from earlier to later, for example, the development of an idea or an entity over time, say, the development of the idea of democracy or the history of the Aztec empire; the latitudinal, or horizontal, study is one which deals with a given historical entity at a given time, say, the Age of Napoleon; in its various aspects, political, social, and so on; the point study, which might be represented on a graph as the intersection of a longitudinal and latitudinal line is comparatively circumscribed; an example might be an account of the imperial bureaucracy in the time of the emperor Constantine. I think this is an illuminating way of putting order into the historiographical field, but, like all schematisms, it has its bumps and gaps. For example, it would be hard to deal with the idea of democracy without latitudinal considerations, and it would be hard to deal with the Age of Napoleon without longitudinal elements. Every subject of historiographical study is multidimensional, extended in space, and time, even a point study. Nonetheless, I think the graph approach has its merits. It is superior, for example, to dividing historiographical studies into those which deal with Minneapolis last Tuesday and those which do not. That dichotomy is superior logically, but leaves much to be desired from the point of view of pragmatics, common sense, and sanity.

A more chaotic approach, but one which might more appeal to the Wittgenstein of the *Philosophical Investigations*, would be to note political, social, cultural, economic, intellectual, military, religious, etc. histories; or periodized histories, such as Ancient, Medieval, and Modern; or national histories, such as Greek, Roman, French, and such. One might also leave room for autobiographies and biographies, and the biographies might be of individuals, say, of George Washington, or Andrew Jackson, or groups, and such, say, of the AFL, the Green Bay Packers, the Red Cross, the local bowling league, the town's chamber-music group, the Ku Klux Klan, the NAACP, and so on. And then there are the "histories of," as well, histories of art, poetry, sculpture, music, dance, theater, philosophy, mathematics, history, baseball, chess, handwriting, child-raising practices, flight, science and technology, law, and so on. And one hesitates to forget the history of pretzels and buttons, for which I would like to reserve a place, being fond of pretzels and buttons, for different reasons. One supposes there could be a history of about anything to which there was access and for which there was evidence. There is even a history of the stone knife, in a way, which has been reconstructed by paleoanthropologists. We have no history, however, of the fellow, or beast, who picked up the first sharp stone.

2. Agendas

Much light is shed on historiography if one considers the purposes for which it might have been created. It is hard to understand the nature of any artifact unless one knows what it is for. In the Nineteenth Century a frequently found primitive artifact was a sturdy wooden stick, some twelve to eighteen inches in length, with a small, round hole in one end. This was referred to a "baton of command," the object's being understood as a symbol of authority, a scepter, of sorts. Later anthropologists, engaged with contemporary stone-age cultures, found the object in common use for a prosaic purpose. It was an arrow straightener. Branches seldom grow straight but, peeled, warmed over a fire, twisted a bit here and there, with that tool, they make excellent arrow shafts. The analogy to historiography is that it is easier to understand a historiographical artifact, what it includes, what it leaves out, how it is written, and so on, if one knows the purpose of the artifact. One may concern oneself simply with its truth or falsity, but it may well have interests beyond its truth and falsity. It may illuminate a culture. It often points beyond itself. And it is likely to tell truths which are not in the text itself.

I am going to list a few reasons why individuals might write history, and, though not explicitly specified, they would be associated, as well, with reasons why individuals might seek out history, read it, and care for it. There is no particular order, either chronologically, or of imputed merit, in the following list, nor is it intended to be exhaustive. Similarly, as most behavior is multiply motivated, these purposes, or agendas, are not mutually exclusive. There is no reason why one might not do something for several reasons, and most of the time one supposes one does. Similarly, one is not supposing that the historian need be fully aware of the purposes involved. Much motivation , it seems, if one is to take depth psychology seriously, may stay out of sight, and, in many cases, might be well advised to do so. A familiar distinction contrasts good reasons with real reasons. It is not impossible that a historian might, with a clear conscience, and a commitment to objectivity, produce a work which to turns out to be grossly tainted. Evil does not invariably elude the grasp of the well-intentioned. Lastly, one might note that an inference is always involved when one attempts to interpret the intentions of another. It is hard enough to know one's own mind, and, supposedly, most of us don't, let alone understand the mind of another, that of a spouse, of a friend, an enemy, a historical personage. There is behavior, and guesswork. And much of history, too, is guesswork, and must be. Without this understanding there can be no understanding, of another, or of history.

1. Reportorial

The work of the great Nineteenth Century German historian, Leopold von Ranke, surely went beyond reportage. On the other hand, his famous remark, to the effect that history should be written with impeccable accuracy, that the historian's job is to tell us what happened, and exactly how it happened, how it really was (*wie es eigenlich gewesen ist*), makes a nice introduction to this agenda. This is, presumably, from the point of view of many, at least a commonly declared and frequently recognized intent of historiography, a foundational or *Ur* agenda of the discipline. Many may feel it is impossible, for a number of reasons, to satisfy the Rankean ideal, but few would deny that it is an ideal worth seeking. Very few historians will proclaim an agenda of intentional distortion and deliberate falsification. Few would read them unless for clinical interest. Cynics, of course, are always at hand. One hears that history is "a pack of lies agreed upon by historians," for which something is to be said, except that historians are in disagreement. A similar remark is to the effect that history is "an account of something that never happened, written by someone who wasn't there." Fontenelle spoke of "*fables convenues*," or agreed-upon fables, as if there was agreement, and so on.[5] On the other hand, as we shall later see, while the cynics have their point and something to say very well worth considering, it is highly probable that there are

---

[5] Fontenelle seems to have had in mind ancient historians. On the other hand, there is no indication that his suspicions would have stopped at a particular point in historiographical time. Presumably questions of degree would be involved. Mistakes and lies come in all sizes. The expression continues to sum up a viewpoint nicely, allowing for some rhetorical leeway.

abundances of historical truths, and that much historical agreement is plausible, rational, and well founded.

The major shortcomings of this agenda are epistemological, reductive, and psychological.

Whereas it is doubtless the case, putting aside subjective idealism, that things exist whilst unperceived, it must be noted that *if* they are perceived, they are perceived by someone from somewhere and his perception is an ingredient in his first-person experience. Accordingly, we never perceive something as it really is, in itself, but always as it seems to us. This is not to deny that it really is, in some sense, only to recognize that its perception, in the nature of things, must be relative to the perceiver. The rose may really exist, but, if it is seen, it must be seen by someone from somewhere, in some light, and from some angle, and the person may know botany or not, may have normal color vision, and may not, and so on. Now a historical event, unless one is present as an eyewitness, is not only more complex than a rose, but it is also less accessible. What one has to go on is not even a perception of the event, but a conjecturing concerning the event, based on evidence. Even in the case of the eyewitness what he experiences is not the event, as it is in itself, if that makes sense, but his perception of the event, if you like, the event *as he sees it*. This is not a counsel of despair by any means but it does mean that the historian cannot write of the event as it really was, in itself. He can only write of it from a direction, from a background, from a perspective. This does not jeopardize the value, or veridicality, of his account, no more than similar considerations jeopardize the value, or veridicality, of science, but it does call attention to what is going on. Accordingly, it is not possible to describe something, *simpliciter*, as it really was. This is simply an epistemological fact of life. No one is denying the Punic Wars took place, or suggesting that they are in some sense observer-dependent. This is not a sort of Schrödinger's War, waiting for the historian's attention in order to exist.

The reportorial agenda, if taken literally, is also reductive. There is a familiar distinction drawn between history and chronicle. Chronicle supposedly contents itself with reportage, that this or that happened, but history includes and transcends that, and attempts to *explain* what happened. Thus the historian is supposedly not merely trying to tell us what happened, but also why it happened, and probably more. Ranke himself, of course, was well aware of this.

Lastly the reportorial agenda leaves open a very important question, which, one supposes, might be best characterized as psychological. Why should anyone be interested in reporting what happened in the past? Why bother? What is the point? Surely there are other things to do, involving less effort, less challenge, things requiring less imagination, less talent, less intelligence.

This leads us then to the purposes beyond purposes, and other agendas.

2. Explanatory

We will later be devoting attention to various problematicities associated with explanation in historiography. Much of what might be said here has already been said, above. We will note here that the historian, commonly, is not content with chronicle, but wants to transcend chronicle and achieve explanation. An analogy might be drawn from science, where the scientist seldom contents himself with observing regularities, cataloging facts, noting similarities and differences, and such, but wishes to develop a theory in virtue of which such things may be understood in an acceptable manner, often in terms of a theory by means of which, given certain initial-condition statements and various auxiliary hypotheses, such things might be predicted, either categorically or to a certain degree of probability. This sort of thing might be something of an ideal of scientific explanation, seldom realized, but, if it were achievable, it would normally be taken as a paradigm case of such explanation. The historian's task, for a number of reasons, is far more complex and difficult than that of the scientist, who is usually dealing with limited, quantifiable, manipulable, repetitious, discernible phenomena, and far less likely to attain certifiable success, but, like the scientist, he normally desires to, and attempts to, explain something. The fact that explanation is a goal of both endeavors does not entail that the endeavors are essentially similar, or that any degree of dissimilarity must redound to the detriment of historiography. Historiography is often concerned to identify realities which elude the current nets of science. Historiography is concerned with more than "material bodies moving through physical space according to mathematical laws," or statistical, laws. for that matter. Outside the laboratory is a large world. That is where, on the whole, the historian is at work.

Lastly, as in the case earlier, of the reportorial agenda, one might note again an important but unanswered question, in this case, why should anyone be interested in explaining the past?

This is not an inadmissible question.

Presumably no one explains the past just to explain the past.

So once again one is led to purposes beyond purposes, and other agendas.

3. Didactic

It is said that even the brown rat has a tradition, that it will warn young rats away from poisons. The old rat has learned from the past, and his imparted wisdom is to the profit of the new generation.

George Santayana remarked that those who do not remember the past are condemned to repeat it. This remark clearly draws attention to a value which may be derived from history, whether or not it was the intention of the historian to preclude the repetition of past mistakes.

In the didactic approach, strictly, the historian intends to advise and warn, as, say, Keynes, in his small history pertaining to the punitive Versailles Treaty following World War I. Do not repeat the mistakes of the past. This lesson, whether from Keynes or not, was well learned and had a considerable effect and influence on the policy of the Allies following World War II. He might also, of course, provide us with noble examples for emulation, doers and deeds. Celebrate these doers and deeds, imitate these leaders, these saints and scientists, and such; go forth, and do likewise.

Here I think it is useful to distinguish between a historian's didactic intent and his didactic value.

Both may be noticed here.

One supposes that many historians hope that others will learn from their works, and that the value of their work will have some influence on society and its views. It is hard to suppose, for example, that Marxist historians are neutral reporters. Another fellow, a Nazi intellectual, say, Walter Frank, might recommend writing history in such a way that history-makers will carry it in their knapsacks, and thus, they, too, the historians, will count as history-makers.

Most historians, one guesses, whatever might be their ideological orientation, hope that their work will have some desired effect upon society, that society will be the better for it. This suggests that there is a sense in which most historians would have in their bones a didactic streak, even if this were strenuously denied. Scratch a teacher, find a preacher. If nothing else his work endorses and expresses a sense of life, which he hopes others will share.

Even if the historian somehow, through lack of imagination or subglandular passivity, has no serious views on life, nor any interest in how it might be lived, his work may have didactic value.

In the ancient world history was often valued for its lessons, for its examples of courage and glory, of cowardice, treachery, and folly. Consider Plutarch. Generals and statesmen from Alexander the Great to Winston Churchill have been, in their ways, students of history. They sought to understand, and learn, from the past. We all take induction seriously, even Hume. It seems inevitable in a natural world inhabited by human beings, with ambitions, drives, natures, and such, that various sorts of situations will recur, and that what happened in the past might suggest, though not entail, what might happen in the present and future; surely one might inquire into the consequences of diverse lines of action having to do with these situations. What worked, and what did not work, and so on. Is there that much new under the sun? Might not the past afford occasional signposts, or guidelines, for present policies? It certainly seems so. Remember the old rats and the young rats. Poison may look good and taste good, up to a point, but it is still poison.

Hegel said that the only thing one learns from history is that no one ever learns anything from history. Hegel is unlikely to outscore Oscar Wilde in the witticism department, but this is one of his best. In the Hegelian jungles one occasionally encounters so unexpected and brightly plumaged a bird. It is obviously false, but to note this seems ill-mannered, if not churlish. Taken in context, Hegel is saying something important, namely, that participants and situations differ, and each should be understood in the light of its own time and context, and it is a serious mistake to read, at least uncritically, lessons for now out of a distant then. The temple of Jupiter had little relevance to the Bastille. The urgencies of Cato and Brutus shed little light on those of Danton and Robespierre. Hegel obviously, in his own work, thought he had learned a great deal from history, what its constituents were, what it meant, where it had been, and where it was going. Thus his own work, if he were to take it seriously, which one supposes he did, would belie his aphorism. To be sure, it is one thing to learn from history, as Hegel doubtless hoped to do, and another to mindlessly ransack it for analogies and stratagems.

It is a part of the received wisdom that didactics is no longer an element in the agenda of the modern historian, who has long ago put such things behind him, but in this respect, as in several others, the received wisdom is in error.

4. Inspirational

I think there is not a great deal to be said here. But, for example, as has been noted, each generation means a new barbarian invasion, the arrival at the gates of literally millions of these new barbarians, small, ignorant, energetic, unsocialized, selfish, and demanding. Somehow these new arrivals, who lack even a language, lest the world subside into chaos, must be socialized. Assuming we have some interest in civilization it is of great moment how this is done. It does not do itself. Even the kitten is cuffed, the puppy nipped. Every civilization, whether it is that of ancient Assyria or Midtown Manhattan, must address itself to this problem. This unpromising raw material must somehow be worked up, at least for the most part, into law-abiding citizens. This is done through conditioning, acculturation, example, education, and so on. The society strives, for its own survival, if nothing else, to encourage an axiological consensus, a set of shared values, a common morality. Without this there is a breaching of the social contract, a lapse into the state of nature, a descent into savagery, a warfare of large and small gangs.

Only in a moral world is there a safe place for those who would sneer at morality and proclaim themselves intellectually above such simplicities. Only within the walls they mock are they sheltered from the beasts outside. The upshot of these considerations is that there will always be a role for inspirational historiography, which may function to reduce division within a society. A Balkanized society is a society in dissolution. Difference and diversity are values only within similarity and unity.

Inspirational historiography, whether the intent is to inspire patriotism, devotion to a faith, allegiance to an ideology, or whatever, has a bad name, and to some extent, justifiably so. On the other hand, the importance of education extends beyond the imparting of information; one of its important roles is to promote the common welfare, to make possible a livable society. Values are, of course involved, and one must choose amongst the values to be promulgated. Some are basically essential to the security and survival of any society; others are particularly germane to given sorts of societies. If one believes in, or hopes for, say, a society of mutual respect, civility, tolerance, discussion, due process, and such, then such values should unabashedly acknowledged, celebrated, and encouraged. Some values will be promulgated. If you refuse to profess, promote, and encourage yours, others will take their place. There are no empty bell jars in this area, no value vacuums. Yours, or others.

Presumably the truth can be inspirational, even the search for truth.

There is nothing wrong with inspirational historiography, *per se*. In any event, whatever one thinks of it, it is a possible historiographical agenda, and one which, at least from a pragmatic viewpoint, is not to be despised.

The trick is to do this in a way which is not self-betraying, to do it, if possible, fairly and honestly.

5. Polemical

Polemical histories abound.

One of the most interesting, famous, and valuable is H.G. Wells' remarkably tendentious "Outline of History," which is well worth reading. From the reader's point of view such histories tend to be memorable, if only for the passion with which they are written. Certainly they are a welcome change of pace from the challenge of compulsively fighting one's way through the sedative prose of a typical, run-of-the-mill yawn producer, written to secure a promotion one supposes. The author cares about what he is doing. He has views, and he lets you know what they are. A wonderful example of this *genre* would be Gibbon's *Decline and Fall of the Roman Empire*. That book is so good one almost forgets it is polemical. To be sure, a book with which one agrees is less likely to seem polemical. Polemical books may be written to denounce religions, political parties, economic systems, individuals, say, Joseph Stalin or Franklin Delano Roosevelt, and so on. Polemical histories need not be false, of course, strictly, but they are likely to be one-sided, with a vengeance. Historiography would be less rich without her polemical books. One can read them in the light of the sparks flying from the axes being ground. There is an analogy here to the law, and the adversarial process, the hope being that the truth will somehow emerge as a result of the fight, a sort of trial by combat. For this to work with the polemical book, of course, one should match, where possible, as in the law, alternative polemics. One gains something here which might not emerge from a carefully balanced account. This is terrible, of course, if, as seems often the case in contemporary academia, only one side is heard. This is something like a trial in which only the prosecution is allowed to speak, or only the defense.[6]

6. Hagiographical

This, in effect, would be polemics in reverse. Whereas hagiography, rather strictly, is associated with the lives of the saints, one supposes the expression might be used more broadly to suggest accounts in which, say, any given individual, faith, idea, institution, or such, might be celebrated and praised, perhaps uncritically, perhaps effusively, perhaps inordinately. There is nothing wrong with this, assuming the historian is sincere in his praise. Certainly we are all entitled to our heroes. Doubtless many things are worth celebrating. Heroes may be in short supply but if one shows

---

[6] The best propaganda, and the hardest to detect, as is well known, is that which tells only the truth, but tells it selectively, leaving out the qualifying truths, or the contexualizing truths, or the counter-truths, and spins its truths in such a way as to induce and support a particular ideological viewpoint. These days, as has been obvious for several years, and has recently been noticed, the academic woods are filled with what are known as "scholar activists." They are soldiers in the culture wars and out to save society, by shaping it into something which they would expect to prefer. These are sincere fellows, most of them, those who are not card-carrying opportunists who will leap on any bandwagon which rolls by, and, like all idealists, they are very serious about what they are doing. Also, they are willing to sacrifice others to their good cause, for example, by ideological discrimination in hiring practices. I suppose they think their scholarship is good scholarship. At any rate, it is supposed to be good for a cause. And that is what is most important. The important thing after all is not to understand the world, but to change it. To be sure, not all propaganda is that which deals only with truth, suppressing most of it and selecting some of it, to tailor it to an ideological objective, truth employed to further falsity. There is a place, too, for the outright lie. Lies are part of the tool kit. Essential equipment. A lie repeated frequently enough is likely to be accepted as truth. Perhaps one might think of this as the Frequency Theory of Truth. One wishes they would let people make up their own minds, but they have no intention of doing so, because people are stupid, and might not make up their minds in the right way. They must be saved from their witlessness, and so education becomes indoctrination, missionary activity supplants scholarship, and conversion trumps truth. One trusts that no contemporary historian has ever used his work in the interests of ideology.

up, it would not be professionally improper to take note of it. Presumably things genuinely worth caring for and celebrating are not to ruled out *a priori*. If so, one is entitled to an explanation as to why, at least. Salutes and banners are no more to be denied to the historian than the knives and pistols of the historiographical assassin. To be sure, one supposes that the best history is not likely to emerge from either parades or homicide. As an example of this *genre* one might propose the three volumes of Ernest Jones's *The Life and Work of Sigmund Freud*, a remarkable work pertaining to a remarkable man.

7. Judgmental

This is my least favorite agenda.

Here the historian's mission, or penchant, is to praise and blame, to set himself up, by what authority it is not clear, as judge and moral arbiter. To my knowledge, the most famous advocate of this possible aspect of historiography is Lord Acton, H.B. Acton, the British historian. Lord Acton apparently regarded himself as qualified to umpire the ethics of historical figures and deeds. Perhaps he was, but, as far as I know, he never disclosed the nature of his credentials, their warrant or origin. We all, of course, have our moral views. On the other hand some of us are more reluctant than others to impose them on others, or insist on their certitude, which comes easy, or on their *right* to certitude, which does not come easy. Perhaps Victorians were more entitled than lesser sorts to righteous pomposity. That is possible. Who knows? Goethe remarked that only the observer has a conscience, not, presumably, the historical participant. Whereas that is false, there is no doubt that the Sunday morning quarterbacks of history's gladiatorial games, who weren't even sitting in the stands, do have a considerable advantage over the fellows sweating and dying in the arenas, sitting in their studies, assigning to themselves a moral high ground. Very few people wake up in the morning and decide to go out and do some evil. They may manage it, but very few people intend it, or find it agreeable. Cultural matters, too, may become involved. Slaughtering infidels, of whatever stripe or type, may be quite evil, but it should be kept in mind that the folks who do the slaughtering may not think it evil, and, in that sense, while doing evil, are not intending evil. I have no objection to regarding them as evil, as they are doing evil, but I am not sure much is gained by calling them evil. Showing what they are doing, the evil, it seems, should be sufficient. It is well to remember that if we were in their place, had been raised as they were raised, had been exposed to the same influences, and had the same false beliefs, and such, we might have behaved similarly. Let us hope not, but it certainly seems possible. To understand is not to forgive, but it is to understand.

Lord Acton's notion here seems to be that the historical personages will tremble before the historian, and fearing his frown will improve their deportment. This doubtless depends on the personage. As the anecdote goes, it was once called to the attention of Joseph Stalin that a proposed action of his would be likely to elicit the disapproval of the Pope. "How many Italians has he?" inquired Stalin. Similarly Bismarck reportedly observed that conducting the affairs of state according to principles would be like trying to run through a forest with an eleven-pole clenched in one's teeth.

On the other hand, presumably there are historical personages who are concerned about their "legacy." In the old days they could carry their own historians with them, on their campaigns, admit them into their circles, keep them in their courts, house them in their palaces, and so on. In these days, about all they can do is to invite them over for dinner, perhaps see that they receive a medal, or such. If the only reason a historical personage would behave in a morally acceptable manner is because they fear the judgment of history, that would be something interesting for the historian to note.

After an account of the oddities and sadisms of a Caligula or Nero there doesn't seem much point in saying they were good or bad. By that time the reader should have caught on.

All one needs to note here, at this point, is that moral judgment is a possible agenda for historiography.

8. Illuminative

"All men by nature desire to know."

That is the first sentence in the *Metaphysics* of Aristotle. It is hard to suppose that that sentence is the result of a poll, or an extrapolation from a representative sample of the human species. One supposes it is an extrapolation from Aristotle by Aristotle. On the other hand, it is also evidence that not all philosophers are pessimists. It seems reasonably clear that not all human beings want to know all that much. There is probably much that the average human being is not interested in knowing, or would rather not know at all. One of the dangers of seeking the truth is that one might find it, and not like it. There is much to be said for delusions, lies, and comfort. On the peaks of truth the air may be thin and the wind blow cold. As H. G. Wells put it, "... One gift that poor ape had to help it in its hideous battle with fact. It could lie. Man is the one animal that can make a fire and keep off the beasts of the night. He is the one animal that can make a falsehood and keep off the beasts of despair." To be sure, the grail of truth is a treasure not to be lightly foresworn.

One supposes that one of the most precious and beautiful values of historiography is its capacity to illuminate, not simply to report or characterize, but to illuminate. If one is searching for a motivation for, or a justification of, historiography, it would not be easy to locate one nobler or more respectable. Some men do, whether by nature or not, desire to know. And to some men, one of the blessings of life is learning, not simply the acquisition of facts, but the understanding of something. Certainly this brings the scientist to his laboratory, the historian to his evidence. This fancy probably is due to nature, actually, constituting a refinement, an extension, and an enlargement of the curiosity of the speculating anthropoid, this beast turning over a rock, perhaps climbing later to a higher branch. While it would be naive to belittle or dismiss the selfishness and belligerence of a gifted, aggressive, murderous ape, and fail to note the survival values and survival dangers of its dispositions and propensities, to see it only in its shadows, as it emerges hungry from its lair, it would be equally or more faulty to belittle or dismiss its merits and charms, amongst them virtue, fidelity, and reason. This ape, after all, has learned to do more than steal food, strike his fellow, and create war; it has learned to strike stones together, and produce fire; it has invented dance, language, song, and science. It has thought about itself, and the world. These are not inconsiderable achievements for a form of life.

The human being is a complex organism, probably the most complex on our planet, even allowing for a certain ethnocentric vanity. Much of what other forms of life can do the human being cannot do as well, but much of what the human being can do other animals cannot do at all. It is not easy to understand the human being; it is multiplex and cognitively elusive. We can photograph it, and weigh it, and note its behavior, that sort of thing; it depresses a scale no more remarkably than flour or grain; rolling down a mountainside it is not that much different from a rock; the human being, however, is not so much on the outside as on the inside. He exceeds his basement, so to speak; one can identify his genes and discover that he shares most of them with chimpanzees and gorillas, and yet, for the most part, not begin to understand him. One can approach him from a multitude of directions, physical, chemical, biological, zoological, and so on, and learn much, and miss much.

To understand the human being better, to move beyond the commonalities he shares with his primate brethren, one turns to other sciences, human sciences, social sciences, such as psychology, anthropology, sociology, and such. But here, too, given commitments to *genera*, to the seeking of the abstract and general, to typical responses to stimuli, to cultural influences, to group dynamics, and such, one predictably encounters preferred limitations, methodological walls, and simplicities, which are not so much handicaps as desiderated conditions for scientific progress. What is missing here, one supposes, is the unique, the special, the different. For this one looks elsewhere, less toward the general than to the specific, from which may spring enlightenments, even general enlightenments, general enlightenments of a special sort, other than those of the laboratory, the culture, the poll. Here one turns to the humanities, to music, dance, art, poetry, literature, history, such things. Here one finds not so much the properties of man, as the meaning of man.

Certainly there are many ways to know man.

One of the most illuminating is history.

It is through history that one has a sense of what it was to wade through the mud of Gaul, to be on the Atlantic with religious dissenters in the early Seventeenth Century, to witness an assassination at the foot of Pompey's statue, to hike through the Alps with Nietzsche, to stand at the foot of a cross on Calvary.

As R. G. Collingwood has pointed out, in my view the greatest of all philosophers of history, history is illuminative of the present, and of human possibilities. "History tells us what man is by what man has done." We know man by his deeds, and through his deeds. Yet what is most important to know is what is known through the deeds, the thought, the hopes, the intentions, the motivations, the purposes. We shall meet this unusual man more than once in the course of his study.

For those who are thrilled to learn, history is an inestimable gift.

9. Recollective

The point of this agenda is primarily personal. Here one is concerned to recall to mind things personally experienced. The paradigm example of this agenda would be the diary, or personal journal. One supposes such things can deepen and enrich a life, and guard against its loss, as it fades from memory. Herewith is the erosion of memory challenged. In the pages of the diary or journal one is reminded of the stranger he once was. One supposes the memoir might be put here, but the memoir is usually intended, as most histories, to be accessible to a public. Is the diary or journal written, too, for such a purpose? Perhaps. Consider the journals of Delacroix. One wonders about the *Meditations* of Marcus Aurelius. Perhaps he thought he might one day edit them. He wrote them in Greek, not Latin. He died on campaign, it seems of fever.

10. Protective

Here the agenda is one of treasuring, of trying to guarantee that memorable doings, and worthy folk, will never be forgotten.

The most beautiful declaration of this sort of thing, at least with which I am familiar, goes back to the history of Herodotus.

It goes as follows:

These are the researches of Herodotus of Halicarnassus, which he publishes, in the hope of thereby preserving from decay the remembrance of what men have done, and of preventing the great and wonderful actions of the Greeks and the Barbarians from losing their due meed of glory; and withal to put on record what were their grounds of feud."

It is to be noted that "great and wonderful actions" are being ascribed here not only to the Greeks, but to the enemies, to the "Barbarians," as well, in this context, the Persians.

Family histories are presumably often motivated by this agenda, the seeking of genealogies, too, and such. Here history is memorial in nature, a way of honoring forebears, an act of piety, in a sense. One wants to remember and pay tribute to the once-living, to remember the fathers and mothers, their joys and sorrows, their deeds, what they did, what they could not do, their struggles and hardships, such things.

And to be sure, this sort of thing can enhance and deepen one's own life, supplying a sense of continuity, and identity, providing a source of respect, or pride.

"Young man," snaps the old lady, "I will have you know I am descended from William the Conqueror."

11. Entertainment

What historians refer to as "pop history" is presumably written primarily for entertainment, or, if that word is unkind or unfair, for at least an entertaining, light read, an easy read. This suggests that such productions are superficial, but that need not be the case. There is no contradiction in supposing that a work is both sound and entertaining. And there is certainly no contradiction in supposing that a work might be both sound and interesting, or even sound and well-written, whatever might be the suspicions of those who might prefer work which is neither entertaining, interesting, nor well-written. History need not be the exclusive province of the yawn *meisters*. It is hard to understand how one can look on the excitements of history and write on them so inadequately, so dismally, so poorly. Do they not understand what they are looking at, what they are doing? And in any event, this motivation or agenda is no worse than a cynical economic agenda, where one writes for money via promotions, or with the plan of enhancing one's career or prestige, say, of writing oneself out of school A into school B, or snagging a prize. One supposes that many biographies are written for their likely popular appeal and, in that sense, to an extent, at least, for their entertainment value.

Entertainment, *per se*, is not to be despised; it is one of the things that makes life bearable.

Only the shallow can be invariably serious.

Where there is no depth one need not fear the penetration of truth and tragedy.

12. Response to Life

Why do people make up songs, paint pictures, write poetry, or compose music?

Presumably these things are done because they are gratifying, because they are fulfilling. In doing such things one interacts with reality, expresses oneself, and makes a mark, scratches the sidewalk, so to speak, in such a way as to say, "I am here." One makes the world a bit different than it might otherwise have been. One might even express one's gratitude to the world in such a way, gratitude that one had a chance to look upon it, and to be alive within it. In a way, one comments on the world, perhaps celebrates it.

The notion here is that doing history may constitute an emotional and aesthetic response to reality, to life. It is surely different from, but may not be entirely disanalogous to, other forms of constructive and creative activity, even forms of art.

It is not that a work of art cannot tell the truth.

Surely one learns from Rembrandt and Goya, from Picasso and Michelangelo, but the learning from history is a different sort of learning, one which, on the whole, in theory, can be stated in truth-bearing linguistic entities subject to confirmation and disconfirmation. It is an enterprise which is more prosaically cognitive. It can founder on the rock of fact. Art, as art, is superior to refutation, immune to disconfirmation. Art may be poor, but it cannot be false, not as a statement may be false. Picasso does not have a contrary, a negation, confirmation conditions, a set of entailments.

In many respects history is clearly distinct from art.

On the other hand, history is one of the few places in which a single artifact can embody truth, art, and personal vision. In this sense history lies at the crossroads of truth and art.

It may have recourse, for example, to the lens of metaphor, as art, but this, in its case, is neither a disparagement nor a diminishment. By means of metaphor one may often say things more simply, more vividly, more realistically, more truly, than by means of clumsier phonetic chunks more conveniently at hand. The point is not literal or figurative speech. The point is how to say things most clearly, how best to convey the truth. The best route to a given destination may not always be by means of roads that already exist. They may not go there. You might have to make new roads. The point is to get where you want to go, to say best and most clearly what you want to say.

It might be nice, from the point of view of utility, of course, to measure in inches and weigh in pounds. That would solve many problems. Is not such clarity a desideratum of cognitivity? Surely. On the other hand it is hard to measure ideas and weigh meanings. Significance is not found amongst the natural numbers. On the grounds of the difficulty of quantifying, or the inability to do so, one might reject history. In doing so, however, one would be rejecting much of what is most important in humanity, in a way, rejecting much of ourselves.

Does history need art?

Not really, only the greatest history.

Art is not frosting on the cake of fact. It is a way of seeing fact best.

Perhaps history might be an art, an unusual art, a cognitive art.

That is something we might think about, later.

13. Contexualization

In cataloging a few of the historical *genres* we mentioned several of the "histories of—," such as the history of art, of baseball, and so on. What one has in mind here is not strictly a "history of—" so much as the use of history to shed light on something or other. Several years ago there was a movement in literary criticism spoken of as the "New Criticism," and its practitioners as the "New Critics." This movement was much justified in its time, it seems, reacting against the substitution of contextualization for the close scrutiny of the work, say, a poem, itself, how it was built, how it achieved its effects, and so on. Here, at least in extreme cases, the biography of the author was to be put to one side, evidence of his intentions, as might be found in letters, and such, might be discarded, or, at least viewed with suspicion; and, so, too, one might dispense with conjectures as to the influence of his contemporaries, of the times, and so on. One would surely agree that the artifact itself should be the primary focus of attention, but it also seems clear that the artifact may not be well understood without a sense of the literary ecology from which it sprang, if it can be understood, at all. These things do not spring miraculously from the forehead of Zeus, but arise within, and, in a sense, are products of, their historical matrix. One gets more out of Chaucer, one supposes, if one has some sense of Medieval society, with its religiosity, hypocrisy, gusto, and so on. It is hard even to read Shakespeare today without notes. Who knows what a "fardel" is? If one abandons intention and influence, one is well on the way to "reader-response criticism," in which arrogance and egocentricity replace research and insight. "What it means" is replaced not even by what I hope it means, but by anything I want it to mean. A document becomes a *tabula rasa* on which one may doodle to one's heart's content. This is particularly embarrassing when one is dealing with a document whose original meaning is quite clear, from its context, the meanings of words at the time, the debates in the light of which it was formed, the literature that preceded its drafting, the literature that expounded it shortly thereafter, and so on. Here, unfortunately, the document is extant, and, worse, one is supposed to be interpreting it, not something else which one would prefer. One would like, of course, to write up one's own document, but this is impractical, and so one must pretend that the document one would like to write up is there in a quite different document, one which one did not write up. Here reader-response criticism comes out of the seminars and into the national courts. One reads policy preferences into the law, and pretends that something means something which it obviously doesn't, something which would have surprised, if not dismayed, the original authors. And so one comes up with "the living Constitution," which is to be substituted for the actual constitution. It would be more honest to simply, openly, abolish the Constitution and enact whatever laws would be fashionable at the time. This is impractical, however, as one would then have to deal with a large group of elected fellows who are accountable to an even larger group of electing fellows. It is easier to get an unelected five out of an unelected nine on your side, particularly if they may not be removed from office, and are unaccountable for what they do.

One thing nice about the New Criticism was that it was concerned with what something supposedly actually said, and not with what it might be nice, or better, to have said. In this way, one may find it innocent of literary wrong doing, certainly of intent, if not negligence, although it might have inadvertently planted seeds the blossoming of which would presumably have proven disconcerting to the original sowers.

There is nothing wrong, of course, with reading anything one wishes into a poem, or whatever. It is just that it should not be confused with what the poem says, or with interpretation, or criticism.

One nice thing here is that, on such an approach, there is nothing to be right or wrong about, though one supposes one could lie about what it means to them.

The point here, of course, is that historical research can contexualize data and thereby render it more comprehensible, perhaps even intelligible.

That is a possible agenda for historical inquiry.

14. The Satisfaction of Curiosity

This is certainly a common motivation for the reading of history.

> How did it come about that there is a place called 'Poland'?
> Between what points stretched the "Silk Road"?
> Did a trireme have three banks of oars or three men to a single oar?
> What were the origins of Greek drama?
> What led to the supersession of the phalanx?

Most of these preceding questions are rather specific, but curiosity often begins with small things. One may be curious about linguistic transformation, the influence of economics on society, the rise of modern science, and such, but usually one's interest is first aroused by narrower puzzles, as in noticing that 'father' and '*Vater*' sound much alike, wondering about the origin of coinage, or how the vacuum pump, or the computer, came about, and so on.

Presumably the same curiosity, the yen to know, which intrigues the reader also intrigues the historian.

Finding out something that is new, that was hitherto unknown, or forgotten, and the delight in such discoveries, is presumably an agenda for the historian, as it undoubtedly is for the reader.

There are, obviously, many agendas for historiography, of which the preceding are a few. In considering such agendas and their intellectual matrices, one deepens and vitalizes one's understanding of the remarkable individual and cultural endeavor that is historiography.

Part Two:
Logic and Semantics

I. Logic

The word 'logic' may be used in a variety of senses, but most of these are not germane to our current interests, which are technical. One may speak of the logic of persuasion, the logic of events, and such. We are not, however, concerned with that sort of thing here, now, at any rate. Hegel, for example, was fond of speaking of logic, but what he was doing, however interesting, had little, if anything, to do with what the logician commonly understands by logic. He seems to have confused causality with logical necessity, negation with opposition or destruction, contradiction with conflict, and so on. The logician commonly thinks of logic as associated with classes, or sets, or linguistic entities, say, sentences, statements, or propositions.

There are three understandings of logic in the more technical fashion, two of which are classical and famous, deductive and inductive logic. Following Charles Sanders Peirce, there is also abductive logic, but this is, substantially, the hypothetical/deductive method, scientific methodology, and such. That, too, will not much concern us, certainly not here.

As far as I can discern, historiography has no unique logic. The logics at its disposal are also at the disposal of other disciplines, as would be mathematics, statistics, and such.

The historian David Hackett Fischer has written a well-known, valuable, and deservedly popular, if controversial, book, entitled *Historians' Fallacies*. The subtitle of the book is "Toward a Logic of Historical Thought." Whereas one joins with Fischer in recommending cogency to historians, and anyone else in sight, his book makes no contribution toward a unique or special logic of historical thought. Most, if not all, of the fallacies to which he calls our attention would be variations of what are often called informal or material fallacies. One detects nothing here which would necessitate an addition to inductive and deductive logic, as usually understood. Fisher's subtitle suggests that there might be something very different or special about the historian's logic, which would distinguish it from that of, say, the physicist, the anthropologist, the ordinary logician, and so on. The only thing that seems different is the subject matter to which the logic is addressed. This in no way denies importance to a wonderful book. It is merely to say that if there is an independent logic of historical thought, somehow different from that of logical thought as normally understood, one must look further for it.

My own view is that there is no unique logic to historiography. Luckily.

What would it be, how would one find it, how would one test it?

I am assuming that the reader is familiar with both deductive logic and inductive logic, and the latter in one or more of its variants.

The logic of most importance to the historian, given the relation between evidence and inference is inductive logic.

Long ago, in an article on the argument from silence, published in *History and Theory*, I discussed a number of problems associated with inductive logic in historiography.[7] At that time I held out the hope that a collaboration between a historian and a probability logician might introduce some order into this realm, largely by way of guidelines or recommendations, not that such things could provide a substitute or replacement for the historian's intuitions. The hope was, however, that some of what the historian does in virtue of his experience and insight might be made more explicit. One advantage of that would be that it might aid the historian to be somewhat more circumspect in his work, to be more aware of, or critical of, his inferences, and so on. Also, of course, it might be of some help to others in understanding what the historian is doing, and, if they were capable, of subjecting it to examination. Over the years I have become much less sanguine as to the possible success of such a project. I suspect the historian would know too much, and the logician would know too little. I think it

---

7 "The Argument from Silence," *History and Theory: Studies in the Philosophy of History*, Vol. V, No. 3, 1966, pp. 288-301. (Wesleyan University Press, Middletown, Connecticut).

unlikely the historian could comfortably generalize, and without these generalizations the logician would lack the foundation to apply his own apparatus and expertise.

The route between an occurrence and an account of the occurrence is seldom one of identity or necessity, unless the account itself is the occurrence. Once noted, such cases may be dismissed. An important link between the occurrence and the account, often a tenuous link, is the evidence. Minimally, five things are involved, only two of which will concern us at this point. The five things commonly involved are the occurrence, the perception of the occurrence, the evidence of the occurrence produced by some individual, who may or may not be the perceiver; the perception of this evidence by the historian, and its subsequent utilization by the historian for the purposes of his account, or "picture of the past." We should note, though we will not be dealing with them in our simplified schematism, that there is an incredible tissue of probabilities involved in these matters. There is a probability as to whether or not an occurrence will be perceived, and, if perceived, a probability as to whether or not the perception will be reliable. There might even be a possibility that the occurrence never took place but a perception occurred, the result of an illusion or hallucination. There is also the possibility that the event never occurred, but was merely alleged to have occurred. Probabilities are also involved as to the likelihood of an event, if perceived, being reported, recorded, and so on. One then has probabilities to worry about as to whether or not the report, call it the evidence, is reliable, distorted, biased, tendentious, or such. Probabilities also arise with the likelihood or not of the historian having access to the evidence, understanding it, and so on. Probabilities would also be involved as to the influence of the evidence with respect to his account, how it might influence it, and to what extent, and so on.

Let us consider the following, simplified schematism.

Let us distinguish, simply, between E and A, or, if one likes, P. E will be evidence, and A will be the account to which the evidence is supposed to be relevant, or P will be the "picture of the past," a lovely metaphor, to which the evidence is supposed to be relevant. We will consider E and A, and the relation between them.

The relationship between E and A is seldom one of logical entailment. E certainly implies E, itself, and if one copies E and then uses that as A, then, since A is identical with E, E would imply A. This sort of thing, however, is rarely, if ever, the case. The usual problem then is how does one build an account on evidence which does not imply the account. It does, presumably, influence the account.[8]

Along these lines it is useful to recall a distinction which was emphasized by R. G. Collingwood, between authorities and sources. A historian who takes earlier documents as authorities, and uses them to construct his account, is to be contrasted with the historian who uses documents not as authorities, to be accepted uncritically, but as sources, regarding them critically. The ultimate authority here is not the document, but the judgment of the historian. He decides what E means, whether it is authentic, whether it is plausible, whether it is to be accepted, or not, and to what degree, and so on. Collingwood

---

8 Technically, logical relations, either deductive or inductive, would be thought to obtain amongst abstract entities, most commonly statements or propositions. Thus the Lincoln penny, so to speak, a nonlinguistic entity, could not, in the nature of things, imply the statement 'The Lincoln penny is an artifact', but, if the Lincoln penny is an artifact, the statement 'The Lincoln penny is an artifact' would be true, and that statement would then, without worrying logic, have logical relationships to other statements, entailing them, being consistent with them, being inconsistent with them, and so on. For example, it would entail the statement 'The Lincoln penny is an artifact or Albany is not the capital of New York State', 'If Chicago is in Illinois, then the Lincoln penny is an artifact', 'If it is not the case that the Lincoln penny is an artifact, then Julius Caesar was a Roman general', and so on. Any statement, true or not, entails an infinite set of other propositions. Not all evidence is statemental in nature, of course. The Lincoln penny is not a statement, but it could be evidence of something to someone, In order to avoid indirection, circumlocution, pedantry, and such, we will usually speak of probability relations obtaining amongst nonlinguistic entities, for example, the probability of a given event being reported, the probability of a given piece of evidence being understood, and such. This could all be put in terms of linguistic entities but it would seem tedious to do so. Also, more interestingly, one supposes that objective empirical probabilities exist, which are independent of linguistic entities. Indeed, these would be the probabilities that linguistic entities would try to state. Otherwise the whole empirical probability enterprise becomes unintelligible. For example, it is presumably empirically improbable that out a thousand tosses of a typical two-headed coin, such as one might pick up in change, that one face, say, heads, would come up only four percent of the time. Mathematical probabilities, on the other hand, can thrive by definition. A fair coin, for example, in virtue of the definition of fairness, will come up heads 50 percent of the time; a fair die, subject to stipulation, will come up six once every six times, and so on.

famously characterized the results of an uncritical reliance on authorities as "scissors-and-paste" history. I recall the distinction here because it draws attention to the fact that the relationship between evidence and account is seldom, if ever, one of entailment. The logic here is one of probability or confirmation. Probability theory and confirmation theory, assuming one is concerned with empirical matters, are much the same thing; probability suggests independent relationships; and confirmation suggests the utilization of such relationships in assessing hypotheses. This sort of thing might be put in terms of the legitimacy of confidence levels, if one is disturbed about the notion of objective probabilities, out there like apples and rocks. On the other hand, the notion of legitimacy of confidence levels requires recourse to an explanation of, or justification of, legitimacy, and this returns us to the notion of objective probabilities, out there like apples and rocks. Metaphysics lurks. On the other hand we expect the rubber ball to bounce and water to run downhill. The most persuasive justification of induction, which is a closely related issue, in my view, is that of Hans Reichenbach, which is neither question-begging nor sunk in someone's notion of the dictates of a transitory semantics. Reichenbach acknowledges that Hume is correct, happily, as Hume is correct, but shifts attention from what one can know or prove to questions of rational strategy. Reichenbach's substantial recommendation, which I am revising somewhat, is that there is either pattern in the world or not. It is an open question both as to whether this exists, or whether or not it will continue to exist beyond, say, the next minute. One now has the option of either acting on the basis of induction or not acting on that basis. If there is no pattern now, or later, it doesn't matter much what you do. You are in a bad way, even if you are a quantum physicist. On the other hand, if there is pattern, then one can either repudiate induction and make a mistake, or bet on induction, and profit. If there is pattern, induction is the key to its discovery. Thus the rational bet is on induction. We live this way anyway, of course, including Hume, but now one can do so with a philosophically clear conscience. One gives Hume his due, salutes him, rejoices, and moves on.

It should be noted in passing that analytic probability theory or analytic confirmation theory is not going to solve the practical problems involved. Those are branches of mathematics, and mathematics, as one knows from Leibniz and others, is safe in any possible world. Reality of the usual sort fazes it not. Tigers either exist or they don't, and in not one of those worlds is there a tiger who falls the least bit short of being a tiger. No wonder that folks eager for intellectual social security are drawn to the condos of Platoville. The world to which the historian addresses himself, on the other hand, is messier, probably because it is real. Too, if there are tigers in his world, it is likely they bite. The point here is that a form of, say, analytic probability theory could let us know, with respect to a given premise set assigned a given probability, that a conclusion drawn from that set would have exactly such-and-such a probability. This is all analytic, all a matter of entailments, of logical necessity, as much as adding two and two and coming up with four. These are amazing and beautiful intellectual constructions but they are of no use to the historian without assigning a probability to a premise-set. That comes from the outside, and is a matter of empirical speculation, of guesswork, if you like, of a hunch. Indeed, it seems there are really two practical problems involved. First, the assignment to the premise-set, or claim, of a probability, which the system itself cannot do, unless the premise set itself is either analytic or inconsistent, and, second, the probability of the inference from the premise-set. The latter could be set into the system analytically, but, as a practical matter, a decision would have to be made as to how to incorporate it in the system.

Let us consider the following:

Our premise-set is:

There is an 80 % probability that A harbored murderous intentions toward B.

Now consider two conclusions:

(1) A arranged the murder of B.

(2) There is a 60 % probability that A arranged the murder of B.

One can well imagine the difficulty of trying to assign a particular probability to the premise-set. We do not even know the fellow. We assign, however, a probability of 80 %. Now a system could be set up in such a way as to allow you to infer the first conclusion analytically from the premise-set, but presumably no rational probability theorist would set up a system allowing one to do that. It might be possible, but it would be absurd. The system might be consistent, and such, but it would be useless, certainly if one wished to apply it in the real world. Not all consistent geometries, for example, map onto physical space, at least without a number of ad-hoc adjustments, transformations, and such.[9] . One could design a mathematics in which two plus two came out to six, but this would require a reordering of operators, necessitate an infinite number of adjustments, and so on. It would not only rock the boat of mathematics, but probably sink it.

This leads us to the second conclusion.

Here we might note, initially, that that would be a very unusual sentence to find in a historical text. One might, however, encounter sentences to the effect that it seems probable, or likely, that A arranged the murder of B, or such.

But how would one go from the premise-set to the conclusion? It seems that another empirical speculation would be involved, in this case that whenever there is an 80% probability that A, or an A, harbored murderous intentions toward B, or a B, there is a 60% probability that A, or an A, will arrange the murder of B, or a B. And, obviously there are a number of other probabilities which would be involved, in arriving at the 60% probability, concerning which it might difficult to conjecture. For example, is A the particular sort of individual who will act on murderous inclinations of that percentile that percentage of the time, does A have the intelligence, motivation, power, cunning, lack of scruples, cohorts, and so on, to arrange such a murder? Would A be likely to arrange such a murder, considering the suspicions likely to be involved, the possible personal and political repercussions, and so on? Now, all of these latter considerations could be packed into the system analytically, given the first probability assignment, that given to the premise-set, but I think it is clear that the historian had best go his own way here, and do the best he can. He will probably have to assess a complex tissue of probabilities here, but it does not seem likely that his work will profit much from an attempt to plug his guesswork

---

9 One could use Euclidean geometry for interstellar measurements, for example, but this would necessitate a number of corrections for gravitational distortions. It is simpler, apparently, to make do with a Riemannian geometry, in which the interior angles of a triangle would total more than 180°, a geometry thus more suitable for a "curved space."

into the socket of a formal system. To be sure, if it would help, more power to him. For most historians I suspect such an endeavor would be uncongenial. It might be more of an impediment than a utility. It seems that in such a terrain the wheels of historiography might spin indefinitely. Too, presumably the only way to test the value of such a system would be to examine its results in the light of one's own intuitions, for which one presumably does not have the system to thank. To be sure, this may be like explaining why the airplane will not work. Perhaps such systems might one day have much value, and a reciprocity might emerge whereby the system might be revised in the light of the historian's intuitions, and the historian's intuitions might be reviewed in the light of such a system. One can always hope for the best.

The primary logic of historiography is inductive, and the articulation, assessment, and formalization of such matters is currently beset with awesome, if not insuperable, difficulties. The variables in historiography are the variables of life. We do not even know exactly, in physics, where the penny will land, dropped from the tall building. In history we may know, so to speak, where the penny landed. What we do not know is the multitude of variables and forces which might explain how and why it landed where it did. Too, the penny may still be in flight. The historian may, in effect, be seeing it on its way past.

Before leaving this subject it seems appropriate to discuss the feasibility of a historiographical calculus. It is easiest to discuss this in the context of a deterministic universe. The reader may add his own qualifications or modifications with respect to probabilistic explanation. The essential points, from our point of view, are points in common. The following would be properties of a deterministic system S. Everything that occurs in S occurs in virtue of natural law. One need not speak of causal necessity here, for one rows softly in those water after Hume's charting of the shoals and reefs. One may content oneself with exceptionless regularity. All occurs in accord with natural law if not because of such law. Invariability serves the purpose. Now, if the universe is deterministic, then it follows that all events in S are in theory predictable, given the satisfaction of condition C. To satisfy condition C four subconditions must be satisfied.

1. One must have complete knowledge of at least one state of S.

2. One must have complete knowledge of all the laws obtaining in S.
3. One must have the capacity, intellectual, technological, and so on, to make predictions based on the complete knowledge of one state of S and complete knowledge of all the laws obtaining in S.

It should be noted in connection with subcondition 3 that one would be capable of both prediction and retrodiction.

4. S must be an isolated system.

Obviously all bets are off if intrusions occur, unless S is a component of an encompassing system S', in which case bets are on again. For example, if one lets a fellow know that he is going to Minneapolis on Tuesday he may go on Monday, or Wednesday, or not go at all. A new factor was thrown into the mix, vitiating the prediction. The system was no longer isolated. In the encompassing system, if it is isolated, one might predict that he will go on Wednesday, and he goes on Wednesday. If, on the other hand, you inform him that he is going on Wednesday, system S' is no longer isolated, and you may have to have recourse to system S", and so on.

Obviously condition C is unlikely to be satisfied. Remember the penny dropped from the tall building. We could not accurately predict its point of landing. To calculate these things out it seems one would need a divine entity and one of a very special sort, namely, one which was omnipotent and omniscient, one who knew everything and could do everything, at least what did not involve contradictions, did not involve going against its own nature, or such. For example, it is not clear that a necessary being could commit suicide, or render itself contingent, and such. To be sure, one might leave such things up to the being in question.

The god of deism, as usually conceived, created the world and then retired; he wound it up, so to speak, and then let it run. It was a clockwork universe, congenial to Newtonians and generations of scientists. In such a universe there is no place for quantum mechanics, unless as a delusion characterizing one of science's more embarrassing moments. Similarly there is no place in such a world for miracles, even if they were plotted in from the beginning, as they would be breaches of natural law. That they might be planned breaches would not alter the case. Hume's arguments against miracles are founded on the conviction that the universe is a deterministic system. It is more likely that people are deluded, or lying, than that a miracle occurred. The universe does not stumble. It is interesting to note that the argument against miracles is founded on a belief in the uniformity of nature, a belief to which it is not clear Hume is entitled, given his epistemology.

In any event, a deterministic universe would make a historiographical calculus feasible in theory, and, to some extent, in certain situations, it might have empirical relevance.

The unity-of-science view and the logistic model of scientific explanation are relevant here.

What would be required for the construction of a historiographical calculus?

A familiar approach to such a calculus would see it as an interpreted logistic system. This system, in a familiar form, would require a lexicon, formation rules, transformation rules, and primitive formulas, analogous to axioms or postulates. Lastly, to supply the interpretation, one requires designation rules. The lexicon supplies the primitive signs of the system, for example, operators, perhaps for negation and disjunction, signs which might serve for individual variables and constants, predicate variables and constants, identity, class membership, and such. One will balance off elegance against convenience. One might do with a single operator, such as one of Sheffer strokes, but, unless one is filled with microchips, one will probably want a few more. The formation rules specify how to combine signs in ways acceptable to the system, thus providing a criterion for assessing well-formedness. For example, in mathematics, as we normally do things, '2 + 2 = 4' is a well-formed formula, whereas '= + 224' is not. The transformation rules provide what one might think of as the logic of the system. These might be rules of inference, such as logical addition and modus ponens, or rules of replacement, such as distribution and transposition. You would now have the makings of a system of natural deduction. The next step on the road to our calculus is a set of primitive formulas. These are the base formulas, and they are internal to the system. These would be, as noted, analogous to axioms or postulates. We now have an uninterpreted logistic system. In order to turn this into an *interpreted* logistic system, one sort of which would be our historiographical calculus, one sets up designation rules. By means of these rules one will supply meaning assignments in such a way as to introduce individual constants and predicate constants. For example:

j : Juliet
r : Romeo
Ax : x is an apple
Lxy : x loves y
Exyz : x is evidence of y to z

An example of an interpreted well-formed formula, then, might be 'Ljr' ('Juliet loves Romeo') or 'Lrj' ('Romeo loves Juliet').

Now, if the world is a deterministic system, and all occurs in accord with natural law, then, in theory, one could use statements of these laws as our primitive formulas, or, now that they are interpreted, as our primitive sentences. Then, conjoining these laws with initial-condition statements, one could logically infer present, future, or past states of the system.

For example, if there was a law to the effect that all empires fall, and an initial-condition statement to the effect that Rome is an empire, one could infer that Rome falls.

So:
r : Rome
Ex : x is an empire
Fx : x falls
Then:
1. $(x)(Ex \supset Fx)$
2. $Er \; / \therefore \; Fr$
3. $Er \supset Fr$ From 1, by universal instantiation.
4. Fr From 2 and 3, by modus ponens.

In English, one might have:
1. For every x, if x is an empire, then x falls.
2. Rome is an empire. Therefore, Rome falls.
3. If Rome is an empire, then Rome falls.
    (From 1, by universal instantiation.)
4. Rome falls. (From 2 and 3 by modus ponens.)

The example is constructed to be radically simple and one

would not expect a Gibbon, Momsen or Rostovtzeff to abandon historical studies in its light, but it does make clear the sort of thing that would be involved in a historiographical calculus, namely, the utilization of laws and initial-condition statements to derive empirical statements. And, in this way, from the point of view of some, this would provide us with a modality of explanation, as well as a modality of prediction and retrodiction. Indeed, we would seem to have here a case in which a particular scientific desideratum is satisfied, namely, that of explanation/prediction symmetry. If you can explain you can predict, and if you can predict you can, and have, explained. The principle of explanation/prediction symmetry has not fared well in the philosophy of science, however, as there can be cases of explanation without prediction, at least in any usual sense, for example, as in deriving the height of a tree from laws and initial-condition statements involving measurements and angles, and prediction without explanation, for example, as in calculating the approximate number of misaddressed letters processed by the post office annually, and so on, but, on the whole. the principle of explanation/symmetry remains a scientific ideal. Certainly the historiographical calculus, as conceived, would in theory provide explanation/prediction symmetry. Of course, if we took explanation/prediction symmetry as a necessary condition for an explanation, the historian would seldom, if ever, explain anything. Nor, in fact, would nearly anyone else. The covering-law model of scientific explanation, of which the historiographical calculus would be a spectacular example, embodies an ideal seldom achieved, not merely by historians, but even in the physical sciences.

Independent questions might be whether or not this sort of thing is to be appropriately sought in historiographical explanation, and whether or not, to the extent it is neither achieved, nor sought, then so much the worse for historiography. Such questions will be engaged at a later point.

In any event, to the best of my knowledge, there is no special or unique logic to historiography. On the other hand, the applications of classical logics to her subject matter present problems which are in themselves sufficiently special and unique, and the possibilities of developing analytic systems which permit precise assessments of her claims and conjectures deserve recognition and encouragement.

II. Semantics

Logic might be considered as a study of abstractions, say, classes, sets, forms, or such. For example, consider the propositional variables 'p' and 'q' and the argument form:

$$\frac{p \& q}{q}$$

That is the form of a valid argument, one form of an infinite number of forms of valid arguments.

In English, 'p and q. Therefore, q'.

Any legitimate substitution instance of that argument form yields a valid argument. On a semantic construal of validity, which is typical, an argument is valid if and only if it is logically impossible for its premise-set to be true and its conclusion false. Thus a contradictory premise-set logically implies all propositions whatsoever, as it is logically impossible for the premise-set to be true, and an analytic, or logically true, conclusion is implied by all premise-sets whatsoever, because it is logically impossible for the conclusion to be false. The expression 'premise-set' is neutral between an argument with a single premise and an argument with more than one premise, perhaps a hundred premises.

This is all a matter of form, though, of course, one has to know what one is talking about, and that will involve meanings.

Semantics, by contrast, is the study not of forms, but of meanings.

We are accepting the existence of meanings.

To most of those who might be reading this book that will not seem a surprising, let alone an alarming, act, probably because they have been familiar with, or will have supposed themselves familiar with, meanings, almost from the cradle. There are views and positions which deny the existence of meanings and expect people to understand what they mean by that, and so on. The notion here seems to be connected with a robust empiricism which, armed with calipers and cameras, has discovered that meanings are unlike marbles, ball bearings, Lincoln pennies, or such, namely, that they are not empirically verifiable, and thus ontologically suspect. It is true that if one must limit oneself to noises and the movements of bodies it will be hard to locate meanings. This is because one would be looking in the wrong place. One must acknowledge that philosophical behaviorism has a real point, namely, that one cannot measure meanings with calipers nor photograph them with the latest digital equipment. That is, of course, because they are not marbles, ball bearings, Lincoln pennies, and such. Consider the meaning of the word 'elephant'. If you understand that word then at least one meaning exists, and perhaps more. Technically, a philosophical behaviorist should not be able to understand the word 'elephant', though we suspect he could find his way around the zoo as well as the rest of us. One could, of course, try to unpack the notion of meaning without recourse to meanings, namely, to unpack "meaning" behaviorally. For example, in this sense, what is the meaning of 'pain'? A classical example of this is that of the fellow mangled under the wheels of the street car. Here, supposedly, all one means by saying he is in pain is that he is being noisy, is thrashing about, and so on. Certainly that seems surprising. There are, of course, numerous arguments and counter-arguments involved here and one is pleased to note that there is no time to enter into them. One wishes that some philosophers would give more attention to the world as they find it, and less to piggy-backing on self-restricting psychological theories. There may be much to be said scientifically and methodologically for psychologists fixing their attention on behavior and ignoring conscious experience, but most behavior would be unintelligible without the supposition of the reality of such experience. While on the subject, how would one prove that other minds exist? The calipers and cameras don't work there either. Philosophical behaviorists, as far as I know, have never let us know what they would take as evidence that meanings exist. Until they do it seems their claim as to the nonexistence of meanings would have to ranked as *"Unsinn,"* to borrow an expression from the great days of the Vienna Circle. So, is the sign lifted again in the back of the room? "*Unsinn?*" "Nonsense?" Apparently they are reluctant to take as evidence what most folks suppose is evidence, namely, being familiar with, or seeming to be familiar with, meanings, and such.

If meanings do not exist, we should invent them as soon as possible, for the order, precision, clarity, simplicity, explanatory power, intelligibility, utility, and such, which they contribute to a variety of human activities, such as thinking and communication.

In any event, we shall suppose, as a convenience, if nothing else, that meanings exist.

It they don't, they should.

So let us suppose they do.

Whereas there seemed to be no special or unique logic to historiography, it does seem as though it relies on, or occasionally has recourse to, a rich, and sometimes troublesome, lexicon.

Our primary concern here is with meanings but, prior to engaging certain semantic issues, we should note, in passing, several functions of language, most of which could characterize historiography. Language may be used informatively, interrogatively, persuasively, expressively, inspirationally, logically, hypothetically, practically, instructively, imperatively, ceremonially, ritualistically, speculatively, anticipatorily, playfully, imaginatively, poetically, lyrically, enactionally, as in performatory discourse, and so on. It may be used to do fiction, to do fact, to arrange and organize, to disarrange and disorganize, to negotiate, to deceive, to confuse, to encourage, to ventilate frustration, to intimidate, and so on. It is equally at home serving conceptual and social purposes. It may even be used for philosophical purposes, and historiographical purposes.

Here are some samples of locutions from the historiographical lexicon, not all of which, of course, are unique to historiography: 'historical period', 'social forces', 'group mind', 'spirit of the age', 'needs of the time', 'will of the people', 'historical destiny', 'world-historical individual', 'stimulus-and-response', 'classes', 'rebirth', 'growth', 'degeneration', 'decadence', 'pattern', 'progress', 'culture', 'nations', etc.

Let us now distinguish between unproblematic discourse, quasi-problematic discourse, and problematic discourse. The distinctions are rough and ready but, I think, helpful. If one wishes to be technical, most discourse, if pressed, becomes problematical. For example, the word 'cat' is unlikely to give anyone much trouble but, under the exercises of imagination, it might. For example, could you have a healthy, functioning adult cat which weighed only one ounce, or, say, two tons? What if the catlike creature could talk with you, or changed colors at will, or walked through walls, and such? It is certainly not an ordinary cat, but is it just a strange cat, or something other than a cat, and so forth? This is sometimes called the open texture of empirical concepts, or, more literally, the porosity of concepts, from the German '*die Porosität der Begriffe*'.[10]

The essential difference, as it is understood here, between unproblematic discourse and problematic discourse is that problematic discourse tends to be philosophically interesting. One supposes that unproblematic discourse seldom provokes the efforts of the analyst. Quasi-problematical discourse, about which category there might be controversy, may or may not interest the analyst, but one supposes, at least today, not much. The terms of quasi-problematic discourse are likely to appear to many analysts as semantic blank cartridges, if not obsolescent garbage, at least literally understood. They tend to elude empirical scrutiny; they seem to explain little, if anything; they do not abet inquiry; they lead nowhere; they do not fit in; they are cognitively useless; and they are essentially verbal, unredeemed by experiential utility or confirmation. Some examples may help.

Some Types of Discourses

Unproblematic:
table, chair, apple, Airedales, mountains,
clouds, unicorns, centaurs, etc.

Quasi-problematic:
gods, spirits, ids, egos, superegos, etc.

Problematic:
numbers, meanings, propositions, rights,
obligations, cultures, nations, etc.

---

10 The concept is from Friedrich Waismann. I have adapted one of his examples here. (Cf. "Verifiability," *The Proceedings of the Aristotelian Society*, Vol. 19 (1945). The article is reprinted variously, e.g., in *Logic and Language* (First Series), edited by Anthony Flew (Basil Blackwell, Oxford, 1960)).

Most terminology encountered in historiography, as elsewhere, is unproblematic. So far, so good. Some discourse encountered in historiography would seem quasi-problematic, namely, such that it is not very illuminating, helpful, or interesting, or, say, that it seems either unintelligible or obviously false. For example, few folks today would take seriously the notion that the state is the Divine Idea on Earth. Doubtless the simplest approach to such discourse would be to consign it instantly to the wastebasket of semantic zeros, but there are very few claims from which one cannot extract some empirical content, if one is willing to put in the effort. And do we not find herein hope for many intellectuals careless of, or above, relating their discourse to a recognizable world? Beneath the verbal plumage there may be no bird, but there is usually something. It seems more likely then that one would wish to assign a truth value to the unusual claim about the state. Dismissing it as nonsense may let it off too easily. If there is some empirical content, however negligible, to the claim that the state is the Divine Idea on Earth, presumably it would be along the lines that, if it is true, we might expect the state to be, at least, all-benevolent, omniscient, and omnipotent. I have little doubt that the state these days is too powerful, too intrusive, too interventionistic, and such, but it seems, as yet, to fall short of omnipotence. It may be able to deprive you of your property, freedom, and life, but it is not yet capable of protecting your property, respecting your freedom, or safe-guarding your life. Too, it does not seem omniscient. The IRS would do better if it were. Similarly it is not clear the state is all-benevolent. Herein the reader might supply his own examples. It seems odd that Hegel, who was in many ways a brilliant man, would think of the state as the Divine Idea on Earth. Surely his own historical studies would have demonstrated to him that most states were founded in conquest and preserved by force. Was he not the one who referred to history as a "slaughter-bench" on which were sacrificed "the happiness of peoples, the wisdom of states, and the virtue of individuals"? Since most of this slaughtering was done by states, which are adept and experienced at such things, would that not cast some doubt on the Divine-Idea-on-Earth notion? All this turns out to be justified from Hegel's point of view, of course, which manages to view the ills of the world with ultimate equanimity, a view obviously not from the "slaughter-bench." To be sure, not all states manifest the Divine Idea on Earth. It was manifested in the "Germanic states," of which Prussia would have been one, England another, and so on. One need not, of course, assign properties such as omnipotence, omniscience, and all-benevolence to a divine entity. It is probably a good ideas not to, as one then encounters the problem of evil, which, one gathers, is insoluble to those who are capable of understanding it. The best solution to the problem of evil is not to find out about it in the first place, and then, if one does, to forget about it as soon as possible. But then, if one has a divine entity, call it Spirit, *Geist*, or whatever, and it works out its will in virtue of hatred, conflict, cruelty, blood, disease, famine, catastrophe, and such, one wonders if it is worth respecting, let alone worshipping. If that is the divine entity which manifests itself in the state, then the worst suspicions of anarchists are well confirmed. It is considerations of this sort which would lead one to say that a claim such as the state's being the Divine Idea on Earth, namely, a manifestation of *Geist* in Objective Spirit, or such, is not so much unintelligible as obviously false, and, to the extent that it might not be obviously false, it would seem to be unintelligible.

At any rate that would be a proposal for a claim from quasi-problematic discourse.

It may be recalled that we characterized problematic discourse as discourse that would tend to be more philosophically interesting than either unproblematic or quasi-problematic discourse.

The lexicon of historiography is rich in problematic discourse.

We suggested, earlier, several examples of what we might take to be problematic terms, 'historical period', 'social forces', and such.

Obviously there is a difference between words and the world, even if we take words to be a part of the world. Obviously there is a considerable difference between, say, the word 'rhinoceros' and the rhinoceros, and so on. Words may provoke duels and cause wars, but they don't gore people, at least literally. On the other hand, if this is all so obvious, why are there verbal thinkers, thinkers whose discourse, at any rate, seems to blur the difference between words and the world, thinkers who speak and write as though the world was under an obligation to conform to words, or that there was some sort of automatic correspondence between words and reality? One of the indisputable discoveries of empirical linguistics is that a plethora of natural languages exist, and that they differ in a large variety of ways, not merely in lexicon, which is relatively trivial, but, more substantially, in the way they map the world, grammatically and conceptually. Many individuals, in effect, see the world through the lenses of language, and different lenses mark out and call attention to different facets of reality, not marking the same categories, not making the same distinctions, one language noting something here, and not there, and another doing it differently. There may be no words for things that are, and there may be words for things that are not. The Sapir/Whorf Linguistic Relativity Hypothesis suggests that thinking itself tends to follow the natural geodesics of the language involved, as water might move within an available terrain. Consider the subject/predicate form of sentence structure in Greek. This leads naturally to a corresponding metaphysics of substance and property, a distinction which, when pressed, leads to incoherence. Is this a trap set by language, into which even an Aristotle might fall? One needs words to get at the world, but words are not the world. The hypothesis of linguistic relativity is not a counsel of despair, but it suggests caution. It is not insurmountable, but it is there to surmount. Awareness facilitates avoidance.[11]

Let us consider a particular example which seems to involve the substitution of an abstraction, associated with a word, for a reality. It is quite possible that this sort of thing is historiographically unavoidable. On the other hand, it seems important to understand what is going on, even if it is impractical or undesirable to alter

---

11 An awareness of linguistic mapping, and the realization of a variety of different mappings, of which yours is only one, is helpful here. Also, as all natural languages are substantially intertranslatable, one realizes one is not hopelessly enclosed within, or handicapped by, the accident of a single linguistic framework. Too, there is some possibility that human beings may share a genetically embedded depth grammar. If that is the case, then any problems that might remain here would seem to be indigenous to the species, and not to particular linguistic groupings.

one's practice in the light of the facts. For most practical purposes, words hold still, and reality doesn't; it changes.[12]

Consider France, first in transition, second, at a particular moment. There are problems both, so to speak, longitudinally and latitudinally.

One would expect a history of France to cover several centuries. It is not really clear where one would begin this history nor what might be included within it. For example, would you include Gaul? Would you include mining, or poetry? The historian would have to decide such things. There would be limits, presumably, to rational decision. He would not be likely to begin it in the Olduvai Gorge in the time of *Homo habilis* nor include in it the contemporary doings of the Japanese Ainu. One thing that would be very clear to the historian, and his readers, or one hopes so, is that he is really treating very different sorts of things, or states of affairs, at different points in his history. The France of Pepin I, if one thinks of it as France, is obviously much different from that of a later figure, say, Charles de Gaulle. Continuities are involved, obviously, but it does not seem that there is any "same thing" which is involved. This is not like, say, a single person. There are great differences between the new-born infant and the child, and the teenager, and the young adult, and the mature adult, and so on, but there is a physical continuity involved. Whereas there is a clear sense in which we note, and might say, that the infant is very different from the adult, there is also a clear sense in which are justified in saying that they are the same person. The physical continuity is there. Also, neural cells, of which there are millions, are the same. Not all of the person is replaced every seven years. For example, one can remember things which occurred more than seven years ago. The ontology of a nation, say, France, is very different from this sort of thing. Whatever France may be, if it is something, it does not seem to be a person, not, at any rate, a person like Pepin I or Charles de Gaulle.

---

12 Interestingly, over time, words are also on the move. Compare the English of Beowulf, and Chaucer, with modern English. Alvin Toffler calls to our attention that some forty percent of the English lexicon has changed since the time of Shakespeare, words lost, words born, and so on. He notes that if Shakespeare were to show up today, he would understand, then, only something like five out of every nine words in English, and would be a semi-illiterate. He notes, too, that this sort of thing seems to characterize all modern languages.

Let us be clear on this longitudinal problem.

It seems then that there could be no history of France, but only, at best, of a succession of Frances, so to speak. Consider a history of "Pierre." There is Pierre^1, Pierre^2, Pierre^3, and so on. Could one then write a history of "Pierre"? There are two problems here, the first, which is formidable enough, is to find out what went on, and the second, which has no single solution, is to conceptualize what was going on. What went on is part of the world; how we think about what went on is up to us. "France" might turn out not to be a thing, so to speak, but more of a linguistic stratagem, or a scholarly convenience, in terms of which to conceptualize, or, more simply, unify, and refer to, a variety of actions and events. In any event it is clear that France is not an unchanging entity which, from time to time, does this or that.

So clearly there are difficulties in dealing with "France" over time and throughout change. Putting these problems aside, there are also difficulties in dealing with "France" at a single moment. This is the latitudinal problem.

We are going to consider an ontological trichotomy.

It will be convenient in the following to take 'existence' as, at least in most cases, an informative predicate. This is in accord with familiar, common-sense English usage. Long ago Kant suggested that 'existence' was not a real predicate, but only a logical, or verbal, predicate. For example, if you knew the coin was gold, worth so much, weighed so much, was in such and such a location, could be used to buy apples, and such, then adding that it also existed added nothing to the concept. This is correct in its way, but it does seem to distract attention from the common-sense distinction, which Kant himself embedded in the verifiable properties of the coin, between the imaginary coin and the real coin, where 'existence' is useful, and a real, or informative, predicate. Usually 'existence' is quite informative. The rhinoceros which exists, and can dent your land rover, is very different from the one which does not exist, and from which the land rover is quite safe. If I tell you that an 1804 silver dollar exists, I am telling you something informative. Similarly, if, in virtue of the principle of significant negation, I tell you that there is no such coin, that it does not exist, you are clear as to what I mean. I am also saying something significant, though in that case false.[13] The upshot of these remarks is that 'existence' is usually an informative predicate when contextualized, though quite possibly an empty predicate considered in isolation, in a semantic vacuum. Consider the following: "A glorp exists." Is "existence" informative here? It seems so, but minimally. It suggests, for example, that something to which the expression 'glorp' refers exists, in some way or another. To be sure it is not clear in what way it might exist, as we do not know what a glorp is supposed to be. There are different sorts of existence. Is a glorp a theorem, a unicorn, a square circle, a grain of sand, the square root of minus one, a meaning, a mind, a planet, or what?. One wants more information. Once one has in mind what a glorp is supposed to be, then an assertion claiming that a glorp exists is likely to make sense. For example, if a glorp is a mythological bacterium, then it does not exist, by definition. If it is a seven-pound bacterium, then presumably it does not exist, for empirical reasons, as bacteria do not come in that size.

The question before us now, latitudinally, is whether or not France exists, and, if it exists, how does it exist.

We would like to fit this question into an ontological trichotomy.

Consider '(x) (Ex v ~ Ex)'. That might be read, in English, as 'For every x, x either exists or does not exist'. This is not fazed by the fact that x might exist at one time and not at another time. For example, in the Cambrian period dinosaurs did not exist; in the Jurassic period they did exist; and in the Pleistocene they did not exist. For those who are alarmed by using 'existence' as a predicate here, and fear this is either vacuous, incoherent, or immoral, let us understand 'existence' in some sense that would be sustained by common-sense English discourse. One might suggest something along the following lines: Let 'Ex' mean 'x exists in the sense that x is an agent which

---

13 In symbolic logic, existence is commonly figured in terms of the existential quantifier, rather than appearing as a predicate. Let 'Sx' be 'x is a swan' and 'Wx' be 'x is white'. Then we might have '(∃x) (Sx & Wx)', which we might understand as 'There exists an x, such that x is both a swan and white.' Here existence does not figure as a predicate, perhaps a heritage of Kant here, but existence is still involved. It is shoved under the logical rug, so to speak. For example, what is the mysterious x which happens to be both a swan and white, which is asserted to *exist*.

can interact with physical objects, which interaction would produce empirically discernable effects'. In this sense, illustratively, a god would count as existing if it could interact with physical objects, which interaction would produce empirically discernible effects. If the god could not do this then it might exist in some other sense, which we leave up to those concerned with such matters, but it would not exist in this particular, limited sense of existence. And, illustratively, the number six, being causally inert, would not exist in this sense either, though one might hope it could manage to exist in some other sense, perhaps a Platonic, or mathematical, one.

In the following, we take 'f' as an individual constant, taking for its value an alleged entity, France.

1. (x) (Ex v ~ Ex) (A logical truth.)
2.   Ef v ~ Ef From 1, by universal instantiation.

From what immediately precedes we know that France must either exist or not exist, and we have a particular sense of 'existence' in mind, and, as logic will have it, France must either exist or not exist in that sense, or in any sense, as long as the meaning of 'exist' is held constant.

The three most likely approaches to this problem, if one wishes to assign the property of existence to France, though surely not the only possible approaches, would be to think of France as an area, a territory, or such, or a people, a citizenry, or such, or as something other than, say, an area or a people, say, something supersensible, an idea, an ideal, an intangible entity, an unusual invisible being, a mystical entity, or something along these lines. Another possibility, of course, would be simply to deny that France exists, at least in certain senses, a possibility which, viewed in certain ways, is compatible, as we will see, with people speaking French, voting in French elections, being proud of France, fearing for the future of France, resenting disparagements of France, being ready to die for France, and so on.

Let 'Nx' be understood as 'x is a nation'
Let 'Ax' be understood as 'x is an area'.
Let 'Px' be understood as 'x is a people'
Let 'Sx' be understood as 'x is a supersensible entity'
Then consider the following formula:

(x) (Nx ⊃ (Ax v Px v Sx))[14]

We might read this in English as 'For any x, if x is a nation, then x is either an area or a people or a supersensible entity.' The 'v' here signifies inclusive disjunction, so the formula would count as true, for any legitimate substitution instance, if any or all of the disjuncts were true.

As we are worrying here, in general, about the concept of a nation, and whether nations might be said to exist, and, if so, in what way, how do they exist, and so on, I think we may take it, as a given, in the context of our example, that France is a nation, which we might symbolize as 'Nf'.

Now if France doesn't exist, then it does not exist, analytically. Accordingly, one would make the assumption that it does exist, and proceed accordingly, and see what happens.

Thus:
1. Nf   (France is a nation.)
2. Ef   (France exists.)
3. (x) (Nx ⊃ (Ax v Px v Sx))   (For any x, if x is a nation, then x is either an area or a people or a supersensible entity.)
4. Nf v ~ Ef   From 1 by logical addition.
(France is a nation or it is not the case that France exists.)
5. ~ Ef v Nf   From 4 by commutation.
(It is not the case that France exists or France is a nation.)
6. Ef ⊃ Nf   From 5, by implication.
(If France exists, then France is a nation.)
7. Nf ⊃ (Af v Pf v Sf)   From 3 by universal instantiation.
(If France is a nation, then France is an area or a people or a supersensible entity.)
8. Ef ⊃ (Af v Pf v Sf)   From 6 and 7 by hypothetical syllogism.
(If France exists, then France is an area or a people or a supersensible entity.)

In the consequent of the conditional formula in line 8 of the

---

14 As the particles are binary, this formula, technically, is not well formed. On the other hand, as 'p v (q v r)' is logically equivalent to '(pvq) v r' by association, I will use the simpler formula, It may be clearer, and, in any event, is less cluttered, and easier to work with. Too, this practice will be generally adopted.

above proof, one has a legitimate substitution instance for the Trichotomy of Historiographical Ontology.

Thus, if one can show that the substitution instance in the trichotomy is false, one will also have shown, via *modus tollens*, subject to how we are going about this, that France does not exist. This is an unhappy conclusion and one we would like to think is obviously false. On the other hand, it is conceptually instructive to discover why it is false, or even if it is false. A disjunction, or, in this case, such a trichotomy, is false, if and only if each of the disjuncts, or trijuncts, in this case, is false.

So now one addresses oneself to this inquiry.

It seems one could have nations which are not territorialized, namely, which are not attached to any particular area. One might suppose a territorialized group which, say, defeated in battle, is evicted from its location. It seems possible that such a group might carry its national identity with it, though it might be widely distributed. If we could continue to think of that as a nation, then the possession of a particular territory would not seem to be a necessary condition for the existence of a nation. Suppose a people loads its wagons and marches, as in barbarian invasions. Are they carrying a "nation" with them? Are the Dorians a nation? One speaks of the Sioux nation, but it does not seem to have a national territory. And the Sioux were not always located in the plains area of the North American continent, and even when they were, their "territory," or hunting grounds, or areas they commanded, were ill defined. There were no borders in the modern sense. One might also think of nomadic "wagon nations," such as those of the Gobi Mongols. Similarly one might think of a maritime nation, so to speak, one with no given territory it can claim as its own, but possessing a number of vessels, access to ports of call, and such. The modern nation state, if only by definition, is a recent historical development. Were the social entities from which these states emerged "nations," or, say, "prenations," or "protonations"? And consider the ancient world, of, say, city states, kingdoms, empires, and such. Was Athens a "nation?" Was Lydia, was Rome a nation? And certainly nations can disappear, even if the territory remains in place. Suppose the territory is taken away, as by conquest, is that the same thing as destroying the nation? Certainly territory can be lost, and territory can be gained. Suppose the population of France were deported, and the land was left without people. Would the remaining land still constitute a nation? As we have seen, an area is not a necessary condition for a nation; there can be nations without areas; and, similarly, obviously, an area is not a sufficient condition for a nation. The areas usually associated with present-day France existed long before there was a French nation; and if, in the wake of some planetary catastrophe, in which, say, the population of the Earth vanished, the area would presumably last long after the disappearance of the nation. Consider a *Gedankenexperiment* in which the population of France is moved to a parallel universe. Or to a far planet, or even to, say, Argentina. Does France move with them? The original area is left behind.

The upshot of the preceding considerations suggest that a nation cannot be identified with a given area, nor is a given area even a necessary condition for a nation. One may have to have a place to be, but a place to be does not seem to be essential for a nation.

The next trijunct in our proposed historiographical trichotomy is 'Px', or 'x is a people'. The notion of people, *simpliciter*, is vague. It can suggest several individual persons, as in 'there are many pleasant people on the New York City subway system', which is true, if surprising; or a locution such as 'power to the people', as though people, *en masse*, could do much of anything without being told what to do, and is usually translatable roughly as 'Give Group G power'; or racially, linguistically, or nationally, as in 'white people', 'the English-speaking peoples', or 'the French people', in which something like a common historical background, or, in later times, even a citizenry might be suggested. It might even suggest an alleged species characteristic, as in 'People are strange'.

We saw that an area is neither a necessary nor a sufficient condition for a nation.

We must now consider whether a nation is a people, or even if a people is either a necessary or a sufficient condition for a nation.

Now, clearly people, as we normally think of them, are not a sufficient condition for a nation, as people have been around much longer than nations. Similarly, most clusters of Neolithic agriculturalists in the Fertile Crescent six thousand years ago would not be likely to count as nations, nor the folks on the New York subways. What then about the notion of "a people"? Here, also, it seems we would not have a sufficient condition for a nation as there have been many "peoples" who did not constitute nations, for example, Paleolithic and Neolithic peoples, nomadic peoples, maritime peoples, peaceful peoples, warlike peoples, Alpine peoples, Mediterranean peoples, brachycephalic peoples, dolichocephalic peoples, black peoples, white peoples, Helladic peoples, Hellenic peoples, Germanic peoples, Scandinavian peoples, Asian peoples, and so on.

So we see that a people does not imply a nation. On the other hand, it seems more plausible that a nation might imply a people.[15]

If that is the case, then a people, in some sense, would be a necessary condition for a nation.

Letting alone the "necessary condition" possibility briefly, we note that a nation cannot be identified with a people. People are organisms, and nations are not, at least in the usual sense of an organism. Similarly, a people has gender. It is male and female. Nations, however fondly or skeptically one thinks of them, are neither male nor female, at least in the usual sense of male and female. Similarly, one usually thinks of a nation as one thing, and a people is many things. If, say, France was to be identified with a people, then it would not be deviant to say, for example, the average age of France is such-and-such, France is such-and-such a percentage neurotic, overweight, color blind, and so on, but it is deviant to speak that way. Similarly one does not think of part of France getting on an airplane, visiting Switzerland, returning by automobile, and so on. Similarly people come and go, but, as one usually thinks of these things, France sticks around. People are born, live, and die in a sense that France does not, and so on.

Putting aside the possibility that France can be identified with

---

15 Entailment relations, strictly, obtain amongst abstract entities, propositions, and such, and not amongst, say, physical objects. For example, rocks do not imply anything. On the other hand, 'x is a rock' logically implies 'x is a physical object'. There is nothing particularly odd, however, in saying that being a rock implies being a physical object. This sort of thing could all be put in the linguistic mode, but there seems no point in doing so. Those interested in doing so are free to do so. They may have recourse to "semantic assent," which is occasionally useful for some purposes, if they wish, but it seems unnecessary here. There is not much point in climbing the stairs when the ground floor will do just as well.

a people as mistaken, or, at least, implausible, one might then consider the seemingly far more plausible possibility that a people might be a necessary condition for a nation, in this case, France.

Could France be France without a people?

To be France, must France have a people?

If the answer to this question is affirmative, then having a people would be a necessary condition for the existence of France.

Here one notes, interestingly, that something could be a necessary condition for a nation not only without being identical with a nation, but without even being part of the definition of a nation. C, for example, might be an *empirically* necessary condition for the existence of N, without being a *logically* necessary condition for the existence of N. For example, the possession of an empirical substrate is not part of the definition of a circle, but there could be no circles were it not for empirical substrates, unless one is a Platonist, in which case circles manage on their own, or, better, the form of "circle," which, interestingly, could not itself be circular, manages on its own. In our case, if it should turn out that a state cannot be identified with a people, and is other than a people, and that a people does not enter into its definition; namely, that a people is not a logically necessary condition for a state, though perhaps an empirically necessary condition for an embodied or enacted state, then one has shown that an actual or existing people is not necessary for France to be France, though a people would be an empirically necessary condition for, so to speak, the empirical embodiment of France in a physical world. In this sense, a people would not be logically necessary for the existence of France, but would be empirically necessary for a manifestation or enactment of France. The analogy here would be that being drawn in the sand, or on a black board, or in a notebook, or such, is not part of the definition of the circle, but is essential to a manifestation or enactment of the circle.

Accepting provisionally the notion that a people is some sort of necessary condition for a nation, either logically or empirically, let us give some attention to the notion of a people.

Obviously, it has to be more than a people; it has to be a particular sort of people.

Perhaps the following *Gedankenexperimente* might be helpful in worrying through this issue.

Consider a new-born infant. He probably counts as a citizen of the nation. Perhaps he should not count a citizen of the nation. Perhaps he should not be accepted into citizenship until he has a certain acculturation, a certain education, an awareness of tradition, is old enough to understand the nature of citizenship, and such. On the other hand, clearly, most of the citizens must be quite different from the infant, or, indeed, the child. If a population was removed from a national territory and only young children were left behind, it seems likely the nation had vanished. Thus we see that a particular sort of people would be needed, assuming that a people counted as a necessary condition, either logically or empirically, for a nation.

Similarly, if we removed a population from a national territory, and imposed a different people on the national territory, presumably the nation would have vanished. It takes time to form a particular sort of people. Similarly, let us suppose that, in virtue of immigration or such, an alien population, with different traditions, and ideas of government, and such, entered the national territory, outbred the original population, took over the country, however democratically, instituted an obligatory national religion, and, in general, remolded it to its own desires, perhaps into some sort of totalitarian, police-state theocracy, it seems the former nation would be superseded, even if the name remained the same. One would then have, it seems, a new nation, under an old name. Though, one supposes, the old name would be put aside, when practical.

What if populations were switched?

Suppose, for example, that the French and Germans exchanged territories, or the French and the Argentineans exchanged territories. One supposes that France would then be where Germany is now, and vice versa, and the same for France and Argentina. The particular people would seem important, not the area.

On the other hand, suppose that the French population was subjected to memory erasure. Would this be the end of France? If so, then the "particular people" has to be far more than a particular set of identical bodies. If France would be thought to survive under these circumstances, then it seems clear that France does not require a people to be France, and thus a people would not be a necessary condition, either empirically or logically, for the existence of France. If France vanishes at this point, then a particular people, of a particular sort, would be at least an empirically necessary condition for the existence of France. The *Gedankenexperiment* is complicated if one supposes that the former French population is then implanted, perhaps electronically, with the backgrounds, traditions, and such, of, say, the Germans or Argentineans. They would then think they were Germans or Argentineans, however mistakenly, and we might be willing to say they were still French, rather as one might say a fellow suffering from delusions was still of this or that nationality, but, if this were general, what would be the consequence for France itself. Could it still exist, if wiped from the minds of its former citizens? This depends on what we take France to be. Suppose every idea of France was removed from the mind of every human being on Earth. What would be left behind but large numbers of unintelligible books, films, artifacts, place names, and such?

On the other hand, suppose that the population of France[1] in Universe[1] is exchanged, via a quantum fluctuation, with that of France[2] in Universe[2]. Then, it seems, France, in either universe, would continue on, without losing a step. So, again, the bodies are not important in themselves, but something about the bodies, or within the bodies.

That is, if a particular people is a necessary condition for the existence of a nation, either empirically or logically.

De jure questions could also enter into these things. Let us suppose the United Nations turns into a worldwide, tyrannical, socialist police state, as many seem to desire, with its own army, navy, air force, and such. Then, with its supreme power, other states being methodologically disarmed, let us suppose it decrees that France no longer exists. Presumably then, *legally*, there would no longer be a France. It was not conquered, merely abolished, by fiat. The people, on the other hand, would still be there, with their traditions, and such, but their country would not be. So we cannot identify the country with the people. Similarly, let us suppose that our tyrannical world government decides to keep France around but removes the current French population, resettling it in some less developed area, say, for the good of the planet, as it sees it, and puts a different population, from somewhere else, in the territory customarily thought of as French, and decrees, by fiat, that that population is now the French population. Presumably then, legally, it would be the French population, but it might not know French, nor anything about anything French. Thus, *legally*, any population could count as the French population, even one in Argentina, *by decree*, and thus the population of France would not even have to be a people of a particular sort. All that would be required would be the act of the overstate, or macrostate, or world government, pronouncing it to be the French population..

We see, thus, legally, one could have a people of a particular sort without having the nation, it having been abolished, and, secondly, one might have the nation without having a people of a particular sort.

Indeed, *legally*, one could have the nation without a people *of any sort*. For example, our hypothesized all-powerful world state could decree that France no longer had a population. Here one would have the case, *in law*, that France existed, but no one was any longer French, thus having the situation of a nation without a people, a people then not being a necessary condition, of any sort, either empirically or logically, for the nation. To be sure, this is not of much interest, as a supreme state could decree anything, for example, that a horse was a senator, following the precedent set by Caligula, and, more intriguingly, that black was white, men were women, and so on. Supposedly the British Parliament has such power. At any rate, whereas this may work for senators, colors and genders would prove recalcitrant. To be sure one could always call rich cream thin milk, and vice versa, and thus, as in the story by Sholom Aleichem, the rich would have to make do with thin milk and the poor would finally get to enjoy rich cream.

Perhaps a people is not a necessary condition, either empirically or logically, for a nation.

For example, suppose that the population of France vanished. There would still exist a network of relations, diplomatic and commercial, with other nations. Presumably treaties, agreements, and such, would still be in effect. Could they be in effect with what does not exist? A territory, too, would still be there, with borders, and such. An individual might think of himself, properly or improperly, as having entered France when he had crossed the English channel at a certain point, and so on.

Most people use the concept of "nation," as nearly as I can tell, without any clear idea of what they are talking about.

This might be a good idea, but it is philosophically problematical.

Let us now turn to an interpretation of "nation talk" which seems to fit best with uncritical discourse.

This brings us to our third trijunct in the trichotomy of historiographical ontology, namely, that a nation is a supersensible entity. A supersensible entity would be something like an idea, an ideal, an intangible entity, an unusual invisible being, a mystical entity, or something along these lines.

Two things seem to be very clear at this point, first, that almost everyone would deny, even scoff at, the idea that they might take a nation, say, France, to be a supersensible entity, and, two, they talk and write as if that were exactly what they were doing.

Did not France do this or that, at this time or that time?

How did she come about?

How has she changed over the ages?

Are there not histories of France, did she not have her kings, her geniuses and heroes, has she not lost and won wars, did she not come to the aid of the young American Republic in the latter part of the Eighteenth Century, did she not have a Revolution which produced the first modern nation state, was Napoleon not once her emperor, was she not the dominant power in Europe at one time, is her art and literature not better known than that of, say, Lithuania, does she not now have a space program, is she not now a nuclear power, and so on. What direction will France go? What will she do next, and so on?

We are trying to consider the concept of a nation. We are trying to undertake, in Whitehead's terminology, "the analysis of the obvious," and, as is often the case, one discovers, under analysis, that the obvious is often subtle and complex, and anything but obvious.

This is new philosophical territory.

One is making the first maps.

At this point it is clear that it is not well advised to think of a nation in terms of a territory, nor, interestingly, is it necessary to think of a nation in terms of a people, even a particular sort of people. This does not deny, of course, that one usually associates nations with a territory and a people, of a particular sort, at a particular time. On the other hand, if we can have nations without territories or peoples, even of particular sorts, at a particular time, this brings us to, as noted above, at least one other possibility, say, the third element in the trichotomy of historiographical ontology.

To this we now proceed.

In order to make more clear what is going on here, because the matter is likely to be surprising and quite unfamiliar to most, let us, in analogy, initially, contrast two senses of form, a Platonic sense and an Aristotelian sense. In the Platonic sense of form there would be, say, a form of horse, which has some sort of existence independent of particular horses. Indeed, even if horses became extinct this form would remain extant, safe in its independent existence. In the Aristotelian sense of form there would be, say, a form of horse, and, as in the Platonic sense, this form, while not a horse itself, would be what makes a horse a horse. But the Aristotelian form, at least of the horse sort, unlike the Platonic form, has no independent existence. It is embodied in matter, forming matter. The union of form and matter produces a substance. There are many conceptual problems connected with both the Platonic and Aristotelian conceptions here, but, at least verbally, the distinction seems reasonably clear.[16] In the Aristotelian view, if there were no horses, the form "horse"

---

16 A sampling of difficulties connected with these conceptions would be the lack of confirmation and falsification conditions. What empirical evidence might be offered for independent Platonic forms? What empirical evidence would disconfirm the hypothesis of their existence? How many forms, and of what sorts, are there? Is there a form for Chihuahua and another for Great Danes, or will "Dog" do? Do women count under the form "Man," or do we need a form "Woman," etc. Is there a form for "impatience," for "jolly," for "motion," for "change," etc. Aristotle might seem to have problems with evolution, as in moving from the three-toed Eohippus to the modern race horse, etc. If the forms are embodied, and have no existence if not embodied, are they then multiplied and disunified, as one is in Stable$_1$ and the next is in Stable$_2$, and both are now, along with their matter, eating hay, etc. Do big horses and little horses, fat horses and thin horses, matter? Does one have, if these are embodied, big and little forms, fat and thin forms, and so on? It is probably a mistake to think of forms pictorially, of course, not just in cases like courage and justice, but even in cases like "horse" and "triangle." Probably one should think of them in terms of logistic criteria. Thus, for example, a given criterion for triangle would handle triangles of all shapes and sizes. It is not so clear, however, that this works for embodied forms. Aristotle criticized Plato for "eternal sensibles," but it seems Aristotle's forms, being embodied, might count as "transitory sensibles." To be sure, there are complex issues here, of various sorts, and much seems obscure.

would be in a bad way, having lost out on existence. On the Platonic view, it remains ontologically secure. On both views, however, we note, the form cannot be identified with any particular horse. That is what is important here. Now let us suppose there is a form of "nation." If all actual nations perished, the Platonic form would be unaffected. And all the Aristotelian form would need to survive would be at least one actual embodiment, one enacted nation. On the Aristotelian view, then, the form is independent of any particular enactment, unless there is only one enactment.

Now presumably in both Plato and Aristotle there are tiers of forms. For example, presumably both would have a form of living being, a form of animal, and a form of horse, the form of horse doubtless incorporating that of animal, living thing, and who knows what else. If this is the case, we might regard, say, France, as a form which incorporates, or is an instance of, the form "nation." Forms, after all, can be instances of other forms, more general forms. France, then, would be a form which might be enacted. On a Platonic view, it would not even require an enactment to exist; on the Aristotelian view it would not require any particular enactment, and thus would be independent of any particular area or population, or such, though it would require, say, at least some population, or such, at any given time, to exist. In the Platonic sense no enactment or embodiment is necessary; in the Aristotelian sense no particular enactment or embodiment is necessary, but some enactment or embodiment would be necessary.

I think these remarks are a suitable introduction to the sort of thing which might be involved in the third element of the ontological trichotomy of historiography. On the other hand, we are not suggesting that the best understanding of "nation" or "France" is in terms of either Platonic or Aristotelian forms. As far as I know there is no form for "nation" in either Plato or Aristotle, though both were interested in diverse forms of government, and there is certainly no form "France."

All forms in Plato and Aristotle, of course, were not limited to entities such as "triangle," "horse," "courage," and such. There would also be forms for, say, "shuttle" and "bridle," which are artifacts. The remarkable, wonderful, and troublesome Ayn Rand, who was less than an enthusiast for Athens' most venerated philosopher, Plato, and was almost more than an enthusiast for her second most venerated philosopher, Aristotle, once asked, it seems rhetorically, if there were forms for "spark plug" and "monkey wrench." Probably the best answer to her question would be, "There are now." If there could a form for, say, "bed," as we learn in Plato's Republic, can spark plugs and monkey wrenches be far behind? The point here is not whether or not the Platos and Aristotles of one day or another anticipated spark plugs and monkey wrenches, but whether or not such things lend themselves to a Platonic or Aristotelian analysis, and if there would be much point in having them do so. A moment's reflection will suggest that Plato has the best of it here. On Aristotle's view the form of the spark plug and monkey wrench would no longer exist if there were no extant spark plugs and monkey wrenches. On the other hand, clearly the form would still exist, enabling folks to manufacture new spark plugs and monkey wrenches. The form need not exist in some eternal Platonic state of being, or merely as a logical possibility, such as erudite purple unicorns, but might exist in human minds, in plans, in directions, and such. Here we see the form would require no enactment, no more than the form of a new artifact which has been conceived, but not yet built, and may never be built.

Forms can be invented.

And they need not be embodied or enacted.

Similarly forms can be unwittingly invented. There is nothing Freudian here. It is something, actually, which is quite common, and familiar. A great deal of light is shed on this matter by the researches of a variety of thinkers, in particular, political analysts and economists. These people are sometimes thought of as spontaneous-order theorists, evolved-order theorists, systemic-process theorists, and such. In this area of inquiry, one sometimes hears of "evolutionary rationalism."

Since ancient times a popular dichotomy has often been drawn between the natural and the artificial, or conventional. For example, the warning cry or hiss of an animal might be regarded as natural but the word 'danger' as artificial, or conventional, a dominance hierarchy as natural, the explicit designation of a leader by means of a token, such as a necklace of bear claws, artificial, and so on. There may be some dispute here as to the borderline, where to put social organization, the family, and such, but the dichotomy is both familiar and popular. Spontaneous-order theorists, on the other hand, have called our attention to the fact that several of the greatest and most important human institutions elude this simplistic dichotomy. These are constructions which are, as the saying has it, the result of human action but not of human design. They are akin to evolution in the sense that they have arisen naturally over long periods, unplanned, in virtue of innumerable social selections, but are akin, as well, to the artificial or conventional in the sense that human beings have had a hand in their formation. Some typical examples of such constructions, amongst many, are language, law, and the market. These things are intricate and, on the whole, work marvelously, but their current forms were not anticipated by the beast who invented the first word, the hominid who made the first ruling, the fellow who first who first exchanged so much flint for so much food.

One encounters in social theory, in Hobbes and Locke, the notion of a social contract. As human social groupings presumably emerged from animal groupings, the notion of a social contract seems unlikely, if understood as an event in human history. For example, crows, as far as we know, never stopped to think about it, called a meeting, and decided to flock together. Nor, so to speak, did humans. Early human groups presumably spent much of their free time not in drafting contracts but slaughtering one another over hunting grounds. The conquest and oppression, and murder and enslavement, of weaker groups would have been more likely than contractual negotiation. Where an armistice was in order, given a balance of power, staying out of one another's way would be more likely than entering into harmonious social arrangements. There is a sense in which one can think of an implicit social contract, or compact, which is the sense that, within a group, a necessary condition for the group's survival is some measure of civility and cooperation. In this sense, any individual who prefers to submit himself to the group rather than be robbed, imprisoned, or killed might be regarded as having chosen to abide by the social contract, or compact. He no longer has a jungle available into which he may, if he wishes, slink away, surreptitiously. This is not to deny that a polity might be devised, such as a nation here or there, such as the United States of America, though in the light of numerous precedents in political theory, tradition, custom, law, and so on. One might also note the League of Nations and the United Nations, but these would count not as nations, but organizations of nations, through which various nations will, one supposes, to the best of their ability, seek their own welfare. For most practical purposes nations still stand to one another in a state of nature. If not, one supposes several nations, by now, would have been voted out of existence.

Most nations have been founded on conquest, or have been the result of war or revolution, and, from that point on, have tended to develop, often in ways that might have surprised, if not distressed, the original captains and bandits, soldiers or brigands, or statesmen, from whose work they first emerged.

Recall that forms can be invented, and now realize that the invention of a form need not be intended. It may emerge in virtue of countless social selections over centuries, or millennia. It may be the result of human action but not of human design. Many are the consequences of actions which are not anticipated by the participants in the action. It is easy to start a war, without anticipating how it will finish. Dropping white and black pebbles into an urn is a long way from voting machines and the Electoral College. Perhaps the Germans were not well advised to send Lenin to the Finland Station.

In the investigation of the supersensible-entity approach to the notion of a nation, which seems to be a default position following upon the failure of the territorial and populational accounts, one would wish to distinguish between two different sorts of "supersensible entities," namely, forms of some sort, and, so to speak, invisible organisms, intangible organisms, mystical persons, and such.

One notes in passing that the most straightforward and least sophisticated interpretation of the overwhelming majority of references to France, both in scholarly and popular literature, would suggest that an invisible organism, an intangible organism, a mystical person, or such, was the subject of the innumerable references. 'France' is, one supposes, a proper name. We might refer to this analysis in general as being an "invisible substance" analysis. Once again, we note that this option would presumably be unwelcome to most commentators, journalists, historians, and such. We suggest it primarily, at least at first, because it is the most obvious interpretation of the literatures in question. Too, one would not wish to dismiss it out of hand. Indeed, one might wish to return to it. It might not turn out to be as stupid and simple-minded a hypothesis as it is likely to seem to most folks with a robust sense of reality.

The other major form of the "supersensible option" would be some sort of "form" option.

This is quite different, at least verbally, from the "invisible substance" option because forms are not substances, at least not in the sense of a thing which can do this and that, change over time, and such.

So, do not think of a form as a substance, or, at least, not as a changing substance. Think rather of a form as a form at a particular time. Eohippus is not Citation. It is convenient to use the term 'horse' to refer to both, but they are different. Similarly one might, as a verbal convenience, use the word 'France' to refer to an entity in the time of Voltaire, and another in the time of Jean-Paul Sartre, but they are not the same entity. France^n and France^{n+1} are not the same, no more than two follows named 'Pierre', say, Pierre^1 and Pierre^2, are the same fellow. Each, analyzed, would have a different form. It is more accurate to think of forms *replacing* forms, rather than a single form undergoing change. Forms are not organisms. In this way any given form may be the result of social selections, the result of human action but not of human design, but it is not identical with preceding or succeeding forms. A form is considered to last until it is replaced. The most likely alternative to this form analysis would be to commit oneself, either implicitly or explicitly, to an invisible substance, a mystical substance, or something along those lines. One may wish to do something like that, eventually; but not at this time.

We will not, incidentally,. concern ourselves with interpretations of the supersensible entity in terms of ideas or ideals, though such might be involved. For example, there is something to saying that France is an idea or an ideal, but that something is not of much use in this context. Ideas presumably require human minds. I do not think we would want to locate France in a variety of minds. Presumably different minds would entertain very different ideas, and we do not want several Frances. Similarly some of these ideas might be logically incompatible, and we do not want France to turn out to be impossible. Similarly many people who are not French may have ideas of France, or think they do. And we do not want to put part of France in Argentina, several other parts in Asia, and so on. Also, if everyone changed their mind, or had a memory lapse, we would not want France to vanish. Similar considerations militate against the notion that France is an ideal, for an ideal would presumably be the object of thought, and thus share the perils of thought. If there were no thoughts, presumably there would be no ideals. Also, France is not an ideal in the mind of many, for example, in the minds of some of its critics, French and otherwise.

This returns us then to the "invisible substance" notion and the "form" notion.

Before trying to evaluate, and recommend or dismiss, either of those notions, it will be useful to briefly consider three other options, each of which is likely to have its proponents, presumably exasperated by now. These are the "look and see," the "language-game," and the "internal/external question" options. All of these have in common something valuable, which is a sensitivity to the word/world distinction. The first two options, which I am adapting and revising for my purposes, are suggested by the work of, so to speak, the second Ludwig Wittgenstein, that of the *Philosophical Investigations*, and such, as opposed to the "first Wittgenstein," that of the *Tractatus Logico-Philosophicus*, a remarkable book more in the spirit of an early Logical Empiricism. The third option is due to Rudolf Carnap. In none of these cases am I attributing my use of these options to the original authors. I am being influenced; I am not explicating.

"What is an x?"

An Aristotelian approach to this sort of question might be to look for an essence, which is presumably something in the entity itself, and a modern version of that sort of thing, though obviously different, as it is semanticized, might be to look for the necessary and sufficient conditions which must be satisfied before we could correctly designate something as an x. Let us suppose, we asked, "What is a human being?" Presumably Aristotle would come up with something along the lines, "a human being is a rational animal." Aristotle, as noted earlier, was an optimist. A more modern philosopher, provided he, too, was an optimist, and had not thought much about dolphins, communicative chimpanzees, irrational human beings, and such, might say something along the lines, "for the expression 'human being' to be correctly applied the entity must satisfy the condition of rational animality, which would be both necessary and sufficient for the correct application of the term." One might, of course, define a human being, or the words 'human being', in a variety of ways, depending on one's purposes, or what properties seemed interesting or important. Purposes become important. 'Essence', if one wishes to retain the term, becomes purpose-relative.[17]

Wittgenstein would seem to suggest at this point that rather than look for necessary and sufficient conditions one should look and see what is involved. Pay attention to the subject matter. His famous example is "games." Rather than try to come up with necessary and sufficient conditions for something being a game,

---

17 One must watch one's step, of course. One science might define a human being as an x with a brain of type B, and another science might define a human being as an x with a posture of type P. Thus, with respect to the first science ,'For every x, x is a human being if and only if x has a brain of type B' would be analytic, a logical truth, and, similarly, for the second science ,'For every x, x is a human being if and only if x has a posture of type P' would be analytic, a logical truth. Also, analytic locutions can imply only analytic locutions, never contingent statements, never falsifiable statements.
Consider the following formulas:
1. (x) (x is a human being ≡ x has a brain of type B)
2. (x) (x is a human being ≡ x has a posture of type P)
3. (x) (x has a brain of type B ≡ x has a posture of type P)
Lines 1 and 2 imply line 3. Line 3 is clearly contingent, clearly falsifiable. It is easy to conceive of an x which has a brain of type B but does not have a posture of type P, say, a centaur, and, similarly, it is easy to conceive of an entity which does not have a brain of type B but does have a posture of type P, perhaps a protohuman, or such. As one cannot accept that analytic statements can generate contingent statements, falsifiable statements, one must regard the conjunction of 1 and 2 as nonanalytic, despite the fact that either, separately, could be held to be analytic. This does not mean logic is in danger; it only means one must be careful how one goes about defining things

examine games, and, as one can, see their interrelationships, their "family resemblances," so to speak. There may not be, one might hypothesize, necessary and sufficient conditions involved. For example, not all games are amusing, not all have winners and losers, and so on. It is not clear that a child's bouncing a ball off a wall and catching it has much in common with World Championship Chess. Games might have much in common without there being anything which all games have in common. A might have something in common with B and B might have something in common with C, but there is no reason to suppose that A and C have anything in common, other than, say, both being called "games." They might have something in common, and they might not. Look and see.

Now this approach, whatever its merits here and there, and one supposes they are many, does not seem too helpful with "France." France is not a set of games. One might, one supposes, look at the French railway system, the French post office, the Louvre, French cinema, French night life, and such, but this does not seem helpful. The approach might seem to work better with "nations," since, as with games, there at least seem to be several around. On the other hand, the "look and see" approach is not helpful here either, for several reasons. First, what does one see when one looks? Railroad stations, stores, taxi cabs, people coming and going, street cars and buses, markets, government buildings, a postal service, perhaps a few airports, and such. What makes something a nation is not likely to be seen when one looks. Nations are not like games. Nations may indeed have many family resemblances; perhaps A has railroads in common with B and perhaps B has a navy in common with C, but perhaps A has no navy and C has no railroads, and such. Second, there may well be some things which all or most nations have, such as an area and a population, but we have noted the difficulties militating against taking such things as definitive of nations. Too, nations are not identified with sets of physical objects. A nation is not a heap, not a collection. This approach, too, is substantially verbal. One just takes the word 'nation' and goes from there. And does not go far. This would not even work with games, if the language was slightly different. Suppose the word 'game' was also applied to bicycles. Then looking and seeing would discover some two wheeled games, but would this shed much light on possible relationships, direct or indirect, as to why hide-and-seek and bridge are both called games? Perhaps all games do have something in common, as Hillary Putnam, claimed, in that they are all played But are Olympic Games played? And things are played which are not games, such as trumpets and violins.

In my view, the "look and see" approach, the "collection" approach, is not helpful. It may not do even for games, a terrain seemingly ideally suited, and perhaps for that reason chosen, for the deployment of its artillery. In any event, perhaps an analysis can be found which transcends what can be filed, cataloged, and photographed.

The "language-game" approach may be more plausible, and in any event will lead us eventually to the Carnapian notion of diverse realms of discourse, which is worth serious consideration.

Wittgenstein uses the notion of a "language game" extremely broadly, to cover, it seems, much, if not all, of what human beings do with language, and, too, language is often closely interwoven with behavior, and that is perhaps the most basic form of the language games, the intertwining of sound with doing. Some examples of "language games" would be what you do when you tell a joke, when you issue orders, when you make believe, when you give an account to someone of a dream you had, when you inform a colleague concerning something you saw on the street yesterday, and so on. One learns to play these "language games," and they involve various ways of interacting with others. Presumably bantering, insulting, persuading, manipulating, threatening, delighting, and so on, would all be ways of using language. It is a complex, supple instrument and it suffices for many purposes. It functions in a variety of ways and Wittgenstein's primary interest seems to be in understanding and describing these ways rather than in evaluating them. One supposes there would be a "historiographical language game," a "philosophy language game," and so on. One gets the impression, hopefully wrongly, that this is more analogous to mood music or humming than to science and strict cognitivity. One makes this verbal move and it is countered by another verbal move. Words float. These endeavors are a form of verbal chess, and the pawns, the kings, and the rooks, never get off the board, do not need to, and have no inclination to do so. One does not ask for the meanings of words, but how they are used, and so on. Wittgenstein scholarship is complex, interpretations abound, and controversy exists. Accordingly, although the view I am presenting here seems to me correct, and fits in nicely with the notion of Wittgenstein's philosophical behaviorism, and such, it may be incorrect. Indeed, I hope that is the case. At any rate, we are less concerned here with the explication of Wittgenstein than we are with the application of one possible understanding, correct or incorrect, of "language games" to our subject matter, an application and understanding which, if accepted, would have considerable relevance.[18]

Basically, the historiographer is playing his language game, and, in this language game, he should feel no compunction, or concern whatsoever in referring to, and utilizing, notions such as destinies, inevitabilities, forces, ages, influences, causes, patterns, cultures, nations, etc. Do not ask for an analysis of this discourse, or what it might mean, if anything. That question may impair, if not ruin, the game. Stay on the board with the kings and queens, the rooks and the bishops, and don't ask questions. Just play the game, and forget it.

One supposes that that might be a good idea, for a couple of reasons. One, it would save a great deal of time which might otherwise be expended in trying to understand what one is doing, if anything. Reflection is always hazardous, and may be confusing.

---

18 Interestingly, a supposed humanitarian consequence of this approach, either one in coincidental attendance or perhaps one literally intended, and constituting a compassionate motivation for the enterprise, is also to be noted. Wittgenstein spoke of language as "bewitching the intelligence," and wished "to show the fly the way out of the fly bottle." The notion here seems to be that the tricky treacheries of language are likely to lead the uninformed or unwary into fruitless labyrinths from which few could return unscathed. On this approach, philosophy, at least as often practiced, would seem to require, as Schopenhauer said of metaphysical solipsism, not a refutation but a cure. Philosophers and others must be saved from themselves, rescued from the pitfalls of language into which the simple and ignorant may so easily stumble. Supposedly the natural uses of natural language, if observed and understood in the context of the "language games" involved, will not lead to tormenting puzzles, and, properly understood, may help in extricating the lost, if not doomed, from their quandaries, which result from a misuse and misunderstanding of language. This is sometimes spoken of as "therapeutic positivism." It is perhaps unfortunate that Wittgenstein was not born two to three millennia earlier; we might have been spared philosophy. Plato might then have made good as a tyrant and Aristotle as a biologist.

Two, it gives us an account of historiographical discourse which is, in effect, that it is a speech activity which for the most part resides in, and thrives in, its own unanalyzed, uncritical, unquestioning, self-contented universe of discourse, or game. The question is to consider how terms are used, not what they mean, if anything. So time would be saved, and the game can go on.

Whereas referring to these things as "games" might seem belittling, and perhaps is, the metaphor is perhaps justified because the notion is that there are ways in which things are done and ways in which they are not done. Therefore, there is some justification, if not much, for speaking of "rules," and where there are rules one might suppose that games would come naturally to mind. Also, calling something a game need not be understood as dismissing it as either trivial or unimportant. Russian Roulette is a game, and many think of war as mankind's most stupid and dangerous, if occasionally necessary, game.

To be sure, this "game" notion of historiography, philosophy, and a variety of other disciplines, is not likely to be universally appealing, or persuasive. Accepting it would not solve our problems, but would dismiss them. In effect, it would say, "Lo, and behold, there is no problem!"

Forgetting about a historiographical or philosophical problem, or a problem in Shakespearean criticism, or such, may not be as dangerous as forgetting about the problem of a famine, a contaminated water supply, or the Huns at the gate, but not everyone can, or desires, to forget about such problems. They seem to persist. Once one has doused them with Wittgensteinian acid, or put them on the Wittgensteinian couch hoping for a remission of symptoms, and they resist the acid, having failed to notice it, and they prove belligerent and recalcitrant patients, clinging doggedly to their alleged delusions, one seems to have two likely choices. The first is to accept that one is benighted and ignorant, and a hopeless case, and that what one is doing is misguided and stupid, and one has failed to grasp this, and the second is that the doctor is mistaken.

Philosophy will survive the second Wittgenstein, just as it did the first, enriched for having known him, but getting on with its business. There is more to philosophy than semantic taxonomy and recipes for curing nonexistent linguistic maladies. There is more to inquiry and cognitivity, and clarification, and recommendation, than an uncritical acquiescence to a linguistic *status quo*, a prescription for semantic conservatism, an uncritical submission to the accidents of casual discourses developed over centuries for purposes independent of philosophical awareness and concerns. The key to philosophical progress, if it is attainable, does not lie in the speech habits of the plumber and grocer, nor in substituting one inquiry for another, nor in giving up the search for truth or conceptual refinement. A technical vocabulary, an articulated, special, customized lexicon, with attention to its development and precision, is essential for a serious intellectual discipline. Physics no longer makes do with earth, air, fire, and water, or, say, the cold and dry, the hot and fluid, the hot and dry, and the cold and wet.

It is true that a historian may be successful with little or no knowledge of, or attention to, the conceptual aspects of his discipline. Indeed, he may pride himself on his ignorance in this area. That is surely possible. It is not at issue. No one denies that it is possible for a historian to be successful, and shallow.

In any event, we are not willing to substitute the description of a "language game," whose relationship to the world is tenuous, if existent, for an attempt to better illuminate, and relate to, the world, an attempt which must necessarily discover, or propose, relationships between words, or concepts, and the world.

We want to do more than use words; we would like to use them meaningfully.

A third approach, the first having been the "look and see," or "collection" approach, and the second having been the "language game" approach, which would be compatible with contemporary speech practice in historiography, pretty much letting it go on in any way it might please, is one suggested by the work of Rudolf Carnap, and has to do with the distinction between what might be called internal and external questions. In my view this approach is far more judicious, and interesting, though ultimately as unacceptable, as the "look and see," or "collection," approach, and the "language game" approach.[19]

---

[19] "Empiricism, Semantics, and Ontology," Rudolf Carnap, *Meaning and Necessity: A Study in Semantics and Modal Logic*. (Phoenix Books, University of Chicago Press, Chicago, Enlarged Edition, Fourth Impression, 1964).

Carnap's famous distinction between internal and external questions is perhaps best illuminated in the context of his own example, which has to do with numbers. This has its relation to the notion of abstract entities, forms, universals, and such, and the alleged ontological status of such entities. Carnap, as a logical positivist, is inclined to be skeptical of such questions. For example, it is clear that raccoons and chipmunks exist, and one knows what it would be for them to exist, and has some sense of how to investigate the issues connected with their existence. On the other hand, it is much less clear what it would mean for an abstract entity, say, a number, to exist. How would one prove that, say, the number two existed. How long has it existed, where does it exist, can it exist without existing somewhere, how does it go about existing, does it need minds, or a notation, for it to exist, would it continue to exist if the universe disappeared, etc. Carnap, as a positivist, naturally, is wary of such questions. Are they not metaphysical questions, questions which seem verbal, at best? On the other hand, clearly one can think of the number two, in some way or another, and there are a number of things which are demonstrably true and false about the number two, for example, it comes between one and three, is more than one, and less than three, is half of four, and so on. Carnap's approach here is to work out a way of giving two its due, while avoiding dubious, even unintelligible, existential commitments.

What one might do here then is to distinguish between questions which are internal to a system and questions about the system as a whole. In this way one might ascribe an intrasystemic existence to the number two, recognizing its ontological status, or place, or function, within a number system, but deny meaning to the external question, which would have to do with the system as a whole. Thus the answer to the internal question, "Do numbers exist?" is affirmative, for two, three, and so on, exist, within the system, but the answer to the external question, "Do numbers exist?" is neither affirmative nor negative; it is an improper question, with no methodology available by means of which it might be resolved.

In the context of our inquiry, then, we might suggest something analogous to what Carnap was doing with numbers. As a historiographical internal question, within the system, so to speak, the answer to a question such as "Do nations exist?" or "Does France exist?" would be clearly affirmative. They figure within the system of historiographical discourse. They are familiar counters, which have their familiar uses. On the other hand, as an external question, "Do nations exist?" or "Does France exist?" is less clear, at least, for one would have to know what one means by 'nations' and 'France', and so on. What is a nation, what is France? It is no longer enough just to use the words in the usual manner. It would be more like asking what is a number, say, the number two, in some sense other than noting that it is more than one and less than three, and so on. For example, is it the class of all pair-classes; is it a type as opposed to a token; is it a form or universal; is it an idea in people's minds; is it the object of an idea in people's minds, and, if so, what sort of object; is it a fiction, an invention, a postulate, a mere notational convenience, a collection of marks on a page, or what?

This approach, which we have referred to, with some license, as "Carnapian," resembles the "language game" approach in that it leaves historiographical discourse in place.

On the other hand, there are different ways of leaving things in place. For example, Carnap is not a philosophical behaviorist. Meaning is important to him, indeed, essential. For example, he might draw a distinction between intension and extension, between properties and classes. For example, the intension of the expression 'dog' would be whatever property would be necessary and sufficient for something to be correctly counted as a dog, whereas the extension of the same expression would be a class, in this case, the class of dogs. Carnap, personally, finds precise systems congenial. This is quite different from taking the linguistic world as one finds it, and stopping. His work is more normative than descriptive, for example, in proposing intelligibilities as opposed to calling attention to speech activity, in addressing oneself to the explication of language rather than observing and cataloging empirical facts of actual usage, and so on. Too, Carnap is a linguistic pragmatist, willing to allow himself expressions such as 'number', or 'property' or 'class', in virtue of their usefulness in discourse and intellection in general. Recall the distinction between the internal and external question. Lastly, one supposes that Carnap would be unlikely to find the "game" analysis of speech activity illuminating when dealing with the cognitive aspects of language, those in which he is primarily interested. The most plausible approach to truth, for example, would have less to do with on what occasions people use the expression 'true' than what accounts for a linguistic entity's being true, presumably some relationship between its meaning and the world.

Thus, in the Carnapian approach, the internal discourse of historiography would seem to be explicitly referential and cognitive in ways one would not require of a language game. The rules of a language game could, in theory, be as arbitrary as those of bridge or chess. That they are not suggests that much more than a game is involved. One could invent a mathematical language game in which two counted as three, if one were willing to accept all the ensuing consequences elsewhere in the system. In a language game one could design and revise the rules in a number of ways, as one fancied. On the Carnapian approach, very little, if anything, is arbitrary. The system exists and there are true and false statements within it. Similarly, Carnapian language involves intrasystemic existential claims. The kings and queens, the bishops and the rooks, come down from their board and mix with the commoners. As an internal statement 'France exists' is clearly true, and 'France does not exist' is clearly false. This does not have to do with how words are used, words that might be used differently, but with their intrasystemic referents. Logic and referentiality are essential here; there is a connection here not with how words might or might not be used, but with what they *mean*. Semantics takes precedence over usage. Also, for Carnap there is an external question, which he recognizes, but, in the case of numbers, at least, is deemed metaphysical, unamenable to empirical assessment. From the language-game approach, it seems the external question would not even exist. If it did come up, perhaps it might be therapized away.

Thus, on this approach, as in the "language game" approach,. historiography's internal discourse would for the most part remain untouched. Historians would continue to go about their work much as usual, just as mathematicians go about their work as usual, without worrying about the ontological status of numbers. It might not even occur to them that there might be a problem there. As long as two and two continue to come up to four, the average mathematician is not likely to worry about whether or not this is possible. For example, if two does not exist, how can it do anything, let alone be half of four? If it does exist, please tell us about it, how it exists and so on.

Internally, one could take the meaning of, say, 'France' to be unpacked in thousands of ways, as in, say, 'the nation once ruled by Louis XIV', 'a country of which Rousseau and Voltaire were once citizens,' 'the nation whose capital is Paris', and so on. Similarly one could unpack the notion falsely, as in 'the nation of which Goethe was a citizen', 'the country whose capital is Berlin', and so on. Internally, cognitivity abounds.

One could then take the more philosophical questions, such as 'What is a nation?', 'What is France?', and so on, to be external questions. And, in a sense, it would be as safe for the historian to ignore such questions as it is for the mathematician to ignore questions about numbers. On the approach of the linguistic pragmatist one might allow oneself expressions like 'nation' and 'France' in virtue of their convenience, or utility, within a realm of discourse. Thus. one could allow oneself the claim 'France is a European nation' to be true, without having the least idea what, if anything, France was, or what, if anything, a nation might be.

It seems, however, that the analogy between internal and external number discourse and internal and external historiographical discourse breaks down. There are a number of important differences between these modalities of discourse which militate against using the one as an illuminating analogy for the other, and thus authorizing, or recommending, or permitting, the internal/external approach to historiography.

It is clear that numbers, as usually thought of, if one thinks about it, are regarded as abstract entities. That is certainly not the case with, say, nations. One might discover that the best analysis of a nation is along those lines, but that would have to be argued, and is certainly not to be presupposed. Secondly, the way in which one learns primitively about nations is quite different from the way one learns primitively about numbers. One learns about nations by empirical inquiry; and, beyond counting pebbles, and such, one learns about numbers by rational inquiry; in the one case, one might consult documents; in the other case one might calculate, derive theorems, and such. One discovers the truths of mathematics in one way, the truths of historiography in another way. The truths of mathematics, are, for the most part, demonstrable; the truths of historiography, if demonstrable, are not demonstrable in the same way. Confirmation procedures in mathematics are quite unlike those in historiography. One can do things with numbers you can't do with nations. For example, you can multiply them by 647. And you can do things with nations you can't do with numbers, for example, conquer them. The entities of mathematics are immune from change; they are independent of the "pollutions of mortality." The entities of historiography, nations, and such, on the other hand, lack neither mortality nor pollutions. They come into being, and it is always possible, though hopefully not inevitable, that they will perish. The number two looks on with equanimity. Lastly, numbers are causally inert. They don't do anything; they just sit there. On the other hand, as we commonly think of nations, they are not causally inert. Like winds, floods, and earthquakes they can produce changes with empirically discernible consequences. In this realm of discourse there is no interesting and dramatic difference between internal and external questions. If there were an external question here, the answer to it would seem to be in the affirmative, namely, yes, nations exist, France exists, and so on. The question then would be, what are these things, and how do they exist. And, one supposes, there are plausible answers to such questions, though answers which might turn out to be surprising.

Recall our proposed formula, involving the trichotomy of historiographical ontology, in which, to have an example, we proposed France as the value for an individual constant, and used that constant as a legitimate substitution instance, within the quantified functions.

Accordingly:

$Ef \supset (Af \vee Pf \vee Sf)$

(If France exists, then France is an area or a people or a supersensible entity.)

Recall that we learned that France could not identified with either an area or a people, even of a particular sort. For example, it might be regarded as still involved in treaty obligations, and such, even if its population mysteriously vanished. Further, if neither an area nor a people are a logically necessary condition for a nation, then the conjunction of an area and a people cannot constitute a logically necessary condition for a nation either. This is not to deny, of course, that we ordinarily think of nations as involving an area and a population. Indeed, one might even be tempted to suppose that a people, at least, might be an empirically necessary condition for a nation, if not a logically necessary condition for a nation, particularly if one were of an Aristotelian cast of mind. On the other hand, the *Gedankenexperiment* of the treaty-bound entity whose population vanishes while the treaties remain in effect, demonstrates that a people is not even an empirically necessary condition for a nation. This does not mean, however, that we, having withdrawn from the Lyceum, must now enroll in the Academy.

As we have rejected the first two trijuncts, 'Af' and 'Pf', in the trichotomy, that means we have only the third trijunct, 'Sf', left, namely, the possibility that France is a supersensible entity of some sort.

The two most likely supersensible entities, as you may recall, are those of a "form" and an "invisible substance," perhaps a mysterious person, or such.

Now, whereas forms may come into being, be invented, be discarded, be forgotten, and such, they are, in their nature, timeless, changeless, and causally inert. Consider the form of "monkey wrench" or "spark plug." One does not think of the form of the spark plug as being eternal, but one does not think of it, either, as appropriately considered in the matrix of temporal predicates. It does not worry about next Tuesday, either in Minneapolis or elsewhere. One does not think of it as having a certain age, and being older tomorrow than it was today, and so on. You do not celebrate its birthdays, or berate if for being tardy for appointments, and such. It is much like a theorem, perhaps one recently derived. Was the theorem waiting for all eternity to be derived? Was the spark plug there from all eternity, waiting to be thought up, etc.? Forms do not watch clocks, nor do clocks tick in the vicinity of forms. They have different ontological habitats. Also, forms do not change, develop, grow, thrive, degenerate, or perish, or such.

They are changeless. If one thinks up a new spark plug one form is replaced by another form. The first form has not changed, but has been superseded, or replaced. Forms do not change. Similarly, forms, like numbers, are causally inert. They do not exist, if they exist, in the special sense of existence which we earlier selected, namely, that of agents which can interact with physical objects, the interaction with which would produce empirically discernible effects.

So we see that forms are timeless, changeless, and causally inert.

They are accordingly ruled out as candidates for nations, as nations, at least as one usually thinks of them, are temporal entities. France is older today than she was yesterday. She can celebrate anniversaries, such as Bastille Day. Similarly France can change, and has changed. Longitudinally there is a succession of Frances, so to speak, but each of them lasted for a time. The France of Philip Augustus and the Third Crusade was not that of Louis XIV, nor was his France the same as that of Danton and Robespierre, nor was their France the same as that of today. But each of these Frances did change. There are historical continuities amongst these Frances, of course, but it would seem somewhat surprising or anomalous to regard them all as a single entity. On the other hand, I will suggest a conceptualization in terms of which that would be possible, if not judicious. Lastly, nations seem not to be causally inert, but causally active. It seems they can produce, and do produce, empirically discernible effects, for example, imprisonments, massacres, bombings, and invasions, and doubtless many nice things, as well, perhaps highways, hospitals, airports, schools, and such, depending on the nation.

So forms are timeless, changeless, and causally inert, and nations are time-bound, change, and are not causally inert. So it seems we should reject the "form" theory of nations.

That leaves, amongst the supersensible entities, the notion of the intangible substance, the invisible substance, the mystical or mysterious person, or such.

I am supposing that this option seems unwelcome.

Let us suppose, then, that we wish to rule out, say, intangible substances, or such. For example, if a substance is intangible how could it have empirical effects? Let us suppose, then, hypothetically, that we do rule out, say, supersensible persons, on whatever grounds, say, on grounds of absolute absurdity.

Then, as we have already rejected 'Af' and 'Pf', we would have completed the falsification of the consequent of our ontological conditional, and, accordingly, we are logically compelled to find the antecedent of that conditional false as well, in virtue of *modus tollens*. The following is a valid argument:

1. Ef ⊃ (Af v Pf v Sf)
2. ~ Af & ~ Pf & ~ Sf
3. ~ (Af v Pf v Sf)   2, De Morgan Transformation
4. ~ Ef   1, 3, *Modus Tollens*

1. If France exists, then France is an area or a people or a supersensible entity.
2. It is not the case that France is an area, and it is not the case that France is a people, of a particular sort, and it is not the case that France is a supersensible entity.
3. It is not the case that France is an area, or a people, of a particular sort, or a supersensible entity.   (From 2, by a De Morgan Transformation)
4. Therefore, France does not exist.   (From 1 and 3 by *Modus Tollens*.)

I am supposing that the derived conclusion is even more unwelcome, and perhaps even more absurd, than the hypothesis that France is some sort of supersensible entity.

At any rate, we seem to have arrived at a troublesome dilemma. It seems we must either see France as a supersensible entity of some sort, which probably we do not wish to do, or deny existence to France, which, one supposes, we are even less likely to wish to do.

One might go a number of ways here. One might look for a different interpretation of 'existence' but then it is likely one would have to deny that France can have effects in the world, and one does not wish to deny that, because France does have, or seems to have, effects in the world. One might also multiply options beyond the three of the trichotomy, but it is not clear what they would be, and the three options seem to cover the most likely possibilities. Perhaps one might have recourse to fragmentation, but this would be to say that France is, say, several thousand things, or several million things, that France is all over the place, so to speak, there in the post box, there in the *gendarme's* cap, there in the child's singing the *Marseillaise*, and so on. This way of thinking about things would make no sense whatsoever of historiographical discourse having to do with France. Another option, of course, would be to forget about the whole thing, but this would be to acknowledge defeat, to regard the problem as insoluble, or too difficult, or something along those lines. I am supposing we would be reluctant, however, to withdraw from the field, and certainly would not care to do so before assuring ourselves that the day has been irrecoverably lost. The problem is surely difficult, as we are well aware, certainly by now, but, interestingly, it is not really insoluble. Indeed, a solution is before us, though one which may not have been anticipated.

One bites the bullet and goes for the alternative which is the least noxious, the supersensible-entity option, and one may find that this option, upon review, may not be as noxious as we feared, but may turn out to be actually quite attractive. Perhaps you remember the movies in which Mabel shyly removes her glasses, which it seems she did not need anyway, and is discovered to be amazingly beautiful.

There is a clue from law here, and the concept of the legal fiction, or the legal person, the corporation, or such. I think it is not helpful, at all, whether lawyers do it or not, to speak of fictitious persons. There is nothing fictitious about, say, General Motors or IBM. They are very real. They may be short on aortas, corpuscles, and such but they are entities which have discernible effects in the real world, which are effected by their transient populations, primarily their officers and employees, and those to whom the transient populations have recourse, craftsmen, advertisers, distributors, clients, customers, and such.

We are looking for a theory of "nation" or "France" here which will cohere with, and illuminate, our discourse, which will make sense of the way one thinks of nations, perhaps France. We want this theory to account for France as an agent, for France to enter the world of time and space, for France to be capable of change, and for France to be causally active, to take her place as a sovereign entity in a society of such entities, and so on. France is not a corporation in the sense one usually thinks of a corporation, but a corporation, considered as a substance, a person, gives us a contemporary metaphor in terms of which we may comprehend and explicate a lexicon and a discourse, by means of which we may unify and justify standing practices and familiar habits. It also gives us a way of understanding how a human being might be loyal to a nation, love a nation, be willing to fight for a nation, be willing to die for a nation. Such dispositions might be elicited for a person, but not for an area, *per se*, of so many square miles or kilometers, nor for a population, *per se*, most of which the individual has never seen, and does not know.

On this hypothesis then, one is entitled to the following sorts of historiographical commonalities earlier noted:

Did not France do this or that, at this time or that time?

How did she come about?

How has she changed over the ages?

Are there not histories of France, did she not have her kings, her geniuses and heroes, has she not lost and won wars, did she not come to the aid of the young American Republic in the latter part of the Eighteenth Century, did she not have a Revolution which produced the first modern nation state, was Napoleon not once her emperor, was she not the dominant power in Europe at one time, is her art and literature not better known than that of, say, Lithuania, does she not now have a space program, is she not now a nuclear power, and so on. What direction will France go? What will she do next, and so on?

So, have we discovered what France is, or have we merely suggested a way of thinking about France which would provide a rational justification for how we think about France, talk about her, and so on? I suppose it doesn't really make much difference. My suspicion, however, is that we have not so much invented something here, which we might take France to be, but have rather discovered, in effect, what she has been all along.

At any rate, *vive la belle France!*

Part Three: Metaphysics

I. Monisms and Dualisms

Positions in ontology, or the general consideration of what exists, may be divided conveniently into Monisms and Nonmonisms, such as Dualism, or some other form of Pluralism. In Monism the notion is that a single kind of substance exists. In Dualism, the notion is that two and only two kinds of substance exist; whereas Dualism is, technically, a Pluralism, in Pluralism the usual notion is that at least three kinds of substance exist, and, doubtless, several other sorts, as well. The most common form of Dualism suggests that the two sorts of substance which exist are material substance and another form of substance, say, mind, spirit, soul, or such. The most common forms of Monism are Materialism and Idealism. Neither of these notions is all that clear, but in Materialism the notion seems to be that the only sorts of entities which exist are those which can produce changes in physical entities. Here the mind, or, doubtless better, consciousness, thoughts, and such, are considered as physical entities. For example, the physical entity which is alcohol could produce changes, however indirectly, in the physical entity which is consciousness; and consciousness, which is a physical entity, can produce changes in other physical entities, such as moving bodies about, say, walking one to the bar and back. As we normally talk of these things, consciousness, thoughts, suspicions, anticipations, noticings, griefs, pleasures, hopes, dreams, imaginings, and such, are not usually thought of as physical entities. Certainly they are unlike trees and rocks. Certainly they have properties quite other than those normally associated with physical objects as usually understood. Certainly a thought and a rock are quite different. Thoughts are private and rocks are public. One knows thoughts, like stomach aches, from the inside, and rocks from the outside. Rocks are easily locatable, and thoughts are not easily locatable, if they are locatable, at all. Some folks think they have something to do, however, with the brain. There are also properties like consciousness, subjectivity, intentionality, and understanding, which characterize consciousness and do not characterize, as far as we know, trees, and rocks, and such. So Dualism certainly has a *prima facie* plausibility. The major problem facing the Dualist is one that he does not really have to worry about, but, if he worries about it, he is in serious trouble. The Dualist might, simply, accept as obvious that there is some sort of interaction or apparent interaction, between, say, the mind and body, and then forget about it. Perhaps it is a bit like knowing it is raining without worrying about meteorology, or accepting as a given that the light goes on when the switch is depressed, without worrying about how that is the case, which he can leave to others, perhaps a Cosmic Electrician. If he does, however, worry about these things, he faces what is called the Interaction, or the Mind/Body, Problem. This problem, roughly, is how a nonphysical entity, a mind, something not located in space, can affect, or be affected by, physical entities, say, why it hurts when he is kicked in the shins, or how it is, when he so wills, that he can pick up a pencil, tie shoe laces, and drive a car. Where does the energy needful to do work come from, or go, and is this compatible with the Law of the Conservation of Matter/Energy, and so on. There are numerous "solutions" to the Interaction or Mind/Body Problem, which have little in common other than implausibility. No wonder many are content to leave this one to one or more gods. Another approach to this problem is to adopt some form of Monism, usually Materialism or Idealism. There seems little to worry about with Materialism, for it is clear that physical entities can knock other physical entities about, without difficulty, though it does seem odd to think of consciousness as a physical entity. Supposedly Idealism, which might maintain that reality consists of, say, Spirits and the Perceptions of Spirits, counts as a solution of the Interaction or Mind/Body Problem. But it is not really clear how that could be. We have some notion of rocks knocking rocks about, without difficulty, but I am not sure we have any idea whatsoever as to how spirits or perceptions of spirits could interact analogously, knock one another about, without difficulty, and so on. What is the relationship amongst the perceptions and perceivers? Could Jones' spirit punch Smith's spirit in the spiritual nose? One supposes this might be less a solution of the Interaction or Mind/Body Problem than an alleged solution, a verbal solution, a solution in name only, substituting one word for another, say, 'Spirit' for 'Matter', without explaining how the problems seemingly solved by the first solution might be similarly solved by the second. To be sure, these issues, which have their literatures, and are replete with complex and interesting arguments and counter-arguments, are, for the most part, outside the scope of this study.

The following observations, however, are quite relevant:

1. At one time there was no human consciousness and, at a later time, there was human consciousness. (Presumed scientific fact.)

2. Let us suppose we wish to be monists. (In this way, one would avoid the Interaction or Mind/Body Problem.)

3. On this approach, there was at one time unconscious x and, at a later time, there was conscious x.

4. If we wish an interpretation of x, two candidates suggest themselves:

(1) Unconscious matter, then conscious matter.
(2) Unconscious mind, then conscious mind.

On this approach the distinction between calling x matter and calling x mind is a matter of indifference. Calling it mind costs matter nothing. Calling it matter costs mind nothing.

Everything stays in place. Nothing is lost.

A nearly as I can determine, a metaphysically plausible historiography would be monistic, given the difficulties attending dualism, and, based on the preceding discussion, it seems it wouldn't make much difference, as, upon reflection, the distinction between materialism and idealism seems verbal, at best. One supposes a historian might be a dualist, particularly if he had never given much thought to the issues involved, but then it seems he should provide some sort of account of the relationships between his two supposed realms of reality. For example, does Caesar's decision to cross the Rubicon take place outside of space and then somehow get registered or noted in space, and thus, indirectly, affect a physical matrix, or does it flash a light, so to speak, not in space, which the body, in space, manages to notice, and then, in virtue of this, engineers a response in space, or what? It is very difficult to talk about this sort of thing, which is probably why people usually don't talk about it. One supposes it would be an unusual historian who would be tempted to explain an act by a historical personage in terms of dualism. "Well, why did Caesar do that?" "Oh, no particular reason. He just made a free-will decision." Try that on a dissertation advisor. To be sure, decisions do not take place in vacuums, but, if one is a dualist, something would have to come into the matrix, or decide amongst the alternatives in the matrix, and it is not clear what that might be, nor how it could affect the matrix. Verbally, of course, free will is all over the place. We would often say x did such and such of his own free will, if, for example, he was not threatened or intimidated, not mentally ill, not having his arm swung by someone else against the champion's jaw, and so on. In this sense free will could thrive in any universe, including one exclusively deterministic.

Reflexes, such as knee jerks, hiccups, and sneezes, happen, but they are not exactly things done. They do not count as acts. This does not mean there cannot be habitual actions, or acts one does not pay attention to, or unconscious acts, but these things are in virtue of accession, in most cases, it seems, rational accession. They are very different from burps, barfs, sneezes, and such. The notion of a gratuitous *act* is a contradiction in terms. Throwing a stranger off a train to prove that one has free will is not a gratuitous act. It is an act done on purpose, for a particular reason, and is thus not gratuitous. Similarly a behavior, say, throwing a stranger off a train as the result of an inexplicable, random quantum fluctuation, or such, does not count as an act. You were not responsible for it. To be sure, it is likely to get you in trouble. Most judges would not look favorably on the random-quantum-fluctuation defense.

Historians are free to speak of acts, but this does not commit them to a dualistic metaphysics. Similarly, choices are made and things occur because of choices made. This, too, does not commit anyone to a dualistic metaphysics. Choices presumably have their causes and become ingredients in the causal nexus, producing effects in turn.

To be sure, there is much controversy pertaining to these matters.

On the hypothesis of a monistic metaphysics, motivations, movements, events, and such, are comprehensible, and, in theory, explicable. Thus, even if a historian is a dualist, he might be well advised, if only for working purposes, to adopt a postulate of methodological monism. He wants to make sense out of the past. On the dualistic hypothesis, it is hard to make sense out of anything.

The question here, incidentally, is not whether free will in some sense or other exists. The question, rather, is what metaphysics seems to be presupposed by a rational historiography.

The answer to that seems to be that a rational historiography will presuppose, or at least proceed as if it presupposed, a monistic metaphysics.

There doesn't seem much else it can do.

Later, in dealing with another issue, we will return, in a charitable frame of mind, to these matters, even making out a case, of sorts, for free will.

All we need here is that free will, historiographically, seems to explain nothing, and might confuse much.

Even if it exists, in some sense, historiographically one is well advised to forget about it.

As an explanatory entity it is worthless.

It does seem to provide a license to scold historical personages from a safe distance, if one wishes to do so.

But as an explanatory entity it is worthless.

II. Ontology: The Basic Ontic Hypothesis

1. Problematicities of Time

Within our Monism or Dualism, we will, of course, have a number of ontic hypotheses, or at least talk as though we do. Most of these will be quite unproblematic, for example, rocks, trees, people, continents, rivers, and so on, and some others may be more problematic, such as the Athenian *ethos*, Feudalism, the Medieval Mind, the Renaissance, the Reformation, Capitalism, Nations, and such. The basic ontic hypothesis, on the other hand, will be the existence of the past.

Does the past exist?

Interestingly, we will note that historiography could get on quite well even were there no past, or not much of a past.

Should it turn out that time is unreal, it seems the past might be in a bad way, not that the future would be much better off.

Let us first examine, briefly, two contrasting views of time which agree, at least, in granting time an ontological status, one in the sense of a metaphysical given, the other in the sense of a consequence of motion. We will call the first "metaphysical time," and the second "operational time." In the first case motion presupposes time, time being a necessary condition for motion, and, in the second, time presupposes motion, motion being a necessary condition for time. Metaphorically one might say, in the first case, clocks measure time, and, in the second, that clocks create time. The differences may be formalized, as follows:

$$C \supset T \quad (\text{If C, then T.})$$

This would give us metaphysical time. The notion of a "clock" here is to be understood as, in effect, something changing or in motion. It might be the growth of a grass blade, the falling of rain, the changing of seasons, the flight of a bird, the movements of planets, and such.

$$T \supset C \quad (\text{If T, then C.})$$

This would give us operational time. Physicists seem to be fond of this sort of thing. For example, one might hear that time began with the "big bang" or something like that. What was going on while the big bang was being set up, or had not yet gone off, is ignored. Similarly, if the universe is cyclical, and we have a continuing "big bang/big crunch" universe, expanding and contracting, as we would have, given a certain amount of dark matter in the universe, it seems time would be presupposed, or that time would have had to have had several starts and finishes, perhaps an infinite number of them already, and to come, and so on. An analogy to this approach would be the notion that space is finite but expanding. This makes sense operationally, if space is defined gravitationally, as in the metaphor of the expanding balloon, where the inhabitants on the surface of the balloon cannot get off the balloon, so their space is balloon space, so to speak, but it is incoherent as one usually thinks of space. What is the balloon expanding into, and so on. Whatever the utilities operational space and time may have for this generation or that generation of physicists, the usual notions of space and time are not operational, though measurements of time, whether by manufactured clocks or the movements of the heavens, would be. Time does not need clocks, but clocks, it seems, need time.

Would time exist in an empty universe, without motion?

The answer would seem to be, "Yes," as the universe is there, and lasting. The following counterfactual conditional seems true. "If there was a clock, which there is not, in that universe, by definition, it might tick, say, x number of times." If that is true, and there is no clock there, it seems the empty universe would not require a clock to spend its time, so to speak. It could last without clocks.

Another such *Gedankenexperiment* is to suppose that all motion in the universe stops, and then starts again. It seems it would make sense to ask how long it was between the stopping and the starting of the universe. Were the lights off, so to speak, for five minutes, or ten minutes, or how long? We would have no way of finding out, but the question is meaningful. We know what would be involved. Perhaps an alien pops into our space from hyperspace and informs us that our universe had been stopped for six minutes. Perhaps he presents us with a motion picture from hyperspace in which we see our universe in motion and then stopping, and then starting up again. And, sure enough, the interval was six minutes, on the button.

These two views of time, of course, whichever you accept, do agree that time is real, whether as a metaphysically necessary condition for existence, whether in motion or not, or that it is a consequence of motion, perhaps "the number, or measure, of motion," as Aristotle seems to have suggested.

There are, of course, arguments to the effect that time is not real, at least in the metaphysical sense.[20]

The following type of argument has occurred in the literature, suggesting not only that time is unreal, as, say, centaurs and unicorns might be unreal, but that it is logically impossible, in the manner of square circles, round triangles, and such. An entity is logically impossible if its existence would require it to possess logically incompatible properties, as, for example, triangularity and circularity. It is now supposed that being past, present, and future are not only different properties but incompatible properties, and, if time were real, entities would have to be characterized by these incompatible properties. For example, the French Revolution, if time were real, would have to be past, present, and future, and

---

20 Its reality is problematical also, though this seems to have been seldom noticed, in the operational sense. How, really, could, say, a clock create time? What is time? What is being created? What is different? What does the creation look like, how much does it weigh, etc. When an artist creates a sketch we see what is created. When a sausage machine creates a sausage, we see what comes out of the machine. But when the clock creates time we see nothing. Perhaps it is merely measuring time, which is already there to measure, as space is already there to be measured. Space is not created by yardsticks. Why should time be created by clocks? Is not the metaphysical sense of time, with all its peculiarities and harrowing problematicities, lurking in the background?

this is impossible. For example, say, at time t_1, at the time of the Punic Wars, the French Revolution possessed the property of being in the future, at time t_2, when it was in progress, it possessed the property of being present, and, at time t_3, say, at the time of the first Moon Landing, it possessed the property of being past. So, since the French revolution cannot be past, present, and future, and this would be required by the reality of time, at least as normally understood, time is unreal, indeed, logically impossible, at least as usually understood. There must be some way to regard this argument as plausible, but it eludes me. What seems to be overlooked here is that an entity is logically impossible only if its existence would require it to possess logically incompatible properties, as, for example, triangularity and circularity, *at the same time*. There is no reason why a piece of wire might not be triangular at one time and circular at another. There is no problem with something's being red and green all over provided it is not trying to be red and green all over at the same time, in the same sense; there is no problem with being red and green all over at the same time if the senses are different. Perhaps the fellow is an unseasoned, amateur Communist.[21]

Before approaching a more interesting argument against the reality of time as one normally thinks of it, it might be appropriate, in passing, to note the puzzle having to do with the length of the present. There are pragmatic senses of 'present' which are clear enough, as in present notions, ideas, and fashions; the politics of the present; the problems and ills of the present; that leeches are less relied on medically at present than formerly; and so on. Psychologists also have a notion of the "specious present," which is supposed to last a few seconds, and such. To be sure, it would seem there is nothing really "specious," or "illusory," about it, unless one somehow were to suppose that the "real present," the nonspecious, or nonillusory, present was some sort of infinitesimally short mathematical present. The argument might go something like this:

How long is the present?

---

21 This sort of argument was suggested by J. E. McTaggart, the British Idealist. The account above, I think, is fair, but it is intended to give a sense of this sort of argument, not intended to be a strict account, or a detailed account, of a particular philosopher's views.

One minute long.

No, half of that minute is gone, and the rest of it isn't here yet.

OK, the present is one second long.

No, half of that second is gone, and the rest of it isn't here yet.

OK, the present is one nanosecond long. (This is one billionth of a second.)

No, half of that nanosecond is gone, and the rest of it isn't here yet.)

This sort of argument is founded on a category confusion, rather analogous to the supposed infinite divisibility of matter. It is confusing empirical quantities with mathematical quantities, which is something like confusing the number two with a pair of shoes. How many pieces are there in a pie? It depends on the size of the pieces. Zeno was into turtles and arrows, but he might as well have been into pies. Mathematically, one pie, or one piece of a pie, could feed the world. For any given size, on the other hand, there is a finite number of pieces. As soon as you assign a unit, the present is that long, exactly. Similarly, an inch is exactly one inch long. The board then is some particular length, in terms of that unit. Similarly, if the unit is one minute, or one second, or one nanosecond, that is how long the present is, and any given length of time is susceptible to treatment in terms of that unit. Suppose we define the present as one minute long. We then have a unit in terms of which one can measure time, and clearly demarcate the present from the past and future. The past is before that minute, the future is in front of it, and the present is within it. Measurement requires a unit, and it is cognitively illegitimate to switch units in the midst of a measurement. How long is the present is an unintelligible question until one specifies a unit of measurement, and then, when that is done, that is how long the present is. Mathematically, there are just as many numbers divisible by 647 as there are numbers altogether. That is fine for mathematics but it doesn't work for potatoes, automobiles, and such. Do not mix the mathematical world with the empirical world. They are different worlds, and never the twain shall meet, which is not to deny that we can pair off potatoes and automobiles with numbers, up to a point, the point where we run out of potatoes and automobiles.

A far more interesting argument against the reality of time, at least as we normally think of it, is due to Immanuel Kant, who would be on almost anyone's short list of great philosophers.[22]

Kant claimed to have been "awakened from his dogmatic slumbers" by the writings of the Scottish philosopher, David Hume. Hume had argued persuasively that the scope of human knowledge was far more limited than was commonly supposed, for example, that there are no universal, necessary truths that can be known with respect to matters of fact, that the notion of causality was an unintelligible verbalism inflicted on experience, that one had no guarantee that the future would resemble the past, and so on.

Kant. who was a scientist, a physicist and astronomer, was predictably uncomfortable with such views, and, unlike most people, who would be content to forget about them as soon as possible, he set himself to discover a ground on which these discards might be restored to their previous credibility. This led to what Kant referred to as his "Copernican Revolution."[23] The original Copernican Revolution involved a radical transformation of astronomical perspective, substituting a heliocentric theory of the solar system for the traditional, common-sense geocentric perspective. We have then two radically different interpretations of the same data, the movements of planets, and such. Kant's revolution also involved a radical shift in perspective, and, indeed, a shift far more radical than that of Copernicus, so radical that it might make some sense to speak

---

[22] Not on Ayn Rand's. Rand, with some justification, saw Kant's work as providing a loophole for faith, a place for the intrusion of superstition and irrationality. Kant says as much in the preface to the second edition of the *Critique of Pure Reason*, "...Ich musste also das *Wissen* aufheben, um zum *Glauben* Platz zu bekommen ..." ("... I have therefore found it necessary to deny *knowledge*, in order to make room for *faith* ...") As nearly as I can tell, Ayn Rand's short list of the great philosophers would consist of Aristotle and Ayn Rand. I hope I am not being too unfair here. I have a great admiration for this remarkable woman. She is clearly, at least to date, the most important and influential of all woman philosophers. If her politics had been different, Woman's Studies departments and programs might acknowledge her existence. Aristotle, it might be noted, in passing, was not short on *chutzpah* either. (The English translation of the German above is from Norman Kemp Smith. (*Immanuel Kant's Critique of Pure Reason*, Macmillan & Company, Ltd., Saint Martin's Press, New York, 1956. P. 29.))

[23] The sage of Königsberg, too, it seems, was not short on *chutzpah*. It is hard to think of a great philosopher who did not have something of this, perhaps Spinoza.

of Copernicus' "Kantian Revolution," for Copernicus considered himself to be dealing with, so to speak, customary external realities, and did not question the ontological independency of, say, space, time, and causality. Copernicus was on the "outside," so to speak, an outside no longer hospitable, following Hume, to a number of things, for example, knowing that there are universal, necessary truths pertaining to matters of fact.

The sort of thing which is going to go on here is of a sort familiar in philosophy. Philosopher[1], perhaps a rationalist, believes something to be indubitably true, and then proceeds to draw out the consequences of what seems to be indubitably true, and may find something entailed which is very surprising, say, that motion does not exist. So Philosopher[1] accepts that motion does not exist. Philosopher[2], perhaps an empiricist, comes along and is more sure that motion exists than that the premise-set of Philosopher[1] is true, or his reasoning valid. So Philosopher[2] rejects the premise-set or the reasoning of Philosopher[1], most likely the premise-set.

Consider the following:

E: Reality is substantially as it is normally understood.[24]

---

[24] Given Hume's phenomenalism, that all a human being has to go on is experiential reality, which consists of impressions and ideas, and what we do with them, it is not clear Hume is entitled to this premise, at least as Kant understands it. Indeed, Kant will, substantially, adopt Hume's implicit orientation, that of a plurality of phenomenal worlds. One does not get to a single objective, shared, phenomenal world until later, beginning, at least in more modern times, with German idealism. In Hegel, for example, it seems the phenomenal world is the only world, so there is no longer any point in calling it phenomenal, and he does not, as there is nothing to contrast it with. Earlier, in Berkeley, on an objectivist interpretation of Berkeley, which does not fit very well with what he actually says, it seems a Divine Entity may produce a shared perceptual world, or a world of shared perceptions. Without denying that a Divine Entity might create a world which it perceives, in which, say, the fire may burn down to ashes when no one is watching, except the Divine Entity, it is not clear how the perceptions of lesser spirits are to be understood as related to that world. As the Divine Entity is presumably omniscient and omnipotent, there would be no problem in letting the fire pop out of existence, and then arranging an individual's perception of ashes when the individual has certain other perceptions, which the Divine Entity would also, it seems, have to arrange, such as opening the door to the library. Here, the individual is not creating the ashes when he opens the door; rather, the Divine Entity is supplying the perception. Too, if the Divine Entity does "perceive," or "hold in

C: Many things cannot be known, for example, universal, necessary truths with respect to matters of fact, that causality involves necessity, that the future will resemble the past, that a self, or soul, exists, and so on.

Kant will wish to maintain that at least some of these things listed in our supposed conclusion, C, can be known.

Kant's basic question is:

How are synthetic *a priori* judgments possible?

There are a number of interesting things involved here, to which one lacks the time to do justice. Briefly, and somewhat inadequately, following a simplification of Kant, propositions are either synthetic or analytic, and either *a priori* or *a posteriori*. All of these properties relate to how one can know a proposition to be true or false; analytic and synthetic have to do with meanings; and *a priori* and *a posteriori* have to do with experience. The analytic proposition is one whose negation is inconsistent, or whose concept of the subject contains the concept of the predicate. An example of the latter would be 'All swans are birds', in which the concept of the subject, "swan," supposedly contains the concept of the predicate, "bird."[25] A synthetic proposition, on the other hand, is one whose predicate concept is not contained in the subject concept, for example, 'All swans are either black or white'. Here the predicate concept, "black or white," is not contained in the subject concept, "swan." An *a priori* proposition, on the other hand,

---

mind," the fire when no lesser spirit is perceiving it, it is not clear how the later perception of the lesser spirit and that of the Divine Entity are related. There seem to be problems in both the subjectivist and objectivist case. Indeed, there are many problems here, which would carry us too far beyond the intended scope of this study. In any event, the concern with phenomena as we are now concerned with it, is more appropriate to Kant, and those whom he influenced, positively or negatively.

25 This criterion is presumably intended to be logistic, although it sounds psychological, and Kant occasionally speaks of thinking the concept of the predicate in thinking the concept of the subject, which sounds even more psychological. Pretty clearly, granting the intelligibility and utility of concepts, concept B might be contained in concept A, without being noted. The inconsistency-of-the negation criterion is unexceptionable. A more modern approach to these things, providing one accepts the notion of meanings, would be that a proposition is analytic if and only if it is true in virtue of its meaning alone. For example, a substitution instance of '$p \supset (\sim p \supset q)$' would be analytic, but it does not seem that the concept of '$\sim p \supset q$' is contained in the concept of 'p'.

looks at these things from the point of view of experience, rather than meaning, *per se*. One can know prior to experience, therefore *a priori*, in this sense, that all swans are birds. One does not have to experience all swans in order to determine that every last one is a bird. One can know only *a posteriori*, or "after experience," on the other hand, that some swans are white or black. One would have to see such a swan, or be told about it, or such. Obviously, even in the case of the *a priori* proposition, some experiences would be essential, being conscious, knowing what one is talking about, and such, but one supposes the point is clear enough. Now, it is clear that all analytic propositions are *a priori*, and that no *a posteriori* proposition can be analytic. That brings us to synthetic propositions. Clearly most, if not all, synthetic propositions are *a posteriori*. Remember our black and white swans. The question then is whether or not synthetic *a priori* propositions are possible. Such would be propositions which could be known *a priori*, namely, known prior to experience, although the concepts of their predicates were not contained in the concepts of their subjects. Kant claimed that all mathematical judgments were synthetic *a priori* but this claim has not fared well. Most people would not see '1 = 1' or '7 + 5 = 12', an example from Kant, as synthetic. More plausibly, Kant suggested things along the line of 'Every event has a cause'. It is to be noted that many of the propositions toward which Hume would have entertained reservations would presumably have counted, from Kant's point of view, as synthetic *a priori*. A synthetic *a priori* proposition would be universally true and necessarily true, *and would pertain to matters of fact.*

Now let us return to Kant's question.

How are synthetic *a priori* judgments possible?

Many might see this as an instance of the fallacy of complex question, where a question presupposes that something is not at issue which is very much at issue. For example, "Do you still beat your wife," "Do you still rob banks," and such. Here Kant is accepting that such judgments exist, and that his problem is merely to explain how they could exist.

He assumes what is at issue.

Here we have another example of something philosophically familiar. A view is developed from which follow surprising consequences. These consequences, as they follow logically from a seemingly indubitable premise-set, are accepted by Philosopher[1], in this case, Hume. On the other hand, Philosopher[2], in this case, Kant, rejects the conclusion, and so, logically, he is forced to reject either the reasoning or the premise-set. In this case, Kant is rejecting the implicit premise-set, Hume's seeming notion of reality. Kant is more sure of the truth of synthetic *a priori* propositions than he is of the account of a reality in which they would turn out not to be possible. Thus, that concept of reality is mistaken. That concept of reality, however, happens to be the one that the human species, including philosophers and scientists, and plumbers and grocers, and basketball players and accountants, has accepted for millennia. Serious things are afoot.

So:

1. $E \supset C$
2. $\sim C$
3. $\sim E$ 1, 2, Modus Tollens.

So, Kant is rejecting a traditional and classical concept of reality, one largely independent of, and external to, the mind, because it entails that one could not possess knowledge which Kant believes one does possess, namely, knowledge of synthetic *a priori* propositions.

Interestingly, Kant, though he does not speak of impressions and ideas, is adopting what it seems should have been at least the general tenor of Hume's phenomenalistic epistemology. It seems he intends to beat Hume on what would seem substantially to be Humean territory.

He is going to propose a radical dichotomy between phenomenal worlds and another sort of world, a world of things-in-themselves, or, occasionally, the thing-in-itself.[26] In the phenomenal worlds the conditions of human experience control what may be experienced

---

26 Hume has to be understood as a phenomenalist, given the impressions-and-ideas epistemology. On the other hand, he wished to do for psychology what Newton had done for physics, and that suggests an uncritical acceptance of a common-sense epistemology. There are differences in Hume scholarship on these matters. When Hume gets into his ethics, his essays, and his history, one would never know he was the "masked epistemologist," so to speak. Kant, too, requires a plurality of phenomenal worlds, one for each center of consciousness. Appearances are individual-dependent and individual-relative. Too, if this were not the case he could not explain differences in experiences of the same objects, illusions, hallucinations, and such. Also, he would need some sort of universal group mind, to supply a universal form of sensibility, and such, which he does not suggest.

and how it can be experienced. Kant has a very complex apparatus for sensibility and intellection, but all one needs here is to note that causality is a category of the mind, and space and time are forms of intuition, or sensibility. This is indeed a "perspectival revolution," as one commonly thinks of these things as being independent of the human mind and its aspects. In Kant, they will turn out to be mind-dependent, in their way conditions without which human experience, as we know it, would be impossible. We could not experience a world noncausally, or nonspatially, or nontemporally, not because causality, space, and time are out there, that they exist, externally, in reality as it is in itself, but because we could not experience at all, were it not in these ways. It is one thing to say color does not exist in an outside world, and is thus sensibility-dependent, and we could not have visual experience, even of shades of gray, without "color," so to speak, and quite another to say that causality, space, and time also have no reality outside of human experience. Would that not mean that there is no causality before or apart from human minds? What about the Kant-Laplace theory of the formation of the solar system? What about churnings in the atmosphere of Titan even now, and so on. Similarly, was there no time before human minds appeared, and is there no space beyond the reach of our telescopes, or where we are not now looking, etc.? One can work out Kantian responses to such questions, but, clearly, there seem to be problems here.

Remember, too, on this approach, space and time cannot characterize reality as it is in itself. Similarly, although reality-in-itself must somehow produce human experience, or be responsible for it, causality *as we think of it* cannot be involved. One is reminded, naturally, of some of the properties typically associated with a Divine Entity. For example, it is sometimes supposed that such an entity would be neither spatial, nor temporal, nor physical.

Why would anyone take these Kantian suggestions seriously?

Kant has two major argument lines to support his position, one positive, the other negative.

The least interesting argument line, at least in my view, is the positive one, from the alleged existence of synthetic *a priori* propositions. Supposedly we know these to be true, and we could not know them to be true if Hume were right, so Hume is wrong, and what follows from that? What follows is that their veridicality, their reliability, their universality, and necessity, is guaranteed not by something outside of us, but by the nature of the mind itself. An analogy, though perhaps not a happy one, would be that we know for certain that '7 + 5 = 12' is universally and necessarily true, but we do not know this in virtue of something alien and unknown, a mysterious exterior reality unavailable to us, which we do not even understand, but by the way that we, with our sort of minds, *must* think. We cannot consistently think it otherwise. So, too, we cannot experience except under the intuition of time, a form of human sensibility, nor practice science or comprehend the world of our experience as a whole without the intuition of extension, another form of sensibility. Similarly we must organize and understand our experiences in terms of causality. This, as much as space and time, is essential to human experience, as we know it. We could not know, say, "that every alteration has a cause," were it not for the fact that causality, as a category of the mind, requires that we so think. We cannot experience otherwise. Just as we cannot consistently think otherwise than seeing that seven and five must equal twelve, so, too, we cannot consistently think otherwise than every alteration's having its cause. Such truths cannot be grounded from without, only from within. Therefore the world of human experience, with its space, time, and causality, and such, must be an experiential, or a phenomenal, world, presumably much different from the "noumenal world," the necessary-to-be conjectured world, the world of things-in-themselves, or the thing-in-itself, a world without space and time, and a world to which causality as we think of it is inapplicable, and irrelevant.[27]

---

[27] It is sometimes objected to Kant that he, as an Enlightenment figure, had uncritically adopted the notion of a single sort of human mind, one which was shared by all members of the human species, in whatever time or place. Moreover, that this view is mistaken. I think there is little doubt that Kant supposed there was a given sort of human mind, which all human beings shared, but it is not at all clear that this view is mistaken. Despite the varieties of human acculturation discovered by explorers, traders, travelers, anthropologists, and others, it is not likely that any of these widely different sorts of folk did not experience spatially and temporally. Similarly, presumably they thought in terms of causes, as well, though some of the causes supposed, gods causing winds, and such, might seem unlikely to a modern investigator. Similarly one supposes that the Homeric oarsmen, the Zulu warrior, the Medieval Japanese potter, the 19th Century French *bon vivant*, and such, would all find it impossible to believe that seven and five

did not add up to twelve. There are problems, but they are less likely to come from anthropology, and such, as from physics and mathematics. It is true that Kant supposed that the shortest distance between two points would be a straight line, namely, that space was Euclidean in nature. Here we encounter a distinction between what might be thought of as "metaphysical space" and "operational space." A Riemannian geometry, in which the interior angles of a triangle total more than 180°, may be more convenient for calculations based on a gravitationally curved space than utilizing Euclidean geometry for the same purpose, and then being forced to correct for a variety of gravitational "deformations," but this does not alter the fact that, if a straight line were possible, which it is not, the shortest distance between A and B would be, and would have to be thought to be, the straight line. This is all Kant needs. This type of consideration would apply, too, to all non-Euclidean geometries, of which, in theory, there could be an infinite number. The rabbit might have to go over the mountain, because he cannot go through the mountain, as in the old German joke, but, if he could go through the mountain, the shortest distance to the other side would be through the mountain, a consideration which also applies to chickens crossing roads. Quantum physics poses a more serious problem. Can we really think of something happening without a cause? Could the universe, for example, simply appear, simply pop into being, from nowhere, for no reason? I suppose this could be imagined, but it is not clear it could be believed. I suspect that quantum physics, in its more philosophical aspects, is a sort of *pis-aller*, a last resort, a counsel of despair, resulting from the minuteness and subtlety of its subject matter and the problems of accessing it instrumentally, with the result that the best that can be managed under the circumstances are statistical probabilities. To be sure, this is up to the physicists, and, one suspects, to the next generation of physicists. It is one thing to say that one cannot determine the cause of x, and another to say that x has no cause.

Kant, of course, does have many problems. A couple might be mentioned, in passing. Given Hume's attack on induction, it seems that Kant would have no way of knowing that the human mind was going to continue to be in the future what it was in the past. Is not Hume still dangerous? On the other hand, it is hard to think of a human mind which would not experience, say, spatially and temporally. Would it be human? To be sure, Kant seems to be willing to postulate the possibility of a human soul, or something, outside of experience, and one supposes that that might count as a thing-in-itself of sorts. It is not clear what its experience might be if it were disembodied. Lastly, one might note that Kant concerns himself with the human mind. But there are presumably many other centers of consciousness, as well. One supposes, for example, that a raccoon, while probably not being too good at arithmetic, would be likely to experience temporally and spatially, and such. Would not raccoons, then, and squirrels, and cats, and such, have their own phenomenal worlds? Presumably. But, if so, it does not seem clear what consequences this would have, if any, for the Kantian view.

What I am calling Kant's negative argument line, to argue for his "Copernican Revolution," is, at least in my view, a far more interesting argument line than the positive argument line just sketched. This is the argument from the "antinomies," and we will limit our treatment to some observations on the antinomies associated with space, time, and causality. An "antinomy," in our context, is an inconsistency, a contradiction, resulting from the conflict of two similarly plausible suppositions. Thus, all antinomies would be contradictions, but not all contradictions would be antinomies. For example, 'Herodotus is a flying horse and it is not the case that Herodotus is a flying horse' would be a contradiction, but not an antinomy, because the two suppositions are not similarly plausible. There is no reason to believe that Herodotus might be a flying horse. Pegasus, perhaps, but not Herodotus. The second preparatory point to be made here is to remind the reader that any proposition or set of propositions which entails a contradiction must be false. No true propositions or no true set of propositions can entail a contradiction. Indeed, if a proposition 'p' entails a contradiction, that not only implies that 'p' is false, but it is literally logically equivalent to '~ p'. Two propositions are logically equivalent if and only if they must, of logical necessity, have the same truth value. Equivalently, two propositions are logically equivalent if and only if they are interdeducible, namely, each implies the other. It might also be noted that only a contradiction can imply another contradiction, and thus, if 'p' implies a contradiction, it itself must be contradictory. Also, all contradictions are logically equivalent, as all analytic propositions are logically equivalent. Similarly the negation of a contradiction is analytic, and the negation of an analytic proposition is contradictory.

Note:

'p ⊃ (q & ~ q)' is logically equivalent to '~ p v (q & ~ q).

('If p, then q and not q' is logically equivalent to 'Not p or (q and not q)'.)

So:

$$\frac{\sim p \text{ v } (q \text{ \& } \sim q)}{\sim p}$$

Here we see that any proposition which entails a contradiction is logically equivalent to its own negation. If the numerator formula is true, '~ p' must be true, as the other disjunct is a contradiction, and must be false. Thus we see that the numerator formula logically implies the denominator formula. Similarly, beginning with the denominator formula, '~ p', we see that it entails the numerator formula, for the numerator formula will be true if even one disjunct is true, and thus, if '~ p' is true, the numerator formula must also be true. Accordingly, the two formulas are interdeducible, and thus logically equivalent.[28]

Consider the following pairs of suppositions. Both conjuncts seem plausible, and yet the conjunction itself seems inconsistent..
Set 1:
Space is infinite.
Space cannot be infinite.
Set 2:
Time must have had a beginning.
Time cannot have had a beginning.
Set 3:
There must be a first cause.
There cannot have been a first cause.

One could, of course, seize on one conjunct or another here, and run with it, accepting, say, that space is infinite, time eternal, and that, say, given the principle of the conservation of matter/energy, the presumed impossibility of something emerging into being from nothing, and such, that there was no first cause.

From Kant's point of view, on the other hand, the classical world view entails contradictions and thus the classical world view is false.

Let 'S' stand for an external, mind-independent space, 'T' for an external, mind-independent time, and 'C' for an external, mind-independent causality. Then, in his view, each of these suppositions

---

28 It is important not to confuse synonymy with logical equivalence. All synonymous propositions will be logically equivalent, but not all logically equivalent propositions need be synonymous. For example, 'p' and 'p v (p & q)' are logically equivalent, as they are interdeducible, but their substitution instances would not have the same meaning. Similarly, all analytic propositions are logically equivalent and all contradictions are logically equivalent, but synonymy need not be involved. For example, 'Herodotus is a flying horse or it is not the case that Herodotus is a flying horse' and "If Thucydides is a unicorn, then Thucydides is a unicorn', both analytic propositions, are logically equivalent, but not synonymous, just as 'Herodotus is a flying horse and it is not the case that Herodotus is a flying horse' and 'It is not the case that if Thucydides is a unicorn, then Thucydides is a unicorn', both contradictory propositions, are logically equivalent, but not synonymous.

involves one in a contradiction, which would demonstrate that each of these suppositions is false.

So, in view of logical relationships with which we are now familiar, we note that '(S v T v C) ⊃ (p & ~ p)' is logically equivalent to '~ (S v T v C)', which, by a De Morgan Transformation, is equivalent to '~ S & ~ T & ~ C'.

In effect, then, each of the classical suppositions with respect to space, time, and causality leads to a contradiction, and thus each of them is not only false but contradictory, and thus necessarily false.

If they are necessarily false, then the classical world view not only cannot be true, but it would be literally logically impossible for it to be true.

This is a fascinating argument but there are at least two serious problems with it. First, the classical view, *per se*, need not be viewed as leading to a contradiction. As suggested, it does not imply that, say, space must be both finite and not finite. Indeed, it cannot imply that. It would imply, if anything, that it must be one or the other, but it does not imply that it must be both. Similarly, even if human thought were led inevitably into contradictions, it does not follow that reality has to have similar problems. It is a typical arrogance of rationalism that reality has to be as we see fit to think it. Reality may not much care how we think it. It may very well go its own way.

To be sure, mysteries linger.

Who has not wondered why there is anything at all, even empty space, or, if you have space, how can it be finite, but, how, too, could it be infinite; and, if you have time, how can it have begun, but how, too, could it not have begun; and, if there is a causal nexus, how could it have had a beginning, but, how, too, could it not have had a beginning, and so on.

Perhaps, as Lord Dunsany suggested, man is small and the night is large, and full of wonders.

We have tried to make out a case for the reality of an objective time, largely by examining and rejecting arguments which would, in one way or another, either rule it out as unreal, or interpret it in such a way that it would be pluralized and subjectivized. One is then trying to intellectually ground what one supposes to be a common presupposition of historiography. Presumably, if either time were taken to be unreal, an illusion of sorts, or if one had to multiply it by the number of perceivers, this would put historiography in a very strange light. In one sense there would be no 14th Century and in another sense there would have been several million of them, one for each perceiver. In a sense, I suppose this is a bit like worrying about "nations." One is trying to come up with a theory in the light of which certain implicit presuppositions and practices might be recognized, explicated, and justified.

In any event, the usual presupposition of historiography would be the reality of an objective time, difficult though it is to comprehend its nature, so difficult that it is often confused with movement, which would presuppose it. Time, it seems, is a lastingness. It does not pass, but it continues. It does not flow, so many gallons per minute, but resides. The usual metaphors are from concepts of motion, but they are inapplicable. In a sense, it is not time that passes, or flows, but the things in the world that pass, that flow, while time watches. Clocks do not measure time; they measure their own movements.

2. Past, Present, and Future

This brings us to the notions of past, present, and future. These notions, as we have seen, are relative to a stipulated present. They are like "now," "before now," and "after now." A given event, such as the French Revolution, as noted, could be thought of as past, present, and future, depending on the reference involved, in the future relative to the Punic Wars, in the present as it was enacted, and in the past, relative to the first Moon Landing.

This demonstrates that while the past, present, and future would presuppose time, they cannot be identified with time. They are relative, whereas time is not, except "operational time," which, as we have seen, is unintelligible without the presupposition of a "metaphysical time." Time may be operationally meaningless without clocks, as length is operationally meaningless without, say, inches and feet, but time is not created by clocks, nor length by inches and feet. Time existed before the first clock, and length before the first yardstick. Operational time requires its frame of reference, but the frame of reference, to exist, requires time.

Past, present, and future may be thought of in two quite disparate ways. First, they may be thought of purely temporally, as relative to a stipulated present, in which case they are historiographically empty, but, more importantly, secondly, they may be thought of in terms of actions, behaviors, events, and such. It is in this second sense that the notion of the past, present, and future becomes historiographically accessible. Here we have a clear analogue to the notion of "operational" or "quantitative" time. The historiographer thinks of the past, acceptably, in terms of what occurred in the past, its changes, and such. These happenings, occurrences, and such are like the "clocks" and "yardsticks" of the physicist. The historiographer thinks of the past in terms of its contents, not, so to speak, in terms of the vessel. He tends to think of the past in terms of what occurred in the past, in terms of its clocks, so to speak, rather as the physicist tends to think, too, of time in terms of the movements of bodies. The great difference between them is that the physicist uses the movement of bodies to speak of what is not a body, time, whereas the historiographer's interest is in the movements of the bodies themselves. It is in this embodied, or actualized, sense of the past that he thinks of the past. And, as soon as he does this, the "paradox of the past arises."

The "paradox of the past" has to do with its ontological status.

R. G. Collingwood seems to have maintained, though this is certainly not obvious in his actual historical writings, that the past did not exist, although remnants of the past might persist in the present, artifacts, documents, and such. Accordingly, as he saw matters, a correspondence theory of truth would be inapplicable to past-referring statements, as the correspondent term, the past, was lacking. Thus, a different theory of truth would be required for historiography. As he took the proper subject matter of historiography to be thought, not behavior, and took the historian's job to be the rethinking of past thoughts, he opted for an identity theory of truth, involving a cognitive Platonism. Thought was timeless, and thus the historian's thoughts were true when his thoughts were identical with those of the historical personage. His famous example was that of rethinking Euclid's thoughts. His thinking, the historian's thinking, did not correspond to Euclid's thoughts; they were the same thoughts that Euclid thought. Obviously there are a number of fascinating aspects to this approach to truth theory in historiography, but we mention it here merely in connection with the "paradox of the past." Here, we have a clear denial that the past exists, and by perhaps the greatest of all philosophers of history. Consider an analogy to the physicist watching the movement of a pointer on some scale on Monday. It would seem to make a great deal of sense to say that on Tuesday, that movement no longer existed. Recall now that the historiographer is working with the "movements," in terms of which time might be measured, or thought. His interest, as noted, is in the "movements of the bodies themselves." It is in this embodied, or actualized, sense of the past that he thinks of the past.

Let 'P' be "The past exists," and '~ P' be "It is not the case that the past exists."

Reasonably clearly, if the past exists, it should be possible to make to make true statements pertaining to the past. For example, consider the following two statements:

S: Themistocles commanded the Athenian fleet at the battle of Salamis.

~ S: It is not the case that Themistocles commanded the Athenian fleet at the battle of Salamis.

Both of those statements are about the past, and one of them must be true, as they are related as statement and negation. Thus, we know there is at least one true statement about the past. If something can be true of the past, then the past must exist.

This would be an argument in favor of the existence of the past. But consider:

The interior angles of a Euclidean triangle total 180°.

That is presumably a truth about the Euclidean triangle. Does it follow from this that the Euclidean triangle exists? Perhaps the theorem is only true of something which does not exist. Could it be true of something which, even, could not exist? How could there be a point without size or shape, a line without width, a surface with but one side? Surely it is strange that a supposed model of necessary truth should seem to involve incoherent assumptions. Can we have truths about the nonexistent? What if the past did not exist? Could we then have truths pertaining to it? Certainly the past, however we conceive of it, would seem quite other than the ideal objects of a geometer, Euclidean or otherwise.

What if, as seems obvious to many, the past does not exist. Indeed, in a sense, only the present exists, which we might quantify variously, depending on our purposes.

It is possible to make true statements about nonexistent objects. Consider:

S_1: Pegasus is a flying horse.

~ S_1: It is not the case that Pegasus is a flying horse.

S_2: Pegasus is a flying turtle.

~ S_2: It is not the case that Pegasus is a flying turtle.

At least three possible interpretations of locutions of this sort are possible.

(1) A literalistic approach in which S_1 and S_2 would be false due to reference failure, there being no Pegasus; and, naturally, the negations, ~ S1 and ~ S2, the negations of false statements, would then be true.

(2) A regionalized, or contextualized, approach, in this case indexed to mythology, in which S_1 and ~ S_2 would be true, and ~ S_1 and S_2 would be false.

(3) The "no-truth approach." due to suggestions by John Austin, in which truth values are denied to locutions in fictional discourse, as, supposedly, no references are intended, or made.

As, clearly, statements in historiographical discourse are intended referentially, or at least it seems so, and are supposedly cognitive, are supposed to be the sort of locutions which can sustain truth values, and such, we can dismiss the Austinian approach here, at least as relevant to our purposes. Historiographical statements might be lies, mistakes, inventions, fabrications, forgeries, such as the Donation of Constantine and the Protocols of the Elders of Zion, or whatever, but, being purportedly true, they cannot be fiction in the relevant sense. Even with respect to fiction itself, it is not clear that the Austinian approach is judicious, as it would, for example, deny a truth value to something like 'Pegasus is a flying horse', which seems, clearly, to have a truth value, false, if intended literally, true, if considered in its own habitat, the mythological matrix.

We see on the basis of the foregoing, that true statements can be made even in connection with what does not exist. For example, if the past does not exist, ~ S, 'It is not the case that Themistocles commanded the Athenian fleet at the battle of Salamis' would be true. Similarly, if Pegasus does not exist, 'It is not the case that Pegasus is a flying horse' would be true. And, on the "regionalized approach" to the literally nonexistent, something like 'Pegasus is a flying horse' would be true, and 'Pegasus is a flying turtle' would be false. The question would be then, if the past does not exist, could one have something like the "regionalized approach" to the past, in which, say, S, 'Themistocles commanded the Athenian fleet at the battle of Salamis' would count as true?

The analogy then would be between the mythological matrix and the historiographical matrix.

Relativizing these matters to a realm of discourse in this manner would allow us to do without an identity theory of historiographical truth, and avoid its difficulties, which are many.[29]

The "paradox of the past" is now clear. One might even refer to it as an antinomy, rather in the Kantian sense, for it seems that a contradiction is involved, and that both conjuncts, the statement and its negation, are equally plausible.

P: The past exists.

~ P: It is not the case that the past exists.

There seem to be equally cogent reasons for favoring both propositions.

For example, it seems that the past must exist as it appears to be a subject matter, and an object of study. Similarly, can it not be remembered? Is it not required in order to explain the existence

---

29 A formal approach to 'Pegasus is a flying horse' could use a "unique x" designator (given here as 'x_u') for "Pegasus," to be understood as the unique x which has the property of being Pegasus, or the unique x which Pegasizes, so to speak, which unique x formula could then be replaced by more formal notation.

Proper name: 'Pegasus'
Unique x: 'Px_u'
Formal notation for the original statement.
$(\exists x) (Px \& ((y) (Py \supset (y = x)) \& FHx))$
(There exists an x, such that x Pegasizes and for every y, if y Pegasizes, then y is identical with x, and x is a flying horse.)
The above would be false if construed literalistically, and true, if regionalized, or contextualized, to the realm of mythological discourse.

of certain documents and artifacts? If it did not exist, would the present not be unintelligible? We certainly believe that, say, the Peloponnesian War took place, and does this not mean that the past exists, etc.

But, how could it make sense to think of the past existing? Is that not like supposing that physicist's pointer movement still exists? If it exists, where does it exist? How could the past exist, in what ontological modality? Presumably the future does not exist, as it is not here yet, so why should the past exist? Is it not the case that only the present exists? How then could the past, or the future exist? If the past exists, where does it exist? In what ontological pigeonhole should we place it?

In what follows we suggest something in the nature of some boxes of being, some cosmic pigeonholes, an ontological card file, or laundry list, or such.

Physical Objects	Mental Objects	Fictional Objects	Properties, Relations
Trees, rocks, tables, chairs, etc.	Thoughts, dreams, memories, afterimages, emotions, pains, pleasures, etc.	Pegasus, Reynard the Fox, Mickey Mouse, Nicholas Nickleby, etc.	Red, obscure, mirthful, smiling, frowning, kindness, cruelty, being fond of noodles, being to the left of, etc.

THE PHILOSOPHY OF HISTORIOGRAPHY

Supernatural Objects	Theoretical Objects	Ideal Objects	Sentient Objects
Gods, spirits, etc.	Selves, minds, ids, egos, superegos, quarks (?), uncaused events, and such.	Numbers, theorems, geometrical figures, etc.	dogs, cats, people, etc.
Constructs	Inconsistent Objects	Possible Objects	Miscellaneous Objects
Legal entities, cultures, historical periods, *Zeitgeistes*, etc.	square circles, swans which are not birds, etc.	Possibilities, erudite purple unicorns, "roads not taken," etc.	space, time, symphonies, plays, chess, magnetism, ownership, rights, duties, moral truths, words, etc.

"Being" of some sort, wisely or not, has been ascribed to most of the above-referenced objects. Some of these objects, such as the square circle, clearly cannot exist. When one speaks of it as a nonexistent object one does not mean that there is such an object which does not exist, but, rather, that the concept of the object is inconsistent, and thus it is logically impossible that there should be such an object. This is a familiar way of speaking about such things.

Ascribing nonexistence is not to surreptitiously ascribe existence. Similarly, when the logician might give us a formula such as:

$\sim (\exists x)\ FHx$

(There does not exist an x such x is a flying horse.)

He does not mean to suggest that there exists an x such that it does not exist, but rather that nothing has the property in question, that of being a flying horse.

Now it could be argued that the concept of an existing past is inconsistent, and thus that an existing past, like the square circle, is an impossible object, and, of course, if it is an impossible object, it will not, in fact, exist.

Let 'Px' be 'x is a past'. Let 'Cx' be 'x is contemporary', i.e., it is here and now; it is currently in effect, etc.

1. $(\exists x)\ (Px\ \&\ Cx)$ (There exists a past and it is contemporary.)
2. $(x)\ (Px \supset \sim Cx)$ (No past is contemporary.)
3. $Py\ \&\ Cy$ 1, Existential Instantiation
4. $Py \supset \sim Cy$ 2, Universal Instantiation
5. Py 3, Simplification
6. Cy 3, Simplification
7. $\sim Cy$ 5, 4, Modus Ponens
8. $Cy\ \&\ \sim Cy$ 6, 7, Conjunction
9. $(\exists x)\ (Cx\ \&\ \sim Cx)$ 8, Existential generalization

(Something exists which is both contemporary and not contemporary.)

Line 9 is a contradiction, ultimately derived from the notion of an existing, or contemporary, past, coupled with the presumed truth, that no past can be contemporary.

If one wants a more logistically transparent contradiction, one might have proceeded as follows:

6. Cy 3, Simplification
7. $\sim Cy$ 5, 4 Modus Ponens
8. $Cy\ v\ (P\ \&\ \sim P)$ 6, Logical Addition

9. P & ~ P   7, 8, Disjunctive Syllogism

The argument is very simple, but I thought it well to explicitly demonstrate its validity. Obviously the argument is not a sound argument as a sound argument requires both validity of form and truth of premise-set, and the premise-set is inconsistent, because it generates a contradiction, and only an inconsistent premise-set can generate a contradiction.[30] Accordingly, as the premise-set is false, as all contradictions, the argument cannot be sound. What it does show, however, is that the notion of an *existing* past, namely, one that now exists, that is now contemporary, is problematical, since, conjoined with what *appears* to be a logical truth, namely, that no past is contemporary, a contradiction is generated.

It is supposed that what exists must exist now, and that the past, as we usually think of it, and perhaps even by definition, does not exist now. And this suggests that the past does not exist.

This is a an unwelcome conclusion.

It seems anomalous to think of historiography addressing itself to a nonexistent subject matter.

On the other hand both propositions, each disjunct in the antinomy, as one would suppose, is plausible, namely, it seems there are good reasons for supposing that the past exists, and there are good reasons for supposing that it does not exist. Things that exist, for example, should exist now, be contemporary, and such, and it seems that this requirement is not met by the past.

One wishes to avoid this conclusion, naturally, but the question is how to avoid it, and at what cost.

Let us consider three possible evasions, none of which, one supposes, are attractive, though all would suffice, these three being "regionalization," "cognitive Platonism," and the self-sufficing "picture of the past."

In the "regionalization approach," one might analogize from the

---

30 The premise set is not only inconsistent, but the most explicit of contradictions, one in which the premise set consists of a proposition and its negation, and no more. The explicit negation of the first premise, in a set of equivalences, is shown to be equivalent to the second premise:
1. ~ (∃x) (Px & Cx)
2. (x) ~ (Px & Cx)   1, Quantifier Negation
3. (x) (~ Px v ~ Cx)   2, De Morgan Transformation
4. (x) (Px ⊃ ~ Cx)   3, Implication

mythological matrix, in which 'Pegasus is a flying horse' is true, to the historiographical matrix, in which, even though the past did not exist, 'Themistocles commanded the Athenian fleet at the battle of Salamis' would count as true. It would count as true because that is the way the literature has set things up. The constructed *mythos* of historiography, so to speak, will have it so. This *mythos* is founded on documentation, tradition, artifacts, and such, rather as the *mythos* of Pegasus, and his brethren, is founded on a different sort of documentation, a different tradition, and different artifacts, say, pictures, sculptures, and such. Surely historiography could be understood in this manner, as being a sort of literary criticism, an explication of narratives, an organization of, and a rationalization of, a literature, creating a coherent and interesting historiographical world, rather as students of mythology might organize and explicate an interesting mythological world, but this would presumably misrepresent and betray the historiographical enterprise as it is normally understood. Indicative of decisive differences between the two approaches is the fact that few, if any, believe Pegasus actually existed, but a great many people believe that Themistocles existed. The historiographer normally takes himself to be dealing with a real world, or, at least, alleges himself to be doing so. In the "regionalization" approach" the real world is irrelevant. In the "historiographical approach" the real world is not only relevant, but crucial. One wants, if possible, some sort of connection with reality. Historiography's light does not come on, so to speak, until its bulb is plugged into the socket of existence.

To be sure, if this connection cannot be made, one must look further. But presumably one will not return to "regionalization."

A second possibility is that of "cognitive Platonism," which is suggested by the approach of R. G. Collingwood. In Collingwood the historian's job is to rethink the thoughts of the past, those of personages, and, indeed, even those of corporate entities, and perhaps, though this is less clear, of groups. History is not to be reduced to a "spectatorism," to a sort of positivistic physics, to, say, the movements of material bodies through physical space according to mathematical laws. Bodies perish, thought does not. History is on the inside. It is internal, and, in its way, it is eternal, or, perhaps better, timeless. What is contemporary, what is still available, is not the movements of bodies which are gone, but the motivations, the dreams, the policies, the hopes, the fears, the ambitions, the thoughts, of the past. They can be re-experienced, relived, reenacted, the same thoughts. If the same thoughts are indeed rethought, then the historian's thoughts do not correspond to the original thoughts, but are the original thoughts; they are identical with the original thoughts; they are the same thoughts. A subjective act on the part of the historical personage enacted Thought T, and, perhaps centuries later, another subjective act, now on the part of the historian, enacts the same Thought T. Enactments are temporal, but what is enacted exists *now*, in a timeless now. To the extent this congruence occurs, namely, that the historical personage and the historian are enacting the same thought, the historian's thinking is true. Thus, the identity theory of historiographical truth.[31]

This approach allows us another way to overcome the paradox of the past. The "regionalization approach" accepted the nonexistence of the past and introduced a new and surprising vision of historiography, one which might replace the classic view. Cognitive Platonism, on the other hand, can accept the nonexistence of the once-actualized or behavioral past, but it retains, almost as though by prestidigitation, what was the true past, the inside past, that of thought, which stands outside of time.

---

31 In German, '*erleben*' is to witness, to experience, and '*Erlebnis*' is an experience, an occurrence, an event, even an adventure. Accordingly, then, say, '*nacherleben*' would be to relive, to reexperience. Similarly '*einfühlen*' is to feel one's way into something, or to obtain a sympathetic understanding of something, and an "*Einfühlung*" would be an "in-feeling," a feeling of one's way into something, in effect, an empathizing. The most common expression here would be '*Verstehen*', which, literally, means to understand, but, in the historiographical context, as here, tends to carry the notion of a knowledge of the thought side of things, a concern with the "inside" of events. It suggests an empathic understanding, indeed, sometimes, more surprisingly, the notion of some sort of an immediate, intuitive understanding, a form of noninferential knowledge or understanding. *Verstehen* historiography seems to have begun with, or to have been anticipated by, the seminal 18th Century Italian philosopher of history, Giambattista Vico. It is most famously associated, however, with German philosophers, in particular Dilthey, Simmel, Rickert, and Windelband. This approach was also favored by the well-known Italian philosopher, Benedetto Croce. Needless to say, many of these views were shared by Collingwood.

This approach allows one to eat one's historiographical cake and have it, as well.

This is a brilliant solution of a problem seemingly inevitable within the matrix of assumptions accepted by Collingwood, and is worthy of his indisputable genius.

In a sense this "solution" would seem, like the "regionalization approach," to introduce a new vision of historiography, and I think it does, but, from the point of view of Collingwood, I doubt that it does; from his point of view, I suspect it explicates what historians, in so far as they have been soundly and profitably employed, have been doing all along. It is what is involved in "understanding the past," as opposed to speculating on irretrievable materialities which no longer exist. Three glories of this approach are that it retains its connection with reality, gives us an access to it, via documentation, artifacts, and such, and allows for meaningful ascriptions of truth and falsity to historiographical claims.

Obviously there are a large number of difficulties, for example, epistemological, connected with this approach, but, on the other hand, it seems one could do far worse. It provides historiography, compatible with the assumption of the nonexistence of the happenstance past, with a path to cognitivity, a modality within which historiographical truth and falsity would still exist. To be sure, it is one thing for a proposition to be true or false, and quite another to find out which, something which Collingwood, as an epistemological fallibilist, clearly recognized.

One suspects, on the other hand, that "cognitive Platonism," whatever may be its attractions, and however natural it might be to find it emerging from the paradox of the past, is implausible, and, happily, unnecessary.

Doubtless every discipline must be freighted with some metaphysics, but one suspects that cognitive Platonism might overburden historiography.

Its great advantage is that it allows the nonexistence of one past while, in a sense, acknowledging the existence of another, one essentially timeless. For example, what Caesar might have thought, while on the northern bank of the Rubicon, is something which another, as well, might think. Thus there is in thought an intersection, so to speak, or a common point, which might be touched, by two times, once long ago, once currently. One has access to the temporal by means of the eternal. In eternity are resolved the problematicities of time.

On the other hand, if it were possible to make out a separate and different case for resolving the paradox of the past, one not utilizing cognitive Platonism, then cognitive Platonism, whether true or false, whether possible or impossible, would be unnecessary.

If there should be, then, serious difficulties with cognitive Platonism, this might motivate the search for a different solution.

There seem to be such difficulties, even putting aside several epistemological problematicities.

First, any difficulties which might beset classical Platonism, which are numerous, would appear to similarly beset cognitive Platonism, e.g., confirmation and falsification conditions, considerations of evidence, intelligibility of the hypothesis, the supposed ontological status of forms, their nature, number, and relations, their modalities of instantiation, the mechanism of instantiation, etc. Whereas one would not wish to see cognitive Platonism in terms of classical Platonism, for they are very different, one might note that classical forms were presumably very different from thoughts; there might have been a classical form "horse" but presumably there was no classical form for thoughts, such as, say, that horses run fast or eat hay.

Problems of infinities also arise. Just as the number of Platonic forms would presumably be infinite, as it seems there would be a form of one, and another of two, and another for three, and so on, so, too, thoughts would presumably be infinite, as there might be the thought that the first natural number was one, that the second was two, that the third was three, and so on. But, in dealing with thoughts, even if they are no more abundant than Platonic forms, as one is dealing with infinities here, it seems they would be surprisingly diverse in ways one would not expect of Platonic forms. Consider the following thoughts, perhaps enjoying their first instantiation, the thoughts that horses are oviparous, and that erudite purple unicorns read Greek. Too, for purposes of illustration, some Romans, it seems, might have objected to their female friends stepping on another fellow's foot, which, it seems, was a form of flirtation. Doubtless there were thoughts of that sort about. What might there not have been thoughts about? It seems strange to think of thoughts waiting in the wings, or hovering about, so to speak, waiting to be instantiated. One might make things a little easier if one supposed that a thought did not enter into timelessness until it was first thought. This could be something like the form of the spark plug or monkey wrench, which we might suppose did not always exist, but exists now, and might one day cease to exist, when people forget about it, or move on into, say, zook plugs and gorilla wrenches. But presumably the thoughts in cognitive Platonism exist prior to being instantiated, and after having been instantiated, even if the universe perishes in the meantime. Too, what about all the thoughts that were thought in languages one no longer knows. Neanderthals had culture, fire, the bow and arrow, cannibalism, and such. They must have had a language, or languages, and thoughts.

At any rate, whether or not the aforementioned possibilities tend to reduce enthusiasm for cognitive Platonism, it seems clear that the position will have a number of difficulties, like classical Platonism, which might encourage a search for a position with a less awesome metaphysics.

So let us consider our third suggestion for an evasion of the paradox of the past, the notion of the self-sufficing "picture of the-past."[32]

This is similar to the "regionalization approach" in not requiring an external reference for discourse, but is different in several respects. First, it rejects the "regionalization" notion, which requires a contrast with nonregionalized discourse; second, it constitutes itself as a base or primitive discourse, which entitles it to literality; third, it openly relies on, and builds openly on, a major theory of truth; fourth, whereas it sees historiography in a way very different from the way in which it is normally seen, it requires no changes whatsoever in historiographical practice; fifth, it could be claimed that this is actually the most plausible account available of actual historiographical practice.

---

32 This approach is suggested by something in Collingwood, but I am not attributing it to him. Indeed, it would be incompatible with the identity theory of truth and cognitive Platonism. The lovely metaphor of "a picture of the past," is, however, from Collingwood. The major motivation here is to consider historiography in the light of a coherence theory of truth.

There are many theories of truth, some rather exotic. Most theories of truth, on the other hand, fall into three major families, so to speak, and, within each family, there will be several variations. These major families are those of correspondence theories of truth; of coherence theories of truth, and pragmatic theories of truth. In what follows we will consider a generic coherence theory, in which the cohering elements might be variously construed.[33]

This approach can, though it need not, accept the nonexistence of the past. With respect to it, however, and the way it understands truth, it is indifferent as to whether the past exists or not. It can get on quite well without the past.

Whereas this is not always the case, one of the nice things about science is that its subject matter is usually available, or can be produced at will. For example, object 3C 295 in the constellation of Bootes, some five billion light years away, or at least its light, is currently available for spectroscopic analysis; we can see it now, so to speak; more prosaically, our physicist may confirm the melting point of copper, whenever he wishes, should he wish to do so, and one piece of copper will usually do as well as another. Similarly, experiments can be replicated, and results checked, that sort of thing.

The historian, of course, pending the development of a means for outdistancing light waves by means of which he might then see if Hannibal really had eighty elephants on hand at the battle of Zama in 202 B.C., or utilizing a time machine, rented from M.I.T., or waiting for a dislocation in the fabric of space-time, lacks these face-to-face advantages which the scientist usually takes for granted. The historian has to put together a "picture of the past," which he will never be able to compare with the putative original. Consider Thais, of the retinue of Alexander. Doubtless she was beautiful. If the historian had a photograph of her he would not know for sure it was really her photograph, and not that of another. Similarly, if he had a painting, he would not know if it was of Thais or not, or, if it was, if it were a good likeness. Suppose there was a verbal description. Is it accurate, and, even so, presumably the same description might fit a variety of different realities, as there

---

33 Some candidates for such elements might be statements, propositions, concepts, objective ideas, subjective thoughts, etc. The coherence relationship itself might also be diversely understood, logically and metaphysically.

are many ways in which a woman can be beautiful. And, as far as I know, in the case of Thais, we do not even have a verbal description. We conjecture, of course, given her reputation and her position in the retinue of Alexander, she was most likely beautiful. Could the historian do more than provide us with an "artist's conception," if he were so minded, and, presumably, he would not be so minded, as, in such a case, perhaps not in others, he would presumably be unwilling to conjecture, lacking the evidence on the basis of which he might support or justify such a conjecture. The case of "Thais" is a useful metaphor for the difficulties faced by the historian.

The historian may visit Marathon, but he cannot observe the Persian landing, the flashing signal, the movement forward of the Greek phalanx.

Except in rare instances, he is "not there."

He cannot manipulate variables, to test his theories. What if, say, the Persians had won at Salamis, or if Alexander had not died when he did? What if Sabotai had not returned to Karakorum, for the election of a new Khan, upon the death of Ogadai, third son of Genghis Khan? Would we have had a Mongol Europe? Suppose the Spanish Armada had been successful, what then? What would have been the future of France had there been no Napoleon? Had Lincoln not been assassinated, how might the Reconstruction have proceeded? How might the history of the Twentieth Century have been different, if there had there been no Adolf Hitler?

In the laboratory the scientist can mix his variables, and manipulate them. He can see what difference this makes, and what difference that makes. The historian, on the other hand, does not even have variables, but accounts of variables, reports of variables, hearsay about variables, dubious or falsified reports about variables, and so on. Sometimes he must use his judgment to conjecture about variables concerning which there is no evidence extant.

Accordingly, it is on the basis of "sources," putative evidences, of various sorts, that the historian, utilizing his intelligence, judgment, and imagination, constructs his "picture of the past."

What then must be the test of truth?

It cannot be correspondence for the correspondent term is unavailable.

The truth test then is coherence. And coherence does not require correspondence, and, not requiring correspondence, it makes no difference whether the past exists, or not.

A metaphor which suggests itself, but is quite misleading, is that of the jigsaw puzzle. In this metaphor, one would try to put the pieces together, to produce the picture. The metaphor is misleading in several respects. First, there is an indefinite number of pieces. Second, the pieces often do not fit together. Third, there is no particular, single picture which they would form. Lastly, the pieces themselves form no picture at all. Their use is to enable the historian to form some picture, a picture which they themselves do not form.

There are many difficulties with the coherence theory of truth, but there are usually taken to be two major objections to it. To be sure, both of these objections presuppose the very theory whose defects the coherence theory is supposed to remedy.

First, one has the "correspondence objection," namely, how do you know that, say, a given coherent set of propositions is true, in the sense of corresponding to an external reality? Classically, the coherence theory, commonly arising in a context of idealism, would maintain that this correspondence either does not exist, as, say, material reality does not exist, or, if it existed, it could not be known, for all that can be known are ideas, or experience, that sort of thing. There is no "outside world," no "mind-independent world," or, if there was, it would be unknowable. Therefore, truth is to be understood, *faute de mieux*, if nothing else, as intraexperiential, as a matter of coherence.

Second, one has the "incompatibility objection." This second major objection commonly leveled against the coherence theory of truth is that incompatible coherent sets of propositions might exist, For example, 'p & q' and 'p & r' are both coherent sets and are logically compatible. They might both be true. On the other hand, the two sets 'p & q' and 'p & ~ q' are coherent separately, but incoherent, incompatible, if conjoined. Thus, how would one choose between 'p & q' and

'p & ~ q', as both sets cannot be true?

There are two major argument lines opposed to this objection, the first accepting that incompatibility is a problem, the other denying it.

The first objection may confuse reality, construed in an

idealistic metaphysics, with propositions supposedly relating to that reality. If reality is construed as a system of ideas entertained by, or identical with, a cosmic spirit, or such, then presumably it has to be coherent, as reality cannot be incoherent. If one then identifies truth with these ideas, then truth, too, must be coherent, and, given the doctrine of internal relations, in which each bit of reality involves reality in its entirety, there is no truth short of the whole truth. For example, if the sewing machine was invented in the early 19th Century, that would not count as truth in this holistic sense, but it would be, so to speak, an aspect of the sphere of truth, and might, say, be spoken of not as true, but as "correct." It could not be understood fully, supposedly, except in so far as it fits into the whole. There is no truth short of the whole truth. On the other hand, what would make for the "correctness" of a proposition, on this approach, would be its coherence with an ideal set of propositions which would adequately reflect the unity of the whole. Thus, coherence turns out to be a "truth-making" or "correctness-making" property. It is here noted that given the unity and coherence of the whole any set of propositions reflecting that unity and coherence would, by definition, be true. It is accepted, of course, that this ideal of a matching set of propositions reflecting the metaphysical coherence of the whole is unlikely to be achieved. It will be remembered here, too, of course, that there is no external material reality, or, at least, not one knowable, so a correspondence relation, as least as usually understood, is not possible. On this view, incompatibility is a problem which might obtain between two particular sets of propositions, at a given time, but would disappear once one had attained the ideal set, which, mirroring reality, must be coherent. The ideal set of propositions must not only be coherent, but, too, adequate, and exhaustive. Ideally each proposition in the ideal set would logically entail, directly or indirectly, every other proposition in the set. It would a bit like '(p $\supset$ q) & (q $\supset$ r) & (r $\supset$ p)', in which each proposition, sooner or later, entails every other proposition. In this way, in such a system, something like 'The sewing machine was invented in the early 19th Century' would logically entail, sooner or later, 'Themistocles commanded the Athenian fleet at the battle of Salamis', a proposition which would normally be thought to be logically independent of sewing machines.[34]

I think the much better response to the "incompatibility objection" is simply to dismiss it as irrelevant. A very different concept of "truth" is involved here than that in the correspondence notion, and that should be accepted, with its attendant consequences. Once that is done a number of difficulties vanish. An analogy would be to one or another of the short-term pragmatic theories of truth in which truth is understood along the lines of utility, for one

---

[34] Supposedly there could be only one exhaustively coherent system. That would follow from the above suppositions, included in the text, but one cannot, naturally, expect everyone to share that set of presuppositions. An argument intending to show that there can be but one exhaustive and coherent system might proceed as follows:
Let A and B be two systems.
1. Either A and B are identical or A and B are not identical.
2. If A and B are identical, then A and B are not two systems.
3. If A and B are not identical, then A and B are not both exhaustive.
4. A and B are not two systems or A and B are not both exhaustive.
(Line 4 follows from Lines 1, 2, and 3, by Constructive Dilemma.)
In this argument the first premise is clearly analytic, and one supposes the second premise should be taken as analytic, as well. The third premise is more controversial, as it seems there might be an indefinite number of systems which might be exhaustive without being identical, differing perhaps in base-language (e.g., physicalistic or phenomenalistic language), in metaphysics (e.g., materialism or idealism), in explanatory discourse (e.g., causal talk or correlation talk), in number and nature of primitive sentences, in theoretical constructs, and such. The argument above is a simplification of an argument line developed by the great coherence theorist, Brand Blanshard. (Cf. Volume 2 of his book *The Nature of Thought*. (George Allen & Unwin, Ltd., London, 1940)).
Even if one took this argument to prove there could be but one exhaustively coherent system, it does not prove that such a system will ever exist, or could ever exist. It is not clear how such a system could be constructed, or what it might be like, if it were constructed, or even if it could be coherent. At any rate it seems that temporally devised, particular systems might indefinitely prove to be incompatible. If that is the case, it seems that coherence might be a necessary condition for truth, but would be an unlikely candidate for a sufficient condition for truth. Given the unavailability of the one exhaustively coherent system, it seems that one will have to continue to face the problem of choosing between 'p & q' and 'p & ~ q', without much help from coherence theory. To be sure, this presupposes the notion that incompatibility is a problem, which suggests an implicit commitment to a correspondence version of truth.

purpose or another. In this way, verbally incompatible accounts could both be regarded as true, provided both were good in the way of belief, say, for one person or another, or for one purpose or another. Similarly, as some theories might work better than others, one might speak of degrees of truth, some theories then being *truer* than others. In this sense both the coherence theory of truth and the pragmatic theory of truth are essentially substituting one kind of "truth" for another, or, even, if one likes, changing the meaning of the word 'truth', for better or for worse reasons. The notion could be that the correspondence understanding of truth is incoherent or unintelligible, or useless, or inapplicable, and must be discarded. One supposes this is possible. Perhaps then it would be better just to use different words, but the word 'true' and the word, 'truth' are familiar and attractive terms and it might be better, if only for evangelical purposes, to retain them, rather than abandon them entirely.

On this approach then two historical accounts, say, with respect to the inevitability or not of the American Civil War, both of which are coherent, documented, and such, might be counted as true. This represents a very different understanding of 'true' from the traditional notion, but it is unexceptionable on this new understanding of 'true'. It is not the case, of course, that one may not adjudicate rationally amongst such verbally incompatible accounts. It is not the case that "anything goes," that there is no difference between good work and bad work, between biased work and less biased work, between cogent argumentation and associational argumentation, and such. Eight sample criteria for evaluating work from the coherence perspective would be:

1. Consistency. An account such as '$p \,\&\, (q \,\&\, \sim q)$' is to be rejected.

2. Logic. Is the account coherent in the sense that its elements are plausibly interrelated, deductively or inductively?

3. Elegance. Are the elements utilized germane to, and adequate to, the purpose, giving the sense of an account which is neither redundant nor incomplete?

4. Documentation. Is the account plausibly related to acceptable sources?

5. Breadth. Presumably the larger the account, and the more

it covers, *ceteris paribus*, the better. Thus the account 'p & q & r' would be regarded, *ceteris paribus*, as better than the account 'p & q', as "more" is cohering.

6. Depth. Presumably the deeper the account, the greater the detail, the better.

7. Explanatory plausibility. A coherent account which is explanatorily persuasive is superior to one which is less so. (Causality is a common route to coherence.)

8. Importance. A coherent account which deals with significant matters is presumably, *ceteris paribus*, superior to one dealing with less important matters.

It will be noted here that "truth" in the correspondence sense does not figure in the criteria for evaluating coherence. Similarly, in the coherence sense of 'truth', verbally incompatible accounts could both be accounted true, and one account could be regarded as, given criteria such as those above, superior to, or "truer" than, another account.

We see here, as well, that a coherence theory of truth does not presuppose an idealist metaphysics. We also note that historiography could get on with a coherence theory of truth, and that the adoption of this truth theory would have little or no impact on historiographical practice. Things would go on much as before. Indeed, if the past does not exist, and there are no correspondent terms, it seems as though the construction of a self-sufficing "picture of the past" might be the most plausible account of historiographical practice. Certainly one would not welcome a conclusion to the effect that historiography is based on a false assumption, the existence of the past, and that most of what historians do is produce false statements. This position, despite the uneasiness which it is likely to generate, does give one a way of attributing truth to historiographical statements.

Take an assertion to the effect that English fire boats wreaked considerable havoc with the Spanish fleet in 1588 in the English Channel. On the correspondence view that assertion would be true if and only if English fire boats wreaked considerable havoc on the Spanish fleet in 1588 in the English Channel. On the coherence view that assertion would count as true if it were an assertion largely accepted in the historiographical community, supported by records, was ingredient in a variety of coherent accounts, and so on. Now let us suppose, as a logical possibility, that the Spanish fleet never encountered English fire boats at all but, say, never left port, or weighed anchor and then turned back, or was recalled, or perished in some other way. But all the documentation, and such, perhaps fabricated for political purposes, was exactly as one finds it today. The historiographical community would then regard the assertion as true, and for very good reasons, although we are supposing, as a logical possibility, that it is false. What this little *Gedankenexperiment* shows is that the historian is at the mercy of his sources. In many cases, he cannot know what took place, but only use his best judgment, based on his evaluation of sources, to conjecture what might have happened. At this point the coherence theorist might suggest that he can never know what happened, can never know the truth in a correspondence sense, so he might as well forget about correspondence, and instead of embracing a misguided and useless theory of truth, content himself with what he does have, namely, coherence. And things are worse, of course, if we deny the existence of the past altogether, for then it seems there no longer exists an object to which the assertion might correspond.

Since truth in the correspondence sense can never be verifiably attained, whether the past exists or not, one should accept a meaningful notion of truth, namely, the coherence notion. It is at least a workable theory of truth. And a workable theory, with a criterion for verifiability, coherence, is better than a metaphysical criterion for truth, never verifiable; a workable theory of truth is better than no workable theory of truth.

So the historian is encouraged to do the only thing he can do under the circumstances, namely, strive to produce a self-sufficing "picture of the past."

Suppose one were to agree that the past does not *now* exist, but insist that it *once* existed, and that that is all the historiographer needs. This is no help. On our current approach, as supposed, the past can *never* exist. The only thing that can exist is the present. So, even in 1588, the past did not exist. And now, of course, on the current approach, 1588 does not exist. It is done with. One might, of course, then try to distinguish amongst presents, so to speak, for example, between $Present_1$, which was, say, in 1588, and $Present_2$, which is now. The problem with this approach is that Present₁ is now past, and thus Present₁ no longer exists. This returns us to the nonexistence of the past and the paradox of the past.

A *Gedankenexperiment* suggested by Bertrand Russell, surely one of the most prolific and influential of 20th Century philosophers, sheds an enormous amount of light on these issues, and is of profound relevance to questions of truth theory and historiography. It suggests a shocking hypothesis, quite at odds with our normal way of thinking about things, and which yet might be true, is precise, clear, and simple, would account for the world as we find it, would explain everything with a minimum of explanatory entities, thus wielding Occam's razor nicely, and, pending unusual circumstances, would never be falsifiable.

This is a very familiar *Gedankenexperiment* but it has, as far as I know, no particular name. We will refer to it as the "Russell Hypothesis."

The hypothesis has to do with the creation of a world, a familiar world, our world. The hypothetical entity or entities responsible for this creation, or production, might be variously conceived, perhaps as one or more demiurges, one or more gods, or, say, a remarkable quantum fluctuation, or such, the sort of thing which might go about precipitating universes into existence, randomly, causelessly, inexplicably, and such, the sort of thing which might appeal to quantum physicists, at least those under the age of thirty.

The point here is not whether the Russell Hypothesis is true or not, but what if it were true, what would be different? And one learns very little, if anything, would be different, as far as we could tell, at any rate.

The hypothesis is that the world came into existence five minutes ago, bearing within itself all the signs of age, including seeming memories of events supposedly having taken place more than five minutes ago. Similarly the physicist's radioactive substances, with half lives, and such, would all be suitably adjusted. The dinosaur bones would be where we find them, and geology's strata, and such, would all be well arranged. Everything would be in place, ancient lake beds, ruined amphitheaters and aqueducts, the pyramids, stars, historical records, all such things.

There are a number of reasons for not accepting the Russell Hypothesis, even should it be true, but these are not of concern in this context.[35] All we need at this point is two observations.

---

35 A sample examination of the Russell Hypothesis might involve both general

and specific considerations. Some of these considerations involve objections to the hypothesis, but it should be noted that several of the "objections" fail if the creation, or production, is not ascribed to something like a god or gods. If a quantum fluctuation, or such, is involved, there is not too much to say.

Some general considerations might be as follows:

Obviously, at least as we normally think of things, the Russell Hypothesis is implausible. What point would there be to it? Why make things look aged, just to fool paleontologists, cosmologists, and such, merely to mislead agnostics and atheists, or what? The hypothesis, too, seems arbitrary. Why not four minutes ago, or seventeen minutes ago, or a nanosecond ago? The hypothesis seems disruptive. It does not fit in. It rocks the boat. It violates the principle of scientific conservatism. Perhaps the hypothesis is even unscientific. Perhaps it is contrary to the laws of nature, its results not having been achieved naturally, in virtue of development, etc. Perhaps there is even some sort of violation of the principle of the conservation of matter/energy, which suggests eternality, not initiation. If a god or gods are supposedly involved this would seem to have recourse to a nonempirical causative factor, something scientifically suspect. The Russell Hypothesis is simple, but perhaps too simple; could such complexity emerge from a single, simple causative factor? An explanation which explains everything might explain nothing in particular. It seems likely that no single explanation could do for a star on the main sequence, for dinosaur bones, for pyramids, and 18th Century manuscripts.

Some specific considerations might be as follows:

It seems simpler to start out with matter/energy, in accord with the principle of the conservation of matter/energy, and go from there than to hypothesize either a "creator," which seems an anthropomorphic supposition at best, and an unintelligible hypothesis at worst, or a "quantum fluctuation," so to speak, which seems unaccountable and inexplicable.

Whereas the hypothesis gives us an alternative explanation for, say, fossils, and such, this sort of alternative explanation would also seem to undermine Revelation, Biblical accounts, and such. Indeed, most classical religious writings, in all traditions, would seem to be at risk. Would not five thousand, or so, orthodoxies be undermined? Might not millions of human beings lose a sense of tradition, and security?

If a god or gods are involved, questions of fairness, and justice, seem to arise. The hypothesis would wipe out many of the noblest and most glorious of human achievements, though, to be sure, as though in compensation, it would also wipe out many of the worst and most embarrassing of human failures. Hitler may never have existed, but neither, too, would have Socrates, Archimedes, Saint Francis, Michelangelo, Leonardo da Vinci, and countless others.

If the Russell Hypothesis were accepted would this not induce global anxiety? Might not the world be "uncreated' as easily as it was created?

If a god or gods were involved, would not the Russell Hypothesis reflect discredit on such a divine entity or entities? Would they not seem then unworthy

First, in theory, though doubtless not in practice, for us, the Russell Hypothesis is both confirmable and disconfirmable. Thus it is empirically meaningful. Even if, in some sense, it should be nonsense, it cannot be dismissed as scientific nonsense. We can well imagine an intelligence other than our own, or, contrafactually, our intelligence, observing empty space, and then, suddenly, noting the appearance of our world. An analogy would be the hypothesis that a flying horse is currently in Jones' backyard. There are presumably no flying horses, but we are well aware of what it would be to see one in Jones' backyard, or note that one was not currently in his backyard. Thus the assertion that there is now a flying horse in Jones' backyard is empirically, scientifically, meaningful. It could be both confirmed and disconfirmed. We know what would be involved. So, too, with the Russell Hypothesis. Second, let us suppose that the hypothesis is true. What would be the consequences for historiography?

If the Russell Hypothesis were true then, on the correspondence view, almost all historiographical statements would be false, due to reference failure. Recall Pegasus, and the literalistic interpretation of the Pegasus mythology. On that interpretation, if Pegasus does not exist, then both of the following statements would be false:

S_1: Pegasus is a flying horse.

S_2: Pegasus is not a flying horse.

S_1 and S_2 are not related as statement and negation. That is clear in the formalization:

S_1: $(\exists x) (Px \& ((y) (Py \supset (y = x)) \& FHx))$

S_2: $(\exists x) (Px \& ((y) (Py \supset (y = x)) \& \sim FH))$

The truth of both S_1 and S_2 would require that Pegasus exists, which is not the case, so they are both false.

The correct, or more careful, statement of the negation of

---

of veneration, as being deceitful. Is the world a joke? A bad joke? The work of the Russell Hypothesis would seem more plausibly attributed to Descartes' demon than to a well-intentioned, benevolent god or gods.

If the Russell Hypothesis were true, would this not be unkind to historians; might it not cause those fellows distress?

Too, do human beings need a past, a past they can at least believe is real? This may be a bit like asking if they need to believe in a mind-independent world, that the future will resemble the past, that other minds exist, and so on. Might not sanity itself rest upon the unknown and unprovable?

'Pegasus is a flying horse' would be 'It is not the case that Pegasus is a flying horse', which might be formalized as follows:

$\sim S_1: \sim (\exists x) (Px \& ((y) (Py \supset (y = x)) \& FHx))$

which would be logically equivalent to the following transformations:

1. $(x) \sim (Px \& ((y) (Py \supset (y = x)) \& FHx))$ From $\sim S1$ by Quantifier Negation
2. $(x) (\sim Px \vee \sim ((y) (Py \supset (y = x)) \& FHx))$ 1, De Morgan Transformation
3. $(x) (\sim Px \vee (\sim (y) (Py \supset (y = x)) \vee \sim FHx))$ 2, De Morgan Transformation
4. $(x) (\sim Px \vee ((\exists y) (Py \& \sim (y = x)) \vee \sim FHx))$ 3, by successive applications of Quantifier Negation, Implication, De Morgan Transformation, and Double Negation.

And 4, which is logically equivalent to $\sim S_1$, might be read as 'For every x, either it does not Pegasize, or there exists a y which Pegazsizes and y is not identical with x, or x is not a flying horse'.

From this it is clear that if the Russell Hypothesis were true, in a correspondence sense, and one opted for a correspondence view of truth, most, though not all, historiographical statements, at least occurrent statements, ones actually made, would turn out to be false.[36]

On the other hand, if one wished to retain a truth value for many occurrent historiographical statements, one might do so by subscribing to either a coherence or a pragmatic theory of truth. Clearly the existence of an actual past in either a case would make no difference whatsoever to historiographical practice. Indeed, what if the Russell Hypothesis were true? Perhaps it is true. Are things not going on as usual?

One might note, in passing, that a coherence view in such a case would seem less suspect than, and presumably morally superior to, a pragmatic view. A pragmatic view, being a value-oriented view, might be easily perverted to particular ends, political or otherwise. What is "good in the way of belief," even "in the long run and on

---

[36] One speaks of occurrent statements, because, strictly, the number of true and false statements would be identical, as for every statement 'p' there is a statement '$\sim$ p'. Accordingly, if 'p' is true, '$\sim$ p' would be false; and if '$\sim$ p' is true, 'p' would be false.

the whole of the course," would seem to depend on who is doing the believing, and what purposes the beliefs are supposed to serve. It is possible that the mistreatment and betrayal of scholarship is not unknown, even in democracies.

We have now arrived at a crucial point in this discussion.

As the discussion has been complex, and the issues, one fears, are even more complex, let us review some points.

1. We wish to retain truth value for many historiographical statements.

2. Historians seldom, if ever, have direct access to their subject matter. This is the case even if they are interviewing a historical personage. The events related are no longer occurrent. The historian works with sources, and inference. He can seldom, if ever, "look and see." He cannot experiment. He cannot replicate experiments. He cannot manipulate variables, and so on. Thus, he has no way to directly confirm his conjectures. He is trying to construct his "picture of the past," a picture he can never compare with the original.

3. It follows from this that he can seldom, if ever, directly verify his hypotheses. He is not present at the time.

4. The correspondent terms are seldom, if ever, available.

5. Problems compound if one includes amongst such considerations the nonexistence of the past. We saw, earlier, that reliance on the past pastness of the past does not seem to help. That the past *did* exist, we saw, might even be seen as a contradiction in terms, as it might seem that only the present exists, and if one speaks of past "presents" one is back where one began, since the alleged "presents" are now past. A metaphysical hypothesis of "didness" is not likely to inspire enthusiasm.

6. Considerations such as the preceding suggested three approaches to historiography which did not presuppose the existence of the past, the "regionalization approach," the approach of "cognitive Platonism," and, recently, that of the self-sufficing "picture of the past."

It is my hope that the preceding discussion has cast considerable suspicion on the "paradox of the past."

The antinomy was as follows:

The past exists.

It is not the case that the past exists.

We saw that there were reasons, even good reasons, to support both claims, and yet, obviously, conjoined, they are contradictory.

At this point it is likely to occur to most that a simple distinction is in order, which would allow one to save both propositions, merely understanding them in different senses. For example, it is not a case of 'p' and '~ p' but a case of 'p' and 'q'. For example, say, Bill is red and not red, but there is no problem because he is a Libertarian native American who loathes Communism, or such.

One might proceed as follows:

When it is claimed that the past does not exist, it is meant, for example, that Caesar is not now crossing the Rubicon, that Charles Martel is not now turning the Moors back at Tours, and so on, and that is true. On the other hand, when it is said that the past does exist, it does not really mean that at all, but means something quite different, namely, that it is true that Caesar once crossed the Rubicon, that Charles Martel once turned the Moors back at Tours, and so on.

No problem!

But, alas, there is a problem.

One must account for the truth of the statements about Caesar, Charles Martel, and so on. It is not enough that they happen to be true, as we suppose they are, but the important point is why are they true, what accounts for their truth. If they are true, there must now be a correspondent term. How could they be true if the past did not exist?

Nothing exists if it does not now exist.

And something exists in virtue of which certain statements are true, and it must now exist, for nothing exists if it does not now exist.

My suggestion here is that the antinomy is an antinomy, that we are dealing with a contradiction, and that the word 'past' must have *the same sense* in both statement and negation.

The antinomy is not evaded by the artifice of such a distinction; it is not evaded by changing meanings.

Consider, space is finite or not finite. One does not resolve that antinomy by taking space to mean two different things, by meaning by 'space' at one time a gravitationally circumscribed space and, at another time, the mysterious space into which this gravitationally

circumscribed space is supposedly expanding. The way around that antinomy, if one wishes to deal with it, is to declare for one option or the other, hopefully for a good reason. One does not change the meanings of 'p' and
'~ p'. One chooses either 'p' or '~ p'.

Similarly I recommend, as the most judicious approach to this matter, that which will preserve the correspondence theory of truth for historiography, and which will make most sense out of the presuppositions and practice of historiography, an unapologetic metaphysical commitment, that the past exists, and, like all existence, exists now. This does not entail, of course, that Caesar is currently crossing the Rubicon, that Charles Martel is still in the saddle at Tours, and so on. It does maintain that the past is real, and that it exists.

Accordingly, the assertion that the past does not exist is false, while the assertion that it does exist, is true.

One accepts one conjunct in the contradiction, which is a real contradiction, and rejects the other. One accepts 'p' and rejects '~ p'.

All the harrowing epistemological problems remain, but now historiography is grounded, explicitly, as it was not before. It may never know whether a given historiographical assertion is true or false but it knows now it *is* either true or false. The historian, to the best of his ability, makes his epistemological wager, as wisely, as judiciously, as he can. We no longer need a coherence or pragmatic analysis of truth. The historian can use the same notion of truth as the grocer, the plumber, the astronomer, the atomic physicist. One retains coherence, of course, as a test of truth, but one is no longer required to see it as definitive of truth, as being a truth-making property. It is a truth-testing property. Usually it does not tell us much. It can tell us that 'p & ~ p' is false, but it does not tell us whether 'p' is true or '~ p' is true. That one has to find out for oneself, to the extent one can.

It is one thing, of course, to say that a rock exists, and another to say that it does not exist. On the other hand, the meaning of 'exists' in something like 'the past exists' or 'the past does not exist' is different.

The existential commitment here is of a different sort.

Indeed, there are many modalities of existence, species of being, whose genus is little more than existence itself.

The reader may recall, from an earlier discussion, a specialized analysis of 'existence', an analysis in terms of which it might intelligibly function as a predicate.

Let 'Ex' mean 'x exists in the sense that x is an agent which can interact with physical objects, which interaction would produce empirically discernable effects'.

That is an explication of a sort of existence, and is not intended to be the exclusive form of existence possible. For example, one usually thinks of theorems, ownership, space, equations, and such as existing, but they would not exist in the specialized sense specified above with respect to agency.

The "agency sense" is not the sense in which the past would exist, or not exist. It might seem so, but it is really different. One might say, of course, the past had discernible effects. Is the present not a discernible effect, and so on. Similarly, one might say that the past has provoked many actions in the present, changes in policy, and such, and thus it has interacted with physical objects, for the bodies of contemporaries are physical objects, are they not, and so on. Similarly one might say the past is an empirical reality for there is much empirical evidence that it exists, documents, artifacts, and so on. It is certainly true that actions and events at one time may have effects at another time, for example, that the light of a star might be visible elsewhere only after thousands of years, perhaps after the star itself no longer exists. On the other hand the modality in which the past exists is not the modality in which past objects produced future effects. The past in the sense we are thinking of it, as a ground for truth in historiography, is causally inert. It is fixed. It is a *Gegenüber*, an "over-and-against," so to speak, something one can be right or wrong about, though one may never know which. The sense then in which the past would exist, or not exist, is not a typical empirical sense of 'exist', in which, for example, one might say a rock exists, a man exists, a team exists, a nation exists.

'Existence', here, has a different sense.

I do not think that this would have alarmed Kant. If he had thought about it, perhaps he would have given it some sort of phenomenalistic status, and hypothesized that a commitment to an existent past was an *a priori* trait of the human mind, like the forms of intuition and the categories of the understanding. Certainly he talked about the past, often enough. Certainly it would have been presupposed, in some sense, in his astronomy and physics.

Many things exist in the way they exist, and not in another way. Space and time seem to me to exist, in a primitive, indisputable way. I would also be willing to suppose that a mind-independent world exists and that the future will continue to resemble the past. These, too, are metaphysical commitments. I cannot see that the reality of the past is in any way more ontologically hazardous, or unintelligible.[37]

---

[37] Willard Van Orman Quine, certainly one of the finest American philosophers, once proposed a criterion of ontological commitment: To be is to be the value of a variable. Obviously this is not what he really meant as there are doubtless many things which might be taken as the values of variables which do not exist, erudite purple unicorns, for instance. Also, there are doubtless many things which exist which have never had the opportunity to be the values of variables, unsung squirrels, for example. What he meant, I take it, would have been more along the following lines: To be claimed to be is to be the value of a variable. He is, after all, concerned with what individuals are taking to exist, not with what might, in reality, exist. We are dealing here with a proposed criterion of ontological commitment. What is involved here is the notion that a given individual, should he be familiar with certain technical logistic apparatus, and desire to make use of it, and then use it, would be committed to hold as existing whatever might be taken to be the values of the variables over which he would quantify, if the quantified statement were to be true. For example, let us suppose that we are thinking about an erudite purple unicorn who reads Greek, and then we formulate a locution to the effect, '$(\exists x) (Ux \& Gx)$', and we were serious about this, and not playing around in Pegasus country; this locution then, following Quine, would commit us to the existence of such a unicorn. It would do this because the value of the variables in this case is the unicorn, and, if the locution were true, such a unicorn would have to exist. Thus, we are supposedly committed to the existence of the unicorn. To be sure, this seems a bit odd because we might not believe in unicorns at all, and yet formulate the locution. It is hard to say that anyone who formulates such a locution is committed to the existence of unicorns. Quine may have overestimated the solemnity of human beings. To be sure, Quine is more worried about abstract entities, such as numbers and classes. A Carnapian view here would, in my opinion, be far more judicious, namely, a view that the utility of a form of discourse takes priority over obscure, and perhaps inexplicable, referentialities. Carnap has a more instrumental view of language; Quine seems to have more of a photographic theory of language, that words, like pictures,

One supposes that a commitment to an existential past might be an unnecessary presupposition of historiographical discourse, as we have seen, given coherence and pragmatic possibilities, but it is surely a familiar and likely methodological presupposition of such discourse, if nothing else. We, of course, see it as far more than a mere presupposition of such discourse, to be justified by its convenience and utility. We see it as a presupposition without which historiography would be evacuated of significance. Without it, historiography becomes an exercise in compilation, or a game of adjustments, and surrenders its claim to be concerned with truth as classically understood, would abandon its claim to truths amongst the mightiest and most significant to the human form of life.

---

should be of something. In any event, as is clear above, I would be willing to subscribe to a formula such as '$(\exists x)\, Px$', namely, I would unhesitantly quantify over a variable which takes the past as its value. If the past exists, the formula is true; it if does not, the formula is false. We think it does exist. If it did not, historiographical statements, at least on the correspondence view of truth, would have nothing to correspond to; nothing by means of which they could achieve truth and falsity.

III. Causality: The Roots of Why

We shall presuppose here, at least tentatively, until we reach Part Four of this study, that past events, their structure, their causal relations, and such, are graspable, namely, that the past is comprehensible. This does not entail that one can achieve certainty in such matters, for fallibilism seems a not only virtuous but, we fear, a fully justified stance in such matters, but it does entail that what went on in the past, at least in theory, lies within the dimensions of a human cognitive capacity. Most of it, any rate. We have here, following Vico, the principle of *verum factum*. History is comprehensible to us because it is something made by human beings. Its truths are truths for which humans are responsible. The truth in history is a human artifact, something which human beings have made, and which is thus comprehensible to other human beings. According to Vico we do not know why nature is the way it is. Only the Divine Entity, the author of nature, its creator, knows why it is the way it is. He knows the "why" of nature. We do not, because we are not its author, or creator. We may describe the way nature works, tell how it is, but we are spectators, observers, not participants, not creators; we are always on the "outside." On the other hand, we are the authors of, the creators of, human history. We know *why* it is, not just how it is. We understand it from the "inside." It is our artifact, our *verum factum*, our "made truth." And thus we discover, a new, different, wonderful, autonomous science, a *Scienza Nuova*. This is, too, one may suppose, the most significant and momentous of all sciences, since by means of it we understand ourselves, not in terms of abstractions and generalities, as might psychology, but in virtue of all the unique, special, diverse, particular, and concrete details of human reality. Through history, as Collingwood pointed out, one obtains self-knowledge, "... it teaches us what man has done and thus what man is."[38]

Philosophical problems are often multifaceted, and often have aspects which might, from one point of view be regarded as metaphysical, from another epistemological, and so on. For example, the question of the nature of a nation, which we treated under historiographical semantics, might have been dealt with as a metaphysical question, or one of epistemology. Similarly, the subject matter to be now addressed has aspects which are semantic, epistemological, and metaphysical. As it is traditionally regarded as a question of metaphysics, namely, a question as to the ultimate nature of the world and its final way of working, we will deal with it here. Presumably, too, science will weigh in on this matter, and the philosopher is well advised to attend to what it has to say, although, naturally, without relinquishing his native criticality, without which he would betray his discipline. For example, if the two major achievements of 20th Century science, quantum mechanics and relativity theory, should turn out to be logically incompatible, as has been asserted, hopefully incorrectly, he has a right to be worried. Similarly he may be reluctant to accept a theory which would evacuate all theorization of significance, at least without thinking about it. Similarly, if it should be the purpose of a scientist to prove that purposes are unreal, this suggests at least a semantic problem. He may, too, worry about things just happening, happening without causes. He knows enough of the history of science to recall that today's science is often "tomorrow's fallacy." Indeed, he knows this if only from the work of the scientists themselves. Where did phlogiston, and the ether, go? Do the counterclockwise vibrations of "strings" of some sort really require twenty-six different spatial dimensions, which is some twenty-three more than we seem to have on hand? Too, what about these

---

38 R. G. Collingwood, *The Idea of History* (Revised Edition, Edited with an Introduction by Jan Van Der Dussen, Oxford, Oxford University Press, 1994, p. 10).

occasional momentous "paradigm shifts" in terms of which one science yields to another science? It is generally accepted that no scientific theory can be definitively proved, nor, indeed, definitively refuted, though surely some are better confirmed than others, and some are disconfirmed, at least for all practical purposes. Theories, too, are underdetermined by data, the data not entailing the theory. Thus, a variety of different theories might, conjoined with the same initial-condition statements and auxiliary hypotheses, account for the same data. Too, it is a logical truism that any statement logically follows from an infinite number of diverse possible premise-sets, compatible and incompatible, so it is logically possible that our awesome science, worked out over centuries by thousands of dedicated, hard-working, highly intelligent individuals, is only one of a possibly infinite number of sciences, all equally useful, all empirically adequate, each explaining things nicely, each yielding the same verifiable predictions, and so on. Some of philosophy's most egregious and embarrassing mistakes have been the result of taking seriously what science was saying at the time. All in all then, the philosopher, and others interested in these matters, is well advised to be scientifically informed, to the extent practical, while, at the same time, realizing very clearly that he may be, so to speak, scientifically misinformed.

The general notion here is that events are causally related. This may, of course, be a false hypothesis, but it is hard to see how historiography could proceed, as more than superficial chronicle, if it did not presuppose causal relations. Indeed, even chronicle, as all narration, presupposes causal relevancies, for example, in its criteria for recognizing events, for selecting events, and for relating events. Several very different chronicles might result from differences here, even if they were all supposedly chronicling what took place at a given place at a given time. The intelligibility of chronicle itself is founded on substantial agreement with respect to meaningful sequences, and what is important and what is not important. Historiography, it seems, unlike this afternoon's physics, must rule out randomness. The historian cannot get away with "this just happened, and it is not that we do not know why, but rather that there was no reason why it happened, at all. It was just an uncaused, random event."

This brings up the topic of "chance" in historiography.

There are at least two senses of "chance" of which we might take note. One of these senses is intelligible and might be historiographically valuable; the other makes less, if any, sense, and, in any event, would be historiographically useless.

Consider three causal systems, System$_1$, System$_2$, and System$_3$. System$_1$ and Sustem$_2$ are systems within System$_3$, which is the "over system," the "containing system," or "macrosystem." Consider a causal sequence within System$_1$ of A, B, and C, and a causal sequence of D, E, and F within System $_2$. Furthermore, let us suppose that System$_1$ and System$_2$ interact, producing event "K," which initiates a new causal sequence, one resulting from the interaction of System$_1$ and System$_2$, consisting of L, M, and so on. For example, let us suppose we have two individuals, Jones and Smith, and that each of these individuals gets up in the morning, does various things, and then starts to drive to work. At a given intersection we shall suppose that these two individuals are involved in an unexpected collision. Fortunately, both are long-separated childhood chums now delighted to renew their acquaintance, and, after their cars are towed away, they repair to a local bar to celebrate their reunion.[39] From the point of view of both Jones and Smith event "K," the collision and reunion, and such, is taken as an accident, a chance event. I think we would usually say that something like this was a matter of chance. There is nothing deviant, for example, in referring to this as a coincidence, a chance occurrence, or such. Now, what is meant by calling this a chance occurrence is that it seemed unlikely, it was unexpected, it came as quite a surprise, it could not have been predicted by either Jones or Smith when they left their respective driveways, and so on. In other words, from the point of view of both System$_1$ and System$_2$, this was a matter of chance. Life is filled with such things, and even begins with such things. What were the chances of Julius Caesar having been born, or of anyone else, for that matter, given some three hundred and fifty, or so, eggs, produced by, say, Caesar's mother and several billions of sperm cells produced by Caesar's father? Leonardo da Vinci's father tried to reduplicate as well as he could the circumstances surrounding the conception of

---

39 In this way, one hopes to allay any apprehensions on the part of concerned readers.

Leonardo, but he never had the same luck the second time. On the other hand, consider the macrosystem, System$_3$, in which System$_1$ and System$_2$ were components. From the point of view of the macrosystem, event "K" was not an accident, but, in theory, could have been predicted, down to the smallest scratch on the fender of either car. Now, if the universe is a deterministic system, in which all events take place in accord with natural law, then we have a macrosystem, in which everything which occurs in any subsystem, such as System$_1$ or System$_2$, is perfectly predictable, and in no way a matter of chance. If chance is involved, as seems unlikely, it might be that the macrosystem itself is a matter of chance, a way the world just happened to be.

What follows from this historiographically, not logically, but practically, seems to be that the historiographer should recognize the reality of chance in the first sense, that of the surprising and unexpected, but, once the chance is accepted, should begin to trace out, as well as he can, the results of the chance, in the case of our example, the interrelationships of events L, M, and so on. He need not, however, accept the second notion of "chance," in which the inexplicable in theory is presupposed. That he can leave to the physicist, or, at least, to some of them. The historiographer is best advised, it seems, at least professionally, as a working postulate, to accept the existence of a causal world, which does not prohibit him from recognizing that some very unexpected and surprising effects might emerge from a causal matrix. The unexpected is to be expected. Let us suppose that one hundred slips of paper, slip number one, slip number two, and so on, are placed in a hat. The chance that any one of those slips is drawn out is a hundred to one. On the other hand, the probability that one of these hundred-to-one-events will occur is "1," namely, certainty. To be sure, if, due to a quantum fluctuation, the hat should burst into flame, all bets are off.

It seems that causality must be a major presupposition of the historiographical enterprise. Obviously this will have its impact on historiographical explanation, but that topic, on our approach, will be considered while dealing with the epistemology of historiography.

Trouble is afoot.

It seems the historiographer is committed, at least professionally, to causality.

How else could he explain, or try to explain, anything?

The causality hypothesis, on the other hand, has some very serious conceptual and perhaps moral consequences.

> With Earth's first Clay They did the Last Man's knead,
> And then of the Last Harvest sow'd the Seed:
> > Yea, the first Morning of Creation wrote
> What the Last Dawn of Reckoning shall read.[40]

The likely possibilities seem threefold here, determinism, in which there would be no freedom, and no responsibility; indeterminism, in which, also, there would be no responsibility; and "agency," in which one would have both freedom and responsibility, in which the individual is a self-moving being, one whose decisions are originated by the self, one who is an initiator of causal sequences, one who is a "first cause" of his own actions. Consider a decision. The decision is either caused or not caused. If it is not caused we would have indeterminism. If it is caused, it would be caused by the self or not by the self, which latter alternative we will refer to as being "other-caused." If the decision is "other-caused," namely, not by the self, presumably it is a function of antecedent conditions, and this would give us determinism. This does not deny, of course, that a decision may be a necessary condition for the next link in a causal sequence. It is understood here that B may come about because it was chosen, and would not have come about had it not been chosen, but it is supposed that the choice itself was determined. One was not free to choose other than as one did choose. Now if we regard the decision as having been caused by the self, *simpliciter*, we have the theory of agency. Some difficulties here are to understand how this decision would have come about, how could it have started, how would it work, and so forth. There are also problems with the nature of a self. For example, there is obviously a brain, and consciousness, and such, but it does not follow from that that there is a mind, or self, and so on.

What is involved here is the Causal Trilemma.

---

40 Omar Khayyám, *Rubaiyat* (Translation by Edward Fitzgerald, New York, Shakespeare House, 1951, Quatrain LIII, p. 114).

Consider the following six meaning assignments.
SC: The act is self-caused (self-initiated).
OC: The act is other-caused.
NC: The act is not caused.
M: The act is mysterious.
D: The act is determined.
I: The act is inexplicable.
The Trilemma might then be formalized, as follows:
1. (SC) v (OC) v (NC)
2. (SC) ⊃ M
3. (OC) ⊃ D
4. (NC) ⊃ I
5. M v D v I

Informally, the notion here is that the only three possibilities for an act are that it is either self-caused, other-caused, or not caused; and, if it is self-caused, it is mysterious; if other-caused, then determinism is the case; and, if it is not caused, then it is inexplicable. The conclusion then would be that the act is either mysterious, determined, or inexplicable.[41]

One is supposing that each of these trijuncts is likely to be disturbing to many individuals, though doubtless not to all. For example, there are doubtless individuals who are untroubled by the notion of mysterious acts, individuals who view determinism with equanimity, and individuals who have no problem with things happening without causes, and thus no problem with inexplicable acts. The self-caused act may be mysterious, but it is not inexplicable in the same sense as the uncaused act, because it is explained as an act of the self. The

---

41 Some problems are being methodologically ignored here. For example, it might be said, with justification, that the concept of an act requires rational accession, conscious or unconscious, and thus that an uncaused movement, or such, could not be an act, but, at best, a behavior. Whereas this is true, I think it is helpful here, for purposes of simplicity, and clarity, to understand 'act' broadly enough to include whatever an organism might do, with or without rational accession. Thus, technically, a sneeze would count as an act at this point. One might also make a case out, of course, that if determinism is true there are no acts either. For example, when a stone rolls down a hill, is that an act? Presumably not. Similarly, if Jones' picking up a pencil is as much an inevitability as the stone's movement down the hill, is his picking up the pencil an act? In any event, one is using 'act' broadly in the above argument.

problem then is how the self could bring about the act, how the act might be explicable. In the "no-cause case," it is supposed that there is no explanation; in the "mysterious case," it is supposed that we simply do not know the explanation. Whereas some might take probabilism as explanatory, it is not explanatory in the sense we require. For example, it may be true that we can predict that x number of letters will be misaddressed annually, but this does not explain why Jones, in particular, misaddressed the letter to his creditor.

The argument is constructed to be valid, of course. It might or might not be sound. The first premise seems very likely to be true. The second premise, as we shall see, seems true. To be sure, such an act might not be mysterious to a divine entity, say, one who created free will. Similarly, one supposes many individuals do not regard their acts as mysterious at all, any more than they regard it as mysterious that they can pick up the pencil when they decide to do it. Such things are familiar, at any rate. The third premise might not be obviously true. Let us suppose that we have a divine entity who, in a nondetermined universe, i.e., one, in this case, in which self-caused acts are possible, causes Jones to pick up the pencil in virtue of a miraculous intervention in the causal nexus. Then we would have an "other-caused act" which would not require determinism, in the sense of being in accord with the laws of nature, because here, *per* the supposition, the divine entity, for a time, suspended the action of such laws, to cause Jones to pick up the pencil. Here, then, we would have an "other-caused act" which would not necessitate a wholly determined universe. Similarly, one might, in a nondetermined universe, have "other-caused acts" of various sorts, with which we are familiar, for example, Sergeant Black suggests that Private Brown pick up Cigarette Butt B or charge Machine-Gun Nest N, $Bruiser_1$ causes $Bruiser_2$ to fumble on the two-yard line, which causes $Bruiser_2$ to utter shocking expletives, $Heather_1$ causes $Heather_2$ distress by wearing a similar dress to the prom, and so on. But these notions of other-caused acts are not pertinent in this context. "Other-caused" in our context carries the notion of being an ineluctable function of antecedent conditions, an act which might, in theory, in virtue of, say, the position and momenta of the gas molecules in the primeval nebula, conjoined with the laws of nature, and such, have been infallibly predicted billions of years ago. The existence of an "other-caused act" in this sense would imply a deterministic universe, thus suggesting that the third premise is analytic.

In any event the Causal Trilemma gives us a valid argument, and one which may very well be sound. A sound argument, as may be recalled, is one which is valid and has a true premise-set. If the argument is sound, the conclusion must be true, for it is logically impossible in a valid argument to obtain a false conclusion from a true premise-set. There is nothing mysterious here. It is just a matter of logistic form, the fixity of meanings, and such. It is no stranger than the fact that if 'p & q' are both true, then 'q' must be true. So, in this argument, as it is valid, if the premise-set is true, the conclusion must also be true. The premise-set seems to be true. Perhaps it is true. In any event, the argument seems persuasive. Accordingly, any given act, it seems, must either be mysterious, determined, or inexplicable.

We shall briefly examine each of these possibilities, and then speculate on what might be the practical consequences for the reflective historiographer. In this matter, as in others, we are not concerned with the unreflective historiographer. Indeed, one might envy his bliss.

The notion of the self-caused act, that act of which an individual is the "first cause," gives us the theory of agency. There is nothing in agency, *per se*, which is incompatible with the act being heavily influenced by an individual's circumstances, experiences, purposes, desires, and so on. All decisions take place in a "decision environment." They are made by individuals who usually have an end in view and a sense of what is practical and what is impractical, what is desirable and what is not. Jones may wish to decide between Stephanie and Courtney, but if sane, he is not going to opt for Thais, Cleopatra, or Eleanor of Aquitaine. In agency, however, the choice, presumably far from arbitrary, is not a simple function of antecedent causal factors as these are normally understood. His choice is not an effect, but a cause. It was not inevitably predestined by "the first Morning of Creation," nor concealed within the bosom of a "super atom" waiting to go off.

How could this be?

We spoke earlier, in dealing with Monisms and Dualisms, of the Interaction or Mind-Body Problem, and that is quite relevant here.

We will distinguish between two ways of trying to make sense of Agency, which we will call the "Intrusion Modality" and the "Conservative-System Modality."

The "Intrusion Modality" involves the Interaction or Mind-Body Problem, as usually conceived. Perhaps it would be kinder, or less controversial, to call it the "Entrance Modality." In either case, the problem is the same, "How does the decision intrude into the causal nexus," or "How does the decision enter into the causal nexus?"

To get a sense of the problem let us return to the environs of Königsberg for a suggestion. Immanuel Kant, a physicist and astronomer of the Enlightenment, or *Aufklärung*, was, with respect to the phenomenal world, a Newtonian and determinist. In the phenomenal world a strict causality obtained; indeed, this was in virtue of a category of the understanding itself. On the other hand, Kant was much impressed not only by "the starry skies above" but by "the moral law within." As the expression goes, "ought implies can." This means that if moral obligations, duties, and such, are genuine, then an individual must have the capacity to act in such a way as to honor his obligations, comply with his duties, and so on. This is an argument from the authenticity of obligation, indirectly, to the existence of free will.

1. O
2. O ⊃ C
3. C ⊃ FW
4. <u>O ⊃ FW</u>   2, 3, Hypothetical Syllogism
5. FW   1, 4, Modus Ponens

On the other hand, if one cannot honor obligations, comply with duties, and so on, then moral obligation does not exist. This is an argument from the inability to honor obligations, comply with duties, and so on, to the nonexistence of moral obligation.

1. ∼ C
2. <u>O ⊃ C</u>
3. ∼ O   1, 2, Modus Ponens

It might be noted, in passing, that the inability to fulfill moral obligations, and such, does not entail the nonexistence of free will. The nonexistence of moral obligations is logically compatible with the existence of free will.

The following argument is invalid.

1. ∼ C
2. O ⊃ C
3. C ⊃ FW
   ∼ FW

Suppose FW is true. Then the conclusion would be false. Then, if O were false, and C were false, one would have a true premise-set and a false conclusion, showing the argument to be invalid.

Kant, of course, regarded moral obligation as authentic, and binding, and so on. He even devised, or discovered, an unusual version of the Generalizability Principle, his famous first version of the Categorical Imperative, which might be used, he seems to have thought, as a test for moral obligation.[42] This is no place to go into

---

[42] Formulations may differ slightly, but there are some three principles that are usually cited here. The first is the famous first version of the categorical imperative, the sense of which is that one should act only on a maxim which one is willing to generalize, namely, one which one could also will to become a universal law, presumably of nature. (This seems to confuse two senses of law, one the formulation of the law, and the other the law itself. What Kant presumably means here is that one should not do x unless one would be willing to will that everyone, in such circumstances, would invariably, and of necessity, act similarly. For example, one should not renege on a debt, unless one were willing to will that all debts should be reneged upon, forever, universally, necessarily, and so on. Presumably one would be unwilling to will that, if only because one might be the creditor the next time around. Society would be reduced to chaos, and so on. Thus, "Renege on this debt," would be a maxim one would hesitate to generalize into "Renege on all debts," and then will that debt reneging should become a universal law of nature.) The other two, or so, versions of the categorical imperative are quite different, but they are obviously imperatives, and one supposes Kant supposed them categorical, for example, not contingent on particular circumstances, such as would be a hypothetical imperative, e.g., 'If you wish to win Stephanie's favor, be nice to her cat', 'If you wish to win Courtney's favor, do not belittle her poodle', and so on. The other two imperatives are, first, to the effect that one should always treat others never as a means only, but also, always, as ends in themselves, and, second, that one should always act so as to achieve a kingdom of ends. It is acceptable, of course, to treat others as a means, but not acceptable not to understand them as, and treat them as, ends, as well. The notion of acting in such a way as to bring about a kingdom of ends seems less clear, but the notion is probably to try to act in such a way as to produce a good society, as one sees it, presumably one in which people treat one another with respect, look out for one another, and so on. (Cf. Kant's *Fundamental Principles of the Metaphysic of Morals*, many versions available.)

Kant's ingenious ethical theory, one of the great contributions to the philosophy of morality, nor to consider whether or not, say, the first version of the Categorical Imperative might suffice to provide one with either a necessary or a sufficient condition for identifying moral acts. All we need to understand here is that Kant recognized moral obligation, understood it to entail the capacity to comply with such obligations, and that this, in turn, committed him to a belief in the reality of some sort of free will.

So how would he fit this into his Newtonian, deterministic world, his phenomenalistic world of strict causality?

Recall the world of the things-in-themselves, or the thing-in-itself, that world in which there is no space or time, and no causality, at least as we think of it. That is the world to which thought seems to drive one, the "thought-to-be world," the "noumenal world." We will call that the N world, as opposed to the P world, or the phenomenalistic world. Suppose there is a strict causal sequence in progress in the P world, say, that sequence consisting of A, B, and C. The Noumenal Self, outside of space, time, and such, as opposed to the Empirical Self, in space, time, and such, makes a decision, which would somehow take effect at C, within the phenomenalistic matrix, and, depending on the decision, might initiate any number of new, strict causal sequences, say, D_1, D_2, D_3, or D'_1, D'_2, D'_3, and so on. The notion seems to be that the spirit, the soul, or something, is a noumenal entity and, as such, is not bound by the strictures of the phenomenalistic world, and may thus transcend causality as one usually thinks it

This is a form of dualism, and seems to constitute an attempt to reconcile the world of science with the world of morality, both of which are likely to be, as they were to Kant, very important to human beings. Some problems attending this approach would be the existence or nonexistence of the N world; the existence or nonexistence of an N self; and the question as to how an N self could interact with, and effect changes within, the P world.

We have already called attention to such problems, for example, in connection with the principle of the conservation of matter/energy. Presumably energy is required to do work, such as pick up pencils, and such. On a dualistic hypothesis where would this energy come from? Is it created somehow, outside of space and time? If it enters the P world would it not add to the quantity of energy Q of that world, which seems to violate the principle of the conservation of matter/energy? Too, would changes in the N world not require energy? Would it withdraw energy from the P world to do its work, this again seeming to violate the principle of the conservation of matter/energy? It seems there is not only an "Entrance Problem," but there may be an "Exit Problem," as well. How can the nonspatial entity affect the spatial entity? As the saying has it, "How can the spiritual hammer drive the iron nail?" And how can the spatial entity affect the nonspatial entity? As the saying has it, "How can the iron hammer drive the spiritual nail?" No theorem has ever groomed a horse; no horse has ever trampled a theorem.

Trying to make sense of Agency in terms of the "Entrance Modality" is clearly difficult, if possible, at all.

One might, then, consider the possibility of making sense of Agency in terms of the "Conservative-System Modality."

What if we had a unified system, a conservative system, in which a given quantity of energy, Q, sufficed for both worlds, circulating, so to speak, between them? This would preserve the principle of the conservation of matter/energy. Mind and matter are here conceived as interrelated, and energy may move from matter to mind, and from mind to matter.

There are two major problems here. The first major problem seems to be that dualism is abandoned, this seeming to favor antecedent-condition causality, and threaten Agency. We no longer have a contrast between the spatial and the nonspatial. We have a now single system, a mind/body system, in which a given quantity of energy, Q, transducible, and such, suffices for both mental and physical activity. It is not clear where one would put a soul, or such, into this system.

We need not, of course, regard the system as physical in any sense which precludes mind or the mental, any more than we might need to regard the system as mental in any sense which precludes the physical.

It might be earlier recalled that the history of the world suggests there was at one time unconscious x and, then, at a later time, conscious x. We noted that if we wished an interpretation of x, two candidates seemed likely:

(1) Unconscious matter, then conscious matter.
(2) Unconscious mind, then conscious mind.

We then noted that on this approach the distinction between calling x matter and calling x mind is a matter of indifference. This assumes, of course, that we are interested in a monistic metaphysics, if only to avoid the Interaction, or the Mind/Body, Problem.

Whichever terminology we decide to use we have abandoned dualism, and accepted a monistic system. The advantages of the "Conservative-System Modality" are that it avoids the difficulties of the "Entrance Modality" and offers no challenge to the principle of the conservation of matter/energy, which, presumably, one wishes to retain intact.

Once, again, one is attempting to make sense of Agency, this time in terms of the "Conservative-System Modality." The second major problem one encounters here might be termed the "Decision-Maker Problem." *Per* hypothesis, no intrusion, or entrance, is here required into the system, lest one be returned to the "Entrance Modality," or the "Intrusion Modality," which would return one to the Interaction, or Mind/Body, Problem. On this approach, how is a decision made? How does it start, or come up, within the mind/body energy loop? First, is there a Decision Maker? Decisions come about, of course, but how? Even in strict determinism, decisions come about, ripples in the flow, whose headwaters are lost amongst the mountains of the past. There is certainly empirical evidence for decisions, but there seems to be no empirical evidence for a Decision Maker. If there is a Decision Maker, where is it located? In some part of the brain? Where? Perhaps, most importantly, how would the Decision Maker made its decision? Does it have a mind/body loop within itself? Does the Decision Maker require an interior Decision Maker, and it another, and so on, *ad infinitum*?

As might be recalled, the first premise of the Causal Trilemma was that the act was either self-caused, other-caused, or without a cause. Self-causation is Agency, and, as we have now seen, Agency is hard to understand, and an act produced by Agency would be mysterious. There is nothing illegal or immoral about being mysterious, but it is not cognitively comforting. Many feel, for reasons now obvious, that the theory of Agency is incorrect.

The second and third trijunct in the premise-set of the Causal Trilemma involved, respectively, the notion of "other-causation," which led to determinism, and the lack of causation, which led to inexplicability.

Surely a historian might putatively subscribe to Agency, and proceed as he wishes. Certainly he is under no obligation to first solve the Mind/Body Problem. On the other hand, this would introduce, at least implicitly, some suspect theoretical entities into his account, spirits, souls, noumenal entities, or such. Ultimately, he would be committed to an unverifiable metaphysics, one perhaps consisting of little more than brave verbiage, and he would have no way of explaining anything in scientifically acceptable terms. Possibly he would be unwilling to hang his narrations and explanations on so dubious and invisible a hook, having decisions motivated by, say, mysterious out-of-sight springs and levers, and who is tripping the springs and working the levers, and how would he manage that?

So one supposes, whatever the personal views of the historian, he will write, and act, as though determinism is true.

In short, he will present decisions as though they were functions of an individual's circumstances, experiences, purposes, desires, and so on, decisions in terms of the "Decision Environment," broadly understood.

Certain aspects of determinism require careful attention. In order to devote appropriate attention to the deterministic thesis, and justify that attention, I think it will be helpful, briefly, to call attention to one or more distinctions. Otherwise the issue may be clouded.

First, certain questions of metaphysics should be separated from certain questions of epistemology. Perhaps better put, certain questions of fact, of independent fact, should be separated from questions as to our knowledge of, lack of knowledge of, or speculations concerning, such facts. Even on a Kantian view, there would presumably be such facts. Let us suppose, following Homer, that amongst the fellows heading for Troy, on some forty or so black ships, those of the Lokrians, presumably accompanying swift

Aias, the son of Oïleus, who was leading the men of Lokris, was the lesser Aias, who was not as big as Aias, the son of Telamon, but was, indeed, far slighter, a little fellow armoured in linen, who, nonetheless, somehow, with the throwing spear excelled all the Achaians and Hellenes put together. Now, what about the lesser Aias? If such a fellow existed, there must be several billion facts, or more, about him, which we will never know. We might, of course, with varying degrees of assurance speculate. Presumably he spoke a Lokrian dialect of Greek, was good with the throwing spear, and such. We would be less sure that he came in for a good bit of ribbing because of his size, or that he spent a good deal of time practicing with the throwing spear, perhaps to make the big fellows take notice. We have no idea whether or not he had allergies, was on a first-name basis with Nestor, and so on. [43]

There is a difference with respect to the fact and the probabilities that we are right or wrong about the fact. On the deterministic hypothesis the facts are fixed, constituting a given *Gegenüber*, and our knowledge is more or less certain, and it may not exist at all. On the deterministic thesis probability is a property not of fact but of speculation, knowledge, that sort of thing. An explanation may have one degree of probability or another, but probability does not pertain to the fact itself. Recall the x number of misaddressed letters each year; that does not explain any particular misaddressed letter, and each misaddressed letter is a particular letter. It does not explain, for example, why Jones misaddressed the letter to his creditor. Similarly, a historian would not be likely to try to explain an event E by saying that in such and such circumstances such events occur twenty percent of the time, or even ninety percent of the time. That is not an explanation; that is arithmetic. One wants to know why event E occurred at that time in that way.

The second distinction I want to note, in order to dismiss it, is that there could be a metaphysical sense of probability, as opposed to an epistemological sense, and that would be the case if certain views of quantum theory were to be taken seriously. In such a case, probability could pertain to the fact itself. The fact just happened, and had no cause. In this case, not only is the world

---

43 Cf. Homer, *The Illiad*, Book Two, Marginal References 525, 530. (Chicago, The University of Chicago Press, 1954, Trans. Richard Lattimore, p. 90).

nondeterministic, in this case, indeterministic, but it also makes no sense. One can obtain approximate predictions, of course, in quantum mechanics and elsewhere, as in the percentage of pittings within such and such an area on an electrostatic grid, that most of the oxygen molecules in the room are not likely to congregate in one place, that so many letters will be misaddressed each year, and so on. The historiographer, on the other hand, is trying to explain particular events which take place at particular times, not, on the whole, at least, predict sorts of events in such and such percentages. Quantum mechanics, even if true, is of little or no historiographical value or interest. An uncaused event cannot be explained. And that an event of type E occurs every so often is not an explanation of any particular event E.

Let us suppose the historian is now set to work.

He has at his disposal three possible presuppositions, or hypotheses, with respect to his work. He may, in theory, choose Agency, Determinism, or Indeterminism.[44]

I am assuming that the choice would lie between Agency and Determinism. Insofar as indeterminism would commit itself to things just happening, happening randomly, happening causelessly, happening for no reason, inexplicably, and so forth, historiography would seem to be impossible, except perhaps as a form of journalism, a way of keeping track of spontaneous, unaccountable materializations or such. Similarly, statistical "explanations" might

---

44 Ruling out free will, it seems there would be three sorts of universe possible, first, a universe which is deterministic throughout; second, a "split universe," in which indeterminism might obtain on the microlevel but, when a certain level of complexity is attained, say, the molecular level, determinism "kicks in," and the world is deterministic from that point forward, or upward, and the microlevel is, in effect, irrelevant to practical life; third, one might suppose, as I think is the standard hypothesis in quantum theory, that the world is indeterministic throughout, and the appearance of laws is deceptive, a result of high probabilities; it is, say, only a high probability that all the oxygen atoms in New York City will not congregate in the Radio City Music Hall, or that erudite purple unicorns will not suddenly become abundant, organize political parties, and rule the world. Historiography, it seems, could get on well with either the deterministic universe or the split universe. It is hard to see how it could deal with the indeterministic universe. I suppose it could just forget about it, and proceed as if either the deterministic universe or the split universe were the case. When science makes life impossible, it may be time to look elsewhere.

provide predictions where large numbers of events are concerned, but would not make it clear why any particular event occurred, and that is usually what the historian is interested in. Even if he is a macrohistorian, so to speak, considering, say, societies, civilizations, cultures, and such, he is usually interested in trying to explain why, say, they rise and fall, not merely that they rise and fall.

Let us suppose that the historian elects Agency. He is then committed to the "M Hypothesis," so to speak, namely, to mysteries, to scientifically suspect theoretical entities, and must accept all the problematicities associated with Agency, confront the Interaction or Mind/Body Problem, and so on.

This suggests that the historian, at least as a working hypothesis, would be well advised to elect determinism, committing himself to the "D Hypothesis," so to speak, namely, to the notion of a deterministic universe. Here, however, interestingly, we encounter certain problematicities before which the difficulties and obscurities of the M hypothesis may pale into insignificance.

As these are seldom brought to light, are seldom noted, and such, but are quite interesting and important, I think they deserve some attention.

We will consider three such problematicities, all of which are perspectivally transformational, what we shall call the illegitimacy problematicity, the moral problematicity, and that of the colossal misunderstanding.[45]

---

[45] We spoke earlier about the concept of a deterministic universe, how it was to be understood, its relationship to theoretical predictability, and such. We are supposing that is reasonably clear. Some other observations, however, pertaining to this supposition might be in order. Most obviously, the thesis of determinism, while it might be confirmed, or disconfirmed, to one extent or another, and is accordingly a synthetic thesis, a meaningful thesis pertaining to the nature of the universe, and so either true or false, is not a thesis which can be proven, nor, one suspects, disproven. Naturally, if the quantum hypothesis is true, determinism is false. But how does one know that there was really no reason for that quark to behave as it did, or for the universe to come into being out of nothingness, and so on? How do we know there are no causes involved? Also, of course, we will never satisfy the conditions for perfect predictability. We do not know exactly where the penny will land, dropped from the tall building. And how would we know in all the length and breadth of the universe that there was not once, somewhere, an exception to the laws of nature? Too, perhaps somewhere, erudite purple unicorns exist, though

they would presumably not speak Greek, unless the quantum people are right, and that improbable event happened to happen, without waiting around for a cause. We might call attention to two common misconceptions of determinism, first, that determinism means we are forced to do one thing or another, that we are coerced by the universe, so to speak, and, second, that the choices we make are inefficacious. With respect to the second misconception, we have already pointed out, elsewhere, that choices are usually efficacious, that such and such would not have come about if it had not been chosen. The choice itself, of course, is seen as an ineluctable link in the "casual chain," a function of antecedent conditions and laws. One was not free to choose other than one did choose. The first notion also involves a misconception, namely, that determinism is forcing us, or coercing us, in some sense typical for such words, to do one thing or another. This is not the case in the sense usually given to such words. We are not being manhandled, threatened, intimidated, seized, shoved, flung about, and such. The plant is such that it turns to the light; it is not being forced to do so; mitosis is how cells divide; small *gendarmes* are not supervising the process; the tides in the sea and the lesser tides in the Earth are part of an integrated, natural, lovely, holistic system; they are not fearfully obeying the moon, any more than the moon is fearfully obeying the Earth; planets go their rounds without policing; does it make sense to say they are forced to do so, or are acting under coercion? We make many decisions exactly as we wish and often do exactly what we want to do; surely we are not being forced to decide exactly as we wish or coerced to do exactly what we want to do; it is all part of the unfolding universal process.

Given the seeming freedom of choice we all enjoy, of course, it might be wondered why anyone would take determinism seriously. There are, of course, a number of reasons, of varying merits, involved in this issue. A few such reasons follow:

Given determinism, the universe is at least in principle comprehensible. Many human beings desire a comprehensible universe.

The seeming nature of the universe is deterministic. Regularities abound. A given theory might account for, say, the falling of an apple, the movement of a pendulum, the trajectory of a projectile, the periodic track of planets, and such. It seems we have a universe of law. If the human is an element in such a universe, does it not seem unlikely that he would be antithetical to, or an exception to, its sublime, encompassing nature?

The knowledge/prediction ratio suggests determinism. The more we know about a system, or a human being, the more accurately we can predict its behavior.

There is a general reluctance to accept "metaphysical explanations," given in terms of, say, entelechies, vital forces, ghosts, gremlins, miracles, witchcraft, magic, and such. Such explanations are often found unilluminating, even disruptive. They do not fit into the world as it is conjectured to be. How would one test for the presence of, say, a will? Is there a will, what would it be, what

The first problematicity connected with determinism to which we will direct our attention is what one might refer to as the illegitimacy problematicity.

Since it is not clear how the historiographer could consistently, or intelligibly, apply the I Hypothesis in his work, namely, that the act is inexplicable, this following from the "No-Cause Option" in the Causal Trilemma, we will suppose he will apply either the M Hypothesis, that the act is mysterious, that hypothesis associated with Agency, or the D Hypothesis, that hypothesis associated with determinism.

Let us suppose now that the historiographer, understandably skeptical of the M Hypothesis, in view of its many problems, opts for the D Hypothesis.

That being the case, he will apply the D Hypothesis. His next decision is how to apply the D Hypothesis. Most simply, he can either apply the D Hypothesis universally or not; he can apply it to everything or not apply it to everything; he can apply it to everyone or not apply it to everyone. He could, for example, exempt himself and his work from its scope. That is, in essence, what most people do.[46] This exemption, as far as I know, is never made explicitly, and,

---

would be its properties, is it free, and how would one know that, and so on. Much psychological theory seems to presuppose determinism, both depth psychology, certainly of the Freudian sort, and behaviorism, certainly of the Skinnerian sort.

Determinism seems to give us a way of avoiding the problems noted with Agency, whether conceived of in terms of the "Entrance Modality" or the "Conservative-System Modality."

And, in historiography, as we have suggested, the presupposition of determinism provides a context in which rationally transparent explanation appears possible, however difficult it might be to obtain in practice.

46 There is nothing immoral about doing that but it does suggest an analogy with the immoral. It is very important to the immoral person that the great majority of human beings behave in a moral fashion; he counts on that; otherwise he would probably stay under the bed. The intelligent immoral person recognizes that the world would become a very dangerous, worrisome, terrifying place if his fellows decided to exempt themselves from the moral strictures he is counting on them to observe. Kant seemed to think that such considerations would oblige the intelligent person to behave in a moral fashion. Indeed, the primary point of the first version of the Categorical Imperative is to be consistent, not to claim for yourself privileges you would be unwilling to accord to others. Of course, the immoral person is not necessarily unintelligent,

I assume, it is done subconsciously, or thoughtlessly. It is not easy being consistent, when consistency is attended with unpleasant consequences. It is easier not to look, or even think about looking. Obviously one cannot very well subscribe to the notion of a deterministic system and then remove oneself from the matrix. It is a bit as though one were standing to one side and observing the universal process without noticing that one was carried along with it, even to the noticing of it. One of the nice things about the Stoics was that they accepted that everyone, including themselves, was on the same trireme, floating on the same sea. That does not explain, of course, why they tried to convert others to their point of view. One supposes they could not help themselves, as they were fated to the effort, just as the results of the effort were also fated. So, so why bother? Simple, it was fated that one bother.

The consequence for the historiographer who commits himself to the deterministic thesis is that his own work, thinking, writing, and such, is then evacuated of cognitive and moral significance. The fact that he feels it is cognitively and morally significant is not because it is cognitively and morally significant, but because he was determined to feel that it was cognitively and morally significant. We know, of course, it was just the inevitable unfolding of the universal process, of which he is a part, and for which he is not responsible; it was all, in theory, set up, and predictable, billions of years ago. The film, so to speak, was in the can, before the sun was formed, before the Earth cooled, before the first division of the first replicator, or protocell. He is not to be credited with the

---

logically lame, or even inconsistent. He is merely immoral. He may be quite intelligent, having discovered a way to, say, commit a crime with impunity, which doubtless requires some smarts; he is not logically lame because he knows very well what he is up to, calculates chances of success weighed against chances of discovery, and such; and he is not inconsistent for two reasons, first, as he exempts himself from the moral community, the consistency requirement does not apply to him; such rules are irrelevant to him, as he is not playing that game; and, secondly, he is not inconsistent because he has excellent inductive evidence that the great majority of his fellow humans will continue to behave morally. The consideration "What if everybody did that," is no rational deterrent when he has an abundance of empirical evidence at his disposal to the end that everybody won't do that. To the charge, "What justification have you for exempting yourself from the rules," he has a simple response, "No justification, and I have." At this point, I suppose one shoots him, or dials 911.

work; which he in truth could not help producing; he is merely the necessary vessel through which it was inevitably revealed, in all its cognitive and moral meaninglessness; he is at best the envelope by means of which the system saw to its delivery, not that the system gave a damn, one way or the other.

The second problematicity to which we shall direct our attention is what we might call the moral problematicity.

It follows from the foregoing that if historiography adopts the D Hypothesis it evacuates not only the work of particular historians of all cognitive and moral significance, and of all historians, but it also evacuates all history and human life of such significance, as well. One will continue to feel these things are significant, of course, and poignantly, but, of course, we now know that the feeling is deceptive, treacherous, a lie, a real feeling surely, but one that is nonveridical. It would be something like the feeling of free will which, if the universe is a deterministic system, may be a real feeling, but it is illusory, in so far as it suggests the existence of genuine options. It certainly seems unfortunate that an inevitability should be preceded by so much inevitable concern, thinking, doubt, and suffering, all of it meaningless. Perhaps one might shake one's fist at the reality and curse it, but that, too, would have been determined. One might lie down and die, I suppose, in passive, craven acquiescence, but that, too, would have been determined.

Just as it would be inconsistent for the historiographer to exempt himself and his work from the D Hypothesis, so, too, it cannot be applied selectively, here and there, as one might choose. The D Hypothesis requires that the world be painted with a single color.

One supposes efforts might be made to preserve a place for morality in the deterministic universe, but such efforts indicate a failure to understand the D hypothesis.

Three such efforts might be briefly noted, what we might call the verbal effort, the things-are-the-same effort, and the indigenous effort.

Analytic philosophers occasionally substitute one problem for another, perhaps because one of the problems seems to them insoluble or unintelligible. This is a bit like proving unicorns exist by producing raccoons, which are called unicorns. A typical example of this sort of thing, supposing the question is the existence of material objects, or the knowable existence of material objects, is to point to tables and chairs, which are called material objects. Behold, they exist! There is one there, and, lo, here is another! The idealist, one suspects, unless resident in an unusual environment, is likely to be well aware that tables and chairs exist. The question has to do with the existence of, or the knowable existence of, transexperiential reality, perhaps a question which should not have been brought up in the first place, but one which is not to be answered by a trip to the furniture store. The notion here seems to be that the answers to philosophical questions are at hand, embedded in one's native language, rather like the diamonds found scattered about in the seeker's backyard, who has for years sought them abroad unsuccessfully. This problem switching occurs also, of course, in moral matters. Does free will exist? Well, one looks in the backyard, and picks up the semantic diamonds which lie profusely about. We talk as if free will existed, so free will exists. We say that someone did such and such of his free will, if he were not at gunpoint, not concerned to rescue his aged grandmother from brigands, not a kleptomaniac, and so on. This sort of free will, as noted earlier, is compatible with the strictest form of determinism. Also, determinism is not a verbal issue, but an issue about the real world, one to which evidence of various sorts is clearly relevant.

A second effort to reconcile morality with the D Hypothesis is similar to the verbal effort, but is considerably less stupid, as it does not pretend that the issue is one dependent on speech habits obtaining in a particular speech community at a particular time. It is more profoundly cultural. It does resemble it, however, in substantially ignoring the real problem by, in effect, denying that it exists. This effort, we might call the "things-are-the-same" effort. The notion here is we find a morality in place, which, statistically, is taken seriously. It is irrelevant whether it is genuine or not. Here we have individuals worrying about their duties, proclaiming their rights, disputing moral issues, dealing with moral problems, worrying about them, trying to resolve them as best they can, frequently attributing merit and demerit, praising and blaming, and so on. This is just what one would expect if morality meant something, so why worry about anything? Things are "just the same" whether in some objective sense morality is genuine or a fraud. This is a bit like saying, if folks believe morality is objective, then it is immaterial, whether it is or not.

I think there is a genuine point involved in the "things-are-the-same" effort, which is that the social effects of a genuine morality and an empty morality would be the same, provided people do not suspect, or do not realize, that the morality is empty.[47]

If morality should turn out to be relative, and subjective, and so on, it seems to me one should think twice before rushing into the streets with this message. One might always hope that in giving Jones a moral *carte blanche*, he will give you one in return, else why would you give him one, but you have perhaps miscalculated. Relativity is sometimes thought to entail tolerance. It does not. Relativity is perfectly compatible with intolerance, tyranny, fanaticism, censorship, restricting and narrowing education, imposing one's views by force, burning dissenters, and so on. Relativity tears down fences and opens gates. Tolerance may not be the only visitor. Accordingly, if morality should be a sham, one

---

47 Nietzsche's parable "The Madman," in *Die Fröhliche Wissenschaft*, recognizes the possibly catastrophic consequences which might afflict society should a similar recognition become general.
The book's title does not translate easily into English. Today, one encounters options such as *The Joyful Wisdom*, and *The Gay Science*. To me 'Wisdom' does not seem a happy translation of '*Wissenschaft*', and 'Joyful' seems to me a bit too jubilant and serious for 'Fröliche', which suggests to me light-heartedness. 'Gay Science' would, in my opinion, be much better, except that the appropriate, original meaning of 'gay' has been lost in English, as the expression is now used to designate a sexual orientation or proclivity, a misfortune as there is in English no synonym for the original meaning. Further, whereas every science is a *Wissenschaft*, not every *Wissenschaft* is a science, and what Nietzsche was up to was not science, or certainly not science as English speakers are accustomed to think of science. As suggested, it does not seem to me that the title translates well into English, but what Nietzsche presumably meant, given the nature of the book, was a sort of intellectual *jeu d'esprit*, a frolicsome exercise, within a *way* of doing things, the result of which would be to introduce a new, light-hearted discipline, a different, unique, and delightful sort of *Wissenschaft*.
As is well-known, what concerns Nietzsche in his "parable" are the possible results of a widespread loss of belief in a divine entity, poetically expressed in terms of realizing that "God is dead." Will chaos ensue, will a new idol be found, perhaps the State? Nietzsche's proposal of a replacement ideal, a comprehensible ideal, one a human being might understand, and in terms of which he might attempt to measure, and improve, his life, would be later widely misunderstood.

should at least think twice before buying TV spots, radio time, newspaper advertisements, and such, proclaiming it. Perhaps it would be a good idea to keep it a closely guarded secret. Perhaps, as the Baron D'Holbach is reputed to have said, "One should never discuss atheism before the servants."

On the other hand, what if it were not a sham.

Would that not be of interest?

Let us suppose that the D hypothesis is true, and society never catches on. Then, as noted, "things will be much the same," whether the D Hypothesis is true or not.

Whereas I think one should grant that things will seem the same, and cameras, and such, will not pick up new or surprising behaviors, and people will continue to feel, act, and think as before, that there is still, objectively, metaphysically, if you like, a great difference between the two possibilities. Morality, as we common think of it, requires the existence of viable options; otherwise, it makes no sense. And, on the D Hypothesis there are, in fact, no viable options.

If the D Hypothesis is true there is no genuine moral heroism, no genuine moral courage, no commendable self-sacrifice, no authentic compassion, no praiseworthy behavior, nor, indeed, any legitimately disapproved behavior, for selfishness, lying, cheating, stealing, murdering, and such, cannot be helped. Nothing can be helped, one way or the other. The hero cannot help being heroic, no more than the washing machine can help running as it does. If the washing machine was conscious it might regard itself as virtuous, but it isn't. It would just be a conscious washing machine. Similarly it is absurd to express moral disapproval of the coward or the criminal, for they cannot help what they are. We will, of course, continue to commend, and disparage, and reward and punish, because we have no choice. That, too, is determined. And we might have to invent the concept of free will and moral responsibility to provide a justification for praising and blaming, for rewarding and punishing, but that, too, would have been determined.

The third effort to reconcile morality with the D Hypothesis is what we might call the indigenous effort.

The verbal effort was superficial; the "things-are-just-the-same" effort really addresses a different issue, one not of the way the world really is, but of the way the world seems to be. That is enough for it. It concerns itself with belief, not truth. As long as people believe in an objective morality, it is immaterial whether one exists or not; as long as people act morally, it is irrelevant whether or not morality is a sham. Pragmatically, there is much to be said for this approach. One would surely prefer for an individual to have a mistaken idea of morality, thinking it authentic when it isn't, and act morally, than have a correct idea about morality, say, thinking it inauthentic when it is inauthentic, and act immorally. On the other hand, as an effort to reconcile the D Hypothesis with morality the "things-are-the-same" approach fails; in fact, it doesn't even bother trying.

The "indigenous effort," on the other hand, takes the view that morality is authentic, that is not a sham; it is very real; and it is part of the unfolding process. It is ingredient in the process. It is indigenous to the system, as much so as hydrogen and stars, as much so as rocks and the weather.

If one accepts the D Hypothesis one accepts everything, with the possible exception of the whole itself, as proceeding in accord with antecedent conditions and law, and, thus, as moral concerns and behavior abound, from conditioning small children to the deliberations of international tribunals, one naturally regards morality as not only compatible with the D Hypothesis, but as being part-and-parcel of its calculable inevitabilities. It is nomologically ingredient. Moral concerns, apprehensions, tribulations, strivings, hopes, and fears, are as real, and as grounded in the system, as electromagnetism and gravitation, as quarks and galaxies, as much so as anything else. If the D Hypothesis is true, this is true. But what is this saying, other than what we already know, that there is behavior we characterize as moral, and that people concern themselves with such behavior, and take it seriously, and it is all part of the system, and believing that options exist and are genuine is also part of the system, and that that belief is determined, as well?

The crucial question here is not whether or not moral language, beliefs, and behavior exist but whether or not such things presuppose authentic options for action, and whether or not such options exist.

Two things are clear.

1. Morality does presuppose authentic options for actions.
2. On the D Hypothesis, such authentic options do not exist.

It follows from these two statements that morality cannot be reconciled with the D Hypothesis.
1. M & D
2. M ⊃ O
3. D ⊃ ~ O
4. M   1, Simplification
5. D   1, Simplification
6. O   4, 2, Modus Ponens
7. ~ O   5, 3, Modus Ponens
8. O & ~ O   6, 7, Conjunction

As a contradiction has been generated, we know that the premise-set is inconsistent. This informs us that the premises cannot be conjointly true. As the second and third premises are both true, even seemingly analytic, the *explicit* contradiction is not to be imputed to them, individually or conjointly, but only to their conjunction with the first premise. The explicit contradiction arises only when the first premise is conjoined with the second and third premise. The problem, thus, centers on the conjunction of M and D, which is an *implicit* contradiction. To be sure, any premise-set containing a contradiction is itself contradictory, just as '(p & ~ p) & (q v ~ q)' is a contradiction, though 'q v ~ q' is not a contradiction, but is analytic, a logical truth. In any event, M and D, as shown, are logically incompatible.

It is thus seen that three strategies for attempting to reconcile morality with the D Hypothesis fail.

In this way it is suggested, forcibly, that if one accepts the D Hypothesis, one must abandon the moral dimension of human existence, at least as it is normally understood, both in one's own case and in that of others. To be sure, one might be determined to find this impossible to do, but that is another question.

This brings us to the third problematicity associated with the D Hypothesis, that of the "colossal misunderstanding."

I suppose that most of us. at least those of us with a calculator at hand, are well aware that 3,418,101 divided by 5,283 equals 647.

Why is that?

Well, presumably that is because 3,418,101 divided by 5,283 does equal 647. On the other hand, in a deterministic universe might not a gas molecule displaced a bit from that other gas molecule, ever so slightly, have arranged things differently?

Is it not amazing the gas molecules would have gotten it right? Of course, the mathematician is the fellow who sets up the system, so it has to come out that way. But why did the mathematician set the system up that way? Might not the gas molecules have set the mathematician up a bit differently? Would it be possible he would then have set up the system differently, perhaps in such a way that the answer would have been different. It does not seem so, but why not? Does 2 and 2 really equal 4, or is it merely that we are determined to see it that way? Might it not equal something else, say, raccoons or orange? Remember we are talking about gas molecules here, entities not noted for their probity, who are supposedly moving the unfolding process in one way or another.

Some determined, unfolding combinations, of course, would be likely to be eliminated by other determined, unfolding combinations, much as one rock rolling down a slope might knock another aside. One of the enormously valuable insights common to several theories of evolution is to notice, so to speak, how the rocks knock one another about. Primitive replicators are presumably eliminated by more efficient primitive protocells, and they are eliminated by more sophisticated protocells, and they, in turn, eventually, by marvelously sophisticated unicellular organisms, many of them predatory, their small bodies rich with millions of complex molecules engaged in billions of interactions with one another. Members of species, and species, compete for resources; continents shift, and climates change; and by far the greatest number of species fail to survive. Many combinations fail to negotiate the environmental lattice. The individual who enjoys feeding on cadaverine alkaloids fails to replicate his genes. The beast who finds their taste bitter, and seeks out fruity esters, survives. As the deterministic system unfolds, wrinkle by wrinkle, selections, and eliminations, take place. Some of its productions do well, as they must, the termite, the shark, the crocodile, and others fare less well, as was inevitable, large reptiles, perhaps unable to adjust after a planetary catastrophe, smaller, less warlike, less intelligent hominids. Some inevitable combinations eliminate other inevitable combinations. The least twitch of the fruit fly's wing, as it crouches, feeding, on the apple peeling, was, in theory, predictable.

None of these things cloud or impede the machine as it rolls on, to its doom, or forever.

So, much is not surprising, and might be expected, even in a deterministic system, the alertness, grace, and speed of the gazelle, the stalking of the lion, the careful approach, the sudden rush and pounce.

But all should be predictable, and all should be expected.

Is 'p' true, or merely the proposition we were determined to call true? It could be true by accident, of course. Is Argument A valid, or merely an argument we were determined to call valid? It could be independently valid, of course. Are we determined, under certain conditions, to have certain thoughts, and to think we are thinking, and feel we are thinking, and to be sure of it, and then assert that such and such a proposition is true? Are we determined, under certain conditions, to have certain thoughts, and to think we are thinking, and feel we are thinking, and to be sure of it, and then claim that such and such an argument is valid? It seems real to us, the thinking, its meaningfulness, but, if the D Hypothesis is true, its reality is only a seeming reality, and it is not meaningful in the sense we might suppose, namely, that it might have been other than it turned out, that we are entitled to take credit for it, and so on. There is, essentially, if the D hypothesis is true, no us. In a sense there is no independent us to be involved, at all. There is only the system, its elements pursuing their predetermined courses, some facets of it conscious here and there, taking themselves seriously.

To borrow a metaphor from film, the motion picture has already been shot. It was in the can, long ago. The movie is now showing, and no one is watching. The characters in the movie, of course, in this movie, have feelings, and aspirations, and loves, and hates, and struggles, and such, but nothing matters, as it is only a movie, and the movie plays on, until the film runs out, or it begins again.

We think that we discern. We think distinguish between good judgment and bad judgment. We encourage people to behave in one way or another. We even reward them when they behave in one way and punish them when they behave in another way. We think we reason things out, and calculate. We engage in serious discussions, and have arguments. We work out theories, we try to explain things. It seems to us that we understand, and we treasure a moment of insight. We try to persuade others to one end or another, and they us. We seem to weigh alternatives and judge amongst options. We think we evaluate proposals. Do we not think we appraise and assess? Do we not prize some individuals for their wisdom, their sagacity, their acumen, and intelligence, and others for their beauty, their strength, their fleetness of foot, their thoughtfulness and compassion, as if any of these things could have been otherwise!

We think things matter, but they do not really matter. Nothing matters.

To be sure, we feel they matter. And the poignancy, the agony, is real enough. There is no mistaking that. Perhaps that is the cruelest twist of the knife, that we are determined to take it seriously, to feel that it matters, so much, and is not that the punch line in a ghastly joke, determined from all eternity?

If the D Hypothesis is true, our views of ourselves, and of others, lovers and friends, enemies and strangers, and of the world, and of everything, is evacuated of all human significance.

The puppets, so to speak, do not know they are puppets. They feel, hope, love, hate, suffer and die, and such, as though such things made a difference. But they make no difference.

The process meaninglessly, blindly, unfolds.

It should be noted, in passing, that indeterminism is no better. There is no meaning, no significance, there either. Thus the third trijunct in the causal trilemma restores nothing, and saves nothing. Freedom in a meaningful sense, involving responsibility and meaningfully sought options, exists on neither the D Hypothesis nor the I Hypothesis. It is achievable neither within a deterministic matrix nor in one of congregated probabilities.

Also, it should be noted, in passing, as it may be of interest, that determinism does nor require a presupposed physicalistic matrix. It could be quite as much at home in an Idealism, perhaps of a Hegelian sort, or within a religious matrix, perhaps involving predestination, prevision, or fatalism. In each of these modalities, everything is evacuated of human significance, and in all, too, the victim is condemned to believe that the world of his dreams, of his cherished illusions, is the one in which he actually lives.

But he is mistaken.

It is all a colossal mistake.

We have been examining the Causal Trilemma. I think we have made it quite clear that the M Hypothesis, that of Agency, is obscure at best and, at worst, perhaps unintelligible. Further, we have suggested that the most likely hypothesis here, certainly from the historiographical point of view, is the D Hypothesis, but that the D Hypothesis involves a number of presumably unwelcome consequences, what we spoke of as the illegitimacy problematicity, the moral problematicity, and that of the colossal misunderstanding.

To be sure, one must be aware of the dangers of the *argumentum ad consequentiam*, the argument from the consequences of a belief to its truth value, one way or the other. Unless one is a pragmatist of some sort, one is likely to distinguish between true beliefs and good beliefs. The truth of the belief and the goodness of a belief are usually discriminable, even when, say, the same belief is both true and good. One supposes that most true beliefs are good in the way of belief, and that most false beliefs are bad in the way of belief. On the other hand, that leaves the possibility that there may be true beliefs which are bad in the way of belief, and false beliefs which are good in the way of belief. The *argumentum ad consequentiam*, as an informal or material fallacy, as opposed to a formal fallacy, or fallacy of form, argues mistakenly from the value of a belief, its goodness or lack of goodness in the way of belief, to its truth value.

Consider the four possibilities.

1. Belief B is good in the way of belief so Belief B is true.
2. Belief B is good in the way of belief so Belief B is false.
3. Belief B is not good in the way of belief so Belief B is true.
4. Belief B is not good in the way of belief so Belief B is false.

These are the four ways in which the fallacy might be committed. It will be noted that possibilities one and four are the most likely occasions for the commission of the fallacy. With respect to possibility two, one might think that some offer or such was too good to be true, and with respect to possibility three one might suppose, pessimistically, that truth is often unpleasant.

For each of these possibilities we have a correspondent argument.[48]

> Argument 1:
> Belief B is good in the way of belief.
> Belief B is true.
>
> Argument 2:
> Belief B is good in the way of belief.
> Belief B is false.
>
> Argument 3:
> Belief B is not good in the way of belief.
> Belief B is true.
>
> Argument 4:
> Belief B is not good in the way of belief.
> Belief B is false.

One contrasts goodness with the lack of goodness in order to obtain a logistic dichotomy. The lack of goodness, then, need not be understood as badness, but, rather, as being either bad or neither good nor bad, namely, neutral. An analogy might be that the complementary property of kindness is not unkindness, but unkindness or the property of being neither kind nor unkind. Trees and rocks for example, are neither kind nor unkind. The complementary properties would be kind and nonkind, nonkind being understood as unkind or neither kind nor unkind, namely, neutral. One supposes that most true beliefs would be good in the way of belief, and that most false beliefs would not be good in the way of belief, though many true and false beliefs would seem

---

48 Strictly, as presented, these are not arguments, but argument forms, as 'Belief B' has no specific meaning assignment, and thus functions as a variable, not a constant. On the other hand, informally, one often thinks of such things as arguments. For example, *argumentum ad consequentiam*, is often thought of as an argument, though, technically, it is a form of argument. The distinction between an argument and an argument form is obviously of great importance, but, in many contexts, as here, at least in my view, it seems convenient and harmless to refer to both arguments and argument forms as arguments.

rather neutral with respect, at least, to goodness and badness. For example, the 64th word on page 486 in Felix Meiner's Edition of Kant's *Kritik der reinen Vernunft* is '*etwas*', which, I suppose, is something to think about, but, on the other hand, that would seem to be a belief unlikely to stir passion one way or the other. I suppose it is good in the way of belief if it supplies a point, or something, but, on the whole, it seems to be a pretty neutral belief. Probably it would not make much difference in global utility calculations if it were actually the 65th word, or even the 66th or 67th word.

In any event, arguments of the first and fourth sort seem to be those of greatest interest when considering matters of *argumentum ad consequentiam*, and, in particular, when goodness and badness are at large, as opposed to goodness and the mere lack of goodness. Obviously, too, there are degrees of these things, for example, degrees of goodness and badness, and, also, the supposed goodness or nongoodness of the consequences of a belief might vary from one observer to another, from one interested party to another, and so on.

There are two issues here which, at least initially, seem to be clearly separate, namely, the truth value of a belief and the consequences of that belief, whether for an individual, a group, a society, a civilization, or even, perhaps, humanity, as a whole.

It is a question, of course, as to whether or not these issues are really separate.

Interestingly, this depends on how one understands truth.

If one defines truth as, say, that which is good in the way of belief, whether locally in given instances, for this fellow or that fellow, or, say, for most people, or for all people, perhaps on the whole, and in the long run, or such, then, obviously, the issues are not separate at all, but one is talking about the same thing. One could certainly go about things along these lines, but it would represent a considerable shifting of perspective and practice, and, one suspects, might not itself prove good in the way of belief. One difference which would follow the adoption of this epistemic revision would be that truth would be subjectivized and relativized, whether individually or specieswise.

It would be subjectivized in being indexed to individuals, or such, and relativized as being indexed to diverse interests.

The departure from traditional views would be considerable. For example, in familiar logic and typical epistemology legitimate substitution instances of 'p' and '~ p' could not both be true, and one must be true. According to the usual truth table for negation 'p' is true if and only if '~ p' is false. Their substitution instances must be related as statement and negation.

It is not the case, of course, under the proposed revision, that 'p' and '~ p' cannot both be true, or cannot both be false. It is rather the case, say, that 'p' might be good in the way of belief for x and '~ p' might be good in the way of belief for y. In this case there is obviously no contradiction, only a difference in goods, or perceived goods. Logic, of course, is not lost because contradiction is possible in the following fashion:

α: 'p' is good in the way of belief for x.

~ α: It is not the case that 'p' is good in the way of belief for x.[49]

A problem for the revised notion, as might be noted, is twofold, first, that contradiction presupposes truth in the supposedly superseded sense, and thus that truth, in the familiar sense, pops up, however embarrassingly, and, secondly, that we cannot start trying to evade this *contretemps* by defining *this* truth in terms of "good in the way of belief" without beginning to generate a hopeless regress.

Is it true that 'p' is good in the way of belief?

It is good in the way of belief that 'p' is good in the way of belief.

Is it true that it good in the way of belief that 'p' is good in the way of belief?

It is good in the way of belief that it is good in the way of belief that 'p' is good in the way of belief.

Is it true that it is good in the way of belief that it is good in the way of belief that 'p' is good in the way of belief?

And so on, *ad infinitum*.[50]

---

49 The negation of '', or '~ α', would assert that either statement or proposition 'p' does not exist, or that person x does not exist, or that it is not the case that 'p' is good in the way of belief for x.

50 It is important not to confuse this disagreeable regress with an innocuous logistic regress, such as:
'p' is true.
It is true that 'p' is true. 'T ('p' is true.)'

THE PHILOSOPHY OF HISTORIOGRAPHY 221

If the familiar notion of truth is presupposed even in the attempt to repudiate it, it seems there is not much to be gained by attempting to repudiate it.

Similarly, the old relationships between, say, propositions and the world would still exist, and would be important. For example, water is essential for organic life as we know it whether that should be good or bad in the way of belief. One might use a different word for this sort of thing, one supposes, but there doesn't seem much justification for doing so. One could, one supposes, use the expression 'truth' ambivalently, in the old sense, and also in the new sense, but, even if this produced no confusion, there doesn't seem much point in doing it. None of this denies, of course, that some beliefs may be good in the way of belief and others not, nor that this fact may not be of momentous personal and social importance. What it does maintain is that these are different properties, and thinking will presumably be best served by keeping them separate in thought, as they are in fact.[51]

Indeed, interestingly, it seems that believing that truth is identical with goodness of belief might not be itself good in the way of belief.

This leaves open the question as to whether or not there might not be areas of human interest in which this pragmatic approach

It is true that it is true that 'p' is true, etc. 'T [T ('p' is true.)]', etc.
This is nothing more that an application of the tautology rule, for example, that 'p' logically implies 'p v p' and 'p & p', and 'p v (p v p)' and 'p & (p & p)', and so on. Epistemically, as opposed to logically, 'p''s truth is a function of some fact, or some way the world is. For example, what makes 'snow is white' true is the fact that snow is white. The proposition, via an intermediary, a mind, confronts or appeals to a nonpropositional reality. In something like 'It is true that 'p' is good in the way of belief' that proposition, if true, is true not in the sense of being good in the way of belief, but true in the in the sense of agreeing with a nonpropositional reality, namely, it would be true in the old, familiar sense of truth. Thus, the familiar sense of truth is presupposed, and reappears.

51 If we identified the notions the two interesting versions of *argumentum ad consequentiam*, namely, Argument 1 and Argument 4, would cease to be fallacies, and every instance of Argument 1 and Argument 2 would be trivially valid, for the same reason that an argument with the premise-set
'p ⊃ q' and the conclusion '~ q ⊃ ~ p' would be a valid argument. The conclusion would be logically equivalent to the premise-set.

might not seem more appropriate, for example, in connection with notions of moral or aesthetic truth. For example, the belief that one should treat other human beings as ends in themselves, and never as a means only, as Kant suggests, is quite different from the belief that the board is four feet in length or the sack of sand weighs four pounds. If one believes it is true that one should treat others as ends, and never as a means only, then that putative truth might be understood along the lines of something which is good in the way of belief, perhaps *simpliciter*, perhaps as a means for contributing to a more civil society, or such. Similarly, if one believes it is true that art should exist for beauty's sake, or for passion's sake, or such, then that putative truth might be understood along the lines of something which is good in the way of belief, perhaps *simpliciter*, or perhaps as a means for increasing beauty, improving civilization, deepening and vitalizing human life, or such.

Most of the obvious problems with this pragmatic approach to truth, one of several possible pragmatic approaches to truth, would seem to have to do with differences amongst individuals, or the same individual at different times. For example, it is true for Jones that the Earth is flat, and false for Smith that the Earth is flat, or it is true for Jones at time t_1 that the Earth is flat, and false for Jones at time t_2 that the Earth is flat, and so on. On the other hand, the same sorts of points are pertinent to groups, societies, civilizations, and so on. It may be less obvious but similar difficulties would afflict even a notion such as a belief which might prove good in the way of belief in the long run for the entirety of humanity. It seems unlikely that there would be a plethora of such beliefs, but let us suppose that there were. The distinction between truth and goodness of belief, at least in most matters, would still obtain.[52]

[52] Charles Sanders Peirce, surely on the short list of the greatest of American philosophers, had an interesting and sophisticated notion of truth which is pertinent here, namely, a view of truth understood in terms of opinion: "The opinion which is fated to be ultimately agreed to by all who investigate, is what we mean by the truth, and the object represented in this opinion is the real. ... the reality of that which is real does depend on the real fact that investigation is destined to lead, at last, if continued long enough, to a belief in it." ("How to make Our Ideas Clear," *Philosophical Writings of Peirce: Selected and Edited with an Introduction by Justus Buchler*, pp. 38, 39. (Dover Publications, Inc., New York, 1955. (The first version of this paper was published in 1878, in *Popular Science Monthly*.))

The major difficulty here is that opinion is not true if it is not a true opinion, namely, one which agrees with facts, or the world. That an opinion should be destined to be accepted, or such, is not a truth-making property, as truth is normally understood. Peirce did want, one supposes, within a pragmatic context, to provide for the singleness of truth and its objectivity, two properties with which truth is commonly associated. One suspects, too, that Peirce was drawn in this direction because of a desire to assure the accessibility of truth, not that this particular characterization is much help in that regard, namely, to eschew unknowable truths, unverifiable truths, truths forever beyond the reach of investigation and experience. To domesticate truth one must bring it indoors, namely, understand it in terms of something familiar and intelligible, in this case, opinion, preferably an opinion arrived at in an appropriate manner. Truth was not to be a relation between a hypothesized, unknowable "outside" and a verbalizing "inside." In such a situation, as envisaged, the besought agreement could never be established or ascertained.

Prima facie, at least, this approach to truth would be extremely uncongenial to historiography. Aside from the fact that one has no assurance as to what the fated opinion is likely to be, the historiographer is unlikely to be willing to define truth in terms of opinion. He will have opinions as to what is true and what is false but he does not take it that truth or falsity, at least in most cases, depends on his opinions. These things are logically independent. Something like 'Microorganisms currently exist in the subsoil of Mars' is now true or false, and its truth or falsity depends on the existence or nonexistence of microorganisms in the subsoil of Mars, not on opinions about it. Indeed, the very notion of an opinion carries with it that it should be an opinion about something which is other than itself, that, say, 'p' is true or false.

Truth requires intelligibility, but it does not require ascertainability.

The notion of an unknowable truth is ambiguous. If it means a truth which will never in fact be known, such truths abound; if it means a truth which is somehow unknowable in principle, to anyone in any way, that one would have no idea as to how to confirm or disconfirm it, would have no idea under what conditions it might be true or false, and so on, then it is unintelligible. We would not know what we are talking about, not because the matter is difficult or obscure, but because we are not talking about anything. The assertion that erudite purple unicorns exist is either true or false; the assertion that erudite purple glorps exist is neither true nor false; it is gibberish. There are many subtle issues here, having to do with expertise, background information, techniques, theories, and such. Many locutions in philosophy, for example, have degrees of meaningfulness, and few are totally destitute of meaningfulness. A classical supposed example of a nonsensical locution was 'The Absolute is lazy'. If this is regionalized to, say, Hegelian dialectic, it would count as false, as whatever the Absolute is supposed to be the activities attributed to it do not suggest laziness; if it were understood literally, presumably it would be false due to reference failure, and so on. To be sure, it would not be out of the ques-

Returning to the *argumentum ad consequentiam*, whereas one would wish to maintain the fallacious nature of such argumentation, which we tried to make clear, it is important to recognize the serious motivation of such argumentation, a motivation which should certainly be understood and one with which one, in certain cases, might sympathize, even whilst forbearing approval.

It is dangerous to seek the truth.

It might be found.

It is generally accepted that children should be sheltered from certain experiences, and understandings, that their lives and activities should be judiciously regulated, that the information at their disposal should be subject to parental or social filtering, and so on.

If this principle is acceptable in the case of children, justified in virtue of familial and, later, societal considerations, it seems a case might be made out for something similar in the case of, say, simpler adults, adults less capable of understanding and dealing with certain forms of information, less likely to cope successfully with certain sorts of social situations, and such. Is it not a question of degree? Are not some children wise and astute, and capable of dealing rationally with a diversity of truths and situations, and are not some adults naive and childish, seemingly incapable of dealing rationally with certain truths and situations?

Consider the following argument:

Teaching the truth causes unnecessary pain.
<u>Causing unnecessary pain is wrong.</u>
Teaching the truth is wrong.
Recall Argument 1 and Argument 4.

---

tion to dismiss it as gibberish either. But the point is that things are seldom simple.

All we need at this point is that if we understand the truth conditions of a locution we understand what would be required for it to be true, or false. Thus, it would be true or false. Whether or not we know which is a completely different matter. Being true or false is one thing; being known to be true or false is another. Much of the past may be unknowable, but this lack of knowability does not deprive the historiographer's work of significance, nor of being right or wrong.

Argument 1:
Belief B is good in the way of belief.
Belief B is true.

Argument 4:
Belief B is not good in the way of belief.
Belief B is false.

What if those arguments were revised, along the following lines?

Argument 1':
Belief B is good in the way of belief.
Belief B should be promulgated in society.

Argument 4':
Belief B is not good in the way of belief.
Belief B should be suppressed in society.

Both arguments are still invalid, of course. On the other hand, validity is cheap, and one might add the contextually presupposed premise behind such argumentation, producing:

Argument 1":
Belief B is good in the way of belief.
If Belief B is good in the way of belief,
  then Belief B should be promulgated in society.
Belief B should be promulgated in society.

Argument 4":
Belief B is not good in the way of belief.
If Belief B is not good in the way of belief,
  then Belief B should be suppressed in society.
Belief B should be suppressed in society.

Given validity, the problem now shifts to that of the truth of the premise-set, and, for our purposes, the acceptability, in particular, of the second premise.

Putting aside questions of censorship, suppression, intimidation, indoctrination, and such, which might be utilized by fanatics, dictators, demagogues, tyrants, and such, in order to preserve and enhance their prestige and power, I think we have an issue here on which even benevolently disposed men of good will might disagree.

Even Kant, who is commonly taken as a paradigm case of a rigid moralist, and believed that only the truth should be told, amazingly, regardless of the consequences, did allow, happily, that not all truths need be told.

For example, if the pope should pronounce *ex cathedra* that God does not exist, few in the papal chancery would feel obligated to bring this to public attention. Perhaps the pope was not himself that day, thus vitiating the pronouncement, and how, too, would the pope know such a thing?

Here we must distinguish between two possibilities, possibility one, that it is not possible to conceal the truth, and possibility two, that it is possible to conceal the truth. One supposes that many people would be upset to learn, or come to believe, that their world is not flat, that it is in motion, that it is not at the center of the universe, that their ancestry includes unicellular organisms, fish, amphibians, apes, and such, that their motivations may be muchly undiscerned, and occasionally of a sort which, if discerned, they might be reluctant to acknowledge, and so on. Truth can be demoting. One's self-image is not likely to be enhanced if one comes to think of oneself as a small, somewhat nasty primate descended from a diversity of undistinguished forebears on an unimportant world somewhere in the periphery of an everyday, run-of-the-mill galaxy. On the other hand, it seems impossible, in the long run, to hide such truths, or, perhaps better, conceal such hypotheses, and the evidence pertinent to their evaluation. In such cases someone is sure to "spill the beans," and the word will get out. Also, there are always those fellows who are so set up psychologically that they are going to seek the truth at any cost. Everyone pretends to be like that, and some folks genuinely are like that. Accordingly, given possibility one, that it is not possible to conceal the truth, or what seems to be the truth, it is obviously the best societal strategy to adjust to the truth, or what seems to be the truth, as successfully and graciously as possible. Distinctions can always be drawn, one can always reinterpret texts, and so on, saving as many of the benevolent beliefs as possible. Indeed, many such beliefs, by their very obscurity or scientific vacuity are immune to empirical falsification under any circumstances. How could one prove that a cunning *Geist* was not utilizing the passions of unwitting humans to bring about its own ends, especially when it is not clear what those ends might be?

The more genuine moral problem arises in connection with the second possibility, namely, that it is possible to conceal unpleasant truths, unwelcome truths, dangerous truths, or that it is possible, say, to promulgate false beliefs which would have beneficial social consequences.

Should that be done?

Remember protecting children, and, possibly, simple, naive adults.

"Let the sheep graze in peace."

Here I think one encounters a moral watershed.

Should, say, comforting, if preposterous, doctrines be promulgated?

Should beliefs with deleterious consequences be suppressed?

Or, should truth, or seeming truth, be sought and, if not broadcast, be at least publicly accessible?

My own view, and, I suspect, that of the great majority of those who might be reading this book, would be to choose truth, which is sometimes disappointing and cruel, over falsehood, which is often flattering and comforting. On the other hand, this is only one option. The kindly, informed, self-tortured shepherd who keeps the truth to himself, who sacrifices himself for the happiness of his flock, is not a despicable example of our species, though perhaps one more to be pitied than emulated.

Context, the individuals involved, and the social situation, and such, are doubtless all relevant here.

In general, however, more abstractly, one supposes a vision of the human being would be crucial. What sort of human being would one choose to be? One is not asking which sort of human being is best, only what one would choose. If the choice were between being, say, informed and disappointed, and uninformed and pleased, supposing no deleterious consequences attended the lack of information, such as not knowing about poison in the drinking water, what would one choose?

As far as I can tell, the vast majority of the human race would, and does, choose being uninformed and pleased. This global conjecture is based on psychological comfort-seeking, discomfort-avoidance, and such. It is a conjecture based on how human beings act, statistically, and do not act, statistically. They are, so to speak, given a sealed box and told that it contains a gold coin. The thought that they may possess a gold coin makes them happy. They would rather not open the box. The gold coin might not be there.

Some individuals, a tiny minority, statistically, will, to the best of their ability, look in the box.

Perhaps the gold coin is invisible, and intangible, it can't be seen, and it can't be felt, but perhaps, somehow, it is there, after all.

But there does not seem to be a gold coin.

The box is empty.

The tiny minority wants to know if the box is empty, or, at least, if it seems to be empty. That is important to them. They are lured by the siren of truth; they succumb to the temptation to seek her. They would rather know than not know.

That is the sort of human being they are.

Indeed, is not the self-tortured shepherd, nursing his secret knowledge, such a human being, at least in his own case?

We may suppose he does not sufficiently respect his flock.

But he may know his flock better than we do.

In this fashion we find ourselves returned to the D Hypothesis.

Now, if the D Hypothesis is true, then all effort and life is essentially meaningless, being nothing more than the inevitable unfolding of an enormous, time-consuming, pointless process. It does not seem meaningless, of course, but that, too, is more meaninglessness, an aspect of the process. It is not even an irony, as irony presupposes intent. It is a bit as if mechanical dolls were designed, wound up, and set in motion, bumping into one another, falling off tables, and such, except that the dolls take themselves seriously, suffer, and such. The suffering may not be meaningful, but it is real. The dolls hurt.

We have suggested that the historiographer is well advised, for several reasons, which need not be reiterated here, to accept the D Hypothesis for the purposes of his work.

He should be, so to speak, a methodological determinist.

On the other hand, if the D Hypothesis is true, all the labor, devotion, and learning which he puts into his work, and all the avidity, care, and sympathy with which it might be considered, are meaningless, as well.

Neither he nor those to whom he addresses his work may legitimately exempt themselves from the inescapable compass, or grasp, of the D Hypothesis.

And similar remarks go, of course, for this work, and for any attentions to which it might be subjected, or with which it might be honored.

But is it not interesting that we should have been determined to look into these issues?

What if the D Hypothesis is false?

Perhaps we are determined to consider that possibility.

Reasonably clearly, neither the M Hypothesis nor the I Hypothesis will well serve the purposes of the historiographer. The first is obscure, and the second fails to explain particular events, and, it seems, doesn't even explain groups of events, though it might describe or record statistical behaviors.

We arrive then at the presupposition of the D Hypothesis, accepting it as a desiderated modality in virtue of which intelligibility may characterize historiographical explanation.

But in virtue of certain hitherto-noted unpleasant problematicities associated with the D Hypothesis, one is entitled to ask oneself if one is forced to accept the D Hypothesis as more than a regulatory principle, more than a heuristic convenience, more than a working postulate.

It seems paradoxical, but it is not impossible that the following two propositions might both be true.

1. The D Hypothesis is false.
2. The historiographer should presuppose that the D Hypothesis is true.

In short, the historiographer should adopt the D Hypothesis as a working hypothesis, but need not accept it as a metaphysical certitude. In short, the historiographer should be a methodological determinist, but need not be a metaphysical determinist.

There is nothing unusual, deceitful, or dishonest about this sort of thing. For example, it is wise to act on the assumption that all tigers are dangerous, but that is probably not true. The metaphysical determinist usually acts as though determinism were not true, trying to persuade people, encouraging them to do one thing rather than another, and so on. And the metaphysical indeterminist commonly acts as though metaphysical determinism were true, recklessly counting on the sun to come up, hot water to emerge from the hot water faucet, and so on.

On the other hand, in order that this distinction be embraced without uneasiness, it might be helpful to note that the D Hypothesis may, in fact, be false.

The following four considerations do not refute the D Hypothesis, but they do suggest, one, that it is not obviously true, and, two, that whatever its explanatory or epistemic utility might be, it is pragmatically absurd.

1. The primary data of consciousness certainly favor the hypothesis of meaningful choice and, in that sense, of free will. We have the sense that we may choose as we will. Shall I pick up the pencil or not, should I move it an inch to the right, or leave it where it is, and so on. We have the clear sense that we can do whatever we want, that we can initiate an action or not, that we are deciding, and so on. If the determinist is correct this sense of things is illusory, and free will does not exist. On the other hand, this sort of thing is exactly what we would expect to be the case *if* free will did exist. Is this not evidence of a sort? Why should it be discounted? If this sort of thing does not count as evidence of free will, what would? In any event, the primary data of consciousness suggest free will, and this suggestion should be neither arbitrarily ignored nor routinely overlooked, simply because it appears incompatible with a particular theory.

2. If the Indeterminist is right, and that seems to be where physics resides today, though who knows where it will be tomorrow, then we have a discontinuous universe. Whereas we cannot identify indeterminism with free will, as free will requires responsibility and indeterminism does not, there being an obvious difference between a responsible decision and something just happening, if indeterminism should be true, then the D Hypothesis is false. If the D Hypothesis is false, then the "block universe" does not exist. If the "block universe" does not exist, then free will might exist. Indeed, if there is one chink in the "block universe," perhaps there

are several, and one of these exceptions to that universe might be something or other which, if we understood it well enough, we might be willing to call free will. Too, if things just happen in the indeterministic universe, perhaps something or other might have come about, however randomly, which, again, if we understood it well enough, we might be willing call free will.

3. It seems to us that argument, judgment, appraisal, and such, are significant. We inquire, we study, we strive to learn; we discuss; we argue; we assess; we try to convince one another of this and that; we suppose ourselves to be listening to reason; we hope we are open-minded; we believe ourselves ready to be convinced if we are mistaken; we think we may choose amongst genuine options; we consider evidence, assessing its relevance; we propose evidence, supposing it is relevant to a conclusion, and so on. We examine propositions, attempting to determine their truth value; we construct arguments; we evaluate deductive arguments for validity; we evaluate inductive arguments for the putative relevance of premises to conclusions, and so on. We strive; we hope; we believe; we live to achieve this, and avoid that; we act.

If the D Hypothesis is true, as noted earlier, all this is meaningless, as usually understood; it is, in fact, a sort of illusion, at least insofar as we think our efforts might have made any difference to an outcome. In this universe, we do not act; we are carried along. Even the universe itself does not act, for an act requires intention, either implicit or explicit. The rock rolling down the hill does not act; it just rolls down the hill. If it were conscious, it might suppose it was acting, but it is not acting; it is just rolling down a hill, thinking it is acting.

On the D Hypothesis none of this, which seems so poignantly important, which seems so momentous and meaningful, is what it seems to be.

On the other hand, do we have any sufficient reason, really, for supposing that things are not precisely what they seem to be?

If these things are what they seem to be, if they are significant, if, say, argument, judgment, appraisal, and such, are significant, if they do make a difference, then the D Hypothesis is false.

They seem significant.

So perhaps the D Hypothesis is false.

4. We may now direct our attention to what we might call life-purposes. Such things are irrelevant, of course, to the truth or falsity of the D Hypothesis. The world is a deterministic system or it is not. Nothing we can do has any effect on that issue.

That has to do with the way the world is, not how we think the world is, nor how we would like the world to be.

Let us suppose that the D Hypothesis is true.

So what?

What does one do?

Let us suppose the I Hypothesis is true.

So what?

What does one then do?

The point here is that neither of these hypotheses provides any guide for action. Suppose the D Hypothesis is true. What do I then do? Do I wait around to see what the universal process is going to do with me, do I just lie down and die, or what? Similarly, let us suppose the I Hypothesis is true. What do I then do? Do I just wait around to see if something happens, or what? Neither of these hypotheses is of the least bit of help in getting on with doing, and living. Neither tells me what to do, or how to live.

I have to do the doing; or it seems so; I have to do the living, or it seems so.

Neither decides for me.

Shall I have A or B for supper?

The universe may have ordered A served up for me from billions of years ago, but I don't know that. Perhaps it has ordered up B, or even C. Similarly, it may just happen that B will show up for supper, or at least a summation over probabilities suggests that, but D is possible, or anything else, like a rhinoceros, belt buckle, or motorcycle.

Uninformed as to the precise nature of the springs and gears of the universe, and deprived of the intuitive capacity to anticipate the random and causeless, the unanticipatable, I decide to have A for supper.

This may have been set up from all eternity, or it may have happened for no reason, even that I prefer A, but I do not know these things.

The upshot is that I must act as though I had free will, as

though the choice were mine, and not that of a universe, either deterministic or indeterministic.

Both determinism and indeterminism are useless for life-purposes. Regardless of the nature of the universe I must act, or seem to act, as though I had free will.

There is no practical alternative.

The human being may be either a determinist or an indeterminist, either a fatalist or a predestinarian, or anything else. But in life and living we are all, and must be, working voluntarists, libertarians, free-willists, or whatever. We must choose so, and act so, or succumb to paralysis and immobility. The adoption of an epistemic stance favoring natural liberty, the adoption of freedom as a working hypothesis, is not an arbitrary commitment. It is the only alternative one has to paralysis, immobility, and death.

We may think as we will, thought is cheap, but we must act as though we were free.

Thus, both the D Hypothesis and the I Hypothesis, whether true or false, are, from the point of view of life-purposes, useless, crippling, and absurd.

IV. Progress, Plan, and Pattern

A small bird, unexpectedly, inadvertently, coming in from the winter, and the night, enters the feasting hall through one smoke hole and, moments later, exits through another, on the opposite wall, near the roof. The flight is brief, and bewildering. The small bird understands nothing. It is startled by the noise, the blazing fire in the long fire pit, the singing, the shouting, the laughing of the warriors. It flutters about, perhaps frightened. Certainly it understands nothing. Then, its brief, peculiar, disconcerting, unintelligible flight ended, it has returned to the winter, and the darkness.

This is a Viking story, in which we have a metaphor for human life.

We have seen, earlier, that the human being is a pattern-seeking animal. Certainly pattern seeking has been selected for in the cruel games of evolution. It is no mere happenstance that inducing animals survive. They see in the past the explanation of the present, and see in the present the auspices of the future, and shape their activities and ends accordingly. Too, it is speculated that the primitive mind, which we continue to bear within us, understands change in the light of action. If something is done there must be a doer. Just as he shapes stone so might a force or god shatter mountains and open the earth. As he casts a spear so, too, might unseen beings cast lightning. As he senses himself within a body so, too, must there not be other selves in other bodies, where movement and life is found, in the rushing brook, in the restless, lovely, shimmering of the laurel? It took a long time, we suppose, for the universe to be dehumanized, deprived of point and meaning.

Few victories are achieved without loss.

We become strangers in our own land.

Following Wordsworth, one might wonder if the world might not be too much with us, and whether or not, getting and spending, we might be laying waste our powers. Certainly one would agree that we see "little in nature that is ours." Perhaps, with him, one might hope to have "glimpses that would make one less forlorn":

"Have sight of Proteus rising from the sea;

Or hear old Triton blow his wreathèd horn."

With apologies to Wordsworth, it seems possible that, genetically speaking, we might all be, as he regretted he wasn't, "suckled in a creed outworn."

Not only would we like to love a world, in a way a machine cannot be loved, but one would like to think it all makes sense, or has some purpose.

It may not.

But what if it did?

That is not impossible, is it?

Unlikely, perhaps, but not impossible, one supposes.

Even today, it is not unusual to hear educated adults ask for the meaning of one thing or another, for them to try to make sense out of happenings, sparings, coincidences, unexpected occurrences, afflictions, and such, in terms of intention.

This is an inveterate human habit, one hard to break.

If anything has meaning, the universe, or such, it seems that history might, that odyssey of an entire rational species, that it might, if anything, have some import, perhaps even a bit of local, if not cosmic, significance, that it might, here and there, have some meaning, and perhaps even—meaning as a whole.

Certainly this has been, historically, a frequently encountered conjecture.

One need not think of plans, and such, of course. Much which is unplanned might be quite meaningful, might exemplify patterns of great moment to the human being. For example, one frequently encounters the outcomes of systemic processes, the emergence of complex adaptive systems, the formation of remarkable spontaneous orders, and such. Sometimes this sort of thing is characterized as evolutionary rationalism.

The ancient division, construed as a dichotomy, between that which is natural and that which is artificial, or a matter of convention, is not exhaustive. The division is incomplete. As has been frequently pointed out, particularly by economists, and as we have noted, many things are "the product of human action, but not of human design." Much of what is most important to human life and welfare eludes the plausible but misleading division between the natural and the artificial, or conventional. Typically, the practicality and efficiency of a self-adjusting, spontaneously emerging market, daily coordinating millions of interactions and exchanges, is cited. Other examples might be the development of natural languages and legal systems. Some small, shaggy genius, hundreds of thousands of years ago, may have first conceived the possible relationship between a noise and a meaning, and invented the first word, but vast, natural languages, like a functioning market, are the product of no single human being, or organized committee, or particular congregation of human beings. Like a functioning market they develop over generations, becoming ever more complex and proficient instruments of communication and expression. Another often-proposed example of the product of human action but not of human design is the growth, over centuries, and millions of cases, of the law. A great many things exemplify this sort of development, traditions, cultures, and, doubtless, moralities. Presumably a practice, an institution, which has evolved naturally has succeeded in evolving precisely because, like an ecology, or a balance of nature, it has managed to produce and sustain systems of almost incomprehensible diversity and complexity. Such systems have withstood, adapting and changing, here and there, as was necessary, the test of time. Such systems, like nature, are not to be lightly disregarded.

The search for pattern in history is not a task to be eschewed, or belittled.

History is laden with patterns, and, indeed, if there were no patterns, it would be unintelligible.

As with many other aspects of the philosophy of historiography, an attempt to deal with the notions of progress, plans, patterns, and such, might be considered either metaphysical or epistemological. We deal with it here under the category of metaphysics, primarily because it deals more with post-conceptualization fact than with the antecedent normativities of conceptualization.

In what follows, we have no intention of trying to argue for either the existence or nonexistence of some form of progress, or of any specific plan, or of any particular pattern in history. Our concerns here are essentially philosophical, inasmuch as we are not so much trying to answer such questions, as trying to understand them, and how one might go about seeking their answers. Our efforts then are neither dogmatic nor partisan, but, rather, ancillary or propaedeutic.

In order to achieve an entry into these issues, which are complex, we will begin with what appears to be a simple, familiar, and plausible candidate for a possible pattern, that of progress. In the discussion, a number of issues may be touched on which, by their very nature, have a more general relevance to our topic.

1. Progress

1. Means/Ends Sufficiencies

In many common understandings of 'progress' it is generally accepted, and, for the most part, quite justifiably, that progress abounds, for example, that, given certain ends, the means for achieving them have become more proficient.

One gathers that Hannibal at the battle of Zama, in 202 B.C., for example, had at his disposal eighty elephants. Pretty obviously he would have done better with one machine gun.

If one wants to get through gates, dynamite is more effective, or, at least, quicker, than battering rams.

It is easier to kill more people in less time with thermonuclear weapons than with bows and arrows, and so on.

Obviously, if one values health and length of life, modern medicine is superior to that of Periclean Athens; if one is wishes to go from point A to point B as quickly and comfortably as possible, depending on the A's and B's, jet airplanes are likely to win over oared galleys and four-horse chariots. If one wishes to communicate with Aunt Susan, and really wishes to do so, a telephone or the internet is superior to trekking overland, though the latter might be preferable if one is not eager to communicate with Aunt Susan. Much depends on context.

Technology, in particular, in hundreds of facets, exemplifies progress.

So progress exists.

2. Not all change is progress.

Karl Marx seems to have regarded socialism as inevitable and, with his Hegelian optimism, took it for granted that what comes later will be better than what came before. Indeed, he seems to have supposed, on the basis of such views, that it was not really necessary to worry about how an economy could function without a natural market, how directors, for example, could feasibly plan, and calculate, relationships between production and distribution, between what should be produced and in what quantities, and how it might be distributed, and in what quantities, and so on. Similarly, he seems to have supposed that the natural human being will be happy to produce according to his ability and receive according to his need, and did not suspect that the optimum strategy in such a situation would be, given the inevitable scarcity of resources and the disutility of labor, to proclaim need and conceal ability. Thirdly, he seems to have viewed with equanimity the subordination of the individual to society, and failed to recognize that the "equality" enforced on a "pancake society," so to speak, would require "equality enforcers," and that this would reintroduce a new, and presumably fixed and permanent, inequality.

The point of these remarks is not to disparage the lethal fantasies of a particular social theorist but to suggest the possibility that change is not always progress.

There seems no logical or empirical reason to suppose that what comes later will be better than that which went before.

It might be the case, but it might not be the case, too.

Socrates had several children. They might have been superior to their father, but, as far as we know, they stirred no Platos.

It does not seem that Commodus, if he was the son of Marcus Aurelius, improved on his putative father.

In some respects, at least, history might miss the Athens of Pericles, the Florence of Michelangelo, the London of Shakespeare, the America of John Adams and Thomas Jefferson.

Old age is not obviously superior to robust youth.

Whereas, currently, it seems that socialism is unlikely to be seriously revived, at least in the near future, as a viable social system, though its rhetoric is likely to continue to have its appeal, particularly to the young and historically uninformed, it seems quite likely that something rather like it, an eventual command economy, an omnipotent state, a substantially fascist tyranny, inch by inch, law by law, may indeed come about. Is this not the "third way"? Given the gullibility of most human beings, and their natural desire for comfort, security, and unearned benefits, and their insouciance as to how these things are to be brought about, and the power of a manipulated majority to emplace and preserve demagogues in power, perhaps a resembling succession of such, it is not clear that the future will be superior to the past.

In any event, not all change need be progress.

3. Criteria-relevant Considerations

Conservative theorists constantly remind us that there are always "trade-offs." Popular wisdom assures us that there are no "free lunches." Somebody, even if it is not you, is paying for lunch. If economics is, for most practical purposes, the study of scarce resources which have alternative uses, it is implicit in the realities of the matter that utility bestowed here is utility withheld there. Obviously it is wiser, from the point of view of a whole, if not from the point of view of a part, to increase a quantity Q of wealth, so eventually there is more for all, rather than distribute it, withdrawing it from wealth-producing enterprises. No country, for example, has ever managed to tax itself into prosperity, to inflate itself into prosperity, to distribute itself into prosperity, and so on. Goods, after all, are the index to wealth; not paper. A dollar, for example, which will buy, so to speak, only three cents worth of goods is not worth a dollar but only three cents. A minimum wage of one hundred dollars an hour which will buy, so to speak, only two dollars worth of goods is, for all practical purposes, a wage of two dollars an hour.

The point to these reflections is not to rehearse a succession of economic truisms usually concealed from an electorate, but to indicate, by means of an intelligible example, something which should be obvious upon reflection, namely, that utility for A is often purchased at a cost to B.

One man's progress may well be another man's stagnation, regress, or catastrophe.

Inverse correlations abound. Where there are gains there are usually losses. Where there are winners there are likely to be losers.

From the point of view of the winners the losses to the losers are not likely to count. Usually they are irrelevant, or claimed to be deserved.

Might may not make right, but it seems to be the usual test of right, and so, for most practical purposes, pragmatically, it does make right.

"*Die Weltgeschichte is das Weltgericht.*"

Certainly the fact that it is the winners who survive and, for the most part, write the history sets a familiar problem to historians, the speculative discernment of fact by means of assessing narrow, incomplete, tendentious accounts contrived for the most part to distort it, if not to conceal it altogether.

Progress for Persians may not be progress for Babylonians; progress for Greeks may not be progress for Persians; progress for Romans may not be progress for Greeks, and so on.

Progress for a jealous god may not count as progress for a

decentralized multitude of tolerant gods who are content to share their divinity with equanimity. Progress for fanaticism does not count as progress for compassion and civility. Progress for totalitarianism is not likely to not count as progress from the point of view of natural liberty, private property, a free market, limited government, and such. Progress for subjectivism and relativism does not count as progress from the point of view of rationality, objectivity, logic, and such.

Obviously, whether or not something counts as progress is likely to depend on one's criterion for progress, and these criteria may differ from person to person, and party to party.

Let us consider a few criteria which might be offered for "progress," some points of view from which progress might be assessed.

4. Some Concepts of Progress

Progress is goal-related, and assessed in terms of the degree to which the goal in question is approached or realized.

It is usually presupposed that the goal in question is one which, if it were clearly understood, would be approved of, if not sought by, most human beings. The effort to attain some goals, for example, might be beyond what a given human being would be willing to exert, or should exert. For example, seriously pursuing some goals of human perfection might well be a route to human misery, resentment, fanaticism, sickness, hatred, and even insanity. Encouraging a congenitally imperfect creature to become perfect is to set it a task which is not only beyond its capacity, and will never be completed, but one which will remind it constantly of its failures and shortcomings, and will afflict it with guilt, as there is always more which could have been done. It is not unusual for goals to be set which are unachievable. It is a common pathology. Why should a cat devote its life to being the perfect mouser, when it is not bad at mousing anyway, and there are other things with which to concern himself, lady cats, for example.

Goals, of course, might be trivial, idiosyncratic, or even, from a customary point of view, evil. An individual's goal might be to win a lottery, impress Stephanie or Courtney, make ten million dollars, or such. It should be easy to track progress in such matters. Similarly, someone might be interested in universally propagating the virtues of peanut butter or Vitamin C, or the pleasures of music or chess, or stamp collecting. A goal, too, might be unusual, or, from one point of view or another, evil. For example, one might wish his particular religion, as it is in his view the one true religion, to be the single, universal religion of the human race, one race, one religion, and be willing, with the usual consistency of the self-righteous lunatic, to impose it "by fire and sword" on the rest of the world, which would just as soon not hear about it. Progress toward such a goal might be tracked demographically. Similarly, let us suppose someone regards the human race as a very serious mistake, and would prefer the planet to be surrendered to carp, cockroaches, and squirrels. Accordingly, the greater the number of nuclear explosions, release of homicidal viruses, poisonous gases, and such, the better. He is willing to do himself in, of course, but not until he is the last survivor, which will presumably guarantee him a considerable longevity.[53]

---

[53] In passing I might note something which is quite obvious upon reflection, but which eluded me for several years. For a long time I found it difficult to understand what seemed to me an almost fanatical concern with subtle doctrinal points, such as the nature of one trinity or another, the possible nature or natures of a given religious figure, the nature and attributes of a divine entity, the necessity of this ritual or that, this sacrament or that, for salvation, divine foreknowledge and free will, justification by works or faith, or both, the efficacy of prayer, to whom one might pray, the role of saints and intercessions, who is a heretic and who isn't, and such. Aside from the fact that none of this admits of much testability, if any, and most of it is presumably nonsense, individuals were prepared kill one another over one verbalism or another. I did not see how or why a divine entity would be in the least bit interested in what anyone thought about these things. Would it really be concerned that folks got it right? What difference could it possibly make to such an entity? If it were interested, surely it could just appear in the sky and set things right with a helpful word to those concerned. These things seemed to me very hard to understand until I realized that doctrinal points were not really at issue, that they were theological red herrings, so to speak, cover-ups, diversions, smoke and mirrors, one might say. What was truly at issue was wealth, prestige, and power. And, of course, people have always been willing to kill, torture, and burn to keep and increase such things. Assuming that the individuals involved are not simply self-conscious hypocrites, which seems unlikely, on the whole, at least,

Here is a sketch of some possible theories of progress:

Progress consists in achieving greatness, say, a great civilization, a great art, a great music, etc.,

... in widening an appreciation of the fine arts,

... in achieving human excellence,

... in deepening sensitivity to human values,

... in achieving security and comfort, in minimizing insecurity and discomfort,

... in achieving happiness, in achieving satisfaction,

... in achieving human perfection,

... in allocating utility as widely and equitably as possible, so that, as far as it can be managed, no one has any more than anyone else, that all will have the same level of housing, the same income, the same level of diet, etc.,

... in raising the general standard of living and health as much as possible,

... in achieving spiritual enlightenment,

... in the universalization of a given set of beliefs,

... in the maximization of human freedom,

... in the minimalization of human freedom,

... in the establishment of a rule of saints, or the kingdom of a divine entity on Earth,

... in the establishment of a planetary caliphate,

... in the establishment of a world of rationality and toleration,

... in the establishment of a single utopia,

... in the establishment of a world of diverse utopias, with a minimum of violence and coercion, in which individuals are allowed life, liberty, and the pursuit of happiness, within limits, as they see fit,

... in apprising as many people as possible of the true nature of the world and reality,

---

it seems one has a case here on which depth psychology might shed some light. In any event, it seemed to me that these things would be of little interest to a divine entity, but might be of much interest to those whose status in society, their position and power, and their very means of livelihood, depended on the offerings of the faithful, a faithful which might, in theory, cross the street or go next door, to another such institution, party, or establishment. Their collection plate, so to speak, is to be the only one in town.

... in making certain that as many people as possible are not apprised of the true nature of the world and reality.

... in universalizing compassion, tolerance, and love,

... in continuing the human adventure, in reaching for the stars, etc.

Obviously there could be an indefinite number of such goals. The above selection is proposed as representative.

5. Some Challenges to Progress Theory

If the D Hypothesis should be true it doesn't seem that there would be much point in speaking of "progress." That notion usually has a normative sense to it, and, in the D Universe, as we have seen, there is no genuine normativity. There is only nomological necessity. There might be "inevitable development," or such, but, as one usually thinks of progress, one would not think of it as inevitable. One usually thinks of progress as a desirable, nonnecessary improvement consequent upon meaningful human choice, significant human action, and such. One would not want to make this a matter of definition, of course. For example, a consistent Marxist might regard the eventual appearance of a classless society as being an example of both inevitability and progress. On the other hand, then progress would mean nothing more, it seems, than an inevitability of which one was determined to approve, as opposed to one which one was not determined to approve, and, secondly, it would deny one the right to legitimately approve or disapprove of those whose efforts preceded this form of society, as they could not help but do what they did. Somehow the whole thing would seem to be evacuated of significance. Also, one should then, it seems, speak of the development of a plant as progress, the inevitable output of a machine as progress, and so on. One would not, I think, wish to do that.

Three major challenges to progress theory would be cyclicity, stasis, and decline.

One requires a criterion for progress here, naturally, in order to assess not only its development, but its lack of development, in one fashion or another. For example, if the development of a global, heavily populated, heavily industrialized world would lead not only to a statistical reduction of the quality of life on the planet, but, perhaps, even to the alteration of the biosphere to an extent that life as we know it would become impossible, this would presumably not count as progress. To be sure, if the cockroach inherits the Earth, this is doubtless progress from the point of view of the cockroach, but presumably not from the point of view of at least several other life forms, unless perhaps they are a particular stripe of environmentalists.

Decline theories are not common but should be mentioned, if only for purposes of completeness. If one regards the ideal form of human life to be a life of simian contentment in a sort of zoological preserve in which there is not much to do but name animals, and such, everything has been downhill since the Garden of Eden. Karl Marx has what might be seen, perhaps unkindly, as a version of this view in his notion of a presumably idyllic "Asiatic" or "stasis" phase of human society, in which all property was tribal property, property held communally, and so on, a phase prior to the emergence of private property, a development which would seem almost unaccountable in such a society. Perhaps some selfish individuals wished to keep what they had worked for rather than give it away to others who had not worked for it. In any event, the placidity of millennia was somehow disrupted and the juggernaut of economic necessity began its cruel, bumpy journey through the centuries toward the classless society, in which the circle would be complete, private property would be again abolished, ownership would be again invested in the collective, and so on. Marx never gives us a plausible reason as to why this situation might not, as was the case with its hypothesized ancient predecessor, give rise, once again, to private property, and begin a new cycle. Supposedly this would not happen because, if class conflict is the mover of history, and there are no more classes, history should stop. But, it didn't before, in the classless society of the "stasis" phase, so there seems no *a priori* reason why it should now. Why should the same process not begin again? At least, the "equality enforcers," the ruling class in the classless society, should be on their guard. The most famous classical decline theory is that of Hesiod, in which a Golden Age is replaced by a Silver Age, and that by a Bronze Age, and that by a Heroic Age, and that by his own age, the Age of Iron, naturally, the worst of all.

There are, of course, cyclicity theories. Perhaps the most famous of these would be that of the Stoics' Cosmic Year in which the world, which is perfect, is born in fire, and proceeds through the produced elements, air, water, and earth, to once again, eventually, be consumed in fire, from which it will be again reborn, Phoenixlike, and once again it will be springtime in the cosmos. As the world is perfect, and perfection cannot be improved upon, each of these cycles is presumably identical. The notion of divergent, equivalent perfections did not seem to be entertained. Friedrich Nietzsche, who referred to himself as "the last Stoic," also had a version of an Eternal Recurrence, based in his case, one supposes, on an understanding of the physics of his day, a finite number of physical particles in constant motion, in accordance with immutable laws of nature, but Nietzsche was less optimistic about the nature of the process than his Stoic predecessors. On the other hand, it did provide a sort of immortality, intermittent though it might be, and guaranteed that some redemptive, precious moments of joy would return, again, and again, forever.

Cyclicity theories of perhaps greater importance in our context would be those of Oswald Spengler and Arnold Toynbee. Giambattista Vico's cyclicity theory, being progressive, and ultimately ascendant, is less relevant here. It would be, in its way, a progress theory, though not one of constant and invariant improvement. It would be, so to speak, a "progress on the whole" theory. a step backward, two steps forward, and so on.

Spengler's gigantic, awesome, and poetic vision of the rise and fall of cultures is clearly one of the most impressive attempts ever undertaken by a human mind to come to grips with the nature of human history. Critics commonly misunderstand the organic metaphor, and carry on as if Spengler were unaware that cultures lack central nervous systems, and such. If one takes Spengler's approach as primarily descriptive, as that of an observer of cycles, of flourishings, subsidences, terrors, disintegrations, and deaths, and not as intended to be explicitly explanatory, particularly in detail, his work is an unforgettable historiographical experience. It is likely to be moving to anyone who has a sense of the ephemerality and poignancy of human life.

Toynbee, on the other hand, who begins with more than twenty civilizations, dead, living, arrested, and so on, and then moves on strangely, years later, to what appears to be an obsession with global religions, is much narrower than Spengler in some ways, as his concerns are more precisely historical than cultural, and much broader in other ways, not only with respect to the much larger number of units considered, but with respect to the detail brought to bear in their consideration. Both men present unusual examples of erudition and scholarship. Toynbee is sophisticated, didactic, organized, learned, guardedly optimistic, and religiously sensitive. Spengler is clearly sophisticated and learned, but his approach is more intuitive, more in accord with *Verstehen* theory, than that of Toynbee. One has the sense that Spengler has looked at his cultures from the inside, insofar as possible, whereas Toynbee was content to observe them from a safe distance. Spengler, too, accordingly, is much concerned with the unity and character of cultures, with their "personality," and the coherence of their elements, how these things hang together, their *Zusammenhang*, so to speak, more so than Toynbee, who is more historically or reportorially oriented. The personalities of the men, too, are, too, quite different, as one would expect, between the optimistic and religious, and the pessimistic and secular. This doubtless flavors and conditions their work. Spengler seems much more consistent than Toynbee, or, at least, seems to take induction more seriously. Spengler, on the basis of fewer units, some eight or so, expects the downfall of Western Civilization.[54]

[54] The title of Spengler's most famous book, *Der Untergang des Abendlandes*, does not translate well into English. It is certainly correct to translate it as '*Decline of the West*', but this, probably necessarily, loses much in the translation. '*Untergang*', in German, means not only an undergoing, or, perhaps better, a going under, or sinking, or subsidence, but it is also a word for "sunset" or "the setting of the sun." '*Abendlandes*', literally, means "lands of the west." The sun sets in the west, so one has the sense of the sun's setting on the lands of the West, the end of a day, the coming of the end, of twilight, the approach of night, the end of a time and reality.

Toynbee, on the other hand, despite much more evidence suggesting inevitability, and such, holds out hope for the West, and the world, perhaps in terms of some sort of new, eclectic, global religion. It is a bit as though Spengler conducted an experiment in which A was followed by B some eight or so times without exception, and concluded from this that A's are followed by B's, and then Toynbee replicated the experiment over twenty times, and remains hopeful that the next A will not be followed by a B. Perhaps Toynbee is right; that might be nice; but, as religions tend to be dogmatic and divisive, and lead to exclusionism, arrogance, hatred, persecution, and war, one might hope, rather, for a new Enlightenment, a stab at civility and tolerance, such anomalies. Too, Toynbee is not a Utopian, primarily it seems because of "Original Sin," which, one fears, he may understand in some theological sense. One may share his apprehensions, of course, without obscuring evolved characteristics with dire penalties, death and such, imposed by a divine entity on successions of innocent generations for an ancient indiscretion which took place long before they were born in a place they never heard of. Toynbee does provide much more in the way of an apparatus for historiographical explanation than Spengler, for example, in terms of responses, effective and ineffective, to various sorts of challenges, physical and human. Though why A responds to challenge C in way B rather than D may remain unclear.

Stasis as a challenge to progress theory is plausible, and apt, but requires two presuppositions, a level of considerable generality, and a particular understanding of progress.

In a general sense things remain much the same; the specifics may differ, but the *genera* preside. Men are born, they live, they die. They seek their best interests; occasionally they sacrifice them. They fall in love; they replicate their genes; families are raised; goods are produced, exchanged, distributed, and so on. One travels, whether on foot, or by ox cart, or train, or bus, or transcontinental aircraft. We read ancient literature and find it familiar, we encounter love and hate, ambition, courage, cowardice, betrayal, loyalty, friendship, enmity. Costumes and contrivances change, and even cognitive fields, and life conditions, but one continues to recognize oneself, and one's brothers. There may be much that is "new under the sun," but there is much, too, and perhaps the most important things, with which the sun is altogether familiar.

Secondly, if we have in mind a moral or spiritual criterion for progress, a case might be made not only for stasis but even for decline. In some respects, of course, we regard our world as morally superior to that of, say, the Greeks and Romans, but it is not obvious that this view would be shared by the Greeks and Romans. For example, is a world in which an enemy is enslaved really morally inferior to one in which an enemy is exterminated? Is a world in which a hundred religions live side by side, each with its own devotees, morally inferior to one in which heretics are hunted down and burned? Is a status society obviously morally inferior to one in which winning is prized in a race which all must run and most must lose? Is a simpler, more leisurely world spiritually inferior to one more harried and complex, in which work and competition, timed and measured, is frenetically incessant? One acknowledges, of course, the inestimable values of a superior diet, more health, less infant mortality, a greater abundance of goods, and so on, who would give them up, but these are not normally understood as moral or spiritual goods, though they might facilitate, one hopes, the attainment of such goods. So we look about, and we see expanding populations, diminishing resources, a threatened planet, global diseases, mutating viruses, widespread ignorance and fanaticism, governments and religions apparently in the hands of madmen, and weapons of mass destruction proliferating unchecked. It is not obvious that our time is morally and spiritually superior to most other times and places; we may only be more crowded, more self-righteous, and more powerful. This is not to argue for a return to a past of famine, deprivation, relentless toil, widespread misery, and such, but, rather, to suggest that, on an overview, all things considered, it is not altogether obvious that our age is characterized, statistically, by much, if any, moral and spiritual progress.

Unlike the optimism of Vico, we may have, so to speak, not taken one step backward and two steps forward, but one step forward, and two steps backward.

6. Some Dangers of Progress Theory

Before moving to considerations having to do more generally with historical pattern, it is natural, and appropriate, to note some dangers, or hazards, which might easily afflict progress theory.

These particularly characterize progress theory when a particular end state is envisaged and sought.

First, such a theory minimizes the importance and value of the present except insofar as it is instrumental in bringing about the desiderated end state. That is the role of the present, to prepare for and bring about the end state. The present is not an end in itself, but a means to an end. Generation after generation, then, is to live in terms of this ideal, willingly doing what is necessary, selflessly, heroically sacrificing their time and utility, and perhaps their lives and happiness, to bring it about, this supposed Utopia, this alleged "promised land," which they, like Moses, will never live to enjoy. This seems an extreme, unrealistic, and inhuman thing to ask of human beings, an unnecessary and dreadful task to impose upon them. Do not people have a right to live for their own sake, and as they see fit? At the very least, it would seem to diminish the importance of the present and to denigrate as selfish those who might hope, in the time at their disposal, to seek their own happiness. Is their happiness not as important, not as valuable, as that of possible strangers in an implausible future?

Secondly, the goal of progress, conceived as some sort of Utopia, seems vague, even inane. From the propaganda point of view it is useful to leave the nature of the end state open, so that each individual, rather as the peruser of Rorschach Blots, may read into things whatever appeals to him, and whatever he would like to see. We do have, however, some conjectures which might be helpful. Following Leon Trotsky, "the average human type will rise to the heights of an Aristotle, a Goethe, or a Marx. And above this ridge new peaks will rise."[55] This would certainly be something to look forward to, but until genetic engineering is more advanced, one supposes that the average human type will have to be content with

---

55 *Literature and Revolution*, translated by R. Strunsky (London, 1925), p. 256. (Quoted by Ludwig von Mises, *Human Action: A Treatise on Economics*, Volume I (Liberty Fund, Indianapolis, 2007), p. 71.)

the average human brain. Karl Marx, whom Trotsky seems to rank with Aristotle and Goethe, and Friedrich Engels, whom he does not seem to include in the ranking, suggest, in *The German Ideology*, that a fellow in communist society might hunt in the morning, fish in the afternoon, rear cattle in the evening, and criticize after dinner, though it is not clear what there would be to criticize, nor if it would be wise to do any criticizing. According to Marx's usual view of things, the revolution, to be followed by the dictatorship of the proletariat, to be followed, somehow, by the classless society, would not come about until an advanced stage of capitalism would be attained, presumably involving heavy industrialization and large urban populations. Thus, activities such as an individual's, or a population's, hunting in the morning, fishing in the afternoon, and such, might require careful planning, game management, and such.[56]

Thirdly, the proponents of Utopias may misunderstand the nature of human beings, the nature of human life, and such. Most seem to be "hollow-body theorists," namely, theorists who see the human essentially as a vessel into which anything might be indifferently poured, or as, say, moist, yielding clay, which may be pounded and shaped to a potter's whim, in short, as essentially a product, a social artifact, to be manufactured according to specifications, to be designed by right-thinking social engineers. Without denying the obvious influence, benign or noxious, of acculturation on a human being, one must realize that the object being acculturated requires acculturation precisely because it is in itself something quite different from the proposed end result of the acculturation process. It is an animal, with inbred dispositions and needs, social and antisocial, extending back not only through a succession of ancestors, but a succession of ancestor species. It is no longer possible, today, given animal studies, genetics, and sociobiology for an informed, candid person to pretend that the human being is a passive *tabula rasa* on which messages and instructions of any sort whatsoever might be successfully inscribed.

Civilization involves, as would be expected, its "trade-offs."

---

[56] Karl Marx and Friedrich Engels, *The German Ideology*, Parts I and III, Edited with an Introduction by R. Pascal, no translator credited (International Publishers Company, Inc., New York, Fourth Printing, 1965), p. 22.

In some respects, it is a cage, within which is confined the human beast, and an oppression, whereby the beast is to be tamed and herded. It would be hard to deny such things. On the other hand it is obviously superior to the jungle and tribal warfare. Without it one might expect cannibalism and chaos.

It does, of course, certifiably, produce its diverse forms of repression and mental illness in many individuals. Indeed, the freer and less socially controlled human being, the one more resistant to rules and constraints, the one less susceptible to induced guilt, supposedly lives longer than his more socially controlled brother. Too, the existence of crime and cruelty, coercion and violence, hypocrisy, discrimination, prejudice, and hatred, on both sides of the law, despite an almost universal education and all the emplaced apparatus of social control, makes clear that human nature, in some of its less pleasant aspects, is not wholly subdued or extinguished, nor wholly an artifact at the mercy of the society's current crop of kings and potentates, programmers and engineers. The existence of lying, cheating, and stealing, of fraud and extortion, of delinquency, vandalism, and crime, of armies and navies, of police departments, of courts and prisons, testify to the fragility of civilization, and its need to defend itself from its own. Considerations of this sort suggest the problems to be faced by any society larger than, say, a small, self-policing village. There is no reason to suppose that in, say, a classless society, were such a thing possible, human beings would be much different from what they are now. They would still be themselves, generous, noble, kind, loving, hard-working, self-sacrificing, ambitious, aggressive, possessive, acquisitive, hating, cruel, ready to inflict pain, frequently irrational, and so on. Given the nature of the human being he seems a dubious candidate for enrollment in the school of perfection. Accordingly, it seems that the first requirement for a workable Utopia would be to deny him admittance. Sheep might do.

A second problem having to do with the progress theorist's possible misunderstanding of the nature of the human being, of human life, and such, with consequences to the practicality of his hopes, has to do with the diversity of human interests and preferences. The very concept of Utopia, as usually understood, involves the projected imposition of a particular set of values on a passive population. "I am smarter than you, and I know what is best for you." "Shut up, and be happy." "You are free—to be just like me." And so on. One man's Utopia might be another man's gulag, one man's heaven another man's hell. "In cat heaven there are many mice; in mouse heaven there are no cats." Would there be an escape from Utopia? Would there be somewhere else to go?[57]

Hopefully, one has now achieved an entry into these issues, having to do with pattern, plan, and such, that via an example, in this case, that of Progress Theory.

We will now devote our attention, first, to the notion of plan, and, thereafter, to the broader notion of pattern.

2. Plan

Initially, one must note the obvious point that the two concepts, that of plan and pattern, are not identical. Obviously, one might encounter patterns which have not been planned, or need not be considered as having been planned, as spontaneous-order theorists have demonstrated beyond any doubt. Similarly, the famous pattern postulated by Marxist theory, founded on the forces of production, namely, the means of production and human labor, and the relations of production, namely, the dialectical relations of conflict between a dominant ruling class and a subservient working class, master and slave in one era, lord and serf in another, and, later, capitalist and proletarian, was not conceived of as having been planned. Rather it was supposed to be the natural, lawlike unfolding of an inevitable material process which must result in the end state of a classless society.[58]

---

[57] The most devastating critique of the Utopia concept in the literature, at least to my knowledge, occurs in Robert Nozick's *Anarchy, State, and Utopia*. The analysis is brilliant and detailed, an intellectual *tour de force* by one of the most imaginative and finest minds to characterize recent philosophy, too, that of a friend, who is much missed.

[58] If this view were taken seriously by Marxists it seems they should just wait around for the classless society to show up. It would seem odd to urge rocks to obey the law of gravity or water to boil at such-and-such a temperature at sea level. One cannot, logically, have things both ways. Either the process is one

Whereas it is obvious that pattern need not involve plan, it might be thought that plan would necessitate pattern, but that, too, interestingly, is not the case. The two concepts are logically independent, neither essentially involving the other. For example, it might be part of a divine entity's plan to include free will in its creation, thus allowing, unless the system were anticipated and rigged, possible exceptions to pattern. Might not a divine engineer's plan endow its mechanisms with random elements, precluding regularity? Might not a planner plan for chaotic torment, and such? A divine entity is presumably under no obligation to comply with the rules of common civility. It might do any number of things, favor Trojans, send plagues, murder first-born children, create hells, and so on.

One thing a plan would require is a planner. A pattern, on the other hand, requires no patterner. Plans require *intentionality*; and pattern does not. A plan, too, need not have a single planner. A number of gods might get together, say, on Mount Olympus, form a committee, and, some months later, after many compromises, come out with a plan, better or worse, a committee product, of one sort or another. Usually one thinks of plans as being unitary, but they need not be. For example, you could have conflicting plans, altered plans, and limited plans. If one has more than one god one could have more than one plan. And some of these plans might conflict. Presumably Ahriman and Ahura Mazda would have different ends in view. Too, a god might be working at cross-purposes with himself, be absent-minded, or perverse, or

---

of material determinism or it is not. Even the notion of "hastening the birth pangs," makes no sense. It would be like urging the rock to fall faster, or water to boil at a different temperature at a different altitude. Obviously the Marxists, in practice, recognized the silliness of their own view, and pitched in, revolting here, assassinating there, and such, to realize their ends. The only consistent position here would be to claim that they were determined to do what they did, and, if this is the case, neither credit nor discredit would be due. One has an analogy to the mind/body's "Entrance Problem" here, namely, how does a free element enter into and influence a nonfree element? At best, the Marxists would seem committed to a form of dualism at odds with their proclaimed materialistic thesis. Similarly, if the nonfree process is subject to influence, for example, to "hastening," then it could presumably be influenced in other ways, as well, to other ends; it might be slowed, stopped, fractured, diverted, or transformed. Thus, for all practical purposes it is not inevitable at all.

something, and produce conflicting plans, as well. Plans might be altered. There is no reason why an omnipotent god should be denied the option of changing its mind, not that one would expect it to do so. Perhaps it relents, and decides to give one or another chosen people a chance to try again, to do better this time, to make good this time, or something. Plans, too, while one often thinks of them as holistic, might be limited in a variety of ways. They might be, for example, temporarily limited or limited with respect to subject matter. Perhaps the plan only goes to 1804, at which point the divine entity may have lost interest, or, perhaps the plan only kicks in at 1804, the divine entity finally deciding that it had better take charge of things. Similarly one or more divine entities might have a variety of diverse plans, say, a plan for each race, each religion, each ethnic group, each nation, and so on. Indeed, might there not be a specific plan for every organism, every person, or every ant, or, say, for every other organism, every other person or ant? In such a case, there might be an abundance of plans, but no particular plan for history as a whole, except insofar as it might emerge as a function of these other plans, or, indeed, it might emerge as nothing planned in itself, but only as a complex pattern, not itself planned, consequent upon these other plans. Obviously there are many possibilities.

The belief that history has a plan, and a purpose, at least in an overall sense, is quite common. Christian historiography, for example, is likely to see history as a momentous purposeful drama, which begins with the formation of the world itself; in it we find the origin of man, the genesis of races and languages, and the recounting of a number of pivotal events, the fall, the flood, the election of a Chosen People, their adventures and tribulations, the Incarnation, the birth, life, death, and resurrection of Jesus, the Christian Messiah, the foundation of a favored Church, its mission, the prospect of a world's end, and so on, all of this indicative of the workings of a divine entity in history itself. Christianity, like Judaism, is a very historical religion; history is in its very bones. Islam, too, and several other religions, as well, have their views of history, what it means, and where it is going.

The planner, or planners, are commonly taken as gods, or, at least, as some sort of unusual, powerful beings. Humans, too, of course, might have their plans for history. It seems clear that individuals such as Adolf Hitler, Mao Tse-tung, and Joseph Stalin had plans for history. One supposes, too, that many inmates of lunatic asylums have such plans, but lack the means to implement them.

Detectability problems will obviously arise.

Naturally, a plan might exist and not be detectable. But an undetectable plan, though doubtless objectively of enormous human importance, as it might be the key to much, or everything, is of no epistemological importance whatsoever; from the point of view of historiography it might as well not exist.

On the other hand, those individuals who see in history the hand of a divine entity, or the results of altercations amongst such entities, must feel they have some evidence, at least, to support such a conjecture.

Our major discussion of detectability problems will arise in the more congenial, familiar milieu of pattern, but a word or two is in order here, given the special nature of plan detectability.

There is a joke to the effect that a roofer begins to slide rapidly down the steep roof and faces the prospect of a long, dangerous fall. Alarmed, he calls out, "Lord, help, please, save me!" At the last moment he catches on a nail, and is safe. He then, dangling there, much relieved, calls out, "Never mind, Lord! I caught on a nail!"

One is not exactly sure what to make of this story, but the most obvious inference would be that the Lord exists, and usually, at least, works his ways through the mechanisms of the world, and that He has saved our endangered roofer, who fails to understand this, fails to understand that the Lord, via a nail, perhaps these things arranged from the beginning of the world, foreseeing the prayer, has saved him.

One of the intriguing problems of philosophy, a discipline frequently given to worrying about things about which it never occurs to most folks to worry, is the "Other Minds" problem. Briefly, we are aware of our own consciousness, or, at least, of our own thinkings, emotions, feelings, imaginings, and such. We have, so to speak, a first-person direct access to such things. We may not understand everything that is going on, and we may be mistaken about it, but, obviously, we have such experiences. Presumably others have similar internal experiences but the philosophical question is how do we know that. We have such a belief, probably, because we are genetically wired, so to speak, to have it, rather as we suppose our confidence in the reliability of induction, our belief in the existence of an external world, and such, are similarly wired in, or, genetically produced. Indeed, individuals who did not have such beliefs would be ill equipped to survive in the world as we know it. The beliefs doubtless have causes; the philosophical question is, rather, how do we know the beliefs are true, how might the beliefs be justified, if at all. Without entering into these matters in any detail, the most obvious epistemological support for such conjectures is the utility of acting on them. In the case of the "Other Minds" problem, we might also, of course, base our conjectures on inference, conscious or unconscious, and analogy. We infer from the behavior of another, the way he acts, the noises he makes, that he, too, has an inner life, feelings, and such. As we have no direct access to the mind of another we infer, then, from the individual's behavior, and its resemblance to ours, that he has a mind, feelings, and such. Analogy, too, might enter into the attempt at justification. We have properties A, B, C, D, and E, and the other fellow has properties A, B, C, and D, so we hypothesize that he also has the property E. It is not likely, of course, that the original belief, which we are concerned to examine and justify, if possible, was arrived at by ratiocination. It seems unlikely that there is an exciting, even startling, moment in the life of the infant in which, after a process of reasoning, it suddenly realizes that his mother has a mind, or, if he is a philosopher, that his mother may have a mind.

The metaphysical solipsist, most of which are likely to have been institutionalized, believes either, if he is a piker, that his is the only center of consciousness in the world, or, if his philosophy is more robust, that he is the only entity in existence. Schopenhauer reputedly remarked that metaphysical solipsism requires not a refutation but a cure. That is fortunate, for it is impossible to refute. Perhaps you are the only conscious entity in existence, or the only entity in existence. For all you will ever know, it might be the case.

If it is the case then you are dreaming this book up out of your own consciousness, which, I trust, is not alarming, and, I hope, not distressing.

The point of all this is that if we cannot establish the irrefragable existence of any mind other than our own, and, as a logical possibility, metaphysical solipsism might be true, then we could never know that another mind, an intentionality, was responsible for an apparent pattern in history.

That the nail saving our endangered roofer was there might be a coincidence, an accident, and so on. Indeed, that seems to be his own view of the matter.

There is always a distinction between data and the interpretation of data. Data underdetermines theory. Any given set of data is susceptible, in theory, to an infinite number of diverse interpretations.. Accordingly, no theory can be conclusively proven. Similarly, for a number of complex reasons, having to do in particular with auxiliary hypotheses, no theory can be conclusively disproven.[59]

Thus, again, the existence of intent or plan behind history could never be proven, or known, or, indeed, disproven.

This is not to deny, of course, that history might be the result of such a plan, nor is it to deny that under certain conditions it might be plausible, or even rationally coercive, to infer the existence of such a plan.

Let us consider three scenarios, so to speak.

First, let us suppose that over a vast extent of territory, one has a common civilization, a common language, an absence of borders, and a unified governance; moreover, one has considerable ease and safety of movement on both land and sea, on land, for example, in virtue of an enormous and marvelous system of roads kept in

---

[59] None of this suggests that science must stop in its tracks. Certainly many theories may be taken to be sufficiently confirmed, if not conclusively proven; and many theories, too, might be taken to be sufficiently disconfirmed, if not conclusively falsified. There is a distinction here of great importance, which is that between truth and "empirical adequacy." Strictly, whereas a theory might be true, why not, it could never be known to be true. What could be known is that it is "empirically adequate," namely, that it does its job, accounts for the facts, yields predictions, and such. Obviously, if this is the case in the sciences generally, then similar considerations would appertain to the hypotheses and theories of the historiographer. He, too, might touch truth, but, strictly, might have to content himself with attaining a good account, one which was, in its way, to the best of his ability and knowledge, "empirically adequate."

good repair, and the substantial elimination of brigandage, and on sea, for example, by the frequent and convenient availability of affordable shipping and passage, and, for most practical purposes, the elimination of piracy. We now note that these conditions facilitate the comparatively easy and expeditious propagation of a particular set of ideas and practices, perhaps a religion, say, Christianity. It seems reasonably clear, too, that if these conditions were not in place the spread of, say, Christianity, would not have been as simply, swiftly, and straightforwardly accomplished. It all came together, nicely, so to speak. Now it is very easy to see how a historian to whom the supposition of a historically involved deity was familiar and congenial might be easily persuaded, and perhaps properly, to see in these facts not a set of fortunate coincidences, but a design, an arrangement. And he might be right.

What seems to be obviously true is that Situation S makes possible, even facilitates, Result R. That, one supposes, is not at issue. From the secular point of view it seems we have an instance here of the Fallacy of False Cause, or that of Fallacious Imputation. Also, causality in a mechanistic sense, as opposed to a classical sense of cause as teleological, might seem to be involved. The Fallacy of False Cause would occur if one were mistakenly supposing S *because* of R, or *in order that* R, namely, that R was the *raison d'être* or the reason behind S, or, in a sense, the cause of S, namely, that S was *for* R. To be sure, the actual cause in this case would be the divine entity's setting up S in order to facilitate R. The Fallacy of False Imputation would occur if one were mistakenly supposing that S was designed or arranged to bring about R. One would be imputing something to S which was no was no part of S. To be sure, here again, the actual cause would be not S or R, but the divine entity, who might cause S in order to facilitate R. Mechanistic cause is cause from A to B, or cause from past to future, from time t_1 to time t_2. That is familiar. Teleological cause, much harder to understand, though easy to verbalize, is end-state causality, or, in a sense, cause from B to A, or from future to past, or from time t_2 to time t_1. Along these lines one might think of the acorn being *for the sake of* the future oak tree, that it is the future state which gives it meaning and purpose, that where it is going and what it will be is more important than where it is now and what it is now. Teleological causality seems to presuppose a universe somewhat alien to that in which the modern mind usually takes itself to live, a universe of implicit purposes, and such, a universe with unfolding potentialities, with destinies to fulfill. The concept of teleological causality does not seem illuminating, or helpful, even in cases where one supposes it would be most at home, where conscious intentionality is involved. Even here, a purpose is at A and its fulfillment would be at B. It is not already, somehow, at B, out there, reaching backward to A. To be sure, as pointed out, the final causal agent here is neither S nor R, but the divine entity who would design or arrange S in order, in the dimension of time and terrestrial reality, to bring about R. If this is actually going on, of course, no fallacies are involved. The historiographical question is whether or not there is good reason to suppose it is going on. On this, observers might differ.

An independent question is whether or not the concept of a divine entity is meaningful, and such.

Obviously some sort of meaning can be extended to such a concept, if only anthropomorphically.

Let us now consider two further scenarios, these being *Gedankenexperimente*.

First, let us suppose that an ancient papyrus is discovered somewhere in Egypt. The dating of this papyrus, we shall suppose, is clearly quite old, certifiably so, scientifically. Perhaps New Kingdom. We shall also suppose that the papyrus itself claims to be the hundredth copying of an original manuscript, each copy having been made at intervals of one or more generations. This would make the putative original much older than the ancient document recently discovered. We shall further suppose that it is claimed in the document that it is the revelation of some god or other, perhaps Thoth, to some priest or other. It concerns the plan for the world, set up by, say, Amon-Ra, the god of the sun. We shall supposes that Thoth, the scribe of the gods, took it down in a professional manner, and thought that the priest might find it of interest. As the manuscript is slowly translated by a team of qualified Egyptologists, copies Xeroxed and circulated to various museums and universities, a shock wave of unprecedented proportion rocks the world of Egyptology, that is, one or two individuals for every twenty million or so being shaken to the core. The manuscript is quite unusual; it lists, in orderly fashion and considerable detail, masses of integrated chronologies, stating thousands of happenings in the past, most of which took place well after the presumed date of the supposed original ms., thus seemingly occurring after the time of writing. There is no indication that the copying priests even knew what they were doing, as much of this material pertained to the future, from their point of view, and dealt with individuals, events, and topics about which it would be presumed they could know nothing. The chronology, of course, insofar as it can be checked, by being correlated with eclipses, and such, and, later, dynastic successions, king lists, archon lists, consul rosters, Olympiads, caliphates, years, and so on, is, as far as one can tell, fearfully accurate. There is much in the ms. which might be fanciful, or, at least, deals with material new to historiography, some of that stuff about the Hittites and Elamites, Cleopatra's troubled childhood, hanky-panky amongst the Sassanids, Theodora's interest in explicit pottery, and such. On the other hand, much that one discovers in the ms. agrees with, and, in a sense, even confirms a number of supposedly established historiographical facts. Caesar's assassination, for example, is there, to the day, though, in theory, given carbon dating, and such, the discovered copy of the ms. was inscribed over a thousand years earlier. If this is a hoax, the least that will happen is that atomic physics must be revised. About this time the copies of the ms. are being kept under lock and key, save for the long hours spent in translation. Things continue on, including even footnotes on the best designs for horse collars and moldboard plows; remarks on the best diet and exercise regimes for hunting falcons; shrewd suggestions for breeding horses capable of carrying two hundred or more pounds of armored rider, etc. We hear later of the financial difficulties of Christopher Columbus, and their impact on his personality problems. A brief reference to the defenestration of Prague occurs, amongst many other things, wars, and such. Judaism, Christianity, Islam, Jainism, Buddhism, Hinduism, Zoroastrianism, and many other religions are huffily dismissed, as inexplicable anomalies and heresies. Ikhnaton, in particular, comes off poorly in the ms. It will be remembered that these accounts are supposedly the revelations of the god, Thoth, to a particular priest, long ago, of the plan of Amon-Ra, the god of the sun, for the human race. Things continue on, of course, and we are now up to date. Should we continue to translate the ms.?

In this case it seems that we have not only an alleged plan for history, but an available, explicit account of the plan, which we can follow, date by date, event by event. So, should we accept this as proof of the existence of Amon-Ra, Thoth, and so on, and should we accept it for what it claims to be, the plan of a god for the human race. Certainly no other plan, *per hypothesis*, can approach this plan in detail and accuracy. If this were, say, a Christian ms, one supposes a number of individuals would take it quite seriously.

What would one make of something like this, particularly if it continued to accurately predict the future, and there seemed nothing one could do to frustrate or falsify its predictions?

We could insist that it was a hoax, but it is hard to see how a hoax could know the future. One could claim that it was all a coincidence, and one might be right, but the coincidence hypothesis, given the extent and nature of the material involved, would seem improbable. To be sure, some very improbable events occur, and daily. Similarly to what we noted earlier, if one hundred slips of paper, numbered from one to one hundred, were placed in a hat, and one were to be drawn out, it would a hundred to one that, say, six, would be drawn, but it would be a certainty that one such number would be drawn. It is highly probable that some highly improbable events will occur. Too, our friends of the I Hypothesis could view all this with equanimity. They could put it down to just another one of those improbable events showing up, events which they do not expect, but insist might happen. Religious individuals might insist that these things might be explained in virtue of the activities of evil spirits, or something along those lines, perhaps malignant entities somehow apprised of the future. One would not expect the pope, for example, to convert to the worship of Amon-Ra. Others might claim that 'Amon-Ra' was just another name for their own deity, and thus that the existence of the ms. confirmed their own religious hypotheses.

In short, even in such a case, in the face of such evidence, supposedly overwhelming, individuals might not accept that a plan was implicit in history, or take the plan at its face value, as what it claimed to be, and seemed to be.

This seems informative.

To be sure, we might expect some to start for Luxor and Karnak.

A third scenario, one simpler, easier to understand, less ambitious, having to do with the interpretation of evidence, might pertain to prayer.

Let us suppose we have two devotees, one of goddess A, perhaps Ishtar, and another of goddess B, say, Isis.

We shall suppose that both devotees feel that their particular goddess is to be preferred over the other, for a variety of reasons, perhaps having to do with character, personality, attentiveness to the faithful, fondness for doves, an open-minded attitude toward temple prostitution, efficiency in answering prayers, and such. As both of these devotees are everyday default pagans neither wishes to deny the existence of the other's goddess, and, for their part, neither goddess is a jealous goddess, to the extent that she feels it important to be exclusively worshipped, particularly to the extent that those who fail to see things in that light should be forcibly converted or, if unconvinced, put to the sword.

Each devotee, fond of her opposite number, as they are childhood chums, save for a temporary disagreement over Publius at the age of eleven, wishes to win her friend over to the worship of her own goddess. We further suppose that both devotees are bright and rational, which had dismayed Publius and sped him into the arms of another.

Accordingly, we may suppose that after listing and discussing the attributes of their goddesses, and failing to persuade one another that either goddess, on paper, so to speak, held the advantage over the other, the devotees decide to undertake a series of experiments of the sort which, several centuries later, would have been approved by John Stuart Mill.

The experiment proceeds as follows. In phase one, each devotee will pray, on five consecutive days, for five things. On the first day, $Devotee_1$ prays that the sun will come up the next day, and $Devotee_2$ that the local tides will come in on schedule. As the sun does come up the next day and the tides come and go as usual, both prayers are taken as answered. This scores one point for each goddess. The next day the devotees switch prayers, $Devotee_1$ praying that the local tides will come in on schedule and

Devotee$_2$ praying that the sun will come up. Once again the sun comes up and the tides behave normally. Once again both prayers appear to have been answered but the devotees are uneasy. It is conjectured, finally, however, that either goddess may handle both the sun and the local tides. One might do it a bit better than the other, perhaps, but the differences, if any, appear indiscernible. A passing Epicurean, young and symmetrical of feature, accosts the devotees with an ulterior motive but, upon learning of their inquiry, its nature, and such, his plans change immediately, and a philosophical dialogue ensues, on the Epicurean's part flavored by atoms, swerves, impingements, strikings, the void, and such. This sort of thing they had never gotten from Publius. The Epicurean suggests that the sun and tides may have done what they did regardless of the praying. He also suggests that they pray tomorrow that the sun does not come up and the tides don't come in, and see if those prayers are answered. The devotees decline to do so as the risk is too great. Also, more importantly, such prayers seem somehow improper, even if motivated in the interests of science. The next three days the devotees pray for different things, Devotee$_1$ that a particular rock which she releases in midair will not descend, and Devotee$_2$ that smoke from a particular wood fire will not ascend. That sort of thing is much safer than involving oneself and goddesses with the sun and tides. Neither prayer is answered. On the last two days each devotee prays for something or other she would like, different things, say, a shawl, sandals, a bracelet, a necklace, such things. Each receives, we shall suppose one of the things prayed for, but not another. If you are keeping score, the goddesses are even so far, each having, it seems, answered three prayers, namely, those connected with the sun and the tides, and one each, having to do with apparel or ornaments. That is not bad, three out of five. The goddesses are tied.

But why were there unanswered prayers? Why did Devotee$_1$ not get, say, her sandals and Devotee$_2$, say, her necklace? Perhaps the sandals were not right for Devotee$_1$ and the necklace not right for Devotee$_2$. Surely the goddesses are the best judge of such things.

In order to standardize variables, which is approved by the Epicurean, despite swerves, who is lingering in the vicinity, actually, interestingly, as he is a philosopher, primarily for philosophical purposes, the devotees, for the next five days, in phase two of the experiment, will pray for the *same* things, a glimpse of the now-matured, dashing Publius, a well-fried fish cake for supper, an encountered, unclaimed *denarius*, a golden apple, and another glimpse of Publius. We shall suppose both achieve their glimpses of Publius, who is often visible locally, particularly in the vicinity of his own home, an area in which the devotees often take the air, and that Devotee$_1$ does discover a *denarius* and Devotee$_2$ obtains her fish cake. The market value of the fish cake, we shall suppose, given inflation, is one *denarius*. Neither devotee obtains a golden apple. Tallying, and summating, these ten days of experiments, it seems possible that each devotee has had six answered prayers, which, out of ten possibilities, is excellent. Discounting, however, at the behest of the Epicurean, the prayers pertaining to the sun and tides, and those pertaining to the activities of rocks and smoke, we have seven acceptable experiments, in which each devotee has, it seems, had four prayers answered, two out of each four being Publius glimpses. If, following the insistence of the Epicurean, we rule out the Publius glimpses as having been casts of loaded dice, so to speak, given the carefully timed strolling habits of the devotees and the predictable daily comings and goings of Publius, then each devotee has had, it seems, two prayers answered, out of five. On this approach there appears to be, then, a forty percent efficacy of prayer, which is quite good, one would suppose.

There seems to be no way of deciding at this point between Ishtar and Isis, with respect to worshipper-friendliness. They might be similarly disposed toward their devotees, and similarly disposed to answer prayers, but this is not obvious. Perhaps Ishtar is more frugal with gifts than Isis, but more impressed with Devotee$_1$ than Isis is with Devotee$_2$, and that Isis, who is more generous with gifts than Ishtar, is not as impressed with Devotee$_2$ as Ishtar is with Devotee$_1$. Balancing these things out we could still have a forty percent figure. But let us suppose, as seems probable, that Devotee$_1$ and Devotee$_2$ are worshipper-equivalent, and that the goddesses, as seems likely, are equally generous or parsimonious. There still seems no way of deciding between the goddesses.

Perhaps we should let it stand that way.

Now the goddesses might exist or not, one or both. If, say, the goddesses do not exist, then there is no prayer answering, at all, and the belief in an answered prayer is mistaken. If the goddesses exist, then they are either interested in people or not. The Epicurean believes, or judiciously claims to believe, the gods exist, but he does not think they have any interest in human beings, or would have anything to do with them. Who could blame them? If the goddesses exist but have no interest in human beings, then, too, there are presumably no answered prayers. If the goddesses exist and are interested in human beings, then they either answer prayers or not. Perhaps they think human beings are best left to solve their own problems. At any rate, if the goddesses exist, and are interested in human beings, but do not answer prayers, then, again, there are no answered prayers. If the goddesses exist, and are interested in human beings, and do answer prayers, then they either answer all prayers or do not answer all prayers. In this case, it would be hard to know if a prayer was answered or not, or if something would have come about, say, anyway. If the goddesses exist, are interested in people, and do answer prayers, and answer all prayers, then they might answer prayers in a way the devotee expects, or not. For example, if a prayer were answered not in the way a devotee hoped, but in another way, then it would be hard to know if the prayer had been answered at all. For example, suppose the devotee prayed for a fish cake but was given a barley cake instead. It would presumably not be clear to the devotee that the prayer had been answered.

If one does not obtain that for which one has prayed, then the prayer, for whatever reason, for most practical purposes, discernible purposes, at least, has not been answered. If one seems to obtain that for which one has prayed, that might be a coincidence, or an accident, and so on, and so, again, one would not know if the prayer had been answered or not. Perhaps the best bet is to let the gods alone or pray that their will, and not yours, be done, which is pretty safe, as they are gods, and are presumably going to do their own will anyway.

These considerations are applicable to all, or most, attempts to discern the will of divine beings, to discover the activity of such beings in the course of human events, and so on.

If a divine entity, of course, appears to one, or speaks to one, that would do the trick. On the other hand, if a divine entity only seems to appear to one, or only seems to speak to one, that would not do the trick. The problem is to distinguish between these two possibilities.

Evidence is relevant of course; if one prayed to Apollo to win the lottery eighty-nine times in succession and one won the lottery eighty-nine times in succession, something would presumably be going on, unless, perhaps, one were a devotee of the I Hypothesis.

Similarly, if a great being appeared in the sky, with drums and trumpets, and informed the human race that such-and-such was his plan for history that might not be logically conclusive, but it would be worth taking seriously.

In order to give our story a happy ending we shall suppose that Devotee$_1$ wins the heart of Publius, who is willing to overlook her high intelligence, in virtue of an abundance of compensatory properties, and that Devotee$_2$ happily elopes with the Epicurean, who, given his youth, thinks little of imperiling his *ataraxia*.

The upshot of the preceding considerations is that it would be difficult to detect a plan in history, and be sure that one had it right. It would be, so to speak, a subproblem of the more general problem of detecting extranatural intentionality or action in the terrestrial world, a problem just touched on. On the other hand, history is laden with patterns, and without patterns it would be unintelligible. This results in a number of interesting problems for the philosophy of historiography, pattern and nonpattern, actual pattern and apparent pattern, types of patterns, the nature of pattern, the detectability and establishment of pattern, or patterns, and so on.

3. Pattern

1. Prolegomena.

In most of what follows, we will adopt the epistemic stance of naive realism.

Naive realism is the thesis that the nature of reality is as it is perceived. One simply opens one's eyes and there is the world, and it is as one looks upon it. Seeing is a bit like looking out the window and being directly aware of the world outside the window, a world whose properties are its own, and absolute, not relative to an observer. The world is as it seems to be.

To be sure, the "outside world" might be organized in different ways, conceptually. That is compatible with the stance of naive realism.

It was clear even to the skeptics of the ancient world that this hypothesis, that of the direct, incorrigible apprehension of an external reality, was demonstrably false. The conflict of appearances made that clear, for example, the object cannot be both large and small, moving rapidly and moving slowly, round and not round; the lamp cannot be both bright and dim, the room cannot be both hot and cold, and so on. On the assumption that reality is consistent, one realizes then that one is dealing in one's experiences not with reality as it is in itself, but with its appearances, and, further, that this is the nature of experience, that it has at its disposal *only* appearances. The nature of that which produces experience is thus transcendent; other than appearance, and, accordingly, unknowable. Later, scientifically, it becomes clear that experience is internal to the organism, and that it is only topologically related to a hypothesized external reality. Happily the topological relationship, selected for in the course of evolution, is generally reliable, else the hominid would be likely to miss the branch for which he leaps, and the flung spear would be unlikely to make contact with the antelope, or saber-toothed tiger. We are quite capable of seeing what is not in nature, and quite capable, occasionally, of not seeing what is in nature. Illustratively , under post-hypnotic suggestion we may see Aunt Susan in Toledo where she is not, and not see her in Bakersfield, where she is. Similarly the best argument for the existence of Apollo is that many people have seen him; certainly we accept such evidence in the case of Aunt Susan. It has long been recognized that color and sound, and taste, and touch, and smell, as we normally think of these things, are sensibility-dependent, not sensibility-independent, that they are "inner-world actualities," not "outer-world actualities." Supposedly, out there in the conjectured world are very different things, light waves, surfaces which differentially reflect and absorb such waves, concussions in an atmosphere, particles drifting about, and so on. If the physicists are right the world is silent and colorless, and, a while back, mostly empty space, and, lately, it seems, a plenum of fields, or such. It is hard to keep up with physics. Bosons and fermions, or strings, if they exist, may account, in part, for trees and flowers but they are not very treelike or flowerlike. And things become more alarming if one begins to multiply spatial dimensions, and such. In any event, there are clear differences between the experiential world and the supposed actual world.

Now, interestingly, if we are sane, we experience the world, basically, uncritically. We are, in effect, at least in our nonprofessional hours, all naive realists. Naive realism may be an illusion, but it is one of those illusions without which life would be impossible. It has been selected for in the course of evolution. It is only on such a premise that life is doable. In this sort of thing we are one with the raccoon and chimpanzee. Even Immanuel Kant, when he took his constitutionals, attended in the evening to his travel books, and such, we may suppose acted as if the world was nonphenomenal, and space, time, and causality, were part of it; just as we have reason to believe that Hume would shelve his skepticism before essaying a game of backgammon or delighting in a comic novel, or, perhaps, writing English history, turning out some remarkable essays, or doing ethics.

In any event, in what follows, we will, for the most part, ignore certain sophisticated epistemological questions, not because they are unimportant, but because they are largely irrelevant to our enterprise, which is the attempt to produce a detailed philosophical analysis of one of humanity's most valuable and important endeavors, historiography. This methodological bracketing, whereas it is important to be noted in a philosophical endeavor, as we are doing, does not preclude, of course, calling attention to certain aspects of human psychology, pattern selection, pattern imposition, and such, without whose recognition the nature of historiography, and that of several other disciplines, is not likely to be well understood.

2. Pattern Potentiality

•
· •

The human being, as noted, is a pattern-seeking form of life, a property favored in natural selection. He is likely to pattern his existence, and to relate to the world in terms of patterning. To be valuable, these patterns need not be sustained by the natural world, as are the patterns of day and night, the seasons, the solar year, and such.

Many patterns are tolerated, so to speak, by nature, but presumably are not of interest to nature, such as gradations of size, weight, and speed, orderings of colors, sortings as to agility, age, sex, and so on. These are ways of introducing order, system, or pattern, into the world, and are founded in nature, but they are not like the metamorphoses of insects, the annual migrations of ungulates, and such. Other forms of patterning may be, for most practical purposes, imposed on nature, usually innocently. Gestalt psychology has made enormously significant contributions to the psychology of perception, in calling attention to the human penchant to group data and interpret experience in terms of such groupings. At the head of this paragraph occur three dots, which are only three small, black marks on the page, little bits of ink, but most human beings will see the dots as forming a triangle, and other formations as squares, circles, and so on. In a sense, one might think of one's imposing a pattern in such a situation, but, if so, it is certainly one thing to impose "triangle" there, which seems very natural, and quite another to impose "triangle" on the set of dots below.

•
•   •

On the other hand, easily enough, one could see a nice right-angled triangle here, with a long hypotenuse.

Often the imposition of a pattern is scarcely sustained by nature, as in several of the classical constellations, where a handful of stars may be colligated and named for mythological figures, Andromeda,

Cassiopeia, Hercules, Orion, Perseus, and so on. Sometimes these points or nodes are connected in such a way as to suggest a picture. Individuals are not the only thing involved here, but animals, ordinary and extraordinary, Ursa Major and Minor, Leo, Lepus; and then Pegasus, Cetus, Draco, Hydra, and so on; and even ornaments, furniture, and musical instruments, e.g., Ariadne's Crown, Cassiopeia's Chair, and Lyra. One supposes that this sort of star-patterning, if implicit picturing is claimed, is cognitively silly, as any number of pictures might be drawn which would be compatible with the points, or dots, so to speak, to be connected. This sort of thing carries us far beyond triangles and squares. The five stars that constitute the constellation Cassiopeia's Chair one supposes might just as well have been associated with Alexander's horse, Bucephalus, or Henry Ford's First Assembly Line Model T.[60]

Considerations such as these make it clear that there should be some sort of distinction, however difficult in practice it might be to draw, between legitimate and illegitimate patterning.

Two problems which beset the historiographer, but certainly not uniquely, are what we might call the Gestalt problem and the nodal-point problem.

The Gestalt problem is, simply, that the human being seeks patterns, and perceives in terms of patterns. Indeed, if it were not for recollections of similarities, resemblances, ordering habits, and expectations, all aspects of patterning, it is not clear that the human being could perceive at all, let alone perceive coherently. This is not a problem in a general sense, for it is the way in which the human being, and many other animals, is built. It is a problem in the sense that a pattern may be imposed which is not well-supported or justified by the data, or, more dangerously, is selected, but is only one of several possible patterns in terms of which the data might be organized; indeed, strictly, any given set of data can be

---

[60] Astronomers, it might be noted, find that grouping stars into constellations is a way of mapping the sky which works very well, given some supplementation with Greek letters and Arabic numerals. For example, Sirius, the dog star, it seems, is alpha Canis Majoris, or alpha of the "Big Dog," or, for short, "αCMa." Some stars, it seems, are both named and numbered. Two examples are 51 Pegasi and 71 Virginis. Most stars, of course, will not be named. There are something like 10^{11} stars in our own galaxy, and there are, so far detected, something like 10^9 galaxies beyond ours.

organized in an infinite number of ways, is susceptible, in theory, to an infinite number of diverse interpretations, and so on.

Data which supports interpretation A might also be compatible with, and, consequently, also support interpretation B, or C, or D, and so on.

The nodal-point problem involves the selection of the "dots," so to speak, on which the pattern will be anchored. In the case of historiography, the nodal points are usually incidents, actions, happenings, events, that sort of thing. Let us suppose, that we encounter, as is commonly the case in historiography, a complex, flowing, relatively seamless, four-dimensional, multifaceted process which contains a large number of interacting, reciprocally influencing elements, many of which are out of sight and will remain so, even for those contemporaries who are literally a part of the process. The historiographer knows this sort of thing is the case, and he also knows that his access to the case is founded on a usually inadequate residue of evidence, primarily documentary. The incredible challenge he faces then is to try to construct, usually long after the process is over, some sort of account of particular threads in that now-vanished, vast, once-rippling tapestry in motion. We shall also suppose he is a normal human being in many respects, a "child of his time," and a creature with preferences and disinclinations, probably a few prejudices, several of which he is unaware, and passion. He then attempts to relate to this incredibly complex object of inquiry. His account must obviously be a simplification of this object, and so the question is how shall it be simplified. What is important, and unimportant, and what caused this and what caused that, and what means this and what means that, and so on. Also, if he is an adult, he approaches the past with a general "picture of the past" in mind, one obtained from his education, his reading, and such. He expects to find certain sorts of things, and will be looking for them, and what one looks for one often finds. In any event, he is not holding a mirror to history, but regarding it, at least at first, through a pair of personal binoculars, given to him by others, and adjusted in certain ways. No one can write history "*wie es eigenlich gewesen ist*," because, if for no other reason, no one knows the way it really was, or, if they did, which is unlikely, they probably kept it to themselves, misremembered it, or lied. In addition, history is too complex to be dealt with as it really is. Too, one must have one's Gestalt, which is inevitable, and one chooses one's nodal points, as one must. An insightful or creative historian is one who, in theory, perhaps finding himself uneasy or dissatisfied, can essay a new Gestalt or select different nodal points. One gathers few historians, like few physicists, and such, are capable, in virtue of a perhaps unusual imagination, of seeing things as they have never before been seen, or perhaps transforming perceptions, or, in any event, of showing that some new and interesting perceptions are possible. History's truths may all be true, but they are not all the same. And doubtless many remain to be discovered. Some historians, like some physicists, can take a fresh look at something and see in it what was not seen before.

In any event, let us consider the following schematism, in which we find twelve nodal points.

$$A \quad B \quad C \quad D$$

$$E \quad F \quad G \quad H$$

$$I \quad J \quad K \quad L$$

The nodal-points, we shall suppose, are given. Actually, of course, they are not given, but must be selected. We shall also suppose that the nature of these nodal-points is established, which might not be the case, and that, in some provisionally accepted sense, they differ in utility, some good, some bad, some pretty much neither. These assumptions are in place to facilitate a point. On the other hand, I think there is nothing unusual or amiss with such assumptions. I think we can count on most contemporary historiographers to be in substantial agreement in certain respects, for example, morally, to regard slaughter as usually bad, peace as usually good, cures as usually good, disease as usually bad, and so on.

Logically, an infinite number of different curves can join the twelve points in our schematism, or any two points, for that matter. But, for purposes of radical simplification, we shall limit ourselves to four possibilities. The top row of points we shall regard as likely to be approved, the bottom row disapproved, and the middle row as largely axiologically neutral. Also, the columns are ordered chronologically, the time line moving from left to right. The four possibilities we wish to mention here would be the selection of nodal points A, F, and K; that of I, F, and C; that of E, F, G, and H; and, finally, that of I, B, K, and D.

The AFK line would suggest decline; the IFC line would suggest progress; the EFGH line would suggest that things are pretty much remaining the same, and the IBKD line would suggest the possibility of cyclicity.

This is a simplified a schematism, to be sure, but it makes a serious point, namely, that history is complex and, depending on nodal-points selected and their nature, and evaluation, one could make out a variety of different historical patterns, in the schematism, decline, progress, stasis, and cyclicity. Historiographers might very well agree on the nature of each of the nodal points and yet, depending on selection, emphasis, and such, come out with a variety of historiographical interpretations, all of which are supported by the data at one's disposal. Coming to grips with the whole is presumably impossible, and it is not clear that, so to speak, an ABCDEFGHIJKL interpretation is possible, or meaningful. At best it would be uninterpreted reportage or indiscriminate chronicle. Agreement on causal factors is likely to be high; the estimation of the causal weight to be assigned each is less likely to be the subject of consensus; and, even if there were consensus, there is no guarantee that the consensus is correct.

Much in historiography depends on judgment, the accuracy of which can seldom be determined.

3. Pattern Triviality

There are two senses in which pattern is trivial, and unavoidable, logically and, putting aside the I Hypothesis, causally.

Any set of objects or occurrences must, in order to exist, exhibit a pattern of some sort. At the very least spatial and temporal patterns will obtain. Take a handful of confetti and cast it from the roof of a tall building and it will, in its fluttering flight, exhibit a pattern, as it will when it lands, this piece here, that piece there.

Similarly, assuming that events have causes, these events must be causally patterned.

On the other hand, individuals who deny pattern in history, or question it, are well aware that events occur in sequences, in different ways, at different times, and they will commonly suppose, as well, that these events have causes.

Accordingly, when one speaks of the possibility of pattern in history, one must, to exceed triviality, have something weightier in mind, something more important,

4. Relevant Pattern

To count as a pattern in the relevant sense, in the usual sense one has in mind when speaking of "historical pattern," we might recommend that the pattern possess the following five characteristics.

1. Be regular and/or directional.
2. Be large scale.
3. Be long term.
4. Be socially significant.
5. Be historical.

Let us consider these characteristics.

1. It must exhibit regularity and/or directionality. Cyclicity and stasis, for example, exhibit regularity, and progress and decline exhibit directionality.

2. The pattern must be one of large scale. For example, a particular life may well have a pattern, but one would not usually think of this sort of pattern as being historical.

3. The pattern should be not only large scale but long term. A pattern, for example, which was exhibited for a short time only would not normally be considered a historical pattern. It might be of considerable historical importance, but it would not usually be thought of as a historical pattern, but, at best, as an instance of such a pattern. For example, the rise and fall of Hitler's Germany would

not count as a historical pattern. Some might suggest that it could be regarded as an instance of a pattern, say, Caesarism, dictatorship, exploitation, demagoguery, the will to power, or such. Much here would depend on how narrowly or broadly one were willing to understand the notion of pattern. A pattern, of course, need not be continuous. Recurrent, intermittent episodes of similar sorts might count as examples of patterns. For example, if revolutions tend to follow a similar track, beginning with, say, enthusiasm, heroism, and idealism, and then proceeding through a period of excess, turbulence, insecurity, cruelty, and persecution, and then concluding with a reaction into oppression and a harsh reestablishment of rank, order, distance, hierarchy, and such, that could presumably count legitimately as a pattern, despite the lack of continuity which one would normally expect in a historical pattern. The existence of a pattern P need not presuppose a law that P. Patterns might arise from the interaction of several laws, or might not require laws at all, at least in the usual sense of 'law', as in "law of nature." Whereas I think the historiographer, for reasons earlier indicated, would be well advised to adopt a hypothesis of methodological determinism for purposes of explanation, this does not commit him to spending his time looking for specific laws in terms of which to understand specific historical situations. Such laws may very well not exist. Aunt Susan may prefer chocolates to Brussels sprouts but there need be no particular law to account for this, or, at any rate, not one worth looking for.

4. The pattern should be socially significant. This is vague, but one wants to put "importance" or "meaningfulness" into our mix. For example, patterns exhibited in the history of buttons, pretzel knotting, decorative sewing, board and card games, and such, may be extremely interesting and well worth discovering, and a delight to apprehend, but such things would probably not count as socially significant patterns, not comparable at any rate, to the development of animal husbandry, agriculture, art, architecture, armaments, religion, science, communication, technology, popular government, and such.

5. The pattern should be historical.

It is obvious that if something *is* a historical pattern it is historical. That is analytic, or logically trivial, a matter of meanings. On the other hand, what is at issue here is what makes a pattern historical, and, for that to be clear, one must have a sense of what will be involved in "historical." Obviously, whereas all historical patterns are historical, it is not the case that all patterns are historical, and one is trying to propose some sensible understanding here of what might be judiciously counted as making a pattern historical.

The sun rises and sets, the earth has its seasons, the heavens turn, the tides come and go, chemistry and physics, and electromagnetism and gravitation, the strong and weak nuclear forces, and so on, carry on as usual, but this sort of thing is not, *per se*, historical. We can think of it as "natural." A subdivision of the natural would be the biological, and subdivisions of that the botanical and zoological. That maple trees, and raccoons, and human beings go through certain cycles, and such, surely exemplifies patterning, but one does not think of this form of patterning as being particularly historical, though it is presupposed, so to speak, by what is historical. Such things are necessary conditions for the existence of the historical. Such things may enter the historical dimension, too, in ways which may affect it in a particular and unusual manner, for example, as in plagues of locusts, hurricanes, droughts, floods, and such.

A "historical pattern" is understood here as a pattern in human history, namely, a succession in which human beings are numerously and significantly active. It is opposed, for the most part, to patterns which are either simply "intrahuman," biologically human, circulatory, metabolic, and so on, or which are "extrahuman," which would not require human beings for their existence, such as the orbits of comets and the life cycle of stars. Historical pattern would be "interhuman," so to speak, requiring interactions amongst human beings, but not all interhuman relationships would count as historical events, and, *a fortiori*, possible exemplifications of historical pattern. For an event to count as "historical" more is usually required than that it happened in the past; presumably it would be something significant that happened in the past, that had significant consequences. To be sure, opinions as to historical significance might vary from individual to individual. It is hard to quantify such a notion, but such notions appear historiographically essential.

In a broad sense, as noted earlier, one can surely speak of the history of the universe, or of the planet Earth. In the narrower sense, however, that with which we are concerned, one usually thinks of "history" as *human* history. In most "history classes" one would not expect to be dealing with cosmology or geology. For example, let us suppose that some hundreds of millions of years ago the land surface of the earth consisted of a single massive continent, Pangaea. In this narrower sense then, an earthquake in Pangaea which occurred hundreds of millions of years ago would not be thought of as a part of history, part of the past, yes, but of history, no. We do not think of it as a historical event. To be sure, natural events and processes can impact a species and affect its development. Climatic changes which forced an arboreal species to adapt to the ground could be important. Evolution is certainly important.

The type of pattern with which we are particularly concerned then would be a pattern which is regular and/or directional, large scale, long term, socially significant, and *historical*, in the sense suggested.

Hopefully, this characterization, rough as it may be, is clear enough for our purposes. Absolute clarity may be unobtainable outside of, say, numbers, and we do not even know what numbers are.

It might be thought that for us to count a pattern as historical it must also be detectable. Now, presumably, if the pattern is regular and/or directional, large scale, long term, socially significant, and historical, it would be detectable. On the other hand it is quite possible that a pattern might have the five suggested characteristics and, one, not be as yet detected; and, two, might never be detected; and, three, might be undetectable.

5. Varieties of Pattern

There is obviously a difference between a real pattern and an imposed pattern, but, just as obviously, it may be occasionally difficult to assess whether a pattern is real or imposed. The pattern of the seasons is obviously real; a fanciful drawing of Hercules connecting a few stars of diverse magnitudes and distances would seem pretty obviously imposed. This is similar to the distinction in statistics between meaningful correlations and interesting but presumably meaningless correlations. For example, should there exist a high correlation between variations in the earth's magnetic field and the behavior of the stock market that would presumably, rightly or wrongly, be discounted as an accidental, or meaningless; correlation; on the other hand, a correlation between happenings in the world, announcements of earnings and losses, and such, and the stock market might well be less than accidental. Similarly, just as there is a distinction between real pattern and imposed pattern, so, too, there is a distinction between a real pattern which is causally significant and a real pattern which is not causally significant, or does not seem so. Such a pattern, not itself causally active, might, of course, be an accompaniment of a causality.

If we are dealing with patterns which are either real or imposed, significant or nonsignificant, and causal or noncausal, we have eight logical possibilities.

1. Real, significant, and causal.
2. Real, significant, and noncausal.
3. Real, nonsignificant, and causal.
4. Real, nonsignificant, and noncausal.
5. Imposed, significant, and causal.
6. Imposed, significant, and noncausal.
7. Imposed, nonsignificant, and causal.
8. Imposed, nonsignificant, and noncausal.

A "real pattern" will be one objectively ingredient in nature; an "imposed pattern" will be one not objectively ingredient in nature. In some cases the distinction is quite clear, but, in others, less so. In so far as ontogeny recapitulates phylogeny, that is clearly a real pattern, objectively ingredient in nature; presumably, too, spatial and temporal relations are ingredient in nature, though their apprehension and measurement may require conventions and frames of reference; counting does not make Earth the third planet from the sun; what makes it the third planet from the sun is that it is the third planet from the sun, whether anyone is around to do the counting or not. To suppose otherwise is to found reality on language, thinking, counting, and such, which, rather, presuppose reality. Some philosophers claim that if there were no word 'cat' cats would not exist. Perhaps they have something in mind here, but it is unlikely to be of interest to cats. Reality is the quarry of language, not its consequence. We may also count as real patterns those patterns which are either sustained by nature, or tolerated by nature. Examples would be diverse forms of ordering, as in relationships of size. It may be true that a dog is large with respect to a flea, and small with respect to an elephant, but it is clear that in an ordering of size, the flea is smaller than the dog, and the dog smaller than the elephant. That is given in nature, not that nature is much interested in it. Patterns which are not ingredient in nature, but imposed on nature, would be minutes and hours, weeks and months, inches and feet, pints and quarts, longitude and latitude, and such. To be sure, it is hard to be adequately clear about this sort of thing. But knives may be useful, even if not perfectly sharp.

A pattern may be either significant or nonsignificant.

There would seem to be a distinction between "objectively significant" and "subjectively significant," and "generally significant" and "personally significant," but it would be extremely difficult, as would be expected by now, to mark such distinctions clearly. It seems as though one might say, without much fear of contradiction, that the career of Lepidus, a member of the Second Triumvirate, was of less objective significance to the subsequent course of events in Roman history than those of his fellow triumvirs, Antony and Octavian, and that this is not simply a matter of how historians might, subjectively, view things. For example, if the community of historians all happened to think his career was more important than those of Antony and Octavian, that would not make it so, and they would presumably be wrong. Pretty clearly a reality is involved here, but it is hard to see precisely what it is. Presumably it is a matter of causal importance, but this introduces the notion of "importance." If an event would not have occurred if it were not for the occurrence of, say, several hundred thousand antecedent conditions, at least, it would require some selections to pick the important causes from amongst the less important, when all were necessary for the result, and then to proceed further and decide which of the important causes were the most important and the least important, and so on. So much depends on judgment!

Similarly, in dealing with the subjectively significant, one would wish to draw a distinction between what was generally subjectively significant, hopefully related somehow to an objective reality, and what might be more idiosyncratically or personally significant. Many things are personally significant which are not generally significant.

Accordingly, in what follows, for want of anything better to offer, 'significant' will have the sense of "generally regarded as important by qualified observers." It is not clear that any independent, testable sense can be given to the notion of significance outside of this notion of a shared subjectivity. Presumably the shared subjectivity is founded on a reality but the ascertainment of this reality, which may in itself be objectively, presumably causally, important, may be difficult to determine.

Lastly the pattern may be either causal or noncausal. The movement of tectonic plates, resulting in the shifting of continents, the billions of chemical reactions occurring within a single cell, and such, are clearly causal. On the other hand, many orderings in nature, to which we have previously drawn attention, are not causal. Also, there may be relationships which are themselves noncausal, but are the result of a causality. For example, day does not cause night, nor night day, but both are the result of an independent causality, consequent on the rotation of the Earth, the position of the sun, and such.

All cognitive enterprises proceed on the basis of pattern detection or imposition. Indeed, without patterning, it is not clear that human experience, as we usually think of it, would even be possible. Certainly it would not be coherent. Dreams, for example, do not do without patterns; what occasionally gives them an unusual aspect is that patterns may be juxtaposed or interrelated in a surprising fashion, unicorns showing up in the backyard, making the game-winning catch against the wall in Yankee Stadium, and so on. In its way, all of this makes sense, and all of it is comprehensible; were it not, we could not understand the dream, that there was a unicorn in the backyard, that the catch saved the game, and such. For example, if one could think "unicorn-game-wall-winning-backyard-Yankee-catch-Stadium-saved," or such, the pattern, at best, would be meaningless, as most likely would be that resulting from the casting of confetti from the tall building.

Let us now briefly return to the aforementioned eight possibilities with respect to pattern, indexed to the parameters of real vs. imposed, significant vs. nonsignificant, and causal vs. noncausal.

None of the eight possibilities may be ruled out as logically impossible. For example, it is not logically impossible to impose a causal pattern, as in Possibilities 5 and 7 (respectively, "Imposed, significant, and causal," and "Imposed, nonsignificant, and causal"). People frequently impose causal patterns where they do not exist. Indeed, a famous material fallacy is the "Post-hoc-ergo-propter-hoc" fallacy, in which B, because it follows A, is mistakenly understood as an effect of A. For example, an aborigine performs a rain dance and it rains, so it is inferred, naturally enough, I suppose, that performing the dance caused it to rain. Assuming contemporary meteorology is for the most part sound, that would be an example of such a fallacy.

Since a genuine causal pattern should be a real pattern and not an imposed pattern, we eliminate possibilities 5 and 7 (respectively, "Imposed, significant, and causal," and "Imposed, nonsignificant, and causal.") as irrelevant to historiography. This is not to deny that historiography might be interested in looking into the etiology of such mistaken hypotheses.

I think we should also eliminate possibilities 3 and 4 (respectively, "Real, nonsignificant, and causal," and "Real, nonsignificant, and noncausal.") and possibilities 7 and 8 (respectively, "Imposed, nonsignificant, and causal," and "Imposed, nonsignificant, and noncausal.") The general reason for rejecting these four possibilities is that we suppose historiography is interested, at least for the most part, in significant patterns. (Possibility 7, also, has been ruled out earlier, independently, in virtue of the claim of imposed causal pattern.) This is not to deprive the antiquarian, or the historiographer, from an inquiry into nonsignificant patterns, which is up to him, but, mainly, to concern ourselves with the sort of thing which is likely to be of much greater interest to most historiographers. One accepts, of course, that differences of opinion may exist with respect to significance, and also that significance is a context-relevant consideration. For example, a pattern of great importance for understanding what happened last Tuesday in Minneapolis may be nonsignificant from the point of view of American history, or Western history, or world history.

The following five possibilities have now been eliminated.

3. Real, nonsignificant, and causal.
4. Real, nonsignificant, and noncausal.
5. Imposed, significant, and causal.
7. Imposed, nonsignificant, and causal.
8. Imposed, nonsignificant, and noncausal.

That leaves us with three sorts of patterning which might be of considerable interest to the historiographer.

1. Real, significant, and causal.
2. Real, significant, and noncausal.
6. Imposed, significant, and noncausal.

The importance of Possibility 1 goes without saying, and represents, presumably, a desideratum for historiographical explanation. Indeed, it is largely in recognition of this desideratum that we proposed, earlier, a methodological commitment to the D Hypothesis. This is not to suggest that the historian must address himself exclusively to explanation. His work may be of great value descriptively, where strict explanation is obscure or inaccessible, and of great value, too, in illuminating the past, which is not identical with explaining it. For example, an anthology of Medieval poetry, songs, *contes*, and such, may not explain much but it is invaluable in enlivening and deepening a sense of vanished human realities, which, for the most part, are not alien to us.

Possibilities 2 and 6, on the other hand (respectively, "Real, significant, and noncausal," and "Imposed, significant, and noncausal"), despite their enormous importance, are seldom given their due. In the analytic frenzy to make sense of historiographical explanation, the role of real and imposed *noncausal* patternings is often overlooked.

Let us consider Possibility 2, that of "Real, Significant, and Noncausal."

Philosophers, at least in the old days, were supposedly "spectators of all time and existence." Since this is impossible, it seems to follow that there has never been, nor ever will be a philosopher. On the other hand, it does suggest something that is common with philosophers, and others who have a philosophical cast of mind, that they wonder, wisely or not, at least occasionally, about large things, like the universe, space, time, existence, causality, knowledge, truth, meaning, morality, beauty, history, and such.

Without wishing to load any axiological dice, one might distinguish between the "forest historiographer" and the "tree historiographer," or even the "microscopic-bit-of-bark" historiographer. As one can have trees without a forest, but not a forest without trees, we see trees as logically prior to forests. It there are no trees, there is no forest. The forest emerges, so to speak, from trees. I think this gives a certain honor of place to the "tree historiographer," whom one supposes is the typical or paradigm historiographer. On the other hand, personally,. I have never known a "tree historiographer" who did not have some notion of the forest, even if it were to deny that there was a forest. One is seldom drawn to history unless one has a deep mind, a remarkable curiosity, and a long view. Accordingly, all, or most, historians, I suspect, have views about the speculative philosophy of history, or, if one prefers, "macrohistory" or "forest history." I think the views are usually not so much that this sort of thing is wrong-headed or impossible, or unimportant, as that it is very difficult and is seldom, if ever, done well.

Please recall that the type of pattern, in particular, with which we are concerned would be a pattern which is regular and/or directional, large scale, long term, socially significant, and *historical*, in the sense earlier indicated.

In the first possibility, the historical elements interact and produce the pattern directly. Event A influences Event B, and Event B brings about, or influences, Event C, and so on. The closest thing to this in "forest history," or at least the most familiar, would be Marxian historiography, in which one set of vague factors supposedly gives rise to a second set, and so on. In most of the familiar, paradigm macrohistoriographical patterns, on the other hand, we have the second possibility, that of real, significant, but *noncausal* pattern, for example, in Hesiod, St. Augustine, Eusebius of Caesaria, Vico, Hegel, Comte, Spengler, and Toynbee. In thinkers such as the foregoing, one has a *description* of pattern, but not, in particular, an explanation in terms of pattern, though an explanation of pattern *is presupposed*. The pattern itself is noncausal, though it is doubtless caused. The causality is elsewhere, perhaps in the activities of a divine entity in history, in those of a Hegelian *Geist*, or such. Comte's Law of the Three Stages, for example, theological, metaphysical, and positivistic, may be interesting and illuminating, and help one to relate to history, though perhaps not very well, but it is not explanatory; it is descriptive, at best. Similarly, the awesome vision of Spengler is primarily descriptive. We hear about the rise, growth, flourishing, and decline of cultures, one after another, but there is little "in the trenches" historical work to spell this out in detail. Even Toynbee, a historian of amazing energy and erudition, of remarkable imagination and phenomenal scholarship, who certainly does supply the elements of an impressive apparatus for interpretation, and applies it seriously, can do only so much, even in ten volumes. The ultimate historiographical hope presumably lies not with single giants but with the community of laboring historiographers. Meanwhile, possibility 2 has enormous value. That something happens regularly, or seems to happen regularly, is momentous. *Why it happens in that fashion is a different question.* In any event, in possibility-2 historiography, where significant pattern is detected, or is allegedly detected, pattern is *noncausal*. The pattern, in itself, is not causal; *it is caused*. Thus we have paradigm cases of pattern which is real, significant, and noncausal, and patterns which are regular and/or directional, large-scale, long-term, socially significant, and historical. The pattern itself is not causal but emerges from a causality. An analogy would be to the real pattern of day and night, which is not itself causal, but the result of causality. There is no reason why pattern may not emerge from the workings of an extranatural entity in history, should such exist, or inevitably from the intersection of countless causal lines in a D universe, should that be the nature of the universe.

All possibility-2 patterns, of course, need not be so ambitious, large-scale, long-term, and such. Indeed, most are not, and examples are abundant. For example, it seems that many artists, even while supposedly drawing from life, are influenced more by other artists, and their training, than they are by their putative subject matter. For example, to quote a famous example, a drawing "from life" of a rhinoceros may turn out to look more like an earlier artist's drawing of a rhinoceros than a rhinoceros, and so on. How do you learn to paint trees? Do you look at trees, or do you look at paintings of trees? This is supposedly a familiar pattern amongst artists, but the pattern obviously, while doubtless caused, is not itself causal.[61]

In possibility 6 we have imposed pattern which is significant and noncausal. There is nothing untoward or suspicious about this, and a moment's reflection will make clear that this is primarily the sort of thing which is accomplished with a native language. A conceptual structure, significantly but not entirely linguistically conditioned, provides a way of relating to, or "mapping," the "phenomenal grid," or nature. The conceptual structure is not *in* nature, in the way trees and rocks are in nature, but it is in large part indexed *to* nature, otherwise it would be fruitless and useless. For example, the distinction between blue and nonblue, is accepted by nature, tolerated by nature, and sustained by nature, but it is not required by nature. Nature bestows colors. From that point on it is up to us.

Such patterns need not be consciously organized or planned, of course, nor need there be a particular, noted imposer, committee of imposers, or such. Here, again, one has the result of systemic processes in action, gradually, over generations, introducing concepts, eliminating them, modifying them, and so on.

The patterns with which one is concerned here are not only of great importance to historiography, but without them historiography would be impossible as we know it. At best, one might be able to do something with drawings, dances, or such.

Consider the concept of Spenglerian cyclicity. If such cyclicity exists, it is ingredient in history, not imposed, but discovered. On the other hand, its recognition, comprehension, supposition, and articulation presupposes a sophisticated conceptual structure, involving notions of, for example, culture, civilization, biology, and cyclicity. Two steps are involved which may be logically distinguished, however intertwined they may be in practice, those of conceptual structure and the application of conceptual structure. To take a simple, but illuminating, example, there are many places in the world in which villages are ranged serially, intermittently,

---

61 This type of thing is found in the work of the eminent art historian, E. H. Gombrich. (Cf. His *Art and Illusion: A Study in the Psychology of Pictorial Representation* (Bollingen Foundation, New York, 1961)).

along the banks of a long river, say, the Amazon, or Congo river. Let us suppose there are ten villages in question. The individuals in villages 1 and 2 have no difficulty in communicating with one another, and so on for adjacent villages, 2 and 3, and so on. On the other hand, it is somewhat difficult for the individuals of village 1 to understand the individuals of village 3. This sort of thing progresses along the river, and it turns out that the individuals of village 1 cannot begin to understand those of village 10. We would certainly want to say that there are at least two languages spoken along the river. The actual question, however, is how many languages are spoken along the river. Obviously there is no clear right-or-wrong answer to such a question without a workable, applicable distinction between dialects and languages. There is no doubt as to the data; the only problem is how to organize the data in a useful, generalizable fashion. The question as to how many languages are spoken along the river does not have a true/false answer until the conceptual structure for answering it is in place. The data are real; the challenge is to organize it, and relate to it, in a rational manner. Similarly, without an imposed conceptual structure in place it is unlikely that a "historical pattern" question could be raised, let alone answered, positively or negatively. Once the structure is in place, we have a comprehensible, if subtle, empirical question before us, to which evidence is relevant. We have the apparatus in hand for asking ourselves if we are, or are not, dealing with a real pattern, either causal or noncausal.

Whereas these particular "sixth-possibility "pattern questions" are not themselves "historical-pattern questions," namely, not questions dealing with patterns which might be regular and/or directional, large-scale, long-term, socially significant, and historical, they are important to such questions, being logically prior to them.

So we are now concerned with patterns which are imposed, significant, and noncausal. Such patterns are not *in* nature, but, ideally, if all goes well, fruitfully indexed *to* nature. If they are intelligently imposed, well imposed, nature does not object to them; they are consistent with nature; and they are, so to speak, tolerated by nature, accepted by nature, and sustained by nature.

They would constitute more or less successful mappings of nature. Obvious examples would be time lines and spatial grids.

Historiography is rife with such patternings. The very notion of history itself is to organize empirical data in a useful but essentially arbitrary way, to select out and call attention to a particular form of phenomena, other than cosmological, geological, meteorological, physical, chemical, biological, and so on. Two familiar examples of patterning in this fashion are periodization and colligation.

The historical sequence, once it is carved out of the universal process, might be chronologically arranged and tracked in any number of ways. Consider the distinction between ancient, medieval, and modern history. It is doubtful that a Martian, or a mathematician, would independently hit on that sort of arrangement. One need not fault this perspective for its Eurocentric parochialism as that is its point; it is intentionally centered on European history, and its more direct antecedents. It is, of course, then, a narrow chronology, but there is nothing really wrong with narrow chronologies. Surely they have their purposes. More dubiously, ancient history turns out to be several times longer than both medieval and modern history put together. That should surprise our Martian and annoy our mathematician. Similarly, as one learns from history, these divisions are not sharp as the river of history not only flows along, but parts of it do not much flow at all, and other parts flow differently, and at different speeds, within the same time frame. For example, Boccaccio, an essentially Renaissance figure, and Chaucer, an essentially Medieval figure, were contemporaries. One supposes that the historical subject matter, even in the West, might have been organized quite differently, for better or for worse. One does have the division into centuries, of course, which is helpful, but obviously arbitrary. Historically, one might make out paradoxical cases, such as the 19th Century really began in the 18th Century, and the 14th Century did not reach England until the 16th Century, and so on.

Chronologically speaking, the year is too short to map trends well, and the century is too large. Using a chronology founded on, say, twenty-year periods would allow considerably more precision, but one would wish to balance out desiderata, and might be reluctant to sacrifice the simplicity of larger units. The important thing, of course, is to have some sort of consistent chronology, and, hopefully, one which is universally applicable and acceptable, and conveniently manageable. For example, from a strictly chronological viewpoint, there seems little justification in splitting history in two in favor of one religious orientation amongst many, and then, rather arrogantly, starting to count backward and forward from a particular moment. One might have to do this sometime, but, presumably, it would be far handier to go back to some ancient calculable eclipse, or such, which would be, at least, religiously neutral, and, two, would allow one to count rationally forward from a long time back, say, six thousand years or so ago. Before that, those who were still interested in counting backward would be free to do so. One might also note that in the current chronology in general use, there is no year zero, and so there are three years between 2 B.C. and 2 A.D., not four. Also, then, the Millennium began not with the year 2000, but with the year 2001.[62] The decimal system is presumably to be traced back to the usual possession of ten digits on a pair of human hands. If the human hand, accordingly, had had six or seven digits, one might then have a base-twelve or a base-fourteen system, and this would doubtless have been reflected in historiographical chronology.

Colligation, of great importance historiographically, is another example of imposed, significant, noncausal pattern. Colligation, or, so to speak, "bundling," is the unification of a diversity of elements

---

[62] It is interesting to note that according to the New Testament, Jesus was born during the reign of Herod the Great, who died in 4 B.C. Accordingly, Jesus, or Rabbi Yeshua of Nazareth, was presumably born some four to seven years B.C. If one wishes to divide history into two parts for some reason, perhaps some date of momentous significance for all humans, regardless of race, religion, ethnicity, or such, might be suggested; one might, for example, suggest July 20, 1969, the date of the first Lunar Landing. As life on the Earth must, sooner or later, inevitably perish, the human race must become a multiplanet species or die. Accordingly, if we wish a dividing point in history, why not the moment in which a representative of our race, the human race, first crossed space and set foot on a new world? To advocate a rational, neutral calendar is not to disparage the keeping of denominational calendars. There is no reason why Christians, like Jews, and Mohammedans, might not keep their own calendar. But, just as Christians might not wish to adopt, say, a Mohammedan calendar, so, too, it might be recognized that some denominations, similarly, might not view the Christian calendar as an unmixed blessing either.

under a particular theme or concept. When fruitful, this is made possible by affinities or resemblances amongst many elements, constituting cultural congruences. One of the fascinating things about a historical period is how so many of its elements seem to fit together, its music, art, fashions, handwriting, philosophies, literatures, and such, how there is a *Zusammenhang* to it all, how a time is likely to have a particular "appearance," a "style," a "personality," so to speak. A colligation begins with an induction from instances, and then proceeds, if plausible, to found a unifying concept, under which such instances, and later instances, may be subsumed. For example, let us suppose that there is a period in Western history in which a variety of new manuscripts, for the first time in centuries, copies of ancient writings, become available, opening a window to other times, worlds, and possibilities; it is a time in which there is a rediscovery of what are supposed to be ancient glories, a time of repudiating ecclesiastical narrowness, a time of growing secular scholarship. There is a growth of cities, travel, and trade; a flourishing mercantile economy is developing; we begin to have a celebration of the robust, independent, secular individual; there is a new sensitivity to the beauties of the natural world and the multiplex potentialities of human life. *Virtu* becomes important; it is now acceptable to be manly, ambitious, proud, possessive, aggressive; men become less miserable, less penitent, less guilt-ridden, less passive, less obedient, less humble; indeed, one notes, lamentably, here and there, an emerging lack of scruples; worldly success becomes important; there are new directions in business, banking, and finance, new directions in painting, sculpture, and architecture. On the supposition, either, that this represents a rebirth of vanished splendors, tragically lost or suppressed for centuries, or the beginning, after a lapse of more than a millennium, of a newer, freer, healthier, more honest, more innocent civilization, we decide to call this remarkable, fruitful episode in Western history, a Renaissance. With this illuminating, organizing concept in mind, the result of associating and ordering a variety of historical instances, we have at our disposal a colligatory vessel, a library of sorts, a cognitive treasure chest, an intellectual pocket, so to speak, in which not only to place the coins already discovered but in which we may now place additional coins, perhaps short-lived, reactionary, religious revivals bordering on hysteria, like the Bonfire of the Vanities, the cosmetic applications of *bella donna*, designs for poison rings, papal corruption, political assassinations, the career of a Cesare Borgia, the patronage of the Medicis, the writings of a Machiavelli, the painting of Raphael, the sculpture of Michelangelo, the notebooks of Leonardo da Vinci, Neoplatonism, NeoAristotelianism, a revival of Epicureanism, and so on, and on, creating and enriching the concept, which is imposed, significant, and noncausal.

Given the nature of the human mind, not only its pattern-seeking penchants, but its dispositions to induce, simplify, generalize, and such, one notes that colligatory conceptualization is not only endemic and profitable in historiography but essential. There is little danger here unless one is unclear as to what is actually going on and succumbs to one of the most common but often unrecognized of human fallacies, that of reification, treating as objects or things what are not, in actuality, objects or things. The Renaissance, for example, is not well understood as a "thing." The notion of a Renaissance mind is intelligible; a notion such as the mind of the Renaissance is not. The Renaissance, for example, is not a cause; it is a unifying concept; thus, the Renaissance does not change Europe, contribute eventually to religious dissension, indirectly promote toleration, and such. One might talk in this way but one should understand what one is doing. The multitude of causal chains involved may well produce substantial cultural alterations, but those are patterns which are real, significant, and *causal*.

The fallacy of reification is common. It is not unusual to hear of such things as social forces, the spirit of the Age, the needs of the time, the will of the people, historical destiny, and such. Much of what one was attempting to illustrate when speaking of the Renaissance, would do, as well, for the Reformation, the Enlightenment, and such. One hears of the Age of Faith, the Age of Reason, and so on. Sometimes value judgments enter into these things, Golden Ages, Dark Ages, and such. Even the notion of history can be reified, as in what history has proven, what history tells us, the lessons of history, and so on. One might, for example, speak of "Greek history." and then learn one is primarily dealing with the history of Athens and Sparta, and forgetting about dozens of other *poleis*, to be sure, *poleis* about which one may know very little. This would seem a bit like identifying American history with what went on in Los Angeles and New York. No one is suggesting that historiographers should abandon this sort of lexicon, but being more attuned to the distinction between a causal element and a conceptual element might put many historiographical conflicts in a clearer light, such as when did the Renaissance begin, did it represent a sharp break with the Middle Ages, and so on.

Whereas reification is a fallacy, it may, like the fallacy of naive realism, be one which is useful and, properly understood, unobjectionable.

Like the D Hypothesis, which may well be true, it is, at least, a way of getting on with one's work.

It should be noted, in passing, that the fallacy of reification is not committed if one deals with a thing as a thing, understands a thing as a thing, and so on. There are, obviously, different sorts of things. For example, a corporation is a thing, but it is not a thing like a tree or rock, or a taste for chocolate or a negative attitude toward Courtney's poodle. It is not clear that one is reifying if one considers a particular Rome as a kind of thing. It would be reifying if one thought a succession of Romes was, in effect, merely a set of beads strung on a single string, if one were to suppose some unified, single, intangible entity was involved, that there was a single biography involved.

Whereas, for example, a given historical Rome might be understood fruitfully, as something analogous to a corporate entity, it would be a mistake to fail to notice that one such entity, if one accepts this perspective, is not another such entity. The Rome of Tarquin is not that of the early Cato, nor that of the early Cato that of victorious Caesar, nor that of Caesar that of victorious Augustus, nor his that of mad Heliogabalus. $Rome_1$, so to speak, is not $Rome_2$, or $Rome_3$, and so on. This does not mean that "Rome" is in fact no more than a word, or a superficial, contentless verbal construct floating loose in historiographical space, but it does mean that the history of Rome is not well understood as the biography of a single, rather mystical, unascertainable entity, beyond all testability or comprehension. We would tend to see it as a succession of resembling but distinguishable creations rather analogous to a set of corporate entities, but that is only one possible analysis.[63]

It is well to remember, in all this, that what is going on, at least visibly, actually, verifiably, in the final analysis, is always "ground-level" actions and interactions amongst human beings. That is where historical causality resides. Even the "corporate entity" which acts, acts, in the final analysis, by means of its officers, employees, and such. To be sure, for the most part, one cannot hope to deal holistically, or even adequately, with phenomena this complex and pervasive, let alone past and often inaccessible. Thus, one selects, one represents, one summarizes, one invents, one interpolates, and such. One constructs a picture which, hopefully, bears at least some topological relationship to one's object of inquiry.

6. Detectability

The three patterns of primary historiographical interest were possibilities 1, 2, and 6, as follows:

1. Real, significant, and causal.
2. Real, significant, and noncausal.
6. Imposed, significant, and noncausal.

With respect to detectability, possibility 6, that of imposed,

---

[63] This sort of analysis is, I suppose, unfamiliar, and surprising, and is doubtless controversial, and may be injudicious. Surely, too, it is not the only analysis possible. I would hope, of course, that it would be taken seriously. It seems that any unhappy or dissenting individual might legitimately be expected to provide his own lengthy and detailed analysis, prove that it is immune to the several criticisms of rejected, familiar, alternative analyses, that it is somehow, hopefully clearly, superior, and so on. What one hopes for is to come out with a judicious understanding of these matters, regardless of its nature or source. I think the matter is difficult. If anyone thinks the matter is not difficult, I suspect he has not thought much about the matter. The usual jejune, imbecilic evasions that, say, France is a set of "relations," or such, is not so much wrong as that it is intolerably vague. What sort of relations, exactly, and in detail? Too, would anyone really love, or die for, a set of relations? It seems surprising to me that people can go about writing histories of "x" without even worrying about what "x" is, if anything.

significant, and noncausal pattern, presents no problem, obviously, because it is invented and imposed. It may be fruitless, useless, stupid, confused, and obscure, but it is at least detectable.

In possibility 1, we encounter the cardinal sort of pattern with which historiography hopes to deal, that which is real, significant, and causal. Insofar as the historiographer is not a mere journalist, concerned purely with reportage, this is the major focus of his effort, the attempt not only to recount, but to explain, the past. The attempt to analyze and clarify historiographical explanation, its difficulties, and its nature, will be treated in the next major section of this treatise, that dealing with epistemology. Here we content ourselves with noting that the detectability problems here are predominantly historiographical and not philosophical. In possibility 6, detectability problems were nonexistent because imposition was involved. The imposition might be illuminating or not, felicitous or not, but it is surely detectable. It is right there in front of one, so to speak, because it has been put there, right in front of one, so to speak. Detectability problems in connection with possibility-1 patterns, on the other hand, are intricate and enormous, complex and challenging, but, too, they are predominantly historiographical, or scientific, and not philosophical, or conceptual. The detection of real, significant, causal patterns is a scientific inquiry, calling for insight, intelligence, imagination, talent, conjecture, perhaps some luck, judicious hypothesizing, gathering and assessing evidence, and so on. It is a task in which the historiographer is often engaged, and one undertaken without many of the techniques and advantages possessed by his opposite number in a laboratory. As detectability problems relevant to possibility 1 are primarily specific and technical, we will turn our attention to detectability problems relevant to possibility 2, namely, those dealing with real, significant, but noncausal pattern. The problems posed to the historiographer by possibility-2 patterns are more conceptual, or philosophical, as they relate less to identifiable causal lines than to inferences claimed to follow from such lines, or patterns alleged to emerge from such lines.

Our discussion here will be general, but let us first remind ourselves of the diversity and richness of possible patternings of this sort. For the purposes of organizing such patterns one might propose the following schematism:

I. Linear
A. Simple Linear
B. Complex Linear

II. Nonlinear
A. Simple Nonlinear
B. Complex Nonlinear

Obvious simple linear patterns would be given in descent theories, as in Hesiod, or ascent theories, linear progress theories, as seem to have been presupposed by the French Encyclopedists. One might also suppose axiologically neutral or ambiguous simple linear theories, either goal directed or not. Perhaps history is moving toward a homogenized humanity, a Utopian totalitarianism, or even to Courtney's niece's next birthday party. It would be interesting if some divine entity, well disposed toward Courtney's niece, had made that the actual point and meaning of the entire historical process, at least to that date, its literal *raison d'être*. Certainly it is the result of a plethora of antecedent conditions, stretching backward in time several billion years at least. History has led up to quite a few things, and, presumably, will lead up to several more.

Some complex linear patterns would "staircase" theory, based on learning theory, and "jagged line" theory. These are both versions of progress theory. Staircase theory is the notion that there is no actual significant decline, but progress proceeds for a time, and then levels off, or "plateaus," and then begins again. "Jagged line" theory is the notion that there are actual periods of significant decline, but that, on the whole, there is appreciable, measurable progress. One or another of these theories seems common amongst many contemporary intellectuals. Two other illustrations of complex linear pattern would be the optimistic "redemptive" theory and the pessimistic "downfall theory." In "redemptive" theory," which is widely held religiously, the notion is that there was a Fall, say, from Paradise, which is a downward movement, but then, hopefully, there is later a turn-around point from which proceeds an upward movement, at least for some, towards redemption, and a new chance at Paradise, or such. In "downfall" theory the notion is that progress carries a rational species upward, until a technological point is reached at which its native aggression and belligerent ethnocentricities turn inward and destroy its civilization, if not its world's life as a whole. This is one proposed explanation as to why, despite a large number of persuasive statistical arguments for the existence of a universe abundantly populated with forms of rational life, we have not received any unmistakable evidence of, or communications from, such forms of life. Given the nature of many members of our own species and the bloody, conflict-ridden history of our planet, and the various advances in weapons of mass destruction, this hypothesis cannot be casually dismissed by a rational mind.

The two best-known simple nonlinear theories are those of Spengler and Toynbee, both obvious *tours de force* of scholarship, even if there should be disagreements about the quality of the scholarship. In Spengler you have *lawbound* cyclicity. In Toynbee you have *descriptive* cyclicity, with some hope held out for the future. I know of no major modern historiographer or philosopher of history who maintains a simple nonlinear pattern of rises and falls, without much changing over the long run of history, but this seems to have been a fairly commonly held notion in the ancient world. Things come and go, and wax and wane, generals rise and generals fall, and so on, and things stay pretty much the same. "Men go and come, but earth abides." —Ecclesiastes.

The best example of an alleged complex nonlinear theory of history might be that of Giambattista Vico, with his *corsi e recorsi*, who is often thought of as understanding history in what might be figuratively seen as an ascending spiral, or, better, an ascending sinusoidal curve, a directional cyclicity, a progressive cyclicity, or such. One can only push these metaphors so far, but, if one wants to utilize them, I would personally think that Vico might be better thought of in terms of a complex linear pattern, of the sort we referred to as a "jagged line." In any event, the general notion is that there is an overall progression interrupted by occasional regressions, but no successive regression, or decline, descends to the level of its preceding regression, or decline; for example, Decline^n is not as low as Decline^{n-1}, nor as high as Decline^{n+1}.

The usual examples of possibility-2 patterning, those which are real, significant, and noncausal, tend to be ambitious, pertaining to times, cultures, and civilizations as wholes. This is perhaps because philosophers, and philosophical historiographers, classically at least, tended to think in terms of a *Weltanschauung*, a world view, a vision of the way the world is, how it works, and what it means, if anything. On the other hand, questions of real, significant, noncausal patterning come up frequently in less large, or holistic, venues. This, naturally, introduces the concept of pattern pluralism. Whereas holistic pattern pluralism is possible, as in a pattern which obtains for so much time, and is then disrupted, or displaced, or such, one usually thinks of pattern pluralism as pertaining less to, say, cultures as wholes, as to elements or aspects of cultures. This affords the historiographer, or philosopher, a field of inquiry less ambitious than global or cultural patterning, but a field easier to measure and manage, difficult though it might be at times to disconnect it from, so to speak, the surrounding countryside. Some examples of elements or aspects which would seem likely to exhibit real, significant, noncausal patterning would be technology, art, bureaucracy, industrialism, urbanization, the development of a service economy, scientific understanding, democracy, statism, and such. In such areas patterns might be detectable which are various. For example, technology seems to follow an upward linear path; but science itself, on the other hand, might exhibit a pattern of paradigm replacement. It is not clear that much progress is made in art and literature. One still wonders at Renaissance and Dutch masters; reads Dostoyevsky and Tolstoy; doubts that Shakespeare will be lost until his English becomes a foreign language, and so on. Morality presents a different problem. One would like to think that one is beyond Assyrian terrorism, the Roman arena, pyramids of skulls, and such. Then one encounters world wars, the calculated, systematic slaughter of innocents, the leveling of cities and destructions of populations, the rise of state-sanctioned irrationality, bigotry, and fanaticism, the murder of strangers praised as martyrdom, and so on. It seems clear that the blood-drinking, homicidal ape so familiar to history is still amongst us; alive and well.

In passing, it should be noted that pattern identifications may be axiologically neutral or axiologically charged. It has been said that science tells the truth because it has so little temptation to lie. A scientist may be extremely interested in the difference between up quarks and down quarks, or such, assuming such things exist, but he is presumably primarily interested in understanding what is going on, rather than lying about it. Scientists do lie, of course, slant research, manipulate statistics, rig studies, arrange polls, and such, to obtain politically desirable results. Similarly, it is not unknown for them to present plagiarized work as their own, to fudge data, falsify results, perhaps to retain grants, and such, but all that is, in theory, extracurricular for the scientist. It is a betrayal of professional ethics, understandable perhaps, but still a betrayal. Also, he might be caught at it. The mathematician is even more to be trusted. Who has heard, even in confidential, faculty-lounge gossip, of a mathematician who lied about the binomial theorem? There are doubtless domains of inquiry in which axiologically neutral detections of pattern, relative to a given set of objective parameters, are possible. Meteorology would be a likely candidate. One supposes that axiological neutrality would be more difficult to achieve in the social sciences, and certainly in historiography, and, if it were achievable, at least in historiography, which will be later discussed, that the results would be of little interest. Much depends on the cognitivity of value judgments.

Northern and Southern historiographers might agree that the first shots of the Civil War occurred in Charleston, South Carolina, on April 12, 1861, when Confederate forces under General P. G. T. Beauregard opened fired on Fort Sumter. Similarly a good deal of chronology would presumably be shared by historians, and, to a lesser extent, doubtless, several matters of causal interaction. On the other hand, history is very different from the behavior of quarks or numbers, and even from the brightness or dim-wittedness of rats negotiating mazes, the operant conditioning of pigeons, and such. History involves human beings acting in ways that are generally comprehensible to us in pursuit of ends which are seldom unfamiliar. It is meaningless without a notion of choice and every choice involves a value judgment, and the entire point of human action is to achieve meaningful goals. Meaning and values permeate history, and history, as we shall see, is humanly meaningless without them. Were it not for meaning and value history would be as pointless to us as recording events in an ant hill, mechanically noting the comings and goings of small insects, whom we seldom differentiate, whose lives we do not feel, and in which we are likely to have no more than a general entomological interest. One of the great insights of the *Verstehen* historiographers was to recognize this unique aspect of historiography, and to celebrate its pertinence and legitimacy. In historiography, we are, in a sense, learning about us. One does not want to know merely what happened, but how it was understood and felt, what it meant then, and what one can learn from it now. This is why a tiny, illuminating detail can convey as much or more than some explicit generalization, such as the promise by a Southern orator to wipe up with his handkerchief all the blood that would be spilled as a result of the Secession.[64] One commonly reads history not only to learn what took place, but to understand, humanly, what took place. One wants to know not only what happened, and how it may have come about, but what it means. One looks for hints, too, in the history, as to what these things mean to the historiographer, and what he wants them to mean to the reader. Too, what should they mean to us, if anything? In this sense one is likely to read historiography very differently from the way in which one reads, say, physics or biology. This sort of thing is to be more properly dealt with in later sections of this treatise, in particular, those dealing with epistemology, ethics, and aesthetics. It is enough, now, to simply recognize, without comment, that axiologically charged pattern identifications are common in historiography. For example, one man's progress, as noted, may be

---

[64] A detail making clear Southern optimism, and the tendency to underestimate, apparently, the likely consequences of Secession. This failure to anticipate the future broadcast devastation and havoc of the war was seemingly common on both sides. When President Lincoln called for his seventy-five thousand volunteers, they were to be enlisted for only ninety days. (Cf. Bruce Catton, *The Civil War*, (American Heritage Press, Inc., New York, 1985.))

another man's decline; one country's loss may be another country's gain; Carthage's loss is Rome's gain. When Rome falls, is this to be understood as the deserved disintegration of a vast, over-extended, corrupt state, or the tragic downfall of one of the great civilizations of all time, or, in ways, both?

Since our concern here is with possibility-2 patterns, those which are real, significant, and noncausal, one should note that, as one is dealing with *real* pattern, the problem arises as to whether or not the pattern is detectable. It is clear, logically, that such a pattern need not be detected, certainly not at a given time, but, more interestingly, that it might never be detected, and, further, that it might be undetectable, undetectable by human intelligence or perhaps, even, by any finite, limited form of intelligence.

For example, returning to plan possibilities, it is possible that a divine entity might have patterned history in a fashion no human being is equipped to grasp. Similarly, even from a secular point of view, there are probably aspects to reality, *Ur* fundamentals, which are beyond the cognitive capacity of any human being, and perhaps beyond that of any finite, limited intellect. Forms of rational life may exist in the universe which are as far beyond human rationality as human rationality is beyond that of hamsters and house cats. Too, their rationality may take a quite different form, one we cannot even fathom. But certain patterns might be beyond even such intellects. There will always be, too, the basic surd, which is given, and cannot be explained, because it is presupposed by all explanations. So even for such a mind, Haldane's remark might be appropriate: "The universe might not only be queerer than we think, it might be queerer than we can think."

Part Four:
Epistemology

I. Historical Statements

Epistemology, the philosophy of knowledge, deals with a wide range of questions pertaining to such matters as the nature, foundations, limits, and justification of knowledge, too, its units, varieties, levels, and such. In it, as well, one might be concerned with the relation of mind to a putative external world, the ascertainment and analysis of inductive inference, of causality, of explanation, the feasibilies of various skepticisms, and so on. Traditionally, too, questions of meaning and truth are considered epistemological concerns. Many of these topics, of course, interpenetrate other philosophical areas, such as metaphysics, logic, the philosophy of science, and the philosophy of language. The internal borders of philosophy are no better defined than her external borders. This porosity is one of her charms. Philosophers, too, profitably and unapologetically, raid such fields as those of science, art, anthropology, sociology, law, literature, and history for whatever grains may prove grist for their mills. As one of the classical endeavors of philosophy is the construction of a *Weltanschauung*, it stands to reason that her cartographical expeditions, analyses, and hypotheses will be diverse and widely ranging. In what follows, we will be dealing with a small, but hopefully illustrative, set of epistemological problems encountered in historiography.

From an outsider's point of view there is a great deal of confusion in historiography, and it seems quite clear that one can be a fine historian without paying much attention to what one is talking about. We noted the ease with which one can write about nations without a theory of what a nation is, and how one can confuse causal with conceptual elements, as in "Renaissance," and so on. There seem to be "ways of talking" which are uncritically accepted, and on the basis of which one just moves ahead, "felicitously doing one's thing." I do not think this casualness vitiates or undermines the historiographical enterprise, but it does cause uneasiness, once noticed. It is probably best not to notice, but once something is noticed, it is hard to unnotice it. Everyone is guilty of this sort of thing, naturally, and it is probably necessary, to get on with life. For example, how much do most people worry about minds and selves, what one can know or not know, and how can one be sure of it, or can one be sure of it, the reality or nonreality of a future, the truth value of future-referring statements, and such? My guess is, not many. And that is probably to the good. To alter a remark from Wittgenstein, one can talk intelligently about plants without knowing what a plant is. I think that is true. On the other hand, it might be nice to know what one is talking about.

Accordingly, an obvious place to begin our epistemological inquiry would be with the "historical statement." What is a historical statement? We shall attempt to develop a theory of historical statements. This would seem pretty basic. On the other hand, as far as I know, this has not been done before.

Please consider the following table:

One is concerned here with statements or propositions, and three principles, those of logical negation, significant negation, and "historical negation." 'T' and 'F' stand for 'True' and 'False'. 'Signif' stands for 'Significant'. 'Hist' stands for 'Historical' '~' signifies negation.

Principle of:

Logical Negation		Significant Negation		Historical Negation	
p	~ p	p	~ p	p	~ p
T	F	Signif	Signif	Hist	Hist
F	T	~ Signif	~ Signif	~ Hist	~ Hist
'p' is true if and only if '~ p' is false.		'p' is significant if and only if '~ p' is significant.		'p' is historical if and only if '~ p' is historical.	

Logically, a statement, or proposition, is true if and only if its negation is false. In short, if 'p' is true then '~ p' must be false, and vice-versa. This presupposes there are only two truth values, the true and the false. "False," it will be noted, counts as a truth value. This is a bit like claiming that there are two false values, one of which is true, but that is not to be noticed. Now there are multivalued logics, in which a proposition may have three or more, even an infinite number of, truth values, but the classical logic is a two-valued logic, with the true and false. This is a matter of definition, not one of looking closely at the world. From this definition it follows that the number of true and false statements is the same, which seems a remarkable coincidence, until one realizes that every statement has a negation, and, if the statement is true, the negation is false, and vice versa. Logic, in this sense, is like mathematics, living in its own world of Platonic comfort. As soon as one tries to map logic onto the world the troubles begin. Yet, logic will triumph. Consider the question as to whether or not Jones is bald.

Bald _____x_____ Not Bald

We shall suppose that if Jones is well toward the left on above line we will call him bald, with confidence, and if he is well toward the right we will, with equal confidence, deny that he is bald. Jones, however, is rather in the middle, where reality often resides. We do not wish to say he is both bald and not bald, as that generates a contradiction. Similarly, but perhaps less easily noted, to claim he is neither bald or not bald, generates the same contradiction.[65] At this point, one might be attracted by the notion of multiplying truth values. For example, if one were to divide the line into three segments, and then, instead of having two truth values, the true and false, having three values, say, 1, 2, and 3, this would solve the Jones problem, as Jones would fall in the middle of value 2, and "Jones is 2" would be true and 'Jones is either 1 or 3' would be false. This

---

65 Understanding 'Bx' as 'x is bald' and taking 'j' to stand for Jones, the contradiction would be 'Bj & ~ Bj'. Using the same apparatus, 'it is not the case that Jones is either bald or not bald' might be formalized as '~ (Bj v ~ Bj)', which, by a De Morgan Transformation, gives us '~ Bj & ~ ~ Bj', which will return us, shortly, following double negation and commutation, to the original contradiction, 'Bj & ~ Bj'.

reintroduces 'true' and 'false', but innocently, as one is now on a higher level, a metalevel. This victory, however, saves one day, but not another, for now we have substituted for the problem of "excluded middle" the new problem of "excluded in-betweens." Obviously the same difficulties we encountered originally would recur with respect to the borderline between 1 and 2, and the borderline between 2 and 3. We would not have solved our problems, but doubled them. As we do not wish to discard logic altogether, we resolve to save the law of excluded middle, and the distinction between the true and false. This means we could be driven to such lengths as specifying how many hairs are required to count as not being bald, the height and condition of such hairs, whether they need to protrude from the surface of the scalp, and how far, whether we wish to count a dried-up follicle as a hair, and so on. How far does one go? The answer is simple. We keep going until it is clear that Jones is bald or not bald. It is true that the laws of logic hold in the universe, but there is a simple reason for that. We see to it that they do.

The principle of significant negation is the claim that 'p' and '~ p' must either be both significant or both not significant. There is a simple and obvious reason for that as the content of 'p' and '~ p' is identical. It is merely the case that in 'p' the content is affirmed, and in '~ p' the content is denied. Some logicians used to use an affirmation sign before 'p' to signify its affirmation. Today that is seldom, if ever, done. It is supposed that 'p''s affirmation will be taken for granted. A disadvantage of this almost universal practice is that it leaves us with no way of representing the content of 'p' independent of its affirmation or denial. It should be noted that the principle of significant negation has epistemic consequences with respect to considerations of confirmation and disconfirmation. A statement which lacks falsification conditions is either analytic or empirically meaningless. For example, an Egyptian priest might claim that whatever happens is in accord with the will of Amon-Ra. On the other hand, if there is nothing he will accept as evidence that something or other was not in accord with the will of Amon-Ra, then his statement lacks falsification conditions, and is, accordingly, analytic or empirically meaningless. This is not to deny that such locutions may be religiously, inspirationally, or emotionally meaningful. Similarly, as far as logic goes, everything might be in accord with the will of Amon-Ra, and Amon-Ra knows it. The problem is just that it is *empirically* meaningless, namely, as far as we can tell, *Unsinn*, nonsense.

Analogous to the principles of logical negation and significant negation, I would like to introduce what we may call the principle historical negation. The substance of this principle is that a statement will count as historical if and only if its negation also counts as historical. This seems like an innocent and obvious supposition, and worth making a matter of definition. It will have, however, as we will note, some surprising and counterintuitive consequences.

Before attempting to develop a theory of historical statements, it is important to recognize, in general, certain logistic aspects which must appertain to almost any such theory. Let us take 'N' as a naturalistic statement, for example, 'Objects near the surface of the Earth fall at $\frac{1}{2}gt^2$', 'Turtles are oviparous', or such, and take 'H' as a historical statement, namely, one of the sort to be later characterized as historical.

Consider the following formula:

$$H \rightarrow N$$

In such a formula, if it is true, 'H' is a sufficient condition for 'N', namely, if 'H' is true, then 'N' is true. And 'N' is a necessary condition for 'H', namely, if 'N' is false, then 'H' is false. The opposite does not obtain. For example, 'H' is not a necessary condition for 'N' and 'N' is not a sufficient condition for 'H'. This is very general, but what we mean to convey is, so to speak, that history presupposes nature, but nature does not presuppose history. For example, one might have nature without history, but one could not have history without nature. History is a sufficient condition for the existence of nature, and nature is a necessary condition for the existence of history. Speaking loosely, history implies nature, but nature does not imply history. Thus, nature is logically prior to history. The '$\rightarrow$' in the above formula is best interpreted as logical entailment.[66]

In the sense of logical entailment it seems clear that natural

---

[66] If the D Hypothesis is true then, in a sense, history does not exist. Everything would be an aspect of nature, and the rolling of a stone down an incline would not, in essence, be different from the fall of the Roman empire. Every state of the system would be nomologically implicated, or implicated in virtue of natural law, with every other state of the system. On the other hand, one would usually distinguish, even in such a case, amongst, say, mathematical statements, geological statements, biological statements, and so on.

statements could not imply historical statements. This will turn out, however, not to be the case, but for reasons which may impress some as less than satisfying. First, let us note that historical statements, however we interpret them, must be contingent statements, namely, statements whose truth value does not depend on their meaning alone. For example, if we take 'Rc' to mean 'Caesar is a Roman', that would presumably count as a paradigm example of what one would wish to count as a historical statement. On the other hand, 'Rc & ~ Rc' ('Caesar is a Roman and it is not the case that Caesar is a Roman'), a contradiction, and 'Rc v ~ Rc' ('Caesar is a Roman or it is not the case that Caesar is a Roman'), an analytic statement, would not count as historical statements, as their truth values are functions of their meaning alone. Logically, a contradiction implies all statements whatsoever, and, logically, an analytic statement is logically implied by all statements whatsoever.[67] If one were to allow contradictions and analytic statements to count as historical statements, then, since all contradictions are logically equivalent and all analytic statements are logically equivalent, then some historical statements would be logically equivalent to nonhistorical statements, and that is injudicious. For example, 'Rc & ~ Rc' and 'Rc v ~ Rc' would be logically equivalent, respectively, to 'Some swans are not birds' and 'All swans are birds'.

The next point which should be made is that N statements, surprisingly, can imply H statements.

For example:
    1. N
    2. N v H 1, Logical Addition

Presumably, 'N v H' is a historical statement. On the other hand, if we do not care for this, let us suppose that we rule that it is *not* a historical statement. Then, however, one faces the following argument:
    1. ~ N
    2. N v H (ruled *not* a historical statement)
    3.   H 1, 2, Disjunctive Syllogism

Thus, N statements can imply H statements.

---

67 This can be shown in a number of ways, but, perhaps most simply, it follows from the definition of entailment itself, which is that 'p' entails 'q' if and only if it is logically impossible for 'p' to be true and 'q' false. Accordingly, if it is logically impossible for 'p' to be true, then it is logically impossible for 'p' to be true and 'q' false. Similarly, if it is logically impossible for 'q' to be false, then it is logically impossible for 'p' to be true and 'q' false.

An even simpler example would be as follows.
1. N & H
2. H   1, Simplification.

Let us suppose, however, not caring for this, that we rule that 'N & H' is a historical statement, and thus that we are merely deriving a historical statement from another historical statement. Then one would have the following difficulty to contend with.
1. ~ N   (Clearly a nonhistorical statement.)
2. ~ N v ~ H   1, by logical addition.
3. ~ (N & H)   2, De Morgan Transformation.

Here, from '~ N', clearly a nonhistorical statement, one has derived the negation of 'N & H' earlier ruled a historical statement. Since, given the principle of historical negation, the negation of a historical statement must also be a historical statement, we have, again, derived a historical statement from a nonhistorical statement.[68]

Presumably not all statements are historical statements. For example, the following statements would not be regarded as historical statements.

2 + 2 = 4.
2 + 2 = 5.
Objects near the surface of the Earth fall at $\frac{1}{2}gt^2$.
A molecule of water consists of two atoms of hydrogen and one of oxygen.
Water assuages thirst.

---

[68] An interesting observation here is that an infinite number of statements containing N components are logically equivalent to any given H statement. It is, of course, a truism that any statement logically equivalent to an H statement must itself be an H statement. Accordingly, there are an infinite number of statements with N components which are H statements. A brief sampling of such statements would be: H v (H & N), H v (N & ~ N), H & (N v ~ N), (H & N) v (H & ~ N),
(H v N) & (H v ~ N), (~ H ⊃ N) & (~ H ⊃ ~ N), ~ H ⊃ (H & N), ~ (H & N) ⊃ H, ~ H ⊃ (N & ~ N),
~ (N & ~ N) ⊃ H, (N v ~ N) ⊃ H, (N ⊃ H) & (~ N ⊃ H), and so on. *Mutatis mutandis*, there would be an infinite number of N statements containing H components, and thus an infinite number of statements containing H statements which would be logically equivalent to any given N statement, and thus, being logically equivalent to N statements, would be N statements.

Fire burns.
Lions are carnivorous.
Turtles are oviparous, etc.

In the following assume that 'Rx' is read as 'x is Roman', 'Ix' as 'x is Irish', and that the individual constant 'c' has for its value Caesar.

We might then have the following four statements.
1. Rc (Caesar is Roman.)
2. ~ Rc (It is not the case that Caesar is Roman.)
3. Ic (Caesar is Irish.)
4. ~ Ic (It is not the case that Caesar is Irish.)

Clearly, statements 1 and 4 are true, and statements 2 and 3 are false. Given the principle of historical negation, a statement and its negation must either be both historical, or neither historical. Clearly statement 1 is a paradigm case of a historical statement. One would be surprised to hear it denied but one could conceive of a historian presenting evidence in favor of statement 2. For example, Gaius Cilnius Maecenas, a valued advisor to Augustus Caesar, whose name currently tends to be taken as synonym for a wealthy and benevolent patron of artists, is commonly taken to be a Roman, at least by most nonhistorians who have heard of him, but it turns out he was an Etruscan, in a time in which one usually thought of Etruria being much in the past. Whereas it is certainly unlikely that Caesar was not a Roman, one could conceive of evidence being found to support that contention. It is not impossible, for example, that a dictator in one country might have had his origins elsewhere, in, say, Austria. In any event, what we need here is merely that '~ Rc' be counted as a historical statement. It will be so counted in the light of the principle of historical negation. If 'Rc' is a historical statement so, too, must be '~ Rc'. And, presumably, if 'Caesar is Roman' counts as a historical statement, so, too, must 'Caesar is Irish', 'Caesar is Polish', and so on. Certainly 'It is not the case that Caesar is Irish' is true, and it is surely a historical statement if 'Caesar is Roman' is a historical statement. Given the principle of historical negation then, we must count its negation, namely, 'Caesar is Irish', as a historical statement. It follows that all four statements above are historical statements.

Two points are worth emphasizing.

First, we are concerned with developing a general theory of historical statements, not trying to limit the discussion to matters which are currently of interest to, or controversial amongst, historians.

If someone is unhappy with counting 'Caesar is Irish' as a historical statement, then it seems he should also be unwilling to count 'It is not the case that Caesar is Irish' as a historical statement, and make clear why he rejects that statement as historical, which is obviously true and pertains to history. He should be consistent, at least. Surely his criterion for a historical statement ought to be clear and general; it should not be occasional, private, specific, undisclosed, sporadic, intermittent, or arbitrary; it should have something better to offer than idiosyncratic whimsy.

Second, one must be careful to allow for falsity amongst historical statements. Historical statements are not to be limited to true statements about history. First, this would make it analytic that all historical statements are true, which is absurd, and, even if it didn't alarm the principles of logical and significant negation, would have the consequence that many historians much of the time would not even know if they were uttering historical statements or not. Too, it seems one should allow for the possibility of a historian being wrong, namely, uttering a statement about history, a historical statement, which is mistaken.

One might define a historical statement as a statement about history which is true, but trivializing the matter in that fashion not only secures no advantage, but would necessitate casting about for a new name or category in terms of which to identify what used to be taken as historical statements regardless of truth value. It would be like defining poodles as even-tempered, brave, and noble, and then discovering that there were not as many poodles about as one had thought.

Few historians are going to be actively concerned with the possibility that Caesar might be Irish, but, if they are interested in a theory of historical statements, the consideration of such locutions, implausible or surprising as they may be, is imperative. One cannot develop a general theory by limiting it either to what historians actively worry about, either now or in the past, or, worse, to statements which are true.

One initial entry into the attempt to develop a theory of historical statements would be to identify such statements with statements about the past.

This, rather clearly, is too broad.

Consider the following statements:

> $2 + 2 = 4$ yesterday.
> $2 + 2 = 5$ yesterday.
> Turtles laid eggs 10,000 years ago.
> In 1054 a supernova occurred.
> The sun orbited the Earth in the time of Ashurbanipal.
> The Earth orbited the sun in the time of Ashurbanipal.
> Bill blinked one second ago, etc.

The above statements all pertain to the past but one is unlikely to see them as historical. The main reason, presumably, is because they do not deal in any interesting or important manner with human beings and their interactions. Recall, that we are dealing with a somewhat specialized sense of 'history', not the broader sense of history, as in the history of the universe, of the solar system, of the planet Earth, of the rise of life forms, and such. Our concerns are with interhuman realities, not intrahuman realities, such as metabolism, and cell division, or extrahuman realities, such as the composition of distant stars, the deposition of sediments in Alpine lake beds, and such.

We may dismiss the two mathematical statements as, if not extrahuman altogether, timeless, or, if one likes, truths which hold for all time, yesterday, today, and so on. "$2 + 2 = 4$" is not an event; it is not caused by "$(1 +1) + (1 + 1) = 4$," or such. It is outside the causal nexus. A historical statement must, at least, have reference to a causal nexus. Recall that a methodological presupposition of the D Hypothesis was recommended, and that the I Hypothesis was ruled out as historiographically unintelligible, useless, and arbitrary, and certainly so where particular cases or individual events were concerned.

The statement pertaining to the oviparous nature of turtles is zoological, and essentially extrahuman.

The statement about the supernova, despite the specific reference to historical time, is astronomical, and not historical. On the other hand, 'The supernova of 1054 was noted by Chinese astronomers' would count as a historical statement. This "guest star" doubtless caused quite a stir in the Chinese society of the time, a time when the sky was thought filled with portents.[69]

Ashurbanipal is a historical figure, and was the last major ruler of the Assyrian empire, which collapsed something like a generation after his death. The two statements pertaining to Earth/Sun relations, however, are not likely to be considered historical even though involved in the causal nexus and including an essential reference to a particular historical figure. This would mostly be due, one supposes, to the fact that the major subject matter is extrahuman, and the reference to Ashurbanipal, while essential to the meaning of the statement, is irrelevant to the naturalistic periodicities involved. Ashurbanipal may need the sun, but the sun does not need Ashurbanipal.

The statement about Bill might be rejected for a number of reasons, some good, some bad. I have included it here because it is a necessary condition for a historical statement that it pertains to the past, and this means one must have some sense of what is to count as the past. This question is much like, and is related to, the length of the present, which we considered earlier. We noted that such a question is absurd unless one presupposes a unit, and, as soon as the unit is posed, that is exactly how long the present is. One cannot, rationally, ask such a question and then refuse to answer it by constantly changing units, endlessly shifting to a theoretically infinite succession of ever-smaller units. If the unit of measurement chosen for the present is the minute, then that is how long the present is, one minute long; if the unit is an hour, then that is how long the present is, and so on. In dealing with the historical present the same principle holds, but one would expect, and discover, that

---

[69] This was apparently quite a remarkable event, as the light was visible for days, even at noon; it was the result of the explosion of a star of such magnitude that its remains now constitute the Crab Nebula. It is difficult to comprehend the amount of material involved and the force of such an explosion.

the unit here might differ from historian to historian, and from context to context. In the sense of present times, or present-day fashions, and such, the present would normally be taken as rather lengthy. An ancient historian might regard the "present" as being a century or more in length. A historian of contemporary life would presumably regard the historical present as much shorter. A journalist might think of the current day as the present, and yesterday's events as the past. I am supposing that 'Bill blinked a second ago' would not count as a historical statement, as it occurs in the historical present. Not every past event counts as an event in the historical past.[70]

In attempting to work out a theory of historical statements one is essentially engaging in a process of explication. There is no true/false answer, but there are presumably better/worse answers, and one is looking for a good answer. Incidentally, that some answers are better than others shows that some value judgments have truth values, or that, since some people think some answers are better than others, that some people think that some value judgments have truth values. If one does not share this view, then, from his point of view, it is not the case that one answer is better than another, for example, that the answer "four" is not a better answer to the question "How much is 2 + 2?" than "five," or "nine." Similarly, in answer to a question as to the quickest way to get from Chicago to Los Angeles, as no answer is better than another, he should remain uncommitted between a number of proposals, say, jet airplane, horse-and-buggy, ox cart, hiking, and such.

An explication is neither true nor false, but is a proposal. If the proposal is accepted, then truth and falsity fall into place. Remember the river, and the villages. Once a proposal, or explication, for the difference between a language and a dialect is accepted, it then

---

[70] Consider the temporal interval between cause and effect. For example, starlight may have taken thousands of years to reach the Earth. Thus we are now seeing what happened long ago. The star may have burned out or gone nova, and no longer exist. But, in a sense, one always sees and hears not what is happening, but what has happened. Let us suppose you hear and see a friend who speaks to you. A time interval is involved, though much shorter, just as in the case of the light of stars. There is a speed of sound, and a speed of light. Hearing and seeing takes time. One hears now what was said in the past; one sees now what happened in the past. We may be in the present, but, in a sense, we live in the past.

becomes an empirical question, with a true/false answer, as to how many languages are spoken along the river.

In undertaking an explication one begins with one's presuppositions, and intuitions, and some awareness of practice. An explication is not a report on usage, but it must take usage into consideration. If it does not, it risks irrelevancy. On the other hand, usage cannot be the ultimate arbiter; if there was no difficulty, obscurity, inconsistency, or confusion in usage, an explication would be pointless. An explication, then, is likely to accept given elements, in particular, those which are fit and useful, add some new elements, delete some old elements, and perhaps modify others. It is a "reforming definition" or "reforming characterization." A good explication introduces order into disorder; replaces obscurity and confusion with clarity; should cover what it is important to cover, and should be as simple as is compatible with adequacy. It should also illuminate a subject matter. One does not expect, of course, that the explication which is underway here, the attempt to develop a theory of historical statements, will be altogether successful. It is, however, doing what has not been done before, and calling attention to a problem, if nothing else. In any event, these are interesting and uncharted philosophical waters.

You may recall that we have considered two lists of representative statements. Let us refer to these lists as List A and List C. In each list we placed some statements which we supposed would not be well regarded as historical.

List A:
2 + 2 = 4.
2 + 2 = 5.
Objects near the surface of the Earth fall at $\frac{1}{2}gt^2$.
A molecule of water consists of two atoms of hydrogen and one of oxygen.
Water assuages thirst.
Fire burns.
Lions are carnivorous.
Turtles are oviparous, etc.

List C:
2 + 2 = 4 yesterday.
2 + 2 = 5 yesterday.
Turtles laid eggs 10,000 years ago.
In 1054 a supernova occurred.
The sun orbited the Earth in the time of Ashurbanipal.
The Earth orbited the sun in the time of Ashurbanipal.
Bill blinked one second ago, etc.

The point of List A was to call attention to a number of statements of a sort which would not, presumably, be regarded as historical statements. None referred essentially to the past. A historical statement must be a past-referring statement. The point of List C was to call attention to the fact that not all past-referring statements are well regarded as historical statements.

It is now time to consider a third list, which we will call List B. List B, not surprisingly, we place between Lists A and C, whose entries, we suppose, were relatively uncontroversial. The test of an explication, of course, is its utility in deciding difficult cases. Too, it is the hard cases, the unusual cases, the borderline cases, and such, which not only challenge an explication, but are often useful in its clarification and refinement. There is an obvious analogy here to the development of the law, which proceeds not simply in virtue of enacted laws and statutes, but in virtue of the rulings of judges in particular cases. It is not always an arrogance, vice, or crime for judges to legislate from the bench; often, they must.[71]

List B:
1. Caesar was born.
2. Someone was born.

---

[71] Bureaucrats must often, as well, given the porosity of law, legislate from their offices. Actual legislation may provide little more than pompous guidelines, and largely blank checks for the bench and office to fill in as best they can. The notion that a country is essentially at the mercy of its judges and bureaucrats is not a total fantasy. Many judges are unelected, unaccountable, and irremovable; and many bureaucrats are, for most practical purposes, the same. Hopefully this relative immunity to replacement will foster dedication, objectivity, and integrity, reducing the necessity to trim one's sails to the prevailing political winds. Trade-offs, in any event, not only exist, but abound.

3. Donald Trump was born five hundred years ago.
4. The world was created 5 minutes ago, bearing within it all the signs of age.
5. The Athenians will win the sea fight tomorrow.
6. Khnum is the god of the first cataract of the Nile.
7. Plotinus merged with the One.
8. Elam was southeast of Babylonia.
9. The Thirteenth Century did not exist.
10. The Claude Glass was invented in the 18th Century.
11. If the legions of Varus had not been annihilated in the Teutoburg Forest in A.D. 9, and Rome had civilized and pacified the barbarian tribes north of the Rhine, the Roman Empire might not have fallen, World War I might not have taken place, and there would have been no rise of Hitler and Nazism.
12. Parrhasios was a better representational painter than Zeuxis.
13. Parrhasios was a better painter than Zeuxis.
14. The Roman *ludi* were morally justified.
15. The sins of the emperor brought about a wide-spread drought in the land.

The fifteen locutions in List B raise fifteen problems, out of a number which might be indefinitely large. On the other hand, one is supposing that most of the serious challenges to a theory of historical statements would be implicit in such a list. In the first exploratory journey into a new country it is likely that a river or mountain may be missed, here and there. Before considering the list one should make seven assumptions clear. First, a historical statement, as any other statement, must have a truth value. Second, this truth value must not be a consequence of its meaning alone, i.e., the statement must be neither analytic nor inconsistent, for reasons already specified. Thirdly, the truth value need not be known. Fourthly, the truth value need never be known, and may forever remain unknown. Fifthly, the truth value must be knowable in theory, namely, one must know under what conditions it would be found true or false. Sixthly, the conditions must be empirical conditions. For example, it is not clear under what conditions a locution such as 'Khnum, the god of the first cataract of the Nile, disapproved of Seti I' would be true or false. That we would be well advised to leave up to Khnum and Seti I. One could certainly imagine stories, and such, in which, say, Osiris might bring something to the attention of Horus, privately, out of the hearing of Isis, and so on, but this sort of thing, even if attested to by a college of Egyptian priests, would not be likely to be counted as historical statements. That the priests might attest to such things might form a subject matter for historical statements. Seventhly, the statement must be a past-referring statement. Interestingly, whether a statement is past-, present-, or future-referring can depend on its expression-occasion, when it is uttered, or such. Too, whether a statement is present-referring or past-referring could depend on the selected present, say, on when one begins the present, for example, a year ago, an hour ago, a microsecond ago, and so on. Much depends on context. One would not wish to have a theory in which any statement other than a future-referring statement would count as a past-referring statement, because, say, the past has begun before it could even be uttered.

So let us now turn our attention to List B. In doing so, two phases are involved, the first in which one consults one's linguistic intuitions, framed and conditioned by a background and approach, as they must be, and the second, in which one attempts to introduce some order and consistency into these intuitions, and perhaps revise them in *media res*, as one attempts to devise a theory which is reasonably precise, clear, simple, and adequate.

1. Caesar was born.

This might be regarded as a biological event, and, thus, not historical, any more than the birth of a raccoon, or such. It might be thought that what makes Caesar a historical figure is not being born, but his subsequent life and achievements. This is doubtless true but the question here is not whether Caesar was a historical figure at birth, as might have been a king's son, but whether or not the statement is a historical statement. It seems it is a historical statement, certainly in view of his later life and career. It is interesting to note, in passing, that his mother apparently shared certain views of the time, had high hopes for him, and wished him to be born on an auspicious day, and so made sure of it, having her womb opened on the day in question, from which action we have the concept of a Caesarian birth. One supposes it might have been better for the Republic, if he had turned out to be a girl.

2. Someone was born.

By existential generalization 'Caesar was born' logically implies 'Someone was born'. On the other hand, it also implies 'If Pompey was Polish, then Caesar was born', 'If Caesar was not born, then Pompey was Polish', and an infinite number of other statements, as every premise-set logically implies an infinite number of other statements. Both statement one and statement two would, as we are understanding the concept, count as "interpersonal," as an implicit reference to human interaction and societal relations would seem implicit. In this broad sense, an account of Robinson Crusoe's adventures would count as interpersonal, even before the arrival of Friday. Similarly, he arrived on a foundering ship, keeps a calendar, and so on. This goes well beyond the "intrahuman" and the "extrahuman." On the other hand, 'Someone was born' would not be counted as a historical statement, at least in most contexts, because of its lack of specificity. It is clear it is empirically meaningful, and we have a good idea as to what would confirm it, but what would be its falsification conditions, other than the fact that no births whatsoever occurred, that nothing was born, or such, which is clear enough, but calls attention to the lack of information supplied by the statement. There may certainly be historical statements which are very general, such as 'Cultures rise and fall', but something like 'Things rise and fall' is too general to be acceptable. Similarly, one expects a historical statement, even a general one, to presuppose a chronology, and 'Someone is born' is achronic; there is no place for it on a historical time line. Historical statements must be anchored in a chronology. Something like 'After the massacres putting an end to the misunderstandings wrought by the great schism, Marshal Amlik arranged to have himself appointed high satrap of the Poonian Martians in the provincial capital city of Poonli in the third year of the reign of Sios Malepius, the Orthodox and Devout, monarch of all the Martians' might well count as a historical statement on Mars, but would not count as one on Earth, as it lacks insertability in a familiar chronology.

Chronological problems often assault the terrestrial historiographer, but he, at least, has a chronology into which to try to place archon lists, old Kingdom dynasties, and such.

3. Donald Trump was born five hundred years ago.

This statement has its unusual aspects, but one supposes it should be counted as a historical statement, as it pertains to the past, deals with an important person, and so on. It is obviously false, but one may not claim truth as a necessary condition for a historical statement. To rule statements of this sort out would seem to narrow and subjectivize the criterion for historical statements, perhaps to those in which one historiographer or another happens to be currently interested, thinks important, or such. Similarly, we do not wish to limit historical statements to those which are germane to a particular historical inquiry, study, or problem. One could not even have such an inquiry, study, or problem to begin with, if one did not have a prior grasp of historical statements. No zoologist, for example, could begin his work without a concept of animals, without knowing what he was about, what he was looking for, what would count as statements about animals, how one would find out if they were true or false, and so on. Similarly, one could always come up with statements that were clearly historical but which were not germane to any particular inquiry, study, or problem, at least to date. For example, presumably 'Alexandrian mariners reached the coast of Central America in the 2nd Century B.C.', 'Julius Caesar had a cousin who was initiated into the Eleusinian Mysteries one year after the battle of Pharsalus', and 'Anthony and Cleopatra had a son, who later, under a false name, came to power in Pontus' would all seem historical statements, and one or more may be true, but, to date, they are not involved, as far as I know, in any historical inquiry, study, or problem.

4. The world was created 5 minutes ago, bearing within it all the signs of age.

It may be recalled that we discussed, to some extent, in a different context, this locution earlier. The problem it raises is particularly significant in historiographical epistemology, because of its impact on theories of historiographical truth. Here, however, we are concerned with whether or not to count it as a historical statement. It is, clearly, a past-referring statement, is heavily involved with interhuman consequences, given the dating, and fits into a familiar chronology, that of recent minutes. It certainly seems significant, as, if it were accepted, it would seriously rearrange our notions of time, the past, science, history, and reality. Against accepting it as a historical statement is that it initiates, rather than integrates with, a causal nexus. It starts the laws of nature, so to speak, rather than complies with them. This would seem a problem, of course, with any particular creation theory. We need not suppose it requires a violation of the principle of matter/energy, for we might suppose the energy was there earlier, but only, perhaps at the word or action of a divine entity or demiurge, or something, it was suddenly formed into a recognizable world, say, five minutes ago. It is also, in theory, confirmable and disconfirmable. For example, some observing intelligence in another galaxy or dimension might note that the world had sprung into existence five minutes ago, or, similarly, note that it had been there for a long time already, say, several billion years. We have a reasonably clear idea of what would be involved in both cases.

I would like, however, all things considered, to rule this out as a historical statement. It is certainly relevant to, and important to, a conceptual analysis of historiography, but it is not itself, as I would wish to see it, a historical statement. It would suggest, rather, a backgrounding metaphysical stance, similar in its way, though certainly less familiar than, the stance that the world, or matter/energy, is eternal, neither coming into existence or passing out of existence, there being nowhere from which it might have come, and nowhere to which it might go. It is, in its way, like global skepticisms, that transexperiential knowledge is unattainable, that an external world may not exist, that our experience may be no more than a dream, or a fantasy generated by an alien intelligence, that we might be only brains stimulated in vats to have our familiar experiences, that our own mind might be the only one in the universe, and so on. These things might be true, but, for the most part, they are not the sort of things which admit, at least on the whole, of empirical inquiry and resolution. These are the sorts of things it might be fun to wonder about, but unwise to worry about.

I suppose one might meet a little fellow claiming to be a Cartesian demon, responsible for our experiences, but we would be less likely to take him seriously than to pick him up and carry him to the nearest psychiatrist.

5. The Athenians will win the sea fight tomorrow.

This example, borrowed from Aristotle, though for purposes other than his, is an example of a future-referring statement.[72] As we have taken it as a necessary condition for a historical statement that it is a past-referring statement, it is clear that it cannot be a historical statement. On the other hand, it is useful in making a rather different point, which is that a given statement might count, depending on its time of utterance, as past-referring, present-referring, or future referring.

Consider the following meaning assignments:

a: the Athenians

Wx: x has the property of winning an important sea fight in 406 B.C. in the vicinity of the Arginusae Islands

The statement 'Wa' may then be understood as "The Athenians have the property of winning an important sea fight in 406 B.C. in the vicinity of the Arginusae Islands."

If this statement were uttered in 405 B.C. it would not be a historical statement, because it would be a future-referring statement; similarly, if it were uttered shortly before the engagement in 406 B.C., during the engagement, or shortly after the engagement, assuming that the present is taken as one hour long, or one day long,

---

[72] The classical puzzle here has to do with whether or not future-referring statements have truth values. If such a statement is true or false now, this suggests that the future is determined. The dilemma is, it seems, that one must either deny truth values to future-referring statements or accept that the future is determined. Logic objects to the first alternative and common sense to the second. Most people, one hopes, will opt for common sense. A similar problem arises in the difficulty of reconciling free will with divine foreknowledge. If one can do so, then it seems moral issues arise. For example, is it moral to create an antelope whom one knows will die a terrible death? There are also difficulties in reconciling the properties of omnipotence and omniscience. If a divine entity foresees that it will do x, then it seems it cannot but do x, and thus is not omnipotent; if it can refrain from doing x, then it seems it is not omniscient, etc. In such issues, it is natural to seek for distinctions.

it would not be a past-referring statement, but a present-referring statement. On the other hand, after the battle is clearly in the past in, say, 407 B.C., it becomes a past-referring statement, and, in this case, a historical statement. Thus, whether such a statement is a historical statement or not depends on the time of its utterance.

6. Khnum is the god of the first cataract of the Nile.[73]

This is certainly a statement of historical interest, and it gives us a claim about the religion of ancient Egypt. The questions that would arise here would be similar to many questions having to do with gods or unusual beings and history. To be sure, there is no claim here that Khnum is active in history, influences it, or such. Like the gods of Epicurus he might mind his own business. On the other hand, it seems likely that he might have been prayed to, might have been thought to answer prayers, and such. If the god Khnum does not exist, one supposes one could put this sort of thing with Pegasus, but if the god exists then an interesting problem arises. Suppose one had something like this: 'In the second year of the reign of Seti I, Khnum caused the Pharaoh to trip over a mislaid sistrum.' Where we may not be too much concerned with the interpersonal relations obtaining between Khnum and Seti I, it is clear that statements about the interaction of gods and men have abounded in history. Are assertions to that effect to count as historical statements? They are usually datable, at least approximately; suggest interaction; presuppose a causality of one sort or another; are usually specific, and are taken to be significant. Indeed, if Khnum did affect history, or any god, that would presumably be significant for the nature of the act itself, if not for what was actually done. A miracle would presumably be significant, for being a miracle, even if it were not much of a miracle, say, causing Seti I to stumble over a mislaid sistrum. Let us suppose one or more gods exist, so the question of fictional entities, such as Pegasus, will not cloud the issue. Now it is very

---

73 This is one of my favorite gods, probably because he was called to my attention by a physicist friend. This friend, when a child, looked up the most obscure Egyptian god he could find, so that when he prayed, or asked for something, he would be assured of the god's undivided attention. Obviously this was a highly intelligent child. It may also cast some light on the childhood of physicists.

clear that many individuals have believed that one or more gods exist, and that they have interacted with human beings, and have declared or stated as much. Similarly, many other unusual entities, of various sorts, benign, malign, or neutral, have been alleged to exist and to be, at least occasionally, interactive in human affairs. For a historiographer who takes such beings seriously, correctly or incorrectly, he will certainly regard at least certain statements pertaining to them to be historical statements. And, from his point of view, he will be correct. They are historical statements from his point of view. Thus, one must admit that a tincture of historiographer-relativity, so to speak, contaminates these matters. On the other hand, as we are concerned with an explication here and not a straight-forward transcription of, nor an uncritical account of, historiographical practice, we are entitled to exercise a certain selectivity in such matters.

If Khnum does not exist, then we will decline to count statement 6, above, as historical. We will put it in with unicorns, centaurs, griffins, flying horses, and such. This is not to deny that such statements may be of great historical interest. On the other hand, I would like to propose that even if Khnum does exist, for who knows about such things, we should not regard it as a historical statement, nor, indeed, the much more detailed statement about Khnum, Seti I, and the mislaid sistrum either. The reason for this is primarily twofold, first, metaphysical, second, epistemic. First, the causal reference is not clear; it is not clear how an assertion of this sort would fit into a causal matrix, either ingrediently, or consequentially, as a result of a causality, as might a pattern. This is not to deny, of course, that such utterances would have their causes, but that is beside the point. An utterance that 2 plus 2 equals four doubtless has its causes, but that does not entail that $2 + 2 = 4$ is an ingredient in a causal matrix. Mathematical formulas do not make noises, set fire to things, roll down hills, fall at $\frac{1}{2}gt^2$, and so on. Second, we are not clear on the empirical truth conditions involved in such assertions. We may observe Seti I stumble over a mislaid sistrum, but we have no way of knowing that this has been arranged by Khnum, nor that it has not been arranged by Khnum, even if Khnum exists.

The criterion which is emerging from our discussion is, to borrow a term from Karl Popper, a demarcation criterion, designed to separate historical statements from nonhistorical statements. In this instance, its point is to separate historical statements from religious statements. As in the case of Khnum, it is not denying that Khnum exists, though I would be personally surprised if he does, nor is it denying that statements pertaining to Khnum might not be true or false. It is simply claiming that such statements are not, in the light of our explication, historical statements. For example, they do not meet the requirement of empirical intelligibility. Accordingly, they are outside the pale of historical statements, as we would like to understand historical statements.

7. Plotinus merged with the One.

Plotinus was a definite historical figure, a 3rd Century Roman philosopher and mystic, and the most famous and important figure in the NonChristian Neoplatonic tradition.

In Plato one finds the supreme form to be the form of the Good, and, somehow, it seems the plethora of other forms is dependent upon, and somehow follows from, this ultimate and foundational form. On the other hand, the relation between the form of the Good and the other forms is not spelled out in Plato. Moreover, the supreme form, the form of the Good, is apparently impersonal, sublime, nonconscious, needless and will-less, eternal, imperishable, and unchangeable, rather like, one supposes, the One of Parmenides, to which it may well be philosophically akin. As far as we know, Plato's relationship to his hypothesized transcendental realities was essentially rationalistic, doubtless humble, admiring, and awestruck, but not mystical. Plato, although denying the accolade of knowledge to matters of perception and other forms of sense experience, and identifying the real with the changeless, with its supposed consequence, necessary truth, took the route to the unraveling of human and cosmic mysteries to be reason, logic, dialectic, geometry and argumentation. As far as we know he did not attempt to approach the real, let alone participate in it, via some sort of immediate contact, in virtue of a sort of transcendental analogue to sense experience, something like an immediate, extranatural perception or touching. The rhapsodies of Plato, one supposes, were more analogous to those which would startle and enthrall the mathematician, silent on his peak in Darien, than those of the saint or mystic, those not of witnessing, recognizing, or inspecting, but those of union, of participation, of sharing.

Clearly, however, the philosophy of Plato offers, if only implicitly, the sense of a horizon beyond which might lie wonders, a country congenial to lure the dispirited and world weary, or the spiritually adventurous, certainly one which would invite the mystical mind to its exploration.

It seems natural then that philosophers of an extraworldly, mystical bent might seek for, and find, gold in the Platonic hills. Plotinus, who was apparently a beautiful person, seems to be the most prominent of these. The One of Plotinus seems to be an understanding of the form of the Good, and realities, even Being, are emanations from the supreme form, directly or indirectly, this giving us at least a verbal account in terms of which one might attempt to bridge the Platonic gap, or relation, between the form of the Good and lesser forms of reality. Moreover, for the worthy, purified soul an access to the Good is possible, in which the ready, aspiring soul may become one with the supreme fountain of all reality, that beyond even Being itself. Plotinus apparently had more than one such experience, which might be spoken of, insofar as such things may be spoken of, as merging with the One.

The situation here is different from the problems presented by statement 6, above, pertaining to the god, Khnum, because we are dealing here with a particular historical figure, and incidents which are specific and datable. Something like 'Porphyry reported that Plotinus merged with the One' is clearly a historical statement. On the other hand, I suspect that, even if Plotinus did in fact manage to merge with the One, whatever that might mean, that statement 7 is not well regarded as historical.

A major reason for denying its historicity is that it is empirically unintelligible; one does not know what one would be saying; it would be verbal, at best. It represents an inference well beyond the data, and an inference to who-knows-what. Compare: 'Plotinus merged with x.' Claritywise, the sentence is incomplete. It is not, so to speak, a well-formed formula. One may very well acknowledge that Plotinus, one or more times, is likely to have had a remarkable and unusual experience, but there is always a difference between data and the interpretation of data. And, in this case, it is not even clear the interpretation is intelligible. To take a much simpler case, an honest individual might sincerely claim to have heard the voice of Apollo, or to have even seen the god himself. I suppose this might be true, but there would usually be alternative explanations for these experiences, which, as experiences, are not denied. Perhaps the individual was the victim of a hoax, misunderstood something actually heard and seen, was hallucinating, or such.

As the statement does not appear to admit of empirical truth conditions, we will rule it out as a historical statement.

One may not save the day for statement 7 along the lines of, say, 'Plotinus tasted Fruit F', where we ourselves have never tasted Fruit F, and its taste, we shall suppose, is quite different from tastes we have experienced. We would not rule out such a statement as unintelligible, even if we are unable to imagine the taste of Fruit F, for two reasons, first, because we are familiar with fruits and tastes, and are clearly ready to accept that tastes unknown to us exist, and, second, one is clearly dealing with an empirical reality here, one which might be confirmed by others, and even ourselves, at least in theory, even if Plotinus had finished off the last surviving slice of Fruit F. If "One Merging," on the other hand, became a common phenomenon, widely shared, like tasting fruit or hearing crickets, we might wish to establish grants for its investigation. It would then be entering into the country of intelligibility. One might hope to devise tests, of course, to distinguish between merging with the One and merely believing that one had merged with the One, or tests to establish that two Individuals, I_1 and I_2, had actually had the same experience. Perhaps one of them merged with something else, mere emanated Being, or such. No one denies that unusual experiences exist; one only continues to insist on the distinction between data and its interpretation.

8. Elam was southeast of Babylonia.

Whereas one might worry a little about the borders of Elam and Babylonia at given historical times, and how southeast, if at all, Elam was from Babylonia, this seems clearly a historical statement. If one were to rule it out, presumably one would do so in virtue of its spatiality, unclear causal aspects, or lack of interhuman reference. On the other hand the spatiality is clearly of historical relevance, conditioning historical relations, which direction to march to do what, and so on; and whereas land itself is seldom directly causally active, except for volcanoes, earthquakes, and such, it does form the platform for all sorts of agricultural, economic, military, social, and political activities; and, thirdly, it has interhuman aspects as it has been named, fought for, invaded, and such.

Accordingly, we will count this as a historical statement.

9. The Thirteenth Century did not exist.

Historiographers often say unusual things, to make particular points. The presupposition is that they are probably uttering historical statements. It would seem that the *onus probandi* would be on the fellow who might be inclined to be skeptical or issue challenges.[74] Accordingly, if one encounters something like statement 9, or, say, metaphorical assertions, which are often striking, illuminating, and valuable, one is well advised to adopt a charitable stance and try to see what the fellow is driving at. To be sure, charity can be excessive. It is almost impossible to put meaningful words together in grammatical sequences and come up with something out of which no one will be able to make anything. With sufficient effort and ingenuity one can almost always come up with something that makes some sort of sense somehow. And herein we may find the salvation of certain poets, philosophers, and such. More than one such fellow has trodden the road of obscurity to fame, if not fortune. To be sure, it helps to seem as if one were saying something or other, and something important. That is of

---

74 With respect to the *onus probandi*, a word or two might be in order, to alleviate a common misunderstanding in these matters. For example, a skeptic might ask how one knows that 'p' is true, but he might, in turn, it seems, be asked how he knows it isn't. Suppose he asks how one knows that other minds exist, but he, in turn, it seems, might be asked how does he know they don't. There would be no reason to put the burden of proof on the fellow who believes other minds exist, rather than on a fellow who might deny it. On the other hand, this is not to understand skepticism. The point of skepticism is not to establish 'p' or '~ p' but to suggest that neither can be proven. The skeptic does not deny that other minds exist, if he is sane; rather he is interested in the nature and limits of knowledge.

great help. Few literatures have been founded on confused and obscure disquisitions having to do with raccoons.

Given the principle of historical negation, and the likelihood that one would accept 'The Thirteenth Century exists' as a historical statement, it seems one should accept 'The Thirteenth century does not exist' as a historical statement, as well, though one presumably false. On the other hand, that is to understand such assertions literally, and it seems no historiographer would be likely to say something like that literally. What might a statement such as statement 9 have in mind? Two interpretations seem to make sense, one conceptual and the other metaphorical, or, perhaps, in this case, polemic. Conceptually, one might be drawing attention to the conventionality involved in chronology, that decades, centuries, and such, are artificial, that they are constructs, and sometimes inconvenient constructs. History does not really come divided up into centuries, any more than boards come divided up into inches and feet. We do not find centuries in history; we put them there. They are arbitrary, like pounds and ounces, like pints and quarts. Certainly the Thirteenth Century does not exist in the sense that trees and rocks, horses and people, exist. On the other hand, one supposes, without a context at hand, that such an assertion, which is striking, arresting, and such, is intended to convey something important, whether right or wrong. Thus one will understand it as metaphorical, or, in this case, perhaps better, as polemical. Some individuals, who have never had the misfortune to live in the Thirteenth Century, have a tendency to romanticize it. Probably they have mostly in mind that Europe was religiously united, at least substantially, in a way that they approved. Civilization, at least of a limited and narrow sort, was flourishing, bringing relative ease, comfort, and security to a tiny fraction of the population, that which is likely to leave the records and write the history; scholars could travel with relative freedom and converse and write in the common medium of Latin; intellectual freedom, at least within limits, existed; the divisiveness attendant on the Reformation, the unconscionable misery of religious wars, the hideous competition of large, warring nations lay in the future. This was, after all, the age of Albertus Magnus, of Thomas Aquinas, of Dante, of Chaucer, and others. A moral compass was in place and its directions were not much contested. Cathedrals soared above tenements and hovels. Chivalry was in flower. The lord was aware of his obligations to his serfs, and they to him. Much was clear, and there was little confusing of up with down. If you dislike popular culture, tabloids, modern music, and democracy, and long for a stable status society, in which you have the luck to be born in the right stratum, this may well be your century. On the other hand, this century, which may well, according to certain parameters, count as the pinnacle of the Middle Ages, or such, is also a century of inadequate sewerage, of widespread ignorance and superstition, of bias and persecution, of almost universal poverty and misery, of high infant mortality, short lives, and so on. Accordingly, one supposes that, in a given context, an assertion to the effect that the Thirteenth Century did not exist might be taken to mean that someone's view as to a particular time is fantasy, that his "Thirteenth Century," so to speak, did not exist. The Golden Age was not a golden age, at all.

'A is good' and 'it is not the case that A is good' have the appearance of statement and negation, and, if they are statement and negation, then, obviously, were they to be conjoined, one would have a contradiction. On the other hand, if 'A is good' really means 'A is good according to criteria x, y, and z' and 'It is not the case that A is good' really means 'It is not the case that A is good according to criteria u, v, and w' no contradiction is involved. Presumably both historiographers would agree, say, that having a common language for scholarship would be to the good and having inadequate sewerage facilities would not be to the good. To return to our current concern, however, it seems appropriate to count statement 9 as a historical statement, which is either true or false. To be sure, the sentence 'The Thirteenth Century did not exist' is, in effect, the first step on the road to what will count as the statement 'The Thirteenth Century did not exist'. This problem, however, is scarcely unique to historiography. For example, presumably 'Jones is bald' would count as a statement, and yet we noticed, earlier, what would be required before, at least in certain cases, we could assess its truth value. Many locutions we count as statements, properly and without demur, are, under analysis, rather like programs, canvases, or frameworks for statements, something like signposts for statements, or plans for statements.

10. The Claude Glass was invented in the 18th Century.

Claude Lorrain, a 17th Century French painter, was noted for soft, gentle, lovely, romantically understated modulations of color, light, and shadow in landscape painting. The "Claude glass," a later invention, was named for him, and presumably its purpose was to aid painters to achieve effects akin to those for which his work was so remarkably notable. The "glass" consisted of a toned mirror by means of which the scene confronting the artist, reflected in the mirror, could be reduced to a set of tonal gradations, apparently rather in the way a black-and-white photograph of a natural scene would call out gradations of tone. Apparently this sort of clarification could aid an artist in his application of colors.[75]

One of the properties which we wished to require of historical statements was significance. This is perhaps the most dubious and controversial of necessary conditions for a historical statement, as significance could muchly vary depending on observer and context. On the other hand, presumably it would be a violation of both historiographical practice and historiographical common sense to count just any statement about the past having to do with one or more human beings as a "historical statement." Historical statements, at least of a preeminent or paradigm sort, are those which might naturally and plausibly be found in a historiographical essay, narrative, or monograph. For example, that Publia the younger, the twenty-third cousin of someone of whom we have never heard, stubbed her toe on such and such a day, would probably not be regarded as a historical statement, nor that so and so tilled his field on such and such a day, and so on.

If we wished to rule out statement 10 as historical presumably we would do so on the basis of its lack of significance. It did little, as far as we know, to alter the course of human history. It may not have had much impact even on the history of art, and, as far as I know, the invention is obsolete, and, for the most part, forgotten, perhaps justifiably so, even by artists, Contrariwise, rubber bands and paper clips abound and thrive.

---

75 This invention is referred to, and described, in the work, earlier cited, by E. H. Gombrich, his *Art and Illusion: A Study in the Psychology of Pictorial Representation* (Bollingen Foundation, New York, 1961)).

On the other hand, given the observer-dependence and context-relevance of significance, I think that one should be generous and charitable. For example, if one were interested in the interplay of technology and art, as one might be interested in the interplay between technology and science, knowing something of the Claude glass would seem germane to such an interest, certainly interesting, and perhaps important, say, as to why the device was invented, was it useful, how it was received, why it became obsolescent, and so on. The line between antiquarianism and history is not clear, if it exists, at all. Similarly, context-relativity is not to be neglected. Something might be important to the history of a family, a neighborhood, or a community, say, which might not make much difference to world history, but, within the context, it would count as historical, just as something or other which occurred last Tuesday in Minneapolis might be historical with respect to Minneapolis. And, from the point of view of the universe, the history of a small planet orbiting a small star on the fringe of a small galaxy, as galaxies go, amongst billions of galaxies, may not be that momentous either.

Let us count statement 10 as historical.

11. If the legions of Varus had not been annihilated in the Teutoburg Forest in A.D. 9, and Rome had civilized and pacified the barbarian tribes north of the Rhine, the Roman Empire might not have fallen, World War I might not have taken place, and there would have been no rise of Hitler and Nazism.

There is no doubt that the terrible massacre in the Teutoburg Forest inflicted a costly and crushing defeat on Rome, which seems to have seriously influenced its subsequent political and military policies, resulting not only in a general cessation of expansion, but the adoption of a primarily defensive posture, involving withdrawal and consolidation, border defense, the building of walls, and even, eventually, the recruitment, in a variety of ways, of barbarians into the armed forces, a practice which seems, at least in retrospect, to have been dangerously imprudent.

Statement 11 is an example of what is known variously as a contrary-to-fact conditional, a counter-factual conditional, a contrafactual conditional, or such. What they have in common is that the antecedent of the conditional, its first term, is false.

Clearly such statements are familiar, and have truth values. Consider a simple example, 'If the match had been struck, it would have lit', an example made famous for its use in the unsurpassed analytical work of the logician and epistemologist, Nelson Goodman. Goodman has shown that we could have a serviceable analysis of the contrafactual conditional if we had at our disposal a serviceable analysis of natural law, and that if we had a serviceable analysis of the contrafactual conditional we could have one of natural law, but that, unfortunately, we have neither, and, if I read him aright, we are not likely to have either. Some sort of primitive given seems to be involved. Most obviously, one cannot read contrafactual conditionals in terms of the conventions of modern extensional logic because, due to false antecedents, they would all come out true. For example, 'If the match had been struck, it would have lit' and 'If the match had been struck, it would not have lit' would both be true, which is obviously unacceptable.[76]

All we need for our purposes here is that such statements possess truth values. It is one thing to possess a truth value, of course, and quite another to determine its truth value.

Statement 11 is complex and far-reaching. It is a long way from 'If the match had been struck, it would have lit'. The logic of the matter, however, is the same. Our problem, fortunately, is not to come up with a satisfactory analysis of either the contrafactual conditional or natural law, but rather, first, to recognize that both contrafactual conditionals and lawlike statements, whatever their

---

[76] The 'if ..., then ...' relationship may be understood in a variety of ways, for example, logically, as in 'If c is a circle, then c is round'; nomologically, as in 'If an object is released near the surface of the Earth, then it falls at $\frac{1}{2}gt^2$'; or materially, as when 'If p, then q' is understood as equivalent to 'It is not the case that p and not q'. ($\sim (p \, \& \sim q)$) 'If p, then q' in the material sense may be symbolized as 'p $\supset$ q'. Such a formula is counted as true if either its antecedent, its first term, is false, or its consequent, its second term, is true. It is false, then, if and only if its antecedent term is true and its consequent term is false. There are many fascinating, and sometimes paradoxical, consequences of this analysis of 'If ..., then ...', including the substitution of a truth-functional relationship for one commonly considered either semantic or nomological. On the other hand, it has indisputable value, and it is almost universally accepted in the logistic community. It has been, for example, implicitly presupposed in this work, except where noted.

nature, analyzable or unanalyzable, possess truth values, and, two, that their consideration is important to historiographical analysis.

That contrafactual conditionals may possess truth values is made clear not only in virtue of our intuitions in such matters, e.g., "If he had dropped the fragile crystal goblet on the cement sidewalk from the third-floor window, it would have shattered," but from the fact that evidence is pertinent to their assessment. For example, one could take the same match, and, at a later time scratch it, and see if it lit. This would not prove that it would have lit the first time, but it would be evidence in favor of that hypothesis. If one cannot get the first match, or it has been soaking overnight in the puddle on the pavement below, one might try other matches from the same box, or similar matches from different boxes, and so on. In the case of the crystal goblet one could drop it later, or if one's wife had spirited it away for safekeeping, one might drop a similar goblet, perhaps purchased or borrowed from a scientifically inclined neighbor.

The second point here is that the consideration of the contrafactual statements, or the supposition of nonactualized states of affairs, may be of great historiographical importance. This is the historiographical analogue to the scientist's manipulation of variables. The consideration of the nonactual is the primary historiographical path to understanding the relevance and importance of historical figures, elements, and events.

Consider the following time line:

$$t_1 \quad t_2 \quad t_3 \quad t_4$$
$$A \quad B \quad C \quad D$$

Here we see, in this one-dimensional, vastly simplified schematism, that D follows A, B, and C. A camera could show us as much. This tells us nothing, in itself, of causality.

To hypothesize causal relations one is, in effect, implicitly or explicitly, asking if D would have occurred if A or B or C had not occurred. Clearly if A, B, and C had not occurred, and D would have occurred, then neither A nor B nor C could be causes of D.

Consider the following table:

#	A	B	C	D
1	+	+	+	+
2	+	+	—	—
3	+	—	+	—
4	+	—	—	—
5	—	+	+	+
6	—	+	—	—
7	—	—	+	—
8	—	—	—	—

A, B, and C stand for causal candidates. A '+' indicates the presence of the element, and a '—' indicates the absence of the element. For example, a '+' in the A column indicates that A is present, and a '—' in the A column indicates the absence of A. The distribution in the A, B, and C columns is merely logical, ranging through the eight logical possibilities with respect to three elements. The D column, on the other hand is quite different. The D column is empirical and a '+' in the D column indicates the presence or absence of D, given the possibilities for A, B, and C. Please note that D is present only in rows 1 and 5. What one gathers from the table is that B and C are conjointly necessary for the presence of D. A is ruled out altogether as a cause of D, and neither B nor C by itself will produce D. Thus, in terms of this little schema, would that things were so simple, one would infer that the conjunction of B and C was necessary and sufficient to produce D. Actually, it would be empirically impossible to list all the necessary and sufficient conditions to produce an event, but such exercises, I think, are instructive and useful. Certainly historiographers, scientists, accountants, plumbers, philosophers, and others, have little choice but to go about providing explanations of one sort or another.

The scientist, or, better, some scientists, can experiment, manipulate variables, and such, and do something which rather resembles what was going on in the small table above.

Historiographers have a much harder time of it. On the other hand, they do, in effect, manipulate variables in their judgment, and, if they did not, they could not begin to seek causes intelligently, and consider and weigh the importance of historical factors.

Causal identification is difficult enough; causal assessment is even more difficult.

Suppose it is accepted, in connection with our schematism above, that B and C are conjointly necessary for D. The question of causal significance remains open. The table is silent with respect to causal significance. It cannot be determined from the table. In the causal matrix are B and C equally weighty, important, or significant, or is one more significant than the other, and to what degree? Such subtleties call for historiographical judgment. To illustrate, again, consider a simple example. Conjecture a switch, which, when depressed, will detonate an explosion. We dismiss explanations of electricity, wiring, the presence of mechanisms, the volume of explosive material, the chemistry of explosions, and such, and, moreover, what the rigging is all about, who set it up, what is its purpose, and so on. Furthermore, in our schematic example, we shall suppose that the switch, in order to be depressed, requires a weight of one ton and one ounce . We might call the one-ton weight B, and the one-ounce weight C. The explosion will not occur unless both weights are added together. Since both are required for the explosion, there is a sense in which they are equally important, but few historiographers, I suspect, would view the matter in this way. If this were a simple matter of common-sense physics, as opposed to an analogy to historiographical explanation, one supposes B would be regarded as most important, as it supplies most of the weight needed to depress the switch. Historiographically, this might be rather like the underlying or major cause, B, as opposed to the superficial or minor cause, or the precipitating cause or the igniting or triggering cause, or the "occasion," C, perhaps a border incident, an atrocity, an insult, an assassination, or such. On the other hand, if B is understood as prevailing conditions, a situation of comparative normalcy, the way things usually are, a given, stable background, or such, then C might well be regarded as the crucial or most important cause. If switches, so to speak, usually bear the weight of B, then the addition of C's ounce would become more significant, more weighty, more important, and so on. C would have made the difference. The problem in considering history, of course, is that there are indefinite numbers of causes involved, most of which are not known, and thus an indefinite number of causes to which causal weights, difficult to measure, and not all of which are known, are to be assigned. The most common "B" in history would doubtless be human nature, but a reference to human nature is seldom encountered in historiographical explanation.

Let us return, briefly, to statement 11.

It is an example of a contrafactual conditional. It doubtless has a truth value. For example, evidence is relevant to it. And, doubtless, logically, if not empirically, the causal connections might be traced. To be sure, its truth value would be difficult, or impossible, to determine. But that is not unusual in history.

We shall regard statement 11 as a historical statement.

12. Parrhasios was a better representational painter than Zeuxis.[77]

As the story goes, doubtless apocryphal, but delightful, Zeuxis painted some grapes, and they were so lifelike that birds swooped down to peck at them. One gathers that Parrhasios took this as a challenge and set himself to equal or surpass Zeuxis. Sometime later Zeuxis was invited to the studio of Parrhasios to inspect his rival's efforts and Zeuxis, attempting to draw aside the curtain to examine how well Parrhasios had done, discovered that the curtain was the painting, that the painting was one of a curtain. Supposedly then the work of Parrhasios was deemed superior, for the work of Zeuxis had fooled only birds, while that of Parrhasios had fooled not only a man, but a gifted fellow artist.

In a later portion of this study, we will be concerned with issues in axiology, or value theory, and will be concerned, in some detail, with the cognitivity of value judgments, and their role, legitimate or illegitimate, in historiography.

On the other hand, in any attempt to work out a theory of

---

[77] One gathers that this story is famous in the history of art. My immediate reference for it is E. H. Gombrich's book, cited twice earlier, his *Art and Illusion: A Study in the Psychology of Pictorial Representation* (Bollingen Foundation, New York, 1961)). His source noted is Pliny's *Natural History*, Pliny, *Hist. Nat.* XXXV, 36.

historical statements, it is clear that some stance, positive or negative, must be taken with respect to value judgments, and normative statements in general.

So we will do so.

An initial observation would be that most human beings, in all times and cultures, have taken value judgments very seriously, and have regarded them as right or wrong, true or false. Accordingly, before deciding that the human race has been mistaken on this point at least since the Olduvai Gorge we should try to understand it. Another interesting fact is that throughout history there has been, statistically, an overwhelming agreement on axiological issues, particularly when dealing with one's own community.

The first point seems easy enough to understand, which is that much of the human being's behavior does not do itself. Most of it is the result of action, and action must be decided, and one decides in terms of values. Action is value-guided. The human being is a self-governing organism, one of volitional self-consciousness, and it governs itself in terms of what it wants to do or accomplish, and what it wants to do or accomplish in most cases is to achieve a state of existence with which it is better satisfied. Action is unintelligible without valuing, as valuing is what makes action meaningful. Evolution has selected for the rational, valuing organism. Accordingly, human beings take value judgments seriously, and take them as being right or wrong, true or false, because they are built that way.

The second point, which is an anthropological truism, is that human beings, statistically, have in all times and places, as far as can be ascertained, been in overwhelming axiological agreement. This agreement, of course, has not been exceptionless, perfect, universal, and so on. For example, animals may not have been viewed as members of the moral community, or, perhaps, the members of that strange tribe in the next valley. As if axiological agreement were not pervasive enough, one might also note that almost all moral disagreement stems either from differences in life conditions or cognitive fields. In a polar environment, with starvation at hand, an elderly parent who can longer keep up with the sled, or hunt, and such, might be a burden, menacing the survival of the family. In such a situation, doing away with the elderly, as compassionately as possible, could be morally imperative. And it was done. Similarly, if one's cognitive field includes agriculture, gods, and such, and a good harvest is thought to depend on the grace of this divinity or that, it might make sense to honor a virgin by sacrificing her to the god or gods, who are supposedly interested in having, and are supposedly suitably impressed by, sacrificed virgins. In our own time, hopefully a transitory aberration in the history of civilization, there are apparently individuals who think that their entry into paradise is guaranteed by the murder of one or more strangers. This is a difference in cognitive field.

The explanation of the widespread axiological agreement amongst individuals is twofold, first, human nature, organic similarities, dispositions, needs, and such, and, second, the practical imperatives of social life. Moralities are social instruments which facilitate the survival of groups. Presumably no human group has ever been without a morality. If there were such groups they do not seem to have survived. Whether the unit of selection is taken as the individual, the group, or the gene packet, there are necessary conditions for survival, for example, restraint, civility, conformity, mutual assistance, and such, or, if one is thinking genetics, the dispositions to manifest such characteristics, or accede to enhancing acculturations which encourage such characteristics.

Let us accept that the human being is a valuing organism, by nature, and that, as an anthropological or sociological fact, there is considerable axiological agreement amongst human beings.

That might not prove anything, but what would prove something?

If facts such as the aforementioned facts, human nature and considerable agreement, are irrelevant to these issues, what would be relevant? What would the moral skeptic accept as evidence that he was wrong, or might be wrong? If no evidence is relevant to his claims, if he would accept nothing as incompatible with them, then his claims are either meaningless or analytic, namely, compatible with any possible facts or any possible states of affairs, and, so, empirically vacuous. Even if there were perfect and universal agreement on moral issues, which there is not, it could always be claimed that the human race might still be wrong. After all, for a long time people thought the earth was flat and the sun went around the earth. But how would one know, if it was right, that it was right? It seems an answer to that question would be relevant to the discussion.

Recall the principle of significant negation:

"'p' is significant if and only if '~ p' is significant.'

Accordingly, if '~ p' is significant, namely, something like 'value judgments are neither true nor false', then 'it is not the case that value judgments are neither true nor false' or 'value judgments are true or false' must be significant. If there is to be evidence that value judgments are neither true nor false, then there must be evidence, as well, at least conceivable, or in theory, to the effect that value judgments are either true or false.

And such evidence abounds.

It is, of course, criterion-relevant, or, to borrow a term from physics, reference-frame relevant. My general position here, which is all I need at the moment, is that value judgments, or most value judgments, are either true or false, and that the truth values of value judgments are criterion-relevant. This shifts the question then to the acceptability or nonacceptability of the criterion. That is an independent question. In this respect the noncognitivist can shift his reservations from value judgments in themselves, giving that up as a lost cause, and center them where they belong, on the criterion or criteria in virtue of which they obtain their truth values. Questions of the criterion or criteria must be postponed until a later juncture in the discussion.

It will be noted that this approach allows for both the cognitivity of value judgments, which is overwhelmingly supported in human conception and practice, and the possibility of final and irresolvable moral disagreement.

As statement 12 I have chosen a value judgment, which would normally be taken as cognitive, and would normally, I think, be taken as true. It is, of course, criterion-relevant, as is the overwhelming majority of axiological assertions. If one's criterion for evaluating painting, or a given *genre* of painting, is representational verisimilitude, then it seems, according to that criterion, Parrhasios is a better representational painter than Zeuxis, as Zeuxis managed to deceive only birds and Parrhasios managed to deceive Zeuxis. To be sure, this statement is a generalization, and perhaps one should have more evidence, or compare the men's works as a whole or something, rather than rest the claim on a comparison of two paintings. Even so, the statement would be thought to have a truth value, either way. That it might be easier to achieve representational verisimilitude with curtains than grapes might be relevant, or questions as to whether or not Zeuxis was a normal observer functioning under standard conditions might be raised, or it might be suggested that additional opinions might be solicited from a representative sample of qualified observers, and so on, but the issue, once the criteria are accepted, becomes one of fact.

If there are problems here, as to whether this is a historical statement or not, they would presumably arise not in association with questions of axiological cognitivity, and its legitimacy or illegitimacy in historiography, but in association with the likely apocryphal nature of the anecdote. This would be, however, to confuse the statement with the evidence on which the statement is based. If the incident never occurred, the statement itself still remains true or false, and would be historical. Thus we see that at least one value judgment can possess a truth value, and that at least one value judgment may count as a historical statement. We may accept this as inductive evidence in favor of the legitimacy of value judgment in historiography.

13. Parrhasios was a better painter than Zeuxis.

This, like statement 12, is a value judgment, but here the criterion for its assessment is unclear. One can conceive of historiographers wishing to avoid such declarations, and who could blame them. It is not so much that such declarations lack truth values *simpliciter* as it is that their truth values will be criterion-dependent, and artists might be evaluated differently depending on the criteria involved.

Consider:
A is a better artist than B.
This could mean several things, depending on the criteria presupposed. For example:
The work of A is more socially relevant than that of B, and is more likely to contribute to the ultimate victory of the global totalitarian state.

A has a better sense of abstract design than B.

A's use of color is more vibrant and exciting than that of B.

A's draftsmanship, sense of proportion, and handling of perspective, is superior to that of B.

A's paintings look more like their subject matter than those of B.

A's work is more morally uplifting than the work of B.

A's work is more of an authentic expression of his subconscious mind than that of B.

A's work is more unique and adventurous than that of B.

A's work is more popular than that of B.

A's work sells for more money than that of B.

A's work is more soothing to view than that of B.

A's work is truer to the anxieties and horrors of our time than that of B.

I prefer the work of A to that of B.

The problem with something like 'A is a better artist than B' is that the criterion presupposed is not spelled out. Accordingly it is unclear; one simply does not know what is meant. Once the criterion is spelled out, most problems should vanish. There is nothing peculiar or damaging in the fact that cognitivity must wait about until one knows what one is talking about. The alternatives here are not limited to either twaddle or Platonism. Something exists between the meaningless and the one true meaning, namely, what is meant when.

In virtue of the semantic opacity of 'Parrhasios was a better painter than Zeuxis' it is best not understood, as it stands, as a historical statement. Most statements, of course, are unclear, to one extent or another. Two examples suggested by John Austen, a remarkably acute British philosopher of the Twentieth Century, are 'The galaxy has the shape of a fried egg' and 'Beethoven was a drunkard'. True or false? Recall the case of Jones. Was he bald, or not?

14. The Roman *ludi* were morally justified.

Statements 12 and 13, having to do with Parrhasios and Zeuxis, were value judgments of a particular kind, namely, aesthetic judgments. It was useful to treat them first because many individuals might view aesthetic judgments as noncognitive, but would be very reluctant to deny cognitivity to moral judgments. For example, it would be one thing to deny cognitivity to 'Parrhasios was a better painter than Zeuxis', if only because few people other than Parrhasios and Zeuxis would be likely to be interested in the matter, but it would be another thing, or would usually be supposed to be another thing, to deny cognitivity to, say, 'Adolf Hitler was a better man than Saint Francis of Assisi'. Most people would regard that as false. To be sure, it, too, is criterion-relevant. An enthusiast for mass murder, for example, might well consider it true. This does not mean it has no truth value; it means only that the truth value is criterion-dependent, but then, too, for most practical purposes, all truths and falsehoods are criterion-dependent. 'That board is longer than four feet in length' is clearly criterion-dependent, involving a procedure of, and a unit for, measurement. If, in the case of aesthetic judgments, where cognitivity is often denied, one can establish a clear, persuasive case for cognitivity, then it seems one should be able to do so, as well, in the area of morality.

Once, again, moral judgments, as aesthetic judgments, and, in effect, all judgments, will be criterion-dependent.

The Roman *ludi*, or games, were various. We will concern ourselves primarily, however, with gladiatorial combat. I suspect that most of us have been conditioned to disapprove of such arena sports, perhaps rather as future generations might be conditioned to disapprove of football, hockey, professional wrestling, and such. In any event, let us take for our criterion something like 'x is right if and only if x produces the most good for the most people'. This recommendation or prescription is one which is familiar, and is obviously extracted from a major ethical orientation, that of Utilitarianism.

Let us suppose that Publius is a healthy, strong young man, not a Roman citizen, who has been found guilty of some crime, perhaps murder, and expects to be sentenced to death by crucifixion, a common form of execution for those lacking citizenship, a terrible death involving a great deal of limitation of movement, which will shortly produce massive bodily pain, exposure, hunger, humiliation, dehydration, and such, and commonly lasting for two or three days of utter misery. On the other hand, the judge, we shall suppose, offers to Publius an alternative, training in a gladiatorial school. Not only does this give Publius a considerable stay of execution, at least, but he may survive indefinitely, depending on his prowess, and, if he wins a sufficient number of fights, he is given a wooden sword and freed, probably to be taken into the service of some aristocrat as a bodyguard, who will prize, and depend on, the skills with arms which he has acquired in the gladiatorial school and his experience in the arena. Moreover, Publius is now recognized by many, has no dearth of feminine companionship, or masculine companionship, for that matter, should he wish, and is now a celebrity. Even in the arena he probably had his fans and following, who remain admiring and loyal, was cheered robustly, idolized, and so on, rather as we sometimes make heroes of our own champion athletes. The people he might kill in the arena have for the most part, like himself, been condemned to death anyway, and are enjoying, at the least, a welcome postponement of their executions, plus the attentions of the crowd, and even, perhaps, of the emperor and his retinue. They, too, are important. And if Publius wins, their death, by his blade or trident, is quick, and merciful, far different from the lingering torture of the cross. Too, if they have put up a good fight, the crowd may order them spared to fight again, for, out there on the bright sand, they were found skillful and pleasing. As for the crowds themselves, they are happy and pleased, follow their favorites, and keep coming back for more, and more. In short, the Roman *ludi* seem to fill the bill for something right very well, clearly producing the most good for the most people, both for those in the arena and for the others, the promoters, the fans, and such. It follows, then, that on this criterion, namely, that that is right which produces the most good for the most people, the Roman *ludi* are morally justified. It is supposed here, of course, as in Utilitarianism, that good is not something unintelligible and mystical but that it involves utility, and is thus understood along the lines of pleasure, happiness, satisfaction, that sort of thing.

So here in statement 14, we have a moral judgment which, according to a traditional and famous criterion for right, is true.

The point of this brief discussion is not to argue that we should approve of the Roman *ludi*, but, rather, to call to our attention, once again, to the matter of criterion-relevance, and its role in cognitivity, whether with respect to empirical judgment, aesthetic judgment, or moral judgment.

Statement 14, a moral judgment, counts as a historical statement. Thus, historical statements may express moral judgments. Thus, the historiographer is under no obligation to refrain from moral judgment. It is recommended, of course, that, if he engages in it, he know what he is doing. He is under no obligation, of course, if he expresses moral judgments, to accept the Utilitarian criterion. I personally find it morally offensive, and would regard Statement 14 as false, but that is because I have a different criterion in mind. We are thus returned to the crucial matter of noting the pervasive dependence of cognitivity on criteria. Whether it is possible to adjudicate differences amongst criteria, and on what grounds, will be considered later in this study. The historiographer, of course, is free not to engage in moral judgment, if he wishes to do so. That is his business. On the other hand, if moral judgments can be true and false, and he denies them to himself, then his work will be incomplete at best, and vapid and sterile, and largely irrelevant to his subject matter, at worst. To be sure, moral judgments, while pervasive, and perhaps unavoidable, are seldom expressed explicitly in historiography. For one thing, that would be crude; for another, it is commonly unnecessary, for the judgments will usually be obvious; and, for another, to do so would be poor art.

15. The sins of the emperor brought about a wide-spread drought in the land.

Let us suppose we have a given historian who explains a devastating drought as brought on by the sins of an emperor which drought, when the emperor had atoned for his sins, ended. This explains the coming of the drought, and its cause, and the ending of the drought, and its cause. Historiographers have not been above propounding such explanations. Historiographers, of various sorts, in various traditions and cultures, have not been above attributing social, political, and military adversities to lapses in proper behavior, either on the part of individuals, say, kings, emperors, and such, or, indeed, of peoples. Proper behavior, similarly, one supposes, say, offering suitable sacrifices, the promulgation of a new state religion, or such, might be supposed to be rewarded.[78]

This sort of thing we can deal with briefly. One of the criteria for historical statements, in the set of criteria which is emerging from this consideration of particular and representative statements, is that a historical statement must be an empirical statement, to which evidence, at least in theory, is pertinent. For example, we do not know if the statement 'Caesar sneezed while crossing the Rubicon' is true or false, but it seems probable it is false. There is no evidence available that Caesar had allergies or was suffering from a cold at the time. More importantly, had he sneezed it might have been noted, and recorded, being taken as an omen, and one clearly inauspicious. Similarly, if a historical figure stumbled before embarking on some venture that would probably call for reviewing some omens, taking the auspices anew, and so on. Psychiatrists have speculations concerning such matters, in terms of subconscious forebodings, and such. More simply, we know very well what would count as evidence for or against the statement, despite the fact that we do not expect to ever have such evidence at our disposal. It is an empirical statement to which possible evidence, at least in theory, is pertinent. Had we been wading across the Rubicon in the vicinity of Caesar we would have been in an excellent position to confirm or disconfirm the statement.

Matters are quite otherwise with statement 15.

It seems unclear what would confirm or disconfirm such a statement, certainly in isolation. It is certainly possible that the emperor behaved inappropriately, a drought ensued, the emperor redressed matters, and the drought ended, but one goes far beyond the data to impose a causality here. This could be a double incidence of the post-hoc-ergo-propter-hoc fallacy. One has not only problems with the empiricality of the statement itself here, but with the empiricality of the explanation itself. As far as we know, this is not the way weather works. It would be a bold historian who would today explain the vicissitudes of the weather in this fashion, let alone a meteorologist.

---

[78] This particular example is suggested by a discussion by Ludwig von Mises in his book *Human Action: A Treatise on Economics*, Volume I (Liberty Fund, Indianapolis, 2007), p. 52.

On the other hand, it would be a mistake to insist that historiographical explanation must, *a priori*, be compatible with any particular phase of, or view of, science. Accordingly, such explanations as the above may not be ruled out *a priori*, as it is *empirically* possible that factual correlations might exist between behaviors of types A and C, and weather conditions of types B and D.

A: The emperor behaves in way w_1.
B: A drought afflicts the empire.
C: The emperor behaves in way w_2.
D: The drought ends.

Let us supposed that the emperor is in the grip of a scientific elite, and, following their instructions, behaves inappropriately forty times in a row, which behaviors are followed by forty droughts; after each of which he gratefully changes his ways, and, each time, the droughts end. Discounting the likelihood of coincidence, it seems clear that something is going on. What is going on, of course, is not clear. Induction suggests that there are causal connections involved. In theory, we see, then, that statement 15, is subject to confirmation; and, too, of course, happily, it is subject to disconfirmation. For example, let us suppose that in the second experiment the emperor behaves in way w_1 and there is a bumper crop that year, and so on. Thus, the hypothesis that the emperor's behavior is determinative of agricultural well-being in the empire is, for most practical purposes, refuted, and that will be good enough for almost everyone except an occasional philosopher of science.

On the other hand, the historiographer, unless he has good reason to demur, is well advised to keep his explanations, and statements, within the bounds of current scientific plausibility. His explanatory excursions, then, should be scientifically conservative, that is, compatible with the laws of nature, and such, at least as they are currently understood. They should not contradict the nature of the world as it seems to be. This is not a hard-and-fast rule, of course, as sciences and plausibilities can change; for example, an explanation quite in accord with, say, Aristotelian science, invoking teleological causality, might not be in accord with a Newtonian science, presupposing a mechanistic antecedent-condition causality. It may be recalled we recommended a methodological commitment to the D Hypothesis as providing a comprehensible framework for explanation. In this respect, it seemed superior to the I Hypothesis and the M Hypothesis, both of which, while possibly true, provided us with little, if any, explanatory utility.

As statement 15 transgresses the currently understood bounds of scientific plausibility, we will rule it out, provisionally, as a historical statement.

II. A Theory of Historical Statements

The following is an explicit explication, constituting a theory of historical statements. As an explication it is a proposal, and, accordingly, is neither true nor false, but more or less useful, illuminating, valuable, and such. It is substantially descriptive of what the author takes to be common understandings of historical statements, but it is essentially, as a proposal, prescriptive. It intends to produce a conceptual structure in terms of which clarity and order, in a rational and acceptable manner, may be introduced into a complex and diverse subject matter.

As what follows is an explication and not a report, characterization, or description, it will be stated in terms of necessary and sufficient conditions. In this way its adequacy or inadequacy may be most easily assessed. An explication consists of an *explicandum*, that which is to be explicated, and an *explicans*, that which does the explicating. In this case the *explicandum* is 'x is a historical statement' and the *explicans* is the list of necessary conditions for a historical statement. The set of necessary conditions, conjointly, constitutes a sufficient condition for a historical statement.

Here and there I will comment on one condition or another, as might seem appropriate, or helpful.

x is a historical statement if and only if:

1. It is a statement. (Thus, analytically, it possesses a truth value.)
2. It is a contingent statement. (It may be neither analytic nor inconsistent, for reasons earlier stated.)
3. It is a past-referring statement. (As noted earlier, much here may be context-dependent. For example, that Bill blinked one second ago would not normally be taken as a historical statement.)
4. It is a statement whose truth value, in theory, may be known.
5. It is a statement whose truth value, in theory, may be known empirically. (One needs this in order to discount statements whose truth value might be known, or claimed to be known, by revelation, prophetic utterance, mystical intuition, and such. It is understood, of course, even within the empirical realm, that the truth value, as noted earlier, need not be known, need never be known, may remain forever unknown, and so on.)
6. It is an interhuman statement. (It is neither extrahuman, as, say, pertaining to events taking place in Pangaea, nor intrahuman, as, say, pertaining to cellular chemistry, or such. 'Interhuman' does not, strictly, require more than one individual, but it does require societal and cultural relationships and such, which would affect the individual. For example, if there were an isolated individual searching for other survivors after a nuclear holocaust, statements pertaining to his efforts would count as "interhuman.")
. It is a statement which can be chronologically located. (This does not rule out speculations about Paleolithic developments, and such. It is designed to rule out unanchored, free-floating statements which one has no way of integrating into a practical temporal framework or time line, for example, the labors of Hercules.)
8. It is a statement which can be spatially located. (This is required to rule out unanchored, free-floating statements which one has no way of integrating into a practical spatial framework, for example, 'Odysseus was detained on Calypso's island for seven years'.)
9. The statement should have reference to a causal nexus. (This requirement is doubtless controversial, and perhaps vague, but it seems important to tie historiography in with empiricality, naturalism, and science. One is interested in ruling out mythological historiography, theological historiography, mystical historiography,

and such. Assertions about the interactions of a god or gods in history, as in the Iliad, and such, would not seem well considered as historical statements, nor statements asserting the existence of miracles, and such. This is not to deny that the gods might exist and might not have favored Achaeans or Trojans, and such, nor that miracles might not occur, but, rather, to say that such statements, true or false, are not well regarded as historical statements. Thus, an assertion to the effect that a miracle did not occur on Tuesday in Minneapolis might be true, but it would not count as a historical statement. If it did count as a historical statement, then, in virtue of the principle of historical negation, we would have to account its negation, 'A miracle occurred on Tuesday in Minneapolis', a historical statement, and, presumably, we would not wish to do that.

More serious problems may arise with condition 9 with respect to the notion of having reference to a causal nexus, which is not identical with, for example, stating or speculating about specific, contiguous links in a "ground-level" causal chain. The reader may recall that the three patterns of primary historiographical interest were possibilities 1, 2, and 6, as follows:

1. Real, significant, and causal.
2. Real, significant, and noncausal.
6. Imposed, significant, and noncausal.

Obviously Pattern 1, that of real, significant, and causal, deals directly with a causal nexus. On the other hand, Pattern 2, that of real, significant, and noncausal, as we are understanding these things, has "reference to a causal nexus." Often patterns are not causal themselves, but emerge as a result of causality. They are effects of causality, or, so to speak, epiphenomena of causality. An example would be an alleged general cycle of the rise and fall of civilizations. Believing in such cycles might have causal effects in its turn, but that would involve a new causal line. Such patterns in themselves are not causal. They are not like the lighting of a fuse, the burning of the fuse, and a subsequent explosion. Pattern 6, that which is imposed, significant, and noncausal, also, as we are understanding these things, has "reference to a causal nexus," as it is intended to colligate, classify, and conceptualize causalities and consequences of causalities, as, for example, the concept of a renaissance is an attempt to organize and illuminate a large number of causalities and consequences of causalities, in a given area over a given time.

If the I Hypothesis is adopted, references to a causal nexus are out of order, unless one wishes to redefine causal nexus in terms of probability summations over large numbers of theoretically random events, in which nothing in particular is explained at all. Similarly the M Hypothesis appears to lack explanatory value, even should it be true. We recommended the D Hypothesis to historiographers, as it provides one with a *modus vivendi* for explanatory intelligibility.

The notion of reference to a causal nexus, too, calls attention to the desideratum of scientific conservatism, that one's work should not contravene established fact, should not be incompatible with the laws of nature, should not challenge, without good reason, well-confirmed scientific theories, and so on. This is not simply a matter of naturalistic, or humanistic, bias, one cognitive posture as opposed to others, but a condition of being able to know what one is talking about. Following Kant, who preached better than he practiced, whereas percepts without concepts may be blind, concepts without percepts are empty.)

10. The statement must be significant. (We have noted that significance tends to be observer-dependent, e.g., someone might be more concerned than someone else with the buttons on Civil-War uniforms, or Cremona violins, or nuclear weaponry, or context-dependent, e.g., important in some way for understanding something, say, what happened last Tuesday in Minneapolis, but still it seems something like this is needed. For example, Caesar's crossing of the Rubicon was significant, but Jones' crossing the street at State and Madison in Chicago is probably not notable, except perhaps for the fact that he arrived safely on the other side. In any event, it is not likely it would be regarded as a historical statement.)

III. Ancillary Observations: Historical Process and Historical Event

Some interesting relationships obtain amongst the concepts of historical statement, historical process, and historical event. Any of these concepts deserves attention, and, obviously, might have been explicated along the lines we pursued in explicating the notion of "historical statement." Indeed, superficially, it might seem that each of these could be explicated in terms of either of the other two, and it would be a matter of indifference where one started. One would, of course, need a serious explication for the base notion, whichever notion one selected as the base notion. This surmise, however, that all these notions might be mutually explicable, plausible as it might seem, is incorrect.

Just as we took 'statement' as a primitive term in the locution 'historical statement', we take 'event' and 'process' as primitive terms in the following. All of these notions, of course, are epistemically subtle. That is presumably clear from the recently proposed explication of "historical statement." Few things are simple once one begins to look into them. Perhaps that is why so many, including philosophers, look into so little of so much. In any event, one must start somewhere.[79]

---

[79] In order to give some sense of various philosophical subtleties ignored, hopefully judiciously, in the foregoing, one might distinguish amongst sentences, statements, and propositions. On one approach to these matters, sentences are verifiable particulars; they may be seen, heard, and so on; also they are in particular languages; on the other hand, they lack truth values. For example, 'I am taller than he is' is visible, meaningful, and in a language. On the other hand, it obviously lacks a truth value. In a suitable context, it might be understood to express a statement, which would be meaningful, in a language, and possess a truth value. The statement is a universal, which might be instanced by any number of sentences. We need a word, too, for what might be being said in diverse languages, the "same thing" that might be said in different languages. We will refer to that as a proposition. It is meaningful, and has a truth value, and is, as the statement, a universal, as it may be instanced by diverse statements. It makes no sense, however, to think of the proposition as being in a language; it is, rather, what might be said in various languages. As sentences may express statements, so, too statements will express propositions. This is a way of drawing some useful distinctions which will illuminate speech practice. It is, of course, an interpretation imposed on data, a way of organizing data, speech data, a way of speaking about speech data. Saying that statements or propositions exist is not like saying that raccoons or zebras exist. In the following diagram, sentences must be used to stand for sentences, statements, and propositions. We have, below, four sentences, two in English and two in German; the two English sentences express the same English statement; and the two German sentences express the same German statement. The English statement and the German statement, should they be synonymous, express the same proposition.

4 Sentences			
The ball is red.	The ball is red.	*Der Ball ist rot.*	*Der Ball ist rot.*
2 Statements			
The ball is red.		*Der Ball ist rot.*	
1 Proposition			
The ball is red.			

Let '≡' be understood as 'if and only if' in the sense of a logistic biconditional, a biconditional asserting logical equivalence.[80]

Consider the following:

x is a historical event ≡ x is an event in a historical process[81]

---

80 Logical equivalence is not to be confused with synonymy. Synonymy requires sameness of meaning. Locutions which are truth-bearing and synonymous will be logically equivalent, but the converse need not obtain. For example, 'p' and 'p v (p & q)' are logically equivalent, but not synonymous. Two locutions are logically equivalent if and only if they are interdeducible, or if and only if they must, of logical necessity, have the same truth value. These two criteria are, of course, logically equivalent. The requirements for synonymy are more rigorous than those for logical equivalence. Very few locutions are synonymous. There is a popular sense of 'synonym' which means, usually, "words of similar meaning." That is not, however, the usual logician's sense of 'synonymy'. A thesaurus at hand, not to be identified, boasts of having over 10,000 entries and 175,000 synonyms. If this were true it seems that very little could be said in English, because so many words would mean the same thing. It would be as though one had a thousand words for "dog" but few, if any, words for cats. At any rate, happily, all that is required for the discussion in the text is logical equivalence.

81 Strictly, as the above formulas are functions, and the individual variables are not replaced with individual constants, nor do they fall within the scope of an appropriate quantifier, one is not dealing with truth-value-bearing entities, and, accordingly, relations of logical equivalence, as usually understood, cannot obtain amongst the locutions. On the other hand, it seems to me acceptable, and certainly convenient, and simpler, to speak of the logical equivalence of functions, as a sort of short-hand way of speaking, understanding that the suitable replacements and/or quantifications may be thought to be, so to speak, "lurking in the wings." This is extremely common. For example, 'p' is, technically, not a proposition, but a propositional variable, and thus lacks a truth value. On the other hand, one would commonly say that 'p' entails, say, 'p v q'. This might be understood as meaning that any legitimate substitution instances for the variables in question would yield an entailment. Similarly, something like 'x is red ≡ x is red', analogous to the functions in the text, would be understood as claiming a logical equivalence for legitimate substitution instances for the variables in the functions involved. It might also be noted that synonymy does not strictly require logical equivalence if the locutions are not truth-value-0possessing entities. For example, in English, in a literal sense, presumably 'brother' and 'male sibling' are synonymous. On the other hand, neither 'brother' nor 'male sibling' possess truth values. On the other hand, any legitimate substitution instance for 'x is a brother' and 'x is a male sibling' would result in truth-value-bearing locutions which would be both synonymous and logically

x is a historical event ≡ x is an event to which historical statements are applicable

x is a historical process ≡ x is a process consisting of at least one historical event
x is a historical process ≡ x is a process to which historical statements are applicable

We will call the first set above Set 1 and the second set Set 2.
Set 1 consists of:
p: x is a historical event
q: x is an event in a historical process
r: x is an event to which historical statements are applicable
Set 2 consists of:
s: x is a historical process
t: x is a process consisting of at least one historical event
u: x is a process to which historical statements are applicable

It seems clear that if x is either a historical event or a historical process it would be an event or process to which historical statements would be applicable. This would not require, of course, that historical statements are in fact applied to them. There are doubtless countless historical events and processes to which historical statements have never been applied, and will never be applied. Indeed, many significant historical events may have occurred in "prehistoric times," so to speak, in times in which a written language was not yet devised, and, perhaps, not even a form of gestural or oral communication which we would feel comfortable in regarding as a language. Animal psychologists, for example, may be interested in a repertoire of noises utilized by house cats but these noises seem more analogous to signaling than speaking. Language is commonly thought to involve a conventional

---

equivalent. For example, 'Bill is a brother' and 'Bill is a male sibling' would be both synonymous and logically equivalent. There are times when exactitude is less helpful than intrusive, and accuracy little less than an encumbrance. Accordingly, we cut an occasional corner in the text. This preference of clarity over precision, and simplicity over pedantry, is not unprecedented in logistic discourse. To be sure, one must struggle somewhat with one's conscience.

relationship between noises and meanings. The word 'chair' neither looks like nor sounds like a chair.

The terms in Set 1 are logically equivalent, namely, 'p ≡ q', 'q ≡ r', and 'r ≡ p'. Each term implies the other two. Similar remarks hold for Set 2, namely, 's ≡ t', 't ≡ u', and 'u ≡ s'. On the other hand, no term in Set 1 or Set 2 is logically equivalent to or implies any term in the other set.

It is important to note that whereas we can explicate historical event and historical process in terms of the applicability of historical statements, as above, one cannot explicate "historical statement" in terms of either historical events or historical processes.

Consider the following:
x is a historical statement ≡ x is a statement applied to a historical event
x is a historical statement ≡ x is a statement applied to a historical process

We will call this Set 3.
Set 3 consists of:
x is a historical statement
x is a statement applied to a historical event
x is a statement applied to a historical process

These terms are logically independent, none implies another.

'x is a historical statement' does not imply that x is a statement applied to either a historical event or process. For example, it might be applied to a historical figure, and historical figures are neither events nor processes, unless in some metaphorical sense. For example, 'Caesar is Irish', which we saw was a historical statement, is not properly applied to either a historical event or process. Similarly, that Caesar was Roman is true, but Caesar's being Roman does not seem to constitute either an event or process, at least as we usually think of such things. Similarly, 'The Thirteenth Century exists', 'Elam was southeast of Babylonia', and such, do not seem applicable to events or processes. Similarly, a contrafactual conditional statement might be a historical statement, but there is no event or process to which it might be applied, since, by definition, the antecedent in such a judgment is always false. At best it could be claimed it is applied to a hypothetical event or process, but then hypothetical events and processes are not events or processes, any more than hypothetical dogs are dogs. No one has ever been bitten by a hypothetical dog. It is true that all real dogs are possible dogs; but not all possible dogs are real dogs, and it is understood in this context, that one would have in mind a hypothetical entity, or a merely possible entity.

Similarly neither 'x is a statement applied to a historical event' nor 'x is a statement applied to a historical process' implies 'x is a historical statement'. For example, there have been many statements which have been applied to historical events which would not meet the criteria for historical statements. For example, an assertion to the effect that a drought, clearly a historical event or process, was the result of inappropriate behavior by the emperor would not, presumably, count as a historical statement. Many historians have claimed to note the influence or interference in history of various gods, or such unusual beings. Recall the gods in the Trojan War. Such statements are statements applied to historical events or processes, but we are not counting them as historical statements. It may or may not be true, say, that history has been characterized by a growth in human freedom, but it is one thing to take note of that, if it is a fact, which seems doubtful, and quite another to ascribe it to the will of *Geist*, or such, some remarkable or unusual entity covertly manipulating historical processes.

> Consider now Set 4:
> x is a historical statement
> x is a historical event
> x is a historical process

Putting aside considerations of strict logicality, it seems that historical statements would presuppose a subject matter, and that this subject matter would be likely to involve, perhaps amongst other things, historical events and processes. Clearly one could have historical events and processes without historical statements. A historical process, now, would seem to presuppose at least one historical event. We have also supposed, as may be recalled, that a historical event could be understood as an event in a historical process. This might seem more problematical. Could one have a historical event which was not an event in a historical process?

No.

As we have chosen to understand "historical event" it must be an event in a historical process; in this sense it is ruled out that there could be an isolated historical event, namely, one which was not part of a historical process. Whereas this is a matter of definition, so to speak, it is not an idiosyncratic or whimsical definition. It has three major justifications, first, the very notion of "historical" seems to imply some duration and progression; historical events would presumably not be instantaneous; second, the notion of an event itself seems to presuppose something like a beginning, middle, and end, and thus process, even if the event is not historical; thirdly, an event is, in a sense, its own process, unless instantaneous, rather like the possibility of a unit class, a class consisting of one member, the analogy being the event must be in process in order to exist, at all. Logically, however, it seems one might have events which did not presuppose process but they would be, at least, unusual. Let us suppose that a divine entity decides to create a world instantaneously, rather than spreading its creation out over several days or several microseconds. That would seem to give us an event without process. It would not count as historical, however, for several reasons, such as, it is not interhuman, not reliably dated, and involves reference to nonempirical causation. Similarly, if, as the I Hypothesis might suggest, the world pops into being instantaneously out of nothingness, with no cause or reason at all, that, too, would not count as historical, as it was not interhuman, not reliably dated, and such. To be sure, such things would be spectacular, indeed, but they would not count as historical, in the proper sense. What if an idea just pops into someone's head, even a remarkable idea? One might suppose it was not a historical event, *per se*, but perhaps a personal or psychological event, which might later have historical consequences, or, rather, one might suppose it was, after all, part of a process, resulting, perhaps, from subconscious incubation, or the surprising firing of various unidentified synapses, or such.

So let us now conclude these ancillary remarks on "historical event" and "historical process."

Hopefully they have been illuminating and thought-provoking.

In order to deal with the problems of history and historiography, one must obviously conceptualize the subject matter, in one way or another. This requires the construction of a conceptual framework by means of which to identify, articulate, and analyze the subject matter. Of the various root concepts possible, such as, in particular, historical event, historical process, and historical statement, we chose to explicate the concept of "historical statement."

We took that as our base notion.

No eye is innocent.

One sees through the lens of language.

IV. Truth

The philosophical skein contains many threads, which are woven together. We have already drawn attention to this interpenetration of philosophical problems, and philosophical issues. In discussing problems connected with the past, in connection with the metaphysics of historiography, we referred to, and addressed, in some detail, the three major families of theories connected with the notion of truth, correspondence, coherence, and pragmatic.[82] Such remarks would be inappropriately repeated at this point. It may be recalled that we recommended a correspondence approach for historiography. It seems most judicious, for reasons considered, and, also, it is generally presupposed in historiographical literature.[83]

---

82 Other theories of truth exist, e.g., the endorsement theory, or "ditto theory," the assertive-redundancy theory, a "no-truth theory of truth," etc., but the types of theories mentioned above dominate the literature.

83 Many problems afflict the correspondence theory of truth. Consider: 'p' is true if and only if 'p' asserts the case. But a proposition does not assert anything; it is causally inert, like a number. People assert things. And what is "truth" to be predicated of, psychological entities, say, ideas, physical entities, say, sentences, abstract entities, say, statements or propositions, or what? And what is this mysterious "case" that 'p' is supposed to assert? Would one not need a theory of "case" or "fact," or such? And what are cases or facts, true propositions, states of affairs, abstract entities, thatnesses, or what? Also, there is animal truth, and nonverbalized truth. Happily, these considerations, important as they are philosophically, need not be resolved for our purposes. Clearly common sense, and historiography, on the whole, take a correspondence stance toward issues of truth. For example, 'Themistocles commanded the Athenian fleet at the battle of Salamis' would be taken as true if and only if Themistocles commanded the Athenian fleet at the battle of Salamis. One can recognize dogs without having an adequate theory of "dog." We are concerned here with contingent truth, of course, not logical truth.

On the other hand, no discussion of truth with respect to historiography would be complete without a recognition of, and some discussion of, one of the most unusual and brilliantly attractive of all such theories, that famously proposed by R. G. Collingwood, one of the most astute, inventive, and learned of all philosophers of history, and one of the few who was also a professional historian, notable in particular for his work on Roman Britain.

Schematically, one might sketch out a summary of major truth theories in terms of a two-place predicate constant 'R' which will stand for the truth relation. The function then would be 'Rxy' in which it is understood that x bears the R relation, however it is defined, to y. We will substitute two individual constants, 'a' and 'b', for the variables to produce the locution 'Rab', to be understood as a and b are interrelated in virtue of the R relation.

So: 'Rab' depending on the understanding of the R relation, and however 'a' and 'b' are understood, might be delineated as follows:

Correspondence: a corresponds to b
Coherence: a coheres with b
Pragmatic: a is useful with respect to b
Identity: a is identical with b

The fourth term in the preceding list should be shockingly unfamiliar. It is a way of characterizing what we might call an "Identity Theory" of truth. It constitutes a very unusual approach to historiographical truth. Most briefly, and this is in the *Verstehen* tradition, the historian's principal endeavor, and his fundamental and essential task, is to attempt to *understand* the past, and this understanding means to grasp the "why" of history, the intentions, motivations, meanings, and thoughts without which history is unintelligible, without which it would be no more than a record of bodies in motion, as emotionally and cognitively incomprehensible and meaningless to us, as indifferent to us, as unrelated and alien to us, as the ebb and flow of tides, the rhythms of day and night, the recurrence of seasons, light and darkness, heat and cold, the eroding of granite cliffs, the movements of stirred, fluttering leaves. The historian is concerned with action and action has, so to speak, an "inside" and an "outside." The "inside" is, generically speaking, thought. It expresses itself by means of the tool of the body.

As Collingwood sees it, the past cannot be known if these

thoughts are not once more thought. It is they which were the essence of the past; in them the past found its meaning, and, in them, if we are successful, we find the meaning of the past. The historian, if he is to understand the past, can do so only by means of these thoughts, which he must, to the best of his ability, in virtue of his scholarship, judgment, and imagination, access, reconstruct, and rethink. These thoughts may be subtle and difficult to apprehend; and may never be discerned; but they have the imperishability of theorems; they are immune to decay.

"We shall never know how the flowers smelt in the garden of Epicurus, or how Nietzsche felt the wind in his hair as he walked on the mountains; we cannot relive the triumph of Archimedes or the bitterness of Marius; but the evidence of what these men thought is in our hands; and in re-creating these thoughts in our own minds by interpretation of that evidence we can know, so far as there is any knowledge, that the thoughts we create were theirs."[84]

Clearly this approach to truth is not intended as a complete theory of truth, even of contingent truth. A claim to the effect that a book is on the table could obviously be true, and would not fit this paradigm. Collingwood sees history as a re-enactment of past experience. This is reminiscent of the *Verstehen* notion of *nacherleben*. In Collingwood's case, however, whatever might have been the case with earlier *Verstehen* theorists, the experience to be re-enacted, as is clear from the preceding quotation, is thought, or, more accurately, the act of thought, which, judiciously or not, is conceived of as a universal, and thus the notion of "cognitive Platonism."[85]

---

[84] R. G. Collingwood, *The Idea of History* (Revised Edition, with Lectures 1926-1928, Edited with an Introduction by Jan Van Der Dussen, Oxford University Press, Oxford, New York, 1944, p. 296.)

[85] There might seem to be an ambiguity between the thought and the act of thought, but, as I read Collingwood, what is re-enacted is the act itself, and, thus, judiciously or not, that would have to count as the universal. Collingwood gives us an example, that of rethinking Euclid. When he selects a theorem from the *Elements*, and understands it, he does not see this as thinking that Euclid thought such and such, or as an act of copying Euclid's thought. Rather, his act of apprehension is supposedly identical with Euclid's act, both acts are

A schematism to represent the Collingwoodian position follows. The notion is that the environmental, historical, physical, psychological, etc. matrix of the act would differ considerably between that of the historical figure, say, Caesar, and that of the historian, say, Collingwood. Despite these considerable differences, however, the "thought" or the "act of thought" are supposedly identical. In the schematism, following Collingwood's usual exposition, one speaks of the thought, in this case, schematically, Thought T. I have spoken of Actualization A and Actualization B. We have to have something of that sort, if only because the historical figure and the historian are different individuals, at different times, with different mental processes, and such. The notion, however, is that the thought, or the act of thought, construed as a universal, is one. The identity is not like that of two cars of the same model rolling off the assembly line, two copies of the same page, or such, there is only one car, one page, so to speak. The identity is not even like '2 + 2' and '4', but is rather like '2 = 2' or '4 = 4'.

Caesar	Historian
Matrix A	Matrix B
Environmental, Historical, Physical, Psychological, etc. ↓	Environmental, Historical, Physical, Psychological, etc. ↓
Actualization A	Actualization B
↓ Thought T	

the same act. The example chosen, of course, is one likely to be favorable to Collingwood's thesis, if any example would be favorable to that thesis. It is much more likely that two acts would be identical in, say, thinking that two plus two equals four, than in rethinking Caesar's thoughts on the north bank of the Rubicon. Plato's forms, for example, the form of "horse," would not be true or false, and such. Plato did not, as far as I know, have forms for thoughts. To be sure, it seems he might as well have had such forms. When Plato's forms are actualized, they are presumably actualized imperfectly, and are thus reduced, distorted, and degraded in their quotidian exemplifications. One supposes that Collingwood's thoughts, or acts of thought, would undergo no such diminishment, as that might impair their capacity to achieve the identity relation.

As noted in an earlier portion of this study, the apparent motivation of Collingwood's "Identity Theory of Historiographical Truth" is his conviction, one, of the nonexistence of the past, and, two, that truth as correspondence requires the contemporaneous existence of both terms in the correspondence relation. Also, as he was an informed philosopher, as well as a historian, he would presumably have been well aware that coherence is no guarantor of truth, and that utility is likely to guide thought into self-serving and comfortable channels, seductively redefining "truth" in terms of the convenient and appealing. So, in great earnest to preserve a place for, and an understanding of, truth in historiography, Collingwood, building on *Verstehen* theory, ingeniously devises his theory of historiographical truth. One supposes, of course, that he would see this as not so much inventing a theory of truth, as explicating what significant truth in historiography is, and has always been. Certainly he would find what he castigates as a "copy theory of truth" impractical and incoherent, that is, the notion that one has a copy of reality in one's mind and can then compare the copy to the reality.[86]

---

86 To be sure, literally understood, this copy theory, or picturing theory, has many problems, e.g., as there are presumably no thoroughly correct copies, it seems that there would be no true ideas; if an imperfect copy is all right, how imperfect may it be? This also, obviously, suggests degrees of truth, and, literally understood, it would seem to put poor visualizers at a disadvantage. It would also have difficulties, presumably, in accounting for the possible truth of propositions such as the following: 'There are no centaurs', '2 + 2 = 4', 'The French Revolution took place in the 18th Century', 'Mount Everest is 29,028 feet high', 'Jones is kind', 'Jones has a mind', 'Sugar is soluble', 'Jones' house will be at the same address tomorrow morning', etc. At least since the time of Descartes, putting aside an appeal to the honesty and benevolence of a divine entity, it has been recognized that reality may not be as it appears. Indeed, in a sense, this insight goes back to Democritus and Leucippus, and is certainly found in Galileo. In John Locke the mind's ideas resemble reality in some ways, e.g., shape and size, but not in other ways, e.g., color, taste, sound, and such. Berkeley called attention to some difficulties connected with this view. Collingwood, in view of his profound awareness of Kant, has additional reasons for skepticism here. There is no assurance that the world of our experience, the phenomenal world, is much like the transpexperiential world. Indeed, following Kant, it is much different. There is no "copy" of reality as it is in itself, and, if there was, there would be no way to compare it with that reality. The psychology of perception has made it clear, too, even within a mainstream

In the case of historiography, if the past does not exist, then, in Collingwood's view, it cannot be copied, no more than a single document which has been long-ago destroyed; it is not there to copy, even if one wished to do so. On the other hand, even if the past does exist, as we tried to suggest earlier, it is not the sort of thing that can be copied. Indeed, even a contemporary journalist writing about a current event he just witnessed cannot copy the event; he does try, we hope, to tell the truth about it. Even a photograph does not copy an event; it would give us a two-dimensional, momentary view from a particular angle, relative to a particular lighting, lens arrangement, choice of emulsions, and such. Similar remarks would hold for a motion–picture record, but there, of course, one would have a succession of momentary pictures, producing at least an illusion of continuity. A historiographical camera might be a valuable addition to the scholarly paraphernalia of a historiographer, but it would not solve his problems. For one thing, it understands nothing. It cannot photograph meaning. It cannot even supply its own captions or commentary. Sometimes a word is worth a thousand pictures.

Collingwood's "Identity Theory of Historiographical Truth" is intelligently and powerfully motivated; more so, I think, than many people might recognize; too, it is not merely ingenious, and brilliant, but I think, as well, elegant, attractive, and beautiful. Certainly I find it dazzling. It seems to me, however, not merely fraught with difficulties, to some of which we will address our attention, but also, in so far as something in philosophy can be just wrong, basically wrong. It seems to me to constitute an awesome, magnificent effort to solve a problem which does not really exist. For

---

Weltanschauung, that the experience of human beings is extremely complex, and a function of a multitude of factors both inside and outside the organism. Physics, too, puts in its oar, insisting that the world of our experience bears little resemblance to whatever it might be that might, with some luck, satisfy its equations, not to mention causeless events, hyperspace, and such. We have adopted, of course, it may be recalled, as a methodological simplification and working postulate, the hypothesis naive realism, or something approximating naive realism. Historiography, it seems, can get on pretty well, as life in general, without addressing, let alone solving, a number of problems which are less germane to its interests than to those of physics, psychology, and philosophy.

example, its basic assumption, the nonexistence of the past, seems to me mistaken, or, perhaps better, unnecessary, and injudicious.

The past exists.

In any event, I certainly attempted to make out a case to that end. It is my hope that I was successful. In any event, the major motivation of my effort was to provide a philosophical justification for the legitimate applicability of a correspondence theory of truth to the subject matter of historiography. It seems to me that historiography, on the whole, presupposes such a theory, and so I attempted to justify this presupposition, and, despite its obvious difficulties, clear the way for a historiographical correspondence theory of truth. I wanted to supply a philosophical ground, and justification, and defense, for what is, in any case, an unquestioned and inveterate practice. I wanted to show that historiography need not be regarded, upon reflection, as skating naively and dangerously over a thin ice, concealing confusion and incoherence. If the epistemological welfare of historiography should depend on Collingwood, if Collingwood is its only hope, it is in a bad way. The alternatives are not Collingwood or fraud, Collingwood or, for those who understand the problem, epistemic catastrophe.

If my arguments pertaining to the existence of the past are sound, or persuasive, or acceptable, then we have shown that Collingwood's Identity Theory of Historiographical Truth is not required. It is not obligatory. It is unnecessary. That is an important point. On the other hand, it is surely a logical possibility that Collingwood's ingenious theory, while not necessary, might be the best, or ideal, theory of historiographical truth. The *Via Appia*, so to speak, might not be the only road to Rome, but it might be the best road to Rome. In any event it is an independent question as to whether or not Collingwood's Identity Theory of Historiographical Truth is or is not preferable to its field of competitors, correspondence, coherence, and pragmatic. To this question we now address ourselves.

Collingwood's theory, as might be expected, confronts a considerable number of difficulties. These difficulties are principally epistemological, metaphysical, and historiographical.

The major epistemological problems have to do with validation and plausibility.

As we will see later, historiography, in general, faces considerable difficulties with respect to confirmation conditions. These difficulties are so obvious and incontrovertible that, on their basis alone, many might deny historiography the status of a science, and certainly such difficulties have their considerable role in motivating the familiar challenges of historiographical skepticism. Without instrumentation, without laboratories, without experimentation, without the capacity to reproduce situations, manipulating variables, without the possibility of replicating experiments, how can the historiographer test his hypotheses? How far would physics get without its paraphernalia and its accesses to its subject matter, if it had to sit in a room, so to speak, and reconstruct its notions of the world on the basis of occasional scraps of paper slipped under the door, if it had to reconstruct its notions of the world on the basis of a surviving, possibly unrepresentative miscellany of alleged reports, many of which were likely to be tendentious and deceitful? If such difficulties attend historiography routinely, and often even with respect to the "outside" of history, so to speak, with respect to what happened, let alone why it happened, how much more acutely must they not afflict the attempt to reconstruct past thought? Indeed, one is often unsure, even in common life, face to face, of what someone is thinking. How much more difficult then would it not be to attempt this act of interpretation with a stranger, from whom one might be separated by continents, centuries, backgrounds, outlooks, and culture?

How would such hypotheses be tested?

Obviously no direct test is possible.

Yet, evidence would seem to be pertinent to the question.

Let us suppose that we have ten individuals, preferably qualified historians, ideally, too, of different times and cultures, who attempt to place themselves in a historical situation and set themselves to reactualize the thoughts involved. Would serious disagreement amongst them be disconfirming to the Collingwood approach? Would serious agreement be confirming to his approach? Would similarities be sufficient? How similar would the interpretations have to be? Perfect agreement, of course, would not guarantee truth, as all ten might be mistaken. They might have all seen what the "likely thought" would have been, and they might all be right, but that might not be what the thought actually was.

How would one know?

Having an interpretation which fits the evidence, and feeling that one is right, would not prove that one was right. Data, as we have seen, underdetermines theory. Data are quiescent; theory is aggressive. And, too, it is possible to feel an interpretation is wrong, which might be correct.

And the entire enterprise might be awry. The agent's thoughts might have been inexact, sporadic, haphazard, random. Thought might not have been much involved; perhaps psychological pressures, perhaps uncritically accepting the judgments of others, perhaps unusual responses to a casual word, or attendance to an unrecorded omen, or sudden impulses in critical situations, might have held sway. Too, if one takes psychiatry seriously, individuals tend to be subconsciously driven, and motivational thought might be subconscious thought. And, if that is the case, the agent himself might not understand his own thought. Indeed, a historiographer, with some understanding of how things worked out, might have a better understanding of what the historical figure should have thought than what he did, in fact, think.

Considerations of plausibility also afflict the hypothesis. How could different matrices, differing in environmental factors, in historical, physical, and psychological factors, and such, not influence and shape the thought? Both of the historical figure and the historiographer. Different cultures might be involved, and often different languages, or the same languages at different times. These factors would obviously infect at least the emotional context of the thought, and, presumably, the nature of the thought itself. Could the thought be truly understood in isolation from such factors? A theorem, such as the equality of vertical angles, an analyticity, might constitute a common object of thought for thinkers of diverse acculturations and times, but it is not clear that such abridged and specialized commonalities, found in artificial or formal systems, could be well generalized to, say, complex political and social situations. In such situations it might seem the thought could not be well separated from its matrix. How could one truly understand the thought apart from its setting? This may introduce artificial distinctions into something whose reality exceeds distinctions. Also, it might be wondered if one could truly understand the thought of Epicurus without understanding the unwillingness to subject oneself to the competitions and humiliations, the pettinesses and vanities, of the common life, if one could understand him without sensing the desire for withdrawal, the yearning for a quiet garden in which flowers grew; and surely, if one has hiked in the Alps, on a bright, cool summer morning, it helps to understand something about Nietzsche, frail, half-blind Nietzsche, with the wind in his hair.

Metaphysical challenges beset almost all philosophical positions, and, one suspects, even positions which find such challenges uncongenial. Even Willard Van Orman Quine, one of the greatest of recent philosophers, found himself unable, in his work in the philosophy of mathematics, to do without an ontological commitment to classes, a form of abstract entity. This was a bit like an atheist who finds himself forced to believe in at least one god, though perhaps not one of great importance. In any event, Collingwood, as many others, I think unavoidably, builds his house in part on the foggy cliffs of metaphysics. Certainly, he, as much as Plato with his forms, or Aristotle with his *in-re* secondary substances, is committed to the existence of abstract entities, of universals. Numbers, classes, properties, relations, words, statements, propositions, etc. have all been understood, here and there, now and then, as universals. Do universals exist? How would you test for their presence? If numbers did not exist, what would be different? If there were no number two, would shoes not exist?

Beyond these general problems, Collingwood has some special problems. For example, what would be the ontological status of his thoughts, or acts of thought? They are, it seems, universals of some sort. Are there unactualized thoughts, or acts of thought? And are there infinite numbers of unactualized thoughts, or acts of thought? In any event, the thought, or the act of thought, is taken as a universal. That is required for the Identity Theory of Historiographical Truth to work, because the thought, or the act of thought, of the historical figure and the historiographer are supposed to be identical, the same, one thing, and presumably that one thing is not to be understood as something which is actualization-dependent; it must exist, in order to be actualized. Analogously, the Platonic form "horse" must exist, or there could be no horses. There would be no form for them. If Plato thought his theory through, it seems he would have to have had an infinite number of forms; to be sure, they might be constructions, in a Pythagorean sense, from basic forms, say, of number, or perhaps they would all derive from a single number, say, the number "one."

If Collingwood's thoughts, or acts of thought, are universals, either they are eternal and imperishable, in the manner of your typical, everyday universals, or they would have their birth at a particular time, and then, presumably, from that point on, begin their career of being eternal and imperishable. As the problems facing these two conceptions are rather similar, we will deal primarily with the first hypothesis, namely, that we are dealing with typical universals. Presumably there are infinities of possible thoughts, and there are surely large numbers of thoughts that have actually been thought. There would have to be a universal, it seems, for at least every thought that had actually been thought, if not for all thinkable thoughts, which would really seem to be required. For example, if you were to think something now, say, that a blue elephant exists, that would seem to either exemplify a universal or create a universal which would then exist, and might be, in theory, re-exemplified. In either case, there would be many universals out there, By contrast, Plato would seem to be an arch-conservative ontologically. He had, it seems, only one form "horse." He did not have, as far as we know, a separate form for anything that might be thought about horses, say, "that is a nice horse," "that is a fast horse," "that is a slow horse," "that is a gentle horse," "that is a wild horse," "that is a black horse," "that is a "blue horse," "that is a green horse," etc.[87]

---

[87] Similar problems are encountered elsewhere, for example, if one would take words, numbers, statements, propositions, and such, to be universals. Supposedly there is an infinite number of natural numbers, and an equal number of even numbers, and an equal number of odd numbers, and an equal number of numbers divisible by 647, and so on. Thus one has infinities hovering about infinities, and such. My own view here is Carnapian, which is to speak as though universals existed, without worrying about whether they do or not. This might be a bit sly or unfair, but it works. Universal talk is handy talk. I do not think, however, that this sort of move would do for

And so we have a problem of the ontological status of thoughts, and of unactualized thoughts. As normally understood, in our first hypothesis, universals do not require a thinker, and certainly not with hitherto unactualized thoughts, nor, given our second hypothesis, the "birth of the universal" notion, would they continue to require a thinker between actualizations. The "objective thought" or "objective act of thought," on both hypotheses, would presumably be the thought, not the actual thinking of it, or the act of thought, not the actual performance of the act. The thinking and the performing would belong to the exemplification, not what was exemplified. Analogously, Dobbin or Citation participates in the form of "horse," or imitates the form "horse," or such, but are not themselves the form "horse."

An additional problem here is the relation between the thought, or act of thought, and the actualization or exemplification of thought, or the actualization or exemplification of the act of thought. This would be analogous to Plato's problem of how to account for the manifestation of eternal, imperishable forms in a world only too different, a world too finite and transitory, "too contaminated with the pollutions of mortality." If a Demiurge, or a *deus ex machina*, or some such agent, handles this, it would be nice to know how it goes about its work.

It seems strange to think of thoughts waiting around, so to speak, to be thought or rethought. Most thoughts, one supposes, would never be thought, let alone, rethought.. Too, it would seem difficult to know if one were thinking the same thoughts as, say, Caesar or Justinian, or Napoleon. An imperfect actualization would presumably not do the trick. It would not be the same universal. Something which is almost a triangle is not a triangle.

To be sure, Collingwood is after something extremely important. Putting aside the metaphysics, and such, is this not rather what one hopes from a historiographer, that he will do

---

Collingwood. His theory seems to presuppose that more is involved than a convenient modality of discourse. His theory seems to presuppose that universals must exist, in some real, if unspecified, sense.

his best to rethink the thought of the past and, to the best of his ability, make it clear to us.[88]

---

88 Before leaving the topic of universals, and their historiographical relevance, I would like to suggest two applications of the "theory of universals" which would allow, first, a possible expansion of a Collingwoodian epistemology, and, secondly, would supply a stance in terms of which a radically new theory of the past might be proposed, one which, perhaps, Collingwood might have found of interest. First, as indicated in the text, the typical universal is not of thought but of "thing," in a broad sense, dog, horse, shuttle, man, temperance, justice, courage, beauty, wisdom, holiness, and such. Plato probably confused meaning with naming, a likely enough error given the time. If a word was meaningful, there had to be something it named, and, pretty obviously, a word like 'horse' was meaningful. Accordingly, it had to name something and, presumably, as horses were big and little, young and old, came and went, and so on, but the word stayed, and was permanent, it had to name something stable, something permanent, as its meaning was stable and permanent. Accordingly, the most likely candidate for the word's meaning would be a sort, a kind, or, better, a form. Plato, too, seems to have been mesmerized by the necessary truths of geometry, which seemed to bespeak a world of purity and perfection, unspeakably superior to a world of disappointment, defeat, frustration, transience, and tragedy. By means of his mind he touched a better world. Now, if there could be universals of things, and, following Collingwood, of thoughts, might there not be universals, as well, of incidents, events, behaviors, and such, the "outside" of history? Is not, say, "stone rolling down a hill" a possible universal? Certainly, it has been enacted many times. Indeed, is this not the way one understands anything, as being a sort of thing? To be sure, this accessing of reality via universals is perhaps not an expansion of a Collingwoodian epistemology so much as it is a recognition of an aspect of that epistemology. For example, if one could not access the "what" of history to begin with, it would be impossible to even begin asking questions about its "why," its thought, and meaning. Now, suppose one were willing to agree with Collingwood that the past did not exist. Even so, just as one might view a stone's movement on a hill as an enactment of a universal, or an event as the enactment of a universal, so, too, one might take the entirety of human history as one vast enactment of, or exemplification of, a prodigious universal. Then, since universals are eternal and imperishable, one could found a theory of historiographical truth on the basis of that universal, which always existed, and will always exist. 'p' is true if and only if it agrees with some aspect or another of that existing universal. In this way, even without the existence of an actual past, one could frame a truth theory in terms of the universal which was exemplified in that past. In this way one could have a nonexistent past and yet preserve a correspondence theory of truth, the correspondence then being between the historiographer's thought and the nature of the actual universal which was, long ago, exemplified. To be sure, I prefer my way of going about things. It involves less conceptual dislocation, and less metaphysical baggage.

To be sure, one expects much more of him, as we shall soon see.

A third major set of problems connected with Collingwood's approach to these matters might be regarded as essentially historiographical. For example, his method, well or not, might be seen as seriously incomplete, overly intellectualistic, or rationalistic, and neglectful of processes whereby, over generations, complex institutions and intricate practices, unplanned and unforeseen, may be evolved.[89]

There are two principal ways in which Collingwood's theory might be regarded as seriously incomplete, one is the too little emphasized treatment of the relation between the matrix and the thought, or act of thought, and, two, the lack of sufficient attention given to the noncognitive factors involved in the historical process.

First, whereas Collingwood is certainly concerned to understand the problems faced by historical figures, and the circumstances of their action, it seems that the thought, in an almost Enlightenment manner, is regarded as essentially detachable from its matrix. In our schematism, we noted that the matrix consists of such factors as the environmental, the historical, the physical, the psychological, and such. It seems unlikely that one can truly understand the "thought" involved, or the "act of thought" involved, without some emotional rapport, without sensing its possible suffusion in apprehension, fear, suspicion, hope, distrust, anticipation, and such. To concentrate on, say, thought, unless thought is understood here in a very broad or rich way, would seem reductive, and result in a misunderstanding of, a distortion of, the historical reality. This sort of thing may not be essential to working through Euclid's elements, but, when one is working through a proof or two, one is not out to understand Euclid; one is out to understand geometry. In a historical situation, on the other hand, one may, indeed, be out to understand, as well as one can, a Hannibal or Scipio, a Richard I or a Saladin. Probably the historian, who has his own, quite-different matrix, can never adequately understand this sort of thing, which, in any event,

---

[89] In a sense, there are two Collingwoods, Collingwood the philosopher of history, and Collingwood the historian. In Collingwood's historical work there is little evidence of Collingwood the philosopher. In the trenches of his practice, one detects little of theory. On the other hand, perhaps one might regard the theory as implicit, or something along those lines.

certainly does not fit the schematism of a shared universal, in the absolute, or identical, sense that Collingwood seems to desire. The Collingwood paradigm is unrealistic and unattainable. This does not make historiography impractical or impossible. It does suggest that the "shared universal" approach is not only unvalidatable, but inadequate, even if it were achievable. It would be only a part of the story. The meaning of history is not only cognitive; it is also emotive.

Second, in Collingwood, we find too little emphasis, at least officially, on the noncognitive elements which so often have so profound an effect on history, disease, famine, floods, location, resources, accidents, battles, demographics, climate, mass movements, gradual social changes, mineral and soil exhaustion, and so on. One of the major occupations of the historian is to find out what happened. One cannot simply resign this sort of thing to the empirical scientist, who may not be much interested in most of it in any event, as it seems local and transitory, and reserve the impact of such things on thought, or acts of thought, to himself. The "what" must be in hand before one can speculate on its "why." There can be no meaning without its occasion, and its vehicle. This brings us to another historiographical criticism, which is that Collingwood's approach appears to be, with its almost exclusive emphasis on thought, or acts of thought, overly intellectualistic.

It might also be speculated that Collingwood's approach to history might not only be overly intellectualistic, but, perhaps, also, overly rationalistic. It tends to be a basic supposition amongst depth psychologists, doubtless founded on clinical experience, that the human organism is fundamentally irrational, that it is predominantly a creature of feeling and impulse, that the "chip" of consciousness, with its corner of rationality, floats on a dark, secret sea, one deep and tumultuous, of unconscious emotion, vanity, self-seeking, desire, and bias. The Id is alive and well; it bides its time. If there is anything to this somewhat harrowing view of ourselves and our neighbors, even if not all that much, I think it should be accepted that the definition of the human being as a rational animal might, by definition, rule out much of the human race. At the very least it expresses an optimistic outlook. If the human being were fundamentally rational one supposes politics, the media, advertising, popular culture, and such, at least as now existing, would soon collapse. This is not to deny that the human being may be a clever animal, but cleverness and rationality are not necessarily the same thing. What we are suggesting here is that trying to understand human beings in terms of rational thought may not carry us much farther, if that, than Euclid, if our friends in psychology are to be credited, even approximately. Now, if this is true of all, or most, human beings, consider the case with a special subset of human beings, those who seek positions of great power, those who will sacrifice anything or anyone to achieve it, and who have the callous pragmatism to do what is necessary to retain it, at any cost. The world-historical individual, Hegel maintained, is different from us. He is above and beyond the common laws of morality, of humanity, and such, and is not to be seen in, nor judged by, the terms of such encumbrances; the rules are for us, not for him. And Hegel seemed to think this was all right. The admonishing *Gelehrte*, for example, proves his superiority to Alexander by not conquering Asia. In any event, one who fights for, and achieves, certain levels of power is not likely to be your typical, everyday fellow. Indeed, power itself is apparently seductive, and has its transformative effects. Lord Acton, it will be recalled, claimed, or, better, speculated, that all power corrupts, and absolute power corrupts absolutely. That is probably wrong, but he was no mean historian. That he might have been five-percent right is alarming enough. What does seem clear is that ambitious kings, tyrants, conquering generals, warlords, religious zealots, dictators, and such, are not likely to be found hovering about the means of human normality. Indeed, have not an unusual number of world leaders, from Caligula to Hitler, manifested unusual psychological profiles? The point of all this is that it might be difficult for a historian to identify with, or even to understand, many historical figures, even apart from differences in time and culture, in life conditions, cognitive fields, and such. The great leader might be, in effect, psychotic. His world might be small, dark, and terrible. If this is the case your average intelligent, professional historian may find it difficult to share such dark universals. Much of history, like much of life, is not rational. Accordingly, an approach to history with the seeming presupposition of its fundamental rationality, the practicality of sharing universals of thought, may be more the fruit of a misguided hope, than of a well-warranted assumption.

One can certainly sympathize with Collingwood that one should not adopt a "spectator view of history," and, so to speak, see it from the outside, as though it were a typical phenomenon of nature, merely, in its way, "the movement of material bodies through physical space according to mathematical laws." Such an approach, if anyone should desire to attempt it, perhaps because of some *a priori* commitment to some unusual or specialized view of science, perhaps based on the eschewing of "inner variables," and an insistence on quantifiable stimulus conditions and behaviors, or such, would replace history with nonhistory, with a facade, a hollow surrogate, a curtain behind which, as in the case of Parrhasios, there was nothing. It would be like trying to understand a painting, even that of Parrhasios, by chemically analyzing its pigments. The inner variables are, indeed, as Collingwood reminds us, the home of history. On the other hand, part of history, as well, are the material bodies in motion. The inside cannot exist without an outside. Collingwood's emphasis, with which one might fervently agree, tends, in its own way, to reduce and diminish history, by according too little merit or importance to the factors with which thought, or acts of thought, must deal. In this sense, one might see Collingwood's emphasis on thought, or acts of thought, as justified as it is, as one-sided, or extreme. There is more to history, as there is to life in general, than thought, acts of thought, and such. Ideas, as usual, come with bodies.

A third sort of criticism which might be proposed in connection with Collingwood is his seeming lack of attention to processes which, in their way, combine the cognitive and the noncognitive. He does, explicitly, call attention to the unforeseen consequences of action, that a historical figure might, say, do such-and-such and expect such-and-such, but that the results might prove to be quite other than were expected. What I have in mind here, however, is something alluded to earlier in this study, namely, systemic processes, evolutionary rationalism, spontaneous order, and such. Here we have a most remarkable form of interaction between thought and circumstances, which, over generations, without planning or foresight, can produce remarkable human achievements, achievements beyond the capacity of any individual, or small number of individuals, achievements such as a market, language, morality, religions, churches, governments, sciences, philosophies, and more.

The preceding suggestions for criticisms or challenges to Collingwood, a most singular scholar and philosopher, and one whom I profoundly respect, are based largely on a "holistic reading" or "interpretation" which, substantially correct or not, if one were addressing a book to this remarkable man, would have to be qualified variously.

Consider, for example, the following four quotations:

"The history of thought, and therefore all history, is the re-enactment of past thought in the historian's own mind."[90]

But the notion of thought can be very broadly understood:

"The ... historical method is the only one by which I can know the mind of another, or the corporate mind (whatever exactly that phrase means) of a community or an age."[91]

This surely seems a difficult notion. For example, if there are considerable difficulties in accessing the mind of a single individual, how exponentially, it would seem, must be the range of difficulties in accessing the minds of thousands of unknown individuals, or, say, a corporate mind, or of the 14th Century, or such. What would a corporate mind be, the mind of General Motors, the mind of France? And Collingwood himself worries about what exactly such a phrase might mean, and he is the fellow using it. If he does not know, how should we know, or is it necessary to know? Similarly, literally, it is not clear that, say, a corporation has a mind, or that an age, say, the 14th Century, has a mind. One rather senses what Collingwood wants to do here, and one is sympathetic, but this seems to be a far cry from trying to understand Caesar's thoughts before crossing the Rubicon.

And later:

"All history, then, is the history of thought, where thought is used in the widest sense and includes all the conscious activities of the human spirit."[92]

---

90 Op cit., p. 215.
91 Ibid., p. 219.
92 Op. Cit., p. 445.

It is not perfectly clear what Collingwood has in mind here. Presumably he does not have in mind everything of which the human being might be conscious, for example, the stream of sensation associated with sight, hearing, smell, touch, taste, and so on, including sensations of the proprioceptive senses, kinesthetic and vestibular, and of the organic senses, whereby one might experience warmth, cold, pressure, pain, and such. And, too, would feeling emotion, fear, apprehension, hope, and such, count as conscious activities of the human spirit? If we take the words 'activities of the human spirit' seriously then, one supposes, one would be dealing with activities, things related to action, and that action would have to be either consciously intended, such as performing an act or refraining from performing an act, or, perhaps, too, one might allow habitual or unconscious activities which would be acceded to by consciousness, if the matter came up, perhaps, say, wearing a ring one has forgotten about, or such. There would seem to be some difficulties in understanding acts of the human spirit. Do they differ from acts of the human body, or such? One supposes that writing a letter or greeting a friend would count as activities of the human spirit. Presumably sweating, digesting, sneezing, and coughing would not count as activities of the human spirit. Would being angry, or suspicious, or jealous, or feeling enraged, or weeping, or putting on shoes, or combing one's hair, count? It seems that very little, or almost anything, might count as activities of the human spirit. I have, in the text above, construed thought, and act of thought, rather literally, as it seems to make the most sense, given the whole picture. It would seem difficult, for example, to re-enact the same thought as a community or age. Too, if one took seriously the notion of re-enacting past *experience*, it seems that smelling the flowers in the garden of Epicurus or Nietzsche's hiking in the Alps would be such experiences, but Collingwood explicitly, as we have seen, rules out such things.

We have suggested above that Collingwood's approach to history might be overly intellectualistic, or overly rationalistic, and called attention to irrational thought, unconscious thought, and such, and the presumed difficulties of re-enacting such things. One should note, of course, that Collingwood was as aware of the irrational in history as anyone else.

Consider the following quotation.

"The idea that man, apart from his self-conscious historical life, is different from the rest of creation in being a rational animal is a mere superstition. It is only by fits and starts, in a flickering and dubious manner, that human beings are rational at all. In quality, as well as in amount, their rationality is a matter of degree: some are oftener rational than others, some rational in a more intense way."[93]

This quotation could be read in at least two ways, first, irrationality is endemic but it is not an appropriate or possible subject matter for history, which is concerned with thought, or irrationality is a form of thought, and may be re-enacted, as, say, the thought of Euclid. If the second reading is correct, then the problem arises of the plausibility of its being counted as thought, and the difficulties of re-enacting it, if it is to count as thought.

In closing these brief remarks on Collingwood, I should like to reference his lovely metaphor of a "picture of the past" and its relation to coherence theory. One must distinguish between a truth-making property and a truth-testing property. The property which would make the historian's thoughts true, following Collingwood, is the sharing of the universals of thought, or acts of thought. This is required by the Identity Theory of Historiographical Truth. This is involved in understanding truly, in successful *Verstehen*. On the other hand, the historiographer has no way of being certain that he has been successful in this daunting task. One may not be certain that one has understood a contemporary, face to face, or even, given the notorious fallibilities of memory, one's earlier self of, say, five minutes ago. Accordingly, one needs a test for truth, and the test will be the consistency, or coherence, of the "picture of the past." This is, of course, a negative test. As with Socratic Elenchus, it may disprove but it cannot prove. Socrates may call attention to the fact that an interlocutor's views are inconsistent, but that does not refute either of the conjuncts, only their conjunction. One knows that 'p & ~ p' is false, and that '~ (p & ~ p)', or 'p v ~ p', is true, but this does not tell us which conjunct or disjunct is true, and which is false. And, in the case of incompatible "pictures of the past," one is dealing not with contradictories, one of which must be true, but with contraries, which cannot both be true, but might both be

---

93 Ibid., p, 227.

false. It is quite possible that there are no true pictures of the past, but, clearly, some pictures are better than others, better warranted by the evidence, and such, and, hopefully, though not necessarily, the better pictures are likely to be the truer pictures.

Please consider the following two quotations:

"... no system is more than a temporary resting-place for thought, the momentary crystallization of something that will dissolve again very soon; and certainly, no system can wholly satisfy any two minds, any more than it can wholly satisfy the same mind at different times."[94]

"... even in the most favourable cases, one's ignorance is infinite, and one's historical knowledge consists only of a few atoms lost in the void of endless space."[95]

---

94 Op. Cit., p. 428.
95 Ibid., p. 484.

V. Skepticism

One of the major threads in the philosophical skein is that of Skepticism, with its perennial challenges not only to various dogmatisms and orthodoxies, but to familiar epistemological complacencies. When one is confident that one does not know, one tends to be suspicious of others, who claim to know. Perhaps they do not know either. Skepticism has had, on the whole, a bad press, but this is probably because the presses were usually in the employ of transitory establishments, who, understandably, justifiably, felt their pretensions, prestige, and power were insufficiently respected, if not threatened, or in actual peril. Skepticism is not an eccentricity, nor an aberration, but an element native to many rational, inquiring minds. It is sometimes more visible than others, usually depending on the dangers of visibility. Few skeptics have been burned at the stake. They would probably not have seen much point in it. There is not much point in dying for something that might not even be true, including your own views. Dogmatists, the religiously and politically correct, are the fellows most likely to murder one another. Skeptics tend to leave people alone.

Everyone is, of course, to one degree or another, and with respect to one subject matter or another, skeptical. Society makes it clear what it is acceptable to view with skepticism and what it is not acceptable to view with skepticism. Today, many people are permitted to be skeptical of Amon-Ra and Khnum, god of the first cataract of the Nile, and even of various Olympian deities, but, depending on location, it is not permitted to be skeptical of this or that.

No wonder Skepticism keeps a low profile, and doesn't get out much.

We may distinguish between global and local skepticisms.

Briefly, global skepticisms, as the term suggests, tend to be more sweeping or general in their denials of knowledge than local varieties. Few skeptics, of course, if any, have ever claimed to know for sure that one could never know anything for sure, which would be odd or paradoxical, to say the least. Too, it would not save the day to claim that only that one proposition could be known, that one, because that would make two propositions, and so on, and, if one thing, or two things, or however many, can be known, presumably others could be known, as well, why not, and, logically, any proposition entails an infinite number of other propositions, and so, if you know one proposition then, at least in theory, you could know an infinite number of other propositions. Similarly, Skeptics, rightly or wrongly, have seldom, if ever, denied that one could know that arguments were valid or not, inferences warranted or not, as they had frequent recourse to such things in developing and defending their positions. Too, they would certainly know what they were talking about. Classical skeptics did claim, in virtue of the premise-problem, referencing disagreement and/or regression, and the enumeration problem, that the enumeration of particulars from which one might hope to generalize could not be complete or, presumably, if complete, could not be known to be complete, that neither deductive nor inductive reasoning could produce incontrovertible contingent knowledge. They similarly denied that sense perception, in virtue of the conflicts of appearances, and its limitations to appearances, could produce knowledge of the transexperiential, that which produced appearances. Few skeptics, if any, denied knowledge of regularities amongst appearances, that, say, fire would burn and water would assuage thirst. I think Hume, with his points on induction, was the first to suggest possibilities of that sort. There have been, of course, other forms of global skepticisms, for example, religiously, if one were to dismiss the world as we think of it as an illusion, as the Veil of Maya, or such.

Similarly, one might note "egocentric predicament" skepticisms, the most famous of which would be that of Descartes, pondering if his experience might be a dream, or the product of a demon, or such. Descartes, perhaps with his eye on the fate of Galileo, saved the day by invoking a divine entity, a sort of *deus ex machina*, who, presumably a good divine entity, would be above misleading him and others in such matters. This solution had little general appeal. The possibility lingered, that one could not be sure of the nature of external reality. Two other sorts of global skepticisms would be Berkeleyan and Kantian Idealisms, Berkeley in denying the material world, and Kant with his denial of the externality of space, time, causality, and such. To be sure, many philosophers, Idealists, have been dogmatic in one way, and skeptical in another. Hegel, Schopenhauer, Fichte, Bradley, Royce, and others.

Contrasted with global skepticisms are local skepticisms. For example, one might be skeptical of the claims of magic, mediums, mind readers, of one or more religions, of evolution, of science, of advertising, of the motivations of a given political party or political figure, and so on. In a world heavily characterized by flim-flam, nonsense, corruption, and deceit, a healthy dose of skepticism is probably a sign less of villainy than of mental health.

The local skepticism with which we are here concerned is historiographical skepticism, skepticism with respect to claims of historiographical knowledge. Is there such a thing as historiographical knowledge? Does it exist, could it exist? Is it, or would it be, plentiful or rare? What is its quality? What are its foundations, nature, and limits? Is it trivial or significant? Helpful or useless? Is it reliable? Are we entitled to have confidence in the claims of such knowledge, how seriously should we take them, and so on?

VI. Evidence: Some General Considerations

Whereas one need not accept some of the more pessimistic assessments with respect to the feasibility of historiographical knowledge, for example, that historiography is an account of something which never happened, written by someone who was never there, or that it is a pack of lies agreed upon by scholars, the latter witticism failing to take note of the fact that scholars often disagree, one would be naive indeed not to recognize that there is some point to such levity. If one were determined to despair of knowledge, it would be hard to find a better place to start than with historiography.

For the most part, historiographical evidence consists of written documentation, which is not to disparage alternative sources of information, ranging from linguistic anachronisms to radioactive dating. Certainly a variety of sciences, social and otherwise, and sciences not limited to traditional auxiliary sciences of historiography, such as epigraphy, numismatics, and sigillography, have provided an abundance of evidence for historiographical judgment and construction. On the other hand, the cardinal and paramount foundation on which the edifices of historiographical conjecture are raised is the document, whether this is found in pictures on the walls of caves, inscribed on clay tablets, carved in stone, recorded on papyrus or parchment, turned out by a hand press, a sheet at a time, or a power press running off its thousands of daily copies, or whatever. A document might be graffiti, scratched on a wall in Antioch, a letter, a diary, a court record, a chancery report, a temple's accounting of taxes delivered in barley, a sacred text, a secular account, a field manual, military instructions, a recipe, a poem, a ballad, advertising, cartoons, films, almost anything. In particular, of course, we are here concerned with historiographical documents, records of events.

1. The Person

Before the document is the person.

Without reiterating, we remind ourselves of the limitations of the person, those of time, place, intelligence, interest, talent, and background, of culture, social position, language, occupation, education, access to information, and such.

Here it is helpful to remind ourselves, too, that throughout most of human history most human beings were illiterate, incapable of either reading or writing. Only a particular and limited elite possessed even the capacity to record events, supposing they were disposed to do so. The accounts of events transmitted to posterity, accordingly, would be essentially of events regarded as worth recording by these particular individuals, and would presumably be presented to the future as these individuals felt appropriate.

Further, as a variety of familiar psychological experiments have demonstrated, it is quite possible for even well-intentioned, supposedly suitably positioned eye witnesses to offer interestingly incompatible accounts of events which have taken place in their immediate vicinity in the immediate past, simple, overt events theoretically in public view. One sees through the filter of oneself, and memory reconstructs an account which is stimulated by the event but, seemingly, in many respects, independent of the event. One remembers through oneself, as well as sees through oneself. One has a schema for recollection, and what does not fit is rejected. What fits is what will be accepted, and will seem veridical, and what fits may or may not have been the case. If such discrepancies can exist amongst the immediate memories of eye witnesses one understands that matters are not likely to be improved with time, recollections after days, after weeks, after months, after years. Sometimes individuals may compare notes, so to speak, which is probably desirable. On the other hand, the more aggressive, more insistent, more confident individuals may shape, honestly, if not coerce, the recollections of others, those less confident of their memories, until the others actually, honestly, have the sense of "remembering" events in the proposed, recommended manner. The desire, or need, to conform sways recollection. Conformity produces comfort, and it is a small thing for a mind, in all honesty, to subconsciously readjust its memories, in order to obtain this comfort. Might one have been mistaken? Now one realizes that one was mistaken, and is muchly relieved that one now remembers correctly. Perhaps this is a new theory of truth, the Democracy Theory of Truth, truth by voting.

In any event, memory is notoriously unreliable. One usually remembers advantageously, one may misremember, one may "remember" many things which never happened. False memories may easily be implanted, favorable or unfavorable, and these newcomers may shortly be indistinguishable from their more honestly wrought brethren.

The psychology of memory does not inspire confidence in mnemonic reportage.

So we realize that very few individuals, in any age, literate or not, will do the recounting, and that each of these individuals is dependent on his own memory, or the memory of others.

At the basis of any chain of reportorial documents, as its origin, is the fallible human, and fallible memory.

2. The Process

No finite mind could hope to grasp the historical process. Its complexity eludes human comprehension.

An infinite number of measurements and observations are possible concerning the present and past of a quiet, unoccupied room.

The unicellular organism contains multitudes.

A grain of sand, a speck of dust, has its temporal biography, its past, its diverse, remote journeys.

How then could a finite mind, or group of such minds, adequately access, explore, map, and comprehend even the surface of any historical reality, let alone detect, establish, and demonstrate the invisible currents, the secrets of historical depths, often intentionally concealed, which affect and churn that surface? Should the D Hypothesis be true the subject matter, with its interplay of thousands of causal lines and intersections, is too complex to fathom; should the M Hypothesis be true, the subject matter is not only similarly complex but additionally problematic; if the I Hypothesis is true, the matter is not only similarly complex and problematic, but ultimately unintelligible.

Thus, there is a clear sense in which history will never be grasped, never be understood, and cannot, for empirical reasons, be grasped or understood, by the finite mind, if only because of its complexity and elusiveness. Beyond this, history scorns repetition; it is inaccessible and singular. It has left the room; it has vanished.

The preceding dismal ruminations are incontrovertible; they are incontestable. Accordingly, historical understanding, "in a fully adequate sense," even in small matters, is empirically impossible. On the other hand, historiography proceeds apace. Accordingly, *sans* abandoning the historiographical enterprise altogether, the historiographer must, and does, reconcile himself to practical, moderate, achievable ambitions. His primary task is not to explain history, in some ideal sense, in terms of initial conditions, auxiliary hypotheses, and laws, but to illuminate history, to make what sense of it he can. In order to do this he will rely on the conceptual device of the "event," a heuristic invention, not a reality in itself, by means of which he relates to process by substituting for process a succession of fabrications or abstractions. He replaces process with a succession of "events," these a substitution for reality in terms of which reality may be analogized. Whereas the analogy is imperfect, this is something like the invention of numbers, the creation of valuable fictions, whereby an empirical reality, the movements of bodies, the expansion of gases, and such, may be approached and described, if not explained.

It is well to remember that what exists is process, and not events. It is convenient to think of process as consisting of events, but this is to confuse, so to speak, length with the units in which length is measured. Process is real; events are constructs. Process has one sort of ontological status; events have another. Analogously, the board has one sort of ontological status; inches and feet, centimeters and meters, have another. But history's reality is obviously quite different from that of length. The fabrication of events is quite different from that of inches and feet, and such. A better case could be made that a board consists of inches and feet, than that history consists of events.

Consider the following schema, ranging over a day, divided into twenty-one periods, each period or set of periods involving various activities, sometimes the same, sometimes different.

Morning	Afternoon	Evening
1 2 3 4 5 6 7 8 9	10 11 12 13 14 15	16 17 18 19 20 21

We shall suppose we know what is going on here, but we wish to divide this process into a set of events. Presumably there would be several ways in which this might be done, depending on our interests and purposes. Is spending the morning playing chess an event or is each game an event, or each move? Is starting the chess clock after a move an event? If writing a letter is an event, that might occupy time periods 6, 7, and 19. Thus, parts of an event might be separated in time, and, indeed, by space, as well. The letter might not only have been written at more than one time but in more than one place. Presumably we would not count moves six through nineteen as an event. Similarly, we would not be likely to count writing half of the letter and eating half of one's lunch, as an event, and so on. Process may be seamless, but, of course, it need not be regarded, cognitively, as seamless. Process can seemingly come in bumps and globs, and parts of it might seem to start, or to stand out, or to be more interesting. Falling downstairs, for example, is likely to seem more noteworthy than descending them in an accustomed manner. Thus, going downstairs in one way might not count as an event; but going downstairs in another way might count as an event.

But now let us suppose that we have at our disposal, contrary to fact, a noncontroversial concept of "event." We shall also suppose, contrary to fact, that events "exist," and that history is composed of them.

3. Selection

Obviously the overwhelming majority of what happens at any given moment is not observed. In this sense much of history and, if one likes, most historical "events" are not observed, and certainly not by any single individual, or small number of individuals. And what is observed might not be observed attentively, or meaningfully. Its occurrence might not seem important. It might occur too gradually to be much noticed at any one time. Much change is gradual, slipping by. The glaciers of history do not race. An empire may fall in slow motion. Of what is observed, much may be neglected, or forgotten. Of what is remembered, how much is thought worth recording? Some things might be too familiar, too well known to be recorded, too much taken for granted to be recorded. It may be supposed, too, that certain things, so obvious, could never be forgotten. But the future may never know of them. Too, some things might be regarded as improper to record, or unworthy of being recorded. They are perhaps things scandalous, news "not fit to print," and so on. Of things recognized as important, how many are intended to be recorded? And of those, how many are actually recorded? Similarly, of what is recorded, how much is representative? How much is trustworthy? How much is honest? And the recountings, obviously, must be by individuals with limited information and particular perspectives and interests. And of that which is recorded, which may or may not be representative, which may or may not be trustworthy, which may or may not be a satisfactory historiographical sampling, how much survives?

Documentation must withstand the hazards of men, nature, and time. Its survival is by no means guaranteed. Much is doubtless misplaced or lost Records perish, from fire, water damage, neglect, physical deterioration, vandalism, censorship, official suppression, the activities of zealots, the activities of insects and rodents, and so on. One age's treasure may be another age's garbage. Petrarch was horrified to discover the monks of Monte Cassino wrapping fish in classical manuscripts. Consider the copying of manuscripts. Will the manuscript be copied or not? A decision must be made, as copying involves resources, both of material and effort. It might take days, or weeks, to copy a manuscript. For centuries manuscripts must be copied by hand, by scholars, by gangs of literate slaves, by monks. Every copying, independently of possible omissions, errors, distortions, interpolations, and such, is a filtering. The sieve of the Medieval monastery, for centuries almost the exclusive citadel of literacy, statistically, would favor religiously congenial manuscripts, and disfavor manuscripts regarded as wicked, dangerous, heretical, unimportant, worthless, trivial, and so on. Plato thrives. We miss the writings of Democritus, fabled to have been, in their time, the equals of those of Plato.

In the following small tables, I have attempted to suggest, graphically, first, the diminishment of documentation over time, and, later, certain restrictions or limitations affecting what one might think of as active documentation, namely, that which actually influences historiographical construction. The major defect in the first table is that it suggests that much more is recorded during $Present_1$ than would be likely to be the case, that much more is suggested to be surviving in $Present_2$ than would be likely to be the case, and so on. The arrows pointing rightward are supposed to suggest the indefinite amount of history, the indefinite number of possible "events," or such, which are not recorded at all.

SD: Surviving Documentation

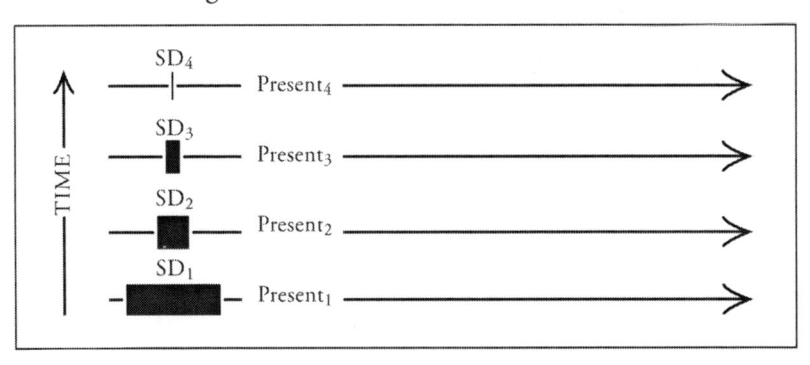

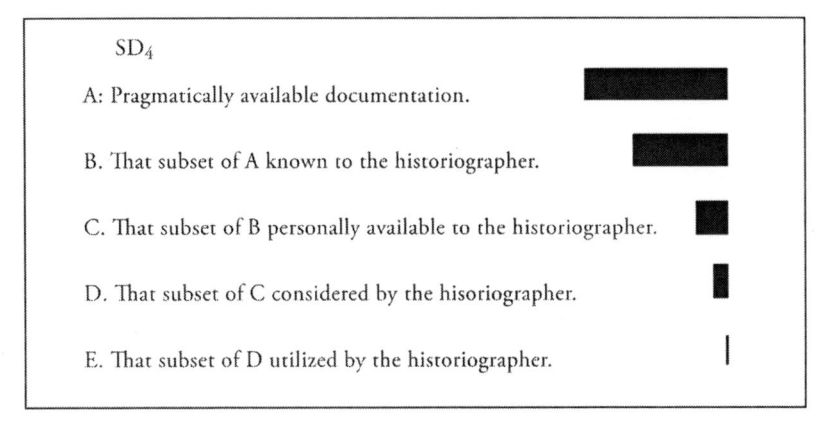

SD_4 — $Present_4$ →
SD_3 — $Present_3$ →
SD_2 — $Present_2$ →
SD_1 — $Present_1$ →

TIME ↑

SD_4

A: Pragmatically available documentation.

B. That subset of A known to the historiographer.

C. That subset of B personally available to the historiographer.

D. That subset of C considered by the hisoriographer.

E. That subset of D utilized by the historiographer.

What one hopes to suggest in this section on evidence are a number of problems characterizing the historiographical endeavor, problems dealing with the person who records, the process on which the recording is putatively based, and the almost innumerable selections amongst possible evidences which take place, both originally, and successively, as some residue of evidence, of whatever quality, reaches the historiographer. This is assuming, of course, that some evidence reaches the historiographer. It may be the case that no evidence whatsoever reaches the historiographer. In such a case, of course, questions might still arise. Would there have been evidence? Is it likely that there would have been evidence? Would it be likely to have survived? If it did not survive, why might that be? The historiographer, in such a case, as any other individual of judgment and imagination, is entitled to speculate on likely or possible relations or connections between A and B, even in the absence of evidence. Indeed, surprising to many, this is frequently done. It is an application, one supposes, of what R. G. Collingwood referred to as the *a priori* historical imagination, *a priori* in a rather Kantian sense, as a presupposed condition of recognizably human experience, analogous to the categories of the understanding and the forms of intuition. Often there are likely relations or connections between an A and B for which there is no specific evidence. In such a case, one speculates. One makes anew the epistemological wager.

Most of the preceding considerations suppose that the authors of documents, whatever may be their limitations and perspectives, are at least trying to tell the truth, at least as they see it. This supposition, on the other hand, is surely naive. If taken seriously it would constitute an unrealistic, even preposterous, concession to an undeserved majesty of authority. The pictures of the past bequeathed to us are often contrivances, vehicles for the conveyance of images, often defensive images, sometimes militantly defensive images, images which may be intended to justify or condemn, to exonerate, to plead, to denounce, such things. Often they are instrumentalities, stories told for a purpose, often a partisan purpose. Sometimes this purpose is local; sometimes it is remote, contrived with an eye to posterity.

This brings us to the Dubiety Dilemma.

VII. The Dubiety Dilemma

The Dubiety Dilemma is a powerful weapon in the arsenal of the historiographical skeptic. It presupposes a distinction between those who are, in effect, in a position to know, the "insiders," so to speak, and those who are not in a position to know, or, at least, are in a much less favorable position to know, the "outsiders," so to speak. The sort of knowledge primarily involved here deals with the "why" of history, the purposes, policies, intentions, plans, and motivations of the movers of history. It also presupposes a distinction between, so to speak, "good reasons" and "real reasons," and the psychological truism that individuals are inclined to present and defend a favorable image of themselves and their actions. Most simply, the notion is that those who are in the best position to know, the "insiders," will falsify, and those who are not in the best position to know, the "outsiders," are to that extent, at least, ignorant. The practical consequence, outside the argument, is that the notion of the present as to the past is imperiled and dubious, as it will be founded on either falsehood or ignorance.

The following argument, set up as a constructive dilemma, will give a sense of its logic.

$$K \vee \mathord{\sim} K$$
$$K \supset F$$
$$\underline{\mathord{\sim} K \supset I}$$
$$F \vee I$$

Let us now consider the Dubiety Dilemma. First, the argument, as a substitution instance of constructive dilemma, is valid. Our questions then must concern themselves, at least on the whole, with the soundness or lack of soundness of the argument. A sound argument requires a valid form and a true premise-set. The argument, as constructed, is valid. Is the premise-set true?

The first premise is an analyticity. Accordingly, any legitimate interpretation of that form will yield a logical truth. We must accept the first premise as not only true, but true in virtue of its meaning alone. To be sure, significant problems would arise with respect to this "meaning" in virtue of which it would have to be true. "K" is a vessel here, which might be diversely filled, and, when filled, it would have to be filled in in such detail and with such exactitude that 'K v ~ K' will be true, an achievement not likely to be easily obtained. To take a simple analogue, everything must be either large or not large, but this tells us little, if anything, about largeness. For example, suppose A might weigh two hundred pounds and be five feet tall, and B might weigh one hundred and fifty pounds and be six feet tall. Who is larger? What weight counts as being heavy, what height counts as being tall, etc.? Recall the dog, large with respect to the flea, small with respect to the elephant. Remember 'Either Jones is bald or it is not the case that Jones is bald'. We know Jones must be either bald or not bald, but which is he? The laws of logic, as commonly understood, prescribe and require dichotomies. Reality, on the other hand, is indifferent. Although we must accept the first premise as a logical truth, in order to comply with the laws of logic, it surely suggests that there is a clear distinction between 'K' and '~ K', and that, at least at present, is not true. There are degrees of knowing, and sorts of knowing. Too, surely "insiders" may be to some extent ignorant, and "outsiders" are doubtless to some extent informed. An "insider" may be an "outsider" with respect to another "insider," and so on. Indeed, not every "insider" need understand his own motivations in psychiatric detail. Accordingly, insofar as the first premise suggests that there is a clear distinction between knowing and not knowing, that suggestion, as noted, would be false, as, analogously, 'B v ~ B' might suggest that there is a clear distinction between being bald and not bald, which is also false. Nonetheless, we must take 'K v ~ K' as a logical truth, at least in the sense that if "K" was precise, then 'K v ~ K' would be true in virtue of its meaning alone, i.e., would be a logical truth. One might think of it, on the other hand, as it stands, as being in a sense a framework for, or a program toward, producing a logical truth.

It may be helpful in understanding the Dubiety Dilemma, and what follows, to consider the groups involved. There are, in one sense, two such groups, contemporaries to the situation, say, in the past, and noncontemporaries to the situation, say, in the present. We may then divide the contemporaries into those who, know, so to speak, and those who do not know. This gives us, altogether, three groups, $Group_1$, the contemporaries to the historical situation who presumably know the "inside" of the situation, but are involved, are partisan, are personally engaged, and such, and are presumed to be untrustworthy; $Group_2$, the contemporaries to the historical situation who presumably are not in a position to know the "inside" of matters, and thus are at the mercy of $Group_1$; and $Group_3$, the noncontemporaries, who are at the mercy of $Group_1$ and $Group_2$, at the mercy of the falsifiers and the ignorant.

It seems likely that both the second premise of the dilemma, '$K \supset F$', and the third and final premise of the dilemma, '$\sim K \supset I$', are false. We are assuming here, of course, that some clear, or reasonably clear, understanding of "K" is specified. It need not be absolutely clear, of course, though logic might like that, but it must be clear enough for '$K \vee \sim K$' to count as a logical truth. For example, in a given case, we could stop worrying about baldness once we were clear enough on the concept to decide whether, say, Jones was bald or not. It is usually possible to preserve the laws of logic this side of absurdity.

Let us consider the second premise, '$K \supset F$'. There is no reason to suppose that $Group_1$, or some of its members, might not tell the truth, either for commendable reasons or not. They need not be heroically or suicidally honest; they might regard the truth, in a given case, as in their best interests. Indeed, telling the truth is a nice way to present a favorable image of oneself and one's actions. Also, falsehood is seldom effective if not placed against, or camouflaged within, a background of truth. An inveterate or pathological liar is unlikely to be an effective propagandist. The best propaganda, as is well known, is true. It is merely selected in such a manner as to convey a view, which is one-sided, if not clearly misleading or false. For example, remarking that Jones was sober today might be true, but it might also be a way of suggesting that Jones, perhaps a teetotaler, is commonly drunk, an alcoholic, or such.

The third and final premise, '∼ K ⊃ I', may also be false, depending on the meaning assignments given 'K' and 'I'. The fact that one might not know in a given sense or to a given degree need not imply that one is ignorant in another sense or to another degree. There are also varieties of knowledge, and one might be informed in certain ways and not in others. For example, it is possible that one who is ignorant of accounting might not be ignorant of astronomy, and vice versa. In our case, an individual who might be unaware of Motivation M_1 might be aware of Motivation M_2. A servant, for example, who is not privy to certain councils, might have a reasonably good idea of what is going on behind the scenes, might divulge it in his cups, in the local tavern, and such. Too, "outsiders," from the behavior of "insiders," might form intelligent conjectures as to the covert principles implicit in certain forms of practice. $Group_2$ would be in a position to know, or to intelligently surmise, much. And those of $Group_2$ are as likely to be as familiar, or more familiar, with the "inside" of the "outside" of history than those of $Group_1$. $Group_2$ will commonly bear the brunt of history, the suffering, the hunger, the fear, the pain. It is the common man who is most likely to encounter Alaric and his Visigoths in the streets of Rome.

One thing we do not wish to do is to regard the third premise, '∼ K ⊃ I' as analytic. One would not wish to understand, for example,

'∼ K' as being synonymous with 'I', or as entailing 'I'. It is true that if an individual does not know p, then he is ignorant of p, but it is not only possible, but likely, that an individual might not know p, but be well aware of q and r. That one knows something does not entail that one knows everything; and that one is ignorant of something does not entail that one is ignorant of everything. In the present case the main difference involved is the knowledge of the "insider," which is direct, and first-hand, so to speak, and that of the "outsider," which, if it exists, might be indirect, and second-hand, so to speak. If this acceptable, then we need not regard the third premise as analytic, but contingent, and thus allow for its possible falsity.

On the current approach, the first premise is taken to be

analytically true; the second premise is taken to be clearly false, if taken as a universal generalization; and the third premise is taken as likely to be false, once again, if taken as a universal generalization. In this sense, on this analysis, one recognizes the plausibility, and force, of the Dubiety Dilemma, which is considerable, but need not accept it as discrediting or undermining the historiographical enterprise.

Its recognition does, of course, call attention to hazards of interpretation, and the necessity of historiographical criticality. As Collingwood famously pointed out, documents are to be taken not as authorities, but as sources. The historiographer is warned against trust. Surely a streak of historiographical paranoia is to his distinct advantage. Suspicion is often a virtue, not always a vice. His job is not to patch together an uncritical picture of the past, sampling and coordinating accounts, picking up this and that, from here and there, in a sort of "scissors and paste" history, Collingwood's term, but rather, detectivelike, again following Collingwood, to construct as best he can, critically and rigorously, a consistent, plausible picture of the past. That a document is false does not impair its historiographical value, for example, but may enhance an insight into an institution or time, as in the case of the Donation of Constantine, the Protocols of the Elders of Zion, and such. It is natural that men may lie, and it is to be expected when it is to their advantage. Most historiography has its purposes, and its agendas; too, it is often subject to a variety of pressures, institutional, economic, social, religious, political, and moral. The Dubiety Dilemma is less a cause then for historiographical despair, than a challenge to historiographical acuity.

How amazingly challenging and interesting must be the work of the historiographer! He is no mere purveyor of the past, no mere file clerk or keeper of records. Ideally, he does not rubber stamp the work of others or mindlessly reiterate the bromides canonized by current establishments. His work, ideally, is to tell the truth about things of significance, where we have been, and how we have come to where we are. His work is amongst the most important to which a human mind can address itself. How much we learn from him! It is through his eyes, in significant measure, that we learn to see ourselves, and our species. Who are we? He will help us learn. He is an active professional from whom truth expects much.

VIII. Knowledge

1. Problematicities

Theories of knowledge abound.

Knowledge remains one of the most elusive beasts still at large in the epistemological jungles.

Our primary concern here, fortunately, is radically delimited, having to do with a specific form of alleged knowledge, historiographical knowledge.

It is common to distinguish amongst varieties of knowledge, sources of knowledge, and degrees of knowledge. For example, a familiar distinction is drawn between skill knowledge and propositional knowledge, for example, knowing *how* to do something, such as tying one's shoes, and knowing *that* something, for example, that one is tying one's shoes, or that Congress will meet next Tuesday. Similarly, within propositional knowledge, where philosophers usually hunt, one commonly distinguishes between empirical, or synthetic, knowledge, for example, that zebras live in Africa, and *a priori*, or analytic, knowledge, for example, that zebras are mammals. And obviously domains of knowledge are recognizable different. Knowledge of history is one thing, knowledge of chemistry another, and so on. There are also a number of alleged sources of knowledge, typically such things as perception, reason, introspection, memory, intuition, testimony, and such. Indeed, one of the most famous distinctions in philosophy, that between empiricism and rationalism, concerns such things, the relative epistemic priority of sense perception and reason. Also, presumably, animals know things. This is not likely to be doubted by anyone who has ever owned a dog or cat. Thus, propositional knowledge, knowledge *that*, does not require a language, as animals lack language but possess knowledge. If one is skeptical about dogs and cats, what about chimpanzees and gorillas, or our own busy, inquisitive, hopefully clever arboreal ancestors? One might wonder if there is innate knowledge, not in the classical sense of innate ideas, say, in the sense of the laws of identity, excluded middle, and noncontradiction, but in the sense of genetically coded knowledge, as, for example, pertaining to induction, other minds, an external world, such things. Certainly there seem to be genetically conditioned dispositions to believe in such things, if not to know them. Much depends on how narrowly or broadly knowledge is to be understood, whether or not it requires conscious reflection and attention, whether or not beliefs have to be explicit, whether or not justification is necessary, and such. A bird knows where its nest is. Does that true belief require justification? Suppose someone infallibly predicts what card will be drawn from a deck, over hundreds of thousands of drawings, over a lifetime. By definition, we shall suppose no justification is apparent, either to the contestant or the onlookers. In such a case, might one speak of knowledge? We might, of course, suggest that a colossal stroke of luck is involved.

Of great importance to the question of historiographical knowledge is the acceptability of the notion of degrees of knowledge. A dichotomy such as 'K v ~ K' suggests that knowledge is an absolute entity lacking degrees, rather as '2' is an absolute entity lacking degrees. Something is either the number two or it is not. If this were taken seriously, little, if anything, would be known. Perhaps one might claim to know there seemed to be a red patch in one's field of vision at a given time, or that two and two equaled four, such things, the probability that one has forgotten or is confused about the meaning of the word 'red' or that one's addition was faulty being minimal. The amount of what is known would seem to depend on where one sets the bar for knowledge. It might be claimed that one does not know, or truly know, or such, if one could conceive of evidence in the face of which one would withdraw the knowledge claim. In such a case one would recognize that one could be mistaken, and, if one could be mistaken, then one would not know, or truly know. For example, one is sure that Queenie is a dog, and has been sure of that for several years, but, should Queenie one day, under constant observation, begin to meow, purr, chase mice, yowl on the back fence, have kittens, and such, one would presumably withdraw knowledge claims in this locality, and begin to hypothesize dramatically, say, that one had been under a misleading post-hypnotic suggestion for several years, that Queenie is an unusual cat, one which was, say, under an evil spell, now broken, that the seeming beast in question is neither a dog nor cat but an investigating alien, who had now slipped up on its disguise, etc. Setting the bar for knowledge so high, however, means, for most practical purposes, ruling out the possibility of knowledge altogether. For example, one might conceive of counterevidence to most hypotheses. What if the world turned out to be an illusion, a dream, the product of Descartes' demon, or such? What if the "Russell Hypothesis," about the recent creation of the world, should be true? Historiographical knowledge, for the most part, would vanish, but it would have plenty of company, just about everything, if not everything. Accordingly, we want to allow for gradation in these matters. Presumably we do not want a theory of knowledge which rules knowledge out.

Allowing for degrees of knowledge fits in well with linguistic intuitions, speech practice, common-sense, and such. We often distinguish between knowing more or less about something, knowing chess better than bridge, baseball better than football; we are likely to claim more secure knowledge for recent memories than for distant memories; we are likely to elevate personal knowledge over knowledge from testimony; we are less likely, in most cases, to be wary of formal knowledge than empirical knowledge, etc. Also, this allowance, this concession to practice and habit, need not jeopardize the analyticity of

'K v ~ K'. "K" might be understood variously, in terms of degrees, and such. If K is understood, as, say, 'K_1', K to such and such a degree, or as 'K_2', K to such and such a different degree, 'K v ~ K' would still be analytic, which is all that logic requires. 'B v ~ B' does not require that we always count hairs in the same way.

If we do not allow for degrees of knowledge, historiographical knowledge would become rare, if not, for the most part, nonexistent.

Classically, there are three requirements for knowledge, the truth requirement the belief requirement, and the evidence, or justification, requirement. This is sometimes summarized with the formula 'K = JTB', namely, knowledge is identified with justified true belief. The most problematical element in the classic analysis is usually taken to be the evidence, or the justification, requirement. In theory, evidence, rather like probability, which can range from 0 to 1, or certainty, can range between extremes. In short there might be no evidence, or justification, or some evidence or justification, which might range from very little to overwhelming, from not much to the pragmatically indubitable. The analogy to mathematical probability is useful, but only an analogy, as a probability of 1, or certainty, is unlikely to be reached except within the context of idealized situations, in formal systems, and such, if even there, as some might insist on the possibility of miscalculation, or such. In any event, in empirical matters, and in historiography, in particular, with which we are here primarily concerned, one does not look for certainty, at least in a mathematical sense, though one will surely encounter it frequently enough in a psychological sense. To be sure, it is one thing to be certain, and another to be right.

Here is a version, semanticized, of the classical, or standard, account of knowledge.

I know p = df. 1) p is true
2) I believe p
3) I have good evidence for p

Whereas some individuals are happy to claim, and feel it correct to do so, that knowledge does not imply truth, this is a minority view. Some feel it acceptable to say that individuals once *knew* the Earth was stationary, flat, at the center of the universe, and such. Whereas one grasps the rationale for such assertions, it is usually thought that one needs more than conviction, assurance, psychological certitude, and such, for knowledge. Knowledge, as usually understood, is supposed to require more than taking something for granted, or being sure of it, even if everybody takes it for granted, and everybody is sure of it. The usual thing here would be to say that individuals *thought* they knew such and such, but they were wrong, as such and such was not the case. In any event, the mainstream view here is that one cannot know a false proposition, though, of course, one could know that a proposition was false. Perhaps the "sociology of knowledge" has its points but knowledge and truth are unlikely candidates for cultural artifacts, as they involve transcultural obduracies, the rocks of fact, so to speak. There is little point in dislocating common discourse, and familiar concepts. If we did that then we would need new words for what knowledge and truth now mean. Too, there is a moral hazard here, which is that a totalitarian society, or any society, for that matter, could create self-serving artifacts, which would then count as knowledge, truth, and such, say, master races, politicized sciences, demon theories of disease, a geocentric solar system, the divine right of kings, and such. In any event, in the classical version, one cannot know a false proposition; knowledge implies truth.

The second requirement for knowledge is the belief requirement. On the classical view, as presented, given the hypothesized identity involved, it would be inconsistent to say one knew p but did not believe it. This could be a problem, one of many, with the classical view, but, surely, it would indeed be at least peculiar, or unusual, if not wildly deviant, to say that one knows something but does not believe it. Perhaps one might accept that the evidence for, say, evolution was overwhelming but, for personal reasons, find oneself unable to believe it, or one might recognize that something was someone's duty but find oneself psychologically unable to accept that, and so on. Here one takes one's leave of logic and philosophy; here one suspects the complexity of human psychology, of levels of consciousness, the possibilities of self-division, and such; here one hesitates, unwilling to enter domains best left to the psychiatrist. Here one turns away, seeking safer precincts. In any event, in the classical view, one cannot know p and not believe it.

The third requirement is the most obscure and porous requirement. Certainly there are serious problems of historiographical interest involving truth and belief, concepts which in themselves own epistemological literatures, but the economies of inquiry encourage us to center our attention on the third requirement: I have good evidence for p.

The following table summarizes the classical account:

#	Belief	Evidence	Truth	Knowledge
1	+	+	+	+
2	+	+	−	−
3	+	−	+	−
4	+	−	−	−
5	−	+	+	−
6	−	+	−	−
7	−	−	+	−
8	−	−	−	−

Classically, one notes, as in Line 1 of the table, that knowledge occurs only when the belief, evidence, and truth requirements are met. Line 2 indicates that one may believe and have evidence for a false proposition. Line 3 indicates that more than true belief is required for knowledge, a point that goes back, at least, to Plato. Line 5 indicates that one may have evidence for a true proposition, and yet fall short of knowledge, lacking belief.

2. Evidence: Some Particular Considerations

1. The Evidence Predicate

Evidence is a relational notion, and the evidence predicate is a three-place predicate, namely, 'Exyz', or 'x is evidence of y to z'. In itself nothing is evidence, and evidence is always evidence of something to someone.

Let us suppose that a certain small metal object is located at certain coordinates. This is, in effect, as it stands now, a part of nature. To it the universe is indifferent, as it is to pebbles, constellations, space, and such things. We suppose a savage, or an alien, finds this object. To the savage it is an unusual and interesting anomaly, wondrous in its way, perhaps evidence of other worlds, of the gods. The alien suspects the object is a token, or coin. For it, the alien, it betokens something of great interest, perhaps that the planet is, or was once, inhabited by a civilized form of life, one still utilizing a primitive form of indirect exchange, conducted in terms of physical objects. On the other hand, an individual, some centuries from now, a distant inheritor of elements of our own culture, might find in this same small artifact an evidential trove. Certainly one has evidence of a complex metallurgy, of dies and engraving; and a monetary system capable of milled coins, which may be conveniently stacked and rolled, this suggesting urbanized banking or complex merchandizing relationships; perhaps the coin shows sheaves of wheat, suggesting an agricultural base for an economy, or at least a romanticizing of such a rural past; or perhaps a form of architecture appears on the coin, reminiscent of a temple, which might suggest a form of religiosity, or, at least, value judgments, and an esteem for a certain form of architecture, contemporary or remote. Perhaps a figure appears on the object, which we take to be a coin. We get some sense, too, from this figure, of racial characteristics, of barbering, of fashions of tailoring, and such. We do not know if the figure was contemporary to the time of the coin's minting, or not. We find English and Latin on the coin, and Arabic numerals. Clearly these are interesting historical associations. Clearly, too, there are references to chronology and geography. There is also some evidence of ideas of a divine entity, and references, too, to liberty and a form of political affiliation. One might also note certain mathematical relationships, and, it seems, rather clearly, the employment of a decimal system. If the coin were a different coin, it might have had tiny, regularly grooved edges, which would make shaving the coin detectable, a precaution suggesting that such practices were not unknown, this providing, in its way, a commentary on the times.

In any event, the evidence predicate is a three-place predicate. Something is not evidence in itself, but is evidence of such and such to so and so. To one person the object is not evidence at all; to another person it is evidence of this but not of that, and to another person, it may be abundantly informative, evidence of several things, even though it might be no more than a small, inauspicious artifact, say, a Lincoln penny.

2. The Transcendence of Evidence

In discussing evidence, it should be understood that the relationship between evidence statements and conclusion statements is almost always an inductive relationship, not a deductive relationship.

In discussing evidence it should be understood that evidence statements seldom, if ever, logically imply conclusion statements. The relationship between the evidence statement and the conclusion statement is almost always, as noted, inductive. This is a case of the familiar underdetermination of theory by data. That the missing money was found in Jones' pocket certainly is excellent evidence that he stole the money, but it does not *logically* entail that he stole the money. In theory, there are an infinite number of other hypotheses which would explain the appearance of the money in his pocket, some of which, given certain circumstances, might even be plausible, or likely, say, that he is being framed, that he found the money, and so on. Most typically, in historiography, that a given source claims that 'p' is true does not logically entail, as is obvious, that 'p' is true. It is important to understand that the "picture of the past" constructed by a historiographer is not a simple function of evidence, no more than it would be a replication of evidence. It is an inevitable product of inference. It has no choice but to go far beyond the evidence, if only because the evidence, for the most part, does not go far, at all. It is, in its way, a work of art, a judicious conjecture, subject to rigorous constraints. It will never be adequate, but, with some luck, it may be true.

3. Evidential Conflict

On the supposition that historiographical evidence could be quantified, a generally contrary-to-fact supposition, one could speak more precisely of evidential conflict. For example, if a Hypothesis H_1 was rated at 40 E-points, and a contrary Hypothesis H_2 was rated at 50 E-points, then one could note that, at a particular time and according to a particular modality of evidential calculation, H_2 would be favored over H_1, but slightly, not decisively, and so on. Indeed, on one approach, H_2 would have a rating of only 10 E-points, and its plausibility would be regarded as having been devastatingly undermined by the evidence for H_1. Calculating evidential support on an ordinal scale, e.g., that H_2 is first in plausibility, or most plausible, and H_1 is second in plausibility, or less plausible, would face similar problems. And, in both cases, subjectivity would qualify assessments, in the first case with respect to the points assigned on a common scale, and, in the second, by the assigned rankings. Historiographical assessment is much unlike drawing balls from an urn, containing a given number of balls of given colors. The historiographer must assess evidence, and assign it weights, but it is not clear what is to be weighed, and how it is to be weighed.

Consider the following:

We have two considerably different accounts of certain events taking place in 255 B.C., pertaining to an incident in the Punic Wars, one account by Polybius, a Greek historian, much interested in the history of Rome, and another by a well-known Roman historian, Cassius Dio. Carthage, it seems, had been defeated in battle, both on land, and, perhaps surprisingly, at sea, where one might have expected her to have held her own, by Roman forces under the command of Consul M. Atilius Regulus. The terms of peace which the Romans wished to impose on the defeated enemy were apparently so one-sided and severe that the dismayed Carthaginians, rather than submit to them, sought and obtained the services of mercenaries, Greeks serving under the command of a Spartan general, Xanthippus. A battle was fought at Tunes and the Romans were defeated. Following Polybius, Xanthippus sailed home, his triremes laden with treasure, bestowed on him by the grateful Carthaginians. On the other hand, according to Cassius Dio, the Carthaginians, jealous of Xanthippus' victory, murdered him.[96]

My bet here is that Polybius is closer to the truth, and that

---

96 I think this is a very nice example of historiographical conflict. It was brought to my attention in a remarkable student paper, by a remarkable student, and friend, Wladyslaw Roczniak, who is now a Ph.D., with a specialty in intellectual history. The references are Polybius, *The Histories*, translated by W. R. Paton, *The Loeb Classical Library* (Harvard University Press), Book I, p. 97; and Cassius Dio, *Roman History*, translated by E. Cary, *The Loeb Classical Library* (Harvard university Press), Book XI, p. 433.

Dio may have been swayed by the stereotype of the perfidious Carthaginian, the hated enemy, if not motivated politically altogether. Too, it seems unlikely that Carthaginians would have been in any position, or would have had the resources, whether so inclined or not, to take on large numbers of professional soldiers fresh from victory. Also, one supposes that some thought would have been given to the possible consequences of defaulting on a debt, depriving mercenaries of their pay, murdering their commander, and so on. To be sure, after the battle, Xanthippus seems to have slipped from the pages of history. But then most people never appear in its pages, at all.

4. Evidential Change
This is an obvious point, important to make, but one which requires little, if any, elaboration.

Each new document, each new discovery, can deepen, shade, or alter the view of the past. An unusual lens, a primitive battery, perhaps used for purposes of religious enhancements, comes as a surprise. A constitution of Athens turns up unexpectedly in Egypt. Secrets of cuneiform are unlocked. A Rosetta stone is discovered, and new linguistic worlds lie within reach. Scrolls are found in caves near the Dead Sea, stirring religious apprehension, demanding integration into a concept of the past, objects of interest, say, journals, turn up in an attic, and one has a new insight into a past century, such things. History is frequently reseen, and rewritten. There are a variety of reasons for this, but amongst them, surely, is the changing body of evidence.

5. The Assessor of Evidence
In assessing evidence there must be an assessor. Presumably, amongst assessors, there would be considerable differences in expertise. There are different sorts of evidence and different skills required for its assessment. What is evidence for one person need not be evidence for another. Smudges on a glass, scratches on a bullet, traces of DNA, streaks in cloud chambers, alignments of strata, the positions

of stars, the displacement of wavelengths in the spectrum of a light source, styles of handscript on Medieval documents, a diminished silver content in Roman coins, the extent of radioactive decay in an artifact, and such, may all be evidence for one thing or another, but, clearly, not everyone is capable of discerning such things as evidence, let alone having the professionalism to interpret them.

In all, or most, fields, there will be considerable differences amongst practicing professionals, differences in experience, maturity, background, training, education, talent, expertise, and such. And it is natural to expect that this diversity will be reflected in their work, in the quality and plausibility of their interpretations of evidence, and such. The results of such diversity, however, it should be noted, are likely to be particularly unsettling in historiography, where they are likely to be abundant, this adding fuel to the fires of historiographical skepticism. Qualified professionals in several disciplines have at their disposal techniques and canons of interpretation which are understood by, and shared with, many colleagues, and thus a consensus of interpretation is more likely to be obtained in some disciplines than others. Such disciplines have a cognitive advantage which is not shared by historiographers, or, at least, not to the same extent. For example, one expects more agreement amongst physicists, chemists, astronomers, biologists, and such, than amongst historiographers. Two individuals are more likely to agree on reading fingerprints, marks on bullets, or DNA, than on the influence of Egyptian science on Greek science, of Christianity on the decline of the Roman Empire, of the American frontier on American culture, and so on.

The secrets of nature may be hidden, but they are not hidden deliberately. One may be interested in molecules without being distracted by motivation and meaning. Nature is more likely to be accessible than the hearts of men.

6. The Assessment of Evidence

We have noted the absence of precise, publicly certifiable, noncontroversial procedures for the assessment of historiographical evidence, and that the historiographer must assess evidence, and assign it weights, but that it is not clear what is to be weighed, and how it is to be weighed.

To be sure, it should be noted that, despite certain comparative advantages appertaining to certain disciplines, as suggested above, the inability to quantify evidence noncontroversially is not unique to historiography, but characterizes to one degree or another most empirical disciplines, including those often characterized as the "hard sciences," such as physics, chemistry, astronomy, biology, and such. It is one thing to weigh an object, measure a velocity, count pittings on a electrostatic grid, read a meter, and such, and another to generate theories, to move from data to its interpretation, and to interpret evidence in such a way as to see it as confirming or disconfirming, and to what degree, a given hypothesis.

Thus, if subjectivity is a noxious virus to be eschewed, which is not as obvious as it might seem, one should at least recognize that historiography is not its unique host, and should not be uniquely scorned. Rather, it seems that one would be dealing with a pandemic here, infecting most cognitive species, including those usually regarded as the most immune, arrogant, and self-satisfied. Only the formal sciences, if any, and that is controversial, are immune to the alleged ravages of subjectivity. The number two, one hopes, remains uninfected. Later, one must consider historiographical objectivity, what it might be, and if it is obtainable. Perhaps it is obtainable. But perhaps it will turn out to be subjectivity in disguise, a particular sort of subjectivity, a sanctioned subjectivity.

Two problems are obvious, the first is the scale of plausibility, in which hypotheses might be ranged between, say, 100 E-points, or rationally indubitable evidence, to 0 E-points, or no evidence whatsoever; and the second, where on this scale is "good evidence" to be located, as required by the evidence requirement of the classical account of knowledge, i.e., 'I have good evidence for p'. It requires no great reflection to recognize that the scale does not exist, at least in any determinable, quantifiable manner; and, second, that it is completely unclear at what point on the scale, if it existed, one would place "good evidence." On the other hand, it is also clear that historiographers, and others, do presuppose gradations of plausibility, rather suggesting such a scale, and do, at certain points, perhaps varying from case to case, claim that "good evidence" is in hand.

3. Levels of Knowledge

Obviously the third requirement, the evidence requirement, as stated above, is obscure. It is not only the case that it is not obvious how good evidence must be to count as "good evidence," but many individuals might feel the third requirement, as given, is too weak. It might be suggested that knowledge requires more than merely good evidence, that it would require evidence which was much better than good, that one would not be entitled to claim knowledge until one had, say, evidence which was coercive, indubitable, incontrovertible, evidence which could not be overturned, evidence concerning which one could not, even in theory, be mistaken. Evidence would have to be, perhaps, conclusive. The problem with this approach, if one is not claiming the theoretical perfection of conclusive evidence, is that it, too, like "good evidence," is obscure, as to its position on a putative scale, and such. On the other hand, if one is serious here, and does claim the necessity of conclusive evidence, then one seems to be ruling out not just all, or most, historiographical knowledge, but all, or most, knowledge altogether. So radical a result is not only unwelcome, but, one supposes, unacceptable.

Accordingly, if cognitive enterprises, and much of human life, as a whole, are not to be epistemically short-changed, knowledge claims reduced and devalued to the point of absurdity, one must presuppose levels or degrees of knowledge.

An approach to this matter, dealing with the quality, or assurance, of belief is clearer, and more manageable, than references to an obscure, perhaps nonexistent scale, and marking some critical point on such a scale, to be identified with "good evidence." To be sure, the following approach to levels of knowledge, in terms of belief ranking, has its own problematicities, and presupposes, or relies implicitly on, the scale and point-on-scale difficulties just considered. In that sense, it provides an approach to, or an interpretation of, those notions, not a replacement for them. It does, however, in my view, have certain advantages. First, it is clearer; we are more familiar with notions of belief and degrees of assurance than we are with mysterious, or nonexistent, E-points, and such; second, belief is closely related to confidence levels, and, in most cases, probability, and such, is measured subjectively, in terms of levels of putatively justified confidence. That is certainly the way it works in most cases, and surely in most cases in historiography. The historiographer, on the basis of such and such, regards such and such a hypothesis as more or less justified. How else, for example, is one to assign weights to causal factors, when thousands are involved, mostly unknown? Thirdly, assurance is ideally indexed to evidence, and beliefs, not evidence, *per se*, informally, judiciously or not, are often taken to sustain truth values.[97]

One approach to these matters, having to do with levels, or degrees, of knowledge would be to distinguish between, say, A, B, and C knowledge. The particular schema which follows is an approach to the third requirement for knowledge, the evidence requirement, in terms of levels of belief; it presupposes, of course, that the first requirement for knowledge, the truth requirement, is satisfied. Without truth there is no knowledge. Accordingly, all the beliefs following are taken to be true, and the only question, then,

---

[97] Technically, the truth value is usually thought of as being borne by the statement or proposition, and the belief is a commitment to the truth of the statement or proposition. It is not unusual, of course, to speak, if obliquely, of beliefs being true or false. There is, of course, the fact of animal belief, which would not be linguistic. The generic characteristic of human and animal belief would presumably be one of "thatness," a notion as to what is the case. In my view, this notion of "thatness" underlies even human belief, and is required for making statements and propositions comprehensible. Humans, too, of course, have nonlinguistic beliefs, things assumed, taken for granted, and such. In this study we are generally taking 'belief' as a primitive, or unanalyzed, expression. I think that is not only judicious, but innocent, as most historiographical belief is reasonably clear, as, say, that Themistocles commanded at Salamis. On the other hand, that history gives evidence of the plan of Amon-Ra, or that history has this or that "manifest destiny" would seem less clear. Many interesting questions do appertain to beliefs, their sorts, truth-conditions, relations, if any, to activity and behavior, and so on. Obviously, as noted, not all beliefs require expression in a language, as animal belief exists. How far down the phylogenetic scale beliefs might occur is an interesting question.

THE PHILOSOPHY OF HISTORIOGRAPHY

is which beliefs should count as justified true beliefs, or knowledge. Obviously a rational person in the 2d century might be certain he could not be mistaken that the Earth was the center of the universe, and take that belief to be rationally indubitable. He would, however, have been mistaken. He could not know that, because it was false. Also, it should be noted that the following approach, rather like common law, presupposes notions such as a "rational person." Something like that is necessary. It does not intend to deny knowledge to, say, maniacs; what it does try to do is give us a general approach in terms of which we can think judiciously about levels of knowledge.

A

A. Rationally Indubitable	Beliefs concerning which a rational person is justifiably certain that he could not be mistaken.

B

B_1 Rationally Coercive	Beliefs concerning which a rational person is justifiably certain that he is not mistaken.
B_2 Rationally Insistent	Beliefs concerning which a rational person is justifiably confident that he is not mistaken.

C

C_1 Rationally Appropriate	Beliefs concerning which a rational person justifiably would not believe that he is mistaken.
C_2 Rationally Acceptable	Beliefs concerning which a rational person justifiably would not think it likely that he was mistaken.
C_3 Acceptable	Beliefs concerning which a rational person justifiably would consider it quite possible that he is mistaken.

Some epistemologists would like to equate knowledge with the A category above, namely, that it would consist only of beliefs which were not only true but warranted to the extent that they were rationally indubitable, that a rational person would justifiably believe he could not be mistaken as to their truth.

In this schema it is to be noted that the normative notion of justification is ingredient, which is independent of the level of psychological assurance. For example, it is possible that a rational person might be certain that he could not be mistaken about p, but his certainty might not be justified. In such a case, his belief, however firm, would have fallen short of knowledge.

For example, let us suppose we have an Alexandrian astronomer who predicts, based on his calculations, the future position of some planetary body. We shall suppose that he is rational and also that he is certain that he could not be mistaken, and we shall suppose, further, that he is not mistaken; that his prediction is correct, this giving us truth. On the other hand, his prediction is based on a Ptolemaic model of the universe, which we shall suppose is false. In this case, given the putative falsity of his model, we could deny that he is *justifiably* certain, and thus claim he had fallen short of knowledge.[98]

---

[98] There are a number of interesting epistemological problems here, lurking in the bushes, so to speak, which it would be inappropriate to engage in this study, but to some of which, I think, it would not be inappropriate to give some cursory attention. In the above case, if the Ptolemaic view should be taken not as an underlying factual claim, but as a heuristic device, a mere convenience of calculation, but one known to be reliable, then one might well claim that the knowledge claim of the putative Alexandrian astronomer was warranted, that he did *know* that the planet would be in such and such a position at such and such a time. One might also argue, contrary to the view expressed in the text above, that the astronomer's view constituted an instance of justified true belief, and thus of knowledge, in virtue of the fact that the Ptolemaic model was, though false, fully entitled in the light of the science of the day to count as justificatory. False beliefs for which there is much evidence might thus provide justification for true beliefs. Indeed, as we shall also see shortly, there could be cases in which true justification beliefs could provide justification for true conclusion beliefs, and yet not produce knowledge. First, let us consider the "false justification" case. Let us suppose that we have three individuals, A, B, and C. A, who is well acquainted with B, knows that B has been the proud owner of a blue Chevrolet for several years. A also knows that B and C are waiting in the office, and are the only folks in the office. On the basis of the belief that B owns a blue Chevrolet, which is a well-justified

One last point seems in order in connection with the classical analysis, before we attempt to consider its relevance to claims of historiographical knowledge.

Let us remind ourselves of the analysis.

I know p = df. 1) p is true
2) I believe p
3) I have good evidence for p

---

belief, A infers that either B or C owns a blue Chevrolet. This turns out to be a true belief. On the other hand, it is the case that B has sold his blue Chevrolet and that C happens to own a blue Chevrolet. Here we have, seemingly, a justified belief which is true, and so an instance of justified true belief. On the other hand, we would presumably not count this as an instance of knowledge. Thus, it seems, not all justified true belief can count as knowledge. If it is objected that the justifying belief is false, one may substitute a true belief for it, namely, 'Someone in the office owns a blue Chevrolet' and then from that premise, plus the premise that B and C are the only folks in the office, again infer that either B or C owns a blue Chevrolet, a true conclusion, following from a true justifying belief. But, presumably, once again, we would not want to count this as an instance of knowledge, in this case, one supposes, because the justifying true premise itself is based on a false assumption, namely, that B still owns his blue Chevrolet. This example is suggested by Gettiertype paradoxes, from the work of Edmund Gettier, on which work a controversial literature is founded. An example which may be more telling is the "lottery example," in which it seems there might be overwhelming evidence for a true belief, which would still fall short of knowledge. Let us suppose that A believes that B will lose the lottery, and that B will lose the lottery, and that A has overwhelming evidence against B's winning the lottery, namely, that the odds of his winning the lottery are millions to one. On the other hand, presumably A does not *know* that B will lose the lottery. As it is said, "Hey, you never know." A common epistemological standpoint, currently, is that knowledge requires justified true belief, but that justified true belief does not necessitate knowledge, in short, that 'K → JTB' is true but 'JTB → K' is false, with the result that 'K = JTB' is false. To be sure, the matter is controversial. Personally, I doubt that the entailment relation exists in either case. For example, we noted at least the logical possibility of "peculiar knowledge," where one seems to know somehow, without requiring justification; also, given the hypotheses of depth psychology, it seems one might know, or realize, something subconsciously, without, on the conscious level, either believing it or justifying it, perhaps even denying it; also, it seems most people know, say, that the sun rose in Athens on April 27th, 802 A.D., but have not spent time either believing or justifying it; also, it seems there is much animal knowledge, without the animals bothering to justify it, at any rate, and so on.

This analysis may not only be obscure, and perhaps faulty, but it may be incomplete, and logically awry, as well.

Consider the following:

We might think we had good evidence for p and not have good evidence for p, and we might have good evidence for p, that is, have that in hand which, if properly interpreted, would be good evidence for p, and not think we had good evidence for p.

These are both obvious possibilities, and an interesting consequence follows from them, pertaining to the classical analysis.

In connection with the first possibility one might glance at the clock at two o'clock, and infer that it is 2 o'clock, and later discover the clock was not functioning, an example from Bertrand Russell; in another case, one might take guidance from a street sign and arrive successfully at one's intended destination, but the sign was loose and rotates in the wind; it just happened to be pointing correctly when one looked at it; or, say, one asks directions from a fellow who intends to deceive one, but he is confused, and accidentally gives one the proper directions. In all these cases, one would think one had good evidence but one would not have had good evidence. Thus, one can be mistaken about that sort of thing.

Similarly, one might have good evidence for p, in the sense that one had in hand that which, if properly interpreted, would be good evidence for p, and not think one had good evidence for p. For example, one might believe a raccoon knocked over the garbage can, and be right, and, further, the ground is covered with raccoon hairs and tracks, but one thinks, mistakenly, they are badger hairs and tracks; in 18th Century crime scenes there were doubtless multitudes of fingerprints about, DNA traces, and such, but this, "evidence" in a popular sense, could not count as evidence, epistemically, as it was not interpreted; or, similarly, one might have in hand a document pertinent to an inquiry, perhaps even a confession, but written in a language one cannot read. In a popular sense of "evidence" then, one would have in hand good evidence, but would not know that one had good evidence.

If these two sorts of possibilities are genuine, then it seems one would have to add a fourth condition to the classical analysis, namely, that it would not be enough to just have good evidence but one would have to know that the evidence was good. In such a case the analysis would become:

I know p = df. 1) p is true
2) I believe p
3) I have good evidence for p
4) I know I have good evidence for p

It seems as though the classical analysis would need some such supplementation, for the sorts of reasons suggested. On the other hand, if it is supplemented along these, or similar, lines, then the analysis becomes logically circular, as the essence of the *definiendum*, so to speak, occurs covertly, or, in the revision, explicitly, in the *definiens*. One is analyzing A not in terms of B and C, but, at least in part, in terms of itself. It is as though a word were being used in its own definition. If one does not know what 'x glorps' means, it is not much help to be told that, say, 'x weighs four pounds, is green, lives in Minnesota, and glorps'. Probably the best thing to do here is to content oneself with having good evidence, period, and acknowledge that one does not have to know that one has it, that one might not have it, and so on. One hopes that all goes well, and counts on a bit of epistemological luck.

Let us return now to the levels of knowledge.

Whereas A-type knowledge is doubtless knowledge, it would be a mistake to limit knowledge to A-type knowledge. This would, in effect, limit it to things like thinking that one seemed to be seeing a red patch right now in one's field of vision, thinking that one was seeming to believe that two and two came out to four, and so on. Certainly most knowledge claims would fall short of so Draconian a criterion.

It seems reasonably clear, then, that we should allow B-level knowledge, knowledge expressed in beliefs concerning which a rational person is justifiably certain that he is not mistaken, and beliefs concerning which a rational person is justifiably confident that he is not mistaken.

There are three levels of what we designated C-type knowledge. Presumably the tiers of C-type knowledge are the most controversial. I would personally recommend that C_1- and C_2-level beliefs, namely, those concerning which a rational person justifiably would not believe that he was mistaken, and concerning which a rational person justifiably would not think it likely that he was mistaken, to count as knowledge bearers. The most controversial tier here would be that of C_3, dealing with "acceptable beliefs," beliefs concerning which a rational person justifiably would consider it quite possible that he is mistaken. Such beliefs might, with considerable justification, be denied the right to convey knowledge claims. My own view here, however, would be contextual, and would depend on the nature of the beliefs in question. I think a great many of our beliefs fall into the "acceptable" category, and do have evidential warrant, though not to the degree that we would *insist* that we knew *p*. But, presumably, one can know *p* without being willing to insist that we know *p*, without being upset, or much surprised, if we learned we were mistaken, and so on. Much of our social knowledge seems of this weak sort, for example, that the next fellow we meet will be civil, pleasant, is honest, will speak our language, and so on. It is quite possible, of course, that we are mistaken. But the hypothesis is backed with a considerable amount of statistical evidence, and this would seem to support a knowledge claim, though doubtless one less defensible and robust than its higher-tiered, more securely ensconced, brethren.

Given the preceding analysis, argumentation, and such, I think a plausible case has been made in answer to the general charges of the historiographical skeptic, abstract and speculative, which are far more carefully argued, thoughtful, and serious than I think many historiographers recognize. If we have been successful, the general case for the possibility of historiographical knowledge has been made, a case which depends largely on latitudinizing epistemic criteria to the point where, despite the complexity, subtlety, obscurity, illusiveness, and experimental inaccessibility of its subject matter, the cognitive credibility of historiography is established.

I think the usual penchant amongst epistemologists is to make knowledge too difficult to obtain. This approach would disallow a great many plausible historiographical knowledge claims. There I think the bar is set too high. It would seem to accept only the low-level or trivial, such as the physical arrival of Lenin at such and such a time at the Finland station, if that, or the colossally undeniable, such as the one-time existence of a Roman empire, the occurrence of a civil war in the United States in the 19th Century, or such. One would lose much of the importance and interest of history which deals with less obvious and tangible processes and events, less discernible realities, say, meanings, motivations, intentions, social and psychological consequences, and such. My own approach, of course, might seem to make knowledge too easy to obtain. In that respect a value judgment would occur. But value judgments, as we shall later argue, are usually cognitive, relative to a criterion, which elevates cognitivity considerations to the metalevel, that of criteria. Criteria, however, as we shall later argue, are seldom arbitrary, and are subject to evaluation in terms of metacriteria. An ultimate criterion would presumably be indexed to considerations of consistency, and relativized to a concept of human nature and the conditions within which it would thrive. At the level of an ultimate criterion, it seems scarcely plausible that the choice would be indefensible or arbitrary from the point of view of a normal, rational member of our species. One might, of course, flip a coin at this point, or deliberately, or indifferently, choose death over life, disease over health, scarcity over abundance, poverty over wealth, suffering over contentment, misery over happiness, enmity over friendship, hatred over love, and such, if one wished. Institutions are provided for such people. In any event, my proposed criteria for knowledge are probably too liberal for some and too rigorous for others. The metacriteria here, in terms of which my proposals are justified, are consistency and clarity, and congeniality to linguistic intuition, common sense, and historiographical practice.

One supposes that many practicing historiographers are not interested in these problems or choose, incredibly, to ignore them. Perhaps, on the other hand, it is rather that many are not even aware of these problems. If one is aware they exist, it seems it would be difficult to ignore them. That, at least, would seem to call for a gritty act of will. In any event, it is my hope that this inquiry into historiographical meaning, truth, and knowledge might give historiography something better to go on, epistemically, than denial, inattention, deliberate obliviousness, unquestioned tradition, and complacent, routine dogmatism.

The historiographical skeptic, of course, is not weaponless, nor would one expect him, at this point, even if convinced by the preceding argumentation, to withdraw from the field. It is one thing, to establish the possibility of historiographical knowledge, though that, I think, is an achievement in itself, and another to establish the likelihood of its confident realization, ascertainability, quality, and reliability. Two major objections to the cognitive value of historiography remain to be dealt with, first, the claim that historiographers seldom, if ever, succeed in producing satisfactory explanations, say, explanations of a scientific level, and, second, that historiographical judgment is irremediably subjective, which fact militates against its cognitive value, which, indeed, precludes its attaining the status of a serious discipline, say, that of a science.

IX. Explanation

We may distinguish, roughly, amongst six varieties of explanation, two of which are usually thought of as causal, and one certainly; and four usually thought of as noncausal, the status of at least one of which is somewhat ambivalent with respect to the causal-vs.-noncausal distinction, i.e., that of rational explanation.

The breakdown might be summarized, as follows:
    I. Causal
    1. Thread Analysis
    2. Deductive/nomological
    II. Noncausal
    1. Elucidation
    2. Explaining How
    3. Rational Explanation
    4. Colligation

We will not discuss these in the above order as we wish to reserve the substance of our discussion for the two major candidates of greatest interest, or controversy, with respect to historiographical explanation, namely, the deductive/nomological approach and that of rational explanation.

1. Causal-Thread Analysis

This form of explanation is the most common form of causal explanation. It recounts a series of events putatively related in a causal manner, namely, that each is somehow productive of, or influential concerning, its successors. This is the A caused B, and B caused C, and so on, sort of explanation. It is familiar from common life, is encountered widely in the media, and so on. It is also encountered frequently in historiography. Indeed, "explanation by narration" is often an instance of this sort of explanation, in which one might delineate, explicitly or implicitly, usually with several innocently omitted lacunae, a hypothesized causal relationship amongst a series of events. A famous literary example is the "for want of a nail the shoe was lost, for want of the shoe, the horse was lost, for want of the horse, the rider was lost, etc." sort of explanation, ending up with blaming the loss of, say, a kingdom on a missing nail. Obviously kingdoms are not lost for want of a nail, as thousands of other relationships would have to be in place before the nail's loss would be anything more than a trivial inconvenience, but one sees what the author is driving at. This is analogous to the straw that broke the camel's back. Surely the overloading of the camel would be more causally relevant to the camel's misfortune than a straw, but one gets the picture. In the horseshoe case one would probably be better advised to blame the kingdom's loss, if one wished to think along these lines, on a careless, hurried, or incompetent smith than a nail. And, of course, someone employed the smith, so perhaps we should blame him, and so on, back to the gas molecules of the primeval nebula.

Given the broad, complex, intricate sweep of causal processes the very notion of *a* causal thread is pretty silly. If a wave thunders against the beach it may be helpful to discuss this in terms of a particular, selected drop of water displacing another particular, selected drop of water, and so on, but this is, at least, more of a mental convenience, than anything else, a way of trying to relate, as best one can, to a phenomenon which is the result, if one wishes to think atomistically and discretely, rather than fieldwise or holistically, of a multitude of causal lines. On the other hand, this is pretty much our only option in causal explanation and has a pragmatic, if not a logical, justification, given our cognitive and informational limitations.

We face the ocean and pick out our drops of water and note that drop one displaced drop two. Were it not for the wave of course, drop one would not be where it was, doing what it did, nor would drop two be where it was, doing what it was doing, in order to be affected by drop one, and so on. Also, several more drops were probably, at least, exerting their effects on both drop one and drop two.

This is not to deny, of course, that some things stand out as being particularly important, and obviously involved in the same causal process, for example, Queenie's biting Bill doubtless has something to do with Bill's bloody leg, Sweden's booming economy of the 1930's had something to do with extensive German purchases of war supplies, taking an economy off the gold standard frees governments for unlimited credit expansion and deficit spending, producing large-scale inflation, and so on.

Perhaps the most obvious, though often overlooked, point to note about causal-thread analysis is that it presupposes causality, and thus, most likely, natural law, and the D Hypothesis. It makes little sense except in that context. Otherwise it becomes a succession of unrelated events mysteriously aligned, something like a list of random numbers which happens, by accident, to mirror the series of natural numbers.

What gives causal-thread analysis its explanatory value, even given the selections, obscurities, arbitrarinesses, and vagaries involved, is the assumption that the universe, and we ourselves within it, are physical processes behaving in accord with natural law. Thus, if we wished to explain particular events, it seems that the ideal explanation, the irrefragable, the adequate, explanation would be one in terms of initial conditions, auxiliary hypotheses, and natural laws. If gods were to explain things to gods, would they not proceed in that fashion? Does not causal-thread explanation itself presuppose that such special explanations, even if forever denied to finite minds with limited resources, would be at least the ideal explanations, however inaccessible they might forever be, those which would be favored by any intelligences capable of generating them, the explanations which would be favored by the gods.

This means that lurking behind causal-thread analysis, so to speak, is the metaphysical foundation without which it would be unintelligible.

This would bring us, then, to an attempt to explicate a concept of ideal explanation, at least in theory, to the deductive/nomological model of scientific explanation, sometimes referred to as the logistic model, or covering-law model, of scientific explanation. A literature has developed about this model, and its cousin, which we will not discuss, the statistical model of scientific explanation, in which the categorical laws of the strict deductive/nomological model are replaced by statistical laws. Our motivations for neglecting the statistical model is that it is in so many ways similar to the strict deductive/nomological model that its independent discussion, at least for our purposes, would not prove particularly helpful or productive, and that, in my view, a statistical explanation is not an explanation, for example, that one hen out fifty thousand hens is born with teeth does not seem to me to explain why this hen was born with teeth, though it does assure me that this hen may well be one in fifty thousand. Similarly, as noted earlier, that so many letters are misaddressed annually does not explain why Jones misaddressed his letter. Similarly if nine out of ten letters, or ninety-nine out of a hundred letters, are misaddressed, that is certainly interesting, but it still does not tell me why Jones' letter was misaddressed.

We must return to the deductive/nomological (D/N) model of scientific explanation later, not because of its practicality, which is negligible, but because of its plausibility as an ideal form of explanation, presupposed by the D Hypothesis.

2. Elucidation

Elucidation is a familiar form of noncausal explanation. For example, there are possible explanations of meanings, say, of words, phrases, texts, poems, looks, winks, laws, paintings, and such; of principles, practices, institutions, symbols, customs, arrangements, procedures, and so on. One might wish to have explained to one the differences between, say, Art Nouveau and Art Deco; or have explained to one the code of Bushido, or the social structure of feudalism; why the English drive on the left side of the road, why dishes are passed from the left to the right, why Chinese waiters serve men before women, and American waiters serve women before men; the meaning of a seal on an official document; the rules for succession in a dynasty; Renaissance banking practices; the etiquette of 18th Century Parisian dueling; the requirements for registering an escutcheon with the College of Heralds, and so on.

3. Explaining How

One seldom finds this sort of explanation in historiography, unless one were willing to count things like an explanation as to how one ascended the *Cursus Honorum* in the Roman Republic, how one became a knight in the 12th Century in France, how the difficulties in calculating longitude were solved, etc. But these "hows" would better fit under elucidation, above, than under what one has in mind here. Similarly, "how" is sufficiently vague that one might claim that historiographers are primarily concerned with explaining "how," for example, how the expansion of the Persian Empire was checked in the 5th Century B.C.; how Rome became an Empire; how the parliamentary form of government succeeded royal absolutism in England, etc., but, again, these are not the sort of "hows" one would have in mind here; one supposes these latter "hows" would be better understood along the lines of causal-thread analysis.

In any event, the sorts of "hows" for which we want a separate category here are "skill hows," "directional hows," and such. For example, how do you shoe a horse, how do you medicate a cat, how do you field a ground ball, how do you refer to a previously cited reference in a scholarly paper, how do you get from 46th and Lexington to the Museum of Modern Art, or the nearest McDonald's, etc.

And one would seldom expect to find these sorts of "hows" in historiography. They should be mentioned, however, in any cursory account of explanation, as they are familiar and important forms of explanation.

4. Colligation

Colligation is illuminating, and it is difficult to think of historiography without it. The word 'colligation' has an etiology suggesting binding, or bundling, together. In the historiographical sense of the word it has the notion of a unifying concept, a concept under which a large number of ideas or entities may be subsumed.

Earlier in this study, in discussing patterning, we noted a form of patterning which we characterized as "imposed, significant, and noncausal." Two examples of such patterning were periodization and colligation. As we discussed colligation at some length there, under forms of patterning, we shall not do so here.

I have included colligation here, under explanatory concepts, primarily because it is commonly considered a form of historiographical explanation. One can conceive a number of epistemologists having reservations about this practice. It might be said that colligation explains nothing, but is rather a summarizing or descriptive concept, under which a number of diverse entities, on one principle or another, perhaps even a principle as explanationally irrelevant as time or place, might be subsumed. Analogously, telling us about the similarities of Alpine plants at various altitudes or noting similarities amongst breeds of European dogs may be interesting but it doesn't explain the similarities; and in the case of the plants and dogs, they are, at least, all plants, or all dogs; it is not like asserting alleged similarities between, say, music, painting, politics, philosophy, and such. The charge then might be that colligation explains nothing, and, moreover, that the entities subsumed may not even be similar; lacking a suitable principle of comparability. Accordingly, the very subsumption itself is irrational and spurious.

When, from time to time, logicians look at the real world they are wont to find it lacking. One cannot blame them, for it is indeed lacking in certain qualities. For example, it has little to compare with the impressive distinction between the number two and the number three, which never misses, with the aristocratic reliability of the Euclidean triangle whose interior angles never fail to equal two right-angles, no matter what, day and night, with the unimpaired perfection of vacuous tautologies, not once refuted, and so on. These triumphs of logistic and mathematical purity, of course, are purchased at the cost of staying out of trouble, and playing it safe. Never playing, they never lose. It is easy to understand why they have nothing to fear from reality. They have nothing to do with it. Historiography, on the other hand, and dozens of other disciplines, live and work in the real world, which is notoriously ill-ordered and messy, and all but indifferent to logic.

1. Subsumption does not require strictly comparable units. Apples and oranges are both fruits; physical objects may be solids, liquids, gases, and such, even oxygen atoms and hydrogen atoms, and so on.

More germane to colligation, one may subsume on diverse criteria, supposing, say, sets of the objects in such and such a room, or the objects that exist in the 2nd Century B.C. or such. Subsumptions may be more or less useful, more or less practical, for one purpose or another. A colligatory subsumption is to be assessed on its merits, not ruled out *a priori* for reasons of misplaced logistic pedantry.

2. Generalizations may be based on colligations, but colligations, such as the Renaissance, the Enlightenment, the Middle Ages, Periclean Athens, Twelfth Dynasty Egypt, the Neolithic Period, the Age of Bronze, the Age of Iron, the Computer Age, etc. are not generalizations, but summarizing, illuminating concepts. Not all logically possible colligations would be of interest. For example, one might interestingly compare and contrast, one supposes, Periclean Athens with Victorian England, if one were so minded, in terms of imperialism and democracy, and such, but a colligation such as Victorian Athens or Periclean England would presumably make little, if any, sense. Presumably it would be not only absurd, but unintelligible. The implausibility of such colligations is instructive, as it calls to our attention criteria of "bundling." Whereas anything might be "bundled" with anything else, as one could have, if one wished, a set consisting of locomotives and sonnets, clearly there are better and worse bundlings, and more or less useful or informative bundlings.

Accordingly, The response to the nonsimilarity challenge is twofold, first, to "bundle" one does not have to have similarity, though, doubtless, to bundle well there should be some rationale to the bundling, and, second, in judicious bundlings there will be, if not similarities, congruences, or fittings together, which may be subtle but which are likely to strike informed observers as real. The fact that an age in a given area, for example, is likely to have an unmistakable character or personality seems to be a fact. If this were not a fact it seems it would be impossible to identify, say, a style of clothing, a form of music, a style of painting, or such, with a time and place. But this sort of thing is often possible. More superficially, it does not require an expert to tell tunics from trousers, lyres from violins, minuets from waltzes, muskets from machine guns, and so on. In a culture and time one expects congruence, a fitting together or a hanging together, a *Zusammenhang*, and one is seldom, if ever, disappointed.. Too, more seems to be involved than simply temporal or spatial proximity. For example, at the time of much of the Renaissance there was, throughout the rest of the world, little or no Renaissance, so more than a temporal period was involved; and, similarly, even in, say, Italy, in the time of her Renaissance, there were doubtless large portions of her population which were living much as they had in the past, who were not particularly touched by her Renaissance, except perhaps for the comings and goings of *condottieri*.

Collingwood could speak of the "corporate mind of an age," and, although this may not be clear, it is certainly not unintelligible. It is not like speaking of the pancreas or pineal gland of an age, or such. Similarly, the notion of a *Zeitgeist*, of a spirit of a time or age, is not clear, but, again, is founded on discernible aspects of consciousness, widely disseminated amongst individuals, particularly elite individuals, leading individuals, a consciousness common throughout the more dominant, powerful strata of society, the strata that give a distinguishing cast to a time and area, the strata which governs and builds, which manages and marches, which leaves monuments and records, which arbitrates values and priorities, which will write the history.

And, clearly, there are remarkable differences amongst historical consciousnesses, between that of Egyptian scribe, the Athenian *archon* or *strategos*, the senator in Republican Rome, the feudal lord, the Florentine banker, the Colonial militiaman, the Victorian painter, the Stuka pilot, and so on. Indeed, one of the marks of historiographical genius, so seldom manifested, is to give a contemporary reader some sense of how others see the world and react to it. Without this, historiography, in the fullest sense, can never adequately engage its subject matter, the life and meaning of history.

And it is absurd to suppose that these differences in consciousness, in life conditions, and cognitive fields will not express themselves in the visibilities of history.

Analogously, one is given to understand that an individual's body language is purportedly indicative of psychological characteristics; one is familiar with the fact that individuals, in their choices and lives, express themselves in a variety of ways, for example, in hair styles, in clothing, in furnishing and decorating their dwellings, in the cars they buy, the pets they keep, the music to which they listen, and so on. Similarly, handwriting, rather in the manner of projective tests, almost in the manner of a seismograph, will reflect traits of character, register taste, track mood, and so on. How could it not do so? If the life of an individual has its *Zusammenhang*, then, given the gregariousness of our species, its penchant to follow leaders, to seek the approval of its fellows, to conform, and so on, it is only natural to expect pervasive similarities amongst groups. There are differences even amongst groups of chimpanzees. In any event, whatever the cause might be of those interesting properties which distinguish cultures, and times, and give them their distinct natures and personalities, whether they are an outgrowth of species characteristics, or inexplicable sociological aberrations, they exist. Accordingly, fact, reality, gives the final answer to the criticism of noncomparability. An objection, which seems plausible in the light of logic, crumbles in the light of reality The bumblebee, oblivious of aeronautical theory, flies, and seemingly without difficulty. Things do hang together, identifiably so. Things fit. Clearly. Cultural juxtapositions are not random. The *Zusammenhang* of a time exists. As Wittgenstein might recommend, were one in doubt, "Go, look, and see."

3. As colligation is historiographically invaluable, and, seemingly, necessary, rather like general terms in common discourse, for purposes of understanding the past, it does not seem particularly important whether we regard it as explanatory or not.[99]

---

[99] Whereas there is an analogy between general terms, say, 'dog', 'cat', 'chair', 'table', 'turnip', 'tomato', and such, and colligatory terms, a colligatory term, in its primary use, is not well understood as a general term. It is better understood along the lines of a proper name, like 'Smith', or 'Jones', provided we know a good deal about Smith and Jones, so much so that the name has a rich meaning for us. For example, if one did not understand the word 'Renaissance', then it would be no more informative than 'Smith' and 'Jones', if one had never heard of them. One is a bit better off if one knows that the word means 'rebirth', but not much better off, because one would not know, technically, what was being reborn. For example, in metempsychosis, a soul, in theory, might be reborn a number of times. Plato, for example, seems to have taken this notion seriously. Normally, when one hears the term 'Renaissance' *simpliciter*, one will think of the Italian Renaissance. One could make out a case, of course, for a French Renaissance, an English Renaissance, and so on. But these would, again, properly qualified, be, or suggest, proper names. There is a secondary usage of 'renaissance' (lower case 'r') in which that term, a different term, actually, would function as a general term, for example, the PTA in P.S. 110 had a renaissance when Mrs. Jones took over the helm, or such.

Analogously, we are all pretty familiar with tomatoes. Presumably, for most purposes, it does not much matter, at least to most of us, whether the tomato is a fruit or a vegetable. On the other hand, apparently this makes a great difference when it comes to shipping produce across state lines, if vegetables may be shipped across state lines but not fruits. Happily, in our case, we have no comparable problem here, with, say, shipping colligations across state lines. On the other hand, as historiographers often regard colligation as explanatory, if to the unease of, say, empiricistically oriented epistemologists or typical philosophers of science, it behooves us, in our general effort to provide explications as congenial as possible to historiographical practice, to understand what they might have in mind, or, at least, to seek a rationale perhaps implicit in uncritical practice.

Clearly colligation is not causally explanatory in a primary sense; although it might be secondarily explanatory, as, for example, helping to account for someone's historical interests; rather, it is something which itself requires an explanation. On the other hand, a colligation can be noncausally explanatory, or illuminatingly explanatory. It can help to tell about, and inform about, and, in such senses, inform one concerning a time or a way of life. If it does not causally explain, which is a different challenge, it does provide answers to questions as to how things were, what things were like, how people thought, what they did, and so on. It produces understanding. It makes sense out of things. It is one thing to explain what Jones is like and another to explain how he came to be the way he is. One way of explaining a Turner or Constable, or a Mondrian or Pollack, would be take someone to an art gallery and show him some pictures. Similarly one might explain manorialism or mercantilism by telling someone about economic arrangements, explain knighthood by telling how people became knights and how they were expected to behave, and so on. Thus, the sort of explanation involved in colligation has its affinities with elucidation, discussed above. The major difference would seem to be one of breadth and complexity. In elucidation, one might explain, as suggested, manorialism or knighthood, or such, but in colligation one is concerned less with parts as parts than with parts as they compose wholes, with interrelated parts, with elements in context. Colligation is, in effect, large-scale elucidation. It intends to inform one of times, and ways of life.

Whereas I think the historiographical inclination to regard colligation as explanatory is well justified, the question, on the whole, seems more verbal than substantive.

Indisputably, colligation, whether construed as explanatory or not, is of enormous historiographical importance. Without colligation the past would be largely unintelligible. It provides the major concepts without which historical understanding, as we think of it, would be impossible. The grains of history would make little sense, would be largely meaningless, if not incomprehensible, save for the continents of colligation.

5. Deductive/Nomological Explanation[100]

The Greek expression for law, transliterated into Roman letters, is '*nomos*', from which expression we have our adjective 'nomological', meaning "having to do with, or in virtue of, law." 'Law' in this context refers to natural law, not prescriptive law. The essence, then, of deductive/nomological explanation is to explain phenomena, or purport to explain them, in virtue of the laws of nature. To be sure, the laws of nature, in themselves, if they exist, explain nothing, but, conjoined with other expressions, for example, antecedent-condition statements, statements describing a situation in the world, and such, an argument might

---

[100] A literature exists pertinent to the D/N model of scientific explanation. A reference of particular importance for our purposes is "The Function of General Laws in History" by Carl G. Hempel, originally published in *The Journal of Philosophy*, 39, 1942, a slightly revised version of which appears in his *Aspects of Scientific Explanation And Other Essays in the Philosophy of Science*, The Free Press, New York, 1965. A famous later article pertaining to this approach to explanation is "The Logic of Explanation" by Carl G. Hempel and Paul Oppenheim, originally published in *Philosophy of Science*, 15, 1948, reprinted in *Readings in the Philosophy of Science*, edited by Herbert Feigl and May Brodbeck, Appleton-Century-Crofts, Inc., New York, 1953, and elsewhere.

be constructed, which might entail a statement describing the phenomenon to be explained.[101]

The D/N model presupposes the D Hypothesis. If either the I Hypothesis or the M Hypothesis should be true, phenomena might exist which, at least in theory, would be incapable of D/N explanation.

In presupposing the D Hypothesis, the D/N Model presupposes strict causality. Beyond this, it presupposes that there are isolable natural laws, which might figure in the explanations in question. Upon occasion, it seems there are such laws, for example, having to do with falling bodies, the expansion of gases, the formation of molecules of water, and such. On the other hand, it is less clear that there are such laws pertaining to the phenomena in which the historiographer is likely to be interested, for example, why the Defenestration of Prague took place, as opposed to the rate of acceleration of a falling body; why Charles Martel was successful at Tours, as opposed to the effects of sharp instruments on organic tissue; what impelled Vasco da Gama to circle Africa to reach India, as opposed to the effects of wind masses on material bodies, such as sails, why, say, a given revolution took place at one time and place and not another time and place; why this empire rose, and that one fell, and so on. It seems highly unlikely that there would be a particular law to explain most particular things, why Jones misaddressed his letter, why the great pyramid was built, and so on. Thus, it seems either one is looking for an interaction of several laws, perhaps countless from a finite point of view, or that there is, in effect, one law only, which is, in effect, the relentless unfolding of the universal process. In short, whereas the D/N model presupposes strict causality,

---

[101] The model is often discussed in terms of sentences, viewed as ascertainable particulars, and such. For reasons suggested earlier in this work, we prefer statements and/or propositions. In this sense, I suppose we are illustrating a model of a model, so to speak. This procedure is justified, in our opinion, given the time-and-place-bound nature of sentences, that they are unsuitable candidates for conveying truth values, that their consistent use seems to presuppose meanings, or meaningfulnesses, or generalities, and such, and thus they themselves seem to presuppose the dreaded universals, to be eschewed at all costs, and so on. Universals are required for intelligible, consistent thought. So it would be nice if they existed. If they do not, we had better pretend they do or, at least, talk as though they did. As a linguistic pragmatist one need not worry whether or not universals cast shadows or depress scales. That universals exist is not an empirical hypothesis; speaking as though they did seems a precondition for intelligible discourse.

as required by the D Hypothesis, its additional presupposition, that of isolable laws specific to a given phenomenon, may be unwarranted. It seems possible that either there would be an unmanageable interaction of numerous, perhaps empirically innumerable, laws, which could never be satisfactorily ascertained, or, in effect, no law, or a single law, that of the whole. This is not to deny, of course, that in some instances, usually of little or no historiographical moment, one might be able to approximate a D/N explanation. For example, one could presumably explain the deaths of Charles I and Louis XVI in terms of decapitation.

The following schematism constitutes a model of a D/N Explanation. The *explanandum*, that which is to be explained, or better, derived, which is a description of the empirical phenomenon to be explained, is supposed to follow logically from the *explanans*, that which explains, or, better, in this case, that which, as premise-set, is to imply the *explanandum*.

It is noted that explanation, on this approach, is semanticized, understood in terms of logistic relationships amongst statements of various sorts. This is not the way we usually explain things, of course. We would usually explain Bill's bloody leg by noting that Queenie did a job on it, not by constructing an argument involving the effects of canine fangs applied with such and such forces on body parts, and then noting that such fangs were applied with such and such forces to such and such body parts, and so on, and then inferring from that the condition of Bill's leg. On the other hand, there is no reason one could not try to semanticize the business, if one wished. In doing so, of course, one substitutes explicit statements of laws for the general background assumption that some such laws must exist, though we probably have very little idea of what they might be, and are probably relieved that no one is likely to ask us to spell them out, as presumably we could not begin to do so. In English, 'law' is ambiguous between the law itself and a statement of the law. In the D/N Model, of course, one uses statements, because logistic relationships obtain not amongst laws and situations, and such, but amongst statements, propositions, sets, and such. A similar ambiguity characterizes prescriptive law. The law is not to be confused with the statement of the law. What the judge states may be the law, but the law is not its statement. Laws survive, though statute books burn.

1. $C_1, C_2, \ldots\ldots C_n$ (Statements of Antecedent Conditions)
2. $L_1, L_2, \ldots\ldots L_n$ (General Laws)
$\downarrow$ ----------
3.   E   (Description of the empirical phenomenon to be explained.)

Lines 1 and 2 constitute the *explanans*. Line 3 constitutes the *explanandum*. The relationship between the *explanans* and *explanandum* is supposed to be that of logical entailment.

The D/N Model, as usually construed, imposes five adequacy conditions on the *explanans*, four logical and one empirical, as follows:

Logical Conditions of Adequacy:

1. The *explanans* must logically entail the *explanandum*.

2. The *explanans* must contain at least one general law.

3. Every statement in the *explanans* must occur essentially. (Every statement in the *explanans* must be required for the derivation.)

4. The *explanans* must have empirical content.

The empirical condition of adequacy:

5. The *explanans* must be true.

In order to clarify, and comment on, the D/N Model, we will suggest a number of considerations. The intent of the first five considerations is to indicate the sort of things which would constitute violations of the conditions of adequacy, and the last four considerations will suggest some problematicities seeming to appertain to the model. We will refer to the logical conditions of adequacy as the LC conditions, so 'LC_1,' for example, would refer to the first logical condition of adequacy, and so on. 'EC' will stand for the empirical condition of adequacy. These nine points will be made as simply as possible, and in the context of a convenient schematism, one useful for making simple points, and one not precluded by any of the requirements of the model. We will make frequent use, in the following, of the material conditional. The justification for this is that it is clear, commonly used in philosophical argumentation, and is not forbidden by the D/N Model. On the other hand, it cannot explicate the nature of law, nor are we supposing it can. Laws imply material conditionals but are not material conditionals; they are nomological conditionals, in which the antecedent implies the consequent not in virtue of either truth-functional relationships or meaning but in virtue of natural relationships. As yet, there is no adequate analysis of the nomological conditional. Logically, to date, it is its own country, and its borders have never been crossed. The relationship is normally accepted as an unanalyzable given. Interestingly, it seems that if one could explicate the contrafactual conditional one could explicate the nomological conditional, and if one could explicate the nomological conditional, one could explicate the contrafactual conditional, but it seems neither of these things can be managed. They go their mysterious way, together, arm in arm.[102]

---

102 In the "entailment conditional" the antecedent logically implies the consequent; in the material conditional, the conditional is true if and only if either the antecedent is false or the consequent true. Nomological conditionals might be understood either as "necessity conditionals" or "invariant-correlation conditionals," 'necessity' understood as natural necessity and 'invariant correlations' understood as invariant correlations amongst natural phenomena. Since David Hume the notion of "natural necessity" has been generally understood to be epistemically unintelligible, the result of an illegitimate inference beyond constant conjunction into semantic vacuity. Accordingly, nomological conditionals, or natural-law conditionals, are commonly understood as invariant-correlation conditionals, and explanation is often seen in terms of "correlation under law." As suggested above, the notion of natural law has never been satisfactorily explicated. Presumably it is best regarded as a cognitive primitive, or an unanalyzable given. Similarly, it seems impossible to provide a noncircular explication of space or time. Whereas it will be convenient to speak of "nomological conditionals," which contrasts nicely with entailment and material conditionals, natural laws, as a technical point, might be understood as nomological conditionals or as the quantification of nomological functions. In the first case, one might have something like 'If a material body is free of impressed forces, then it travels in a rectilinear path', and, in the second case, 'All material bodies free of impressed forces travel in rectilinear paths', which, strictly, is not a conditional. It might be read as, 'For any x, if x is a material body, then x travels in a rectilinear path' or formalized along the lines of '$(x)(Mx \rightarrow Tx)$', which would be the quantification of a nomological function. In this study, we will normally speak of both readings as "nomological conditionals," for the sake of simplicity and to avoid distractions, though the second reading, technically, is not a conditional but the quantification of a conditional function. Referring to lawlike statements as nomological conditionals seems justified as law and conditionality characterize both readings. The '$\rightarrow$' above symbolizes the mysterious notion of "nomological entailment," not logical entailment. For the point pertaining to the interrelated problematicities of the contrafactual conditional and the lawlike statement, one is indebted, as indicated earlier, to the work of Nelson Goodman.

In what follows, please accept the following meaning assignments:

H: Hannibal wins at Cannae.
L: Some laws of astronomy. (Suppose them spelled out.)
N: Napoleon loses at Waterloo.

Summarizing the logical conditions of adequacy, we have the implication requirement, the general-law requirement, the essentiality requirement, and the empirical-content requirement. The empirical condition of adequacy is the truth requirement.

Considerations:

1. H
   L̲
   N

   Violation of LC_1; the argument is invalid.

2. N̲
   N

   Violation of LC_2; valid argument, but no general law or laws.

3. N
   L̲
   N

   Violation of LC3; valid argument, but second remise is not essential.

4. All things occur in accord with the will of Amon-Ra.
   It is in accord with the will of Amon-Ra that Napoleon loses at Waterloo.
   Napoleon loses at Waterloo.

   Violation of LC4; valid argument, but empirical content lacking.

5. $\underline{H \& L) \& \sim (H \& L)}$
    N

> Argument valid, antecedent-condition and law statements in place, and all statements occur essentially. Violation, however, of the EC condition, as the *explanans* is false.[103]

Whereas the adequacy conditions do not specifically require an antecedent-condition statement or statements, as they do a statement of a law or laws, such a statement, or statements, is surely assumed, if only because laws, in themselves, would not suffice to imply the desiderated "E" statement. Too, the schematism of the model shows antecedent-condition statements to be in place. *Sans* this, taken as a requirement, one could have arguments of the following sort, which are sound arguments, i.e., arguments with a valid form and a true premise-set, given the use of material conditionals, but which would presumably be uncongenial to the model.

6. L
    L ⊃ H
    $\underline{H \supset N}$
    N

> Here we have a sound argument, not precluded by the model's adequacy conditions as stated, this suggesting the advisability of an addition to the set of conditions.

One might consider a somewhat similar case, one again involving a sound argument, but one easier to dismiss.

---

103 As earlier noted, an argument is valid if and only if it is logically impossible for the premise-set to be true and the conclusion false. In this case, it is impossible for the premise-set to be true, so it is impossible for the premise-set to be true and the conclusion false. Similarly, a tautology, or logical truth, is implied by all premise-sets, as it would be impossible for the premise set to be true and the conclusion false, as the conclusion cannot be false.

7. H
   H ⊃ L
   L ⊃ N
   ———
   N

> Here, again, we have a sound argument, in which all premises occur essentially. And here an antecedent condition is present, but there is nothing here which is equivalent to a law. Although laws occur here in both an antecedent and a consequent position, there are no independent, or free-standing, laws. Whereas the model does not explicitly forbid this sort of thing, it seems judicious to rule in favor of the model here, and see this as a violation of the LC2, the "law or laws," requirement.

8. H
   L
   (H & L) ⊃ N
   ———
   N

> Here we have validity of form, an antecedent condition, laws, essentiality, empirical content, and truth of premise-set. Accordingly, it seems this argument meets the conditions of the D/N Model of scientific explanation. All that seems to be missing is relevance. Interestingly, relevance, pertinence, making sense, and so on, do not seem to be required by the D/N Model.

Let us now consider a case utilizing a "nomological conditional," at least in the broad sense suggested earlier, having to do with conditionality and law, rather than a material conditional, and a case in which relevance is obvious, and see if the D/N Model fares better.

9. Napoleon is at Point P and marches in Direction D at 3 MPH for 3 hours.
Anyone who is at Point P and marches in Direction D <u>at 3 MPH for 3 hours is at Waterloo.</u>
Napoleon is at Waterloo.

This satisfies the D/N Model, but one supposes it would satisfy little else. For example, what is Napoleon doing at Waterloo? Why is he at Waterloo in the first place, and not somewhere else which, as things turned out, might have been a better idea. What does he hope to accomplish at Waterloo? Who else is likely to be at Waterloo, and what might they be up to? Is what might occur at Waterloo likely to be of importance, and why? What is going on? What might depend on what is going on, and so on.

Presumably there could be an infinite number of "explanations" of this sort, and similar sorts, involving all sorts of things, all of which might fit the D/N Model and few of which would be interesting. It is not even clear that they would count as explanations in the sense in which one commonly thinks of an explanation, namely, as something that answers a question whose answer we are interested in obtaining, something that makes sense of something that has puzzled us, something that supplies us with a comprehensible reason or cause, in terms of which we better understand something, or seem to better understand something, and so on. Often we do not ask much of an explanation but we do ask that it explain something, in a sense that we accept as an explanation. We may want to know why Billy threw a mud pie at Susan. We later learn that Bobby gave him a nickel to do it. That may not be much of an explanation, leaving several loose ends at large, but it is an explanation. We can leave out of it, unless we are interested, the laws governing childhood greed, the influences of materialistic civilizations on the young, the intricate interpersonal relationships between Bobby and Susan, genetics, the nature of evolution, the mechanics of constructing mud pies, the trajectories of their flight, and so on. However interested we are we will presumably stop somewhere short of cosmology.

It is clear that the D/N Model, as currently understood, is flawed, and can be easily satisfied in a variety of ways which seem to fall far short of what one would like to think of as scientific explanation. It seems too permissive. On the other hand, it is clearly a remarkable, and profound, intellectual structure. It would be a terrible mistake to lose sight of that. It is worthy of a high rationalism, of a Descartes, a Leibniz, a Spinoza. It is a triumph of prescriptive, or normative, philosophy of science. If one were concerned not with how scientists do go about explaining things, which would be a matter for philosophical tape recorders and video cameras, philosophical journalism, description, note taking, reportage, and such, what would an ideal scientific explanation be? One for the gods? One supposes it would be very much something along the lines of a reformed or narrowed D/N Model. If the D Hypothesis is true, the tragedy of the D/N Model is not that it is inappropriate or misguided but that, on the whole, particularly in interesting cases, it cannot be applied. We know too little; the world is too complex.

Before discussing four major difficulties of the D/N Model, particularly pertinent to historiography, let us review a point or two, with respect to explanation in terms of law.

Presumably there is no single law in terms of which, conjoined with antecedent conditions, one could explain a historical event. It seems, rather, there would either be no law, but only the unfolding universal process, a "one-law universe," so to speak, or that an event would be the product of an indefinite number of causal lines, most of which would not be known. It seems then that lawlike explanations would be either impossible or incomplete. A possible approach here would be to proclaim a unique law for each unique event, but that would seem to deprive the notion of law of its general sense, as something which would appertain to sets of actual events, not possible events, or events in parallel universes. Consider what would be involved:

Situation S consists of at least elements $E_1, E_2, ... E_n$.

Out of Situation S emerges Result R.

These, we suppose, are the facts. It would seem silly, but not incomprehensible or obviously irrational, to suppose, in a D Universe, that the same result, Result R, would emerge from the same situation, if that situation ever recurred, which, presumably, would never happen. One might suppose a law to the effect that if Situation S was the case, consisting of its plethora of specified elements, that Result R would recur. This would be, so to speak, an *ad-hoc* law, a law with only one actual instance, and so on. Perhaps there is such a law, a unique law pertinent to every unique event, and, in a D Universe, that might be the case. But, is this really illuminating or helpful? It doesn't seem to do much more, really, than affirm the D Hypothesis. That law is like a cartridge, which, once expended, is useless. Too, it may very well have missed its mark, because the next seeming Situation S may turn out differently, which, as we do not even know all the elements involved, would be likely. Would one then suppose a new "one-shot law"? Would the universe not be overburdened with laws, requiring one per happening? One suspects that so many laws the universe does not need, nor have.

This is not to deny the D Universe; it is to suggest that requiring, say, historiography, to explain in terms of law may be to deny to her the capacity to explain, at all.

Three last points, prior to considering four major reservations pertaining to the applicability of the D/N Model to historiography, might be briefly made.

First, the desire to extend the D/N Model to historiography, as in Hempel's classic article, "The Function of General Laws in History," seems, rather clearly, to result from a commitment to, and an endorsement of, the unity-of-science program. Briefly, this is the notion that, as the universe is one, science should be one, and that scientific explanation, aside from the particulars being explained, should be of one sort, for example, that of the D/N Model or its statistically conceived cousin, Probabilistic Explanation. It is ironic that Hempel should have been subjected to such an abundance and intensity of criticism with respect to his suggestion, as the suggestion is well-intentioned, fits in nicely with the notion of a naturalistic universe, in which history may well take place, and, in its way, is profoundly flattering to historiography, by way of making a place for it, at least potentially, within the prestigious and esteemed fold of the sciences. This is a remarkable tribute to the cognitive status of historiography, and all the more impressive as its source was one of the greatest of the philosophers of science in the 20th Century. This is a far cry from the notion that historiography is a lowly humanity, at best, ranking with subjective reactions to life, art, and literature, and a pretentious fraud at worst.

Second, at least with respect to limited aspects of the physical world, there is much to be said for the D/N Model. Whereas most scientists would regard the attempt to construct an explicit D/N explanation of a phenomenon as tedious, pedantic, and unnecessary, there is little doubt that their explanations, at least independent of the I or M Hypothesis, generally presuppose something very much like the D/N Model, namely, that the universe is reliable, that it works in certain ways, and so on. This is the sort of thing that the D/N Model tries to make explicit. How could one make sense of the cracking of radiators on a cold night or the expansion of metal jar lids under streams of hot water, or the future position of Mars or the effect on climate of continental drift and Earth/Sun relations, without presupposing that the habits of the universe are such and such, and, in virtue of these habits, it will affect such and such objects under such and such conditions in such and such ways?

Third, it is generally recognized, and certainly Hempel himself recognized this, that few, if any, perfect, unassailable D/N Model explanations have been constructed, even of such circumscribed, pinpoint events as a cracking radiator. And he was acutely aware, in the cited article, of the difficulty of producing such explanations in historiography. His recommendation to historiography was, in effect, to do the best it could under its limitations, and approach, as closely as possible, the ideal of a D/N Model. *Faute de mieux*, one might produce an approximation to, or a "sketch" of, an explanation, the famous "explanation sketch," in which one would specify some conditions, suggest relevant laws, and so on, and then indicate the likely results of these conditions and laws with respect to an *explanandum*, say, an event to be explained. One would, so to speak, construct an invalid argument which would suggest, at least, a perfect argument which, were it perfect, would constitute an explanation. Needless to say, this suggestion has little relevance to what historiographers do, or what they would care to do. Like their colleagues in the field, in laboratories, observatories, and elsewhere, they do not do things in this fashion. Needless to say, Hempel's well-intentioned recommendations were not popular with historiographers. For example, they, as many others, did not view explanations in terms of constructing arguments, and worrying about the logical relations amongst statements. They were more concerned with events and processes, rather than statements about events and processes. Moreover, Hempel's suggestion of the "explanation sketch," while cordial, civil, and well-intentioned, suggested that the best historiographers could manage would be to produce sketches of explanations, rather than explanations. Naturally, historiographers thought they were producing explanations, did not care to be informed otherwise, and were not interested in adopting a model of explanation which would, if only for practical reasons, preclude them from ever being able to explain anything. Hempel, pitching in with high hopes, a good heart, and a ready will, trying benevolently to show historiography the way to the temple of the sciences, seemed, rather, to have proved that the holy road was not for them, and, in effect, slammed shut the door. To historiography, the gates to the sacred precincts must be forever barred. Such help it could do without.

Four major difficulties of the D/N Model with respect to historiography are as follows. It is impractical, unnecessary, untestable, and possibly inappropriate. If one were to make the satisfaction of the model a necessary condition for a science, there would be very few, if any, sciences, and certainly historiography would not be one of them.

1. Impracticality

It is not clear that there are covering laws for historical events. Causalities are seemingly multiplex and interactive. If there are such laws, they seem illusive, and unavailable. How would such laws be ascertained? And how could one know that the supposed lawlike statement was true?

Consider the two following short arguments, the first from Aristotle.

All men are mortal.
<u>Socrates is a man.</u>
Socrates is mortal.

All empires fall.
<u>Rome is an empire.</u>
Rome falls.

Pretty clearly, we are more sure that Socrates is mortal than that all men are mortal. We have specific historical evidence pertinent to the mortality of Socrates, but we have only indirect evidence, founded on induction, that all men are mortal. We are more sure, for example, that this swan is white than we are that all swans are white. We are not inclined to doubt that all men are mortal, but it might be false. There might be a genetic anomaly somewhere, with self-restoring tissue; the elixir of life might have been discovered in a basement of the Sorbonne in the 15th Century; a miracle might have taken place in which, say, some devotee has been blessed with immortality by some deity, say, Amon-Ra; a secret medical experiment in 1920 in Paraguay may have turned out well, and so on. Too, there are many living men about today. For all we know, one or another may prove to be immortal. This may be improbable, but it is possible, and it does lie within the scope of the I Hypothesis, to which, it seems, many physicists subscribe. In any event, one plays one's epistemological cards closer to the vest in betting on the mortality of Socrates than on that of all men. If a lawlike statement such as 'All men are mortal' might be false, then it, conjoined with 'Socrates is a man', does not guarantee that Socrates is mortal. The argument is valid, but the conclusion might be false. Compare:

All men are green.
<u>Socrates is a man.</u>
Socrates is green.

Now the first premise in the second argument, that having to do with Rome, is far more dubious than the first premise in the first argument, that having to do with Socrates, and if we cannot, really, with logistic certainty, trust the first premise in the first argument, then we must be even more uneasy given the first premise in the second argument. Once again, we are more sure of the fact that Rome fell than we are that all empires fall. Most historiographers do not regard the fall of empires as inevitable, but will consider particular causes of a fall, and might even speculate on what, if done, might have prevented the collapse. Too, there may be nonfalling future empires, and, in the galaxy, and in all the other galaxies in the universe, for all we know, there may be millions of nonfalling empires. Besides, presumably no historiographer in his right mind would try to explain Rome's fall by deriving it from a general law, such as all empires fall, and an antecedent condition, such as Rome was an empire.

In short, as general laws in historiography either do not exist, or, if existing, are seemingly unascertainable, and, if seemingly ascertainable, might prove to be false, it is impractical to require them as an explicit element in historiographical explanation.

2. Unnecessary

On the assumption that historiography is not cognitively bankrupt, it is clear that general laws, as required by the D/N Model, are not necessary for historiographical explanation. Historiography has managed quite well without them up to now, and may be expected to maintain this track record of success indefinitely. It is not even clear that the possession of such laws, were that possible, would prove to be an epistemic treasure. They are surely dispensable, and might not, even if in hand, prove to be of much value. Certainly causalities might be more easily determinable than the laws in terms of which they might be supposed instances. Given historiographical explanations, as in considering the outcomes of battles and the fall of empires, would be likely to be more plausible than any covering laws related to such things. Laws, if one wished, might be presupposed. They need not be discovered and stated. Presumably, causality is operative, whether understood in terms of law or not. If there is only an unfolding, universal process, the search for specific laws governing specific historical complexes might be unrealistic. Causal-thread analysis, obvious to common sense, warranted by millennia of human experience, familiar in historiography, proceeds apace, unapologetically.

3. Untestable.

If laws are to be relied upon presumably we would wish them to be true. Indeed, the D/N Model's empirical condition of adequacy requires that the statements of the *explanans*, among which are the lawlike statements, all be true. Certainly one might gather experimental evidence pertaining to the expansion of gases, the interactions of chemicals, and such, and hypothesize laws based on documenting and reviewing the results of such testing. How else, for example, would one discover the melting point of copper? On the other hand, if there are laws pertaining specifically to historical events, it would seem that such laws could not be confirmed. Historiography is not an experimental science, in which experiments might be conducted, examined, reviewed, repeated, and later, if it seemed desirable, replicated by others elsewhere, and so on. Presumably historical events are unique concatenations. Thus, it would be difficult to hypothesize general laws from one such event, in its complexity. And, if one did hypothesize such a law, it is unlikely it could be confirmed or disconfirmed. It is not as though one could try running French history with Napoleon, and then try running it without him, or running it once with him as a Corsican and once with him as a Parisian, and once with him as an artillery officer and once with him as a journalist, and so on. The gods might experiment in that fashion, with a set of almost parallel universes, but we cannot.

Accordingly, given the uncertainty of historical laws, their inability to be confirmed, let alone proven, even if they existed, it would seem anomalous to require them as components in historiographical explanations.

We are likely to be more sure of causalities than of laws pertaining to such causalities.

One must do the best that one can with what is available.

4. Appropriateness?

We have seen, I trust, that the D/N Model is not a practical model of explanation for historiography, and that it, happily, is not necessary for historiographical explanation. We have also suggested that deductive reliance on unconfirmed, or inadequately confirmed, lawlike statements places explanations which require such deduction in jeopardy.

But, beyond these things, one might wonder whether or not

it would be appropriate, even were it possible, to apply the D/N Model to the historiographical subject matter. The answer to this question would depend largely on the scope of its laws. Clearly the D/N Model has its seeds in the physical sciences, in particular, in physics. If one conceives the world largely in terms of "material bodies moving through physical space according to mathematical laws," one is surely in territory

congenial to the D/N model. Similarly, one supposes, if one sees the human organism as a machine ineluctably and perfectly responsive to, and governed by, stimulus conditions, rather like billiard balls on felt tables, much might be said, at least in theory, for the D/N approach to explanation, though in such a case it seems surprising that anyone would be interested in explaining anything, unless, of course, this, too, was an aspect of an evolved automatism pinballed about, consciousness and all, by more stimulus conditions.

Much in history, much in which we are interested, seems to exceed behavior, bodies in motion, so to speak. Indeed, it is not clear, really, that mere bodies in motion would be of great interest. Is anyone interested in the billiard balls themselves, rather than in the game, the purpose, how it will come out, what depends on it, and so on?

One might try, as an experiment, to see history from the "outside," as a facade, a surface with no back, a vacant shell, hollow and empty, never occupied, to see it in terms of complex, ingeniously contrived manikins, moving about, without purpose, meaning, or feeling, as designs without intent, as masks behind which there was no face, as a dark torrent of shadows, cast by nothing, but it would not be easy.

The hare detects a sound, and is wary. Hunger sharpens the hawk's vision. What is a body but the coat of thought and meaning?

Nature stirs, variously.

It is doubtless possible, in theory, for something like the D/N Model to extend its range, and encompass psychological and social laws, if they exist. I suppose there is no reason, at least in theory, why the D/N Model might not be capable, at least as employed by the gods, of dealing with consciousness, thought, hope, intent, willing, purpose, emotion, motivation, meaning, ideals, love, duty, and other things which make life significant, precious, and worth living, but, at present, it is incapable of doing so. And, of course, even if it could do so, the model, no more than a theorem, or a law, could understand anything, or know what it was doing. It might predict the delight of an insight, forecast an emotion, and calculate infallibly the next word spoken, but it would never know the insight, feel the emotion, nor speak the word.

Only the human can grasp such things and without their grasp there can be no grasp of history.

Even were the D/N Model practical it would seem unable to engage the realities of history, as it is an onlooker, not a participant. It does not live, so it cannot relive. It remoteness, its chilly disdain of meaning, would render it at best ancillary to historiography, if that. It sees process in terms of falsifying staticities. It is as far from history as the Platonic horse from the stallion of Adonis who "the bearing earth with his hard hoof he wounds."

History is process, turbulence, and flow.

Its explanatory analog is narrative.

If the D/N Model were practical it might serve for a pinpoint explanation here and there, an explanation of an arrested this or a halted that, isolated and bracketed for scrutiny, if it were helpful, but the thises and thats of history are generally incomprehensible without their context, incomprehensible outside the historical habitat within which they find their meaning, and the D/N Model cannot establish the context without which its application would be useless or pointless. In historiography the D/N Model presupposes an environment which it itself cannot establish and by which it is radically transcended; an environment which cannot itself be produced by the model, nor determined in terms of the model, but is established and grounded by other means, by other modalities of knowledge.

Whatever might prove to be the value of a reformed and narrowed D/N Model, if such could be devised, and one might hope for that, it would provide no substitute for, and would provide, at best, a supplement to, classical historiographical explanation.

The thread of causality winds its way through the hearts of men.

In any event, with all due respect to the D Hypothesis, there is phenomenologically, if not physically, a radical gap between body and thought, behavior and action.

At present, it is unthinkable that any satisfactory comprehension of thought and action, of purpose and meaning, could be achieved in terms of "material bodies moving through physical space according to mathematical laws."

And, again, with all due respect to the D Hypothesis, this will be forever unthinkable. Different orders of reality are involved. What is required here, where historiography resides, is not quantification and measurement, not instruments and experiments, but understanding, *Verstehen*.

Which brings us rational explanation.

6. Rational Explanation

Rational explanation, essentially, is explanation in virtue of reasons. This seems most apt, naturally, when one is dealing with single human beings, but may be extended to the rationale of law, the point of policies, the principles and ideals of institutions, the recommendations and prescriptions of customs, of an *ethos*, and such, anything which may be understood in terms of reasons. Many things, as noted, may be "the product of human action, but not of human design." A market, for example, produced over generations in virtue of innumerable interactions, may not have been reasoned out, but may be comprehensible in terms of such things as prudential interest, human desires, incentives, the exchange of information, processes of distribution, and such. Rational explanation is explanation in terms of purposes, and purposes served, consciously or unconsciously, explanation in terms of ends sought, in terms of teleologies, conscious or unconscious. It does not have in mind, however, the explanation of purpose in the sense one might speak of the purpose of the appendix or pancreas, of the eagle's beak or the lion's claws, matters of physiology, of biology, and such. Similarly, the teleology involved is a rationally comprehensible teleology, not one such as that of the oak tree or butterfly, attributed to the acorn or caterpillar. Similarly, rational explanation may be misapplied, or seemingly so, as in attributing the rise of the Nile to the intent of benevolent gods or the destruction of cities to the wrath of displeased deities. Such things are rational explanations, to be sure, but they are, one supposes, implausible rational explanations. Similarly, the fact that rational explanations are explanations in terms of reasons does not presuppose that the reasons are rational. The religious lunatic, the homicidal zealot, the psychopath and sociopath, the hallucinating schizophrenic, the general delaying the withdrawal of troops from an island death trap because of omens, the dictator astrologically attentive to the supposed messages of planets and stars, all have their reasons.

A major question here, of course, is whether rational explanations, explanations in terms of reasons, are explanations, at all.

This has its analogue to the mind/body problem.

How could a reason, which does not seem to be a material body, exert an influence on a material body?

The mind/body problem was detonated in modern philosophy most conspicuously by René Descartes, who drew a distinction between extended substance, matter, in a broad sense, including gases and such, and thinking substance, soul or spirit, which was nonspatial and intangible. Having raised a question which, on the terms he raised it, seems to be insoluble, it was not surprising that his own solution, in terms of the alleged mediation of mysterious "animal spirits," the existence and nature of which was unclear, failed to secure general approbation. Within the plethora of solutions offered over centuries to the mind/body problem, several of which are fascinating, the one which seems most germane to this objection to rational explanation, namely, that reasons are not causal, is epiphenomenalism.

Epiphenomenalism is the theory that consciousness is an epiphenomenon of, or a causally inert product of, physical processes, a mere accompaniment of such processes. The causal arrow, so to speak, moves in only one direction, from the physical to the mental. The human being is an unusual automaton, one which is conscious. His consciousness can effect nothing, influence nothing. Speaking in terms of physics, it cannot exert energy; it cannot do work. A familiar metaphor for this unusual relationship is that mind is to matter as shadow is to body. The notion that consciousness can affect body is supposedly an instance of the *post-hoc-ergo-propter-hoc* fallacy, namely, the mistaken idea that because B follows A, A must be the cause of B, in our context, something like the movement of the hand follows the decision to move the hand, so the decision must be the cause, or part of the cause, of the hand's moving. On the other hand, the epiphenomenalist would maintain that both the decision to move the hand and the movement of the hand are the consequences of antecedent physical conditions, and the decision to move the hand had nothing to do with the hand's motion. It is essentially associated with it, of course, being a precipitate of underlying causal processes, but it itself was causally inert.

Epiphenomenalism appears to be an inconsistent materialism, namely, a materialism which seems to maintain that the immaterial can be produced by the material, immaterial consciousness, immaterial substance, by material substance, which would betray materialism, and return us to something like Cartesian dualism, to be sure, a unidirectional dualism. On the other hand, a better understanding of epiphenomenalism would be monistic, and consciousness would be material, but causally ineffective. On this approach, a convenient metaphor might be mind is to body as smoke is to fire.

Epiphenomenalism has at least three things going for it, a basic or qualified monism, a congeniality to explanation in terms of physicality, likely to appeal to many scientists, and a concession to common sense, in making a place in its scheme, if not much of a place, for consciousness.

In our context, the epiphenomenalist would recognize the existence of reasons, but see them as epiphenomena, and, thus, see them as causally inert. If they are causally inert, then they are not causally effective, and cannot explain anything. Rational explanation would be pseudo-explanation, more instances of the *post-hoc-ergo-propter-hoc* fallacy.

At this point, assuming that epiphenomenalism is correct, two interesting questions arise. First, how is it that reasons exist, at all, and, second, what, if anything, is their justification.

At this point it is relevant to call attention to the "intentional stance." A nice illustration of this arises in the situation of a chess match, a series of games, between a human being and a computer. Let us suppose this is a very unusual human being, even, say, the chess champion of the world, and that this is also a very unusual computer, something along the lines of the famous Deep Blue, though perhaps even more brilliantly programmed. Who wins the match is not of immediate interest here, though my species chauvinism inclines me to root for the luckless hominids who find themselves cast into such arenas, at the mercy of silicon-sinewed beasts of prey. What is of major interest, whether one wins or loses, is how one plays a machine. One cannot play the machine on its own terms. The machine is not conscious; it cannot think; it cannot understand. What it does do is function. Given a particular board situation we shall suppose that our unusual machine, following its programming, in a second or so, flashes through the possible moves for white or black, whichever it is playing, so to speak, and the possible continuations, involving possible responses and responses to responses, for both white and black, to the extent of several moves. Supposedly, a world-class chess master can anticipate a forced continuation to something like twenty moves. For a human, this is a remarkable achievement. Let us suppose the machine can do this sort of thing not only for a forced continuation but for various plausible continuations to the extent of some thirty or forty moves. It is then programmed to output that move which will produce the most favorable board position for white or black, whichever it is playing. And this continues, until the game is finished, win, lose, or draw. For each move, the machine in, say, a second, flashes through several million possibilities, stopping at the best outcome for its color. This sort of thing the human being cannot match, any more than he can read the Encyclopedia Britannica in ten seconds or outrun a racing car. Unless he is a computer expert he is probably not even aware, except in a very general sense, of what is happening inside the machine, and how, electronically, a given result emerges. Even the computer expert cannot grasp this emotionally, as opposed to mathematically. It would be like understanding what it would feel like to run at the speed of light. Now, as suggested, the chess champion, conscious, and deliberating, plays with an end in view, plays purposively. The machine, on the other hand, is not conscious, does not deliberate, does not play with an end in view, is not purposive. It is no more purposive than a wheel barrow or shovel. It does not really play, at all. It functions. How does our champion match wits with the machine, as it has no wits? It would be like trying to match wits with the weather. The machine cannot be outguessed, as it has no plans; it cannot be outthought as it is not thinking; it cannot be tricked, or misled, or confused; it is never in time trouble; it does not tire; it gives no thought to either supper or Susan; it has no attention which might lapse, wander, stray, or waver; it has no ego to be threatened; however the game turns out, it will feel no embarrassment or shame; no chagrin, frustration, or disappointment; similarly, it will take no pleasure in its victory. It is a machine; all it does is function.

So how can the chess champion relate to this opponent, which does not know it is an opponent, or know anything?

The champion adopts the "intentional stance."

The only way to play the machine is to play it as if it were another human being, as if it were a thinking, deliberating, purposive opponent, as if it were rational, as if it had reasons.

Consciousness is "intentional," it intends, it has a focus; it is always "about" something or other. Trees and rocks, the revolutions of planets and the movements of continents, are not about anything; consciousness is, always. Wheel barrows and shovels are not about anything; so, too, the machine is not about anything. It is not an alien form of intelligence, as some engineers might be pleased to think; it is not a form of intelligence, at all.

Yet, the only way to deal with the machine is to relate to it as though it were intelligent. Without adopting this posture, this pretense and fiction, this radical simplification, the game could not be played.

One must act as though the machine had reasons.

What could it be up to, with that surprising rook move to Queen's Rook Six? Have I missed something? Is that a flaw, a brilliancy gone wrong, or a brilliancy afoot? I must think carefully about that. Perhaps the game depends on it.

If epiphenomenalism is correct, reasons lack causal efficacy. On the other hand, what is really going on in a human being, given the D hypothesis, and the influence of multitudes of complex, interacting chemical and physical causalities on behavior, over years, both within and outside the organism, most of which are unknown, is beyond the capacity of any human being, himself or another, to understand. Accordingly, one would expect evolution, in a social organism, to select for simplifying mechanisms, pretenses or fictions, if you like, which would enable individuals to interact and relate to one another. This evolved invention, the reason, would facilitate human interaction, and the interpretation of human behavior. It would substitute the reason for the actual causes, which would, *per hypothesis*, be too complex and deep for human understanding. Reasons are no more than flags signifying the presence of invisible armies, and one responds to the flags, as the armies are innumerable and unseen. Thus, one says a given action was done because of greed, another to preserve honor, another in virtue of ambition, and so on. And we reify such verbalisms, entitling ourselves to interpret and explain human behavior in terms of them. We adopt, as we must, the "intentional stance" toward ourselves, and our fellows. Only in this fashion can we make sense of ourselves and others. Such fictions, like the hypothesis of naive realism, may be illusions, but they are illusions without which life would be impossible.

In this way we see how "reasons" could emerge in the context of evolution, and their justification, if one were needed, would be their social utility, their value in providing intellectual devices which could stand in lieu of actual causalities, and enable us to seem to understand ourselves and others. And there is nothing arbitrary here, no more than in naive realism, for these fictions, like the perceptions of naive realism, presumably have their topological relationships to independent realities. The flags may be mistaken for the armies, but it is the armies which brandish the flags.

If this analysis is correct, as it might be, then reasons are causally inefficacious, and, literally, rational explanation, as usually considered, is impossible. The best that could be said for it is that rational explanations are false, but familiar and convenient, perhaps indispensable. But an indispensable falsehood is still a falsehood.

To be sure, this conclusion presupposes that epiphenomenalism is correct, and that reasons, and consciousness, as a whole, are causally inert. That might not be true.

Let us consider four aspects of this matter.

1. Consciousness might be without causal efficacy, or causal relevance, but, given the data of consciousness, that claim would seem implausible. It certainly seems to us that consciousness is causally relevant to behavior. The epiphenomenalist, of course, is as well aware of this as anyone else. This relevance he denies, presumably on theoretical grounds. In any event, the data of consciousness suggest the causal relevance of consciousness, reasons, and such. This evidence may not be conclusive, but it is evidence and, as evidence, it should be neither lightly dismissed nor ignored..

2. The justification for ruling out consciousness as causally efficacious appertains to an inconsistent epiphenomenalism, one which sees a materialistic base as capable of somehow generating a nature quite unlike itself, one which would be nonspatial, intangible, and so on. It is rather as though Descartes' extended substance managed, somehow, to produce nonextended substance, spirit, or mind. As soon as one adopts a more consistent epiphenomenalism, consciousness will have to be, in some way, "physical." If we reject the metaphor of mind is to matter as shadow is to body, which might be associated with an "inconsistent epiphenomenalism," and accept the metaphor that mind is to matter as smoke is to fire, or such, which might be associated with a more plausible epiphenomenalism, then a place has been made for the "physicality," and, consequentially, the causal efficacy of consciousness, reasons, and such. To put this in terms of the latter metaphor, smoke is real, and, as real, might have effects, participate in causal chains, and so on. The causal arrow, in such a case, might go both ways, not only from the physical physical to the physical mental, so to speak, but from the physical mental to the physical physical, so to speak. In short, two physicalities, two sorts of physicality, or a single physicality with two sides, so to speak, might be supposed. Or, similarly, an Ur substance might be presupposed, which one might, if one wished, think of as an "x." As we saw earlier, if we have a monism, then it is immaterial whether one thinks of unconscious matter followed by conscious matter, or unconscious mind followed by conscious mind. We will generally think, however, of "physicality" here, as that fits in better with the presuppositions of epiphenomenalism, with which position we are, at this point, particularly concerned.

3. Cybernetic theory, like common sense, presupposes the

causal efficacy of consciousness. Whatever values consciousness might have it seems there is at least one which is undeniable. It constitutes an element in an organic feed-back loop.

The driver adjusts to the road conditions, avoiding, say, a fallen tree; the quarterback leads his receiver; the fielder judges the fly ball; Jones, seeing Courtney's frown, refrains from poodle comments, and so on.

The notion that consciousness is inefficacious is not only incompatible with cybernetic theory but it is incompatible with common sense, and familiar facts of human life.

It is possible to evade this objection but only at a cost which I think few would wish to pay.

One might presuppose a whimsical deity or the I Hypothesis at its worst. In the case of the deity it likes to fool people; consciousness is inefficacious; but the deity is busy fooling people into thinking it is efficacious; for example, the driver sees the tree lying in the road and stops the car, and thinks, mistakenly, that his seeing the tree and wishing to avoid an accident had something to do with his stopping the car. It did not. Rather the whimsical deity either provided an on-the-spot miracle, stopping the car, or, if more clever, set up the universe, say, some eighteen billion years ago, in such way that the car would be stopped when it was, and the driver be fooled, in virtue of a pre-established harmony. Similarly, such innumerable coincidences, making it seem that consciousness was causally effective, might in theory be produced by an unlikely, but possible, random act. Following the I Hypothesis such things might happen, although, as they are improbable, one would not expect them to. Descartes' demon might be active, as well. If it can produce a seemingly real world which isn't real, why not? And so on.

But it seems more plausible to suppose that consciousness is genuinely efficacious.

4. Lastly, one might note the evolutionary argument against epiphenomenalism.

Why would consciousness have been evolved and preserved if it had no purpose, if it had no function?

That seems incredible.

It is certainly possible that there may be genetic riders, so to speak, genetic linkages amongst elements in which, randomly, perhaps an eccentric or unnecessary, even useless, characteristic might be an accompaniment of another characteristic, one more pertinent to the survival of an organism and the replication of its DNA, but consciousness seems an unlikely candidate for such a role. Even the peacock's unwieldy and gaudy plumes have, one supposes, been important in sexual selections, despite likely shortcomings with respect to intimidation, aggression, flight, escape, or camouflage. Most properties have presumably been selected for, in one way or another, though it is possible that some properties owe their survival to a fortunate linkage with such properties. Presumably consciousness, in view of its seemingly enormous value, would belong to the first class, to the majority of properties, rather than to the second class of properties, a minority of supernumerary, genetic fifth-wheels. Supplementing the plausibility of this conjecture one notes the presumed pervasiveness of consciousness throughout the animal kingdom. Despite the claims of Descartes who, presumably for religious reasons, saw animals in terms of cogs, wheels, and springs, as clockworks, as machines without consciousness, most of us would not suppose that "the howling of the tortured dog was no more than the sound of breaking glass." If consciousness is indeed pervasive throughout the animal kingdom it seems obvious that it actually serves, as it seems to serve, a multitude of purposes.

Epiphenomenalism, in one variety or another, seems to present the most serious challenge to rational explanation.

On the other hand, in virtue of considerations such the preceding, I think we can accept that epiphenomenalism is false and consciousness is efficacious.

It is an independent question whether or not reasons are causally inert.

If they are causally inert, then rational explanation is a mistake.

It should be noted that it is important to discuss the question of rational explanation, *simpliciter*, which is independent of the question of possible laws pertaining to reasons, and the possible extension of a D/N Model to cover explanations in terms of reasons. Clearly, to make the possibility of rational explanation depend on its possible incorporation into a D/N Model would, in effect, given the difficulties of the D/N model, deprive historiographers of rational explanation altogether. Thus, one hopes to establish the legitimacy of rational explanation, *simpliciter*, as it seems to be understood by historiographers, and, certainly, as it is commonly utilized in historiography.

Can that be done?

I think so.

It may be recalled that we earlier distinguished, however roughly, amongst six varieties of explanation, two of which are usually thought of as causal, and one certainly; and four usually thought of as noncausal, the status of at least one of which was somewhat ambivalent with respect to the causal-vs.-noncausal distinction, i.e., that of rational explanation.

Why should rational explanation be commonly regarded as noncausal? Why is there a common distinction drawn between reasons and causes?

If reasons are causally inert, one cannot explain in terms of them. Yet one often does just that. It seems then that they are often thought of as causes, and treated as causes. The ambivalence here seems to be between categorization, where reasons are often contrasted with causes, and use, where reasons are, on the other hand, commonly treated as causes.

One supposes the common contrast between reasons and causes is based, ultimately, on the distinction, possibly fraudulent, or misleading, between body and mind, between matter and thought, and such. For example, a causal explanation of an act might be expected to restrict itself to quantifiable variables, things occupying space and involving measurable forces. Causes would be publicly ascertainable; reasons would be private. Causes might be the material bodies moving through physical space according to mathematical laws. Reasons, on the other hand, do not seem to fit that sort of paradigm; they do not seem to be material bodies moving through physical space, whether according to mathematical laws or not. How much do reasons weigh, are some heavier than others, how wide are they, are some wider or narrower than others, are there fat and thin reasons, are some rounder than others, are some more triangular than others, how fast are they moving, are there slow reasons and speedy reasons, or do they move, at all, really, or do they just sit there, perhaps ready to move, and what are their laws, if any, and are there different laws for different reasons, and so on?

A causal explanation of the assassination of Caesar would presumably consist of an account of moving bodies and material forces, and, in a sense, would explain nothing. Causally it would be on a par with any other account of material bodies, dislodged pebbles, falling leaves, floods, earthquakes, chemical interactions, the rotation and revolution of celestial bodies, and so on. A rational explanation might try to explain why the bodies were moving as they were, what they had in mind, what they hoped to accomplish, what they saw as the justification for their movements, and such. Causes deal with behavior; reasons with action.

Please consider two arguments, the first an instance of *modus ponens*, the second an instance of *modus tollens*.

> If reasons explain, reasons are causal.
> <u>Reasons explain.</u>
> Reasons are causal.

> If reasons explain, reasons are causal.
> <u>It is not the case that reasons are causal.</u>
> It is not the case that reasons explain.

We should accept the first premise as true. There are noncausal explanations, but they are not explanations in the sense one has in mind here. They would be elucidations, colligations, instructions, or such. When one explains, or tries to explain, in terms of reasons, one is not telling what something is like, or how to do something, but is telling, or trying to tell, why or how something came about.

Now it seems, at least prior to reflection, that the second premise of the first argument is true, that reasons do explain. One is reasonably sure of the truth of that premise, and would be likely to question it only on the basis of some theory, presumably one committed to a cause/reason dichotomy, possibly mistaken, and restricting explanation to causes, understood in terms of bodies and their motions, bodies large and small, bodies of the sort dealt with by, say, physicists and chemists. The presumption then is that reasons do explain and, since they explain, they are causal.

Accordingly, the burden of proof here rests on he who would deny the efficacy of rational explanation. If he wishes to convince us that the common presupposition here, that reasons do explain, is mistaken, it seems he would have to give us some reasons, in some sense, if not a causal sense, to support his position. In any event, we do not expect him to respond in terms of material bodies moving through physical space according to mathematical laws, or such. In short, we would expect him to make out a case for the truth of the second premise in the second argument, namely, that it is not the case that reasons are causal.

In so far as his position is based on epiphenomenalism, or a similar position, it would seem to be committed either to an untenable dualism or a claim that some physicalities are incapable of entering into causal relations. The first alternative is incoherent and the second is dubious. We have also seen that there are excellent reasons for rejecting the sort of base theory on which his claim is founded, in virtue of cybernetic theory, common sense, evolutional likelihood, and such.

Too, obviously, he cannot, nor would he wish to do so, make it a matter of definition that reasons, generically, are without causal efficacy, as that would render his theory eccentrically analytic. His thesis, to be taken seriously, must be empirical. One cannot define one's way to victory.

At this point we have called attention to the general presupposition that reasons do explain, to be sure, a presupposition which might be mistaken, and have noted that if this presupposition is correct, then reasons must be causal. We have also established that certain reasons for supposing that reasons do not explain are not conclusive.

It is now necessary to make out a positive case that the general presupposition is correct, namely, that reasons do explain.

This requires demonstrating their causal nature.

First, one must call attention to two points, which should be recognized, and then disregarded. First, there can be, and doubtless often are, false rational explanations. No one is claiming that all explanations in terms of reasons are even plausible, let alone correct. Just as classical physical explanations can be wrong, so, too, can rational explanations. Just as classical science can resort to its vital forces, humors, phlogistons, ethers, and such, so, too, rational explanations can be framed in terms of entelechies, blood thinking, the Prussian spirit, racial minds, the cunning of Reason, intervening deities, vengeance-seeking ghosts, and such. The claim is that reasons can explain, not that all reasons are explanatory. Second, rational explanations, by their very nature, involve epistemological perils. They are too easy to come by, and they are difficult to confirm. This does not mean, however, that they cannot be true, and cannot, in some cases, for most practical purposes, be known to be true.

Consider two possible motivations, M_1 and M_2, which might or might not obtain. The logical possibilities are as follows:

$$M_1 \,\&\, M_2$$
$$M_1 \,\&\, \sim M_2$$
$$\sim M_1 \,\&\, M_2$$
$$\sim M_1 \,\&\, \sim M_2$$

It is easy to suppose four historiographers who might see the motivations for a given action on the part of a given historical figure in four different ways, ranging from the historiographer who attributed the action to both M_1 and M_2, to the fellow who feels that neither M_1 nor M_2 was involved. Logically, one and only one of these fellows has to be right. On the other hand, in the real world, what is going on would be likely to be more complicated. For example, the action might be motivated by M_1 and M_3, in which case the second fellow is right, but there is more to it than he knows, or the action might, say, be motivated by M_4, M_5, M_6, through M_n, in which case the fourth fellow is right, but is still far from understanding what went on.

It is one thing to track the trajectory of a cannon ball, observe the weather, and note the time of the first shot fired at Waterloo, and another to deal with thoughts, motivations, intentions, reasons, and such. One can understand why behavioral scientists, baffled by the mysterious relationship of consciousness to brain states, annoyed by the fleeting subjectivities of personal experience, and dismayed at the vagaries of introspective reports, would desire to substitute pubic for private variables, observables for nonobservables, stimulus for meaning, response for understanding, behavior for action, the measurable for the immeasurable, and so on, in order to "scientize" their discipline, to replace it actually, substituting for it a physics of sorts, something respectable and manageable, if largely irrelevant to a species hitherto thought to be interestingly and uniquely distinguished from the coelenterate and raccoon by just those properties and variables now to be methodologically neglected. Whatever information about the human being which might be gained from pigeons and rats is surely welcome. And so, too, would be welcome any information on pigeons and rats which might be gained from the biographies of Mozart and Einstein. But the pigeon wants its seed and the rat its cheese and inner variables once more intrude. To be sure, they may be ignored.

Rational explanation is surely suspect.

It is safer outdoors than indoors, but part of the human being lives indoors, and that is the part which makes him uniquely and interestingly human.

In any event, reasons, and such, are the key to understanding the human being, not meter sticks, clocks, and scales. Reasons, of course, are private, and subtle, and are often concealed, even from the reasoner. One speculates on the inner world from messages encountered in the outer world.

How does one understand another human being?

One may never succeed in this task. That is possible. But, if it could be done, how would it be done?

It would be done in the same way, essentially, that one understands oneself, namely, in terms of reasons.

This is the only way one can understand a human being as a human being, and not as an object in space, as an assortment of chemicals, mostly water, and such.

This returns us, of course, to the nature of reasons, their existence or nonexistence, their causal efficacy or inefficacy.

Might rational explanation be no more than the adoption of the "intentional stance," the grasp of an enabling fiction, to produce a sense of understanding where, actually, there is no understanding?

My defense of rational explanation, aside from noting its presuppositional plausibility, and rebutting, hopefully successfully, arguments against its possibility, is threefold. First, one must develop a theory of reason; second, demonstrate that, in the light of such a theory, rational explanation is epistemically acceptable; and, third, show that rational explanation is not only epistemically acceptable, but historiographically indispensable.

1. A THEORY OF REASON.

First, we must distinguish between reasons and the verbalization of alleged reasons. If one were to identify reasons with their expression, then reasons would be indeed inefficacious. If someone does something and we inquire as to his reason, and he says "R" is the reason that may or may not be true, but, clearly, the statement of the reason is not causally efficacious as a reason, though it might figure in a different causal chain. This is no different from a standard bodies-in-motion sort of explanation. Obviously the statement of the cause, correct or incorrect, cannot be the cause. Once this verbal confusion is dismissed, one of the common reasons for rejecting rational explanation is put aside, namely, that such explanations are merely verbal, are superficial, are convenient rationalizations, are epiphenomenal in nature, and so on.

Second, one must reject the cause/reason distinction as bogus. That distinction not only confuses the issue, but, as usually understood, suggests that reasons cannot be causes. It loads the question; it prejudices the outcome. Subtly, it attempts to transform an empirical issue into one of semantics, and secure a victory by means of a question-begging definition. Obviously there is a phenomenological difference between an explanation in terms of bodies in motion and an explanation in terms of intentions, reasons, and such, but this difference, which is a real difference, is, in the view I wish to develop, a phenomenological difference which would, at most, commit us to a difference amongst causalities, rather than a difference between the causal and the noncausal. Beyond this I would wish to argue that both sorts of explanation presuppose a generic sense of causality, in terms of which both sorts of explanation, properly understood, may find a place in, and be understood as expressions of, a monistic naturalism. In short, I wish to develop this theory within the compass of the D Hypothesis. The M Hypothesis would do, surely, but it is too much involved with the difficulties of the mind/body problem to be scientifically reassuring. In this context, the I Hypothesis, even if true, seems epistemically absurd and pragmatically useless. Recourse to the D Hypothesis, as might be recalled, whether true or false, is a useful postulate on which to found historiographical explanation. It is justified by the pragmatics of explanation. The project, then, is to make a place for rational explanation within the context of the D Hypothesis.

The crux of this theory, then, is the metaphysical hypothesis of monism. Given monism we noted that the Ur substance is unitary, "x," if one wishes, and, if one wishes, beyond this, to think in terms of matter and mind, then it is a matter of choice, a matter of semantic or ideological preference, whether one thinks of unconscious matter followed later by conscious matter, or unconscious mind followed later by conscious mind. With a trivial verbal adjustment, enlarging our usual notion of matter, to include conscious matter, or enlarging our usual notion of mind, to include unconscious mind, science, and all its triumphs, hazards, fallacies, and such, remains in place. One can still predict the interactions of chemicals, the future position of Mars, the effects of continental drift and Earth/Sun relations on climate, and retain, as well, ball point pens, drip-dry shirts, jet engines, penicillin, nuclear reactors, and so on. Nothing is lost, and something is gained, at least a possible role for rational explanation, a possible causal role.

Beyond the monistic hypothesis, we are accepting the reality of consciousness, and its obvious role in causal sequences, as made clear in cybernetic theory.

Let us approach the point by means of mechanical devices, first, one developed during World War II, a product of the theory of cybernetics. The device in question is a type of antiaircraft weapon. This particular weapon tracks its target, calculating its range and speed, and feeds this information back into the elements which adjust the weapon's aim and permit its discharge. The weapon does not fire at the target where it is but fires to a location where it isn't, but may be in the future. In short, the shell is aimed not at the present position of the target but at a projected rendezvous point with the target. To be sure, this is much what an antiaircraft gunner with a more traditional weapon does, by means of his own judgment. Presumably the sophisticated weapon performs, or is likely to perform, better than at least the average gunner, which justifies its production. Note that both the weapon and the gunner are, in effect, doing the same sort of thing, but in different ways. Both are tracking, estimating, and behaving, or, in the case of the gunner, acting. Now the antiaircraft weapon is not conscious and it would not make much sense to say it has its reasons. On the other hand, it does respond to its environment, and, in the light of its task design, adjusts its behavior accordingly, and reacts on the environment. It is a goal-oriented, or an end-oriented, mechanism. If the machine was conscious, one might think of this goal, or its end, as a "reason," in terms of which its task design is constructed. The machine has its purpose, which is to strike moving, aerial targets. No one would suggest, in the case of this machine, the antiaircraft weapon, that one could give a rational explanation of its behavior. It lacks consciousness, reasoning, desires, intentions, and such. One might suggest a rational explanation for the behavior of the engineers and scientists who conceived and designed it, but not for the machine itself. Now let us suppose that we have a very different sort of machine, one conceived rather in the manner of "bottom-up" robotics, in which the machine is programmed to adjust its behavior as a result of its environmental interactions, following programmed goals, as opposed to "top-down" robotics, in which the machine is preprogrammed to respond to anticipated situations. The "bottom-up" type of machine does not meet its environment with a battery or encyclopedia of preprogrammed responses which, with luck, will fit the environment, but, rather, it tends to fit itself to the environment. Its behavior is an analogue to "learning" and an engineer or scientist who has a penchant for anthropomorphic enthusiasms might claim that it is actually "learning." In any event, whether or not it is "learning" in some sense, it is not conscious, does not reason, does not want or desire, does not have intentions, and such. And its goals, or such, are not self-conceived, but are imposed on it, and from the outside. But, whether these goals are imposed on it from the outside or not, it does have goals. Namely, it is designed to achieve certain ends under certain circumstances. The weapon is designed to bring down moving aerial targets. The "bottom-up" robot may be designed, at least, to keep itself from falling over edges, such as stairs, pressing indefinitely against solid surfaces, such as walls, and such. The weapon and the robot both have their goals, which are part of their design. One cannot weigh or clock the goal, but, as a result of the design, it is very real. A is larger than B, and to the left of B. One cannot weigh the relationship "larger than" or "to the left of," but A is in fact, we shall suppose, larger than B and to B's left. Similarly, goals are real, and empirical. Such relationships do not require a distinction between mind and body, nor do they jeopardize a monism, of whatever sort. Fifi's *being* Courtney's poodle, for example, cannot be picked up, photographed, bathed, groomed, fed puppy chow, or whatever, but, on the other hand, it does not entail a dualistic metaphysics.

Now, let us suppose we have a very different machine, or something very much, in various ways, like a machine. The machine, or machinelike thing, we have in mind now is composed largely of carbon and water; it is a natural result or product not of a manufacturing process, but of an organic process, evolution. It does not come off an assembly line but it is hatched from an egg or, in the case we have mostly in mind, it is the result of a viviparous parturition. We will call it an animal, and it may be, if sufficiently complex, a human being. Certainly to some extent it comes endowed with a plethora of dispositions, proclivities, possibilities, and potentialities, many programmed to become active at given levels of development. It may not come into being with the Pythagorean theorem in mind but it is such that, if it starts thinking along those lines, it might come up with it. In any event, it is no *tabula rasa*, nor, as far as we can tell, is it invariably a mindless hollow body inert until filled with memes and activated by the local social engineers. To be sure, it often is. Some bodies, however, probably due to internal idiosyncrasies, felt criteria of appropriateness, genetics seeming to have supplied them with a modicum of deviant responses, thought, rationality, and such, are, to one extent or another, self-programming, a feature sometimes useful, sometimes embarrassing, to a too-uniform gene pool. In such cases, it is a bit as though the antiaircraft weapon, on its own, due to some unforeseen design flaw, began to prefer flower arrangement to shooting down airplanes, or the "bottom-up" robot were remain stationary, devoting itself to the contemplative life.

The point is that, however it is to be explained, there are arrangements, of neurons or whatever, which produce dispositions to respond in certain ways under certain circumstances. There is something in the human body, presumably in the human brain, which is functionally equivalent to the dispositions to respond in certain ways under certain circumstances of the antiaircraft weapon and the "bottom-up" robot. That the task design is incorporated in "organic hardware" rather than in silicon chips, and such, is immaterial to the general point involved. Whether the door is opened for Courtney and Fifi by Jones or an electric eye, the door gets opened. There is the task-design mechanism and the task, one of which is quantifiable and the other not, yet both are real. If we are dealing with a conscious human being, whose feed-back loops are complex and hierarchical, it would seem appropriate, and familiar, to speak in terms of intentions, motivations, purposes, reasons, and such. If we need a causal role for "reasons" it is only necessary to identify the reason with the organic hardware in terms of which the goal is achieved. As an analogy, although one can measure oxidation and dissolution, one cannot weigh combustibility or solubility. One cannot weigh kindness and cruelty, courage or cowardice, hope or despair, ambition or sessility, but one can see them as dispositional properties of bodies which produce activities and displays which we would characterize in terms of such words. In this way we can as meaningfully claim that Hannibal was brilliant, Fabius Cunctator cautious, Caesar ambitious, Mark Anthony infatuated, Caligula deranged, and so on, as that the wood of triremes was combustible or the pearl of Cleopatra soluble. The best way to guarantee a causal role for reasons is to identify the reason with that which causes the behavior to be explained. Analogously, the cause of the combustibility of wood are those properties in virtue of which it can burn. Similarly, ambition, as a reason in terms of which to explain, are those empirical properties which produce behavioral manifestations of the sort we might attribute to ambition. Obviously human beings possess real properties which produce various phenomena. How else could they be produced? And, given the monistic hypothesis, those properties are as real as any others, say, those which result in combustibility, solubility, and such. Accordingly, within the context of a naturalistic monism, rational explanation is epistemically legitimate. One may explain then in terms of purposes, motivations, intentions, reasons, and such. It is an independent question, of course, as to how purposes, motivations, intentions, reasons, and such, come about. That is an independent inquiry. Similarly, why a given object is combustible and another not, or one soluble and another not, why, say, sugar is soluble and iron not, is an independent inquiry, to which, one supposes, physicists might address themselves. On Humean grounds one could certainly imagine noncombustible wood and soluble iron.

2. Explanation in terms of reasons.

With a naturalistically founded theory of reason in place, in which reasons are identified with givens of "organic hardware," which have dispositional properties to produce behaviors of one sort or another, in various contexts of circumstance, reasons become indisputably causally effective. Indeed, a sufficiently advanced science, within a monistic metaphysics, might be able to ascertain the organic givens in question, though one suspects that the mystery of a precipitated consciousness would remain as strangely marvelous and inexplicable then as it is now, and has always been.

Given the complexities and obscurities of the organic givens presupposed, explanations in terms of reasons are likely to remain quantifiably elusive. In one sense they seem less comprehensible than explanations in terms of weights and pressures, but, in another sense, that of familiarity, they seem more comprehensible to us. As suggested, we explain ourselves to ourselves, and others to ourselves, in terms of intents, purposes, motivations, reasons, and such, not in terms of four-dimensional empirical bodies in motion. Indeed, to us, such an explanation, a bodies-in-motion explanation, on the conscious level, would be misdirected, inapt, and unintelligible. It would be as silly as trying to explain combustibility in terms of solubility. Reason talk now, as conceived, has an indisputable, if subtle and elusive, causality behind it, a causality sensed in, or recognized in, consciousness, in a phenomenological awareness of data.

If the preceding argumentation is correct, or substantially correct, it is epistemically legitimate to rely on rational explanation in appropriate contexts, most obviously when dealing with the actions of individuals or groups, less obviously, but plausibly, when dealing with institutions and practices incorporating, or resulting from, human action. This is a desiderated outcome because historiography, without which we would be boxed in the present, unable to understand our past, our time, or our world, requires such explanations. Without them she would be worse than crippled; she could not exist.

This is not to deny that many problems appertain to rational explanation. For example, they deal with inferred variables, "private variables," the dreaded "intervening variables," rather than public variables, such as external stimuli and overt behavior; they may be difficult to ascertain, and they are surely difficult to confirm; they do not, at present, lend themselves to quantification; was Caesar more or less ambitious than Tamerlane; when does zeal slip into zealotry; pride into arrogance, and so on; the vocabulary in which we relate to them is insufficiently precise; it is reasonably clear what is meant when we say that Caesar had the "falling sickness," presumably epilepsy, and less clear when we speak of his alleged dishonesty, greed, charm, tactical skills, literary talents, ambition, and so on. Similarly, a scales-and-meter-stick approach to reality is less likely to suffer from unwonted subjectivity than rational explanation, in which there is a natural tendency to color interpretations with the hues of one's personal preferences, as, for example, with respect to socialism or capitalism, religion or secularism, and so on. It might also be maintained that rational explanation would become progressively less reliable when dealing with distant times or unfamiliar cultures. What is rational or acceptable under certain sets of life conditions or given certain cognitive fields may seem less so under different life conditions and within different cognitive fields. Presumably, that is to be expected. None of these considerations, of course, suggest abandoning rational explanation, as if that might be possible. What they suggest, rather, is that it should be used with as much sensitivity and common sense as possible, that one should retain a wariness in its application, that one should cultivate an acute sense of its often perilous and precarious nature, and that one should, accordingly, with a generous recognition of the complexity of the subject matter and one's own fallibility, tread softly.

3. THE INDISPENSABILITY OF RATIONAL EXPLANATION.

Let us consider a simple example of a possible rational explanation, one which might be proposed to account for an interesting discrepancy between likely facts, as inferred from documents, and alleged facts, or an authorized version of facts, explicit in sanctioned accounts, pertaining to the same train of events.

The battle of Kadesh took place in Western Ancient Syria in 1288 B.C. in the fifth year of the reign of the young pharaoh, Ramses II. It is the first battle in military history, thanks to surviving manuscripts, which can be reconstructed in detail. The manuscripts make clear that staples of warfare such as deception, troop screening, surprise attack, flanking movements, division of enemy forces, and such, were already well understood and developed. There are many accounts of this battle amongst modern historians, military and otherwise.[104] For our purposes, we need not describe the battle, and its phases, in detail, accounts of which are readily available, but only allude to some general features, in terms of which we can make our point.

The Egyptian forces, consisting primarily of four major divisions, were led personally by Ramses. He drew near the city of Kadesh. There was no sign of the enemy, Hittites and their allies. His scouts had reported nothing. The Hittite king, Metella, sent agents to the camp of Ramses, posing as deserters, who informed the pharaoh that he had withdrawn northward. Perhaps he feared to give battle. In any event, it seemed he had abandoned the city of Kadesh to the mercy of the pharaoh. Given the inability of his scouts to make contact with the enemy, and relying on the accounts of the

---

[104] I am relying principally here on James Henry Breasted's *A History of Egypt from the Earliest Times to the Persian Conquest*, Second Edition, Fully Revised. (New York, Charles Scribner's Sons, 1950). P. 425, ff.

supposed deserters, Ramses presumed that Metella and his forces were far distant, and did not prepare for battle.

Kadesh lay before him.

Eager to reconnoiter and begin the siege of Kadesh, Ramses crossed the Orontes River at the ford of Shabtuna in advance of his first division, no vanguard before him, accompanied, it seems, by only household troops. His first division was outdistanced and the other three were eight to ten miles behind.

Unknown to Ramses at that time Metella's forces were drawn up behind Kadesh and, as Ramses moved north and formed a camp, his first division now with him, the enemy kept the city between them, screening their position, circled about, outflanked the Egyptians, and fell on Ramses' second division, his third and fourth far behind, the fourth so far behind it took no part in the day's action. The second division was cut to pieces, and the survivors sought the pharaoh's camp, where the first division, disconcerted, seems to have broken apart and fled. Metella's forces overran the camp and, if better disciplined, might have turned a rout into a massacre, but they fell to plundering the pharaoh's camp. Meanwhile, the pharaoh, pathetically outnumbered, sent word to his third division to come up with all haste. Then, like a man without hope, driven to desperation, he, with a handful of troops, seeking an opening, counterattacked the enemy where his lines were thinnest, by the river. There seems to be no doubt whatsoever about the personal valor of the pharaoh, who plunged into the enemy's ranks again and again. A total catastrophe at Kadesh was averted when unexpected reinforcements from the coast fell on the unsuspecting, plundering enemy in the pharaoh's camp and apparently destroyed them to a man. These reinforcements, abetted by reformed remnants of the scattered first division, now participated in the action, and, later, finally, the summoned third division arrived on the field, and the Hittites, who might have been caught then on two sides withdrew into Kadesh. In any event, Ramses survived the battle, and, as the Hittites withdrew to the shelter of Kadesh, held the field. On the other hand, it is quite possible that his losses were greater than those of the Hittites and their allies, and it is supposed that Ramses either lost the battle, or that it was drawn. In any event, as Ramses pressed on no further, did not follow up a victory as one might expect if he had won a victory, apparently neither besieged nor occupied Kadesh, and promptly withdrew to Egypt, one supposes he was grateful to leave the valley of the Orontes behind him.

Although there are some discrepancies amongst the Egyptian reports the above account, partial as it is, seems to be substantially correct. It will be noted that the historiographical inferences, as is usually the case, are based on the reports but go beyond the reports. A typical example of this would be that from the absence of an account of a victory being followed up, one might, invoking the argument from silence, presume that there was no victory to be followed up, and thus that the battle had either been lost or drawn, or, in any event, had been so costly that an attempt to capitalize on the victory would have been impractical or perilous. If the victory had been followed up, given the military relevance and value of such an action, it seems obvious this would have been noted in the records. As it was not, one supposes no victory took place, or, in any event, no victory susceptible to exploitation.

Considering what one supposes actually took place, as suggested above, it is interesting that numerous monumental and commemorative inscriptions, large numbers of which are still visible in Egypt, suggest unmistakably that the battle of Kadesh was a spectacular Egyptian victory, indeed, one largely owing to the personal heroism and prowess of the pharaoh himself. One of his now-assumed titles is that of "Prostrator of the lands and countries while he was alone, having no other with him," and so on.[105]

The remarkable discrepancy between what seems to have taken place in the vicinity of the city of Kadesh in the late May of 1288 B.C. and the glowing claims of large numbers of inscriptions commemorating the battle as a glorious Egyptian victory, owing almost exclusively to the brilliance, courage, and might of the pharaoh himself, lends itself naturally, and, one fears, almost too easily or obviously to rational explanation.

In any event, in the context of this incident and its aftermath, we would like to suggest some general observations pertinent to rational explanation.

First, the discrepancy between the inferred facts and the

---

105 Breasted, p. 435.

proclaimed facts, however we chose to explain it, would be in terms of rational explanation. Even the gods, in possession of one state of the system of the D Universe, to the position of the last subatomic particle, with a full knowledge of the laws of the system, and with access to batteries of divine computers, could not explain what occurred, as we understand it, or try to understand it, in terms of material bodies. They could predict the least movement and the tiniest sound of the battle, every hoofbeat, every jangle of harness, every rotation of each chariot wheel, everything, to the least particle of dust raised or pebble moved, every noise of every human and every beast, living and dying, could describe everything, but would understand nothing—until resorting to rational explanation. Analogously, the gods could equally and infallibly predict assemblages of letters but, without rational explanation, there would be no difference between 'nrocinu' and 'unicorn', between 'yrotsih' and 'history'. Thus, without rational explanation even gods could have everything before them and see nothing, could hear but would be unable to listen, could know everything but would understand nothing. The distinction between history and nature is marked by meaning.

Second, as noted earlier, many difficulties appertain to rational explanation. Such explanations may be indispensable to historiography, but they are inferential, and thus peculiarly vulnerable to error. Moreover, given the distinction between data and the interpretation of data, and the knowledge that any given set of data is capable, in theory, of an infinite number of interpretations, one becomes, if informed, appropriately chastened by the hazards of inference. The chances of being wrong, even within the compass of plausibilities, is not negligible, and the chances of being wrong to one degree or another are considerable. And there is small comfort to be gathered from the recognition that, even if one were right, to the least minim, one will never be epistemically entitled to certainty. The complement of this fact, of course, is that it is unlikely one could ever be proven wrong, but this, in a discipline allegedly cognitive, is a liability, an occupational misfortune, not an advantage.

In the context of our example, the rational explanation of the noted discrepancy between presumed facts and alleged facts seems so obvious that most historians would be unlikely to explain it at all, but would rather leave it to the common sense of their readers. It need not be regarded, however, as all that obvious. The standard interpretation would seem to be that Ramses is a creature of boundless conceit, of colossal vanity, a vainglorious liar, an egotist of megalomaniacal proportions. And, one supposes, that may well be true. Certainly one could imagine his household troops defending him to the point of lunacy in a number of his sallies against the enemy, and, without disparaging his bravery, leadership, and importance, one is well aware that few battles, involving thousands of men, chariots, and such, are likely to be won single handedly by one warrior, which would seem to be suggested by the official monuments dealing with the matter. Common sense supports the standard interpretation, which may well be true. On the other hand, it also tends to reflect the likely views of law-abiding, peace-loving, violence-loathing, power-envying, comfortable, middle-class, sedentary scholars who, happily, never had to duck a Egyptian javelin or leap from the path of Hittite chariot trying to run them down. Their views of Ramses seem to suggest that he might have had his childhood in Minneapolis, presumably in a dysfunctional family, and, in any event, is in desperate need of therapy.

First, it is logically possible, if not likely, that the monumental celebrations of the battle are substantially correct. Perhaps the battle was a stellar Egyptian victory. The better accounts of the victory may have perished, perhaps at the hands of Ramses' critics, leaving behind only an incomplete record, and an inconsistent one, at that. Too, in Ramses' time there seems to have been little objection to his claims, even by traditional foes, safely beyond his reach.. Not much historical revisionism, muck-raking, or such, seems to have been about. Indeed, later on, he even married a Hittite princess. Too, whereas I should like to think that there is a human nature, and that it is logically possible for the local grocer to understand an Egyptian pharaoh, a Hebrew prophet, a Viking berserker, a Sioux warrior, a Napoleonic grenadier, and such, we should also recognize that this might take a bit of doing. One of the important insights of *Verstehen* historiography is the recognition of the need, insofar as it is possible, to "feel one's way" into the past, to try to understand the way historical figures understood the world and found themselves within it. One supposes there is an analogue here to the Stanislavski theory of acting in which the actor becomes absorbed in the role, becomes the character, and so on. One need not go as far as Benedetto Croce, encouraging one to "become a blade of grass," that one may understand a blade of grass, but, if one is to gain a sense of history beyond its surface, something beyond the names and the dates, it would probably be useful to try to feel one's way into an alien time and culture. Otherwise, one will be forever a spectator, a baseball fan at a cricket match, and never a vicarious participant. It is easy to assume one's own moral superiority and the superiority of one's own views and culture, and criticize other views and cultures in those terms, from the outside. This is easy enough to do, and reassuring to one's self-conceit. On the other hand, if one is to understand another culture, or time, it is imperative to try, as one can, to see it from the inside. This does not mean that one must ultimately approve what is so understood, but it does mean, at least, that one will then, in virtue of understanding, be entitled to one's disapproval. It will be rationally grounded. It will have been earned, from the inside out, not from the outside down. In any event, one will no longer be likely to judge a Ramses in terms of Minneapolis.

There seems little doubt that the pharaoh thought well of himself. Few pharaohs, as far as we can tell, suffered from a lack of self-esteem or underwent an identity crisis. The pharaoh, after all, was divine. None of that humility or democracy nonsense here, or "being a servant of the people." The people were his servant. His major worry was probably the powerful Egyptian priesthoods, because then, as now, those who can manipulated the superstitions of the masses are to be reckoned with. Ikhnaton's sublime and benevolent heresy crossed that line, and perished. In any event, if one honestly and sincerely takes oneself as divine, as a god, or such, and one's whole community accepts this, and reinforces it, it is easy to see how naturally, given such a cognitive field, one might see a battle's outcome as a function of a leader's divinity, and the leader might see it himself in such a fashion, with all innocence, as well. Similarly, in such a community, presumably favored by the gods, and supposedly under divine leadership, a battle's loss, or even an admission of incomplete success, a balanced account, an attempted objective rendering of events, might be subversive of the very beliefs on which depended the security of the kingdom. Even if the pharaoh preferred to be candid about certain events taking place in the late May of 1288, how he was ambushed and nearly wiped out, and such, which is unlikely, he would have been well advised to forget about it, and, in view of the likely consequences of publicizing inconvenient and embarrassing truths, incompatible with the image of "the great house," set his masons to work on a major public-relations project. Too, one supposes that then, as well as now, some historical figures would be concerned with their "legacy," and would not be above altering the facts a jot here, a tittle there, or, essentially, rewriting history, and, in the pharaoh's case, in stone.

None of the above claims that the traditional views of Ramses II, that he was a creature of boundless self-conceit, and such, are incorrect, but they do suggest that the traditional views may be mistaken or, at least, in need of some qualification. He seems to have successfully ruled one of the greatest kingdoms of the ancient world for some sixty-seven years, through thick and thin, through war and peace. One supposes that took intelligence and discretion, leadership and flexibility. As one of the greatest of all the Egyptian pharaohs, ruling for more than a generation in perilous and troublous times, he is a figure perhaps more to be understood than unwisely dismissed.

Too, if nothing else, it seems that in his youth, leading men, he fought well at Kadesh.[106]

Whatever the truth may be concerning the nature and character of Ramses, truths which will presumably remain forever unknown, his exploits and career must be approached, and can only be approached, by means of rational explanation. Certainly a bodies-in-motion explanation would be unilluminating. That neurological situation N_1 is followed regularly by neurological situation N_2 would not be helpful, unless one had the conscious correlates in

---

[106] There is speculation that Ramses II may be the pharaoh of the Book of Exodus. Personally, I think this doubtful. I suspect this identification is largely motivated by the desire to search out a pharaoh of great importance for the role in question. If the pharaoh had been Ramses, it seems likely that he would have been explicitly named. In any event, the historicity of the Book of Exodus, with its plethora of apparently mythical elements, and its lack of independent corroboration in Egyptian sources, is profoundly suspect.

mind. It would be like explaining a passage of poetry by measuring the arrangements and depth of ink marks on a page.

Explanation in terms of reasons, rational explanation, is not only epistemically acceptable but appropriate. It is not a substitute for explanation, the best that historiography can manage, but a form of authentic explanation, felicitous, suitable, judicious, and comprehensible, and that even within even a monistic metaphysics presupposing a D Hypothesis. Moreover, it is indispensable. It is the only way we have to understand ourselves and others. It is not only historiography which would be impossible without it. We, too, as we think of ourselves, as we understand ourselves, as human beings, would be impossible without it. Without it we could understand neither ourselves nor others. Without it we would be alienated from ourselves, and others, would be as innocent and uncomprehending as idiosyncratic electric eyes and thermostats reacting to environmental stimuli. The human being, in this sense, curious and questioning, speculating and inquiring, differs from, and exceeds, the forces of nature, large and small.

4. Addendum: Multiply Explanatory Prose

It might be recalled that we earlier suggested a taxonomy of explanation, as follows:

I. Causal
1. Thread Analysis
2. Deductive/nomological
II. Noncausal
1. Elucidation
2. Explaining How
3. Rational Explanation
4. Colligation

I think this taxonomy is familiar, and that justified the initial breakdown, as above. Our major departure from the standard view, obviously, has been to shift rational explanation into the causal category, where, if the theory of reason propounded in the text is acceptable, it belongs.

Those familiar with historiographical prose will recognize, however, that actual historiographical explanation often involves an interplay of causal and noncausal explanation. Further, even the generally accepted distinction between description, or chronicle, and explanation is seldom viable. It is surely hard to draw a sharp distinction, for example, between description and elucidation, which is a form of noncausal explanation. One man's description can be another man's elucidation.

In any event, whereas the distinctions between description and explanation, and between causal and noncausal explanation, are important, and surely have their point, and historiography would be the less comprehensible and coherent without them, it is a matter of record, so to speak, that a working historiographer often approaches his subject matter by means of narrative, and that narrative seldom, if ever, divides itself up into description and explanation, or explanation into causal and noncausal explanation. In the living organism of historiographical narrative, the "flow narrative," so to speak, in explanations by "telling," as one might think of them, which supply backgrounds and contexts, and trace causal threads, explicate sequences, and account for developments over time, these elements are blended, and, in the case of a talented historiographer, effortlessly, subtly, and sometimes powerfully, even beautifully. Historiographical narrative, as will be seen later, is a unique form of literature, albeit it one which, ideally, can take pride in its adherence to austere moral and cognitive standards.

We had earlier, if successful, in virtue of considerations having to do with truth, evidence, and knowledge, established the possibility of historiographical knowledge. We had then noted that it is one thing to establish the possibility of historiographical knowledge, and another to establish the likelihood of its confident realization, ascertainability, quality, and reliability. We had then recognized that two major objections to the cognitive value of historiography remained to be dealt with, first, the claim that historiographers seldom, if ever, succeed in producing satisfactory explanations, say, explanations of a scientific level, and, second, that historiographical judgment is irremediably subjective, which fact militates against its cognitive value, which, indeed, precludes its attaining the status of a serious discipline, say, that of a science.

Given the previously developed theory of reason, we have demonstrated, if successful, that rational explanation, on which historiography muchly depends, is real explanation, not pseudoexplanation, that it is, in its way, as causal as an explanation in terms of physical objects in motion. We brought it securely within the fold, even, of the D Hypothesis. The difficulties that attach to it, then, are difficulties not in theory, but of practice. That such explanations are difficult to establish and confirm is notorious, but this has to do with the subtlety of the variables in question, as we have seen in the example of Ramses and Kadesh, not with their lack of reality. It is easy to be mistaken about such things, but they are not figments of the imagination, not illusions, not fictions. Empirical reality is there. One is dealing with variables as real, in their way, as pressures and temperatures, not with the mythical or insubstantial. There are frequent analogues to this sort of thing throughout science. Presumably we will never know the weather on a given afternoon at certain coordinates on Pangaea some 550 million years ago, the colors of the Archaeopteryx's plumage, the lexicon and cosmology of the Neanderthals, and so on, but these things were real. We may never know why Jones misaddressed his letter, but one supposes a cause, and psychiatrists might judiciously speculate on whether a reason was involved or not, and, if so, the nature of that reason, and speculate correctly or incorrectly. "Inner variables" may not lend themselves to quantification, but without them there would be no interesting behavior to quantify. One would be limited to hiccups, belches, sneezes, twitches, and such.

Rational explanation, correct or incorrect, is not arbitrary guesswork, but, when true, believed, and founded on appropriate evidence, constitutes knowledge. In this sense one can know, though one may never know that one knows. This is a concession to fallibilism. There are few cases, if any, where counterevidence is not conceivable. Knowledge would become meaningless if it were defined out of existence.

X. Historiography and Objectivity

So far, then, we have established that historiographical knowledge is possible, and also that there is no reason to suppose that it is not abundantly and frequently achieved.

To be sure, our inveterate and determined skeptic might suggest that this seeming exoneration of historiography, this *apologia* for a practice, is seriously, if not irremediably, flawed, due to an overlooked *de facto* and endemic subversion of, or contamination of, the third element required for knowledge, the possession of appropriate evidence. Here the charge would be that historiographical judgment is irremediably subjective, which fact militates against its cognitive value, and that this fact precludes historiography's ever attaining the status of a serious discipline, say, that of a science. In short, evidence is invariably gathered with a thesis in mind and interpreted from an ideological perspective, say, religious, political, national, social, ethnic, economic, or racial. Accordingly, historiography is not, and, in the nature of things, cannot be, objective. One supposes that typical sciences have commonalities which are shared by, and accepted by, all qualified practitioners. This does not seem to be the case with historiography. Even outside of trained observers, and such, one would expect St. Anthony, the Desert Father; Petronius Arbiter, the Master of Ceremonies at Nero's court; Saint Francis of Assisi; Richard the Lion-Hearted; Karl Marx; and Friedrich Nietzsche to agree on the length and width of tables, the weights of rocks, the time of day, and so on, if on little else. But, alas, the complaint goes, *sans* instrumentation, agreed-upon and ascertainable units of measurement, techniques of experimentation, the control of variables, and such, historiography can be no more at best than a harmless, gentlemanly hobby, a repository for interesting personal responses to the world, and is likely to be at worst a fraudulent pretender to one of the thrones of science and a covert weapon by means of which to wage ideological warfare.

So, one must consider the issue of historiography and objectivity.

1. A familiar riddle goes as follows:

Q: Why do scientists tell the truth?
A: They have so little temptation to lie.

I am not a scientist, but I gather, from a number of sources, that scientists are seldom at risk of canonization, and not merely for reasons having to do with the heliocentric theory of the solar system, or such. Rather, it seems scientists can, and have lied, have misrepresented experiments, fudged data, falsified reports, plagiarized articles, stolen results from other laboratories, engaged in research espionage, swiped theories without acknowledgement, undermined the reputations of colleagues, engaged in character assassination, overstated budgetary needs and manipulated grants for personal gain, bent theories and produced studies to obtain political acceptance and/or patronage, embezzled funds, chased lovely technicians around laboratory tables, past Bunsen burners and graduated cylinders, and so on. The preceding allegations, of course, are uniformly false, because, as we all know, every scientist is a paragon of virtue. All we need for our point here is that a scientist might upon occasion be tempted to lie, say, when his reputation, prestige, standing, position, work, and career might depend on it. Presumably, however, even in such extreme circumstances, he would not succumb to this temptation, as he is a scientist. On the other hand, he might be tempted.

The point of the riddle, of course, is that there is usually no reason for the scientist to lie. There would not be much point in it. Virtue is easy in a world where vice is without profit. Most of us do not much care whether there are up quarks and down quarks, or sidewise or diagonal quarks; whether there are eight or ten chromosomes in your typical fruit fly, how long it takes for a spore case to pop, and so on. Such things are surely interesting, and well worth inquiring into, but most of us could accept, say, either eight or ten chromosomes in *Drosophila melanogaster* with equanimity, without having one answer ruin our day, darken our life, or induce suicidal impulses, or another answer elevate us into jubilation and reassure us that we have not lived in vain. This is not necessarily the case with respect to questions having to do with religion, politics, morality, and so on. These things can make a serious difference in one's life, how one views things, how one lives, what one will do and not do, and so on. And the historiographer deals with such matters, and is a human being, with a stake in such matters. Clearly he is more likely to be tempted to lie, or, better, to see things in a predetermined perspective, than the scientist. It is an ordinal matter, a question of degree, but, on the whole, there is a point in our lovely little riddle. Can one be a proper judge in one's own case, in matters that matter?

2. The charge that historiographers begin their work with a thesis in mind and then gather evidence for and against the thesis might be denied. It might be claimed that historiographers, unlike physicists, chemists, and such, just, so to speak, "go and look," just "round up the facts," and so on. They just see what happened, and then tell us about it. They just find out, and then report back. Without wishing to deny radical differences between historiography and laboratory sciences, or that some historiography might fit the suggested paradigm, it is not the case that the charge could be well denied. Rather, it should be accepted, and with equanimity. First, it is clear that some historiographers do have theses in mind, for example, Saint Augustine, with divine intentionality, Karl Marx, with economic determinism, and Oswald Spengler, with organic destiny. Second, though less obvious because so taken for granted, because so familiar as to be almost invisible, many historiographers, particularly in the past, took politics, religion, and war to be the primary movers of history, rightly or wrongly, and this led them

to gather their facts, see importance, and construct their work in the light of such elements. Their hypothesis was to the effect that these were the predominant causalities in history and thus evidence tended to be selected in terms of these causalities, and history was seen largely as a result of them. The explanatory power of this implicit theory was so dazzling that counterevidence, or qualifications, for example, cultural, economic, geographic, technological, social, and such, were largely marginalized.

3. Let us suppose then that it is true that evidence in historiography is invariably, or at least generally, gathered with a thesis in mind and interpreted from a perspective. Let us hope so, at any rate. It is not clear how it, or any other cognitive discipline, could proceed in any other way, at least fruitfully. One does not gather facts, indiscriminately, as one rakes leaves. Nature is silent until questioned. In science one formulates a hypothesis, which is a thesis, and then gathers evidence, as one can, for and against the hypothesis, in several sciences by controlled observation, testing, experimentation, and such. Similarly, this evidence is seen in terms of, and interpreted in terms of, a perspective, usually that of naive realism, the reliability of sense perception and instrumentation, the objectivity of a reliable universe, and so on. In most sciences, too, this perspective is ideological, namely, that of quantitative materialism, ruling out elements common in a number of other perspectives, mysterious forces, interventions by demons, ghosts, gods, and so on. Given the principle of significant negation, if, say, "R" is an ideological perspective, then "It is not the case that R" would also count as an ideological perspective. One should also note that "perspective" is epistemologically unavoidable, for an organism whose consciousness is intentional. As it is said, "There is no view from nowhere." The very notion of "view" entails a viewer and a view from somewhere. The evasion of perspective is possible, of course, but the cost is high, for example, being a purely material object, say, a rock, or being unconscious.

4. The problem then is not the avoidance of perspective, but an adjudication amongst perspectives, presumably founded on pragmatic considerations. Not all perspectives are created equal,

or, if so, under review, stay equal. Perhaps some perspectives are better than others. Perhaps some perspectives are simply false, and provably so. Perhaps some others are simply false, but not demonstrably so. Indeed it might be claimed that they are not false, but unintelligible, or meaningless. Presumably being either false or meaningless would not count in favor of a perspective. It is another problem, of course, to prove that the false is false, or that the meaningless is meaningless.

5. Presumably, given the preceding observations, being "objective," whatever it is to mean, cannot mean being without a perspective, or being without an ideology, in one way or another, or to one degree or another. For example, if physics and chemistry have their perspectives, and their ideologies, there seems no reason to deny such things to historiography. That being the case, it seems incumbent on the skeptic who would deny objectivity, rather selectively, to historiography, to make clear what he would accept as objectivity. What is it, specifically, that historiography lacks, if it is not objective? If the only thing we are to know about objectivity is that historiography lacks it, we know nothing about what the skeptic has in mind, assuming that he has something in mind. Similarly, if the only thing we know about "goozsis" is that historiography lacks it, we have learned very little about either historiography or "goozsis," only about historiography that it lacks "goozsis" and only about "goozsis" that it is lacked by historiography.

6. It would be very difficult to give a nonarbitrary meaning assignment to 'small'. Weighs less than one ounce, is less than two inches high, would fit in a one-foot-square box, etc? Remember the flea, the dog, and the elephant. Similarly, it would be very difficult to give a nonarbitrary meaning assignment to 'objective', and, surely, the skeptic has not succeeded in doing so. On the other hand, consider the relation 'is smaller than'. This is much clearer. We know what we are talking about when we say that the flea is smaller than the dog, and the dog smaller than the elephant. Similarly, I think we know what we are talking about if we were to say this account is more or less objective than that account. Objectivity is best thought of as a relative notion. Just as

it would be unintelligible to speak of something which is absolutely small so, too, it would be unintelligible to speak of something as absolutely objective. When one does think of an account as being "objective" one is usually thinking that it is, so to speak, "pretty objective," or "very objective." Now, there is no reason in the world why "objectivity," in such a sense, as an understood relative notion, could not characterize historiography. Historiographers should not be taken to task for failing to achieve some hypothetical Platonic objectivity any more than Citation should be criticized for not exemplifying the Platonic horse, which, in any event, doesn't exist anyway. There is no reason why historiography, in any meaningful empirical sense that can be given to the notion, cannot be objective. Thus, even if historiography has never, as yet, succeeded in being sufficiently objective, perhaps due to the malfeasance of iniquitous historiographers, there is no reason they could not turn over a new leaf, or, if necessary, be replaced with a new, and more virtuous, crew. There is nothing, in theory, precluding historiography from being objective, in the only meaningful sense that can be assigned to 'objective', that of being judicious, honest, and fair.

7. No one claims, of course, that being judicious, honest, and fair, is easy. And the skeptic is surely right in pointing out that it is easier to be open-minded about such things as the chromosomes in *Drosophila melanogaster* than, say, one's personal values and political vision.

8. Being objective does not mean being true to the facts, though being objective is probably the best route to being true to the facts. It does mean doing one's best, rationally, intelligently, and informedly, to be true to the facts. It is quite possible to be objective and wrong. Science furnishes many examples. One thing that is important here is trying to be right. There is a watershed here between scholarship and propaganda, between seeking the truth and trying to change society, between science and activism. This is largely a matter of the agendas pursued, knowledge, say, as opposed to politics, truth as opposed to victory. If all this should truly be no more than a secret war, a conflict of class interests, one might at least note which class favors logic, truth, and, as far as it

can be achieved, objectivity, as opposed to which class finds such things not in its interest, so much as fallacy, falsehood, and bias. But then some feel that rationality, and such, is classless.

9. Clearly, if, as suggested, perspective and ideology are unavoidable, one must see if it is possible to adjudicate amongst perspectives, and on what grounds such adjudication might proceed.
That is important to do, and we will attempt to do it.

Before our attempt, however, it is important to clear some brush from the path, to note how objectivity presupposes, in certain senses, subjectivity.
We have noted, hitherto, the problems of "event carving" and "factor weighting." Without denying the problematicities of these two endeavors, neither endeavor, though involving subjectivity, militates against the possibility of objectivity. These two endeavors may be done as judiciously, honestly, and fairly as possible. The fact that choice or decision enters into such things does not jeopardize objectivity. There are better and worse choices and decisions. Subtleties are involved here, not subjectivities in any objectionable sense. One is not measuring tables and weighing rocks. Treating the American Revolution as an event would presumably be objectively justifiable; not treating it as an event would be possible but unusual, and would require some explanation; and, say, in factor weighting, discussing the military advantages of shorter lines of communication and supply, an aroused and generally supportive population, French military support, and such, would presumably be objectively more important to the outcome of the American Revolution than, say, possible deficiencies in British generalship. The fact that things might be done differently by different historiographers does not indicate a lack of objectivity; in the case of event carving, one segmentation of the universal process might be more illuminating than another, and might be preferred on that account; in the case of a difference in factor weighting this would make it clear only that at least one historiographer was wrong, something may have been missed, facts may have been misread, there may have been an error in judgment, and so on. Objectivity does not guarantee being right. Physical science would provide a

relatively outstanding example of objectivity, and its ascension is built largely on errors overcome, and, occasionally, on revising its very notion of the universe.

Objectivity is not a yes/no concept, but a more/less concept.

A perfect objectivity could not be achieved even in fantasy, as in the notions of the "historiographical camera" or the "impartial scribe." In the case of the camera, someone would have to decide what to photograph, and from what angle, and when to turn the camera on, and off, and so on. Too, the camera would miss the "insides" of events, and, having no concepts, and no hypotheses pertinent to the application of concepts, it would understand nothing. Its film would have to be developed, and read. We would have to supply the captions, the commentary, the interpretation, and thus return to historiography proper. Matters are rather similar with the myth of the impartial scribe, in his way much like the camera. If he were actually impartial he would have no criteria for events, and no criteria for selecting particular events, and no criteria for separating the important from the unimportant, the relevant from the irrelevant. In automatistic recording there would be no explaining, and no understanding. There would be chronometric limitations, too, as what happened is often clarified by its consequences. Following Hegel's marvelous metaphor, "The owl of Minerva spreads its wings only with the falling of the dusk." For example, one would not expect to find in the scribe's chronicle sentences such as 'This was the first day of the Punic Wars', 'Today Leonardo da Vinci's grandfather was born', 'The Enlightenment began today,' and so on.[107]

We may not know why Rome fell, but it seems likely that we know more about it than the Romans.

Before engaging in perspective analysis, in an effort to prove that

---

[107] Cf. With respect to certain elements in this paragraph, the notion of chronometric limitation, suggestions for certain examples, and such, I am indebted to Arthur Danto's *Analytical Philosophy of History* (Cambridge University Press, London and Colchester, 1965). Professor Danto is an unusual philosopher, even a maverick, would there were more, and his book is a brilliant, different, creative, ever-surprising work.

historiographical perspective does not jeopardize historiographical cognitivity, we would like to note, succinctly, in passing, two familiar factors involved in these matters, both of which involve choice and selection, and thus subjectivity, but neither of which jeopardizes objectivity. These two factors are cognitional diversity and purpose-relativity. Both are important, and neither, properly understood, constitutes a challenge to historiography's epistemic legitimacy.

10. Cognitional Diversity

Any phenomenon may be cognized under different descriptions. There is no single correct description of an empirical phenomenon. Even in the case of mathematics any entity may be characterized diversely. It is not merely that the number two is the natural whole number between the number one and the number three. It is also the number twice as large as one, the number half of four, the difference between 647 and 645, and so on. Two empirical examples follow:

That is an object.
That is a material object.
That is a wooden object.
That is a hand-crafted object.
That is a piece of furniture.
That is a chair.
That is a throne.
That is the throne of the King of England.
That is King John's throne.
That is King Richard's throne.
That is a symbol of tyranny.
That is a symbol of rightful governance, of tradition, of order, of stability, etc.

A number of objects are in motion over there.
A number of organic objects are in motion over there.
A number of vertebrates are in motion over there.
A number of primates are in motion over there.
A number of human beings are in motion over there.

A number of Romans are in motion over there.
A number of important Romans are in motion over there.
A number of important Romans
are sticking narrow, pointed objects into someone.
are sticking knives into someone.
are killing someone.
are murdering someone.
are assassinating someone.
are murdering a great man.
are assassinating a tyrant.
are trying to save the Roman Republic.
are trying to advance their own interests, etc.

Whereas not all descriptions are compatible, as noted above, many are compatible. There is no one way to look at an object. Perspectives are innumerable. Subjectivity, in the sense of choice, of selection, and such, is not only innocent, but necessary. Without subjectivity nothing can begin; without subjectivity objectivity is impossible.

11. Purpose-Relativity

As noted, above, any phenomenon may be cognized under many descriptions, and, in theory, one might add, under an infinite number of descriptions. This might suggest, at least prior to reflection, that the more detailed and complex a description the better, as being that description most adequate to its subject matter. The *prima facie* plausibility of this surmise is undeniable, but it would be a historiographical catastrophe to act upon it, even to the extent possible. It would destroy historiography as an informative, intelligible, meaningful discipline. The intent of historiography is to illuminate and explain the historical world; in no way is it an imitation of that world, let alone, in some sense, a facsimile, duplication, or reproduction of that world.

The word 'lion' lacks teeth and claws; it is not a lion; it is not an imitation of a lion, not a facsimile, duplication, or reproduction of a lion; it is not even like a lion. Similarly, historiography is not history; it is not even like history. But from language we can learn about lions, and history. And from appropriate words, marvelous words, we can fear the lion approaching in the arena, sense the tragedy of Cannae, the triumph of Zama.

Perhaps you are familiar with the following story.

A fellow is accused of stealing a watch, and, after a trial, he is found not guilty. The judge informs him that he is free to go. He then asks the judge, if it is all right to keep the watch.

This story would not be improved by describing the courtroom. We do not need to know where it was located, or the number of people in the room. Knowing the day of the week, and year, and such, would not be relevant, and so on. The color of the necktie worn by the prosecuting attorney is not needed. We do not even need a description of the former defendant, nor whether the judge wore glasses, and so on.

The moral of this little story, for our purposes, is to call attention to the difference between relevance and irrelevance, and note the purpose-relativity of an account. Similarly, the historiographer is unlikely to indulge in indiscriminate reportage, which would be distractive at best, and misleading and counterproductive at worst. If one cannot find the point there is no point in making it. The thief's question and the judge's gavel have an equal reality, but one belongs in the narrative and the other doesn't. The historiographer, and no one else in his right mind, attempts to verbally photograph reality. The wholeness of reality he can leave to the gods. He wants to give us a sense of a part of that reality, germane to his own purposes. This is subjective, but, within that subjectivity, he can pursue his purpose more or less fruitfully, more or less objectively.

As we have seen, first, an account is not well viewed as a replication of a reality, and, second, often, very little of a reality is germane to an account. Thirdly, we now note that a given reality may be addressed with a variety of purposes in mind. One reality, many purposes, many accounts.

Let us suppose, for purposes of manageability, if nothing else, something simple; an article is to be written, based on a particular film, one putatively based on a book. The same film, frame for frame, might be approached in a variety of ways, depending on the author's interests. The film is an object; it may preclude some interests, but it dictates no interest. Obviously a number of plausible, even valuable, articles might be founded on the same film, differing with respect to content, treatment, intended readership, projected market, and so on. A small, but illustrative, number of possibilities are the following:

1. One might be concerned with film as an art form. In such a case one might deal mainly with the aesthetics of the film, and, primarily perhaps, with its cinematography, the nature of the visuals, the mood induced by these, the editorial work, the use of establishing shots, close-ups, long shots, angles, dissolves, collages, scene flow, cross-cutting, and so on.

2. One might be concerned with the technology of the film. the physics and engineering utilized, the color processes, sound recording, computer graphics, models, special effects, and such.

3. One might be concerned with the film as cinematic theater, in which case, one might be concerned primarily with the quality of directing, writing, and acting.

4. As the film is putatively based on a book, its fidelity or lack thereof to the book might be of interest. A number of questions and observations might be pertinent. The book might be a better book than the film is a film, or the film might be a better film than the book is a book. Or each might be fine and remarkable, or poor, in their way. One thing is certain; they are very different; except in gross features they are likely to be quite dissimilar. Names might be preserved, and a period. But the dynamics of character development and action are likely to be considerably different, due to constraints of time and the requirements of the medium. Prose and film are different art forms, each with its own strengths and weaknesses. Prose may have depth and, when it wishes, it can philosophize, ruminate, ponder, and tell; the film is surface, and it can show, as the prose cannot, setting its own rhythms, supported by sound and music; the reader is alone with the book and his imagination; within certain parameters he is free to construct his own visions; he can come and go, as he pleases, linger or hurry on; the film viewer is presented with the product of another imagination. a *fait accompli*, with which he has little to do; he is a spectator, of a public project, not the author's collaborator, and so on.

5. The film might be subjected to a commercial analysis, its expense, resources, platforming, the timing of its release, its

distribution, and such. This would concern itself largely with the business side, the economics, of the film, the attempt to analyze its success or lack of success at the box office.

6. A sociologist might be interested in the film from the point of view of its demographics, the nature of its audience, with respect to age, race, socioeconomic status, and such, or he might find it informative with respect to cultural values and viewpoints, seeing it as an index to, or a reflection of, such things.

7. A psychologist, educator, politician, reformer, or such, might be interested in the film from the point of view of its possible effects on viewers, say, how it might alter or influence their behavior.

8. One might be interested in the film's impact on other arts, for example, film has apparently affected popular writing, with respect to chapter length, scene shifting, and such, and, presumably, even mobile visual art, or, more likely, one might be concerned with its impact on other films. A successful film predictably generates the sincerest form of flattery.

9. A film historian might be concerned with the film's place in the history of cinema, how it has been influenced, how it has influenced, what it might have contributed to the development of the film as a *genre*, and so on.

10. One might also see the film as a career vehicle for a director, or actor, in terms of its likely effect, positive or negative, on his career.

11. One might also see the film relative to the production schedule of, and ambitions of, a particular studio or producer. A film is occasionally made with an eye to prestige and awards, and the enhancement of the image of a studio or producer. A given film may be produced knowing it will not, in itself, recoup its costs, but may be regarded as justified from the point of view of reputation and public relations. Too, a film might occasionally be produced largely for reasons of vanity, or ideology. The market is not exclusively economically driven. That common perception is incorrect.

We noted that film is an object; it may preclude some interests, but it dictates no interest. This, too, is the case with a historical period, a set of events, an institution, a historical character, and so on.

Accounts are purpose-relative. So, too, are scientific observations and experiments. Purpose may, but need not, jeopardize objectivity.

12. Perspectivism

Initially one might distinguish between perspective pluralisms and perspective monisms, and one might consider them, schematically, as follows:

I. Perspective Pluralisms
A. Compatible Perspectives
B. Competitive Perspectives
C. Cumulative Perspectives
II. Perspective Monisms
A. Actual
B. Ideal
C. Practical

We will be principally concerned with the possibility of developing a practical perspective monism. The motivation for this is to bring about, at least in theory, a unity-of-historiography position, an ideal suggested by the unity-of-science movement, in terms of which a diversity of sciences were to be accepted and reconciled, though in our case, surely, without its paradigm tool, the D/N Model. The notion here is that reality is one and thus that all truths, relative to whatsoever they might be, are compatible.

The object in flight may be moving at a thousand miles per hour relative to reference platform one, and two thousand miles per hour relative to reference platform two, and it might not make sense to ask how fast it is moving, or if it is moving, except relative to a reference platform, but it exists, independent of reference platforms. There is, thus, a reality, to which all truths may be indexed.

Whereas we will be interested in developing a perspective monism, primarily to see if it should be possible, one should recognize that it is by no means clear that such a monism is in the best interests of historiography. There is much to be said for a free market of perspectives; what cannot be said for it is that it is historiography's best route to science, should historiography choose to seek that route.

It seems unlikely that a single perspective would emerge from such a market. None has, as yet. Too, there is no guarantee that the emergent perspective, if it should emerge, would be the best perspective. One well-known definition of a camel is that it is a horse designed by a committee. One does not poll oneself to truth. Democracy is of great value; it gives us a way of changing leaders without killing people; it is of less value in evaluating theories.

To be sure, being a science may not be in historiography's best interest. It might have better things to be.

Amongst perspective pluralisms we distinguished those which are compatible, competitive, and cumulative. Compatible pluralisms are pluralisms which, whether true or false, are consistent with one another. To count as pluralisms they must have recourse to different subject matters, or objects, or different "explanatory handles," for example, emphasizing institutions, climate, race, geography, technology, ideology, resources, psychology, foreign influences, historical personalities, economics, or such. Presumably most such pluralisms, due to narrowness, would be false, but they do not contradict one another as they are, by definition, not explaining the same subject matters, or objects, in incompatible manners; accordingly, they are logically compatible. 'p' and 'q' are compatible, even if they are both false. Competitive pluralisms, on the other hand, are logically incompatible. For example, if Pluralism$_1$ explains Event E as exclusively or primarily due to Factor F and Pluralism$_2$ denies this, for example, explaining E as exclusively or primarily due to Factor G, then the Pluralisms are incompatible. Compatible and competitive pluralisms are both independent pluralisms. Each exists, so to speak, in its own world. Cumulative pluralisms, on the other hand, a Nietzschean notion, are brought together, each welcomed, all useful, supplementing one another, agreeing, differing, harmonizing, clashing, contradicting one another, and such. Here we have "warfare for the sake of one's thoughts." It is hoped, one supposes, that errors will somehow cancel one another out, or qualify one another, or point to a third possibility, which is truth, or such. Hegel would probably like that idea. This seems to be an adversarial notion of historiography in which somehow truth may emerge from conflict. There are analogies here to the notion of the free marketplace of ideas, that truth will somehow surface, or such. "Truth crushed to earth will rise again," but, of course, as suggested earlier, if it didn't, no one would know it. This is certainly an invitation to open-mindedness, and listening to all sides. That is much to the good. If there is a flaw here, or a dubious assumption, it might be the notion that truth will emerge as a sort of compromise, that it will lie in the middle, so to speak, which is not at all obvious. If one person thinks that two and two is four and another thinks that it is six, it does not follow that it is five. Similarly, if one fellow thinks it is eighteen and the other twenty, nineteen is even farther from right. An implicit notion here might be the "center of a distortion series" notion. For example, the round coin looks radically elliptical from one side and, similarly, but differently, from the other side. One then produces a less radical ellipticity, and one even less radical, on one side, and then the same on the other. Eventually, as these distortions converge, the coin looks round. This works pretty well for coins, but its extrapolation to historiographical explanation is unlikely to inspire confidence.

Another assumption involved seems to be that the truth is there, already in the accounts, and one needs only thrash through the accounts, and find it. A much better approach to veridical historiography, for those to whom it is practical, would be to revisit the evidence and begin anew. One might then come out with one of the perspectives, or, more likely, with none of them, with something different.

With all due respect to the robust, healthy, zestful, adventurous diversity and delight of multiple perspectives, presumably there are some who, uncomfortable with such stimulating, lavish chaos, would like to emerge from the jungle and find security and shelter within the palisade of a perspective monism. There might be several psychologies but this is seldom thought to be a virtue of psychology. We do not have several chemistries or several bacteriologies.

Amongst perspective monisms we called attention to three varieties: actual, ideal, and practical.

No actual perspective monism exists at present, and one may hope that one never will. Such a monism would be likely to exist if and only if it was imposed by authority. It is easy to conceive such historiographical monisms being imposed, as, for example, was the case in Nazi Germany, Fascist Italy, World War II Japan, the Soviet Union, and so on. It is natural for a totalitarian regime, local or global, political, military, religious, or whatever, to control education, communication, information, scholarship, and such. Tyrannies do not do well in the light of day. Sheep must be pacified, and reassured that all is well. Freedom imperils oppression.

The practical perspective monism, shortly to be discussed, is not an actual perspective monism, nor is it desirable that it should ever become such. It is an attempt to produce a common-consensus monism which might serve to unify historiographies, though , of course, only voluntarily, only freely. It would never impose itself by force, nor could it do so, if it wished, and it is not the sort of monism, given its openness and its emphasis on freedom, which would be of use to those who would be willing to impose a monism by force. So it is not authoritarian, not coercive; hopefully, it is interesting, comprehensible, judicious, moral, and useful.

But, first, let us consider an "ideal" perspective monism. This is based on Charles Sanders Peirce's notion of replacing or redefining the idea of truth with that of "fated opinion" or the belief which would be ultimately agreed upon by qualified observers, presumably those of the scientific community, if inquiry could be indefinitely continued. The notion here is that there would be an eventual convergence of belief, an asymptotic approach, ever more closely as research and inquiry is prolonged, and indefinitely continued, to the opinion fated to be agreed on, which we may as well think of as a serviceable replacement for truth, or, if one wishes, as truth itself.

The following three quotations are classical statements of the Peircean position:

> So with all scientific research. Different minds may set out with the most antagonistic views, but the progress of investigation carries them by a force outside of themselves to one and the same conclusion. This activity of thought by which we are carried, not where we wish, but to a fore-ordained goal, is like the operation of destiny. No modification of the point of view taken, no selection of other facts for study, no natural bent of mind even, can enable a man to escape the predestinate opinion. This great hope is embodied in the conception of truth and reality. The opinion which is fated to

be ultimately agreed to by all who investigate, is what we mean by the truth, and the object represented in this opinion is the real.[108]

Our perversity and that of others may indefinitely postpone the settlement of opinion; it might even conceivably cause an arbitrary proposition to be universally accepted as long as the human race should last. Yet even that would not change the nature of the belief, which alone could be the result of investigation carried sufficiently far; and if, after the extinction of our race, another should arise with faculties and disposition for investigation, that true opinion must be the one which they would ultimately come to. "Truth crushed to earth shall rise again," and the opinion which would finally result from investigation does not depend on how anybody may actually think. But the reality of that which is real does depend on the real fact that investigation is destined to lead, at last, if continued long enough, to a belief in it.[109]

You only puzzle yourself by talking of this metaphysical "truth" and metaphysical "falsity," that you know nothing about. All that you have any dealings with are your doubts and beliefs, with the course of life that forces new beliefs upon you and gives you the power to doubt old beliefs. If your "truth" and "falsity" are taken in such senses as to be definable in terms of doubt and belief and the course of experience (as for example they would be, if you were to define the "truth" as that to a belief in which belief would tend if it were to tend indefinitely toward absolute fixity), well and good: in that case, you are only talking about doubt and belief. But if by truth and falsity you mean something not definable in terms of doubt and belief in any way, then you are talking of entities of whose existence you can know nothing, and which Ockham's razor would clean shave off. Your problems would be greatly simplified, if, instead of saying that you want to know the "truth," you were simply to say that you want to attain a state of belief unassailable by doubt.[110]

---

108 "How to Make Our Ideas Clear." (1878) Reprinted in *Philosophical Writings of Peirce: Selected and Edited with an Introduction by Justus Buchler* (Dover Publications, Inc., New York, 1955), p. 38.
109 "How to Make Our Ideas Clear." (1878) *Op. Cit.*, p. 39.
110 "The Essentials of Pragmatism." (1905) Op. Cit., p. 257.

The ideal of a perfect historiography, understanding historiographical truth as a predestinate opinion, ultimately to be achieved if research, and such, could be prolonged indefinitely, has three immediately obvious and serious flaws; first, it is useless; it provides no guidance as to how to proceed; second, it requires an implausible supposition, that some such opinion would be predestinate; and, third, it provides no guarantee, let alone even a modest assurance, that such an opinion would be true.

As an ideal perspective monism involves many of the difficulties attending Peirce's interesting recommendations pertaining to truth, some attention might be brought, briefly, to those recommendations. This will also clarify, and perhaps qualify to an extent, the three major objections suggested above.

1. Belief and doubt make no sense without the notion of something to doubt and an object for belief. Belief and reality are independent. Reality was about long before anything was around to believe anything. To define reality in terms of that which is believed, however ultimately, and so on, is to conflate two very different things. Our beliefs might correspond to reality or not, but they do not create reality. We might take for reality what is believed, which makes sense, but to claim that reality, as opposed to an idea of reality, is belief-dependent is confusing, and deviant. The entire Peircean approach seems to presuppose what it seems to wish to dismiss, namely, truth and reality. It seems to presuppose that the predestinate opinion is an opinion about something, the real, and that the opinion would be true.

It may be true psychologically that what human beings really want is merely a fixed opinion and not truth, and that they are happy to stop looking once they are satisfied. But they stop looking and are satisfied if and only if they think their fixed-opinion is true. An individual might be conditioned, religiously or otherwise, to have a fixed opinion that 'p' is true, but they believe, and think it to be the case, and want it to be the case, that the opinion is true. When a human being has a fixed opinion he may be content, and lapse into epistemic serenity or lassitude, but that is because he thinks the opinion is true. If he did not believe that, he would not have fixed the opinion. It would still be "unfixed."

2. For a pragmatist, or pragmaticist, a term he coined for his

position, allegedly because its ugliness would render it safe from theft, Peirce seems surprisingly metaphysical. One learns, for example, that the "fated opinion" may never be entertained, and does not depend on whether anyone ever has the opinion or not. It is as remote, unreal, and hypothetical as the Platonic horse. It is an act of faith, and scarcely a rational one, that such an opinion is out there, waiting for science to catch up, if it can, and that it is always, doubtless, a step or two ahead, as it is to be asymptotically approached, science then presumably like Achilles, never quite managing to overtake Zeno's incredible tortoise. The metaphysics here makes traditional notions of truth and reality, which it is designed to replace or redefine, seem tame indeed.

It is not at all obvious that traditional correspondence notions pertaining to truth are unintelligible, and in need of replacement or redefinition, particularly with notions which presuppose them, and would be unintelligible otherwise.

Drawing distinctions between, say, truth and belief, thoughts about reality and reality, and so on, is likely to be more illuminating than blurring them.

3. There is no assurance that a single opinion, even under ideal conditions, would be foreordained. That involves another act of faith. That such an opinion exists is one act of faith; that there would be only one of them is another. There is no assurance that scientific views will ever converge, nor that, if they do converge, they will converge on the truth. Peirce himself points out that an arbitrary proposition might be universally accepted as long as the human race should last. To be sure, that doesn't seem to concern him, for he is off again into Plato country, where such things do not matter. And if another race should arise to investigate, and such, there would presumably be no reason why it, too, might not subscribe to an arbitrary proposition as long as it lasts, and so on. How would this sort of thing be confirmed or disconfirmed? Might not even Plato himself shiver in the cold of so dark and windy a metaphysical night?

4. We shall suppose that Peirce has in mind qualified investigators, and reliable methodologies of investigation. Presumably they, too, would be conceived of in terms of ideals, for example, new, perfect, hitherto-unconceived, break-through instrumentation, and such.

He also seems to presuppose a large, budgetarily supported science happily independent of political and social pressures. More ideals are involved, and ideals of a given sort, Peircean ideals. Whereas one is willing to suppose, and this is tacitly supposed by Peirce, that there is an independent reality to be right or wrong about, the notion of other races, which he mentions, is interesting. It is not obvious that a race of intelligent fish, intelligent birds, intelligent insects, intelligent aliens, as far above us as we are above, hopefully, alley cats, raccoons, and poodles, would develop identical sciences, converging on identical fixed beliefs.

5. Several of the basic orientations of contemporary philosophy of science suggest that Peirce's ideal of science may be unrealistic, in particular, the underdetermination of theory by data; the impossibility of logically conclusive proof of theories; the impossibility of logically conclusive falsification of theories; and the infinite-accounts hypothesis, to the effect that any given set of data may in theory be compatible with, and explained by, an infinite number of different theories, this entailing that an infinite number of diverse sciences is logically possible. Such considerations lead to a familiar distinction between truth and empirical adequacy, namely, that the scientist may establish that a certain theory is adequate to the data to be explained, generates reliable predictions, and such, but, as any number of other theories, and, in theory, an infinite number of other theories, would also be adequate, generate the same predictions, and such, one cannot be assured that any given theory is true. Such considerations suggest that the notion of a "fated opinion," or such, at least, may not be fated.

I think that the above considerations pertaining to Peirce's fascinating proposals, attempting to replace or redefine notions of truth and reality in terms of belief, support the second and third suggested criticisms of an ideally conceived perspective monism, namely, that there is no reason to suppose that a single historiography, however conceived, would be likely, even ideally, and that there would be no guarantee, nor would there be even a modest assurance, that it would be true.

The first criticism was to the effect that the ideal perspective monism would be useless; that it would provide no guidance as to how to proceed.

Suppose one did accept the ideal of the perfect historiography. What would one do then that one would not have done otherwise? Presumably one would try to argue logically, to research conscientiously, to be honest, judicious, fair, informed, and so on. But one might do that anyway. And presumably one would regard one's views of the moment as true, because they were true, right now, in an ordinary way of being true, not because they might be numbered amongst the propositions of an ideal historiography which might be achieved if research, and such, could be prolonged indefinitely, and so on. Would not such a belief be remote from your interests or concerns? Might not your view be true, and the "fated view" false, and so on? Many ideals might influence one's behavior, but it is not clear how the ideal of a perfect historiography would change anyone's behavior. To be sure, if one convinced oneself that the perfect historiography was that in the best interest of, say, a particular ideology, political party, economic system, race, class, sex, or religion, and one was not already subverting and playing fast and loose with traditional scholarly standards, then one might begin to do so. But this would be to subscribe to a particular version of perfection, and the notion of the ideal historiography is essentially vacuous. For example, if one is encouraged to be perfect, what is one to do? Be a perfect Nazi, a perfect Fascist, a perfect Communist, a perfect anarchist, a perfect liberal, a perfect libertarian, a perfect conservative, or what?

The ideal perspective monism provides no guidance for behavior, unless one has an independent notion of perfection which one then imposes on the monism in question, and then behaves accordingly. But then one did not need the notion of perfection in the first place. It did not influence your behavior. You did not shape your behavior by the ideal; you shaped the ideal in terms of your behavior. Too, on this approach, there could be innumerable ideal perspectives, and that undermines the whole point and value, if any, of the notion. An empty ideal is no ideal; it is a *tabula rasa*, to be written on as one wills; it is a moral blank cartridge.

If we are interested in a cognitive discipline, one which sees historiography in terms of a science, or a sciencelike discipline, as opposed to a historiographical pluralism, in which it might be likened to art or literature, creations as innocent of logistic incompatibilities as the works of Rembrandt and Picasso, or those of Thackeray and Dostoevsky, then it seems one must subscribe, at least in theory, to some perspective monism. Also, on the assumption that reality is one, it follows that all truths, however various, must be logically compatible. This, too, suggests the advisability of, if not the necessity of, at least in theory, a perspective monism. We called attention to three forms of perspective monism, an actual monism, an ideal monism, and a practical monism. We have suggested serious objections to the first two monisms, the actual and ideal monisms.

The "actual monism" involves disadvantaging disagreement, and requires, in effect, a particular party line. One cannot have an actual monism, except by accident, without censorship, policing, and an enforcement procedure. This requires imposing external constraints, presumably political or religious, on historiography, the imposition of certain viewpoints and the preclusion of others. This demonizes dissent, precludes debate, trammels the pursuit of knowledge, and transforms historiographers into agents of an ideology. Presumably no one favors a monism of this sort unless they either possess the coercive apparatus of society or anticipate its possession. Otherwise, with a different monism, they would be ruled out of the running, save insofar as they could redeem their position with assassination, arson, and such.

The "ideal monism," on the other hand, apart from being founded on implausibilities, and being afflicted by a number of logistic and semantic obscurities and deviancies, possibly including inconsistency, is substantially vacuous. Unless one has a clear notion of what being ideal, or perfect, consists in, there is not much point in being told to be perfect, and, as noted, if one defines perfection in terms of one's own preferences, this is likely to produce a number of competitive perfections, and, as one might add, amongst competitive perfections no adjudication seems likely save by coercion, ultimately, presumably, by force of arms.

By process of elimination, given the three most likely versions of perspective monism, one arrives at what we have spoken of as a practical perspective monism.

As a monism, one is supposing that reality is one and, accordingly, as noted, all truths, however various, must be compatible. This intellectual commitment is one historiography would share with classical sciences. Similarly, as with sciences, as classically conceived, questions of truth are not to be prejudged in terms of ideology, either political, religious, or whatever. Truth, as far as possible, is to be sought freely and independently. If the evidence suggests that the earth orbits the sun, rather than the sun orbiting the earth, go with it. You might be right.

A practical monism, as here envisaged, is fully compatible with cognitional diversity and purpose-relativity. It is incompatible, however, with purpose-relativity in any sense which would forsake the truth-commitment. All purposes, on this approach, must be compatible with that commitment. Scholar activism, for example, or any attempt to turn historiography into an instrument of ideology, to use it as a deliberate weapon or tool by means of which to substitute indoctrination and conditioning for the honest pursuit of truth is discouraged, however noble the end of this activity is deemed.

In particular, the truth commitment is not to be betrayed by truth itself, by using truth to lie, for example, by judiciously selecting truths with an intent to favor a particular political or religious goal; this is as objectionable as the neglect of truths relevant to a helpful historiographical assessment of an event, institution, policy, or personality.

Crime is not acceptable, even if committed in the name of law; vice is not acceptable, even if committed in the name of virtue; evil is not acceptable, even if committed in the name of good.

One who lies should realize that others may lie as well, and possibly they may be better armed. Accordingly, the chips of truth are to be allowed to fall where they may; they are not to be selected with an eye to prejudged and preapproved outcomes. Lies may be found out. They make poor timbers with which to construct the house of the future. Both truth and falsehood may sway, but truth sways legitimately and falsehood illegitimately. Those who intend to subvert a discipline to promote an ideological end do not share this particular view of a practical monism. In a practical monism, as here conceived, truth may never be achieved, but it is ever sought. In a practical monism such as conceived here disagreement is to be expected. Liberty does not encourage conformity. Given the complexities and obscurities of the subject matter of historiography it would be remarkable if there were not considerable disagreement amongst the most honest, informed, and fair-minded of scholars. Mutual agreement is not required; mutual respect is encouraged.

All in all, this turns out not to be so very different from an endorsement of, and a recommendation to adhere to, traditional scholarly standards of historiography. It has, of course, its perspective, as it must, and the perspective herein recommended is one of humanistic naturalism.

'Naturalism' suggests an empirical view of a reliable universe. 'Humanistic' suggests an avoidance of unverifiable modalities of explanation, and a seeing of history in terms of human beings, their efforts and works, and the consequences of these, realistically explicable as comprehensible developments, involving human agents, as opposed to such things being, say, the manifestations of the devices and machinations of gods and demons, the embodiment in sorrow and blood of a abstract dialectic, that it is all no more than a pointless theatrical, devised by a bemused deity, performed by human puppets, or such.

This is a recommendation, then, essentially, of a practical "common-denominator historiography," a "core historiography" which, for the most part, should be generally acceptable. It provides a methodological postulate for doing historiography, as suggested earlier in this study. It gives us a way of explaining things in ways which will be intelligible. It is eschewing, as explanatory devices, whether true or not, things like miracles, organic destinies, social forces, secret metaphysical plans, the interventions of extranatural forces, and such. If such things exist, they exist, in some sense perhaps intelligible to gods if not to men, but they do not belong in a "core historiography" as they are not acceptable generally to informed, professional individuals.

If this recommendation to honesty, fairness, open-mindedness, clarity, objectivity, reason, logic, and such is no more than a bias itself, rather than a common platform, on which biases may war as they will, so be it.

Surely this is an ideology, but it is one in which, generally, human beings may meet in civility, and without bloodshed.

It seems to me that this is a useful proposal for a common-denominator consensus, a "core historiography."

It also makes possible the consideration of a question which could not be meaningfully raised except upon the foundation of some practical perspective monism.

Is, or could be, historiography a science?

To that question we now turn.

XI. The Cognitivity Status of Historiography

1. Preliminary Considerations

We have already, if successful, established that both historiographical truth and historiographical knowledge exist. Accordingly, in a minimalist way we have established that historiography is a cognitive discipline. To be sure, similar claims might be made for catalogs, inventories, journalistic investigations, police inquiries, polls, phonebooks, and such. Accordingly, we must here be concerned with questions pertaining to the nature of historiographical cognitivity, in particular, its level and extent. An avenue into this question would be to compare and contrast it with certain alleged paradigm instances of cognitivity, such as physics, chemistry, biochemistry, and such. When one asks if historiography is scientific, or a science, two different questions, incidentally, these are the sorts of science which are commonly held in mind, not, say, geology, cosmology, astronomy, psychology, sociology, and such. Obviously historiography is quite different from, say, physics, but then, so too, are zoology, botany, paleontology, and any number of other acknowledged sciences. Accordingly, one needs here some generic sense of 'science' which might have to be discovered or, more likely, invented.

Before entering into these issues, three points should be noted.

First, it is a simple matter to define 'science' in such a way as to either include or exclude historiography. In that sense, the question, objectively, is rather trivial, more semantic than substantive. However one resolves such matters by rulings, historiography, science or not, is of momentous importance and of indisputable societal value. Few things could compare with it along such lines. Historiography, properly understood, is neither diminished nor enhanced by being placed in Column A or Column B. It is true that certain psychological consequences might appertain to such a classification, with respect to prestige, pride, self-esteem, access to grants, where departments are placed within an academic structure, and so on. No one denies that image can be significant with respect to one's sense of worth, dignity, self-importance, and such. One cannot define irrationality out of human beings; it seems to be built in. Being irrational is one of the things in which the human being excels.

Second, whereas not much, at least in a rightly ordered universe, would hang on whether one puts historiography with the sciences or not, it can be informative and interesting to examine similarities and differences amongst sciences, or, if you like, between historiography and science. We will give some attention to that, as it is relevant to any attempt to delineate a philosophy of historiography.

Thirdly, it is not at all obvious that being a "science" is something to which all right-minded disciplines should aspire. Poetry, art, music, theater, literature, and such, are amongst the deepest and most wonderful creations of the human species, and are none the less precious for not counting as sciences.

Perhaps historiography is more than a science, something better than a science.

Interestingly, sociological matters enter into these things. Views of science vary from culture to culture, and can change from one generation to another. Scientists have occasionally run afoul of establishments from Anaxagoras to Galileo, from Darwin to Freud. On the other hand, the usual view of scientists in the community at large, generally, historically, when they were not suspected of flirting with dark forces, seems to have been that they were on the whole quirky individuals with unusual interests, say, trying to transmute lead into gold or brew an elixir of life, certainly understandable objectives, build a perpetual-motion machine, and so on. Even in the early 18th Century science seems to have been primarily viewed as an avocation of eccentric gentlemen with time on their hands, something of not much interest to the community at large. To be sure, the values of engineering and technology have been recognized and celebrated throughout history, from the working of metals to the building of galleys, from catapults to pottery wheels, from pyramids to aqueducts, from bridges to fortresses, from temples to cathedrals, and such, but one usually, for some reason, tends to put such things to the side, and think of them less as the products of science than of craftsmanship. Later in the 18th Century, following the skirmishes of the 16th and 17th Century, an image of science, if not science itself, became a public player in the open culture wars, a weapon of the Enlightenment, leveled against perceived oppression. In the late 19th and early 20th Century the public image of science, putting aside evolution and depth psychology, was generally favorable, generally optimistic and benign. The achievements of applied science, now no longer categorized with the productions of mere artisans and mechanics, were impressive and indisputable. Advances in sanitation, medicine, communication, transportation, and such, seemed harbingers of a future of comfort and abundance, one which might even lead to the adventures of a multiplanet species. Science, now, was "good." Whereas Livy might have regarded being a scientist as unintelligible, and Gibbon might have been embarrassed to have been considered a scientist, J. B. Bury, in the early 20th Century, on succeeding Lord Acton as the Regius Professor of Modern History at Cambridge, would insist in his inaugural address that history was "a science, no less and no more." Then came the middle and later 20th Century and a rather different picture of science began to emerge, one less exclusively cloudless. Poison gas, lethal chemicals, flame throwers, industrial pollution, radiation, global warming, tanks, bombers, G agents, nuclear weapons, intercontinental ballistic missiles, plastic explosives, the possibility of bacteriological warfare, and so on. And science has now progressed to the point where it can bring about the extinction of the human species, several times over. Moreover, there is abundant evidence that there is no lack of individuals who would prefer this alternative to the failure of their plans. One might wonder what Hitler would have done in his bunker in Berlin, if he had had the power to take the planet with him.

In any event, after a nuclear holocaust, an irradiated world, a poisoned soil, and such, one supposes that a frail, sickly, deformed humanity, amidst rubble and ashes, managed by witch doctors and chieftains, might turn its hand to hunting down scientists, and burning them alive. In such a world, if historiography should survive, one supposes there would be no eagerness to include it amongst the sciences.

The point of these dismal reflections is to note how sociological considerations may influence, as I think they now do, a classificatory endeavor which might be better off without them. The issue should not be decided in virtue of "science good, so historiography is a science" or "science bad, so historiography is not a science."

So one will attempt an axiologically neutral approach to the question, insofar as that might be possible.

The difficulty of pursuing such an approach is obvious when one realizes the issue is often clouded by partisanship, sometimes a partisanship minimized, if not denied. One suspects this might be the case with Edward Hallett Carr, a British socialist historian.

" ... Nowadays these questions of classification move me less; and it does not worry me unduly when I am assured that history is not a science. This terminological question is an eccentricity of the English language. In every other European language, the equivalent word to "science" includes history without hesitation."[111]

Whereas I am not familiar with "every other European language," this claim is incorrect with respect to German, a language not unfamiliar to Kant, Fichte, Hegel, Schopenhauer, Windelband, Simmel, Rickert, Dilthey, and others. The most likely word here is '*Wissenschaft*'. This is not an easy word to translate into English without a context, but it could stand, surely, for a science, but it could also stand for a sort of learning, a kind of knowledge, a discipline of one sort or another, even some sort of "wisdom." In German one distinguishes between the *Geisteswissenschaften*, where one

---

111 Edward Hallett Carr, *What Is History?* (Vintage Books, a Division of Random House, New York, 1961), p. 70.

would be likely to put the arts, the humanities, and such, and the *Naturwissenschaften*, where one would put physics, chemistry, and so on. The question, then, in German, would be whether history belongs with the *Geisteswissenschaften* or the *Naturwissenschaften*. This would put us back where started.

All sciences may be *Wissenschaften*, but not all *Wissenschaften* need be, or are, sciences.

Schopenhauer spoke German. Here is his view on the matter.

"In every class and species of things the facts are innumerable, the individual beings infinite in number, and the multiplicity and variety of their differences beyond our reach. With one look at all this, the curious and inquisitive mind is in a whirl; however much it investigates, it sees itself condemned to ignorance. But then comes *science*; it separates out the innumerable many, collects them under generic concepts, and these in turn under specific concepts, and so opens the way to a knowledge of the general and the particular. This knowledge comprehends the innumerable individuals, since it holds good of all without our having to consider each one by itself. In this way it promises satisfaction to the inquiring mind. All the sciences then put themselves together and over the real world of individual things which they have parceled out among themselves. But philosophy excels them all as the most universal, and thus the most important, knowledge, promising information for which the others have only prepared the way. *History* alone cannot properly enter into this series, since it cannot boast of the same advantage as the others, for it lacks the fundamental characteristic of science, the subordination of what is known; instead of this it boasts of the mere coordination of what is known. Therefore there is no system of history, as there is of every other branch of knowledge; accordingly, it is rational knowledge indeed, but, not a science. For nowhere does it know the particular by means of the universal, but it must comprehend the particular directly, and continue to creep along the ground of experience, so to speak. The real sciences, on the other hand, excel it, since they have attained to comprehensive concepts by means of which they command and control the particular, and, at any rate within certain limits, foresee the possibility of things within their province, so that they can be reassured even about what is still to come. As the sciences are systems of concepts, they always speak of species; history speaks of individuals. History would accordingly be a science of individual things, which implies a contradiction. It follows also from the first statement that the sciences all speak of that which always is; history, on the other hand, speaks of that which is only once, and then no more. Further, as history has to do with the absolutely particular and with individuals, which by their nature are inexhaustible, it knows everything only imperfectly and partially. At the same time, it must allow itself to be taught by the triviality of every new day that which as yet it did not know at all."[112]

This quotation does not resolve the issue, even in German, as we shall see, but it does clearly suggest that a reluctance to place historiography amongst the sciences need not be regarded as a reservation idiosyncratic to English, one which is merely the consequence of an Anglo-Saxon eccentricity.

There are at least three problems with Schopenhauer's view here. First, he seems to confuse historiography with something like chronicle. Surely most historians are interested in doing something more than present a "mere co-ordination of what is known." Presumably they would like to explain things, not simply report them, list them, or such. Secondly, historiography can, and occasionally does, speak of kinds, just as certain sciences speak of individuals. Thirdly, it is, at this point, not obvious that speaking of a science of individuals is a contradiction in terms. That would presuppose that all sciences must, *a priori*, aim at facts which are explicitly general, rather than, say, singular, or, possibly, and more likely, implicitly, general.

There is an echo here in Schopenhauer of a famous distinction in Aristotle, between poetry and history, where, once again, the crucial distinction is between generality and specificity, to the detriment of history, or, better, as we would rather put it, to mark the distinction, between poetry and historiography.

---

112 Arthur Schopenhauer, *The World as Will and Representation (Die Welt als Wille und Vorstellung)* Translated from the German by E. F. J. Payne. (The Falcon's Wing Press, Indian Hills, Colorado, 1958), Vol. II, Chapter XXXVIII, "On History" ("Über Geschicte"), pp. 439, 440.

"From what we have said it will be seen that the poet's function is to describe, not the thing that has happened, but a kind of thing that might happen, i.e. what is possible as being probable or necessary. The distinction between historian and poet is not in the one writing prose and the other verse—you might put the work of Herodotus into verse, and it would still be a species of history; it consists really in this, that the one describes the thing that has been, and the other a kind of thing that might be. Hence poetry is something more philosophic and of graver import than history, since its statements are of the nature rather of universals, whereas those of history are singulars. By a universal statement I mean one as to what such or such a kind of man will probably or necessarily say or do—which is the aim of poetry, though it affixes proper names to the characters; by a singular statement, one as to what, say, Alcibiades did or had done to him."[113]

The primary distinction is between the universal and the particular, or, here, between the universal and the singular, or individual. And, clearly, the universal is favored, perhaps even exalted, as worthier, and more important. I think this is less to be seen as a heritage from Plato, his respected friend and teacher, who seemed to have had little taste for the world in which he lived, a world "contaminated by the pollutions of mortality," than as a function of a particular form of mind, or bent of personality or character. Whereas Plato seems to have preferred the form of horse to anything he could saddle and ride, Aristotle's horse could be stabled, groomed, petted, and fed, could be expected to produce its quota of manure, and so on. Aristotle's universals were embodied, and a substance, for the most part, was to be understood in terms of both form and matter. Three exceptions seem to be the supposed unmoved mover, without which the world would just sit there; the celestial intelligences, presumably managing planetary and stellar motions; and the active intellect, for which there was no empirical evidence. Aristotle recognized that the real world was real, really real, the boldness of which conjecture would alone have

---

113 Aristotle, *The Poetics*. (Cf. Chapter 9, Marginal Reference 1451^b.) *The Basic Works of Aristotle*, Edited and with an Introduction by Richard McKeon (Random House, New York, 1941), pp. 1463, 1464.

separated him from an annoyed Plato. On the other hand, clearly, he favored generalities over specificities, universals over particulars, sorts over singulars, and so on. Woman is more important than Stephanie and Courtney, dog than Fido or Rin-Tin-Tin. Aristotle starts off in the real world but forgets about it as soon as possible. The historiographer, on the other hand, is likely to start off in the real world and, to the best of his ability, stay there. This does not, in itself, decide the issue, as to the status of historiography as a science or not, unless one defines science, as does Schopenhauer, in terms of universals. It is true that public understanding requires general terms with more or less clearly understood meanings, but it does not follow from that that universals are the desiderated object of knowledge; rather they, or meanings, are devices by means of which to relate to, and understand, the world. If they did not do this they would be of less interest than the meticulous fantasies of pure mathematics. For example, the laws of motion would be meaningless were it not for, say, falling apples, swinging pendulums, cannon balls in flight, orbiting worlds, and tumbling elephants; the value of such things, and their justification, is not to provide examples by means of which to illustrate abstractions; the value of the abstractions, rather, is to help us understand the things, the concrete, the real. To see the form of "horse" as more important than the horse, is to miss the point of the form, which is to enable us to identify and relate to a reality, animals of a certain sort. Let's call them "horses."

The historiographer is interested in reality, reality in its concreteness, complexity, and richness. It is not clear that this, *per se*, should count against his discipline being a science. If it does, then it seems so much the worse for science.

Some philosophers of history, or historiography, have distinguished amongst different sorts of sciences, for example, Wilhelm Windelband and Collingwood.

A famous distinction drawn by Windelband divides sciences into nomothetic science, in which a knowledge of universals is sought, and idiographic science, in which a knowledge of individuals is sought. Physics would be nomothetic; historiography would be idiographic.

This is a valuable distinction, and, if it is important to one to have historiography count as a science, this will serve the purpose. On the other hand, as is usually the case with distinctions, it has its difficulties. Whereas it is substantially correct to see historiography as primarily concerned with particular individuals and events, and certain sciences, contrariwise, to be substantially concerned with "kinds," universals, the establishment of laws, and such, exceptions abound. For example, historiographers have been concerned with such things as "the anatomy of revolutions," class dynamics, the impact of material forces, base/superstructure generalities, the rise and fall of civilizations, and such, and so, too, many sciences have been concerned with matters of individuals, or kinds of individuals, for example, the biography of the universe, the formation of the solar system, the break-up of a land mass, the development of a kinship system, the development of a language, the demise of a form of life, the evolution of a particular species, and so on.

We noted earlier that it might be informative and interesting to examine some similarities and differences amongst sciences, or, say, if one wishes, between historiography and science. Such an examination, even one relatively cursory, should shed light on the issue of classification, and, in any event, would be important in any attempt to produce a philosophy of historiography.

So let us compare and contrast historiography with a classical view of a paradigm science, for example, a science such as physics, or chemistry. We will consider this matter briefly from nine perspectives: methodology, intent, time-and-place stance, subject matter, law-boundedness, explanation, outcome statements, objectivity, and accessibility.

2. Particular Considerations

1. Methodology

Certainly there are striking differences between, say, P and H, taking P to be a paradigm science and H, historiography. In the case of P, one would expect to find complex theories; a technical vocabulary; mathematical formulations; the hypothetico-deductive method; direct and indirect observation; available, relevant instrumentation; precise measurement; experimentation; testing; variable isolation and manipulation; public, accepted confirmation procedures; the possible replication of experiments; and so on.

Although H would commonly avail itself of whatever help P might provide, for example, in the radiological dating of artifacts, it is clear that H has little to offer to compete in the spheres of P's greatest strength. H has no historoscopes, no Cliometers, or such. It cannot measure to microns, or even weigh in so gross a unit as grams. There is little in H which can be photographed, which can stain microscope slides, which can depress scales, and such. For most practical purposes, the subject matter of H cannot be observed, cannot be reproduced in laboratories at will, and does not possess variables which might be isolated and manipulated, except in the imagination. H must do without experiments, except in the imagination. The gods might run experiments through a number of parallel universes, subtracting something here, adding something there, but historiographers cannot do so. Confirmation procedures in H are largely up to personal judgment, which is notoriously unreliable. H is not P. It is far from P.

There is no simple account of H methodology, just as there is no simple account of P methodology. For example, bacteriology and astronomy are quite different. The historiographer does have at his disposal a number of auxiliary disciplines, sometimes referred to as auxiliary sciences, for example, paleography, chronology, epigraphy, sigillography, genealogy, heraldry, and numismatics, but these would share many of the problematicities associated with historiography itself. Clearly the historiographer is more likely to be found in the archives than in the laboratory. He is more likely to be engaged in scholarly research than in experimentation.

He will attempt to discover, authenticate, and evaluate documents, in a manner that would be unusual for his colleagues in the P sciences. Like his colleague in the P sciences he is likely to bring hypotheses to his work, but the tests to which he can subject them are seldom external, as those of measurement and instrumentation, but generally internal, as those of judgment and understanding. He will be involved in the location of, and the interpretation of, evidence, but this evidence is usually unlike that of his colleague in the P sciences. It is primarily found in documents, of one sort or another, documents broadly considered, as in accounts, inscriptions, newspapers, letters, diaries, drawings, paintings, maps, myths, legends, poetry, songs, and such, and even in linguistic practices, lexicons, place names, customs, superstitions, and such. Archaeological evidence, too, artifacts, ruins, and such, can be of great value.

Relevant to historiographical methodology are a variety of techniques to which we earlier alluded, involving such things as the attempt to "feel one's way into a historical situation," to seek to obtain a participatory understanding, even a perhaps sympathetic understanding, of another time and culture, to seek to penetrate the mind, the character, personality, and motivations of a historical figure, and such. I think there is little doubt that this attempt to achieve an empathetic insight is historiographically critical. Indeed, how else might a historiographer proceed, how else gain a sense of a past which was living, and alive with action, feeling, and thought? Familiar expressions in the *Verstehen* tradition are *Einfühlung*, *einfühlen*, and *nacherleben*, a feeling of one's way into something, to feel one's way into something, to relive, or to reexperience, and so on. In modern times this tradition, as noted, might be traced to Giambattista Vico, was regenerated in German historiography, remarkably in Dilthey and others, and is found in Benedetto Croce and R. G. Collingwood.

Carl G. Hempel, whose controversial attempt to extend the D/N Model of explanation to historiography, earlier discussed, respected the *Verstehen* tradition as of heuristic value with respect to the generation of hypotheses, but, sensibly, was skeptical of the technique, were it to be construed as a methodology of proof. The claim that *Verstehen* might constitute a proof procedure rests classically on "intuition" as a source of knowledge, indeed, a source of indisputable, infallible knowledge. The case for intuitive knowledge, unmediated or direct, or immediate, knowledge, is best made in the formal sciences, logic and mathematics. For example, given an understanding of the concepts involved, it is clear that if both 'p' and 'q' are true, then 'p' is true, that if A = B, and B = C, then A = C, that 1 added to 1 produces 2, that vertical angles in Euclidean geometry must be equal, and so on. Even in complexly constructed proofs, it is usually the case that each step is the result of an immediate insight, justified by one intuitively obvious rule or another. Whereas proofs may be produced for such immediate inferences, such proofs are more complex than the inferences, and less obvious than the inferences themselves. Here, in logic and mathematics, one may, upon occasion, simply "see" that such and such is the case. If intuitive knowledge exists, these would be its paradigm instances. Outside the formal sciences, however, which deal with analyticities, it seems clear that intuition, whatever its values, which seem considerable, does not constitute a proof procedure. It may, of course, produce evidence relevant to a hypothesis. A supposed, common example of allegedly infallible intuition, or direct, unmediated knowledge, would be just "seeing" that someone is pleased, disappointed, sad, or such. Rather, it seems that we have here a swift inference, an interpretation of data, an inference which may be conditioned, even automatic, from, say, expressions and body language to mood or emotion. One cannot define such things in terms of externals, with all due respect toWittgenstein, without losing the distinction between authenticity and pretence, between the person who is happy and one who seems happy, or is pretending to be happy, and so on. Other usages of "intuition" are even more obviously inferential, and mediated, as in linguistic intuitions, the suddenly available results of subconscious processing, and such. There may be genetically coded intuitions, having to do with, say, induction, other minds, an external world, and such, but the intuition, *per se*, does not guarantee the truth of the conjecture. It is not like seeing that 'p & q' must entail 'q'. If these considerations are correct then it seems clear that *Verstehen*, whatever its historiographical value, does not constitute a proof procedure. Assurance does not guarantee accuracy. That something seems obviously true does not make it true. A hypothesis may be psychologically coercive, even rationally coercive, and be mistaken.

Let us briefly consider the Hempel view with respect to *Verstehen*. That view, as I understand it, is that *Verstehen* may have heuristic value with respect to the generation of hypotheses, but it does not constitute a proof procedure. Presumably, then, the testing of these hypotheses, arrived at by *Verstehen*, is an independent matter, one calling presumably for the objective techniques of empirical science.

While recognizing the plausibility of Hempel's point that *Verstehen*, however coercive the understanding in question is, is not a proof procedure, one would like to call attention to certain problematicities associated with this view. First, if the claim that *Verstehen* is not a proof procedure means merely that it does not guarantee truth, that is doubtless true, but, on the other hand, by parity of reasoning, there are no proof procedures outside the formal sciences. As we saw earlier, in discussing considerations leading to the distinction between truth and empirical adequacy, there is never, even in the most mathematically enriched, instrument-laden sciences, a guarantee of truth, and, in that sense, no proof procedure either, if such a procedure requires the guarantee of truth. Second, on the Hempelian approach, it seems that a great deal of what is taken to be historiographical knowledge, if not all of it, would disappear. How would one, for example, using the objective techniques of empirical science, looking for empirical evidence, three-dimensional physical objects, and such, and disregarding tradition, documentation, and such, establish that, say, the Peloponnesian War or the Punic Wars took place, let alone what might have been their antecedents and developments, the motivations, policies, and actions of their predominant figures, and such? If we believe that historiographical knowledge exists, and presumably most people do, then we cannot require that historiographical hypotheses require for their testing the "objective techniques of empirical science," at least in the usual sense given to that notion, techniques involving instrumentation, quantification, experimentation, and such. Thirdly, it seems plausible that the outcomes of *Verstehen* analysis, depending on their nature, and their relation to empirical evidence, may constitute empirical evidence. Take a case of the sort alluded to earlier, in which one seems to just "see" that someone is pleased, disappointed, sad, or such. We suggested that an inference is involved in such a situation, and that one's "hypothesis" may be mistaken. Perhaps the person is acting, and so on. On the other hand, his expressions, body language, and such, are evidence as to the mood in question, whether reliable or not. Similarly, if we ourselves had no understanding or experience of being pleased, disappointed, sad, and such, the subject's expressions and movements would be unintelligible to us. We hypothesize his mood on the basis of what we see, and what we know, in our own case, of the sort of things involved. Clearly, we would have before us evidence, and evidence of an empirical nature. We are not simply randomizing, or coming up with hypotheses arbitrarily. Given our latitudinizing of the notion of knowledge earlier, removing it from the precincts of inaccessibility, to make it more realistic, and more in accord with what is commonly taken as knowledge, I think we could say that we know the individual is, say, pleased. Namely, if it happens to be true, and we believe it, and we have good evidence for our belief, that constitutes knowledge. If it is not true, we do not have knowledge. But if it is true, and the other two conditions are met, we would have knowledge. One may legitimately claim to know 'p' without claiming that counterevidence is logically, or even empirically, impossible. One may legitimately claim to know that cats do not bark, without denying the possibility that one might one day, doubtless to one's great surprise, encounter a barking cat.

So, based on the analogy of interpreting the moods of human beings on the basis of empirical evidence, and allowing that we can know, in certain cases, the mood of another human being, namely, in those cases when our belief is true, and justified, then it is merely a short step, and not so different a step, to form a view of his mood from, say, a letter. It seems clear from the letter that he is pleased, disappointed, sad, or whatever, at least when he wrote the letter. Once again, if the belief is true, and justified, one would have knowledge.

The analogy to *Verstehen* in historiography is clear. On the basis of evidence, documentational or situational, rather like reading the letter, one, in virtue of one's own understanding of situationality and human nature, infers likelihoods, motivations, moods, intentions, and such. One tries to understand the historical situation, the character of the persons involved, what they wanted, how they sought to obtain it, and so on. One tries, as one can, to "feel one's way" into the different world, to participate imaginatively in the situation, to relive, or reexperience, another reality, another time.

No one claims this is easy, nor that there is any guarantee of success. An underlying assumption is the Viconian assumption of *verum factum*, that we can understand history, as we cannot understand nature, but merely describe it, or measure it, with no sense of its "why," because history is ours; it is our product, our artifact; it is something humans have made, and, being human, we, as human, can understand it. It and we are akin. We have access to its "why."

This is not an "Enlightenment superficiality."

We can understand Egyptian aphorisms and Greek drama, Viking mythology, Medieval miracle plays, 19th Century novels and melodramas, and so on. Similarly, it seems we have a sense, however, imperfect, of Socrates, Plato, and Aristotle, of Alexander and Darius, of Scipio and Hannibal, of Richard I and Saladin, of Napoleon and Nelson, and so on. Humans may be very different from one another, but there is seldom much in one man which is so alien as to be wholly incomprehensible to another.

Verstehen must be rationally founded on evidence, but it, itself, in its plausibility, is in part evidential. It, with its insight into motivation, its recourse to principles of human nature, adds to and abets the evidence. That a discrepancy might exist between the claims of a document and a likelihood, or between one or more documents, adds to the justification which might transform a hypothesis into a justified true belief. Justification is not simply a matter of documents; it is, as well, the interpretation and assessment of documents. Understanding a historical situation, what it admits and prohibits, what it means and does not mean, is evidential in the sense of producing the justified beliefs without which there can be no justified true belief.

Verstehen is essential to historiography and justificational with respect to its claims. It is essential in historiographical knowledge, in forming the desiderated epistemic triad of truth, belief, and justification.

Too, what alternative have we?

No mathematics exists for vanity and ambition. Equations fail to encompass the human heart. Measuring the meaning of man can be done only with the meter sticks of the mind. The meaning of man is not outside, but inside, and that is where it must be sought, and that is where the historiographer seeks it.

If it is worth seeking, one must seek it rationally, intelligently.

Sensitivity and understanding, whatever their frailties and limitations, their weaknesses and inadequacies, are tools at least adept to the task, at least relevant to the task. Something which may not work is better than something which will not work. As the proverb has it, in a palace filled with rats, a lame cat is to be preferred over a fine horse.

And in this case, happily, the cat is not lame.

2. Intent

In so far as one can speak of the intent of enterprises, as opposed to those of individuals, the P sciences and H seem to have much in common. Surely both are concerned to understand the world, or elements within the world, and would desire to establish an organized body of systematically related truths. The P sciences are concerned predominantly with the natural world, as one usually thinks of it, from atoms to galaxies, and H with the historical world, as we usually think of it. If one accepts the D hypothesis there is only one world, which might be thought of as natural, or, if one likes, as historical in a broad sense. The usual distinction between the natural world and the historical world, on the other hand, is a useful distinction, marking out differences within the natural world, broadly considered, or within the historical world, broadly considered. It might be thought that the P sciences are interested in "systematically related truths" and H not, but this seems incorrect, from at least two points of view. First, most scientists are not interested in systematically relating their truths to other truths, for example, those of bacteriology to astronomy, though presumably, given the D hypothesis, they might suppose some such relationship exists. Even the fellows who hope to produce a "theory of everything" usually have some pretty limited objectives in mind, for example, a single theory in terms of which one might explain gravitation, electromagnetism, and the weak and strong nuclear force. They do not seem much interested in paramecia, algae, social insects, the rules for dynastic successions, and such. Secondly, the historiographer, like the P scientist within his own discipline, is likely to be interested in "systematically related truths." Certainly one would expect him to be opposed to isolated or inexplicable truths, "pop-up" truths, so to speak. Without this assumption of reliable, or systematic, relationships, the attempt to explain would be incomprehensible.

3. Time-and-Place Stance.

The P sciences are often thought of as "time-and-place free," whereas H would be "time-and-place bound." As with many such distinctions, this is a useful distinction, if not an unexceptionable one. In the early Precambrian period, as well as now, bodies, at any point on the earth's surface, would fall at $½gt^2$, an atom of oxygen and two atoms of hydrogen would combine to form a molecule of water, copper would melt at 1083° Centigrade, and so on. This has nothing to do with peninsulas or islands, religious festivals, the birthdays of potentates, or such. The truths of the P sciences, on the whole, are supposedly independent of location and are not uniquely datable. There are sciences, of course, which are muchly concerned with particular places or objects, ecology, oceanography, climatology, astronomy, and so on, and with developments, changes, and such, over time, for example, cosmology, geology, biology, and such. Substantially, of course, historiography has a much more marked time-and-place stance. Historical events are uniquely locatable and datable. Historiographers, as noted earlier, may generalize, but they are much more likely to have recourse to generalizations than to generalize themselves. Given the fact that there are many sciences involved with time-and-place considerations, and that historiographers occasionally attempt to transcend such considerations, there seems no reason to rule historiography out of the sciences based on its usual time-and-place stance. Too, even if the distinction was unexceptionable, which it is not, it is not obvious that a particularistic time-and-place stance, despite the Schopenhauers of the world, precludes a discipline from a place amongst the sciences. Being strict about this matter would depopulate the sciences. If one were to claim that the particularistic sciences are merely accidentally particularistic, there being only one universe about, for example, rather than being essentially particularistic, like historiography, the same point could be made in favor of historiography, there being, for example, only one historical world about. In a particularistic science one acknowledges richness and complexity, and deals with it as one can, rather than overlooking it, and subtracting from it. It is not obvious that the first endeavor is less interesting, less worthy, less important, or less scientific than the second.

4. Subject Matter

Here we have several dramatic differences between the P sciences and H. Typically associated with the P sciences are material bodies and their properties. The P sciences are physicalistic and behavioral. Their subject matter is quantifiable. What cannot be quantified tends to be ignored, if not denied. Their nets will catch only what the mesh allows. Other realities, if they exist, escape the net. Here we have a methodological limitation to "externals," to the "outside" of the world, so to speak, to that which can be counted, to that which can be measured. In H, on the other hand, one is concerned most often with actions, and the actions are not understood as behaviors alone, as mere movements of bodies in space. In H, one is concerned with thoughts, with "whys," with the internal, with the inside, with conscious reality, the reality of meaning and motivation, the reality which makes us intelligible to ourselves, the reality without which we are incomprehensible. This sort of thing is not quantifiable. It may be methodologically overlooked, or bracketed, perhaps intelligently so, but it cannot, rationally, be denied. To the extent it lies outside of the P sciences, to that extent the P sciences miss man. Man exceeds the molecules on which he is founded. Historiography hunts his meaning in the only place it can be found, in the internal, particularistic, personal world. It is there that is found the subject matter of historiography.

5. Law-Boundedness

The P sciences are currently divided on the question of law-boundedness, given the I Hypothesis. We have suggested, as a methodological postulate, that historiography subscribe to the D hypothesis, largely to rationalize explanation. It is possible that this hypothesis is false, for example, if the I hypothesis is true, or free will, whatever that might be, exists. Our primary problem with the I hypothesis is its lack of intelligibility and that it cannot explain particular events, which are what historiographers are usually trying to explain. Our primary problem with free will is understanding what it might be in the first place, and, in the second place, how it might work. It might exist in some sense, one supposes, but it would seem to be difficult to understand, perhaps like trying to understand a fifth, or sixth, or twenty-sixth, spatial dimension, or such. One can use the words, easily enough, or, in the case of the supposed spatial dimensions, the mathematical notation, but what would the words mean, or what would the equations signify? One thing we do know about free will is that it requires personal responsibility, and, thus, it cannot be confused with indeterminism, with randomness, with things just taking place, things popping into and out of being, and such. In short, it would be independent of the I hypothesis, which is, hopefully, a transitory fable of physics, an ill-thought-through fantasy consequent on misinterpreting the inevitable inabilities, limitations, and frustrations connected with measurement and detection.

We have suggested, as noted, primarily for explanatory purposes, as a working postulate, the D Hypothesis. Also, this, if nothing else, would align historiography with a classical presupposition of empirical science. If we take A, B, and C, and only A, B, and C, as the cause of Event D in the first instance, it makes no sense to take the same A, B, and C, and only that A, B, and C, in the second instance, to be the cause of Event Non-D, say, E, F, or such.. The principle is "identity of cause results in identity of effect." This is not true by definition, as we know from the I Hypothesis, but it is not clear how one could have intelligible explanation without some such presupposition. That, say, one letter in every 137,000 letters is misaddressed does not seem a satisfactory explanation as to why Jones' letter was misaddressed. Nor, if two letters out of every three letters are misaddressed, that, too, would not tell us why Jones' letter was misaddressed. We might like to know that. Similarly, in a logic of explanation, "free will" would seem an unsatisfactory, even inadmissible, theoretical entity. It seems an unintelligible concept, even if it has a mysterious, undetectable referent. However real it might be, in the eyes of the gods, or such, it is for us an explanational vacuity. It is not an explanation. It is the absence of an explanation.

6. Explanations

In the P sciences one expects explanations to be causal or probabilistic. Given the D hypothesis, explanations in historiography would also be causal, but presumably not probabilistic. The major differences here would be with respect to the entities which might figure in the explanations. As noted earlier, explanations in the P sciences would pertain essentially to material bodies in physical space moving in accord with mathematical laws, whether these material bodies are subatomic particles, interacting chemicals, locomotives, or stars. The entities are to be quantifiable, physically detectable and physically measurable in one way or another, whether they are precipitating chemicals, tropisms, responses to stimuli, or erupting volcanoes. On the other hand, as noted earlier, explanation in historiography is, at least frequently, rational explanation, that is, explanation in terms of reasons, in terms of ends sought, and such. Phenomenologically, this sort of explanation is familiar, so familiar that we commonly explain our own actions in its terms, as well as those of others. Also, as we pointed out, and suggested a modality whereby it might be accomplished, reasons might be brought within the causal net.

At this point, it seems relevant to make one last remark pertaining to the D/N model of explanation.

We have seen that the D/N Model is too permissive, that it would allow a number of entities to count as explanations which we would be unlikely to regard as scientific explanations, or interesting explanations, or, in many cases, in theory an infinite number, explanations, at all. It is also possible that the D/N Model may be faulty not merely in its permissiveness but, also in that, should it be conceived as the single sort of acceptable explanation, it may be too restrictive. If rational explanations are epistemically acceptable, as, hopefully, we have established, and the D/N Model cannot handle them, and it claims to be the single sort of acceptable explanation, then it is obviously too restrictive. On the other hand, even if the D/N Model could be extended to cover such explanations, utilizing laws explicitly framed in terms of reasons, or physical laws with reasons as their consequences, which seems unlikely, it could not, it seems, account for another sort of explanation familiar in historiography. Here we do not have in mind explanations in the sense of elucidations, instructions, colligations, and such, for they are explicitly noncausal, and the D/N model never pretended to be pertinent to such sorts of explanation. Rather one has in mind the sort of thing we referred to as causal-thread explanations, which often figure in historiographical narrative. Causal-thread explanations are usually embedded in what one might speak of as "flow explanations," or explanations by "telling," taking place in a context illuminated by elucidation, commonly within a colligated background. Thus, if such things are explanatory, and outside the scope of D/N Explanations, D/N Explanation is not only too permissive, but, too, again, if it is regarded as the only sort of acceptable explanation, even in the causal sense, it is too restrictive; in short, it not only lets in too much, but it would keep out too much. Causal-thread explanations may well presuppose laws, or, perhaps better, a lawful universe, but they do not require the statement of such laws or their incorporation in the explanation. Indeed, such explanation usually presupposes little more than a universe which works in expected ways, ways which are, for the most part, familiar to the historiographer and others. One way to explain something, for example, is to tell a story, a rational story, one involving reasons, and that is something at which historiography excels.

7. Outcome statements

In discussing Schopenhauer and Aristotle, the questions of universals vs. particulars, universals vs. singulars, nomothetic vs. idiographic science, and such, we noted that the P sciences tended toward generality and H toward particularism. On the other hand, we also noted instances of particularism amongst P sciences and instances of generality amongst historiographers. In view of this, while noting the rough-and-ready justification of, and the usefulness of, such a distinction, we do not find in it, contrary to Schopenhauer, a justification for barring historiography from the sciences. Such an act would depend on too narrow a view of science, one which should not be allowed to prejudge the issue.

8. The Objectivity Problem

The canons of professional ethics prescribe objectivity. This is a point in common amongst the P sciences and H. Clearly, in the P sciences the cost of objectivity and the perils of pursuing it are generally less than in historiography. That the fruit fly has four pairs of chromosomes or five is cheerfully left up to the fruit fly, letting the chromosomes fall where they may. On the other hand, to tell the truth in historiography, concerning issues soaked with partisanship, in a community preferring falsity to truth, fallacy to validity, and myth to reality, can be dangerous, indeed. To be sure, science, too, runs its risks, in shattering world views congenial to political and religious establishments, in revising views as to human origins and what it is to be human, in exploring surprising and perhaps disturbing psychic depths, and so on. But, on the whole, there is less political and cultural pressure placed on the practitioners of the P sciences than on the historiographer, who is expected to produce a flattering, congenial picture of the past, or, perhaps, one severely critical in order to promote a particular ideological agenda. Certainly community expectations weigh more heavily on the historiographer to reinforce viewpoints and serve particular purposes than on the chemist or physicist. Must he not be concerned, in ways the chemist and physicist usually needs not be concerned, with what people wish to hear, with how his work will be received, with how it will reviewed by entrenched, powerful critics with particular political viewpoints, with his employability and occupational security, with his perceived standing and merit, with the ideological bents of a publishing establishment, and so on? It is no wonder that historiography, consciously or not, is often perverted into propaganda, that it panders to those in a position to pay or punish, and so on. In such an environment, it is no wonder, too, that scholar activism, of one sort or another, thrives. Many a historiographer, like many an evangelist, celebrity, or politician will seek the rewards provided for partisanship, following the money, the prestige, and power.

No wonder, too, given some sense of what they doing, that the more sensitive, the less callous and blasé, rationalize such activities, justifying them to themselves by assuring themselves that no alternative is possible, that everyone is doing it, that objectivity is impossible, or, if possible, immoral, and that their appropriate mission is not to tell the truth about the world, but to improve it, according to their particular lights.

But objectivity tends, on the whole, to remain an ideal, however frequently it may be honored only in the breach. Even the most arrant scholar activist is likely to claim he is objective, and, interestingly, in some cases, he may believe this, even if no one else does. In his historiographical cherry picking he is confident, at least, that he is picking the right cherries. And no one, of course, can pick all the cherries.

Supposing, however, that the practitioners of the P sciences and the practitioners of historiography are both morally committed, to the best of their ability, to objectivity, and that both have enough self-perception to be reasonably well aware of their success or lack of success in fulfilling this commitment, there are marked differences between the disciplines, which facilitate objectivity in the one and put it at great risk in the other.

On the whole, the discoveries of the P sciences are unlikely to threaten moral, political, and religious views. They are largely independent of such things. Thus, it is easier for the P sciences to seek and follow facts, so to speak. It is less dangerous for them to do so. Objectivity is more likely to be found where its habitat is neither professionally nor personally hazardous.

Recourse to quantification, instrumentation, measurement, and such, abets objectivity. Race, class, sex, ethnicity, ideology, and such do not affect pointer readings. Controlled experiments, with verifiable results, can be checked, and replicated. This provides a mechanism for review and self-correction. The community of the P sciences is more a community than the community of historiographers. There is much more pervasive agreement in the P sciences with respect to methodology and results. A discovery in one laboratory can become the property of every laboratory. Consensus is important and sought in the community of the P sciences in a way that it is not important and sought in the historiographical community. Disagreement in the P sciences tends to be susceptible of resolution. One is right or both are wrong. A new experiment may help to decide the issue. There are no experiments in historiography. The results in the P sciences, despite occasional, even radical, shifts in viewpoint, tend to be cumulative. In historiography, views may change and results may be revised from period to period. In the P sciences, there is likely to be more continuity, more substantiated agreement, more objectivity, due, for example, to shared presuppositions with respect to subject matter, understood constraints on the nature of acceptable hypotheses, and appropriate procedures for their examination, testing, and evaluation. These marvelous advantages, of course, have largely to do with the subject matter of the P sciences, that they are concerned with physical objects and their properties. It is much easier to be objective when one is dealing with atoms or galaxies than when one is dealing with morality, politics, religion, value, war, peace, race, class, sex, ethnicity, ideology, history.

Objectivity in historiography is less a matter of apparatus, methodology, and techniques than of moral commitment. In this sense it is more analogous to the efforts of a sympathetic but impartial judge, attempting to adjudicate a case on its merits, than to a manipulator of measuring devices, a clocker of light, a calculator of distances, a designer and interpreter of experiments.

The objective historiographer, and this is always, as noted, a matter of degree, is one who, to the best of his ability, as his colleague in the P sciences, who has an easier job of it, usually subject to fewer temptations and pressures, is judicious, honest, and fair.

These are not empty notions but notions which are familiar and comprehensible. Most ethical notions have an ascertainable empirical content. So, too, do the above. Whether one approves or disapproves of theft, the notion of theft is reasonably clear. Similarly, whether one approves or disapproves of lying, the notion of lying is reasonably clear. Theft approved remains theft; a lie endorsed does not thereby become truth.

It might be maintained that being judicious, honest, and fair is a tendentious political stance, an ideological commitment, chosen to advance an agenda, an agenda favoring particular groups, those who have the least to fear from truth and objectivity. That may be true. One also supposes that being injudicious, dishonest, and unfair might also count as a political stance, and another ideological commitment, one chosen to advance another agenda, an agenda favoring other groups, those having the most to fear from truth and objectivity. One supposes that that may also be true. In any event, one must choose one's commitment. The truth commitment has the advantage, as meter sticks and scales, of simplicity. Lies are more hazardous, as they may be found out.

One may maintain plausibly that moralities are incommensurable, or, say, that one morality takes precedence over another, but it is hard for anything human to do without a morality, some morality.

Can any human being honestly believe that ways of acting, in a world where one must act, where the need to choose is unremitting and unavoidable, make no difference to anything, that they are indifferent with respect to ends sought, and can he honestly believe, too, that no one end is better than another end?

That seems to me unlikely.

Every morality has its moral commitments, its moral truths.

A value-free physics or chemistry is doubtful, but is at least arguable; a value-free historiography, as we will see later, is not only doubtful, but might be impossible, and, in any event, would betray and misrepresent its subject matter.

Earlier we suggested the historiographical adoption of a perspective of naturalistic humanism, as a common-denominator perspective. Associated with this perspective is the phenomenon of a pervasive, basic, rather limited, rather simple, rather elementary, but surely effective transcultural morality, a common-denominator morality, so to speak, presumably evolved because without it no viable society, tribal or otherwise, is possible. This morality is not perfect, and it does not solve all moral problems, resolve all moral dilemmas or such, and, although it is essentially transcultural, not every tenet would necessarily be shared by every culture, but, without an overwhelming amount of agreement with respect to these tenets, and their acceptance by social majorities, cultures would be impossible. The alternative would be unthinkable. Without it one would scarcely dare venture out of doors, nor, in all likelihood, would one have lived long enough to consider it. One would have had Hobbes' cruel and surprising fantasy of a *bellum omnium contra omnes*. Indeed, given animal studies, it seems likely that some of this might be genetically coded, selected for in the course of primate evolution, in virtue of its enablements with respect to group survival, with respect to gene replication.

The cognitivity of a morality is indexed to its ends accepted. That something is believed to be moral does not entail that it is moral, any more than a belief that the world is round entails that the world is round. Similarly, that a moral view should be conditioned, or even genetically coded, does not prove that it is correct, but, if it should be genetically coded, that would be of zoological interest, if nothing else. What provides moralities with their diverse cognitivities is their conducibility to ends, which might vary. For example, if one end is, statistically, to further human life, health, happiness, and such, then precepts furthering such ends, such as respect, consistency, justice, and such, would be empirically ascertainable, as practical instrumentalities furthering the desired ends. The end accepted bridges the alleged gap between the "is" and the "ought." On the other hand, different ends, different moralities. For example, if one favors the ends of death, disease, misery, and such, then different precepts would be found conducive to such ends. Different ends, different moralities.

To claim that there is no difference amongst ends, or that no end is better than any other end, is an interesting claim. A lunatic might take it seriously. To be sure, there is no noncircular way to prove that one end is better than another, if one should desire such a proof; but, on the other hand, there is no noncircular way, either, to prove that no end is better than any other, if one should desire such a proof.

He who would genuinely look for, or require, a proof that life, health, and happiness are better than death, disease, and misery is urged to look into the matter. May he succeed. One wishes him well.

In any event, the notion of an honest, judicious, and fair historiography, embedded within a common-denominator morality, produces a situation in which one can reconcile objectivity and morality.

One requires a perspective.

This approach provides a perspective, one which I think is both practical and useful, indeed, one which seems to be implicit in much historiographical practice, at least of a classical sort, a sort hopefully neither obsolescent nor currently unacceptable.

9. Accessibility

One is concerned here with a discipline's intelligibility for, or accessibility to, nonprofessionals. Here, it is clear that the P sciences tend to be far less intelligible for, or accessible to, nonprofessionals. To understand a paper in mathematical physics, written for mathematical physicists, it surely helps to be a mathematical physicist. To comprehend such a paper usually, properly, would require a very serious technical background, one often developed only after years of training and study. On the other hand, though the question is one of degree, an interested, intelligent citizen in the Republic of Letters, is likely to understand, for the most part, your typical work in historiography. Further, the better the historiographer, statistically, the more likely he is to understand it, for the better historiographer's work is the more likely to be rationally constructed and clearly expressed. Some historiographers, like Gibbon and Hume, wrote not only clearly, but luminously, and were master stylists, producing works achieving the status of literature.

Obscurity in writing, pretension, deliberate obfuscation, shoddy logic, muddy structure, maze construction, inexplicable transitions, pompous terminology, gobbledygook, and such, whatever may be their values here and there in academia, do not count as historiographical virtues.

Two aspects of historiography tend in particular to contribute to its intelligibility and accessibility, First, it is typically written in a native language likely to be familiar to its readers. In this sense, even the layman brings years of readiness and preparation to the work. Secondly, the historiographer typically deals with a subject matter akin to the reader, a subject matter with which the reader is familiar, either through personal experience or vicariously, in his own life, the lives and doings of men and women, ambition, temptation, greed, power, love, hate, thought, desire, love, lust, courage, fear, violence, savagery, sacrifice, benevolence, and so on. The historiographer is writing of life and meaning. These things are not alien to his reader. Nothing human is alien to human.

This matter of comprehension is, however, as suggested, a matter of degree. An educated layman, for example, however sympathetically and intelligently he reads a given book or article, would be quite unlikely to have the same meaning fulfillment as a professional in the area. This is not because of an unfamiliarity with a technical lexicon of special-purpose terms, as might be the case in anthropology, economics or sociology, but rather because he has less of a framework of already established understandings within which to place and interpret the new material. The more one knows the easier it is to learn, and understand.

Sometimes the seeming cognitive transparency of historiography is deceptive. One should accept its relative lucidity gratefully, but understand that this lucidity is not likely to have been easily purchased. Behind it may lie a lifetime of application and study.

The relative intelligibility and/or accessibility of historiography to the nonprofessional does not militate against its cognitive status; such things are not a function of its superficiality or lack of importance. Rather, history is as deep as humanity itself, for it in it we find the actions of humanity, telling us what humanity is by recounting what it has done, and for humans there seems little that could approach this in importance.

In it we come to know ourselves.

In that surely we find a sufficiency of importance.

So, after this journey shall we classify historiography as a science or not? And, if so, what sort of science?

3. The Classification of Historiography

Six major positions are familiar with respect to these choices.

I. Science
    A. Assimilationism
    B. Autonomism
II. Not a Science
    A. Proto-science.
    B. Applier of Science
    C. Modality of Reportage
    D. An art, a Humanity.

The position of Auguste Comte, as noted earlier, is either that historiography might become a science, or, more strictly, that a science might be founded on its data, presumably some sort of sociology. In this sense, historiography would never be a science but generalizations, perhaps in a Baconian manner, might be extracted from it. This is reminiscent of the universal/particular distinction discussed earlier, in virtue of which historiography was to be excluded from the sciences. Karl Popper, a famous and controversial philosopher of science, as well as a controversial social philosopher, thought of historiography rather along the lines of engineering, namely, as a discipline that was not a science but which utilized the discoveries of science, applying them in various ways. It is reasonably clear that Popper's heart was with the P sciences, and that he construed science essentially in terms of such paradigms. Whereas historiography would presumably, at least for the most part, be unwilling to contravene the principles of the P sciences, it does not seem that it is in the business of applying the P sciences, except in the general sense that we might all be thought to do so. For example, recognizing that deep mud is likely to slow down a marching column or that fire is not likely to do the palace of Darius much good, and so on, does not really seem to be applying science. Certainly it is not like applying physics in building bridges. To be sure, historiography would doubtless be grateful for whatever help science might provide, as in radiological dating, as in analyses of debased coinages, as in producing evidences of climatological change, as in working out the pitches of cross-country aqueducts or conjecturing plausible devices for moving large weights overland, as in calculations of logistical practicalities dealing with the movements of armies over terrain, the likely positions of rowers on galley benches, and such. But, as suggested, there seems nothing much here closely analogous to, say, architecture, civil or electrical engineering, computer science, or such. A third position here is the Schopenhauerian position that history, or, as are putting it, historiography, is a "rational knowledge," but not a science. It may not be clear what an "irrational knowledge" might be but, if anything, perhaps it would be a direct, intuitive, nondiscursive insight. In any event the position might be termed, as above, "a modality of reportage." Here, historiography is seen as coordinating facts, so to speak, as a form of high-class chronicle or journalism. I think there is little doubt that historiography does this sort of thing, and builds upon it, but it seems to ignore not only historiography's explanatory role but to minimize or misunderstand illuminations provided by historiography. In reading about, say, the French Revolution, one has the sense of learning about revolutions, about human conflicts, about life, and death, about the ideals that can motivate men and the cruelties and horrors which may follow in their wake. If it were not for this sense of enhancing our understanding of our own nature and that of our species might we not see it as no more than a transient episode of strangers taking place in a far time and place? It grips us and terrifies us in its reality because it is akin to us. We are participants in terrible times. We do not see it with indifference, as one might see the falling of leaves, the movements of ants. A fourth way to see historiography is to see it as a form of art, as a humanity. Perhaps this categorization is intended as a sort of consolation prize for losers in the race to the sciences. Certainly such a prize would be precious, and, from the point of the *Geisteswissenschaften*, perhaps imminently preferable to being situated amongst retorts and alembics. Without the arts and humanities we are less than human. The world is inexhaustibly indebted to its Newtons and Einsteins and one rejoices in their reality which so enriched and inspired the world, but, one supposes, had a gamete misfired here or there, and they had never been born, it seems likely that other great minds, sooner or later, addressing themselves to similar problems, might have in time produced similar marvels of insight and conjecture. On the other hand it seems unlikely that another might have duplicated the work, or followed the same paths, or given us the same things, as a Michelangelo, a Rembrandt, a Bach, a Beethoven, a Shakespeare. In any event, the arts, and the humanities, are infinitely precious, and their gifts all the more valuable for being unanticipatable, and unique. On the other hand, with all due reverence and respect for the arts and humanities, in which a niche might well await a deserving historiography, it would seem a mistake, a serious misunderstanding, to set historiography amongst them, at least without considerable qualifications, or without expanding their borders.

With regard to the Comtean position, however construed, either that, say, historiography is reduced to a collector of data, on which a science might eventually be founded, or that it is on its way to becoming a science itself, say, sociology, historiography is not a science. Both interpretations suggest a clear misunderstanding of the nature of historiography. It is not a rudimentary clerical endeavor, primitive and unimaginative, exhausted in cataloging facts, nor is it aspiring to serve, or become, a propounder of abstractions and generalities. It is usually concerned to understand and explain specific events in which specific individuals participate. The question then is whether or not such an endeavor counts or does not count as a science. Historiography, now, is either a science or not. On Comte's approach it is not a science, at least now. On the Popper approach, it would not count as a science, though it may apply science. But this seems trivial. Many activities apply science, for example, gardening, plumbing, umbrella manufacturing, and so on. This sheds little light on the basic question, which is whether or not what historiographers do counts as science or not. Following Popper, it would not, but it is not necessary to follow Popper. Thirdly, if historiography were merely a modality of reportage, it would presumably not qualify as a science. That seems acceptable. On the other hand, this position fails as it is founded on a mistaken assumption; historiography, though it involves reportage, is not a mere modality of reportage. The fourth view, that historiography is a humanity, is magnanimously hospitable, and doubtless well-intentioned; it is even flattering, in its way, given the importance and preciousness of the humanities. On the other hand, historiography, despite affinities with the humanities, given its interests and objectives, is either not a humanity, or it is a very different and unusual humanity. If it is either not a humanity, or a very different and unusual humanity, it remains an open question as to whether or not it is a science. In any event, none of the preceding four objections resolve the question; none of them succeed in ruling historiography out of the sciences.

One might consider the following complex disjunctive syllogism:

$$\frac{\begin{array}{c} A \vee B \vee C \vee D \vee E \\ \sim A\ \&\ \sim B\ \&\ \sim C\ \&\ \sim D \end{array}}{E}$$

is a valid argument, but it may not be a sound argument. The second premise might be true, but the first premise might be false. Simply because four arguments against a position E, say, that H is a science, fail, it does not follow that E is true, that, say, H is a science.

If H should be a science, which has not been proven or disproven, what sort of science might it be?

Two major positions are classical, that of the assimilationist and the autonomist.

Carl G. Hempel's view, for which he argued in the aforementioned article on the function of general laws in history, or, as we would prefer, historiography, would be assimilationist. My own sense of that article is that Hempel was well disposed toward historiography and was, in his way, trying to do it a favor. In his usual astute and generous way, he was challenging the skeptics and pooh-poohers who would tend to ridicule, scorn, and belittle not only historiography, but the social sciences, in general, and classical psychology, as well. Hempel, in my view, recognized that these disciplines all possess an empirical subject matter, and thus, in his view, required only methodological revisions by means of which they might certify themselves as genuine sciences. This fits in nicely, as noted, with the unity-of-science movement, in which Hempel participated and for which he was an enthusiastic and prominent spokesman. In a sense, one truth, one world, so one science. I think he was genuinely surprised at the explosion which his little article detonated. What was the problem? Was it not simple, straightforward, and unobjectionable? What had he overlooked? On what grounds should it have generated a literature, one often intensely critical and negative, if not violent?

In any event, if historiography is a science, it is surely not a typical science, certainly not in the sense of the paradigm sciences, the P sciences, such as, say, physics and chemistry. At least five major differences would make it difficult to assimilate H to the P sciences. First, the historiographer, almost always, is unable to observe his data, even if it is contemporary. He can seldom, for example, have it before him, or reproduce it at will. It is not the sort of thing one can locate in a test tube nor examine in a Petri dish. Second, as a corollary, his evidence is almost always indirect, usually derived from documentation, which is often meretricious and unreliable. Thirdly, he cannot experiment, establish controls, isolate and manipulate variables, and such. Fourthly, the absence of experimentation logically precludes the replication of experiments, so important in corroborating and authenticating results. Fifthly, the P sciences profit from instrumentations, ranging from meter sticks and scales to electron microscopes, X-ray diffraction machines, orbiting telescopes, and cyclotrons. Historiography lacks these ancillary devices, without which the contemporary P sciences would be almost unrecognizable. As a result of these and other differences historiography lacks most of the self-correcting mechanisms associated with the P sciences, and, accordingly, is far less likely to be able to confirm, to one degree or another, its hypotheses. Lastly one might note that historiography is largely concerned with understanding in the sense of *Verstehen*, understanding in terms of rationality, intuition, and sympathy, as opposed to understanding in the sense of measurement, description, mathematical and otherwise, and correlation under law.

In view of considerations such as the above, it seems that if H is a science, it is not a typical science, and that its assimilation to the typical sciences, as we usually think of them, would be something possible only in theory, if at all. Indeed, even to raise the question as to whether or not historiography is a science is to suggest that it is not a science. For example, few people seriously ask if physics or chemistry are sciences. Indeed, it would be hard to even understand such a question, unless it involved an unusual presupposition, such as the nonexistence of sciences altogether, perhaps in virtue of a Russell-type hypothesis, a notion of a radically stochastic universe, a world of dream or illusion, or such. Accordingly, it seems likely that, if H is a science, or we wish to consider it a science, we must find it to be, or consider it to be, a very different sort of science, an autonomous form of science.

The autonomist position has its champions, perhaps most famously, Windelband, Croce, and Collingwood. It fits in nicely with the *Verstehen* tradition, and it is likely to be popular amongst historiographers who recognize the difficulties of assimilating historiography to the P sciences and yet, perhaps feeling the dignity or prestige of their discipline is at stake, would wish to count it, somehow, as some sort of science, say, a special sort of science, a unique form of science.

On the autonomist approach to these matters, then, historiography is its own science, a singular form of science unlike other forms of science. It is not an abstract science, but a concrete science, dealing with individuals and particular events. Unlike the natural sciences, which, for their own purposes, partition the world, abstract from the partitions, and, on the whole, strive for generalities, laws, and commonalities, aspects of reality beneath which selected portions of the real world, in their complex particularities, may be subsumed, historiography is commonly concerned with the very particularities which constitute the world as it is in fact, not with particularities considered as convenient, happenstance examples by means of which to illustrate hypothesized regularities. Metaphorically, the typical sciences would seek the Platonic form of horse, not horses, the form of elephant, not elephants, and so on. The historiographer, on the other hand, finds it interesting that a city would be named after Bucephalus, that a horse would be appointed to the Roman senate in the time of Caligula, that cavalrymen often dismounted and fought on foot, that stirrups facilitated shock attacks of lancers in the early Middle Ages, that the theft of Spanish horses radically transformed aboriginal American cultures, and so on. Too, how did

Hannibal manage to bring an army and thirty-seven elephants of war over the Alps? And of what military value, on the whole, were such beasts? What were the psychological effects of their presence? Did they frighten horses? Did they require a revision in the tactics of infantries? One might consider a war in terms of material bodies moving through physical space according to mathematical laws, and, in theory, so account for each footstep, glance, stroke, wound, and utterance. Such a treatment would account for everything, and explain nothing. In terms of it we could depict everything, and understand nothing.

It is sometimes said that historiography, as opposed to the usual partitioning and abstracting sciences, deals with reality in the "fullness of its being." That, of course, though worth saying, is incorrect. No discipline, unless it be one of the gods, can deal with reality in the "fullness of its being." But historiography does occupy the habitat of reality; it marches through the mud of the world in which we live; it concerns itself, as it can, with the very exactitudes, concretenesses, and particularities scorned by a Plato and acknowledged, but demoted or disparaged, by an Aristotle; it finds what Alcibiades did, or had done to him, of interest, perhaps even of relevance, of importance. What an unusual person! Such, with its complexity, its promise, its advantages, its patriotism, its ambition, its treachery, a human being might be. This is where reality resides, in the particular, where particular avalanches thunder down slopes, where particular volcanoes irrupt, where particular storms break at particular times, where particular chemical reactions take place and particular stars fall, where particular men march and camp, where particular voyages are charted, where particular cities are built, where particular human beings plan and strive, fight, love, hate, win, lose, hope, live, die. Aristotle, in the Metaphysics, his First Philosophy, claimed, or speculated, that all men desire to know. Clearly Aristotle was optimistic, and, in any event, was not acquainted with all men. Many men, it seems, would just as soon not know, indeed, would rather not know. Some men, though, do desire to know, and the past is amongst what many would choose to know, if only because of an eager, undislodgable primate curiosity, if only because we cannot understand our surroundings and ourselves, our own realities, without having some sense as to how these things came about.

Accordingly, then, how are these matters to be resolved?

Is historiography a science or not?

It is instructive to have examined this question, not so much with an idea of resolving it, as with an idea of comparing and contrasting disciplines, and, in the process, better understanding similarities and differences.

It is an intellectual tour worth taking.

Clearly, without much difficulty, for several good reasons, historiography could be ruled a science, or, for several other reasons, seemingly equally good, not ruled a science.

Which ruling would be most judicious, most fair?

In my view it would be a mistake to include historiography amongst the sciences. This in no way diminishes the value and importance of historiography, but, if anything, calls attention to its difference, its specialness, its uniqueness and indispensability, its preciousness, its importance. It is a cultural endeavor of momentous significance. What could compare with it? In it we find the diary of humanity. In it we learn ourselves. It is no disparagement of physics that it is not psychology, nor of music that it is not sculpture. Different ends are sought, appropriately with different tools and techniques. I think there is little doubt that historiography is closer to human life, and human reality, as it is experienced in all its first-person immediacy, than the P sciences. One is likely to learn more of human reality, as it is lived, from historiography, or even from poetry and literature, than from psychology, and certainly more than from physics and chemistry. What our species is capable of, for better or for worse, for good or for evil, is awesomely delineated in its deeds, and these constitute historiography's domain of inquiry. We learn what humanity is, in virtue of what it has been, and what it has done. In view of this, the nature of the truths involved, the difficulties pertaining to their discovery, the importance of the endeavor, and the dreadful responsibilities entailed, it seems clear that historiography's significance is indisputable and secure, and is in no way dependent on its location in an administrative structure; it is neither disparaged nor enhanced, neither reduced nor improved, is in no way changed, either diminished or bettered, by its placement in one niche or another, one container or another, in an academic taxonomy.

My major reason for wishing to hold historiography independent of the sciences, and certainly of the P sciences, is that I believe the historiographer must, and is entitled to, and should, deal with axiological issues in his work, actively and concretely, and that this cannot be done in a morally neutral manner. Not only does he have no genuine alternatives in this particular, but should he attempt to evade these issues and responsibilities, should he attempt to maintain a Martian detachment, so to speak, he would not only render his work humanly meaningless and sterile but he would, in effect, betray his discipline, and, in a sense, render it impossible.

We will examine these issues in some detail.

One of the results of our inquiry will be that historiography is not only more meaningful than the P sciences, in the sense of being more pertinent to human interests and concerns, but that it is broader and deeper than what we normally take to be the sciences. Value is at the core of human reality; accordingly, to deny it is to fail to deal with, or refuse to deal with, human reality.

Historiography must, reluctantly or not, remove itself from what we normally take to be the sciences. It cannot emulate them without abandoning its nature. It has its own responsibilities; it has its own, and a very different, work to do.

We must now address ourselves to questions of historiography and axiology, wherein one deals with questions of ethics, morality, and value.

Such concerns, as controversial as they may be, and as reluctant as many are to engage them, are central to a viable, authentic historiography.

Part Five: Axiology

I. Preliminary Considerations

To begin with, let us distinguish between what we might term intrinsic and extrinsic ethical concerns, and, for most practical purposes, acknowledge, and then dismiss, the extrinsic concerns, because, at least explicitly, they are seldom denied or challenged. Even the most arrant scholar activist or political propagandist is likely to at least pretend to subscribe to the extrinsic ethics of a discipline, if only to avoid self-disqualification as a scientist or scholar, if only to claim legitimacy for his efforts, if only to mask deception and conceal a suspect agenda. Did he not do so he would find himself enmeshed in pragmatic paradox, in rather the famous style of Epimenides, the Cretan, who initiated his discourse, to which we were readying ourselves to attend, by reminding us that all Cretans were liars.

All disciplines, and all games, have their extrinsic ethics; these may be occasionally, perhaps even often, violated, but they survive their subversion intact, and are often associated with sanctions attendant on their violation, for example, ostracization, loss of standing, fines, imprisonment, disbarment, being shot dead across a gambling table in Dodge City in the 1870's, and so on. Only Napoleon, for example, could get away with the Napoleonic Diagonal, in which a bishop manages to change color as it makes its way across the board. Physics and chemistry, for example, would normally be regarded as value-free sciences; certainly little moral attention is devoted to what might be taking place in those cloud chambers or beakers, even after hours; molecules are not subjected to reproach; quarks are seldom commended, no matter how well they behave, and so on. On the other hand, physics and chemistry certainly have their extrinsic, their external, ethics. For example, misrepresenting the results of experiments is frowned on, even if grants are at stake. Similarly, historiography, as most people see it, has an extrinsic ethics. For example, one should inquire into a subject matter professionally, seriously, and honestly. One should not knowingly and intentionally pervert one's work to sustain a dubious or poorly supported thesis. One should not suppress or ignore relevant evidence, even if it points to unwelcome conclusions. One should not plagiarize the work of others. One should argue as cogently as possible. One should try to represent things as accurately as one can; one should try to tell the truth, and so on.

We shall take it as a given that historiography, as physics and chemistry, as banking and accounting, as poker, chess, baseball, and so on, has a reasonably well-established and well-understood extrinsic, or external, ethics, whether observed or not. The most interesting questions are found elsewhere.

Initially, let us dispose of a common misconception, namely, that a clear distinction obtains between normative and nonnormative judgments, or between judgments of fact and judgments of value, with the consequence that it is possible, or at least desirable, to write morally neutral, nonjudgmental accounts. For example, it might be said that that an evangelical Christian account and a radical Islamic account of the Fourth Crusade might be identical, save where the Christian and the Islamic historiographer pause in their proper work to commend or scold, to praise or denounce, and so on. This would be a bit like switching between languages or between colors of ink, distinctions which are clear, and would signal a shift between factual and axiological discourse. This misconception is founded on two assumptions, both false, first, that value judgments are not factual, and, second, that that they are avoidable, or irrelevant, to the historiographical enterprise. The falsity of these two assumptions will be established, as one proceeds.

A second common misconception is that the historiographer may properly report, or describe, value judgments, but may not, or should not, make such judgments himself. Whereas one might surely agree that the historiographer may properly report, or describe, value judgments, and, indeed, that his work would be profoundly and pathetically incomplete if he did not do so, it does not follow that he must, or ought, as a matter of professional reserve, or discipline, or such, refrain from such judgments himself, that, for example, whereas he might properly note that the extermination of alleged heretics was approved in such a time and place, that he himself should express no view on the matter, should remain professionally neutral, and, in the event he disapproves or approves of burning people alive for religious or ideological reasons, he should allow no hint of this to appear in his work. To be sure, in the faculty lounge, he might privately express his views, one way or the other, to colleagues. To be sure, only a poor craftsman would be likely to express a moral judgment explicitly, which would be crude and ineffective, and generally unnecessary. Consider the following:

> In such and such a time and place alleged heretics were burned alive. That was a bad idea.

> In such and such a time and place alleged heretics were burned alive. That was a good idea.

Just as the media analyst, by means of the selection of his material, by means of its presentation, by means of his tone of voice, and his facial and bodily expressions, intentionally or inadvertently, makes clear his value judgments, so, too, might the historiographer, in his selection of his material, its presentation, and his choice of language, intentionally or inadvertently, make clear his own value judgments. It seems unlikely that a human being, a creature who must make constant choices based on values, ends, and such, could deal with a value-laden subject matter, such as that of history, and have no axiological response to that subject matter. That would be something like asking straw to walk through flame and not notice. Even a robot would require its programming. Even a camera has its viewpoint, and must be started and stopped at one point or another. One can ask the historiographer to be judicious, honest, and fair, but one cannot ask him not to be human.

Indeed, as we shall see, he cannot betray his humanity without betraying his discipline.

To be sure, there are value-free subject matters, and some individuals may be drawn to them partly in virtue of their neutral and nonthreatening nature. Dealing with them does not require personal responses, personal risks, and, occasionally, painful choices. It is not necessary to take a moral stance toward constructive dilemma or *modus ponens*. Even the world of physics can constitute an Epicurean garden, a refuge from the tumult of an unpleasant, unpredictable, disarranged world.

Treating a nonaxiological world, a value-free subject matter, as though it was value laden would be unusual.

Here is the binomial theorem:

$(a + b)^2 = (a^2 + 2ab + b^2)$

One might describe this in value-laden language in a large number of ways, theoretically in an infinite number of ways, all of which, one supposes, would be similarly inappropriate, even absurd.

For example:

"With a broad smile, a dashing *a* conjoined with a normally suspicious *b* were dynamically squared in such a way that they, to their astonishment, discovered that they were actually equal to not only a cynical *a* squared but, not one, but two *ab* conjoined with a bemused *b*, himself ineluctably, gratifyingly, squared, as well."

And it seems possible, though it is less likely to be noticed, that treating a value-rich subject matter, such as that of history, in a value-free manner, should that be possible, might be similarly inappropriate, even absurd.

Four possibilities present themselves:

Possibility Matrix

Value-Free World (Physics, Mathematics, etc.)	Value-Rich World (History, Culture, Civilization, etc.)
1. Value-Free Language	2. Value-Free language
3. Value-Rich Language	4. Value-Rich Language

The values of two of these possibilities seem clear. For example, in the case of the first possibility, treating a value-free world with a value-free language seems appropriate; the third possibility, treating a value-free world with a value-rich language seems obviously inappropriate, even silly, as we saw in the case of the personified binomial theorem; the values of possibilities two and four might seem less clear. Possibility two, treating a value-rich world with a value-free language might seem to be an ideal, but, we shall argue, it is inappropriate, and is impossible, if one is concerned to develop accounts adequate to the data; possibility four, treating a value-rich world with a value-rich language, despite its apparent threat to objectivity, will be seen to be not only permissible, but appropriate, and, if one is to do justice to the subject matter, necessary.

Our first observation is an obvious one, namely, that natural language is value-laden.

A familiar distinction is drawn between emotive and cognitive meaning. Consider the following example, from Bertrand Russell:

I am firm.
You are obstinate.
He is pig-headed.

Presumably the personality or character trait referred to here might be identical in the three individuals cited. Accordingly, the cognitive meanings of the terms are presumably identical or, at any rate, similar. On the other hand the emotive meanings involved range from commendability, as in the case of firmness, to the seriously derogatory epithet of 'pig-headed'. Charles L. Stevenson brought a very useful concept into philosophical discourse related to this sort of distinction, the concept of persuasive definition. In persuasive definition a word of presumed favorable emotive meaning is evacuated of its usual cognitive content, which is then replaced, under the cover of darkness, so to speak, with a different cognitive content, usually for purposes of rhetorical persuasion. When one hears of such things as "true democracy," "true freedom," "real culture," "actual justice," and such, one may be surprised that one could have been so wrong, up to now, about such things; on the other hand, it might be suspected, too, that one is being treated to an exercise in persuasive definition. Persuasive definition is an activity of great value to the advertiser, advocate, polemicist, activist, and such. A famous and classical example of persuasive definition occurred with the word 'liberal', which used to connote such things as a passion for individual freedom, a commitment to private property, an endorsement of the free market, and a favoring of limited government, notions now commonly, interestingly, associated with conservatism, even arch-conservatism. In any event, when it became clear to most individuals, including socialists, that classical socialism, with its requirement of state ownership of the means of production, was simply a failed system, that it did not work, and it could not work, that it could not calculate without a market, that its diminishment of incentives reduced productivity, that it required pervasive societal management and coercion, and led to totalitarianism, it was time to reinvent socialism, to turn it into something that might work, however expensively and lamely, to turn it into some sort of selectively exploitative, heavily regulatory, multiply interventionistic state, one circumscribing freedom and centralizing authority, and, for that, a new word was surely in order. As 'liberal' was a good word, with a favorable emotive meaning, it was a natural, if surprising, choice. This was an interesting societal phenomenon because, in this instance, the cognitive meanings were almost opposite to one another. Perhaps one day, "true cats" will turn out to be dogs. That this shift took place without much public notice suggests that the advertiser's view of humanity may have much to it. Surface is substance. Perception rules; image is all. Most men think in terms of boxes, and ribbons, not contents. Responding is easy; thinking is hard. In any event, this is a nice example of persuasive definition, and a useful, remarkably clear illustration of the difference between cognitive and emotive meaning.

Consider the following scale:

```
         | 5
         | 4
Emotive  | 3
         | 2
         | 1
         |_0__1__2__3__4__5
              Cognitive
```

Presumably most words in a natural language, which would be nouns and verbs, or their analogues, could be ranked on a scale of this sort. For example, in English, 'hurrah' would presumably be low in cognitive content and high in emotive meaning, perhaps approximating an E5/C zero word. A word like 'desk' would presumably, generally, be high in cognitive content and low on emotive meaning, perhaps approximating an E zero/C5 word, and so on. To be sure, individual relativities enter into these matters. For example, to a manual laborer 'desk' might have favorable connotations, suggesting an easier and more comfortable way of making a living, and to a pilot, on the verge of being removed from the cockpit and placed in an administrative position, the same word might have a negative connotation, as in 'flying a desk'. Whereas it is difficult to be precise about these matters, it is obvious that a natural language is far from being value-neutral. It is a long way from 'p' and 'q' and '2' and '4'. With respect to value-neutrality, should this be taken as a desideratum, perhaps because of a particular view of objectivity, a desire to emulate the P sciences, or such, the historiographer faces at least two major problems which, so to speak, come with the territory.

First, his subject matter is value laden; it is likely to be rich, provocative, stirring, poignant, challenging, moving, jubilant, thrilling, horrifying, disgusting, pathetic, and tragic. It is difficult to be value-neutral toward human life, and that is the common subject matter of historiography. A history of sewing machines or shoes is likely to be quite interesting and well worth looking into. On the other hand, such inquiries are not typical in historiography, and would often be dismissed as antiquarianism, and left to amateurs. To look upon the ills of the world with equanimity, professionally or otherwise, is not easy, and is perhaps immoral. Second, the primary means by which the historiographer understands himself and communicates with others is a natural language, which, despite its marvelous wonders and powers, is scarcely a value-free device. It is a means, or tool, which has its own dramatic, intimidating, often-coercive, unalienable properties. A language's semantic geodesics, as water in a terrain, is likely to guide thought not only into particular cognitive channels, as is often recognized, but into emotive channels, as well. It is hard to put a value-laden device to value-neutral purposes, should that be desired. Recourse to an "artificial language," incidentally, provides no recourse in such a situation. As an uninterpreted logistic system, a purely formal system, its predicates and constants without meaning assignments, it has no more relevance to historiography than a set of rules for arranging Lego blocks or tinker toys. And, as soon as meaning assignments are given, if they are given in a natural language, or are even pertinent to the subject matter, one is back, so to speak, where one started.

One might also consider the possibility that a value-neutral language, in so far as it might be possible, might be inadequate for historiographical purposes, even inappropriate, even improper; that it might, in its way, betray the discipline.

The following examples are based on a game which we shall call "Baby Catch."[114]

1. System 1 removed System 2 from System 3 and elevated System 2, after which System 4 acquired System 2 by means of a an implement.

2. Soldier 1 removed the baby from its mother's arms and threw the baby into the air, after which Soldier 2 caught the falling baby on his bayonet.

3. The Turkish soldier tore the screaming infant from the clutching fingers of its shrieking mother. Part of the baby's shirt remained in her grasp. Another soldier clubbed the mother back, striking her in the face with the stock of his rifle. Her jaw was broken, and her mouth was bleeding. The tongue had been half severed against her teeth. The first soldier then threw the infant into the air, as high as he could, for that improves the game. Another soldier waited, poised, intent, and caught the falling child on his bayonet. It had been expertly done. Much skill is required, as the infant must be caught through the belly or back, and it has a tendency to twist in the air. That makes things more difficult. "Well done," said another soldier. The successful contestant removed the baby from the bayonet by thrusting it free with his boot. The bayonet had

---

[114] Cf. "Ivan's Rebellion," in F. M. Dostoevski's *The Brothers Karamazov*.

wedged itself between the ribs of the infant. That often happens. "Next," said a soldier. Another soldier stepped forward. "My turn," he said.

The first example here would seem about as close as one could come to a value-free or value-neutral description of the game in question. From the first description, of course, it is not even clear what is going on. If historiography could be dealt with in the manner of the P sciences, in terms of material bodies moving in physical space according to mathematical laws, it might provide us with something of the sort suggested.

In the second example, at least we have some sense of what is going on. It is substantially value-free, unless one objects to impaling infants on bayonets. Whereas the description is designedly neutral, and rather value-free, what is going on is not really value-neutral or value-free. There is a sense in which the second description, telling the truth as it does, is lying. It lies by minimizing. To be sure, the author might view the game with detachment, regard it as interesting example of humans at play, or even approve of the game. Perhaps he wishes he could play it. Perhaps he thinks he might be good at it. In such cases, the description is not a bad one. Much depends on viewpoint. On the other hand, value judgments enter into all such accounts, even if "off-camera," so to speak. For example, one decides what will be noted, its placement in a context, which will shade its understanding, and suggest its importance or unimportance, how it will be treated, and at what length, and so on. Why should it be dealt with, at all?

In the third example, whatever its faults, we have a reasonably clear idea of what is going on, and what it means to the participants. It is the most detailed of the three accounts. It is the best, I think, in conveying an understanding of what was taking place. The description, though detailed, is relatively clinical. It does not explicitly interpolate emotions. The details recounted, what is seen and heard, could all have been picked up by a camera. In a way it is neutral, and not neutral. If there are moral chips here, they are allowed to fall as they may.

It is not clear that being nonjudgmental is always a virtue. Similarly, it is not obvious that all cultures are equivalent. Certainly that is not taken seriously by the many individuals within a culture who wish to change it. One need not, for example, find the casting of infants to crocodiles morally acceptable.

In this section of our treatise, that having to do with ethics, our main concern is the permissibility or impermissibility of moral engagement on the part of the historiographer, supposing, provisionally, that such engagement is avoidable, at all. Whereas an internal, or intrinsic, ethics, as opposed to an external, or extrinsic, ethics would be irrelevant to a value-free subject matter, such as addressed by the P sciences, it is not at all clear that a historiographer, who deals with a value-rich subject matter should, or can, adopt a similar moral insouciance. Indeed, this, as noted, is our major reason for preferring to dissociate historiography from the P sciences, and locate it closer to the center of human meaningfulness, closer to things that matter most, closer to the heart of human reality.

As suggested earlier, there are many moralities, and many of them are presumably noncommensurable. This fact, however, as we shall see, while it suggests an interesting relativity of moralities, indexed to a diversity of goals, does not entail that moralities are subjective, equivalent, unimportant, arbitrary, or noncognitive.

Obviously there is a distinction between 'Group G designates Act A as right' and 'Act A is right'. The first sort of locution would commonly be regarded as descriptive and the second as normative. The first sort of locution has a truth value, that is, it is either true or false, and the criteria for determining its truth or falsity are reasonably clear. Indeed, one need not even have an idea of what 'right' might mean to the group in question, or at all. It would be enough to note that Group G applies the word 'right' to Act A. Similarly, one might investigate 'Group G designates Act A as glorp'. The second sort of locution is more troublesome. It is not clear to everyone that it has a truth value, and it is not clear to everyone how to determine that truth value. Also, in this case, the second case, one needs some understanding of what is meant by 'right'. In this case, 'glorp' will not do.

II. Ethical Taxonomy

Before entering seriously into a presuppositional, largely shared morality, one resulting over generations from systemic-process developments, one which might be neutrally described, without evaluation, it will be useful to delineate, however briefly and inadequately, some major ethical orientations, as they have a considerable bearing on the issues involved. Most of these orientations, however incompatible they might be, one with another, have something important to be said for them, or they would not be as well known as they are, and would not, over the years, have continued to attract adherents and champions. Too, most are extracted from, or suggested by, elements found in evolving moralities. Indeed, it is difficult to consider what might count as a morality which would be both plausible and independent of such antecedents.

        Cognitivism   Noncognitivism
        I. Objective   I. Emotivism
          A. Intuitionism   II. Imperativism
          B. Utilitarian   III. Prescriptivism
            1. Act
            2. Rule
          C. Ideal Observerism
        II. Subjective
          A. Natural
          B. Supernatural

The major distinction here is between cognitivity and noncognitivity, with respect to normative judgments. Do normative judgments, for example, judgments essentially containing normative terms, have truth values? The cognitivist position maintains that at least some normative judgments are either true or false. The noncognitivist position maintains that no normative judgments are true or false.[115]

Within the cognitivist position one might distinguish between objective cognitivism, in which the truth value of the normative judgment is independent of individual- or group-relative considerations, such as approval, decreeing, and such, and subjective cognitivism in which the truth value is individual- or group-relative. In intuitionism, "good" or "right" might be conceived of as nonnatural properties, properties which are not empirical, as we usually think of empirical properties, such as salty, square, yellow, and such, properties of a uniquely ethical or moral sort. Here, rather as in seeing that something is, say, yellow, one sees, or recognizes, intuitively or by rational inspection, or such, that such and such a situation is good, that such and such an act is right, and so on. There is little doubt that, phenomenologically, this seemingly immediate apprehension is a characteristic of much moral experience, at least in clear cases. The major difficulties here seem to be the dubiety of the analogy between sensory experience or logical insight and moral apprehension, that there is no obvious way to resolve moral disagreement, given the conflict of intuitions, and that such seemingly incorrigible apprehensions, in many cases,

---

115 'Judgment', as used here, does not presuppose truth-value possession. For example, 'Act A is morally proper behavior' would normally be taken as a judgment. The noncognitivist, on the other hand, would deny that it was the sort of "judgment" which could be true or false. 'Locution', 'utterance', 'linguistic form', and such, would seem to cover too much ground, to be too broad, and perhaps too vague. There are, incidentally, many fascinating and subtle issues involved in these matters which lie beyond the scope of this treatise. For example, is the distinction between normative and nonnormative terms and/or judgments viable, what might be the criteria for normative terms, when does a term occur essentially in a judgment, what might count as a normative judgment, what are the logical relations, if any, obtaining between normative and nonnormative judgments, and so on. Major candidates for normative terms would be 'right', 'wrong', 'good', 'bad', 'obligation', 'duty', etc. Happily, the overwhelming majority of normative terms, being less general, are much clearer. Analogously, 'red' is less general than 'color' (is black a color?), and 'color' is less general than 'property' (is nonexistence a property of, say, Pegasus?), and 'property' is less general than 'being' (do possibilities have being?), and so on.

may be the consequences of a conditioning process, which might vary, from person to person.

In act utilitarianism that act is right which produces the most good for the most people, whereas in rule utilitarianism that act is right which is in accord with the rule or principle which, if followed generally, would, statistically, produce the most good for the most people. For example, robbing Smith and donating the spoils to charity might produce the most good for the most people, so, if that should be the case, the robbery would be morally acceptable, perhaps even obligatory, in act utilitarianism; on the other hand, widespread, indiscriminate robbery, even with the best of intentions, would presumably reduce the quality of life in a society, so the same act, the robbery, would, under most circumstances, be prohibited in rule utilitarianism. It is generally supposed that what is "good" is clear and quantifiable, without which understanding and quantifiability, the implementation of utilitarianism would be impractical. Needless to say, many problems occur here. Usually "Good" would be understood in terms of pleasure, happiness, satisfaction, such things. Both act and rule utilitarianism run counter to the moral suppositions of most individuals, as it is easy to conceive of acts or rules which would produce the most good, pleasure, happiness, or such, for the most people which would seem, unless one adopted the utilitarian view, morally heinous. Such objections abound, the most famous perhaps being the utility of the "unjust hanging," sacrificing innocent individuals in order to frighten a society into law-abidingness. On the other hand, there is no doubt that the utilitarian viewpoint is often morally relevant. For example, an act which harms no one and produces much good would usually be preferred to an act which harms no one and produces less good. Interestingly, the long-range consequences of taking utilitarianism seriously, which, hopefully, no one will ever do, in either of its versions, have been seldom projected. For example, how could one divide the goods of the world evenly, even if one wished to do so; who would decide how the division was to be made; who would be the beneficiaries, your society, all societies, including future societies, all primates, all forms of sentient life, or who or what; and how could the distributions be supervised and enforced without a totalitarian state; and what would keep the enforcers from favoring themselves; similarly, utilitarianism, if taken seriously, would seem to be not only impractical, but unnatural, immoral, and dangerous. Life would be one of endless self-sacrifice; there would always be more to do, more to give; productivity would decline with the absence of incentives; effort would be pointless, accruing no advantage, lest it be to avoid sanctions; society would become a prison, a penitentiary with millions of subdued, reduced, managed, equivalent inmates, with all power centralized in the wardens and armed guards. A consistent utilitarianism would lead to immobility and stagnation; no longer would men look to the stars. They would then be forever beyond their grasp.

Ideal observerism presupposes a moral consensus. On this approach, the right act is, for example, that act which would be approved by an ideal observer, one who, for example, is informed, impartial, consistent, rational, benevolent, and so on. This makes some sense as a contrafactual proposition is involved, which would presumably have a truth value. Were there an ideal observer, presumably he would have such-and-such a view of the matter. This is somewhat like subjective cognitivism, except that no actual person is required. It is a bit like saying, if there were an ideal batsman he would bat 1.000; if there were an ideal pitcher, he would have an earned run average of 0.00, and so on. One need not concern oneself with the outcome should the ideal batsman face the ideal pitcher. Obvious problems appertain to this view, for example, aside from our own moral views, which we impose on the ideal observer, we have no way of determining what would be the views of such an observer; similarly, it seems we have no way of rationally resolving possible disagreements between A's ideal observer and B's ideal observer.

In subjective cognitivism the truth values of normative judgments are individual- or group-relative, are usually ascertainable, and are almost certainly ascertainable by the individuals or groups involved. In a simple case, something like 'Act A is Right' or 'Experience E is good' would be understood along the lines of 'I approve of Act A', 'I like Experience E', and so on. Such locutions then would clearly possess truth values, being either true or false. If, say, the individual claims that Act A is right, but does not approve of it, he is saying something false; if he claims to like Experience E and really doesn't, then he is lying, and so on. This is certainly a simple, foolproof way to obtain cognitivity for normative judgments, but it is likely to seem dissatisfying to both the cognitivist and the noncognitivist; from the cognitivist point of view it is likely to seem reductive and oblique, a victory which misses the point of cognitivity, and is scarcely worth winning, and the noncognitivist is likely to see it as a cavil or quibble, a timidity, a reluctance to bite the bullet of noncognitivism. Such cognitivism would seem noncognitivism at heart, or in disguise. More charitably, one might see this position as a plausible semantic hypothesis, a way of making sense of normative discourse, of accounting for seeming normative discrepancy, and of retaining a role for truth values in such matters, this agreeing with the pervasive societal view that such judgments are properly to be regarded as true or false. This view, as others, of course, has its problems. As G. E. Moore pointed out, it makes moral disagreement impossible. For example, if 'Act A is right' and 'It is not the case that Act A is right' are to be understood as statements of approval and disapproval, respectively, there is no real disagreement. Both judgments are logically compatible. For example, if Jones says 'Apple pie is good' and Smith says 'It is not the case that apple pie is good' and these locutions are to be understood along the lines of 'I, Jones, like apple pie' and 'I, Smith, do not like apple pie' we know something about Jones and Smith, but we know little about apple pie. If genuine moral disagreement can exist, this position is mistaken. On the other hand, the existence or nonexistence of genuine moral disagreement is what is at issue. It is worth pointing out, in passing, that the Moorean point would also obtain against any noncognitivist position. The subjective cognitivist position, intriguing with respect to high-level, extremely general moral predicates, such as 'right' and 'good', is much less plausible with most moral predicates. For example, it is hard to understand 'x is honest', 'x is fair', 'x is truthful', 'x is compassionate', 'x is industrious', 'x is tidy', and such, along the lines of simple approval and disapproval. Indeed, one supposes one might acknowledge that, say, x was honest and truthful, or industrious and tidy, and, from time to time, wish he wasn't, or not so much so.

Supernatural subjective cognitivism is also individual- or group-relative. In its usual form an individual is involved, a law-giver, whose word, so to speak, is definitive in moral matters. Let us suppose, for example, that Hammurabi's Shamash or Thutmose III's Amon-Ra promulgates a set of laws, and that the respective faithfuls accept these laws. What, then, would make Act A right would be that it was decreed or commanded by one deity or another. Most effectively, the deity did not decree the law because it was right, but the law was right because it was decreed by, desired by, approved by, the deity in question. Surely we do not want an independent right, outside the deity, which it merely recognizes and endorses, indeed, to which he might be obliged to conform. That would seem to reduce or demote the deity and elevate the objective, independent right. In group supernatural cognitivism, the laws, moral code, or such, would be the result of an agreement amongst gods. If there is one god, there might as well be more than one, and most religions have taken that for granted. Happily the gods, though perhaps having their favorites in one war or another, seem to have been in substantial moral agreement. This is not always the case, of course. Some have approved of sacrificing virgins and casting infants to crocodiles, and others have entertained moral reservations pertaining to such practices. One encounters a problem when the gods disagree. This problem is usually addressed by exterminating the devotees of one god or another, usually the god with the fewest devotees.

In noncognitivism, normative judgments lack truth values. These positions can be subtle and complex, with interwoven elements, but, in our brief survey, for purposes of simplicity, we distinguish amongst emotivism, imperativism, and prescriptivism. In emotivism, a normative judgment is understood not as a *statement* of approval or disapproval, which would be either true or false, as in subjective cognitivism, but as an *expression* of approval or disapproval. For example, something like 'Murder is wrong' would be understood as an expression of disapproval of murder, and expressions are not true or false, no more than smirks, grimaces, grunts, hisses, snorts, and chuckles. In imperativism, something like 'Murder is wrong' would be understood along the lines of 'Don't kill people'. Moral judgments are a tricky, or subtle, way of issuing instructions, admonitions, commands, and such. It sounds as though one is saying something true, something which is just the case, is indisputable, is to be taken seriously, and so on, while actually one is making use of a rhetorical device to influence behavior, in a way, to give an order, an order not obvious, an order concealed or obscured, one veiled, one uttered under the guise of something quite different, interestingly, a statement of fact. The most sophisticated form of noncognitivism is prescriptivism, where moral judgments are not reduced to expressions of feeling, analogous to smiles and frowns, sighs or sneers, or covert commands, but to prescriptions, in a broad sense, say, commendations, recommendations, endorsements, urgings, warnings, disparagements, and such. One might take things like 'x is right', 'x is a good watch', 'x is a good car', or such, as examples. To say that 'x is right' is to prescribe or recommend, or urge, behaving in such a way as to bring x about; to say x is a good watch or x is a good car is to commend the x in question. If the prescriptivist left things in this simplicity his position would be no more plausible than emotivism or imperativism. For example, when someone asks a jeweler if x is a good watch or a mechanic if x is a good car, one is certainly interested in knowing something more than whether or not the jeweler or mechanic is going to commend the x in question. One is interested in things like durability and accurate time keeping, safety ratings, gas mileage, and such. Accordingly, the prescriptivist is likely to add what he might choose to call "secondary meaning" into the equation, primary meaning being prescription, commendation, or such, and secondary meaning being the qualities usually associated with the entities commended, these varying with the entity in question. For example, the primary meaning, say, prescription or commendation, would be identical in 'x is a good watch' and 'x is a good car' but the "secondary meanings" would be different. Even within a category, secondary meanings might vary. Different purposes, different desires, different cars. A car which is affordable, reliable, safe, and fuel-efficient may not be the same car as would serve to excite peer envy and dazzle young women of a given I.Q. level. Considering that 'good' usually means 'good for something', 'satisfactory to achieve certain ends', and such, and that 'right' usually means 'right for something', or 'appropriate to realize certain purposes', and such, one might suspect that the prescriptivist may be putting the cart before the horse or putting his eggs in the wrong basket. Nothing is good because it is commended; it is, rather, hopefully, commended because it is good. On this approach commendation is not primary, but secondary. Whereas it would be expected that good things, people, watches, cars, or whatever, would be commended because, in one way or another, they are good, and whereas it would be expected that entities not good would not be commended, because, in one way or another, they were not good, it is certainly possible that good entities, say, good watches, or whatever, are not commended, and that bad entities, say, poor watches, or whatever, might be commended, either meretriciously, say, to bring about a sale, or by mistake. The point here is that the concepts of good and commendation are logically independent. Things are commended for reasons, and the reasons are primary, if anything is primary. Adjudication amongst ends may not be always possible, but it is usually possible.[116]

---

116 Attention might be drawn to an apparent difficulty with prescriptivism, or, perhaps, to my proposed taxonomy. First, prescriptivism is normally understood as a noncognitivism, and a noncognitivistic position is one which denies truth values to moral judgments. That is why I have set the taxonomy up as I have. Commending, for example, is neither true nor false. So far, so good. On the other hand, as soon as secondary meaning enters into the equation, problems arise. For example, if 'p & q' is a conjunction, it would be false if either 'p' is false or 'q' is false. Now, let prescriptivism's 'p' count as the commendatory aspect of moral judgment, and, accordingly, it would be neither true nor false. The residue 'q', then, would be the secondary meaning and that, presumably, is either true or false, whether the watch keeps good time or not, and so on. Accordingly, 'p' is irrelevant and the truth value of the "conjunction" thus reduces to the truth value of 'q', which, *per hypothesi*, is true or false, and thus cognitive. Accordingly, prescriptivism would turn out to be a variation of cognitivism, not noncognitivism. I think this point has been seldom noticed. Perhaps one might save the day by suggesting that secondary meaning is not meaning, but something else, say, a transitory, particularistic presupposition of, or motivation for, commendation, or such. In any event, however this apparent difficulty might be resolved, I think the nature of prescriptivism is reasonably clear.

Given the terrors and horrors of the real world, riots and wars, suffering, disease, hatred, cruelty, starvation, hardship, misery, and such, noncognitivism may seem to be little more than an academic frivolity, one unlikely, happily, to be taken seriously. Indeed, it seems that only robots, psychopaths, sociopaths, or such, would be likely to subscribe to it. It suggests nihilism. It suggests that nothing matters, that nothing makes a difference, that it is not true that starvation is bad, that it is not false that slaughtering innocent human beings is good, and so on. Such views would seem not only false, but heinously immoral. On the other hand, there is nothing in noncognitivism which suggests that the real world is unimportant, or how one lives makes no difference in the world. The noncognitivist may not permit himself to believe that 'cancer is bad' has a truth value, but he will see the doctor. Most noncognitivists, interestingly, live the morality to which they deny truth values. It is difficult to suppose they believe what they preach. It would be easier to understand their position if they could make clear under what conditions, if not those of the real world, the world in which they actually live, it would be false. Under what conditions, even in theory, in what possible world, would they regard their views as false? Perhaps if one could measure morals with meter sticks, if there were 100-percent moral agreement in all cultures at all times? It is hard to know. We shall later argue that cognitivities are conditional, but real.

The preceding survey of some familiar ethical positions, however brief and inadequate, and perhaps somewhat tendentious, will be useful in understanding, and clarifying, various issues in which we shall be shortly enmeshed, such as subjectivity and objectivity, cognitivity and noncognitivity. However remote academic ethics, with its almost Platonic tidiness, may be from the massive, confused, inconsistent, evolving moral geologies of a real world, it doubtless began in that world, rather as horses preceded the form of horse. And, hopefully, it will serve, in its simple way, from time to time, superior, we fear, to the form of horse, to shed some actual light on its world of origin.

It is our hope, in these matters, I suppose obviously, that we shall eventually succeed in entitling the historiographer to tell the truth, all truths, if he wishes to do so, regardless of the sort of truth to be told.

If there are axiological truths to be told, in one way or another, and the historiographer refuses to tell them, or imply them, or show them, then, to that extent, at least, his work is incomplete; it is less than it might be; it would be an inadequate portrayal of his subject matter; it would be a misrepresentation, if not an outright falsification, of his data.

Let us look into these matters.

III. Systemic-Process Morality

The moralities which are taken seriously in the world, and which are likely to influence actual moral choices by large numbers of human beings, are not the inventions of armchair moralists but moralities which have been selected-for in moral evolution, largely for their practicality in facilitating group survival and welfare. Their justification, if one is requested, is their generally beneficent effect, at least statistically, on human life, in making it possible, in prolonging it, and improving its quality. In short, they are instrumentalities, analogous to what Kant would have understood as hypothetical imperatives, e.g., "if you want A, do B." Even Kant's "categorical imperatives" need not be regarded as unconditional directives with which one must comply, for some absolute, unquestioned, and unintelligible reason, "though the heavens fall," but might be brought within the compass of rationality on grounds of societal prudentiality. To be sure, ends are presupposed, but, given the ends, the means to bring them about may be rationally sought. Different ends, different means. This is a useful picture, but it is also one which is overly intellectualized. In a systemic-process morality, as in other evolved orders, we have a structure which is, substantially, a "product of human action but not of human design," analogous to a market, to language, to law, and so on. Much of this, doubtless most, is not thought out. It emerges, often unrecognized explicitly. Much takes place on the grounds of feelings, of emotions. It is probably the seeming spontaneity of many moral responses which led to the intuitionistic version of objective cognitivism.

Before we enter into these issues it is important to return, briefly, to the distinction between descriptive and normative. Obviously a morality may be treated descriptively. Anthropologists do this regularly. One can certainly be right or wrong about something like 'Group G designates Act A as right'. That is descriptive. On the other hand,' Act A is right' is normative. The criteria for evaluating the first locution are reasonably clear. The criteria for evaluating the second locution are less obvious. Indeed, in Group G most individuals, one supposes, might not even understand, at least at first, what was being asked, if a criterion for the evaluation of 'Act A is right' might be requested. Suppose Act A was defending the city in time of danger, feeding one's children, paying homage to the gods, keeping out of the path of racing chariots, or such. Presumably only an idiot, or someone with a trick up the sleeve of his tunic, would ask such a question. Given an invitation to the next symposium or a drachma or two the citizen might address himself to the question. In each case, presumably, an answer would be given in terms of ends to be realized, for example, protecting one's home, nourishing one's children, keeping on the gods' good side, avoiding a mangling beneath hoofs and chariot wheels, and such. Now, even from the outside, one could recognize that the citizen, given the ends in view, was right. This is not a matter of mere description; it is a matter of fact. One need not accept the ends, of course. If the end is ingratiating yourself with Macedonians, exasperating your wife, annoying the gods, or committing suicide, different acts would be right, or correct, in the instrumental sense. We shall later consider whether or not ends may be adjudicated. All one needs at this point is that, relative to ends, cognitivity obtains.

I suppose that all of us, or most of us, including self-identified noncognitivists, behave reasonably morally, according to our lights, and, in any event, take morality seriously. Certainly we regard some behaviors as better than others and, usually, if the question came up, for reasons. Most of us, for example, I hope, would regard sacrificing virgins and casting infants to crocodiles not only as stupid, but wrong. And, if so, most folks would regard something like 'Sacrificing virgins is wrong' and 'Casting infants to crocodiles is wrong' as being true, and 'It is not the case that sacrificing virgins is wrong' and 'It is not the case that casting infants to crocodiles is wrong' as false. The noncognitivist would have to deny that 'Sacrificing virgins is wrong' is true or, say, would have to deny 'It is not the case that casting infants to crocodiles is wrong' is false. To be sure, he is simply insisting that such locutions lack truth values, not that he is insane, or seriously uninformed about the nature of the world. He would probably reassure us, if he felt we were in doubt, that he was not in favor of sacrificing virgins, perhaps because of negative emotions having to do with the matter, or a fondness for virgins, and that, similarly, he did not approve of casting infants to crocodiles, perhaps because they are cute little things. What he could not do is claim that one should not sacrifice virgins or should not cast infants to crocodiles, because that would suggest that there is a right and wrong in such matters, and that would being us back to those eschewed truth values.

Certainly one is justly suspicious of individuals who, perhaps dazzled by their own virtue, or uncertain of it, make much of morality. For the most part, morality is not to be made much of, but practiced. Its effects are more properly manifested in action than garrulity. Indeed, as the saying goes, when someone begins to assure you of his honesty, that is a good time to start counting the spoons. Morality, too, can be a bother, sometimes a real spoilsport. Also, there might seem something unwonted or pretentious about articulating moral views. Too, what would entitle us, with all our own weaknesses, lapses, and faults, to even approach such matters? Who are we, nonvirgins and mature adults, to object to the sacrifice of virgins and the casting of infants to crocodiles, when, obviously, here and there, such things were accepted, approved, and perhaps even prescribed? Would not the expression of a moral reservation in such matters be an implicit imposition of our own values on others, denying them their right to differ and scorning their legitimate moral autonomy in such matters?

Who so bold to rush in, "where even angels might fear to tread"?

I think that most people would agree that the historiographer has a right to moral views in his private life, and might even be permitted to express them privately, on his own time. But there is a view, it seems, which would encourage him, at least to the extent possible, to avoid them in his professional endeavors. One can sympathize with that view to an extent, as few things are as embarrassing and annoying as finding oneself subjected to, and being insulted by, the vociferations of your average moral zealot, concerned to win you to his point of view, whatever it is, say, hopefully, that it is not a good idea to sacrifice virgins or cast infants to crocodiles. It is not necessary, of course, to leave morality to the pests, the nuisances, and zealots. The major question is whether or not there are moral truths. If there are moral truths, then their inclusion in historiographical properties, however it is done, if they are relevant, should be as legitimate as the inclusion of any other form of relevant truth, and their exclusion, if they are relevant, should be as inadmissible as the omission of, if relevant, any other form of truth. The dichotomy between the private and the public life seems unrealistic, unnecessary, and unacceptable. If moral views are unacceptable in public life, then, so, too, should they be in private life. And if they are acceptable in private life, then, so, too, should they be in public, or professional life.

It is hard to understand a well-motivated denial of this, unless one is haunted by the specter of, or obsessed with an image of, the paradigm sciences, the P sciences, unless one feels obligated to succumb to their siren songs, even though the bark of historiography be dashed on the rocks of an alien shore.

One hears much of tolerance.

Tolerance is not a value-free choice. It involves an axiological commitment, as much as its denial. In many respects, and in many contexts, tolerance is acceptable, even desirable. Surely this lesson emerged, if none other, from the horrors of religious wars. On the other hand, it should be clearly understood that tolerance is a blank check on which you may allow others to write, and that you may not receive such a check in return. One should beware of tolerance, for it is not clear what gates it might open. One need not be benignly accepting of the views of those who hate you and intend to kill you, often for absurd reasons, which to you, supposing you are not a psychiatrist, may be scarcely comprehensible. One might more easily understand the motivations of a rabid animal. One need not be tolerant of intolerance. There is a general supposition that tolerance will beget tolerance, and the consequences will be benign. This is a *non sequitur*, logically and empirically. Tolerance may be the veil beneath which the assassin bides his time, the wall behind which, the schoolrooms within which, the houses of worship within which, the end of a civilization is patiently planned and prepared. An unconditional tolerance is insane, and a denial of the right to self-defense.

The historiographer, a human being, is likely to have moral views. That pretty much goes with the human territory. There seems no reason to deplore this, or conceal it. As he is a value-rich human being dealing with a value-laden subject matter, by means of a value-laden language, one expects this to influence his work and appear in his work. It is probably impossible, or at least extremely unlikely, that this should not be the case. The more interesting question is whether or not he should do his best to remove all traces of axiological orientation from his work, and aim to achieve a value-neutral, axiologically sterile, robotic outcome, or, to the best of his ability, accept, but hide, the elements which so profoundly affect that outcome. The choice, of course, is his. The first alternative, treating a value-laden subject matter in a value-free way, given the imperatives of selection, event-carving, factor-weighting, description, and reportage, would presumably be impossible, or, if possible, would render his work incomplete, inadequate, shallow, tepid, and jejune; it would, by minimization and misrepresentation, betray the complexity and richness of the subject matter; and the second alternative would be dishonest. If the historiographer has moral reservations about, say, genocide, mass crucifixions, religious persecutions, human sacrifice, or such, there seems no reason that he should feel guilty about this, or that he should refrain from describing and reporting such things, despite the fact that this is obviously an axiological choice, which need not have been made, and might have some effect on a reader. Indeed, one might see this as a duty of the historiographer, that he should tell the truth, that he should do his best to be honest to the past, to show it as it was, empirically, morally, and so on.

Explicit value judgments are usually unnecessary and counterproductive. At the least, they are poor art; and, at the worst, they are intrusive and distractive, oversimple, or even false. On the other hand, historiography, as we usually think of it, would be unthinkable without implicit value judgments. It, like its subject matter, is redolent with value. Value judgment frames and colors historiography. There is no point in lamenting this, or denying it. There are, of course, competitive moralities. This is not an excuse to avoid morality, but is rather an encouragement to be as honest as one can to one's own. He who is not honest to his own moral vision leaves the field open to those who are honest to theirs. He who does not enter the fray will find himself beaten. The health of historiography lies not in its fear of moralities but in their competition. This competition, by means of reviews, criticisms, articulated alternatives, and such, is the nearest thing in historiography to the self-correction mechanisms of the P sciences, most obviously, the replication of controversial experiments. In historiography, this competition is more than a replication surrogate; it is a route to diversity, dialogue, and greatness.

But if this is not to be more than a liberation to chaos, a license for anarchy, an entitlement to unbridled idiosyncrasy, a case must be made for moral cognitivity. If there is no moral truth, there can be no duty to seek it, successfully or unsuccessfully. If value judgments lack truth values, historiography collapses into a fantasy of pretentious subjectivities. If there is no better or worse here, no good or bad, no right or wrong, historiography has no more cognitivity, axiologically, than the weather, or Oswald Spengler's "flowers of the field, growing in their superb aimlessness."

IV. An Examination of Some Arguments Pertinent to the Cognitivity of Value Judgments

1. Background Considerations

1. Fact/Value Dichotomization

A view occasionally encountered in the matter to which we shall shortly address ourselves is that there is a sharp distinction between judgments of fact and judgments of value, the presupposition being that judgments of value cannot be judgments of fact. That is, of course, what is at issue, and a point whose importance should not be resolved by definition, but, if at all, by an examination of discourse, its semantics and pragmatics. There are surely contexts in which judgments of one sort should not be confused with judgments of other sorts, say, clearly analytic judgments with clearly synthetic judgments, but it is not obvious, to say the least, that what are commonly thought of as judgments of fact and judgments of value are separable in the same way. In any event, the general societal presupposition here, correct or incorrect, is that judgments of value can be better or worse, mistaken or correct, right or wrong, true or false, and so on, and are thus judgments of fact.

The wholesale denial of cognitivity to axiological propositions tends to be founded, for the most part, on selectivity and decontextualization. For example, one selects extremely general predicates, say, 'good' or 'right', and takes them out of context. For example, 'x is good' is less clear than 'x is a good book', 'x is a good rifle', 'x is a good meal', and so on. Similarly, 'x is right' is less clear than 'x is the right choice in this situation' or 'x is the right way to act in that situation', and such. In both of these cases, the criteria involved, or the ends to be sought, would be relevant. On the other hand, the great majority of axiological predicates are ground-level predicates, so to speak, and, for the most part, are much clearer than many familiar, nonaxiological predicates, such as 'small', 'large', 'tall', 'short', 'near', 'far', 'higher', 'lower', and so on. Consider such axiological predicates as 'brave', 'cowardly', 'friendly', 'unfriendly', 'pleasant', 'unpleasant' 'diligent', 'careless', 'reliable', 'unreliable', 'honest', 'dishonest', 'truthful', 'meretricious', 'straightforward', 'sneaky', 'sly', 'cunning', 'selfish', 'sensitive', 'insensitive', 'generous', 'ungenerous', 'kind', 'cruel', 'trustworthy', 'untrustworthy', and so on.

In most instances, axiological propositions involve verifiable matters of fact. Courts of law seem to think so. And so do most people.

We are usually cognizant of what would tend to confirm or disconfirm such judgments; we are usually aware of the sort of evidence which would be relevant to their assessment.

As judgments of value are almost always judgments of fact, facts relevant to criteria, and ends to be sought, a distinction between judgments of fact and judgments of value is unwarranted. A better distinction might be drawn between axiological judgments and nonaxiological judgments.

2. Is/Ought

In a famous passage, in Part III, Section III, of Book II of his *Treatise of Human Nature*, David Hume claims "'Tis not contrary to reason to prefer the destruction of the whole world to the scratching of my finger." Putting aside our relief that Hume did not have a nuclear arsenal at his disposal, this interesting claim has, of course, a purely instrumental view of reason in mind, that it is concerned purely and simply with means/end relationships. Reason is as morally neutral as arithmetic. Doubtless this view would be likely to find favor with some computers and robots. Also, given the restrictions placed on reason, there is much to be said for it. It would come out as true, given how Hume chooses to use words. On the other hand, societally, at least, as most of us choose to use words, some ends are understood as rational, or reasonable, and others not. For example, let us say that someone desires to use peanut butter rather than metal in the construction of automobiles. Given this end, it is certainly reasonable to lay in large quantities of peanut butter. On the other hand, given the laws of physics, chemistry, and such, the end would be regarded as idiotically irrational. Reason is generally useful in adjudicating amongst ends, as well as in helping one to either realize or avoid one end or another. To be sure, this adjudication is usually in terms of accepting one or another end as being preferably instrumental to the achievement of a further end. The pragmatic adjudication amongst ultimate ends, however, to give Hume his due, is not likely to be achieved by ratiocination but by choice, preference, desire, commitment, "passion," or such. Evolution has doubtless seen to it that certain ends, or inclinations to certain ends, have been favored in biological competition, selected-for in the biography of a species. Were this not the case doubtless the species would be extinct, if it ever began. Genetics doubtless has its role in such matters. Let us suppose that it is natural, statistically, for human beings to prize, and seek the realization of, a given Value V. This would then be as real as anything else in nature. This would be a matter of simple fact. One might always ask, of course, if human beings, statistically, should prize, and seek the realization of, Value V, but this would seem, at best, a surprising question. Should a human being value nourishment, hydration, comfort, fellowship, and such, or prefer starvation, thirst, misery, isolation, and such? Let those who would ponder such questions. In any event, properly or improperly, statistically, and with all due respect to Hume, ends such as nourishment, hydration, comfort, and fellowship are regarded as rational ends, and, statistically, ends such as starvation, thirst, misery, and isolation would be regarded as irrational ends. In any event, this is implicit in societal practice. Society, it seems, and not armchair theorists, is the arbiter of what ends count as rational and which do not.

In Book III, Part I, Section I, of the aforementioned treatise, the famous Is/Ought distinction is found:

" In every system of morality, which I have hitherto met with, I have always remark'd, that the author proceeds for some time in the ordinary way of reasoning, and establishes the being of a God, or makes observations concerning humans affairs; when of a sudden I am surpriz'd to find, that instead of the usual copulations of propositions, *is*, and *is not*, I meet with no proposition that is not connected with an *ought*, or an *ought not*. This change is imperceptible; but is, however, of the last consequence. For as this *ought*, or *ought not*, expresses some new relation or affirmation, 'tis necessary that it shou'd be observ'd and explain'd; and at the same time that a reason should be given, for what seems altogether inconceivable, how this new relation can be a deduction from others, which are entirely different from it. But as authors do not commonly use this precaution, I shall presume to recommend it to the readers; and am persuaded, that this small attention wou'd subvert all the vulgar systems of morality, and let us see, that the distinction of vice and virtue is not founded merely on the relations of objects, nor is perceiv'd by reason."

To return briefly to Book II, Part III, Section III, of Hume's *Treatise*, we discover the following claim:

"Reason is, and ought only to be the slave of the passions, and can never pretend to any other office than to serve and obey them."

Hume, here, does not seem "of a sudden surpriz'd" to encounter what might "seem altogether inconceivable." To be sure, we might regard the *is* and the *ought* here to be independent. For example, material objects fall at $\frac{1}{2}gt^2$, and, in addition, should do so.

Hume's "Is/Ought Challenge" is both interesting and important. It will be addressed shortly.

3. Open-Question Argumentation

The *locus classicus* for Open-Question Argumentation is G. E. Moore's *Principia Ethica*. One of the main themes of that book was the claim that "good" was a property, a simple property, a unique property, and a nonnatural property, analogous to, though very different from, the property of, say, "yellow." Supposedly, one could just "see," or recognize, somehow, whether or not "good" characterized, say, a situation or action, rather as one might just "see," or recognize, that a given object was yellow. Clearly, at this point, Moore was an objective cognitivist with respect to "good," though not, as it turned out, with respect to right. "Good" was fundamental, and independent of "right," but the converse was not the case. "Right" would be that which would be productive of "good," subject to some qualifications, in a form of ideal utilitarianism. Not surprisingly, Moore's views did not sweep, overwhelm, and conquer the world of ethics, but they did prove to be of great value, as they stimulated a storm of attacks, analyses, and reactions, the reverberations of which echo in philosophy today, over a century later. Many people apparently lacked Moore's intuitive powers and failed to detect any nonnatural properties. Others did not think it likely that good, whatever it might turn out to be, was simple, or unique. Others doubted that "good" was well understood as a property of any sort, either natural or nonnatural. Indeed, though this is historical conjecture, it seems likely that Moore, a convinced ethical cognitivist, ironically, and unintentionally, did much to precipitate the rise of noncognitivism. His book was largely aimed at ethical naturalism, the view that sense can be made of normative predicates, normative propositions, and such, in natural terms, for example, that normative predicates are naturalistic predicates, taking for their values natural properties. A simple example would be Jeremy Bentham's interpretation of the predicate 'good' in terms of pleasure. For example, on Bentham's analysis, there would be nothing to choose from, "between push pin and poetry," provided that the amount of pleasure produced was the same. In this way, the citizen would be provided with a foolproof way of deciding between reading William Butler Yeats and going bowling.

Moore's particular version of "open-question argumentation" was leveled against what he considered "the naturalistic fallacy," namely, in this case, understanding "good" to be a naturalistically comprehensible predicate.[117] The notion behind the "open-question argument" is that if, say, "good" were identical with pleasure, then asking if "pleasure" were good would be a "closed question," with an obviously affirmative answer. For example, if a circle is a plane figure bounded by a single curved line every point of which is equally distant from the point at the center of the figure, then asking if a plane figure bounded by a single curved line every point of which is equally distant from the point at the center of the figure is a circle, is a closed question, with an obviously affirmative answer. On the other hand, suppose someone were so confused,

---

[117] Philosophers are fond of labeling views with which they disagree "fallacies." Strictly, the views alluded to are seldom fallacies, e.g., errors in inference. They might be "mistakes," of one sort or another, but, strictly, they are seldom errors in inference. For example, deciding to manufacture automobiles from peanut butter is clearly a bad idea, a mistake, but it is not, strictly, a fallacy, as, for example, the fallacy of undistributed middle, the fallacy of denying the antecedent, of affirming the consequent, and such. Versions of the "naturalistic fallacy" may be divided into "analysis versions" and "derivationist versions." In "analysis versions," for example, a normative predicate, say, 'good' might be regarded as being definable, analyzable, or understandable in naturalistic terms, say, as a natural property of some sort, perhaps pleasure. In "derivationist versions, it is claimed that normative propositions can be derived from nonnormative propositions. Most attention is properly devoted to "analysis versions," if only because there are many ways in which, given the nature of logic, normative propositions can derived from non-normative propositions. (Moore, wisely, or luckily, is concerned with an "analysis version" of the alleged fallacy.) The sort of thing going on in the alleged "naturalistic fallacy," incidentally, would be going on in any attempt to analyze, say, 'good', at all. If "good" is truly a simple, unique, nonnatural property, then any attempt to make sense out of it in any other way must be a mistake, or "fallacy." For example, 'x is good = df. x is decreed by Deity D', 'x is good = df. x forwards the class struggle', 'x is good = df. x is approved by such-and-such a moral arbiter', and so on, would all commit the alleged "naturalistic fallacy." For this reason, the alleged fallacy might better have been called "the definist fallacy," or such, as was pointed out, long ago, by William K. Frankena. Hopefully the alternatives here are not that "good" is either a simple, unique, nonnaturalistic property or that it does not exist. Not only have Moore and others not proved that ethical naturalism is mistaken, but it is difficult to see how much empirical or scientific sense could be made out of axiological matters, as commonly understood, on any other approach. To be sure, these matters are extremely subtle and complex, and, ultimately, an existential commitment is undoubtedly necessary, for example, that health and happiness is preferable to disease and misery, and such.

as Moore might have supposed someone would be who might confuse a nonnatural property with a natural property, that he said that a plane figure having four equal sides and four right angles was a circle. Then it might be noted that one might agree that the figure in question was a plane figure with four equal sides and four right angles, but sensibly ask if it was a circle. Its circularity would surely be in question, and the question as to its circularity would be an "open question," and one which, in this case, obviously had a negative answer. Similarly, in Moore's case, one might agree that x was pleasant, but maintain that it was still an open question as to whether or not it was good. If that question was an open question, then pleasure could not be identified with good. Since the question remained open, it would have to be resolved negatively. If good was a unique property then it would be a mistake to identify it with anything different from itself. The entire line of argumentation, of course, at least in this instance, collapses if good is not some sort of simple, unique, nonnatural property, which it does not seem to be. Accordingly, one might, one supposes, now speak of the "nonnaturalistic fallacy." In any event, neither Moore's open-question argumentation, or later versions of similar argumentation, for example, that associated with R. M. Hare's Prescriptivism, have managed, at least in the eyes of many, to remove ethical naturalism from the field, and it stands today as the most likely alternative to axiological nihilism. Certainly there is a difference between 'x is the case' and 'x ought to be the case', a difference recognized by ethical naturalists, as well as others, but it does not follow from this, as we shall try to show, that nothing is better than anything else, that nothing is good or bad, that nothing is right or wrong, and so on.

There are several arguments pertinent to the cognitivity of value judgments, some better than others. We will, following, consider a representative selection amongst such arguments.

The point of this is to demonstrate the provisional acceptability of value judgments in historiography. The historiographer need not eschew a moral stance. Concerning such a stance he need not be timid, diffident, or embarrassed. In such matters there is truth, whether he attains it or not. It is probably impossible to do historiography, even shoddily, without a moral stance. In any event, the following arguments are intended to suggest that the historiographer is entitled to such a stance, without which, at least in my view, his work will fail to do justice to the richness and complexity of his subject matter. Historiography is not an ersatz physics, not an obscure, remote, and impecunious relative to the P sciences. It is something very different, something sturdy and independent. It is not an ugly duckling amongst the sciences. It is something different. It is its own swan.

2. Some Arguments[118]

1. Linguistic

The linguistic arguments call attention to parallelisms between axiological discourse and nonaxiological discourse, parallelisms which one would expect if both forms of discourse were cognitive. For example, both axiological and nonaxiological judgments are expressed in the indicative mood, which is the standard assertive form of discourse, e.g., 'x is good', 'x is right', etc.; both may be reworded as questions, e.g., 'is x good?', 'is x right?', etc.; both can be the subjects of cognitional verbs, such as 'know' and 'believe', e.g., 'I know x is good', 'I believe x is right', etc.; cognitive appraisal terms can be applied to them indifferently, such as 'true' and 'false', 'probable' and 'improbable', and so on, e.g., 'It is true that x is good', 'It is false that x is right', etc.; and the associated predicates can support indisputable noun forms, e.g., 'good' to 'goodness', 'right' to 'rightness', etc. In the way that one can say many things about "loud" or "blue," so, too, one can say many things, and seemingly very similar things, about, say, "good" or "right." Furthermore,

---

[118] Most of these arguments are, so to speak, in the public domain. It would be hazardous and unrewarding, to try to sort out what might be original here, if anything, and what unoriginal, to attempt to locate provenances, and such. In some cases, however, the source is clear. For example, the linguistic arguments are based on the work of Peter Glassen; the anthropological arguments are based on the work of Richard B. Brandt; and the self-governance arguments are found in work by theoreticians as different as C. I. Lewis and Ayn Rand.

disagreements in axiological matters often result in discussions, arguments, debates, and such, which seem to be authentic discussions, arguments, debates, and such. Certainly many provocative similarities obtain between nonaxiological discourse, which is indisputably cognitive, and axiological discourse, which seems to be, and is normally taken as, cognitive.

The linguistic arguments, in themselves, of course, cannot prove that axiological judgments are cognitive, as it is logically possible that two forms of discourse might share several, even most, properties, and yet differ with respect to cognitivity, with respect to truth-value possession. For example, most of the similarities noted here, between nonaxiological and axiological discourse could also be noted with respect to judgments whose cognitivity is likely to be more suspect, for example, judgments with respect to taste in furniture and clothing, and judgments with respect to music, art, literature, and such. Whereas one supposes that an interesting case could be made in such areas, a case for aesthetic cognitivity, for example, that Rembrandt was a good painter, Beethoven a good composer, Jonathan Swift a good writer, and so on, it would presumably be a different case, subject to different criteria, and different ends to be sought. In any event, cognitivity, say, choices between better and worse, is less likely to be suspect in dealing with things such as war and peace, health and disease, than in choosing upholstery and wall paper. The position of axiological cognitivity requires that some axiological judgments possess truth values. It does not require that all axiological judgments possess truth values, whether they do or not. Which judgments do or do not possess truth values would be a function of context, criteria, ends to be sought, and such. It might be noted that this sort of thing, though in a less subtle fashion, also appertains to nonaxiological judgments. For example, 'this board is four glumps long' or 'this rock is six bimiks in weight' are not cognitive either until one has some sort of framework in place that specifies glumps and bimiks, their relation to length and weight, how to apply such notions, perhaps in virtue of instrumentation, how to make particular determinations in particular cases, and so on. Too, moralities, as noted, may be incommensurable, with the result that the consequent diversity of cognitivities might tend to obscure the fact that all cognitivity is inevitably conditional. The incommensurability of some moralities does not entail, of course, that this is a situation which must, or will, or should, endure indefinitely, resulting in permanent, irreconcilable disagreement, resentment, hatred, conflict, and such, nor that there is nothing to choose from amongst such moralities. Given certain criteria, certain ends to be sought, and such, some will be demonstrably preferable to others. It is not known whether or not, indefinitely, diverse moralities will exist. That is an interesting question, on which one might speculate. We do know that there will be at least one morality. Without morality human life is impossible.

The linguistic arguments, though not decisive, as what arguments would be, do present an interesting *prima facie* case for cognitivity, and a case additionally formidable when conjoined with societal presuppositions in this area. For example, it seems unlikely that human populations would be confused or mistaken in a matter of such familiarity and importance. In any event, the linguistic arguments suggest that a burden of proof here, if one wished to think in such terms, would seem to be on the deniers of cognitivity rather than on its defenders.

Also, it seems that one would be owed some explanation for the remarkable parallelisms obtaining. Perhaps the denier of cognitivity might work something out in terms of linguistic conveniences, geodesics or economies, a natural, if unwarranted, transference of linguistic devices in one realm of discourse to a different realm of discourse, or such.

2. Intuitional

Intuitional arguments draw attention to a familiar fact of moral, or, more generally, axiological experience, the first-person felt forcefulness of value judgments, which, at least in clear cases, or cases taken to be clear, is an undeniable datum of consciousness.

For example, many people would react critically to the torture of small animals, to the abuse of a child, to the physical robbery of the weak and helpless, as opposed, say, to their legal robbery, and so on. Similarly, it would seem evident to many people that particular individuals would be unjustified in exempting themselves from rules by which others are expected to abide, and so on.

Sometimes these reactions, which often seem spontaneous and unmediated, are explained by, or attributed to, an inborn moral sense or sentiment, a faculty of intuition, a deity-bestowed conscience, a rational capacity to recognize such things, perhaps in virtue of the "eye of the mind," or such.

However such experiences might be explained, there is little doubt, phenomenologically, that they exist. They are quite real. The overwhelming majority of human beings have had such experiences.

Given the nature of such experiences and their pervasive familiarity, it is easy to understand the warrant for, and the persuasive power of, intuitionist-type arguments. To many people, such experiences are not only familiar and indisputable, but, beyond this, they are taken as revelatory of realities, almost as though, though in a different way, one might have the experience of "yellow," and then take this experience as revelatory of a reality, that of the color yellow.

Obviously there are a number of difficulties associated with this view, which, at least in our opinion, would encourage one to seek a better account of normative cognitivity.

1. Whereas a broad consensus might obtain amongst intuitions, the truth warrant here is individual-relative. If there is an objective, even if conditional, truth and falsity in these matters, one does not want the putative determination of the truth values involved to be relegated to personal intuition, which is a private matter. One would prefer something more public, more open to review. As an analogy, that one sees something as yellow is well and good, and is surely evidence that it is yellow, but it would be desirable, as well, to have some public correlates in place by means of which to confirm or disconfirm the claim. In the case of yellow, given putative, accepted correlations between the differential absorption and reflection of light waves in relation to a surface, and the visual experience of yellow, one has a check on whether or not the surface was actually yellow, or was not yellow, but was merely experienced as being yellow. In the normative realm the empirical correlates are not as transparent, though, given ascertainable instrumentalities,

the acceptance of ends, and such, they would also be, to a larger or smaller extent, publicly determinable. It is a bit like Mark Twain's observation that one praises freedom of speech and hopes that people will have the common sense not to use it. It is easy to do what one thinks is right, even when it is wrong.

2. Intuition works best with clear cases, but many moral situations are troublesome, and sometimes painfully, even tragically, unclear. In these situations, in cases of authentic moral incertitude, intuition is likely to be of small help. It may fail. In such cases, one wants to go beyond individual-relativity; one desires a more open, a more public, decision procedure.

3. There is probably something to be said for the notion of an inborn moral faculty or conscience, genetically coded moral traits which appear at given levels of maturation. Certainly animal studies suggest something of the sort. On the other hand, particular socializations, or conditionings, would seem to be of undeniable importance, particularly when a morality is generalized beyond an in-group. Primitive moralities, those, say, informing the social practices of groups anthropologically classified as primitive, are often ethnocentric and xenophobic. Human beings, as other animals, can be clearly conditioned variously. It is not only dogs which can be conditioned to be suspicious and savage, or trusting and gentle. The problem for intuitionism here is that intuitions, for all their seeming spontaneity and naturalness, may be the results of enculturation, of social engineering. An intuition, seemingly indisputable and infallible, may be a cultural product, a social artifact. Once again, one would like to move beyond intuitions, or, at least, to generate a methodology for adjudicating amongst them.

4. Lastly, intuitions may differ, and, when they differ, it seems that intuitionism, in itself, offers no procedure for resolving such disagreements, other than, say, intuiting again, or more deeply, and such.

It seems clear that one must move beyond intuitionism. On the other hand, it is possible that should an ultimate choice amongst ends arise, which it may not and need not, that one might choose amongst visions of how one would wish the world, and, if that surprising moment should occur, one might once more encounter intuitionism, or something much like it, an ultimate commitment, in virtue of which conducive, facilitating cognitivities might obtain.

3. Anthropological

Whereas selected anthropological findings often figure in arguments against cognitivity, for example, that this group thinks highly of virgin sacrifice and casting infants to crocodiles, whereas, interestingly, the next group does not, and so on, it seems seldom noticed, at least by enthusiasts for subjectivity, relativity, and such, that the great majority of anthropological findings in such areas run very much counter to the conclusions they draw, or would like to draw. Rather, and not surprisingly, given the necessary conditions for viable societies, there is massive cross-cultural agreement on moral matters. The agreement is not perfect, of course, but it is more than substantial; it is overwhelming. Let us suppose, contrary to apparent fact, that there is no single moral practice or idea which is universal. One conclusion which one might draw from that putative fact would be that morality is arbitrary, random, capricious, a mere matter of historical accident, or such. On the other hand, such a conclusion might overlook something even more obvious, something for which one need not search, something so evident it might not even be noticed, and that is the enormous amount of agreement which obtains from culture to culture, and time to time. It is a bit like looking either at the doughnut or the hole. If one looks only at the hole one might miss the doughnut. The following little schematism hints, however inadequately, at what is apparently the actual state of affairs in these matters. 'C_1' indicates Culture One, 'C_2' represents Culture Two, and so on, through five cultures.. The letters represent moral practices or ideas. The shaded letter may represent either the acceptance or rejection of a particular practice or idea. For example, the shaded A in the first line might represent the moral acceptance of a given practice. If that is the case, the unshaded A's would indicate the nonacceptance of the practice. If the shaded A is taken as representing the moral nonacceptance of the practice, then the unshaded letters would represent the acceptance of the practice, and so on. Thus, if the shaded A in the first line indicates a moral acceptance of, say, virgin sacrifice or casting infants to crocodiles, the nonshaded A's in the other lines would indicate a nonacceptance of that practice, and so on.

$$
\begin{array}{ll}
C_1 & A\ B\ C\ D\ E \\
C_2 & A\ B\ C\ D\ E \\
C_3 & A\ B\ C\ D\ E \\
C_4 & A\ B\ C\ D\ E \\
C_5 & A\ B\ C\ D\ E
\end{array}
$$

In the above schematism we are dealing with only five cultures and five elements in each culture. There are, of course, several thousand cultures, supposedly something in the neighborhood of five thousand. Similarly, whatever may be the case with the number of cultures, and how they are divided up, there would be a great many more moral practices or ideas in a culture than the five suggested in our small schematism. Now, it will be noted that, whereas there is no single practice or idea which is, say, accepted in every culture, or repudiated in every culture, something of which the subjectivist, or relativist, will take note, it should also be noted that a great deal of cross-cultural agreement exists, in our small sample, 80-percent agreement. If there were ten cultures and ten items in each culture, there would have been 90-percent agreement; if there had been a hundred cultures, and a hundred items in each culture, there would have been 99-percent agreement, and so on.

Beyond this it seems likely that much of the moral disagreement which does exist might be indexed either to differences in life conditions or differences in cognitive fields. If one could use regression analysis, or somehow screen out these differences, it seems likely moral agreement would be even more overwhelming. For example, if 19th Century Eskimos dropped elderly parents, who, say, were blind or feeble, and could no longer keep up with the sled, through holes in the ice or abandoned them, after sealing them up in igloos with some food, to keep them from polar bears, this might make moral sense, for example, as a means of making the survival of the group, and its children, more likely. On the other hand, a Roman *pater familias* would be less likely to look with favor on such a practice. Similarly, if a group seriously believes that good harvests, presumably essential for survival, require sacrificing virgins, who will presumably then enjoy a pleasant afterlife with the gods, or that casting infants to crocodiles is the best way to impress the gods on whom the welfare and future of the city depends, one can, at least, see the point of such practices. They make moral sense, however unacceptable or disgusting to others, given the cognitive field in question.

I think we may take it as a datum of anthropology that there is considerable cross-cultural moral agreement, and that it is a reasonable supposition that there would be even more moral agreement if one could screen out differences in life conditions and cognitive fields. 19th Century Eskimos, for example, doubtless loved their parents as much as 20th Century Eskimos, or anyone else, perhaps more, and, one supposes, Carthaginian mothers, as most mothers, were maternally solicitous for the welfare of their children. That seems to be a species characteristic, and not one limited to human beings. One supposes they thought that moral or religious duties, however onerous or terrible, were involved. Perhaps, too, they thought the sacrificed infants were destined to enjoy eternal bliss. It is hard to know. One supposes, incidentally, that differences in cognitive field account for most differences in moral practices and ideas, where they exist, probably much more so than differences in life conditions. Today, in a time of global communication, easy access to information, and such, one of the major factors tending to preserve the independence of cognitive fields, with its consequent effects on moral practices and ideas, is religion.. One of the interesting things about the average human being is that it can be taught anything, and, if encouraged, will manage to believe it.

Let us suppose the anthropological situation is, as we have suggested, one of large-scale agreement, and agreement which, presumably, would be even more substantial were it not for differences in life conditions and cognitive fields.

What results, then, if any, would such facts have on issues of cognitivity?

One supposes that this amount of agreement, and rationally

presumed potential agreement, suggests cognitivity. It is exactly what one would expect to be the case if cognitivity obtained. To be sure, the agreement is not perfect. Moreover, it seems possible, too, that even if life conditions were somehow standardized and a common cognitive field obtained, some residual differences might linger, or develop. That is not so hard to suppose. On the other hand, if the moral skeptic, nihilist, subjectivist, relativist, or whatever, before taking cognitivity seriously, will be satisfied with nothing less than 100-percent agreement in moral practices and moral ideas in all cultures, in all places, and at all times, past, present, and future, he has little to worry about. But, let us suppose, now, contrary to fact, that there was such agreement, everywhere, at least in the past, and now. That, in itself, again, would suggest cognitivity, indeed; how better might such a situation be explained; but it would not prove it. Agreement, obviously, does not entail truth. Agreeing that the Earth is flat does not make it flat, nor does agreeing that it is round make it round.

In any event, it seems that the noncognitivist position, if an empirical claim, should, at least in theory, be falsifiable. Otherwise, it is either analytic, a matter of definition, so to speak, and thus trivial, or it is gibberish, and thus meaningless. Presumably 100-percent agreement in all places and at all times, at least up to now, as we have seen, would not falsify it. What then would falsify it? It seems the noncognitivist should give us some help here. If he cannot, then he does not understand his own position.

On the other hand, it is fairly easy to see the sort of thing which would tend to confirm cognitivity, not some sort of pretentious, unverifiable, nonnatural, mystical cognitivity, but the practical cognitivity that most people take for granted, namely, a cognitivity dependent on ends generally accepted.

This brings us to species relativity.

4. Species Relativity

John Stuart Mill may have confused two senses of 'desirable', though this is not all that clear. He is frequently taken, and not irrationally, given the texts involved, to have committed an elementary "Is/Ought" fallacy, rather along the following lines.

<u>x is desirable</u> (x is capable of being desired)
x is desirable (x ought to be desired)

A famous passage pertinent to this occurs in Chapter IV of Mill's *Utilitarianism*, as follows:

"The only proof capable of being given that an object is visible, is that people actually see it. The only proof that a sound is audible, is that people hear it: and so of the other sources of our experience. In like manner, I apprehend, the sole evidence it is possible to produce that anything is desirable, is that people do actually desire it."

It is certainly true that not everything which is desirable, e.g., which is capable of being desired, is desirable, e.g., ought to be desired. Presumably no one, including John Stuart Mill, would believe that. The passage actually occurs in a larger context where the question of justifying ends is considered, not means to ends, but ends themselves. In such a situation, does it make sense to speak of proof? Mill is particularly concerned with "happiness" as such an end; how could one "prove" that happiness is good, or a good?

Later in the same passage, one finds:

"No reason can be given why the general happiness is desirable except that each person, so far as he believes it to be attainable, desires his own happiness. This, however, being a fact, we have not only all the proof which the case admits of, but all which it is possible to require, that happiness is a good: that each person's happiness is a good to that person, and the general happiness, therefore, a good to the aggregate of all persons. Happiness has made out its title as *one* of the ends of conduct, and consequently one of the criteria of morality."

Considering just the aforementioned passages from Mill, it seems several difficulties occur, first, the move from "capable of being desired" to "ought to be desired"; second, the notion that "proof" is involved here; at all; third, an apparent instance of the fallacy of composition, that if x if good for one person, it must be good for all persons; fourth, it is not clear that "general happiness" is an intelligible notion; fifth, a high level of "general happiness," whatever we take that to be, might be best attained by requiring a reduced level of happiness on the part of many; and, sixth, the notion of "happiness" may not be all that clear, or quantifiable, as Mill himself seems to recognize, distinguishing amongst different sorts, or higher and lower forms, of happiness. One might also note the vulnerability of this sort of thing to "open-question" attacks of the Moorean sort; for example, one might grant that x produces happiness, but still regard it as an open question whether or not x was good.

The above-quoted passages do not constitute Mill's finest hour.

One might suggest, however, that if his logic is in the wrong place, so to speak, his heart may be in the right place. One might wish he had not spoken of proof at all, let alone tried to supply one. On the other hand, if the way human beings are is not relevant to what is good for them, what would be relevant to what is good for them? Might there not be selected-for, evolved, genetically coded sets of dispositions, wants, desires, values, and such, and, if so, why should these things be regarded as irrelevant to axiological inquiries, proposals, recommendations, and such? If desire is not at least a clue to the desirable, what would afford such a clue? If the fact that human beings like water, and die without it, is not relevant to questions of the value of water to human beings, what would be?

That x can be desired and is desired does not entail that x is either prudentially or morally desirable, but it is not a bad place to start looking. In a sense, Mill is asking a question which cannot be answered, but his mistake is not in trying to answer it, but in asking it in the first place.

Ultimate ends, life, happiness, satisfaction, health, or such, whatever we take them to be, are not proven, but chosen, or accepted. They are that in terms of which demonstrability becomes possible; they themselves are existentially prior to demonstration; they are presupposed in demonstration; they, themselves, are indemonstrable.

Nature may have predetermined a human being to value life. That is quite possibly a biological given, that life will be valued. To choose life, however, as a value, in effect to say, I will that life should be valued; I choose it so; I will have it so; effects the transition from biological fact, that something is desired, to normative commitment, that something is desirable. The connection is not one of logic, but one of decision. And once, say, the end is accepted as desirable, then the relation of an x or a y, or whatever, to the end becomes a matter of fact, a matter of fact in terms of which cognitivity is epistemically emplaced.

Let us now return to "is" and "ought."

Hume is certainly correct, that something like 'x is the case', if a nonaxiological function, does not logically entail 'x ought to be the case', an axiological function. On the other hand, if it were true that "in every system of morality which he had hitherto met with," he had "always remark'd" and "had always been surpriz'd" to note the "imperceptible " move from "is' to "ought," one supposes he might have, one, given the alleged frequency involved, eventually been less surprised at the move from "is" to "ought"; two, pondered how he had managed to perceive an "imperceptible" change; and, three, asked himself if it was really likely that so many authors, indeed, all with which he was familiar in the area, were naive, ignorant, simplistically confused, or illogical, or if, rather, possibly, something was afoot which he might have overlooked.

The most likely explanation for so allegedly frequent a logistic phenomenon seems less likely to be an epidemic of inferential lapses, an inexplicable plague of invalidity and inattentiveness bordering on global amnesia, than a presupposed relationship between the nonnormative and the normative, one it might be thought unnecessary, even embarrassing, even insulting, to spell out, a relationship so obvious that it might be taken for granted. In short, if one is thinking in terms of argumentation, the connection would be implicit, and the argument would be an enthymeme. One of the enormous values of Hume's inquiry here, and one of a great philosopher's great contributions to philosophy, was to call attention to the problematicity of the interrelationship of the nonnormative and the normative, the nonaxiological and the axiological, and, in effect, ask for a disclosure of, and an open, rational defense of, or explanation for, what seems to be presupposed, or taken for granted.

I think the most plausible response to Hume, if one wishes to propositionalize the matter, is to see the linking premise in the argument, that which links the categorical nonaxiological singular or general premise with the axiological conclusion, as a hypothetical imperative with a nonaxiological antecedent and an axiological consequent. We will illustrate this hypothesis with two arguments, one with a narrow, specific purview and one whose purview is general, even universal. In both cases, an analogue to Hume's problem is evident. In Hume the question was how one could move, presumably validly, from an "is" statement to an "ought" statement. The analogue, in the hypothetical-imperative situation, is how might one justify the linking premise, with its "is" antecedent and its "ought" consequent. The answer to that, of course, as suggested earlier, is in terms of criteria accepted, or ends sought. As suggested earlier, the transition from fact, perhaps biological fact, say, that something is desired, to normative commitment, that something is desirable, appropriately desirable, should be desired, and such, is the result of a decision, or choice. To be sure, this "choice" need not be explicit or articulated, no more than a social contract needs be drawn up, witnessed, and signed. An acceptance of the criteria, or the end, implicitly or explicitly, is all that is necessary. Tropism, automatism, reflexivity are not pertinent; action is pertinent. The action must, as other forms of action, be either conscious, or such that it would be, upon reflection, consciously accepted. Choice is essential, implicit or explicit; without it action is impossible. And without choice, without action, normativity is impossible. Whereas normativity implies choice and action, neither action nor choice imply normativity. One might choose, for example, to ignore, avoid, or repudiate normativity. This would be a surprising choice, but it is logically possible. In theory, the noncognitivist, if consistent, makes such a choice. On the other hand, although choice does not imply normativity, one can choose normativity, and bring it into existence by choice, implicit or explicit. Once that is done, normativity does imply both action and choice.[119]

Once the commitment to normativity is made, which need not be made, but which is commonly made, one has an answer to Hume's puzzle.

By way of illustration, let us consider two arguments.

Argument 1:

In this first argument, our "is" statement, referred to by 'H', is 'Striking newborn babies heavily on the head with sledge hammers is likely to cause harm.' Our second statement, our "ought" statement, referred to by 'O', is 'You ought to refrain from striking newborn babies heavily on the head with sledge hammers.'

Recognizably, if our argument were:

$$\frac{H}{O,}$$

we would have an invalid argument, and Hume might continue to be "surpriz'd," and so on.

On the other hand, I think the argument which most people would be likely to have in mind in some such instance might be along the following lines:

$$\frac{H}{H \supset O}$$
$$\frac{H \supset O}{O}$$

which is a valid argument, a substitution instance of *modus ponens*. The second premise in the argument has an "is" antecedent and an "ought" consequent. It would be justified, generally, in terms of some value commitment or other, for example, perhaps in virtue of a general goal of promoting human flourishing, health, safety, life, or such.

One might, of course, question why one opts for human

---

119 For an analogue to the logic involved, putting aside modalities, one might consider the following two arguments, which are equivalent hypothetical syllogisms. 'A' stands for action; 'C' for choice, and 'N' for normativity.

$$\frac{\sim C \supset \sim A}{\sim A \supset \sim N} \qquad \frac{N \supset A}{A \supset C}$$
$$\sim C \supset \sim N \qquad N \supset C$$

It will be noted here that the arguments imply neither action, choice, or normativity, but only specify relationships amongst them. On the other hand, to put this in the material mode, although neither A nor C imply N, once you have N, say, by fiat, or commitment, then you will have both A and C.

flourishing, health, safety, life, or such, and not for human degeneration and debilitation, disease, fearful risk, death, or such. How do we know, for example, that Silenus, the satyr, was not right when he said that the best thing for a human being was not to be born at all, and the next best thing was to die as soon as possible. Perhaps from the satyrs' point of view, Silenus would have something. Perhaps humans were encroaching on their habitat, were dangerously competitive with respect to resources, were annoyingly voyeuristic, or such. But the answer to the question, of course, at least if the ends were taken as ultimate ends, would be that we so decreed desirability, that that was the way we liked it, that that was our choice. Biology may have predisposed us to such choices, and probably did, but that would be an independent consideration. We would still have chosen and with that choice normativity has come into being.

Let us now consider a second argument, which is much like the first, save in its greater generality.

Argument 2:

In the second argument, we have the following meaning assignments:

    Dx: x is detrimental to human flourishing
    Rx: Refrain from x
    h: The act of striking newborn babies heavily on the head with sledge hammers

1. (x) (Dx ⊃ Rx)
   (For every x, if x is detrimental to human flourishing, then refrain from x.)
2. Dh
   (The act of striking newborn babies heavily on the head with sledge hammers is detrimental to human flourishing.)
3. Dh ⊃ Rh   From 1, by universal instantiation.
   (If the act of striking newborn babies heavily on the head with sledge hammers is detrimental to human flourishing, then refrain from striking newborn babies heavily on the head with sledge hammers.)
4. Rh   From 2 and 3, by Modus Ponens
   (Refrain from striking newborn babies heavily on the head with sledge hammers.)

Here the first premise, a universal generalization, is axiological, reflecting a value commitment, as above. The second premise is a statement of empirical fact, an "is" statement. The conclusion is, in effect, an "ought" statement, e.g., 'You ought not strike newborn babies heavily on the head with sledge hammers'.

One trusts that this argument, however annoyingly explicit, will convince skeptics, dissuade any from striking newborn babies heavily on the head with sledge hammers who might be thinking of doing so, and resolve any doubts on the matter. To be sure, much depends on the first premise, which accepts human flourishing as an end and, in all consistency, the end accepted, enjoins refraining from acts which would frustrate that end. The relationship here is not one of entailment but of common sense, of rational consistency. As noted, one need not accept the end but, if the end is accepted, it is rational to act in terms of it. One might, one supposes, disapprove of human flourishing, and, if so, presumably the first premise might be replaced with another, perhaps to the effect that if an act were detrimental to human flourishing, then one should hasten to perform such an act, perhaps, in a given instance, supplying delivery rooms with sledge hammers. Moralities do differ, of course; for example, the morality of the criminally insane from that of those differently constituted or conditioned.

This approach clearly, though conditionally, as it involves choice, solves Hume's problem. It was extremely important to resolve that question, because it has enormous bearing on the relevance of what might be termed "natural good" and species relativity. Although normativity, at least in the human situation, transcends the nonnormative, as it must to ground a realistic and practical "ought," the realistic or practical "ought" would be capricious and unanchored, even implausible or meaningless, were it not founded in, and related to, the nature of, the needs and desires of, a relevant form of life. To make this sort of thing more clear, consider plants and animals. Clearly, from the point of view of, say, flourishing, there is a "natural good" from the point of view of all forms of life. Nature is such that it determines under which conditions a plant or animal will thrive, and under what conditions it will not thrive. This is a matter of nonaxiological fact. This "natural good," in the sense of what conduces to species flourishing, species thriving, species health, and such, is given by nature. It is not to be rationally argued with, no more than the number of appendages, the existence of a tail or not, the existence of fur or not, claws or not, and so on. Similarly, in this context, concepts such as "natural good," "flourishing," "thriving," and such, should be regarded as value-neutral. Obviously the "natural good" of a parasite may not conduce to the health of its host, the "natural good" of the lion to its prey, and so on. It makes little sense to say that a bacillus has an obligation to infect, a lion the duty to pull down zebras, that a barracuda should attack smaller fish and a snake to strike. Obviously, often, the flourishing of one species is detrimental to that of another. "Natural goods," in this value-neutral sense, differ considerably. Clearly, the "natural good" is species relative.

As the human being is a form of life it, too, has, in the sense specified, a value-neutral sense, a "natural good," what will contribute to its flourishing, thriving, health, and such. There is no doubt that this "natural good" would predispose a human being to axiological commitments, that it would exercise a considerable influence in such matters. It would be incomprehensible if it did not. The whole business of human normativity would be unintelligible were it not for its intimate and indisputable relationship to a human value-neutral "natural good." One moves from the nonnormative to the normative level when one accepts one or another value-neutral "natural good" as an end to be sought. That choice, or acceptance, made, it becomes a matter of common sense, of rational consistency, to seek to realize the end. Not to do so would result in pragmatic paradox, a self-defeating, or self-frustrating act. In such a way is the transition effected between the "desired' and the "desirable," by choice, by commitment, by having it so. The "ought" is contextually justified as a rational expedient to attain the desiderated end. "If you want A, do B." The relationship here is not one of logic, but of practicality, of common sense, of rational consistency.

Accepting that for all forms of life, and all animals, there is a "natural good" and accepting, further, that in a rational animal, one in whom choice exists, this natural good may be elevated to the status of an end to be pursued, not necessarily reflectively, but by choice, implicit or explicit, one recognizes a plausible nonaxiological foundation, on which it is natural to erect an axiological superstructure. Given the nonlogical, but plausible, natural relationship between these two moments, the nonaxiological and the axiological, an implicit cognitivity exists, a cognitivity which is grounded in choice, a choice indexed to "natural good."

Let us suppose, in contrast, something absolutely arbitrary, which could ground a cognitivity, though frivolously. Let us suppose, as suggested earlier, that someone wishes to manufacture automobiles from peanut butter. Given that end, it is true, and thus cognitive, that one should lay in large amounts of peanut butter. If cognitivity can obtain in such a case, then it is obvious that cognitivity could obtain in a case where one accepted a "natural good" as an end to be desired and consequently sought. In such a case, it would then be true or false, and thus cognitive, that such and such a practice, or ruling, would conduce to the realization of the end, say, human flourishing, thriving, health, or such. And, in this case, the end is not frivolous, or capricious, or random, but one founded in the realities of nature. In this way, species relativity, facts of nature, can ground a morality, deeply and importantly, by constituting its first moment, an end given, prior to its second moment, an end accepted.

A cognitivity is thus produced which takes human nature, biology, and evolution seriously.

This seems not inferior to denying them, or forgetting about them.

Whereas the notion of flourishing, species relativity, nature, and such, seem considerably important in these matters, and germane to any plausible understanding of them, it is not surprising that problems abound. For example, there is nothing here which would require any interspecific considerations, any references to consistency, any distinction between individual flourishing and group flourishing, or any reservations with respect to modalities of flourishing, or thriving.

For example, we would not expect the barracuda to express concern for the welfare of small fish, nor lions for zebras, and such. They would not be members of the same species. There is little worked out here, as well, pertaining to moral consistency and generalizability. One might encounter conflicts between, say, social utility and individual rights, between the general welfare and justice, and such. It might also be the case that what is conducive to the flourishing of a given individual or group might be inimical to what would be conducive to the flourishing of another individual or group. Intraspecific aggression is common amongst species. For example, amongst humans, force, war, expropriation, oppression, hatred, and such, have been endemic. Lastly, who knows what might contribute to flourishing. Perhaps a species might thrive best, or be healthiest, and least inhibited, and sleep most soundly, if it founded its life on lies, and dreams, if it lived materially, if it abandoned inquiry, if it forswore the search for truth, if it ceased to see the stars.

5. Presupposition of Science and Technology

A familiar and clear example of axiological cognitivity is furnished by science and technology, for example, medicine, clinical psychology, engineering, agriculture, and such, all recognize, and seek to achieve, agreed-upon, ascertainable goods. Presumably noncognitivists are as well aware of this sort of thing as anyone else, but it seems they seldom consider the relationship of these facts, if any, to their denial of truth values to normative assertions. For example, a strong, safe bridge is presumably a better bridge than one which is likely to collapse shortly, and unexpectedly. On the other hand, one supposes someone might prefer thrilling bridges which will soon collapse unexpectedly. Different cognitivities would be involved. Perhaps that is the sort of thing noncognitivists might have in mind. On the other hand, this sort of thing would not would not prove the nonexistence of cognitivities but rather, their diversity.

To be sure, not all instrumentalities need be approved. Surely some burglar tools are better than others, some making, say, jimmying windows easier than others. Similarly, given the ends in view, doubtless there are good bayonets, good machine guns, good poisons, good torture devices, good bacteriological weapons, good hydrogen bombs, and such.

Cognitivities may appertain to even bad goods, so to speak.

6. Human Consciousness and the Imperative to Action

The human being is a creature of volitional self-consciousness. Much of his behavior is not automatic. He must do; he must decide his own actions. This necessitates a criterion for action, and this criterion involves goals, which involve perceived betters or goods. Otherwise human action would be incomprehensible. This suggests that value judgment is implicit in the human condition.

This is an argument well worth noting, but it may suggest more than its proponents might wish. Whereas there are doubtless risks involved in an attempt to understand animals, say, dogs and cats, it seems likely that they, too, are creatures of volitional self-consciousness, and so, too, for squirrels and sparrows. They give every indication of being conscious, with all due respect to René Descartes who, presumably for religious reasons, at least pretended to regard them as insensible mechanisms, ingeniously constructed automatons. Similarly, although one doubts that they are much given to introspection, it seems likely that they are self-conscious, as well, for example, that they are well aware when they are hungry, angry, in pain, tired, contented, frightened, and so on. It is hard to say how far down the phylogenetic scale this sort of thing might go. As one ascends the phylogenetic scale, approaching the top, where we place ourselves, volitional self-consciousness seems even more likely, as, for example, with monkeys, chimpanzees, gorillas, and such. Indeed, some of these primates, it seems, can converse in one or more sign languages, which is more than I can do.

The important question here, of course, for our purposes, is not how widely spread volitional self-consciousness might be, but its bearing on normativity. Whereas normativity, as we usually think of it, would require volitional self-consciousness, it is not clear that volitional self-consciousness, as we normally think of it, must involve normativity. For example, let us suppose we have four organisms, O_1, O_2, O_3, and O_4.

O_1 sees an object, say, food, and, instinctively, automatically, approaches the object.

O_2 sees an object, say, food, feels an inclination to approach the 0object, and yields to that inclination.

O_3 sees an object, say, food, feels it is appropriate to approach the object, feels it "ought," as a *natural* biological sensation, to approach the object, and does approach the object.

O_4 sees an object, say, food, feels it is appropriate to approach the object, feels it "ought," as a *natural* biological sensation, to approach the object, and then *chooses*, implicitly or explicitly, to approach the object.

I think that normativity is well thought of as occurring only in the fourth case, that of Organism O_4. Presumably, in the fourth case, first, an end is recognized and accepted; second, it is decided that the end will be then pursued; third, it is understood that the end cannot be achieved without action, and thus, since one wishes to realize the end, one ought to act; and thus, fourth, one decides to act; and, fifth, one acts. Presumably, in an actual situation, all this would take place in a flash. The big difference in the fourth case is that the "ought" is axiological rather than nonaxiological. It transcends pure behavior, mere natural response, and requires action, not simple action, a mere doing, but action chosen, or willed, implicitly or explicitly. Note that, in this example, the fourth case builds upon the third case, presupposes it, and would make no sense were it not for the third case, but, involving choice, implicit or explicit, we have a rational or normative "ought" involved, as opposed to an automatic, nonnormative, simply biological "ought," which is only a sensation.

Thus, with respect to this famous argument, it seems to me, at any rate, that volitional self-consciousness does not, in itself, unless we understand words in a certain favorable way, entail normativity. Thus we cannot derive normativity, and normative cognitivity, from volitional self-consciousness, *per se*, although there is little doubt that normativity presupposes, or entails, to speak loosely, volitional self-consciousness. If one were to build normativity into volitional self-consciousness, it seems to me that that would beg the question, and also, that we would then be obliged to attribute normativity to, say, squirrels and sparrows, and I am not sure it is well found there. This in no way denies, of course, that squirrels and sparrows have feelings, and natures, might experience genetically conditioned imperatives, act in terms of such feelings and sensations, and so on. I would not be surprised if they functioned, and perhaps often, at the level of our case three, above. To be sure, who understands these things? Perhaps they might have their own responses to a Hume with feathers or a fluffy tail.

So, let us try to assess this famous argument, that from volitional self-consciousness.

It is impossible to assess any argument, unless its premise-set is inconsistent, or its conclusion analytic, without a clear understanding of its projected conclusion. Only with some idea of the putative conclusion is it possible to consider the relationship of the premise-set to the conclusion, whether the conclusion is entailed or not, or supported or not.

Unfortunately exactly what might emerge from the argument, which would be relevant to our concerns, is not all that clear.

The essence of the premise-set seems to be that the human being is a self-governing creature, that such a creature must choose amongst alternatives, that such choices will be made in the light of criteria or goals, and that criteria or goals require judgments between the better and the worse, and so on.

Accordingly, we might take the conclusion to be that value judgment is implicit in the human condition.

A number of problems suggest themselves.

1. Given supposed phylogenetic continuities, alluded to earlier, dealing with volitional self-consciousness, the need to choose amongst alternatives, and such, this approach would seem to generalize normativity to a surprising, and perhaps unwelcome, extent. For example, it seems possible that, say, Norwegian rats and raccoons choose, make decisions, and act in terms of goals, perceived goods, and such, as well as human beings. This approach, then, unless the rats and raccoons are mere automatistic, stimulus-response organisms, would seem to argue for, say, Norwegian rat normativity, raccoon normativity, and such. Certainly we cannot limit value judgments to judgments actually expressed in a language, first, because linguistic formulation seems unnecessary to value judgments, as animals appear to make them, and, second, human beings make value judgments constantly, which they have not bothered to articulate in one language or another. I, personally, have no objection to animal normativity, but its possibility makes

clear the problematicity of trying to distinguish between the natural and the nonnatural, the biological and the axiological, the nonnormative and the normative. If we wish to deny normativity to animals, it is not clear we have the right to claim it for ourselves. Is value judgment natural or nonnatural, a form of the nonaxiological or a form of the axiological? The problems which so recently engaged us, in trying to overcome Hume's is/ought challenge, Moore's reservations, the supposed difficulties of the "naturalistic fallacy," and such, would seem to arise within this approach.

One could accept, say, that value judgment is implicit in the human condition, and other conditions, and still puzzle about the grounding of a more-than-descriptive axiological "ought." It seems that one has not, here, moved beyond the "desired" to the "desirable."

2. Even a committed proponent of the D Hypothesis would presumably accept the data in question, but would presumably doubt the interpretation. In short, he would presumably accept that value judgments *seem* to be implicit in the human condition, but that what seem to be independent, rationally derived value judgments are actually no more than the playing out of the universal tape. The plausibility or implausibility of this hypothesis would be a function of the plausibility or implausibility of the D hypothesis itself. As suggested earlier, regardless of the truth or falsity of the D Hypothesis, if one is to live, as one usually thinks of living, one must live as though it were false.

3. One supposes that noncognitivists are as much aware of value judgments as anyone else. In theory, however surprisingly, it seems they would deny truth values to such judgments. Thus, in order to abet the project of a normative cognitivity, one would have to enlarge on, or supplement, the volitional self-consciousness argument in such a way as to allow for truth-value possession on the part of at least some value judgments. Truth-value possession, naturally, is taken for granted, in context, by proponents of the volitional self-consciousness argument. It is just not explicit in the argument, as I have presented it. It is easy enough to argue for it independently, for example, as I have done, in terms of criteria- or goal-focused instrumentalisms, of conditional cognitivities, and such.

Despite its difficulties and shortcomings, or seeming difficulties and shortcomings, the volitional self-consciousness argument makes it clear, at least, that a self-governing creature will, and must, act as though value judgments are necessary, important, authentic, and cognitive.

That may not be coercive, but it is something to think about.

7. The Possibility of Axiological Error

It is a common human experience that value judgments may be mistaken, for example, that a perceived good does not materialize, and such. Error points to truth. Without truth error is impossible.

8. Nonaxiological/Axiological Belief Convergence

The most common of way of attempting to resolve ethical disagreement, short of force, physical or psychological, is to explore, marshal, and compare nonaxiological beliefs. Such beliefs are commonly taken as having a bearing on normative disputes. For example, if a given practice tends to have positive effects, for example, resulting in a general, or group-relative, increase of happiness over unhappiness, that is usually, *ceteris paribus*, taken as a point in its favor, whereas, if a given practice tends to have negative effects, for example, resulting in a general, or group-relative, increase of unhappiness over happiness, that is usually, *ceteris paribus*, taken as a reason for doubting or suspecting, abolishing or revising, the practice. Similarly, changes in nonaxiological beliefs pertaining, say, to the existence of, or the nature of, gods can make a difference in ethical matters. As these views shift so, too, might views with respect to sacrificing virgins, casting infants to crocodiles, and such. Similarly, one's nonaxiological views about Macedonians, Persians, Hittites, and such, would presumably have a considerable bearing on whether or not it is a good idea to open the gates of the city. It seems undeniable that axiological views are influenced by nonaxiological views, and sometimes dramatically; for example, the heliocentric theory of the solar system, the theory of evolution, the discoveries of depth psychology, and such things, have shaken up world views, and the ethical universes associated with them.

There is, statistically, clearly, an indisputable relationship between nonaxiological and axiological views. Similarly, on the whole, the more agreement on nonnormative matters, the more agreement on normative matters. That is probably why some establishments, presumably in order to protect their power, position, status, wealth, prestige, and such, attempt to control, as far as possible, nonnormative awareness and knowledge, to control, as far as possible, inquiry, research, access to information, education, travel, contact with strangers, and so on.

This nonaxiological/axiological belief convergence suggests cognitivity, e.g., that morality, ethics, value judgment, and such, are intimately correlated with a nonaxiological belief system and are not mere matters of idiosyncratic commitments, historical accidents, random occurrences, inexplicable whims, or such. Accordingly, as nonaxiological, or nonnormative, belief systems converge, one could expect a similar convergence of axiological, or normative, orientations.

This hypothesis is schematically represented in the following diagram, where a positive correlation is projected between nonaxiological and axiological beliefs, or nonnormative and normative beliefs.

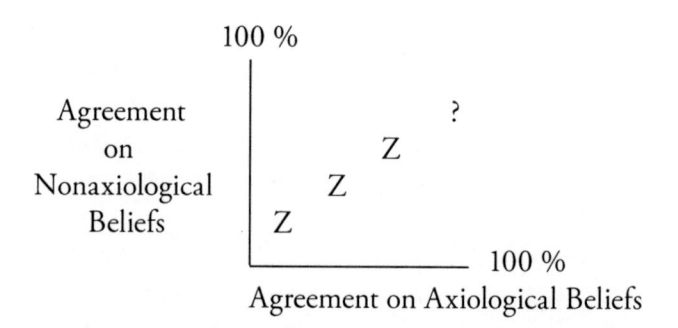

```
                    100 %
                      |
  Agreement           |              ?
     on               |         Z
 Nonaxiological       |      Z
   Beliefs            |   Z
                      |_____ 100 %
                    Agreement on Axiological Beliefs
```

Whereas there is little doubt, given the evidence of history, of social evolution, of cultural interaction, and such, that the correlation projected above is real, that it demonstrates an important bearing of nonaxiological beliefs on axiological beliefs, that it anchors morality, and such, in the "real world," that it favors empirical inquiry into ethical concerns, that it favors ethical naturalism, that it suggests cognitivity, and such, it does not demonstrate, nor guarantee, nor even make likely, the eventual emergence, in itself, of a single, universal, global moral or ethical stance.

First, although it is a matter of established anthropological fact, as we have seen, that there is considerable cross-cultural agreement on axiological matters, and, furthermore, as we shall shortly note, this agreement is easily explained, in terms of the social conditions requisite for the existence and continuance of a society, it is nonetheless true that there are various portions of existent normative spectrums which are not essential to the existence and continuance of the society in question, perhaps portions dealing with homage to the gods, dietary practices, pilgrimages, ornamentation, human sacrifice, or such, which are, for most practical purposes, immune from direct refutation, having withdrawn themselves into inaccessible precincts, where they may linger indefinitely, beyond the perils of encountering the scalpels of empiricism. Such beliefs may eventually collapse, be forgotten, be abandoned, perish from neglect, die of boredom, be replaced, or whatever, but, being unreal, nothing real can touch them. Saying nothing, making no real difference in the world, they cannot be falsified. They remain secure in their remote semantic fastnesses. This being the case, one could, in theory, have incommensurable moralities endure to the end of time.

Second, axiological beliefs can be conditioned, controlled, engineered, manipulated, rigged, and such, and this fact, tilting the moral field, so to speak, could delay, if not preclude, the effects of a rational examination of axiological beliefs in the light of their compatibility with, or relationship to, nonaxiological beliefs. For example, if someone is taught that it is immoral, even hazardous, to look into the facts of, say, astronomy, biology, psychology, or whatever, then he may never do so.

On the other hand, it does seem to be true that there is this positive correlation between belief sets, nonaxiological and axiological.

For example, if one climbs Mount Olympus and fails to detect gods this does not prove the gods do not exist, as they might be elsewhere, say, out to lunch, or on another mountain, or behind some star or other, or perhaps they are invisible, but it does give one something to think about.

9. Societal Prerequisites

Several times, in the course of this work, we have called attention to axiological cognitivity, noting its reality, indexed to criteria or ends. Even an arch noncognitivist. such as A. J. Ayer, acknowledges that one might address moralities objectively, inquiring into them, presumably in the fashion of the anthropologist, sociologist, historiographer, and such. He would certainly have acknowledged that a given individual might, in a given culture, take something like 'Stealing is wrong' to be cognitive, and true. Going beyond the data, an Ayer might then interpret 'Stealing is wrong' as, say, an expression of disapproval of stealing. That is certainly a possible interpretation of the data, but it is only one interpretation of the data, and it seems an unlikely interpretation of the data, certainly from the point of view of the moral agent in the culture in question. It does not account for the agent's viewpoint, which, it seems, should be relevant. Does the agent not really understand what he is doing? Is the agent really misinformed about his own practice? Perhaps an Ayer, if he should be so careless as to let slip an utterance such as 'Stealing is wrong', not to remonstrate with a mugger, but to let the mugger know he disapproved of having his wallet taken, is only expressing a feeling, or such, but it is unlikely the mugger, or anyone else, would understand it along those lines. One could well imagine an apprehended mugger pointing out to a judge that 'stealing is wrong' merely expressed a feeling, and, accordingly, stealing not being wrong, no truth value involved, no crime had been committed, or a repentant mugger lugubriously lamenting not that he had done something wrong, but, rather, that he had once occasioned the expression of a negative feeling. In any event, there seems no reason not to accept the victim's, the mugger's, the judge's, and the society's interpretation of 'stealing is wrong' as being both cognitive, and true. One needs, then, an interpretation as to how it might be both cognitive, and true, or, possibly, cognitive, and false. What one is looking for here is not a observation that under certain conditions a particular locution occurs, merely that particular words are said, say, the words 'Stealing is wrong', but an account of why, in the society in question, such a locution, such words, are taken as expressing a truth-value-bearing entity, and why, relative to that culture, given its criteria .and ends, the locution is, in fact, true, or false. An account of this is easily given in terms of conditional cognitivities, social ends in view, and such, and this interpretation is not only plausible, but has the good sense to take seriously the viewpoint of the agent, the society, in question, and such. One need not accept the criteria, and the desiderated ends, and such, but, in the light of those criteria, and such ends, the locution is cognitive, and true, or false. One need not accept the criteria, the ends, and such, as noted. One might favor stealing, rejoice in theft, express enthusiasm for thieves, feel morally obligated to pick pockets, and so on. One might design a society with such zests and ardors in mind, a society in which 'stealing is wrong' is false, and 'stealing is right' would be true. But that would be a different society.

Beyond questions of a particular society, one encounters questions fundamental to any possible human society. Rather clearly, the statistical adherence to certain basic moral principles, e.g., honesty, fairness, civility, truthfulness, cooperativeness, reliability, industriousness, responsibility, and such, is a necessary condition not only for the thriving of a society, but for its actual existence.

One need not accept the end of a stable society, and perhaps so, if one is either a beast or a god, as Aristotle speculated, but if one accepts the end of a society, that one wants a society, with its comforts, securities, and productivities, then it is rational to recognize and accept the instrumentalities essential to its existence, and continuance. And, once these ends, certain ends, are accepted, morality becomes largely a matter of what must be done to realize the ends in question. There is nothing mysterious or mystical, or arbitrary or capricious, about this. Things are the case, or not. The noncognitivist seems to miss the point of all this. "If you want A, you ought to do B." That can be true, prudentially, surely. I think that is indisputable. And the prudential "ought" becomes a moral "ought," by fiat, by acceptance, by decision. Thus, once, again, by choice, implicit or explicit, individuals accept, and act, and we have anew the institutionalizing of a normativity.

There is no doubt, sociologically, that a morality is a necessary condition for the viability of a society. Accordingly, relative to the end of preserving and enhancing a society a variety of means, moral and otherwise, are relevant, and, in terms of these means and their relationship to the desiderated end, cognitivity obtains, as much as in weaving, building walls, and designing aircraft. That a morality is a societal prerequisite guarantees the cognitivity of a number of criteria- or end-related axiological judgments, a fact pertinent to these matters, and one which it is important to recognize. On the other hand, societal viabilities, beyond a core of basic moral necessities, may be variously purchased. The societal-prerequisite argument, even when accepted, carries one only so far. It leaves a great deal of moral latitude, particularly in theory. Beyond a basic core of moral necessities, it is certainly possible that some significant moral differences might be found, for example, with respect to blood sacrifice, the treatment of foreigners, and so on. Given the possible latitude in theory, beyond a basic core of moral necessities, it is interesting that the amount of cross-cultural agreement is as high as it is. One supposes this is due in part to genetic predispositions in human nature, cultural diffusion, and the evolutionary rationalism resulting from practical social selections, these associated with long-term systemic processes.

10. The Implausibility of an Alternative

That there is no reason to prefer health to disease, happiness to misery, comfort to discomfort, and so on, seems implausible. What would a proponent of the "Hume Indifference Principle" accept as evidence that he was mistaken? If there is no possible counterevidence to his claim, his claim is not an empirical claim, but one which is covertly analytic, and thus empirically vacuous. Human nature, biology, rationality, logic, and such, set things up. One supposes they could have been set up differently, but they weren't. Moral principles, involving what works and what doesn't, are analogous to the principles of medicine, agriculture, and engineering, not to the customs pertaining to cuffs or no cuffs, hemlines, table settings, china patterns, the width of neckties, wallpaper patterns, and such.

3. The Relevance of Axiology to Historiography

Most human beings live moral cognitivity. If they did not, differences of opinion in these matters would be decided not with guns and knives, but rocks and clubs. Rationality and morality have turned packs into peoples, and groups into societies. The massive thrust of opinion in all cultures and societies, historically, and probably prehistorically, and there is some suggestion of this sort of thing in animal studies, has been in favor of cognitivity. Certainly it is society's position. Accordingly, in an effort to make the most sense out of pervasive opinion and practice, we have suggested the hypothesis of cognitivity, that as the best interpretation of the data. In view of this, we have set forth evidence in favor of that hypothesis, and, frequently, with at least some fairness, tried to give a sense of counterevidence. These matters remain controversial, and I am unaware of any account which can pretend to be the last word, the definitive view, in these important, subtle, complex matters. Too, I suspect that the crucial thing here is that moral cognitivity is lived, not that it is proclaimed. Thus, whether or not one believes that axiological judgments are true or false, or neither, is less important than the fact that one lives as though they were.

We have, of course, tried to make a case that they are.

That seems to me, for several reasons, the best case.

For those of you who are familiar with these matters, it will be recognized that what we have presented here is a case for ethical naturalism, supplemented with an existential conception of criteria and end choice. Beyond this, the existential commitments suggested, while existential, are indexed to human nature. Human nature does not logically entail particular commitments, but, given human nature, some such commitments are more practical, more sensible, and, I should like to think, more rational than others.

Ethical naturalism has at least four significant values here. First, it fits in well with empiricism, and requires no dubious or unverifiable commitments to either mystical or unusual routes to knowledge, special moral faculties, the views or decrees of hypothesized supernatural entities, and such. Second, it provides a way of accounting for the cognitivity presupposition of all cultures with which I am familiar, namely, provides a comprehensible interpretation of normativity congenial to the data. Third, it provides a platform for a naturalistic, common-denominator humanism, which, given the significant amount of cross-cultural moral agreement, hitherto noted, allows for a common moral ground, one likely to be shared, up to a point, even by nonnaturalistic systems. And, four, with the establishment of cognitivity in axiological matters, it entitles historiographers, should they be so inclined, to deal unreluctantly and unapologetically with all aspects of their subject matter, in both its nonaxiological and axiological dimensions.

The primary problems of ethics in historiography, as noted earlier, are not in the ethics of practice, which are generally accepted, and scarcely controversial, unless perhaps in the case of scholar activists, political sycophants, frauds, liars, propagandists, and such. There is general agreement, for example, that historiographers should try to be informed, judicious, honest, and fair, that they should familiarize themselves with relevant evidence, should not neglect relevant evidence, should not betray their work by twisting accounts, by deliberately misrepresenting facts, should try, as they can, to argue cogently, and so on. The primary problem of ethics in historiography has to do with the legitimacy or illegitimacy of allowing value judgment into the work itself. For example, is there a legitimate role for axiological orientation and conviction in historiography?

We have tried to suggest that there is.

Three observations would seem in order.

First, for reflective historiographers, which I fear is a distinct minority, this is an extremely important matter. That is the justification for the time we have spent here, dealing with questions of normative cognitivity, to develop a premise-set from which certain procedural and methodological conclusions may be cogently drawn. Most historiographers, as nearly as I can tell, are uncritical and unreflective. They do not ask themselves about such things. They do their work, and don't worry about it. Perhaps that is best for those who can manage it. Certainly life is less complex that way. Over thin ice they skate rapidly, not noticing, or perhaps pretending not to notice, the ice is thin, perhaps very thin. They manipulate terminologies without inquiring into them; they seem innocent of historiographical ontology, epistemology, and so on. They seem little interested in the nature of the entities they allegedly deal with, and seem unconcerned, or little concerned, with time, truth, knowledge, causality, criteria for pattern, tests for their claims, and such, as if all this had nothing to do with their work; they seem oblivious of profound challenges to the very credibility of their discipline, do not explicitly address its limitations and nature, and so on. Perhaps that is the way to live. Who, other than Socrates, has ever supposed the unexamined life is not worth living? Certainly unexamined lives are well worth living, like other lives. Why not? Especially when examining one's life can be a bother. But some individuals, historiographers and others, for better or for worse, will examine their lives. If they do not live better, they will live more profoundly.

We think an important question facing the historiographer, indeed, perhaps the single most important question facing him, is the legitimacy or illegitimacy of axiological orientation and conviction in his work, the role, say, if any, of an intrinsic ethics, or an intrinsic normativity, in his work. The answer given to this question will essentially determine the nature of his discipline.

Second, one of the dangers facing historiography, partly an understandable consequence of the general prestige in which "science" is held today and partly a result of the uneasy attempt to ensure oneself, and society, of the intellectual credibility and integrity of one's discipline, is its ambivalence vis-à-vis the paradigm sciences, the P sciences, such as physics, chemistry, biology, and such. As noted, one can narrow or enlarge the borders of "science" in such a way as to accommodate or exclude historiography. Given the obviously radical differences between historiography and the P sciences, this is little more, then, than a semantic exercise. A definition is not going to make historiography more or less like physics, and such sciences. The integrity and importance of historiography, where it is responsibly practiced, is unassailable, as much so as the integrity and importance of physics, where it is responsibly practiced. Both, where honestly and responsibly practiced, are to be esteemed. The risk here is that an attempt on the part of historiography to emulate the P sciences will result in a betrayal of its own best and highest nature. In the P sciences, as they deal with a value-free subject matter, there is no role for an intrinsic, as opposed to an extrinsic, ethics. Such an insertion would be irrelevant, pointless, distractive, and intrusive. On the other hand, should historiography attempt to adopt a similarly antiseptic and disengaged methodology it would falsify and undermine any adequate approach to its subject matter. It would, in so far as possible, treat action as though it were behavior, motion as though it were meaning, an inside as though it were an outside, understanding as though it were description. It would sterilize and reduce its discourse, substitute surface for depth, and, ultimately, shrink from truth. It is important for historiography to put aside what is honorable but alien, and address itself to what is honorable and akin.

Thirdly, is it possible for historiography to repudiate or eschew the normative, even if it wished to do so? Perhaps, at its own cost. But I think it would be difficult, perhaps impossible to do so, at least if one wished to emerge with a treatment which was recognizably historiographical. We have noted that historiography deals with a value-rich subject matter, that its tool, a natural language, is value-laden, and that the historiographer himself is likely to be a creature with profound axiological views and commitments, which he presumably takes with great seriousness and, if moral, will not betray. He then confronts history. How can he see it except through his own eyes? Presumably we would not expect him to be, nor ask him to be, dishonest to his own vision.

If moral judgments are warranted, it seems the historiographer should be entitled to make them. If they are warranted and he denies them to himself, then he is presenting an incomplete, distorted picture of history. If they are not warranted, then he may make them or not, as he pleases. It is not wrong to do so, as, in such a case, right and wrong would no longer exist.

If there are normative facts in history, why should they not be acknowledged, why not be reported, and, to the best of the historiographer's ability, as they were? We have noted that value judgment, in many ways, enters historiography, and must do so. One carves events, with something in mind, one weights factors as one assesses them, one chooses what one will report, and in what length, and in what detail, with what neutrality, or implicit partisanship, with what remoteness, or poignancy and vividness, and so on. One may try to conceal one's views, even from oneself, but they are likely enough to be evident to others. What is one to do, present a historical horror, as though it were not a horror? Is one to look upon the costs of history, the shed blood, the misery, and suffering with clinical indifference? Supposing that it were possible to view the dislocations and cataclysms of history as though they might be no different, in essence, from the shiftings of geological strata in distant epochs, is it morally appropriate to do so? There is no escape here into the charade of pretending that one can separate the nonaxiological from the axiological, that one can neatly distinguish between "factual judgments" and "value judgments," as though "value judgments" could not be judgments of facts, as well, that one can simply report what happened, and then leave it up to others, who might, should they be so inclined, evaluate it. This is not possible, because one must choose what to report, how it is to be reported, and so on. I doubt that it is possible to do value-neutral historiography, but, in so far as it could be done, should one attempt to do it? I do not think so. I think that that would be no more than an attempt to adopt a methodology and an ideal inappropriate to the subject matter of historiography. It would be an attempt as act as though historiography was not itself, but a pretentious and fuzzy physics.

I think the historiographer is entitled to write as honestly, richly, and fully, as he wishes.

This does not mean, obviously, that he should misrepresent his subject matter. Rather, it means he should represent it to the best of his ability.

He cannot tell the whole truth, as it will never be known, but he can attempt to tell the truth and nothing but the truth, and, in this way, at least suggest the whole truth.

Clearly, questions of proportion and taste enter into these matters. Explicit value judgments can be annoying. Surely they are generally unnecessary. No one wishes to have the value judgments of others forced on him, but one does expect others to have them, and to be honest to them.

Sometimes the most powerful of value judgments are expressed as though they were not value judgments, at all, but mere reports. This is done through understatement. The seemingly neutral presentation of a horror, or its seemingly casual dismissal, interacting with the reader's imagination, can be the most influential and potent of value judgments.

What artist does not know this?

The key to a great historiography is not the suppression of value judgments but their competition.

This brings us, given the putative legitimization of value judgment in historiography, to the final portion of our work, the aesthetics of historiography.

Part Six: Aesthetics

It might be suggested, and not implausibly, that a consideration of the aesthetics of historiography is pointless, either because historiography has no aesthetics, or because, as historiography is a cognitive discipline, its aesthetics, if it has one, is irrelevant to the discipline.

Strictly, aesthetics is a branch of philosophy, an area not well defined, but one typically concerned with beauty, art, music, poetry, literature, creativity, expression, form, and such. It would be unusual to think of disciplines as having an aesthetics. Usually one thinks of individuals or schools as having an aesthetics, for example, Aristotle and Schopenhauer both had an aesthetics, and the Classical French Academy, the Impressionists, the Cubists, had their aesthetics, and so on. Normally, one would not think of disciplines, such as, say, mathematics and physics, as having an "aesthetics," but there are certainly aesthetic aspects to such disciplines, some proofs being more striking and lovelier than others, some theories being more elegant than others, and so on. Professionals in such fields are often sensitive to such things. In logic, for example, a deft, perhaps unexpected, surprising, demonstration is likely to be favored over a more labored, clumsier competitor, though both are equally correct. In chess, an economical, clean win is preferred over a circumspect, prolonged butchery, and so on.

So, although one would not think of historiography as having an aesthetics, as an individual or school might have an aesthetics, a theory of art or beauty, or such, presumably historiography might, if only extraneously, have its aesthetic aspects. If physics, mathematics, logic, and chess, as well as, say, medicine, architecture, engineering, and such, might have their aesthetic aspects, there seems no reason to exempt historiography from such a possibility, or peril. Let us suppose, then, that historiography, if only inadvertently, might have aesthetic aspects. That far, it seems safe to go. On the other hand, we shall later argue, given the affinities of historiography with the humanities, its value-rich subject matter, and the desideratum of accurately representing the past, that aesthetic considerations are significantly, perhaps even essentially, involved in the best practice of historiography. In such a sense, then, one might state that historiography would have its aesthetics, in a sense more essential than one might ascribe to physics, mathematics, or such. That, of course, is controversial.

Let us suppose it is granted that historiography, similar to other disciplines, may find it difficult, at least, to escape aesthetic elements. This is particularly the case when it is understood that not all aesthetic elements need be positive. For example, if beauty is an aesthetic element, it seems ugliness would also count; if clarity is an aesthetic element, then obscurity would seem to be so, as well. The only way to avoid aesthetic elements then would seem to be to strive for, and achieve, some middle ground, perhaps by means of a careful value-neutral prose, insofar as that might be possible. On the other hand, I suspect, for reasons already given, that such a prose may not be possible, or, if possible, might not be desirable. Some "positive" aesthetic elements, or elements which would commonly be taken as positive aesthetic elements, might be rational organization, clarity of exposition, illuminating detail, communicative imagery, and such. That such properties, often commended in historiographical discourse, are legitimately aesthetic is made clear, when one thinks of, say, disjointed organization, muddy writing, irrelevant detail, excessive generality, and such, as being unaesthetic.

The first objection to considering the aesthetics of historiography, namely, that historiography has no aesthetics, has now been addressed. In one or two senses mentioned, it, indeed, no more than mathematics or physics, has an aesthetics. Nonetheless, as any discipline, it would not be immune from aesthetic elements, and, in a rather innocent fashion, might be expected to accept, and even cultivate, some of them, for example, clarity of exposition. To be sure, one expects that more than such innocuous concessions are in mind when one might speak of an "aesthetics of historiography," and caution would appear in order.

The second objection to considering an aesthetics of historiography is that historiography is a cognitive discipline, dealing with facts, and such, and, therefore, even if it is in some manner blessed by, or afflicted with, an aesthetics, this is essentially unimportant, as aesthetic considerations are accompanying characteristics, at best, of historiography; to resort to an Aristotelian figure, aesthetics would not be an essential property of historiography, but an inessential property, an accident, of historiography. For example, being a rational animal may be an essential property of Socrates, but standing up would not be an essential property of Socrates, as he is still Socrates even if he is sitting down.[120]

The general notion here is that aesthetics would be no more or less relevant to historiography than it is to, say, mathematics or physics. Whether the formulas are written in blue ink or black ink is immaterial. To ask of, or expect of, the historiographer anything

---

120 Whereas one sees, one hopes, the sort of thing Aristotle would be driving at in something like this, things are not really so simple, at least verbally. For example, Socrates does not have to be standing up to be Socrates, but it seems, if he exists, he would have to be standing up, sitting down, lying down, in between, or in some other attitude, and so on. Thus, Property P_1 might not be essential to Socrates, but it seems that he could not be Socrates without possessing the property "P_1 or P_2 or P_3 or ... Pn." Similarly, being in Athens may not be an essential property of Socrates, but either being in Athens or not being in Athens would seem to be an essential property, indeed, one logically necessary, not only for Socrates, but for Plato, Alcibiades, and so on. Perhaps one could rule out "logically necessary properties" on the grounds that, say, 'Socrates is in Athens or it is not the case that Socrates is in Athens' is analytic, empirically vacuous, true in all possible worlds, and so on, and thus, in a sense, tells us nothing about Socrates or, at least, nothing usefully informative. On the other hand, if it is logically necessary that a human being is a rational animal, that, too, it seems, being logically necessary, would tell us nothing about human beings. Logical necessity, in Aristotle, however, is not a matter of language, but one of metaphysics, or reality. If that is the case, again, however, one is returned to the earlier problem, namely, now, that Socrates must be standing up, or whatever, being in Athens or not, and so on. And such properties would then, as well, characterize many other things, and metaphysically, for example, raccoons, rocks, trees, etc..

other than truth is to impose on him a burden both unwonted and inappropriate.

There is a sense in which one would surely agree with this view, namely, that what one wants of a historiographer, at least particularly, is truth.

A poorly organized, poorly written, obscure, muddy account written in post-modern, sociological gobbledygook which is, as far as one can tell, after diligent, lengthy perusal, correct, is surely superior to a nicely organized, well-written, clear account written in an English intelligible to native speakers which is, as far as one can tell, wrong. Whereas there are many criteria in terms of which one can evaluate historiographical literature the primary one is surely truth, fidelity to the past. The mistaken book may be a pleasure to read, and be well worth reading; indeed, it may be invaluable in its way, and one may learn much from it, but, strictly considered, as truth trumps lucidity, interest, plausibility, and such, it is obligated to yield the palm of victory to its more dismal, tenebrous competitor.

In several respects, of course, matters are not as simple as suggested. Presumably, unless guided by the gods, or risking little, most histories, well-written or not, will miss much of the truth. Whereas historiography can certainly tell the truth, there may often be no way to determine whether or not the truth is being told. Thus, separating historiographies into the true and the false is naive, and pretentious. Given the subtleties, difficulties, and inaccessibilities involved, the necessities of speculation and the hazards of inferences based on insufficient data, it is likely that the best of historiographies will contain much that is false and quite possible that the worst of historiographies may contain much that is true. If that is the case, to paraphrase a saying, it behooves neither to throw rocks at the other, unless with some thought, and then with careful aim. At least, in view of such a situation it would be advisable to employ pompous dichotomies with appropriate circumspection. Often the most that can be realistically expected is that, in the light of evidence, marshaled facts, and such, it seems plausible that the truth is being told. Similarly, it would be a mistake to evaluate historiographies in the light of a single parameter, however important that parameter might be.

Consider the following two statements.

1. Columbus sailed the ocean blue in 1492.

2. Columbus, an Italian navigator, commissioned by Ferdinand and Isabella, monarchs of Spain, with three small ships, the *Santa Maria*, the *Pinta*, and the *Niña*, setting forth in early August from Palos de la Frontera, Spain, sailed the ocean blue in 1493, discovering what was heralded as "the New World," opening a new era in world history.

The first statement is true. The second statement is false. On the other hand, the second statement is more informative.

Some of the major classics of historiography contain materials which are presumably fabrications. A familiar example is the history of Thucydides, which contains a number of elaborate speeches, addresses, and such, which were probably never given, or, if given, were not given as reported. Thucydides himself does not pretend they are true, but proposes them as what would have been appropriate under the circumstances. They are illuminating, and contain intelligent speculations. Even presumed historiographical exaggerations or distortions like Livy's romanticization of early Rome or Tacitus' views on Gothic tribesmen in his *Germania* shed light on history and, in their way, on the Rome of Livy and Tacitus. Even agenda histories like those of Caesar, Plutarch, Eusebius, Procopius, and others deepen and enrich our sense of the past. Historiographies, as well, may be valued for their role in generating hypotheses, for putting forward new or interesting perspectives on the past, better or worse, dubious or plausible, geographical, economic, military, industrial, racial, ethnic, social, psychological, religious, and so on. Clearly, as well, some visions, aside from their specific credibilities, such as those of Hegel, Marx, Spengler, and Toynbee, dare encompassing perceptions, some extraordinarily impressive and beautiful, seeking history's broadest lineaments, prospecting for her deepest wells and springs, her least visible engines. Too, in the work of some historiographers, such as Hume and Gibbon, historiographical writing, exceeding the typical, expected merits of scholarly effort, may become historiographical literature.

Truth is not the only parameter in terms of which to evaluate historiography. Its capacity to open up vistas, to stimulate thought, to enlarge the mind, to enrich and deepen human beings, is obviously of great value.

Analogously, one of the great values of philosophy is its capacity to open the eyes of the human being who is ready for the experience, to help him to see that data is capable of a multitude of interpretations, that the world may be, and has been, diversely understood. A hundred *Weltanschauungen*, actually thousands, each in its own day and in its own place uncritically accepted by most, have been proclaimed as the single truth. Surely to the rational mind this is a humbling discovery, somewhat unsettling in one way, and refreshing, even reassuring, in another. At the least it suggests the unwariness, the arrogance, of dogmatism, the advisability of caution. There are many ways the world can be, and we may not have it right, even now. That helps one to look about himself. The world then looks different. Similarly, one of the joys of historiography is its capacity to show us diverse worlds and times, to introduce us to ourselves, to show us what human beings have been, and done. And thus to tell us about them, and ourselves.

Historiography and philosophy are both events of an intellectual morning, of a time of awakening. Both are ways of coming alive, and being alive. Doubtless, so, too, are the arts, and the sciences. Values arise here which, even in the case of the paradigm sciences, the P sciences, exceed adhering to a putatively well-warranted set of propositions.

But let us return to truth.

The fear, or uneasiness, likely to be generated when one refers to an aesthetics of historiography is the apprehension that there may be some sort of incompatibility, perhaps even an inverse relationship, between truth and aesthetics.

Is not the "unvarnished truth" the ideal, truth stated as clearly, and as simply as possible?

History, of course, so to speak, comes varnished, comes spattered with thousands of colors. It might take some doing, for example, to provide an unvarnished, tepid, flat, plain account of something which in itself was far from tepid, flat, or plain, but one could always try. An independent question would be whether or not such an account did, or could do, justice to the subject matter. Similarly, whereas there is presumably something to be said for accounts which are as clear and simple as possible, it should also be understood that the clearest and simplest account of an incredibly subtle, complex event might be as clear and simple as possible, but, given its subject matter, it might not be all that clear, and certainly it would not be likely to be very simple. It might not even be clear, at all, unless it was clear about what one could not be clear about, and so on. Being clear about something about which one cannot be clear might be a way of lying.

Scholarly prose is well known for its tedium. How might this be explained? It is unlikely that many graduate schools offer courses in boring writing, that their students may be better prepared to compete in academia. Rather, one suspects, again, that the halls of historiography, and those of a few other disciplines one might mention, such as philosophy, may be haunted by the specter of the P sciences. The fact that it might be peculiar or silly to talk about, say, molecules or the binomial theorem in value-rich prose does not entail that value-rich subjects, so to speak, are best treated like molecules or the binomial theorem. One may do as one pleases, of course. Whereas a given scholar may pride himself on his no-nonsense, sober prose, on writing in the most tiresome and uninteresting manner possible, and going through draft after draft until he has achieved this ideal, he need not elevate his proclivities into a model of scholarly discourse, utilize it in his reviews of the work of others, enforce it on his vulnerable graduate students, and so on. It is hard to know what the presupposition of such a paradigm might be. Perhaps it is, as just conjectured, a misapplication of an alien paradigm, say, from physics to historiography. Perhaps it is a puritanical notion that passion is embarrassing or best concealed. Perhaps it is a pursuit of nondescript anonymity, as a way of fitting in, of not standing out, of avoiding envy, or possible censure. Perhaps it is a notion that the subject is boring, and so that should be reflected in its scholarship. It is hard to tell. It might be, of course, the notion that aesthetic elements are dangerous, or out of place, in scholarship, that they might introduce distortion or misrepresentation. Even if innocent, perhaps they should be eschewed as distractive or irrelevant. Perhaps that might explain much.

Let us consider such possibilities.

It is certainly true that aesthetic elements can be dangerous, that they might introduce distortion or misrepresentation, and it is also true that they may be distractive or irrelevant. It does not follow from these possibilities, however, that they are out of place in historiographical writing. Fire and knives can be dangerous, too, but that does not suggest that one should sit in the cold and tear one's meat with one's teeth. By the light of a fire one might see what otherwise would have remained in darkness; and the knife is a tool which might be used variously; it may have effected the transition from apes to men.

Two presuppositions of the negative view, that aesthetic elements should be eliminated from, or minimized within, historiographical work, appear to be, first, that such elements are easily avoidable, and, thus, given the putative hazards involved, are best avoided; and, second, that their role, when occurrent, is not substantive, but ornamental, at best.

These two presuppositions are both false.

Aesthetic elements, those associated with art, in a broad sense, are not avoidable, or, at least, are not easily avoidable. Indeed, it is hard to see that they are avoidable, at all. The choice here is not likely to be between art and no art, but between good art and bad art.

It is certainly possible that the best art is that which conceals art. But this view, obviously, does not recommend the absence of art. Rather it suggests that the ends of art are best achieved when the art is not obtrusive, or distractive, when it does not get in the way of what it is up to.

In this fashion, interestingly, good art may be mistaken for no art.

Let us address the avoidability issue.

Aesthetic elements, considerations, and such cannot, as a practical matter, be avoided. This is so for two reasons, first, the nature of language, and, second, the necessity of choice in expression.

As noted in our discussion of language, most words, certainly nouns and verbs, have psychological resonances, familiar associations and connotations, emotive meanings, and such, often individual-relative. As it is difficult to paint without colors, so it is difficult to write, or to speak, without colors, whether one wishes to do this or not. This being the case, aesthetic aspects, or penumbras, are likely to accompany even the most determinedly arid of lexicons, as cold follows ice or light flame. Aesthetic elements abound, for the most part, pervasively. It seems clear one cannot eliminate them, and still speak a natural language. If one has little choice but to put up with them, if, as a matter of practical fact, they cannot be avoided, the rational response is to accept this, however reluctantly, resignedly, begrudgingly, bravely, stoically, or graciously, or, I suppose, to welcome it, perhaps as placing at one's disposal a gloriously rich instrument of human expression, one developed and refined, improved and honed, over generations.

Second, aesthetic choice figures in expression, in everything from grunts and snarls to lyric poetry and expositional prose.

One cannot say something without saying it in some way. There are twenty-four ways to translate the English sentence 'Bill gives the book to Susan' into Latin. Presumably, depending on the context, his feel for the language, and such, a Latin speaker would prefer some of these formulations to others, but there is no way he can say it without saying it in one way or another. The form of the triangle and the form of the horse may not have a shape, and, logically, they could not have a shape, but any triangle and any horse will have a shape. Similarly, if anything is to be actually said, it must be said in one way or another. If there is anything to choose from amongst equivalent formulations, one being preferable to another, then the discrimination, if not random, or audience-addressed, is likely to be made on aesthetic grounds. More importantly, as noted earlier, a natural language is a value-rich language; its nouns and verbs are likely to be rich with association and suggestion, to carry emotive meaning, and so on. Accordingly, aesthetic criteria, such as clarity, precision, connotation, emotive resonance, vividness, aptness, and such, would be likely to figure into the formulation. For example, writing well, saying something well, and so on, are aesthetic properties, usually commended. Similarly, poor writing, boring writing, and such, are aesthetic properties usually not commended, outside, perhaps, of certain circles, where they might be regarded as indicative of professionalism. In any event, it is not clear that one can avoid aesthetic choices, easily or otherwise, choices amongst aesthetic elements. We had suggested the attempt to develop a value-neutral prose, but we also expressed doubt that this was a feasible project, particularly given the language at one's disposal. One could, of course, do one's best to do this, do one's best to write colorlessly of what is multicolored, to represent the spectrum in shades of gray, and so on. One does not wish to make it analytic that value-neutral prose is impossible; surely it, or something much like it, exists in certain fields, such as logic, mathematics, physics, chemistry, and so on. Similarly a gray, polysyllabic, generality-laden, remote, disengaged, detached, uninteresting, boring, untouched-by-human hands-or-heart prose in historiography would be a candidate, at least, for such a distinction, one perhaps even coveted as a token of academic respectability. It is also possible, at least in theory, as noted earlier, to develop an artificial language in which to do historiography, but one supposes few historiographers would be interested in such a project, at least on this planet. Too, given the subject matter of historiography the new lexicon would presumably begin to take on the emotive and connotative aspects of the very language it was designed to replace. Too, if one were to translate an account in the new language which was adequate to the subject matter into the old language, and the translation was a good one, one would find oneself back where one had started, and thus might as well have stayed home to begin with.

Expression involves choice, and choice may be legitimately influenced by, and often is influenced by, aesthetic considerations. Are not some formulations more apt, more economical, more expressive, more tasteful, more exact, more appropriate, more clear, sharper, more provocative, more vivid, more satisfactory than others? Some might prefer ink or charcoal sketches to water colors or oil paintings. There is nothing wrong with that. So, too, quite possibly, some might prefer one form of prose to another. There is nothing wrong with that, either. But it seems likely some sort of aesthetic choice is involved, even if it might be denied. To be sure, one might draw words from a hat, or have recourse to another sort of random-selection device.

More important than the possibility, however remote, of dealing with a value-rich subject matter in a value-free manner is the question of the desirability of this project, even if it were somehow achievable.

That question must shortly be addressed.

But let us turn, first, to the second presupposition of the negative view, that aesthetic elements are not substantive, that they are embellishments, that they are analogous to the difference between white paper and yellow paper, between blue ink and black ink, that they are superfluous, frivolous, unnecessary, trivial, irrelevant, decorative, ornamental, at best, or such. This is, in its way, too, the "sauce or condiment notion" of aesthetic elements, They are not the cake, but, at best, the frosting, not the meat but, at best, the gravy. Supposedly they would affect not what was said but, at best, how it was said, as though one could say something without saying it in one way or another.

If our earlier argumentation is correct, attempting, in effect, to demonstrate the unavoidability of aesthetic elements and considerations in historiographical discourse, the question of the substantival or nonsubstantival nature of aesthetic elements and considerations takes on a new aspect or complexion. One would have to maintain, it seems, that elements and considerations which are pervasively ingredient in what you are doing, and with which it is impossible, or improbable, that one could dispense, are somehow of little or no consequence in what one is doing.

This claim would have to be based on some sort of a form/content, or form/matter, distinction, perhaps, say, on the hypothesis that form and content, or form and matter, can exist independently, that, say, a content or a matter exists, and a variety of forms exist in which that same content or matter might, so to speak, become visible, be clothed, be materialized, be expressed, or such. In our context, the notion would be that how something is expressed is irrelevant to what is expressed, and that aesthetic considerations pertain to how something is expressed, and are thus irrelevant to what is expressed.. Accordingly, it would be claimed that even if aesthetic elements, considerations, and such, are unavoidable, they are of no substantival importance.

Let us consider some form/content possibilities.

A typical way of thinking of form and content might be, for example, that a wad of clay might be molded into diverse shapes, a ball, a triangle, a square, and so on. Here, as far as we can tell, the clay must have some shape, if only that of a nondescript blob, and any shape must be the shape of something. In short, unless one is a Platonist, there is no matter without form, and no form without matter. This is a typical Aristotelian notion, though he did not carry this view through consistently, attributing form but not matter to the Unmoved mover, Celestial Intelligences, and the Active Intellect, three entities for which, luckily for the view in question, no empirical evidence exists. Our concerns, of course, deal not with wood, clay, bronze, paper, and such, but linguistic entities.

One might consider the following three sets.

Set A:
1. p
2. (p v q) & (p v ~ q)

Set B:
1. (x) (Rx ⊃ Bx)
2. (x) (~ Bx ⊃ ~ Rx)

Set C:
1. Bill gives Susan the book.
2. The book is given by Bill to Susan.

The two items in each of these three sets are logically equivalent to one another. That means, however, only that they are interdeducible, or, equivalently, that they must, of logical necessity, have the same truth value. If two locutions are synonymous, they must be logically equivalent, but, as noted earlier in this study, they may be logically equivalent without being synonymous. For example, substitution instances supposed, one could give the meaning of the first line in Set A without giving the meaning of 'q' but one could not give the meaning of the second line without giving the meaning of 'q', and thus the two lines, though logically equivalent, do not have the have the same meaning. This could be important in our context because logical equivalence and synonymy are often confused. For example, line 1 in Set A does not say the same thing as line 2. They do not have same content. Form affects content.

A clearer example of the distinction between logical equivalence and synonymy would be the following:

Set A':
1. p v ~ p
2. q v ~ q

Set A":
1. p & ~ p
2. q & ~ q

Since all tautologies are logically equivalent, and all contradictions are logically equivalent, line 1 and line 2 in Set A' are logically equivalent, and line 1 and line 2 in Set A" are logically equivalent. On the other hand, presumably, given legitimate substitution instances, none of the lines in either set would have the same meaning.

The situation in Set B is more problematical. The logical equivalence is indisputable, the quantified function in one of the formulas being the simple contrapositive of the quantified function in the other formula. It is not clear, however, that they have the same meaning. For example, if we interpret the formulas in Set B along the lines of Carl G. Hempel's famous Raven Paradox, we might have something like 'All ravens are black' and 'All nonblack things are nonravens'. These are logically equivalent formulations. Clearly a black raven, and more of them, would be evidence to the effect that all ravens are black. On the other hand, say, a yellow canary, a red rose, a blue baseball cap, a white piece of chalk, and such, would not normally be thought to be evidence pertinent to the blackness of ravens. However, such things would clearly be evidence in favor of the nonblackness of nonravens, and, thus, if one accepts the principle of confirmation symmetry, namely, that evidence in favor of, or against, a hypothesis H is also evidence in favor of, or against, any hypothesis logically equivalent to H, and presumably to the same extent, then one must accept that yellow canaries, and such, is evidence in favor of the hypothesis that all ravens are black. Accepting the logical equivalence of the two locutions, and putting aside the question of confirmation symmetry, our concern here is with the synonymy or nonsynonymy of the two locutions. It seems to me that they are best regarded as nonsynonymous. I would be surprised, for example, if most native speakers of English would regard 'All ravens are black' and 'All nonblack things are nonravens' as having the same meaning, as saying the same thing. Talking about nonblack things and nonravens does not seem to be talking about black things and ravens. Similarly, that a yellow canary would not normally be taken as relevant to the claim that all ravens are black, but would normally be regarded as relevant to the claim that all nonblack things are nonravens, suggests that the two locutions are not well regarded as synonymous. Let us suppose, however, that we keep the synonymy or nonsynonymy of the two locutions an open question. All we need here is the fact that equivalence may be indisputable and synonymy problematical.[121]

I would suppose that most native speakers of English would see the two locutions in Set C as two ways of saying the same thing. In short, I would suppose they would be likely to see them as not only logically equivalent, but as synonymous, as well. One might prefer the active voice to the passive voice, or, perhaps, in a given linguistic matrix or environment, one locution might seem more apt, or suitable, than the other, say, soundwise, but, even so, I suspect most native speakers would see them as synonymous. That "seeing," however, in my view, is likely to be a result of the isolation of the locutions. Whereas we could stipulate that the two locutions are synonymous, holding the meanings steady, so to speak, it is easy to conceive contexts in which they would be used differently, would convey different items of information in different ways, and so on. For example, in line 1 attention is focused on Bill and what he is doing, and, in line 2, attention is focused on the book, and what is being done with it. Second, let us suppose in the first instance, that we are interested in whether Bill or Bob will give the book, and whether it will be given to Susan or, say, Phyllis. We then find that Bill, and not Bob, gives the book, and that it is given to Susan, not Phyllis. We shall suppose, in this instance, we are interested in who is giving the book, and to whom. In the second instance, which we shall suppose occurs in a different context, we are more interested in, say, what will change hands, say, the ring or the book, and in whether or not the object will be given, or sold. We would then, in that context, note that it is the book, perhaps surprisingly, which is going to Susan, and not the ring, which we

---

121 Hempel, whose paradox it is, accepts the paradox, consistently adhering to the principle of Confirmation Symmetry. I think he was correct to do so. On the other hand, it is easy to understand why there is more than one parade on this street.

might have expected, and learn, too, that the book is being given, rather than sold, as we had anticipated.

If we allow that meaning, like color, can vary in context, and that meaning is, at least in part, a function of what is conveyed, then it is not obvious that line 1 and line 2 in Set C would always have the same meaning, at least in a practical, everyday sense of meaning.

Analogously, let us suppose we have three situations, first, a situation where it is supposed the garage is empty; second, a situation in which one knows something is in the garage, but is not sure what; and, third, a situation where one thinks a hippopotamus, whom one is boarding for a friend, is in the garage.

In these three situations it seems the meaning of 'There is a rhinoceros in the garage' would convey different meanings to the three individuals involved, e.g., no, the garage is not empty; yes, there is something in there, a rhinoceros; and, third, your friend's hippopotamus is missing. In isolation, it seems 'There is a rhinoceros in the garage' could have only one meaning, but, in diverse contexts, it might convey different pieces of information to different individuals. To be sure, much here could depend on whether one wished to hold to a static, Platonic, mathematical sense of meaning or a dynamic, context-relative, pragmatic sense of meaning. There is much to be said, and much has been said, for both views. All we need here is that the form/content view seems to presuppose the Platonic view, that an independent, static content exists, to the expression of which form is irrelevant, that how something is said is irrelevant to what is said.

We will challenge that.

As noted earlier in this study, distinguishing amongst sentences, statements, and propositions gives us a practical, illuminating way to approach a variety of linguistic complexities, a way I would be reluctant to discard; on the other hand, we also endorsed this as a way of speaking, a way of making sense out of speech data. In the spirit of linguistic pragmatism such discourse is justified by its convenience and utility, and need not be regarded as ontologically committing anyone to the existence of mysterious, nonempirical, unverifiable, metaphysical entities, no more than arithmetic commits one to adding the number 647 to the furniture of the universe, along with rocks and trees, planets and stars.

In our current context, however, that of actuality, a form/content distinction, or a form/matter distinction, is not viable, no more than a triangle without a shape or a horse without a size and color. Similarly, in our current context, the notion of an independent proposition, independent of formulation, is not only an unlikely hypothesis, but one scarcely intelligible, even as a manner of speaking.

One does not sort through pure propositions before dressing one in a sentence; it is the sentence from which one learns the thought, the sentence in which the thought is discovered; commonly, one does not know what one will say until it is said. The exception to this is saying it first to oneself, and then to another. These matters are more complex than these brief remarks suggest, but the general point is simple, namely, we learn what is said from how it is said. If there is a chronological distinction here one learns what was said only after it was said. We do not move from propositions to saying, but from saying to the hypothesis of propositions, to that which was said.

Accordingly, one cannot, as a practical matter, set aside or marginalize how something is said, separating it from what is said. Logically, verbally, they may be divisible; in the real world, however, it is not so much that they are conjoined, even indivisibly, as that they may be two ways of looking the same thing, one thing. Analogously, concavity and convexity are different properties, but, in a given case, they might be two ways of looking at the same thing, as in the following figure, '⌒'. In any event, aesthetic considerations pertain to form; and, as we have suggested, form is not irrelevant; indeed, without it content cannot exist.

Form and content do not simply go together; they are a unity. There is no distinction between what one says and how it is said. If it seems so, then one does not really know what one wants to say. There is only one way to say exactly what you want to say.

We have tried to make clear the falsity of two presuppositions of the negative view, the view that aesthetic elements should be eliminated from, or minimized within, historiographical work, first, the presupposition that such elements are easily avoidable, and, thus, given the putative hazards involved, are best avoided; and, second, the presupposition that their role, when occurrent, is not substantive, but ornamental, at best.

For most practical purposes, aesthetic elements, aesthetic considerations, and aesthetic choices, art, in a broad sense, is implicit, for various reasons, in historiographical discourse; the choice, as suggested, is not between art and no art, but between bad art and good art; similarly, for various reasons, a distinction between content and form, or matter and form, or how something is said and what is said, in an actual instance, is not viable. Accordingly, aesthetic elements cannot be relegated to the category of the irrelevant or merely decorative.

These considerations are to be taken as arguing that aesthetic elements , aesthetic choices, and aesthetic considerations are important to historiography, and that, in such a sense, historiography has an aesthetics, and, for most practical purposes, ineradicably, unavoidably. This is not an argument for prettiness, for labored conceits, for embellishment, for redundancy, for "high style," for purple prose, or such. Such things, in our view, may be as counterproductive, as subversive of the possibilities of a liberated historiography, as the misguided attempts of well-intentioned historiographers to emulate the prose, detachments, and habits of colleagues in the paradigm sciences, the P sciences. Historiography is different, profoundly different, and this should be unapologetically reflected in its practice, and philosophy.

It is our hope that what we have done to this point has been persuasive, arguing, in effect, for the unavoidability and essentiality, of aesthetic elements, art, in a broad sense, in historiography. These concessions, however, if granted, would seem relatively innocuous. We would like to now traverse into a more controversial terrain, namely, the claim that art is not only implicit within and essential to historiography, but that historiography is best understood as an art, an unusual art, a cognitive art.

There is a literature on art and truth, or truth in art, but that literature, provocative and profound though it may be, is largely irrelevant to what we are concerned with here. One might well learn more about human beings from Dostoyevsky than B. F. Skinner but Skinner's pigeons are real in a way that the Karamazovs are not, just as, one supposes, the Karamazovs are real in a way the pigeons are not. There are different realities. Similarly, if one wishes to attribute truth to art, and I think one would wish to do so, it would be a different sort of truth than one would have in mind in historiography. Truth, in its usual senses, analytic and empirical, does not seem to pertain to music, drama, theater, sculpture, or painting, even representational painting, such things. The ending of Hamlet may be dramatically inevitable, but it is not logically necessary, in the sense of analytic. Perhaps it is true that in the presence of the torso of an archaic Apollo one must change one's life, but it would be difficult to make out a case for the empirical truth of that claim. How would a skeptic be convinced? How would it be publicly confirmed, or disconfirmed? Similarly, how would one falsify the claim that, in the presence of an empty coke bottle one should under no circumstances change one's life, and so on? Truth in art goes far beyond "true to," or "representationally faithful," but, however one understands it, it seems very different from, and irrelevant to, truth in historiography.

These considerations do not preclude, however, that historiography would be well understood as a cognitive art.

What it says is true or false, and herein we discover its cognitivity, and in how adequate or inadequate it is to the depth and wealth of its subject matter we find its art.

The primary obligation of the historiographer is to tell the truth.

This said, it seems plausible that historiography should be free to proceed in a manner adequate to, and befitting, its subject matter.

Clearly, words are not things, but words are the means by which things may be spoken, they are the hints which might enrapture the imagination. A bright image might unlock a mystery, turning a horse's head so that it is not frightened by its own shadow, a boy's seeing that, when grooms and riders do not, and we learn something of his perception and astuteness, even in youth, and his love for an animal, for which cities may later be named.

"... the most glorious exploits do not always furnish us with the clearest discoveries of virtue or vice in men; sometimes a matter of less moment, an expression or a jest, informs us better of their characters and inclinations, than the most famous sieges, the greatest armaments, or the bloodiest battles whatsoever."[122]

There is a saying that the Russian Revolution began under the belly of a Cossack's horse. Obviously, literally understood, that is false. On the other hand, it is a striking figure of speech and conveys much, oppression, brutality, the arrogance of power, the absence of dialogue, the unwillingness to compromise, or even listen, the ruthless reliance on callous force, the futility and hopelessness of peaceable protest, the vulnerability of unarmed civilians, and such. So we have a statement there which is literally false, but which, as a figure of speech, is arresting, and in a broad sense, might be regarded as true, metaphorically.

Historiography, as a cognitive art, should we so choose to regard it, is entitled to trenchancy, lyricism, vividness, imagery, to figurative discourse. It, like poetry, an art which once claimed cognitivity, and achieved it, prior to its reduction to conceptual music, Pavlovian associationism, word clinking, and such, is entitled to metaphor, wherein one finds so much of the mitotic or meristematic vigor of language, the fresh visions of connections and resemblances caught in sound. It is said that a picture is worth a thousand words; a metaphor may be worth more.

Consider:

"We live ephemeral lives in the shadow of great ideas."
—Yevgeny Yevtushenko

Try saying that in literal prose.

One discovers in many historiographers a willingness to speak metaphorically, presumably because what they wish to say may be best said in that fashion. One resorts to metaphor because literal prose cannot so well enkindle the flames of understanding. It is not easy to say new things, if one has them to say, in old ways, if only because there are no old ways in which to say them. Some metaphors are so familiar one no longer sees them as metaphors, such as "the Renaissance" or "the Enlightenment." Some are as awesome, and troubling, as Spengler's biographic archetypes, others as surprising and insightful as Toynbee's references to internal and external proletariats.

---

122 *Plutarch's Lives*, "Alexander."

The difficulties, naturally, once one goes beyond books on the desk or cats on mats, is to determine the truth conditions of metaphorical discourse. To be sure, the difficulty of determining the truth conditions of even literal prose are often daunting. Is that object a desk, or a different piece of furniture, if the books are on a box which is on a desk, are the books on the desk, or box, what if only the tail of the cat is on the mat, or, say, its head, and half of its body, etc. What about claims that morale is more important to the success of an army than equipment, that an assassination caused a war, that a given conflict was inevitable, that a policy was doomed to failure, that a particular leader was brave, or ambitious, or such?

In logic, a statement is either true or false, another statement either entailed or not, a given disjunction either analytic or not, a given conjunction either contradictory or not, and so on. Similarly, in mathematics, a given number is either the number two or it isn't, and so on. The logician and mathematician construct worlds which are, to the best of their ability, clear, secure, and safe. But even here, in the gardens of these fenced-off, sheltered worlds, serpents may coil, undecidable formulas, and classes which must, and cannot, belong to themselves, and so on. The most harrowing problems arise, naturally, when one ventures beyond the fence, entering upon a world so cluttered, changeable, and messy that Plato refused to regard it as real, a world in which it may not be clear at all that that object is a triangle, that that horse is brown, that the box has a width of two feet, and so on, let alone that a policy was doomed to failure, or a historical figure was ambitious, brave, or such. In such a world, one of imprecision and compromise, truth conditions are often allowed latitude, sometimes a considerable amount of latitude. Presumably few boxes, if any, have a width of two feet given the irregularity and raggedness of edges, the empty spaces or subtle fields obtaining in physical systems, and such. It would be difficult to determine, even at a given point, whether the width was 2 feet or, say, 1.9999999999 or 2.0000000001 feet, and so on. Similarly, the foot ruler's or tape measure's markings, considered microscopically, are extended, blurred terrains of no-man's land, and so, too, on other, subtler scales, would be the criteria utilized by even more sophisticated paraphernalia. Tolerances are invoked, and measurements would be recorded as accurate which were not accurate, but close enough, at least for us, at a given time, for a given purpose, to count as accurate. F.C.S. Schiller, the English pragmatist, spoke of "true enough," and, for most practical purposes, this rough-and-ready notion, with its usefully vague borders, is one on which we commonly rely. This is not to deny that absolute truths and absolute falsities may exist. For example, it may be absolutely true that the box's width is between one and three feet, and that it is absolutely false that it is between one and two inches, or more than ten feet, and so on. Similarly it is absolutely true that Epaminondas was born before Napoleon Bonaparte, and absolutely false that Napoleon Bonaparte was born before Epaminondas. On the other hand, usually, there are two problems which arise in these matters. First, it is often the case that what counts as the specific criteria for a particular truth is not clear. Earlier in this study we noted the "porosity of concepts." The resolution of "middle-ground" cases may be controversial. Secondly, even in cases where the criteria are reasonably clear, as in measuring the width of the box, normally, and without cavil, approximations to "truth" are regarded as acceptable. One counts the width to be two feet, for convenience, when the width is about two feet, if only to avoid a situation where 'The width is two feet' would be almost invariably false, and, if the case, could not be known to be the case.

A third problem which may also arise in these matters has to do with "middle-ground" variation amongst individuals. Given the vagueness, as noted, of many concepts, the criteria involved in their application may legitimately differ from individual to individual. For example, two historiographers, equally experienced and talented, and in possession of the same evidence, might differ in their judgments with respect to individuals or policies, events or polities, largely in virtue of their semantic predispositions, differently understanding, say, bravery, ambition, astuteness, loyalty, leadership, importance, success, value, or such. There might be disagreement on when Rome fell, the continuity or discontinuity between the Middle Ages and the Renaissance, the beginnings of the Reformation, the significance of the horse collar and moldboard plow, and so on, different criteria being employed. Obviously, if one were to claim that Socrates was a greater man than Alexander the Great, that Hippocrates was more important than Pasteur and Lister, that Michelangelo was a better artist than Leonardo da Vinci, that Europe contributed more to civilization than Egypt and Asia, different criteria would be involved. Something which is true according to one set of criteria may be false in the light of a different set of criteria. The clarification of criteria may not produce agreement, but it should render disagreement comprehensible.

In the light of the "middle-ground" realities noted; the acceptability, and practical inevitability, of approximations recognized; and individual relativity operative within permissible boundaries duly recorded, the alleged hazards of figurative discourse begin to appear less perilous, and more intriguing.

Let us agree that most natural-language communication is imperfect, in the sense of not being perfectly clear. In talking of numbers, and uninterpreted predicates, constants, variables, and such, we may not know what we are talking about, but we can at least be clear in talking about it, whatever it is. In natural-language discourse one can range from the reasonably clear to the unreasonably obscure. Items of figurative discourse, like their more prosaic brethren, may lie anywhere along this spectrum. The following two items might be suggested.

1. We live ephemeral lives in the shadow of great ideas.
2. Reason is the *substance* of the universe.

Item 1 is clearly figurative, and Item 2 is not figurative, at least as normally understood. The first item, as will be recalled, is from the Russian poet, Yevgeny Yevtushenko. The second item is, in effect, a quotation from G. W. F. Hegel's *The Philosophy of History*. Both items are out of context, but the first item, for our purposes, needs no context, and the second item is probably better off without the context, being one of the clearer remarks in the context. If push came to shove, I think we could annoy the lovely remark by Yevtushenko by paraphrasing it in prose. This would take some time, I think, be clumsy, and would probably be less clear than the original, but it could be done. It could, for most practical purposes, be explained, in terms which would be empirically intelligible. I rather doubt that the second item could be as satisfactorily dealt with. For example, reason, as we usually think of it, is not a substance, and, if it were, it does not seem likely the universe is made from it. The universe seems to be made from other things, rocks and trees, atoms and such. The "Hegelian statement" is either obviously false, rather like vanilla ice cream is made from iron ore, or, if true, is true in some surprising and unusual sense. In any event, if it were to be true, how would it be confirmed or disconfirmed? Too, what would falsify it, if it were not regarded as false, and obviously so, already? Supposedly Hegel, on his deathbed, said that only one man had understood him, and then added, later, that that fellow, whoever he was, did not understand him either. Such an intelligence is not likely to embolden potential expositors. What we need here, of course, is that the first item is clearly figurative, and the second item is clearly nonfigurative, at least as normally understood. But, I think the first item is much clearer than the second item. Thus, if we had a spectrum, as below, one supposes the first item would be toward the left side of the spectrum and the second rather toward the right side of the spectrum.

Clear ———————————————————— Unclear

The point of course, is that figurative discourse may be clearer than literal discourse. In both cases, the individual item is important, not the category.

The vagueness of natural language, whatever its form, is often regarded as a defect, but this assessment is one to be qualified. Whereas there is no doubt that discourse may be needlessly vague, and thus manage to undermine its most likely end, which is to communicate, it is not at all the case that a margin of indeterminacy, or an "open texture," *ceteris paribus*, is either a defect, or a disadvantage. Rather, a certain indeterminacy or open texture in language facilitates communication and increases the power, flexibility, and expressiveness of language. It facilitates communication in virtue of being "clear enough," being adequate for most purposes, as more precise terms might not be. Its implicit generality is a virtue. The word 'cat', as noted earlier, is not clear, for example, if it talks, is it still a cat, if it changes sizes and colors, is it a cat, if it is as large as an elephant, or as small as a gnat, is it a cat, if it can walk through walls, is it a cat, and so on, but this does not prevent one from talking about cats, reading books on cats, and such. Also, the vagueness, or indeterminacy, or open texture, involved allows the extension of words into new application ranges, the noting of relations and resemblances, the making of new and illuminating connections, and such. In the context of our example, one might be able to extend the cat concept in such a way as to deal with new phenomena, perhaps talking cats, chameleon cats, macrocats, microcats, transcats, and such. Similarly, much language had its origin in metaphor, one of the major means by which language increases in power, flexibility, and expressiveness. Thus, one would not need new terms, technical terms, for, say, the foot of a mountain, the leg of a table, the eye of a needle, and such. 'Vagueness', of course, is a word with a generally negative emotive connotation. Perhaps it might be reserved for noxious or unhelpful indeterminacy. One would then need another word for beneficent or enabling indeterminacy, for empowering indeterminacy. Perhaps Friedrich Waismann's 'porosity' or '*Porosität*', or, possibly, 'power' or 'puissance'.

These considerations suggest that figurative discourse, say, metaphor, far from being irrelevant or ornamental, may be wonderfully valuable to the historiographical enterprise, enabling it to speak as it has not hitherto spoken, occasionally lending it wings wherewith heights might be attained, from which new things might be seen. Metaphor is less likely to interfere with communication than to set it free, to enable it to better realize its most profound ends. In any event the historiographer, should he be so inclined, is entitled to its communicative power. To forswear it on some *a priori* grounds would be a gratuitous self-inflicted wound, a self-crippling deprivation. Better might the eagle forswear its wings, to better please local lemmings.

The primary case for figurative discourse is that it is sometimes the best way, perhaps even the only way, to say some exact, particular thing, something perhaps well worth saying.

As noted, determining the truth conditions of assertions, whether literal or figurative, may be difficult, or problematical, and, sometimes, the truth conditions of figurative discourse, as we have seen, are clearer than those of normal, standard, literal discourse.

In both literal and figurative discourse there are frequently ranges of interpretation, areas within which truth may be ascribed, outside of which it would be denied. In both cases, locutions subjected to challenge may be defended by means of criterion clarification, often by means of expansion, or paraphrase. Accordingly, the truth conditions of figurative discourse labor here under no onus that is not shared by those of literal discourse. Sometimes, as well, as we have seen, there is no clear distinction between literal and figurative discourse.

This is not to deny that there are better and worse metaphors, no more than to claim that all nonmetaphorical discourse is, *ipso facto*, clear.

If one were to characterize a historical figure as "lion hearted" or "mouse hearted," the first metaphor having become almost a cliché, having been associated with Richard I, of England, and the second deriving much of its meaning in virtue of its implicit comparison with the first, I would suppose, in virtue of the connotations involved, more would be conveyed than by "courageous" or "cowardly." For example, in the case of the first metaphor, one would presumably gather aggressiveness and pride, as well as courage, and, in the second case, one would presumably think less of cowardice than of timidity. One of the advantages of metaphor is the capacity to enhance, multiply, and blend meanings in a way that literal prose does not. Metaphor is likely to inform effective communication. It is not easy to forget Shakespeare's "tiger's heart wrapt in woman's hide." On the other hand, I am not at all sure what would be conveyed if a historical personage were to be characterized as "horse hearted," "giraffe hearted," "raccoon hearted," and so on.

Clearly metaphors may be striking, and illuminating. By means of them much may be expressed well, and succinctly. They can point up resemblances and connections that might be otherwise unnoted. Considering them, pondering them, unpacking them, may be stimulatory to inquiry. They may open doors hitherto closed, and shed light where, earlier, there was not even an awareness of darkness. Metaphor is the cutting edge of language, the place where language moves, explores, and grows.

In ruminating on these issues I have become aware, as never before, of the frequent openness or indeterminacy of truth conditions, particularly with so-called normal, standard, or literal discourse. Once one moves beyond feet and pounds, dates and places, the pragmatics of communication begin to assert themselves, incontrovertibly and indisputably, even to the point of occasionally superseding and overwhelming the common presumptions of intelligibility, namely, the public ascertainabilities of meaning, the public presupposition of precise, shared truth conditions. Specific meanings seldom exist. Often it seems the historiographer is less interested in enunciating particular propositions than in persuading us to a viewpoint, one which, to be sure, he takes as true. Taking an innocent, straightforward approach to hundreds of seemingly clear claims in historiography and elsewhere, claims couched in what would be universally regarded as normal, standard, literal prose, little considered before, allowed to pass without question or challenge, I have been puzzled, upon reflection, if not troubled, by a simple question: Under what conditions would this claim be true, or false? I think it is usual to ask a secondary question first, out of order, namely, is the claim true? This presupposes that we have some reasonably clear idea of what the truth conditions of the claim are, and are primarily concerned with whether or not those conditions are met. A deeper analysis, however, reveals that this unchallenged presupposition, that of an awareness of the truth conditions involved, is seldom warranted, or satisfied. It is sometimes said that what appears deep and dark may be only shallow and muddy. Conversely, one might well wonder if that which seems clear, whether deep and clear or shallow and clear, is clear, after all. One suspects, of course, that, under challenge, truth conditions might be invented, or certainly gathered together and spruced up, under which the challenged claim would come out true. Were they there in the first place? Perhaps. Perhaps, not. Some sense of truth conditions might be presupposed on an intuitive, or subconscious, level, which would lead one to accept or reject a claim. It might be difficult to invent, or discover, or clarify, those conditions. Perhaps in the attempt to do so, one might even be induced to withdraw or qualify the claim. In some respects communication seems more analogous to body language and mood music than arithmetic; in the communicative act, it is not clear that objects, let alone standardized objects, change hands. Changes, of course, are effected.

In the real world of discourse, one cannot stop continuously to invent, or discover and reveal, truth conditions. Occasionally one might do so, but this would be rare. Much charity is involved in communication. Much latitude is commonly extended. Blank checks are handed out, on street corners, as it were. One may hope to receive some back. One usually does not consider the truth conditions of one's discourse, unless challenged. An associational thinker might be a stranger to truth conditions altogether, might not even be concerned to inquire into them, and certainly would not be likely to have given them much thought, or to have much worried about them. Perhaps he doesn't even have truth conditions, but, if arrested in midflight, might stop to look for some. Just as the speaker is unlikely to consider truth conditions, though, hopefully, he is carrying some about with him, so, too, the auditor, in considering claims, is more likely to accept or reject them, than to understand them. This acceptance or rejection is, presumably, based on whether or not the claim seems right or wrong to him, and that would be with respect to some sense of his own, some sense of the sort of truth conditions which it would, or would not, satisfy. This sense of truth conditions is relative to himself, and is presumably as inarticulate and indeterminate as that of the speaker, in virtue of which the claim is taken to be true. We thus have two indeterminacies, one on the part of the speaker, and one on the part of the auditor, which are numerically different, and quite possibly substantively different, and neither of which is likely to be clear, or even thought out. These problems are usually overlooked because of a presumed public sharing of truth conditions, at least to a workable degree, which might or might not actually be the case. These ruminations are not supposed to be a counsel of despair, nor the issuance of a license to dismiss considerations of clarity and truth in historiographical discourse. They are intended, rather, to convey a realistic consideration of the pragmatics of communication with respect to such discourse. In historiography, given the frequent unavailability of absolute truth, recall the width of the box, the existence of public middle-ground meaning, and of individual-relative middle-ground meaning, given the indeterminacies of meaning and the variations in truth conditions, and sometimes their nonexistence or practical inaccessibility, the historiographer is less well understood as a stater of particular, exact truths, embodied in clear, verifiable propositions, than the conveyer of a vision of truth. To see historiography as it is commonly seen, in terms of particular propositions, is to see it in terms of the essential indeterminacies, inadequacies, and flaws of discourse; it is to see it in terms of its problematicities and inevitable weaknesses and faults; it is to see it in terms of the mire of its imperfections. Obviously, it is better to countenance these than abandon the project. What does emerge here, then, is the preeminence of the historiographical vision. This vision is less a mathematical function of particular integers than a mightiness to which they point. It is achieved less in virtue of the semantics of discourse than the pragmatics of communication. To a large extent, listing and counting are not so much involved as painting and persuasion. The whole here is not a collection, but something beyond that, to which it would point, something which is communicated, something which it allows us to see. And this is what we hope to receive from the historiographer, a sense of the past, a vision of the past.

And so, in this sense, let us speak of truths.

I have spent this time on expression, of various sorts, at this length, because of a way of seeing historiography. Involved is the vision of historiography not as an amateur, unequipped, inept, impoverished, neglected, scorned, distant, bumbling fourth or fifth cousin of a distinguished and noble line, that of the family of true sciences, but rather as a special sort of discipline, its own sort of discipline, a unique discipline, a cognitive art, one whose truths may be told with specificity, detail, richness, and meaning. In historiography we are talking about ourselves, and how we see ourselves. This is not like measuring height and weight, but a way of sharing in human experience. The historiographer must tell his truths as he sees them, not as instruments would measure them. In this sense historiography involves a relation to its subject matter which is far closer, far more intimate, and meaningful, than that which could be afforded by scales, meter sticks, clocks, and such. This role, this mission, this vocation, is unique, different from, other than, the business of the paradigm sciences, the P sciences. What it owes the P sciences is respect, neither emulation nor impersonation. Its identity is different. Its job is not to quantify, but to understand, not to measure but to grasp. As history is human, it is well seen only through human eyes. In no other way can it be understood. The truths that it must tell are amongst those which most matter. It tries, however feebly or inadequately, to understand what history meant, and means. And these are truths well worth telling, and worth telling as exactly, and richly, and adequately, as can be managed. Cognitivity involves telling the truth; art involves telling it as well as possible.

Epilogue

As earlier suggested, more important than the possibility, however remote, of dealing with a value-rich subject matter in a value-free manner is the question of the desirability of this project, even if it were somehow achievable. We suspect, as has been clear, that this is not achievable. Beyond this, however, we suggest that it is not desirable, even should it be achievable. We suggest, though this is obviously up to the individual historiographer, that he accept the challenge of confronting, and attempting to do justice to, his subject matter. This, in our opinion, necessitates being true to his own insights, and his own mode of truth telling. In our view truth to a value-rich subject matter requires the modality of a value-rich response, and permits the utilization of a value-rich mode of discourse. The historiographical engagement is legitimately axiological. If there are axiological truths, they have a right to be heard. In art truth is more commonly shown than told. But showing is a way of telling, and one should not be afraid to tell the truth, as one sees it. If another differs, let him tell the truth as he sees it. It is hard to see what might induce an individual to become a historiographer were it not for an avid curiosity concerning the past and a desire to relate to it in the fullness of his humanity, intellectually, emotionally, and morally. It is in the light of such beliefs that we have tried to make a case for axiological truth, an adequate historiographical modality of discourse, and an active, personal engagement on the part of the historiographer.

His discipline is one of the most important to which a human mind can address itself. It is also one of the noblest, and most beautiful. He touches the past. His responsibilities are manifold and profound. One wishes him well.

Breinigsville, PA USA
21 March 2011
258141BV00001B/37/P